STUDIES IN BRITISH ART

Terry Friedman

# JAMES GIBBS

*Published for the*
*Paul Mellon Centre for Studies in British Art by*
*Yale University Press · New Haven and London*
*1984*

*For my nephew*
*Joshua*
*and my nieces*
*Lieza, Shoshannah and Martha*

Designed by Faith Brabenec Hart
Filmset in Monophoto Baskerville and printed in Great Britain by
BAS Printers Limited, Over Wallop, Hampshire

**Library of Congress Cataloging in Publication Data**

Friedman, Terry.
  James Gibbs.

  Bibliography: p.
  Includes index.
    1. Gibbs, James, 1682–1754.     2. Architecture, Modern—
17th-18th centuries—Great Britain.     I. Title.
NA997.G5F73     1984     720'.92'4     84–40184
ISBN 0-300-03172-6

Frontispiece. John Michael Rysbrack, Portrait of James Gibbs,
1726, marble (St Martin-in-the-Fields, London)

# PREFACE

THIS UNDERTAKING would have proven immeasurably less satisfactory without the encouragement and hospitality of many institutions and persons, not least of all my parents and other members of my family. I also owe a particular debt to Howard Colvin and Derek Linstrum, who read the typescript and made many helpful suggestions, and, with George Clarke, John Harris, Peter Murray, Sir John Summerson and the late Sir Nikolaus Pevsner, generously discussed Gibbs with me on many occasions over the years. I appreciate the assistance of the Department of Western Art of the Ashmolean Museum, Oxford, the Drawings Collection of the Royal Institute of British Architects, and the Department of Prints and Drawings of the Victoria and Albert Museum, London, which together hold the majority of Gibbs's surviving drawings; the Bodleian Library, Oxford, which houses most of the books from Gibbs's library; and the Trustees of Sir John Soane's Museum, London, for permission to quote extensively from the Gibbs manuscript in that collection.

I have received valuable help and information from many more scholars, librarians, archivists, owners and custodians of Gibbs buildings, and friends than I can mention here individually (their names are recorded in the Notes and Catalogue of Works) but I would like to express my gratitude to Patricia Astley-Cooper, the Athenaeum Club, London, the Marquess of Bath, Geoffrey Beard, the late Duke of Beaufort, E. G. W. Bill, Michael Bourne, the British Library, Anne Buddle, S. Bywater, Cambridge University Library, Chetham's Library, Manchester (by courtesy of the Feoffees), George Clarke, the Corporation of London Records Office, Mary Cosh, Coutts Bank, London (by permission of the Duke of Argyll), the late Edward Croft-Murray, Elizabeth Darby, Derby Cathedral (by permission of the Dean and Chapter), Kerry Downes, John Dunbar, Katherine Eustache, Michael Fairbain, Janet Foster, the Guildhall Library, London, Leslie Harris, the Principal of Hartwell School, the Historical Manuscripts Commission, C. Hoare & Co., London, Margaret Hudson, Timothy Hudson, Ralph Hyde, Gervase Jackson-Stops, Bruce Jones, John Kerslake, Anthony Kersting, Pamela Kingsbury, King's College Library, Cambridge, Lambeth Palace Library, London, Susan Lang, Leeds Reference Library, James Lees-Milne, the Headmaster of Leighton Middle School, Leighton Buzzard, Lincolnshire Archives Committee (by courtesy of the Dean and Chapter of Lincoln Minster), Bryan Little, Jill Low, Lady Lucas, the Library of Magdalen College, Oxford (by courtesy of the President and Fellows), Sarah Markham, Marylebone Public Library, Edward Medlicott, Michael Moad, Carol Morley, National Register of Archives, Scotland (by permission of the Duke of Buccleuch, the Marquis of Bute, the Earl of Mar and Kellie), the National Trust, Mr and Mrs D. W. Neilson, North Yorkshire County

Record Office (the representatives of the late S. H. Le Roy Lewis and Mr G. H. Marwood), Hugh Pagan, Carlo Palumbo-Fossati, Brenda Parry-Jones, John Physick, the Pontifical Scots College, Rome, the Public Record Office, London, the Trustees of the Radcliffe Library, Oxford, Stewart Ramsdale, Rijksbureau voor Kunsthistorische Documentatie, The Hague, John Martin Robinson, the Royal Bank of Scotland (Drummond's Branch), London, the Royal Commission on Historical Monuments (England), the Royal Hospital of St Bartholomew's, London, the Royal Society, St George's Hospital, London, Edward Saunders, Leo Schmidt, the Scottish Record Office, Jacob Simon, Michael Snodin, the Society of Antiquaries, London, Dorothy Stroud, Glenn Taylor, W. T. C. Walker, Peter Wallis, the Chief Executive, Warrington Borough Council, B. Weinreb Architectural Books, Ltd, the Muniment Room and Library, Westminster Abbey, Westminster Public Library Archives Department (by permission of the Vestry of St Martin-in-the-Fields), Adam White, Peter Willis, Vilhelm Wohlert and Wolverhampton Area Health Authority. I am grateful for permission to reproduce drawings, photographs and documents from many of these and other sources.

Leeds City Council's generous grant of study-leave to complete my research must be recorded and, finally, I thank most warmly the Paul Mellon Centre for Studies in British Art and Yale University Press and their staff, especially John Nicoll and Faith Hart, for steering the typescript safely to this final destination.

Terry Friedman

Leeds, 1984

# CONTENTS

Had this fam'd Pile in days of yore
Been rais'd, each mortal would have swore,
It was a prince, at least some peer,
Who did the gorgeous palace rear;
And must have thought the brick and stones
Thus neatly rang'd by *Wren*, or *Jones*;
The structure no ignoble part,
Of *Boyle's*, or of *Palladio's* art.

    *Troy's* wall was built, else *Homer* lies,
By two Free-Mason Deities;
For hireling Gods in antient time
Blush'd not to work in sand and lime;
Handled their trowel and their spade,
Each a learn'd artist in his trade.
Had *Gibbs* then liv'd, he had been chose
Their foreman, when the Turrets rose;
*Vulcan* had own'd the Briton's Skill;
And *Neptune* paid him all his Bill;
With him divided all their gains,
And bowing, thank'd him for his pains.

from *A Satire Upon Physicians, or an English Paraphrase, With Notes and References, of Dr. King's most memorable Oration, Delivered at the Dedication of the Radclivian Library in Oxford,* 1755

# INTRODUCTION

JAMES GIBBS was born in 1682 in the remote north of Scotland, of obscure ancestry with no evident history of artistic inclination. By the time he was forty he had studied with a leading architect in Rome, designed two of the most beautiful churches in London, established himself as a pioneer of the new classical style in town and country houses, villas and church monuments, helped create the English landscape garden, 'engross'd all the business' at the two universities[1] and became 'the architect most in vogue'.[2] He was hailed as among 'the greatest architects in the Kingdom'[3] and, indeed, enjoyed an international reputation at the time of his death in 1754 at the age of seventy-two. Horace Walpole, who admittedly liked neither Gibbs nor his buildings, reported in 1771 that 'no man talks of one edifice' by him.[4] However, the chronological bibliography on pp. 351–2 shows that he has been the subject of more or less continuous public discussion from at least the early 1720s, with Sir James Thornhill's exaltation of the 'man of great Fame',[5] through the Victorian age, when he was regarded as 'perhaps the most considerable master of English architecture since Wren',[6] to the present day, with Sir John Summerson proclaiming him as 'one of the most individual of English architects'.[7]

It is apparent in looking at Gibbs's buildings that he rarely exhibited the marvellous visual invention of Vanbrugh and Hawksmoor, or Burlington's and Campbell's uncompromising commitment to classicism. He was professionally more successful than they just because of his willingness to design in the Rococo and Gothic styles as well as the Baroque and Palladian. In this respect, and in the variety of his building types, which include churches and chapels, town and country houses, garden, civic and university buildings, as well as sepulchral monuments, domestic and ecclesiastical furniture, all sorts of decorative embellishment and the production of fine illustrated books on architecture, he is closer to his near-contemporary William Kent and even more so to his Roman teacher Carlo Fontana and, in turn, to Fontana's master Bernini. He was, like them, an architect for all seasons.

> GIBBS may be said, most Times in Dress to please
> And few can decorate with greater Ease[8]

This is the first book to chart fully the architect's long and prosperous career. Much of what we know comes from 'A Manuscri by Mr. Gibbs Memorandums, &c.' in Sir John Soane's Museum.[9] Begun in 1707 while he was a student in Rome (then later supplemented by a now unidentifiable hand obviously privy to both personal and professional information), this 161-page manuscript is divided into two main parts. 'A few Short Cursory Remarks on some of the finest Antient and modern Buildings in Rome, and other parts of Italy, by Mr Gibbs while Studying Architectur there. being Memorandums for his own use. 1707[crossed through] and not intended to be made public being imperfect' includes comments under the headings 'Of the Roman Antiquitys in general', 'a few observations of Some of the Modern Buildings in Rome, and other parts of Italy, &c.', 'Some Remarks on the rebuilding of Rome and of its having layen in Rubbish many hundreds of years', together with brief biographical notes on Brunelleschi, Palladio and Sixtus V. Clearly part of this section dates after 1707, since it mentions Fontana's book *L'Anfiteatro Flavio*, which was published in 1725, the Trevi Fountain, 'a Magnificent peece of modern Architectur, the design of Nicola Salvi', which was begun in 1732, and the 'new fine' front of San Giovanni in Laterano by 'Sigr Galilei', which was built in 1733–5. The second part, 'A Short Accompt of Mr James Gibbs Architect And of several things he built in England &c. affter his returne from Italy', written in its present form sometime after 1754 (since it records his death) but probably no later than 1760 (when some information was used in the *Scots Magazine* obituary), provides the primary evidence of the events of his personal life and professional career and detailed descriptions of the majority of his works; the latter are quoted in the relevant entries in the Catalogue of Works. Of approximately one hundred and twenty-five buildings, church monuments, furnishings and decorative accessories which Gibbs designed and executed, more than half survive. Many of these are mentioned in contemporary literature.

To this material can be added a number of letters to and from clients, a personal Will attested in 1754, three influential publications—*A Book of Architecture*, 1728 (reissued 1739), *Rules for Drawing The several Parts of Architecture*, 1732 (reissued in 1738 and 1753) and *Bibliotheca Radcliviana: or, A Short Account of the Radcliffe Library, at Oxford*, 1747; a library which was exceptionally comprehensive among such holdings by British architects for its day (see Gibbs's Fine Art Library, pp. 327–30) and an equally impressive group of working drawings, numbering in the hundreds. Since Gibbs had no heir he bequeathed both the library and drawings, together with a print collection, to the University of Oxford in 1754.

This book is a study of only the architect's documented work; attributions based solely on the evidence of stylistic similarities or the appearance of a houseowner's name in the list of subscribers to *A Book of Architecture* have been discarded. To the general reader this may seem a particularly rigid approach, but it is necessary in dealing with an artist who was admired throughout his working career, who published some of the most influential pattern books in the history of British architecture and who, therefore, made a strong impact on his contemporaries. I have drawn heavily on contemporary documents, which are helpful in assessing reactions to Gibbs's work, and have paid special attention to his drawings in analyzing the development of his ideas, particularly where groups of drawings for individual commissions survive, as is fortunately the case with many of his major works. Emphasis also has been placed on Gibbs's sources of inspiration because in an age when both the designer and his clients were artistically erudite as a matter of course, it was not thought improper that a judicious borrowing of 'some hints [such as a] door or window-case', as one contemporary observed, 'may perhaps give a good air to a building'.[10]

# I

## 'A MAN OF GREAT FAME'

GIBBESIUS. . . a man of great Fame
Who formerly from Calidonia came
An Aedificator was his Profession[1]

THE THREE DAY CELEBRATION in April 1749 to mark the opening of the Radcliffe Library was one of the most festive Oxford had ever seen.[2] On the 12th, following a degree ceremony at which James Gibbs, the sixty-seven year old architect of this 'most magnificent structure',[3] was made a Master of Arts, there was an entertainment given by the Radcliffe Trustees, who had been responsible for erecting the building. A huge crowd attended a performance of Handel's *Esther* and on the two succeeding evenings they heard *Samson*, the *Coronation Anthem* and the *Messiah*. On 13 April the entourage proceeded from St Mary's church to the new Library, where the Duke of Beaufort officially opened the building. This last event forms the subject of the *University Almanack* for 1751 (Plate 1) which shows the Trustees assembled in the great rotunda-shaped reading room delivering the keys to Alma Mater attended by the genii of Anatomy, Botany, Chemistry and Physick.[4] The company then proceeded to the Sheldonian Theatre to the 'flourish of Musick' and more degree giving. Then, 'amidst the Thunder of the Theatre, rose the great Oxford Orator, & Patriot' Dr William King, Principal of St Mary's Hall, to deliver an hour long oration in Latin. Praising the late Dr John Radcliffe for providing funds to build 'that immense and magnificent Library', he then considered the 'Agent in this great Undertaking . . . the most famous Architect; whose consummate Skill both this very Work and the other sumptuous Edifices, as well publick as private, which he has raised in *London*, in *Cambridge*, and in other celebrated parts of our Island, sufficiently point out and display'. King continued: 'But as for me, I love the Man, for he deserves to be beloved; for he was formerly my Host, and one, whom I knew to be the most humane and friendly Person living, and not only versed in Architecture, but in the knowledge of all Antiquity, and Learning in general', and he praised him as 'clarissimum architectus'.[5]

Gibbs's beginnings were in no way so glamorous. He was born on 23 December 1682 at Fittysmire in the old town of Aberdeen, 'a pretty place [with] good entertainment' and 'a great Air of Trade' on the north-east coast of Scotland.[6] Almost nothing is known about either his family or his early life. Apparently a William Gib or Gibb, the son of another William of Tillyfourie, some miles west of Aberdeen, was bound as a tailor's apprentice in 1648 and admitted a free Burgess of the town in 1655; this second William's son Patrick, a prosperous local merchant, was James's father. His mother, Ann Gordon, was 'a gentlewoman of a good family' and there was another son, William, by Patrick's previous marriage probably to a woman named Isabel Farquhar.[7] James was educated

1. George Vertue, 'Representation of the Solemnity at the Time of Opening' the Radcliffe Library, Oxford, pen and wash drawing for *The University Almanack*, 1751 (Ashmolean Museum, Oxford)

at Aberdeen Grammar School and then Marischal College, matriculating some time between 1696 and 1700.[8] The family, however, was Catholic and had not entirely escaped the persecution that followed the revolution in 1688. An incident, first reported in an account of the architect's life published in the *Scots Magazine* in 1760, relates how 'old Mr Gibbs . . . named two puppies *Whig* and *Tory*, in derision of both the parties [and the] magistrates of Aberdeen . . . ordained the two favourite dogs to be hanged at the cross'.[9] The events of the next decade, which saw repressive Acts against Catholics, coupled with the deaths of James's parents, left his future uncertain. But 'being of a rambling disposition' and wanting 'to go abroad to see other Countrays [he] aquanted his friends with his intentions', raised some money and just before 1700 left for Holland to visit relatives, with whom he stayed for some time.[10]

'A Short Accompt of Mr James Gibbs', in part an autobiography, implies that as a young man he had a great genius for drawing, and the *Scots Magazine* goes further in suggesting that he spent some years in the service of an architect and master-builder in

Holland who, however, has not been identified, although on good authority it was reported in 1713 that he had studied architecture in Rome and elsewhere for sixteen years.[11] His brief comments on Dutch buildings reveal the uncritical yet perhaps already converted eye of the architectural enthusiast. 'As for the Dutch', he observed, 'they are very singular in their buildings, and in every thing else, altho ther are some very fine Buildings at the Hague and Amsterdam, as for their common fabricks they are so like one an other, that if you see one town you may guise at all the rest'.[12]

Some time after 1700 Gibbs moved on towards Italy. His general itinerary was notable in that France, while closed to his Protestant countrymen during the years before the Treaty of Utrecht (1713), was accessible to him. In 1691 Thomas Archer had been obliged to travel by way of Holland and Germany or Switzerland and in 1709, after sailing from Spithead, John Talman and William Kent arrived safely at Pisa only 'by God's blessing after . . . a voyage of 3 months & . . . in danger of being taken by the French'.[13] 'In the great City of Paris' Gibbs found 'numbers of large buildings, palaces, Hotells, churches & other Fabricks . . . which have a particularity in them that distinguishes them to be built by French architects, yet there are some very fine in their kind'. The Louvre, the Luxembourg Palace and several seventeenth-century churches are mentioned in passing. Surprisingly there are no references to either the Invalides, the most spectacular recent addition to the city, or Versailles; but Gibbs owned a number of engravings of these buildings as well as travel books, some of which he may have already acquired by this time, and it is easy to imagine his opinions were reflected by their characteristic rhetoric. 'The Germans,' he observed, 'if they have any grand Building to be erected, they send to Italy for some of the best Masters, in Order to give them propper designs . . . and indeed some of them are very fine'; here he cites the palaces at Schönbrunn, Munich, Bonn and Mannheim.[14] Since the last was not proposed until 1720 this is likely to be a reference to the unexecuted design published in *Le grand œuvre d'architecture de Jean Marot, c.* 1665.

A drawing by Gibbs of one of the early seventeenth-century pilgrimage chapels by Giuseppe Bernasconi on the Sacri Monti at Varese in the foothills of the Alps (Plate 2) suggests that he came into Italy by this route and that he already had some professional training.[15] Of his movements once there more is known. Buildings in Milan, Venice, Bologna, Florence, Genoa and Naples are noted, some enthusiastically, yet 'A few Short Cursory Remarks on some of the finest Antient and modern Buildings in Rome, and other parts of Italy, by Mr Gibbs while he was Studying Architectur there' convey little of the excitement which a young Scottish provincial first discovering Italy must have felt, or of his daily activities. He was 'highly pleased with the fine Buildings, pictures, and Statues he saw in the great towns' but found Rome 'surpassed all the rest in Magnificence and grandeur; And as he was a lover of Architectur, painting, and Scuptry, those arts did shine in perfection there.'[16]

Nevertheless, on 12 October 1703 Gibbs registered as a student at the Scots College in the Via Rasella, near Borromini's church of San Carlo alle Quattro Fontane. He found life under the Jesuits hard; a fellow student, James Gordon, later Bishop of Nicopolis, wrote on 12 August 1704,

> We are still apprehensive of what may fall out, so violent is this Rector [of the College] and so disposed as much as people can judge to do some mischief. Poor Mr. Gib . . . is so terrified with his rudeness that he cannot resolve to take the oath [requiring candidates to confirm a willingness to proceed to the priesthood within the prescribed six months of admission and after ordination to work in Scotland as a secular priest for

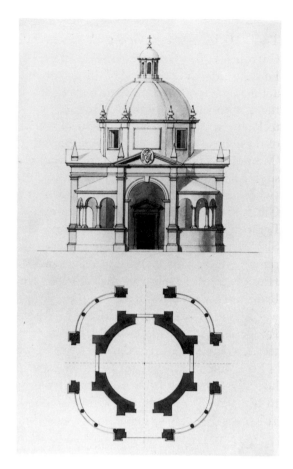

2. James Gibbs, Drawing of Giuseppe Bernasconi's pilgrimage chapel on the Sacri Monti, Varese, Italy, early seventeenth century, plan and elevation, pen and wash (Ashmolean Museum, Oxford, Gibbs Collection III.129)

at least five years]; he should have taken it months ago, but then the Rector did not tender it to him, and he has been in such broils since, that he won't go under it at any rate.

Towards the end of the letter Gordon remarked that Gibbs intended leaving the College and required financial aid. In a second letter, of 19 August, he added,

This youth is of good parts and vertuously inclined and well disposed, and though he leaves the college may be usefull one day, and therefore we think it not amiss to do him some kindness, besides that his father, having suffered much for his faith at the revolution there seem to be more than ordinary reason of Christian Charity and friendship to assist him, especially where there is no great trouble or loss to us. He resolves to stay some while here and apply himself to painting, seemingly to have a great genious for that employment.

Soon after, Gibbs left the College.[17] The 'Short Accompt' does not mention this episode, only that he was so taken with the beauty of the fine churches and palaces, and the noble remains of the ancient buildings, that he resolved to make architecture his principal study. Probably late in 1704 he was recommended to Carlo Fontana, then the most influential architect in Rome, so becoming the first British architect to receive a professional training abroad.[18] Fontana (1638–1714) had been a pupil and assistant of three of the greatest Baroque architects, Bernini, Cortona and Rainaldi, and was himself the master of a number of leading European architects, among them J. B. Fischer von Erlach, Lucas von Hildebrandt, Filippo Juvarra, Francesco de Sanctis, Alessandro Specchi and Nicodemus

Tessin. Gibbs's friend George Vertue relates that he was also taught by Pietro Francesco Garroli (1638–1716), Professor of Perspective at the Accademia di San Luca; and since Fontana was the Principal of this academy between 1686 and 1700, with his son Francesco acting as Vice-Principal until 1708, it is almost certain that Gibbs began his training there.[19] At the same time he frequently visited the British nobility and gentry who came to Rome to see the antiquities, some of whom employed him to make drawings;[20] none of these has been traced. A note that the 'Cursory Remarks', which is dated 1707, were 'Memorandums for his own use . . . and not intended to be made public being imperfect', suggests that he may have guided these tourists as a means of supplementing his income (whose source is now unknown) but also undoubtedly with an eye to future patronage. Gibbs mentions some of these visitors in a letter to Sir John Perceval, later 1st Earl of Egmont, dated 3 December 1707 (soon after Perceval visited Rome): Robert Furness and Sir Thomas Samuel (who later subscribed to his *Book of Architecture*, confirming Gibbs's remark that these men were 'of service to him when he returned to England'), Simon Harcourt, John Molyneux and others.[21] He asks that correspondence be directed to Robert Brown, who is mentioned in another letter of the same year as the host of a concert which was attended by John Blathwayt of Dyrham Park.[22] The Blathwayt brothers arrived in Rome in April 1707 and during the summer received instruction from an unnamed architect hired at a monthly salary of £3 to 3 guineas; perhaps this architect was young Gibbs.[23]

Soon after Perceval returned to London, by October 1707, he wrote expressing the hope that 'the English gentlemen I left at Rome are well, and that Mr Gibbs finds scholars to his mind'; yet although Gibbs claimed in the 'Short Accompt' that he loved to live at Rome, his reply to Perceval in December tells a different story:

> I heard . . . that you are not as yet forgetful of your humble servant; that you hope I have a great many scholars . . . I believe there will come to Rome very few that will leave such a notable character behind them as your worthy person has done. When you went away I am sorry I did not go along with you, though it had been to carry a livery in your service, for things go so ill here, and there is such a pack of us, and so jealous of one another, that the one would see the other hanged, that for my part, if it pleases the stars, I will make my stay as short here as possible. The reason why I did not beg of you to take me along with you was that I must stay some short time longer to perfectionate myself in this most miserable business of architecture. However, Sir John, if I can be any way serviceable to you here, or in England, I will be very proud to have the honour to be enrolled amongst the very lowest of your servants.[24]

In 1708 Gibbs received letters from his friends that his brother was in a very bad state of health and wished him to come home. By November he had arrived in London, but not before William had died.[25] Writing to Perceval, who had moved on to Ireland, he explains how, 'being come now over to England, I shou'd be glad to hear of the Welfare [of] One from whom I have received so many favours' and again on 10 February 1709:

> I have indeed a great many very good friends here, and that of the first rank and quality in England, and with time I do not doubt but are able and willing to do me very great service in my way; but their promises are not a present relief for my circumstances, and it is even uncertain what time itself may produce, for great men's promises are not to be depended upon, when there are so many gaping and pretending for any little place that is vacant, whether in my way or otherwise, so that it is seldom or never considered if a man be qualified for such a post, but what friends or money he has, which never fails, without any regard, or seldom, to merit.

Apparently Perceval had invited Gibbs to Ireland, for the letter goes on:

> So truly, I think it best not to lose certainty for good hopes, and embrace your most kind favour and prefer your most honourable patronage and protection before the promises of the greatest quality here in England. It is true I wish the thing was greater, by *Felix qui potuit contentus vivere parvo* . . . so that I will do my endeavour to set out the first of March [for Dublin].[26]

Two days later we hear from Gibbs that Perceval and a Richard Tighe 'are both about building', the former preparing to rebuild the family mansion, Burton House, Cork, which had been burned in 1690 by Jacobite troops retreating after the Battle of the Boyne.[27] This seemed an ideal opportunity for Gibbs because, despite the fact of his unique training and wide travelling, his position of authority as an interpreter of current Continental architectural ideas was far from secure and did not go unchallenged. He himself acknowledged that St Paul's Cathedral, which was nearly completed in 1708, was 'a very fine building, and shews very much the skill of that great man [Wren], who was not only famous for Architectur, but for many other arts and Sciences'.[28] There was competition, too, from Vanbrugh and Hawksmoor, who were then collaborating at Castle Howard and Blenheim, from Thomas Archer, who had travelled to Italy in 1690 and was now busy at Heythrop and Wrest, from John Talman, who was just setting out for another visit to Italy, this time with William Kent, to acquire designs for a new palace at Whitehall, and from a host of lesser men, some of whom were also foreign-trained, like the Berlin-based architect Johann von Bodt, who designed the spectacular wing at Stainborough Hall (Wentworth Castle) in Yorkshire in 1710. In contrast, at this time Ireland was starved of talented architects working within the European mainstream but apparently had little taste for the arts.[29] Gibbs informed Perceval in a letter of 12 February 1709 that he had acquainted John Erskine, 11th Earl of Mar, with his intention to go to Ireland.

> He told me that I was very much obliged to your honour for the service you had done me, and that he did not doubt . . . I might do very well in Ireland, but that England was the only place to raise a man of my employment, so that if I pleased to accept of a commission in a garrison of his at Sterling Castle it should be at my service. He added that I could be always, or for the most part, here in London . . . that I might follow out my business; and that if you thought fit he would give me leave to come over and see your honour in the summer time for a month or two . . . This post will be about four shillings a day, but his lordship has promised to make it as yet more . . . In fine, my lord has expressed too much kindness to doubt anything of the goodness of his intentions, and is one of the best friends I have in the world next to your most worthy person. This offer being so very advantageous I thought I could not do better than to take your advice upon it.[30]

The Irish expedition was cancelled.

Lord Mar proved a sympathetic patron. He was by his own admission 'infected with the disease of building and gardening'.[31] In 1710 he and Lord Loudoun, as joint Secretaries of State for Scotland, had Gibbs remodel their houses in the Privy Gardens at Whitehall and probably in the same year he designed a lodge on Mar's estate at Alloa in Clackmannanshire, a few miles away from Stirling (Plate 98). Gibbs also prepared but never realized an eccentric design for Mar's brother-in-law George Hay, Lord Dupplin, at Dupplin Castle in Perthshire (Plate 97). Later he attracted other Scottish clients, the Drummonds, Duffs, Montroses and Campbells, including John Campbell, 2nd Duke of Argyll and

Greenwich, to whom *A Book of Architecture* is dedicated for the 'early Encouragement I received . . . in my Profession, upon my Return from *Italy*'. Occasional excursions were made into Scotland, but Gibbs was undoubtedly early aware that his countrymen 'proceed soo slow . . . with everything of that nature [building] that one is allmost wearied before its well begun';[32] in any case the Stirling commission was soon withdrawn as a result of the trimming of military activities which the Lord High Treasurer, Robert Harley, introduced with the Restricting Orders in 1712. But if these ambitious projects slipped away Mar was instrumental in establishing his architect in London in the following year. Rumours had reached Gibbs secretly in August 1713 that William Dickinson intended resigning his post as one of the surveyors (with Nicholas Hawksmoor) to the Commissioners for Building Fifty New Churches, the most important architectural activity in early eighteenth-century London. On 3 August Mar wrote to Harley (whose daughter Abigail was the wife of George Hay) that that very morning 'poor Gibbs' was told of Dickinson's decision; but the soon-to-be-vacated post was not won without considerable struggle, and the events of the following months indicate Gibbs's precarious position within the architectural establishment.

> If it were not that Mr. Gibbs is perfectly well qualified for such a post I would not presume to recommend him . . . He studied architecture at Rome and elsewhere sixteen years, so has had more occasion of improving himself in that way than most of the Architects in this island. He is in great want of some support, and had it not been for a little thing I gave him in Stirling Castle, which he lost last year by the reduction, he had starved four years ago. If this vacancy be once known a great many will be putting in for it, therefore may I beg that you will be pleased soon to recommend this poor (though fit) man to the Commissioners for this post, which will be an act of charity as well as filling the place with one that is rightly qualified for it.[33]

Other powerful friends also rallied. Sir Christopher Wren's son delivered two letters to the Commissioners on 12 August. One was from the amateur architect Robert Benson, Lord Bingley, 'recommending Mr Gib [as] one that I beleeve will be found every way capable of tenury in the imployment'; the other was from the Aberdonian-born physician-in-ordinary to the Queen, Dr John Arbuthnot, in which he praised 'Mr Gibbs The person who made the tuo last Models [for the Commissioners' churches]. I believe your Lo[rdshi]ps will find him very capable to serve you'.[34] These men would also have known Gibbs's engraving dedicated to Prince George of Denmark, the Queen's husband, designed for the first volume of John Flamsteed's celebrated book of stellar observations, *Historiæ Cælestis*, 1712 (Plate 74). Dickinson finally resigned on 13 August and Christopher Wren immediately wrote to his fellow Commissioners that he had been 'for some time acquainted with Mr. Gibbs, and have had opportunity's to observe his knowledge in Architecture and what relates thereto; I believe him to be very well qualified'.[35] Harley had still not done enough directly to promote Gibbs, who now wrote to him in desperation on 13 September:

> I thought indeed that the least intimation in your name by anybody besides so great a man as my Lord Bingley would have been sufficient to the Commissioners for electing the person recommended, but it seems that my antagonist has got the majority upon his side, and unless your Lordship renew your goodness by a line or two from your own hand, I shall certainly lose it. These little places do not fall out everyday, and I may starve before another opportunity presents itself.

Gibbs added a note regarding this 'antagonist': 'Only my friend Mr. Vanbrugh was against me, I suppose because I was recommended by your Lordship, and got the Commissioners to defer the nomination of a surveyor these two months as yet, and it may be longer, which I believe may be dangerous', concluding that a further recommendation would 'contribute . . . very much to my advantage . . . and add a new obligation upon me'.[36] A few days later Mar again pressed Harley:

> The bearer, poor Gibbs, hopes your Lordship will be so good to keep him from starving till he get his place to which you recommended him, that commission not meeting till October. He is a broken officer and gets no half-pay, and he has lived so long in expectation that he has no more credit nor anything to live on. If you be not pleased to give him something he'll be in a starving way, and 'tis pity one who can do his business so well should be so.[37]

The Commissioners vacillated. After John James, Assistant Clerk of the Works at Greenwich Hospital and Master Carpenter at St Paul's Cathedral, delivered a petition forwarding his own candidacy Gibbs followed with another letter stressing that he had 'studied Architectur abroad for several years under the greatest masters at Rome, and especialy that parte that relates to churches, wher of he hopes he is able when required to give sufficient satisfaction to compitent judges'. All this material was considered by the Commissioners on 21 October but no decision was made until 18 November when 'upon Ballating, the Choice fell upon Mr Gibbs'.[38] He was then thirty years old.

His responsibilities as a surveyor included not only designing churches but assessing the proposed sites, the quality of materials and the work of the craftsmen. Between 1713 and 1716 he succeeded in building St Mary-le-Strand (Plate 20), which he described proudly as 'the first publick Building I was employed in after my arrival from *Italy*; which being situated in a very publick place, the Commissioners . . . spar'd no cost to beautify'.[39] About this time we catch a first glimpse of Gibbs's appearance (Plate 3).[40]

Although complimented on his 'fair daughter in the Strand', which would prove 'the most complete little damsel in town' and do 'honour to the parent',[41] Gibbs's professional progress was overtaken by political events. Soon after Queen Anne's unexpected death in August 1714 and the Hanoverian accession, the Tory government was defeated by the Whigs, Robert Harley was dismissed as Lord High Treasurer and imprisoned in the Tower, and Mar was dismissed as Secretary of State for Scotland and by the summer of 1715 was marching south with his Jacobite army, only to be defeated decisively in November by the Duke of Argyll's forces at Sheriffmuir. It was probably Argyll who dissuaded Gibbs from joining Mar's ill-fated troop during those months.[42] Nevertheless, after the Tory dominated Church Commission was replaced by Whigs in December 1715, Gibbs was deprived of his surveyorship. Mar reckoned it 'was certainly Signor Gibbi's performances making the others of the profession ashamed of theirs, that was the cause of his being dismissed, and Toryism only given for the reason, being ashamed to own the true one'[43]; but in a letter to the Commissioners of 13 January 1716 Gibbs mentions 'a false report of a Countrayman of mine that misrepresented me as a papest and a dissafected person, which I can assure you is intirly false and scandalous, and done purly out of a designe to have gott him self into the place I have now lost'. This adversary was almost certainly the Scottish Palladian architect Colen Campbell, who had already tried unsuccessfully to attract the Commissioners. His dislike of Gibbs was compounded as much on professional jealously as condemnation of the Strand church; it can be assumed he placed it with those 'affected and licentious' works of Bernini and Carlo Fontana and the 'wildly Extravagant' designs of Borromini, 'who has endeavoured to debauch Mankind

3. Peter Pelham, after Hans Hysing, Portrait of James Gibbs, by 1723, mezzotint (private collection)

*Iacobus Gibbs, Architectus*

with his odd and chimerical Beauties', in the Introduction to one of the earliest and most persuasive of the Palladian manifestos, *Vitruvius Britannicus*, which appeared in 1715. In desperation Gibbs petitioned the Commissioners:

> I hope you will not be against my proceeding with the Church in the Strand, since I have caryed it up so farr to the intire satisfaction of every body, the Building can not be too fine for the situation, since it's so much in vive [view], and I will ingage it will answer the estimat, you yourselves shall state the prices of the workemen, your surveyours [now Hawksmoor and John James] shall measur and inspect the work to save you from being cheated, all the advantage that I propose by it, is to gain me a reputation to recommend me to other business.[44]

His request was granted. Although he denied it publicly, Gibbs remained a Catholic throughout his life. He had begged John Perceval in a letter of 1709 to 'conceal [my religion] as much as possible, and I can assure your honour that there shall be no trouble ensue to myself or others'.[45] This discretion was maintained, for Father Alexander Grant, a Scottish priest in the Venetian Ambassador's employ in London, reported on 31 August 1754:

> You have probably heard that our countryman, James Gibbs Esqre from Aberdeen dyed here August the fifth; he was a Catholic but always under a mask for fear of losing a pension of 150lbs. per annum [as Architect of the Ordnance]. He had an estate of 500lbs. per annum by which he might live independently but auri sacra fames wou'd not allow him to profess openly what he believed. He kept no correspondence with any churchman, but with B—— Peters [Bishop Benjamin Petre, Vicar Apostolic of the London District], who was his director, and gave him the last rites of his principles.[46]

Gibbs's secret correspondence with Mar, who fled into exile after the defeat at Sheriff-muir, suggests the uncertainty of both their positions at this time. Writing from Avignon on 16 April 1716 the Earl advised Gibbs to appear ignorant of what the heavily disguised political messages in his letter mean for fear it may draw trouble upon him; but he added, 'let us hope still that there are more polite days a coming when arts will thrive and good performances be cherished by those who have a right taste and then I am sure Signor Gibbi will not only be encouraged but courted'. The letter also reveals that Gibbs was then remodelling Lord Burlington's house in Piccadilly (Plate 228) and building at Richmond (probably Sudbrook Park at nearby Petersham for the Duke of Argyll, Plate 140), in Hertfordshire (unidentified) and 'a round room in the middle' of an unnamed building, based on a sketch supplied by Mar, which he believed Gibbs was 'executing since with some improvements of your own'; this is probably the octagonal garden building for James Johnston at Twickenham (Plate 167). Mar also invited Gibbs to join him in visiting 'your old southern habitation [Rome] again'.[47] Gibbs answered on 22 August, 'I though to have seen Paris this season for six weeks, but find it impossible because of the close attendance I am obliged to give to my business. I should be glad to see Versailles and Marly', and in a further letter of 11 August 1717, replying to Mar's persistent invitation, reported that 'Were I not tied by the leg here, I should have been over with you before'.[48]

Mar had enquired in the same letter about teachers of architecture at Rome. Gibbs informed him:

> Just now I cannot remember any acquaintance at the old place, for Fountana is dead, and so is Signor Abramo Paris, my old masters, so that I know none that are good for much. What young men are grown up these 10 or 12 years I dont know . . . I have

a great deal of business on my hands, which I hope will turn to some account. I live the same single life, only a little loose sometimes. I thought to have seen Paris this summer for a month, but shall not have time, being obliged to go to the North. Necessity requires to prefer a little profit to pleasure.

In a final letter of 9 January 1718, he informed Mar that he had 'just come to town, after a very tedious journey from a very barbarous place [Cumbria] . . . I thought to have stolen a month to have come and see you, but have been dissuaded from it on several accounts';[49] maybe Gibbs, losing hope of preferment under a renewed Jacobite clique, was attempting to break with the Earl despite expectations of a second, victorious rising which would return him to power, but which never came. During the next fourteen years Mar wandered across Europe, making dozens of eccentric unbuildable designs for royal palaces, houses and gardens, finally dying in exile at Aix-la-Chapelle in 1732. Long before this he seems to have abandoned Gibbs, subscribing to the second and third volumes of *Vitruvius Britannicus* (1717 and 1725) but not to *A Book of Architecture*. After 1717 Gibbs moved surreptitiously on the fringe of Jacobite circles, probably hopeful of their eventual success yet careful not to prejudice a professional career he was struggling to re-establish under the new regime. He made proposals for Witham Park in Somerset for the Jacobite Sir William Wyndham (Plate 101) and Lowther Hall in Westmorland for Henry, 3rd Viscount Lonsdale (Plate 106), and remodelled Cannons House in Middlesex for the wealthy and powerful Earl of Caenarvon, later 1st Duke of Chandos (Plate 108) and Wimpole Hall for Robert Harley's son Edward, Lord Oxford, and his wife Henrietta, the Newcastle heiress, with whom he was particularly friendly (Plate 113). Although his list of patrons was increasing steadily, the commissions were mainly from Catholics and deposed Tories, and they were exclusively domestic in character, often only improvements to existing houses far from London. A number never reached beyond the design stage. Then about 1720 Gibbs became, in Horace Walpole's words, 'the architect most in vogue'.[50]

In 1719 he had been commissioned by the parishioners of St Clement Danes to complete the steeple of the church left unfinished by Wren, who was then a very old man. In the same year he was honoured with the Stewardship of the Virtuosi of St Luke, a notable London club of artists, which entailed paying for part of the annual dinner held at one of the celebrated London taverns, itself an indication of his growing wealth and professional status.[51] On 27 July 1720, the Radcliffe Trustees thought of inviting Gibbs and six other of the 'ablest architects' (Wren, Vanbrugh, Hawksmoor, Archer, James and Thornhill) to prepare designs for the new Oxford library;[52] and on 13 October General Steuart wrote to the Commissioners for Building Fifty New Churches accepting their recommendation of Gibbs as architect of St George's, Hanover Square, and related that the 'Cheife persons of quallity' living in the parish have a 'very good Oppinion' of his performance and feel he would be 'diligent to the Last degree, for our satisfaction, as well as his own Creditt'.[53] His name was coupled with those of Burlington, Handel, Pope and others as subscribers to John Gay's *Poems on Several Occassions*, 1720. But undoubtedly Walpole's reference was in connection with Gibbs's appointment in November 1720 as architect for rebuilding the parish church of St Martin-in-the-Fields, one of the most prestigious ecclesiastical commissions of the eighteenth century (Plate III). Although this was not so difficult to secure as the New Churches surveyorship seven years earlier, nevertheless he was not free of rivals. Nicholas Dubois, John James, George Sampson and Sir James Thornhill also competed for this coveted post and although Gibbs was finally recommended on 14 September, his election was for various reasons postponed until 24 November.[54] Other public work emerged as a consequence of the prestige attached to this commission: in February 1723 he was appointed architect for rebuilding All Saints (now the Cathedral) at Derby (Plate 61) and in April of the same year his election as a governor of St Bartholomew's Hospital in London led to preparations for rebuilding the medieval fabric in 1728 (Plate 240). In this same year his fellow-governors sitting as City aldermen and common council-men invited him to make designs for the new Mansion House. Such influential acquaintances strengthened his practice. Work came from some of the parishioners who financed the building of St Martin's, from the many distinguished contributors of money to the Derby scheme and from fellow-governors at St Bartholomew's. A group of the last also commissioned church monuments, works of art British architects had previously left to sculptors and master-masons but which Gibbs, the disciple of one of Bernini's outstanding pupils, now made his own. By 1723 he had erected three of the most important recent monuments in Westminster Abbey: to John Dryden and Matthew Prior, among the earliest to embellish Poets' Corner, and to John Holles, 1st Duke of Newcastle (Plates 77, 92, 94). The talented young sculptor John Michael Rysbrack, newly arrived from Antwerp in 1720, was employed on Prior's tomb and its success in demonstrating a new, sophisticated awareness of current Continental trends was celebrated in a contemporary poem:

> While Gibbs displays his elegant Design
> And Rysbracks Art does in the Sculpture shine
> With due composure. & proportion just
> adding new lustre to the finish't Bust
> Each Artist here, perpetuates his Name
> And shares with Prior an Immortal Fame.[55]

The Abbey monument to James Craggs (Plate 95), one of the Secretaries of State, commissioned by his sister and Alexander Pope in 1724 and finished within three years, firmly established Gibbs's leadership in this field. James Ralph in *A Critical Review of the Publick Buildings, Statues and Ornaments In, and about London and Westminster*, 1734, thought 'many tombs have more beauties, none fewer faults'.[56]

Meanwhile, Gibbs was remodelling Wimpole for Edward and Henrietta Harley and supervising their new London estate in Marylebone—the proprietory chapel in Vere Street was consecrated in 1724 (Plate 59). He also rebuilt Shipbourne church in Kent for Henrietta's relatives Lord and Lady Barnard (Plate 55), and remodelled their nearby mansion at Fairlawne. He was working for the 2nd Earl of Lichfield at Ditchley (Plate 116), the Cornish Jacobite Sir William Carew at Antony (Plate 135), William Duff of Braco at Balveny (Plate 155) and Robert Harley's old political partner Lord Bolingbroke at Dawley; the Long Gallery at Stainborough was completed in 1725 (Plate 124) and from this year the first garden buildings began to appear at Whitton (Plate 170), the Middlesex estate of Lord Ilay, the younger brother of the Duke of Argyll, for whom Gibbs had already built Sudbrook Park (Plate 140). In 1726 he replaced the recently deceased Vanbrugh as Viscount Cobham's architect at Stowe, the greatest landscape garden of the age (Plate 199). In 1728 Kelmarsh Hall was begun (Plate 126). Gibbs was by now one of the leading domestic architects in the country.[57] In 1721 he made his debut at Cambridge, in the following year initiating his grand design for the Public Building, the administrative and ceremonial nucleus of the University, of which only the Senate House was realized (Plate 253); between 1724 and 1730 he erected the Fellows' Building, one-third of an even more ambitious scheme for King's College (Plate 258), establishing himself as Hawksmoor's only serious metropolitan-based rival at the university.

4. Bernard Baron, James Gibbs's bookplate, 1736, engraving (author's collection)

In 1723 Gibbs opened an account with the Jacobite banker Andrew Drummond, his first year's credit balancing at £1055.11.4, and encouraged by this new prosperity and independence, he sat for at least three portraits by Rysbrack between 1723 and 1726, the sculptor receiving a total payment of £111.[58] The terracotta bust mentioned in 1723 as 'a bald head . . . extreamly like him' is untraced; but the unflattering version in marble of 1726, with its wigless, egg-shaped skull and naked shoulders, confirms a contemporary verdict that Rysbrack's portraits possessed 'superior meritt to other Sculptors . . . none equallizing for truth of Likeness'.[59] A second marble portrait, also missing, described in 1723 as a bas-relief, and as portraying him with a wig, is probably reflected in the bookplate engraved by Bernard Baron in 1736, with its elaborate cartouche designed by Gibbs himself (Plate 4).[60] Yet another marble bust of 1726, perhaps Rysbrack's earliest portrait masterpiece (Frontispiece), shows the architect full of confidence, in a pose which must have been intentionally reminiscent of Edward Pierce's celebrated bust of Wren (1673). This portrait of Gibbs has an especially interesting provenance, for Horace Walpole, hardly the architect's champion, purchased it at Christie's in 1783 for the Star Chamber at Strawberry Hill; eventually it made its way to St Martin-in-the-Fields.[61]

St Martin's attracted public attention even before its consecration in 1726: 'The inhabitants are now supplied with a decent tabernacle, which can produce as handsome a show of white hands, diamond rings, pretty snuff boxes, and gilt prayer books as any cathedral whatever. Here the fair penitents pray in their patches, sue for pardon in their paint, and see their heaven in man'[62]—and it was a tremendous popular success:

> O *Gibbs*, whose Art the solemn Fane can raise,
> Where *God* delights to dwell, and *Man* to praise[63]

Guidebooks hailed it as 'indisputably the most magnificent Parochial Church in London [the] Fabrick is looked upon as a masterpiece', and it was undoubtedly this which led the Dean of Lincoln in 1726 to proclaim Gibbs one of 'the greatest architects in the kingdom'.[64] The Scots antiquarian Alexander Gordon also praised the church in the preface to *Itinerarium Septentrionale*, 1726, a book which Gibbs subscribed to and not unnaturally helped to promote, for we find him already in 1725 collecting the subscription fee from the King's College authorities.[65] Another distinguished antiquarian, Maurice Johnson, included Gibbs in a contemporary list of the most notable English architects.[66] Both Johnson and Gordon were members of the Society of Antiquaries in London, which had shown interest in the archaeology of old St Martin's at the time of its demolition, and in March 1726, just before the consecration of the new church, Gibbs was elected a member of this august body.[67] His friendship with some of its members, among them Alexander Gordon, George Vertue, Humfrey Wanley (Harley's librarian at Wimpole) and William Maitland (author of the *History of London, From Its Foundation By the Romans, to the Present Time*, 1739, which describes many of Gibbs's metropolitan buildings), and their common interest in both classical and medieval artifacts was significantly to enrich Gibbs's architectural ideas. In 1729 he was elected a Fellow of the Royal Society.[68]

Two years earlier Gibbs had been appointed to the only government post he was ever to hold, Architect of the Ordnance, through the favour of his old patron the Duke of Argyll, who was Master-General. The post was for life at an annual salary of £30, rising to £120 after 1729. It was reported that Gibbs 'found it almost if not merely a Sinecure'[69] and what contributions he may have made remain unclear, but certainly the appointment reinforced a growing sense of both professional and domestic security. This is reflected, for instance, in his places of residence in London. In 1713 he had lodgings in Chandos Street, Westminster; in the next year he may have been living in Burlington Street, north of Piccadilly, but by 1725 had moved to 18 Gerrard Street near Leicester Square, presumably in order to be near St Martin-in-the-Fields. Then from Michaelmas 1725 he took long leases on several terrace houses in Henrietta Street, opposite the Marylebone Chapel on Harley's newly formed estate (Plate 231). His own residence (demolished unrecorded in the mid-nineteenth century) was located on the north-east corner with Wimpole Street, its back garden overlooking the grounds of Lord Bingley's Cavendish Square mansion.[70]

During the next decade Gibbs's reputation increased. The *Daily Post* in 1731 linked him with Henry Flitcroft and Edward Shepherd as 'three famous Architects',[71] and while James Ralph censured the Strand church as 'nothing but a cluster of ornaments [which] will always please the *ignorant*, for the very same reasons that it is sure to displease the *judge*', he regarded the portico of St Martin-in-the-Fields as 'at once elegant and august', and its steeple as 'one of the most tolerable in town', while most of his Westminster Abbey monuments were also well received.[72] In the same year, 1734, Dr Richard Mead, the royal physician, proclaimed Gibbs 'eximio architecto' in appreciation for building his library at 49 Great Ormond Street, Holborn (Plate 238). This reputation depended to a considerable extent on Gibbs's method of instruction on classical design demonstrated in *Rules for Drawing The several Parts of Architecture*, which he published in 1732 and again in 1738 and 1753. In this capacity, as we shall see, he is mentioned often in Robert Morris's *The Art of Architecture, A Poem. In Imitation of Horace's Art of Poetry*, 1742.[73]

Meanwhile, he was building or improving a number of country houses and gardens; from 1726 to 1738 he collaborated at Stowe with the Royal Gardener Charles Bridgeman and later with 'Capability' Brown. In London he built 16 Arlington Street (Plate 234) and 25 Leicester Square. From 1728 until shortly before his death he was occupied with rebuilding St Bartholomew's Hospital, which Maitland described as 'the most stately and magnificent of its kind of any in *Europe*, and probably upon Earth' (Plate 240).[74] Vertue reported in 1746 that he 'has fortund very well ... by his industry and great business of publick & private works'.[75] Yet many schemes were aborted: houses at Arundel, Down, Kedleston, Kirkleatham, Kiveton, Lowther, Milton, Raby, Sacombe, Weston Underwood and Wiston went no further than preparatory drawings; Hampstead Marshall was begun in 1739 but abandoned soon after on the death of the owner; Adderbury and Whitton were lost to another architect, Roger Morris, Catton to William Smith, Kirtlington to John Sanderson and Trewithen to Thomas Edwards. Ostracized publicly for his involvement in corruption arising from the disastrous attempts to rebuild medieval Bishopsgate in London, Gibbs lost one of the outstanding public commissions of the period, the new Mansion House for the Lord Mayor of London, to George Dance the elder. Nevertheless, in 1737 Gibbs succeeded the recently deceased Hawksmoor as architect of the Radcliffe Library and created over the next decade what a later biographer considered 'perhaps the grandest feature in the grandest of all English architectural landscapes' (Plate 283).[76] The occasion of his appointment in 1737 was celebrated with sittings for two portraits, one by the celebrated Florentine painter Andrea Soldi, who settled in England in 1736, the other by a little known portraitist named John Michael Williams (Plate 5). Both show Gibbs holding preliminary plans for the basement and first floor of the Library; since these correspond to plans engraved in 1737 and issued as *Bibliotheca Radcliffiana* in 1737 and 1740 and differ in important features from the building as erected, both portraits must date sometime between those years and not later. Now in his middle fifties, a corpulent double-chinned Gibbs wears a full-bottomed powdered wig and a velvet coat over

5. John Michael Williams, Portrait of James Gibbs, *c.* 1737–40, oil on canvas, (National Portrait Gallery, London)

6. Bernard Baron, after William Hogarth, Portrait of James Gibbs, 1747, engraving (author's collection)

JACOBUS GIBBS ARCHITECTUS.

a brocaded silk waistcoat; his arm rests on a volume of *A Book of Architecture* and nearby is the slimmer *Rules for Drawing*. The early provenance of the Soldi portrait is unknown but Williams's was probably painted for the Duke of Chandos, who died in 1744.[77] A third portrait (Plate 6), engraved by Bernard Baron after a lost drawing by William Hogarth, was first shown framed in a surround of the architect's own design as the frontispiece to his book *Bibliotheca Radcliviana: or, A Short Description of the Radcliffe Library, at Oxford*, 1747. The form was probably suggested by van Audenaerd's engraved portrait of Carlo Fontana of 1691 and the format by the vignette on the title page of Kent's *Designs of Inigo Jones*, 1727, which uses the celebrated Van Dyck portrait. But the idea of incorporating the image of the living author in such an ostentatious manner was unheard of in British architectural publications up to that time and is a further indication of Gibbs's unflagging self-confidence.[78] Lady Luxborough, in writing to thank William Shenstone of The Leasowes for lending her his copy of *A Book of Architecture*, remarked that she 'never yet could admire his taste in Architecture . . . even his genteelest things he disgraces commonly with some awkward ornament. His building at Cambridge [probably the Senate House] I have seen, but never could like. Pardon me for giving my opinion, which is of no value: it cannot hurt Mr Gibbs'[79], so unassailable was his position by this time. A version of the 1747 portrait, also engraved by Baron but with a different surround and showing the architect placed in a columned room, was issued in 1750 to commemorate the events at Oxford of the previous April described at the beginning of this chapter. Gibbs presented an oil portrait by an unknown painter to St Mary's Hall, Oxford, in 1749 and three years later a replica by Williams of his earlier portrait was given to the Bodleian Picture Gallery. Subsequently James McArdell issued mezzotints after these.[80]

Designing and supervising the building of the Radcliffe Library demanded much of Gibbs's time from 1737 until its opening and seems to have impeded the growth of other areas of his practise. Nevertheless, work also continued unabated at Stowe until 1748 and at St Bartholomew's into the next decade; but when on 6 July 1749 the Governors wished to confer a letter of appreciation for the great services performed by him towards the Hospital, they were informed their architect had set out for Aix-le-Chapelle at the beginning of June.[81] He had been advised to attend the baths there, having been long afflicted with kidney stones, an extremely painful disease which caused loss of appetite and weight, sometimes leading to dropsy, and which could be relieved by morphine but was at that time incurable.[82] Its effects are visible in Soldi's second portrait (Plate 7), which seems to have been painted around 1746,[83] and helps to explain Gibbs's sudden relinquishment of the St Bartholomew's surveyorship. By 1745 workmen were already submitting estimates to George Dance the elder, a newly elected governor, and in 1748 the Hospital's steward took over the role of surveyor although, because of his inexperience, William Robinson, one of the City carpenters, was appointed in March 1749.[84] Gibbs remained at Aix until September 1749 and then returned to London.[85] Nevertheless, around this time two impressive new houses were begun, Bank Hall at Warrington (Plate 159) and Patshull Hall near Wolverhampton (Plate 161). The latter had to be completed by a local architect William Baker, and the splendid interiors at Ragley Hall, begun around 1750, remained unfinished for several decades (Plate 164). Little more is known about Gibbs's final years.[86]

On 9 May 1754 he made his Will, bequeathing 'the worldly goods which God has given me', including £1,000, all his plate and three houses in Marylebone with a total annual rent of £280 to Lord Erskine 'in gratitude for favours received from his father the late Earl of Marr'. To John Sherwine of Soho he left £1,400, two houses in Marylebone and Argyll Ground, Westminster, having rents of £125 per annum ('the houses and money

7. Andrea Soldi, Portrait of James Gibbs, *c.* 1746, oil on canvas (National Galleries of Scotland, Edinburgh)

to be disposed of as he shall think proper'), £100 'for a private charity which is to be expended as his [Sherwine's] daughters shall direct', and 'the residue of my money which shall be left over and above the payment of my debts legacies and funeral expenses'. To Robert Pringle of Clifton he left £400 and a Cavendish Square house valued at £120 and to Cosmo Alexander, a Scottish painter, 'my house I live in withall its furniture as it stands with pictures bustoes etc'. John Borlack, 'many years my draughtsman', received £400, as did William Morehead; £100 each went to William Thomas, Dr William King of Oxford, St Bartholomew's Hospital and the Foundling Hospital. The Radcliffe Trustees were given 'all my printed books, Books of Architecture books of prints and drawings

books of Maps [totalling nearly 700 volumes] and a pair of Globes with leather covers
to be placed . . . in the library . . . of which I was Architect . . . next to my Bustoe'.[87]
A few months later, on 5 August, Gibbs died at his house in Henrietta Street. The obituaries
praised him unanimously as 'an eminent architect', 'well known for his great Abilities
in Architecture. as appears by his printed works, as well as publick and private Buildings'
and 'justly esteemed by good men of all persuasions, being courteous in his behaviour,
moderate with regard to those who differed from him, humane and charitable'.[88] He was
buried four days later, according to his Will 'in a leaden coffin [the body] whole and
intire', charging his executors not to 'exceed one hundred and twenty pounds or
thereabouts' for the funeral, and commissioning Walter Lee, a local mason, to make a
modest marble wall tablet, which was set up in Marylebone parish church[89] 'with a short
Inscription . . . as shall be thought fit by my Executors':

> Underneath lye the Remains of JAMES
> GIBBS Esqr. whose Skill in Architecture
> appears by his Printed Works as well
> as the Buildings directed by him,
> Among other Legacys & Charitys
> He left One Hundred Pounds towards
> Enlarging this Church.
> He died Augt. 5th. 1754.
> Aged 71.

An obituary in the *Scots Magazine* in 1760 praised his buildings as 'lasting evidence of
this great man's superior abilities as an architect',[90] and John Gwynn's important book
*London and Westminster Improved*, 1766, claimed that 'No architect, except Sir Christopher
Wren, ever had a better opportunity of displaying his genius in the great stile of architecture than Gibbs . . . and he has acquitted himself upon the whole tolerably well'.[91] His
work also attracted the interest of Continental writers. In *L'État des Arts, en Angleterre*,
published in Paris in 1755, André Rouquet praised St Martin-in-the-Fields (the only
church discussed in the book apart from St Paul's Cathedral) and its architect for 'l'élé-
gance de son goût, et la solidité de son jugement'[92] and Francesco Milizia published an
enthusiastic account of the Radcliffe Library and Gibbs's book about it 'ad esempio anche
in ciò de' buoni Architetti antichi, imitazione che gioverebbe parimenti ai moderni', in
*Le Vite de' piu celebri Architetti*, 1768.[93] A few condemned Gibbs's work. In *The Grecian Orders
of Architecture*, 1768, Stephen Riou thought he had 'a better opportunity than most artists,
to display his talents in the great style of architecture . . . But [his] taste . . . has thrown
no new light upon the art',[94] and James Dallaway imagined Gibbs, 'aware that he was
censured for want of grace, [therefore] determined . . . to obviate all objections [and]
aimed at elegance, but could not accomplish even prettiness [He] indulged his love of
finery in architecture, and has crowded every inch of surface with pretty decorations.'[95]
Horace Walpole felt in 1771 that his buildings, 'without deviating from established rules,
proved . . . that meer mechanic knowledge may avoid faults, without furnishing beauties;
that grace does not depend on rules; and that taste is not to be learnt . . . no man talks
of one edifice of Gibbs'.[96] On the contrary, he became the most widely discussed of
eighteenth-century British architects, and accounts of his life and achievements, derived
mainly from Walpole but usually discarding his adverse criticisms, appeared frequently
throughout the nineteenth century. And one edifice in particular, St Martin-in-the-Fields
(Plate III), became the most widely quoted model in the English speaking world.

# II

## 'WITH YOUR FRIEND JEMMY GIBBS ABOUT BUILDING AGREE'

MUCH OF WHAT Gibbs's contemporaries regarded as his most important contributions to the architecture of his time was summarized by Robert Morris in *The Art of Architecture, A Poem. In Imitation of Horace's Art of Poetry*, published in 1742. He reckoned, for example, that

> GIBBS may be said, most Times in Dress to please
> And few can decorate with greater Ease[1]

Certainly few British architects of this generation were better trained or more erudite. In 1711, a few years after settling in London, he was among the sixty founder members of Sir Godfrey Kneller's Academy of Painting, which provided a drawing class in a house in Great Queen Street near Lincoln's Inn Fields at an annual subscription of one guinea. There he mixed with Steele's 'ingenious Sett of Gentlemen', a cosmopolitan world of native and foreign artists, of whom Gibbs seems to have been the only professional architect. Some of its members were to become friends and collaborators: the painters Michael Dahl, Hans Hysing, John Smibert and John Wootton, the sculptor Francis Bird, the engraver and diarist George Vertue.[2] Then, on 18 December 1716 at the Three Tun Tavern, Gibbs was admitted to one of 'the Tip top Clubbs of all, for men of the highest Character in Arts' (called 'Vandykes clubb' in respect to its founder, or the Club of St Luke for 'Virtuosi [in] London'). Members included William Aikman, who was soon to paint Gibbs's portrait, his collaborator in gardens Charles Bridgeman, his chief sculptor Michael Rysbrack (as well as Grinling Gibbons, Sir James Thornhill, William Talman, William Kent and again Dahl, Vertue and Wootton). Three years later Gibbs served as the club's annual Steward, who was obliged to provide on the name day at one of 'the greatest Taverns in London, in a splendid Manner' a dinner of Westfallen ham, although often 'generous minds added more [with] every person paying a Crown [and] the Surplus . . . pay'd by the Steward'.[3] This was apparently not the same company to which Gibbs belonged in the next decade (although it shared some of the same membership) called the Rose and Crown Club or 'Rosa Coronians', which also 'mostly consisted of the Eminent Artificers in this Nation', who met at a tavern in Covent Garden piazza on Saturday nights. Vertue has left sketches of a lost conversation picture of 1724–5 by the Scots portraitist John Smibert showing groups of gentlemen with 'Jacopo Gibbs' and Alexander Nisbet, an Edinburgh painter, paired on either side of a stove.[4] Another club member, the Swedish

8. (above) Gawen Hamilton, 'A Conversation of Virtuosis', 1734–5, oil on canvas (National Portrait Gallery, London). From left to right: George Vertue, Hans Hysing, Michael Dahl, William Thomas, James Gibbs, Joseph Goupy, Matthew Robinson, Charles Bridgeman, Bernard Baron, John Wootton, John Michael Rysbrack, Gawen Hamilton and William Kent

9. Sir James Thornhill, Edward Harley's Virtuosi, c. 1721, pen and wash over pencil (Art Institute of Chicago, The Leonora Hall Gurley Memorial Collection). From left to right: James Thornhill, Humfrey Wanley, Matthew Prior, Michael Dahl, James Gibbs and John Wootton

artist George Englehardt Schröder, painted Gibbs's portrait some time before 1725.[5] In the 1730s we find him involved in yet another gathering of artists and connoisseurs that usually met at the King's Arms, New Bond Street, a noted tavern. Gawen Hamilton painted two conversations of this group, dated around 1730 and 1734–5 (Plate 8). Both are set in handsome, if probably imaginary Palladian interiors which Gibbs could well have designed.[6]

This last group seems to have been an offshoot of the Virtuosi formed by Edward Harley, 2nd Earl of Oxford just before 1720, as Kneller's Academy splintered into various factions. Vertue praised the Earl's 'noble generous mind and ample fortunes [which] he freely spent to raise emulation and the encouragement of Arts in every kind. especially those of Painting Sculpture & buildings'.[7] Harley had been introduced to Gibbs early in 1713, perhaps through a kinsman, Lord Mar, and he remained his chief patron until his death in the early 1740s. Gibbs also worked for other members of the Harley circle: Lord Dupplin, Lord and Lady Barnard and the Duke of Leeds. Christian Richter, a Swedish miniaturist in watercolour, painted Gibbs's portrait around 1724 and he also sat to Christian Frederick Zincke and Michael Dahl, all of whom belonged to this clique.[8] Thornhill, yet another member, in a sketch for a large conversation piece probably intended for Wimpole Hall, shows Dahl painting a portrait of the Earl's poet Matthew Prior flanked by Thornhill himself, Wootton and Humfrey Wanley, while Gibbs points to an arcade reminiscent of St Mary-le-Strand (Plate 9).[9] This group was a particularly amicable one, for there is Thornhill's testimony of their uproarious journey from London to Wimpole in 1721 as well as meetings at Matthew's 'Palace' in Duke Street and at Down Hall, where they drank Harley's 'healths over and over, as well in our civil as bacchanalian hours' and talked 'of building, pictures and—may be, towards the close—of politics or religion'.[10] Gibbs was also involved in the formation of the famous Harleian library at Wimpole, not only as its architect but in a more modest way, for in 1724 he sent Wanley nine books 'desiring to know if any of them are for my Lords turn'.[11] It seems likely that this early involvement with the family kindled his interest in collecting books and works of art.[12]

A visitor to Gibbs's house and office in Henrietta Street, Marylebone, some time after 1725 would have seen an impressive collection of some 117 paintings by various old masters, although probably not all these were authentic, for it was the custom of the time not to 'disdain to place In the same Room Coppys of such famous pictures as are not to be purchased'.[13] There were also contemporary works by Canaletto, Panini, Sebastiano Ricci and Watteau. Of this collection only a seascape by Willem van der Velde can now be identified from a blue mezzotint engraving by Elisha Kirkall (Plate 11).[14] There was as well some notable sculpture: a 'Masterly' copy of a bust of *Flora* by François Girardon which Gibbs had received by Matthew Prior's Will of 1721, and in the same year he had a version made of Antoine Coysevox's marble bust of Prior; the original he subsequently incorporated in the poet's Westminster Abbey monument (Plate 94).[15] These pieces were joined by two other marbles commissioned from Rysbrack: the disconcertingly wigless bust of the architect himself carved in 1726 and the fine bust of Alexander Pope (Plate 10). Gibbs had been the great poet's architect at Twickenham in 1719–20 (Plate 148) and at first their friendship flourished but even before the portrait's completion in 1730 it was attacked as one of the sculptor's 'Monsters from the Parian Stone'.[16] Pope's disappointment seems to have been taken out on his architect, for he commented soon after, 'I am persuaded that by S-d . . . this Nobleman's Builder [is] meant to be *Gibs*'.[17] Nor did Pope subscribe to *A Book of Architecture*.

10. John Michael
Rysbrack, Portrait of
Alexander Pope,
1725–30, marble
(Athenaeum Club,
London)

Gibbs's membership of these art clubs and especially Edward Harley's Virtuosi per-
formed an important function beyond providing introductions to prospective clients.
Throughout his career he tended to collaborate with the artists and craftsmen who moved
in these circles, a number of whom not coincidentally either lived or speculated on Harley's
Marylebone estate. There was Bridgeman, Rysbrack and Wootton, the architects Roger
Morris and George Shakespeare, the masons Walter Lee, George Mercer and Alexander
Rouchead, the joiners and carpenters John Lane, Thomas Phillips and Benjamin Timbrell,
the smiths Thomas Goff and Thomas Wagg, and the plasterers Henry Elkins, Isaac
Mansfield and William Wilton.[18] Some of these artists, as well as others with whom Gibbs
worked, subscribed to *A Book of Architecture*.

Gibbs seems not to have had any pupils, with the possible exception of Lord Mar, nor
did he maintain an office in the strict sense of the term. But his bank account at Drummonds records a fledgling payment of £10 on 17 July 1724 to one Burlock, who emerges
in subsequent entries as John Borlach and is undoubtedly the same person rewarded in
Gibbs's Will with £400 for being 'many years my draughtsman'. Nothing is known about
Borlach's career before this association. He supplied a perspective view of Kinross House

near Edinburgh which was engraved and eventually published in William Adam's *Vitruvius Scoticus*, 1812, although originally it may have been an independent job associated with John Slezer's *Teatrum Scotiæ* of 1693.[19] Later Borlach issued a set of ten small engraved *Designs of Architecture, for Arches or Gates* which shows his debt to Gibbs (Plate 12). Borlach's sudden appearance in 1724 coincided with the preparations for publishing *A Book of Architecture* (Plate 111 is dated 1725), and his chief responsibility during the next three or four years must have been to prepare the finished drawings for engraving, and presumably in subsequent years also for *Rules for Drawing* and the Radcliffe Library publications. This was certainly his role with regard to the designs proposed by Edward Holdsworth and revised by Gibbs for remodelling Magdalen College, Oxford, which were intended for the *University Almanack* of 1730 or 1731. Holdsworth mentions in a letter of 1729, 'Berlow, who draws the designs ... What [he] will expect for his work I know not. Mr Gibbs who might have inform'd me, having been out of town almost ever since I have been here ... I can only say He [was] at a great deal of trouble, wch you will soon be convinc'd of when you see the draughts.'[20]

Few sketches by Gibbs survive, for they must have been discarded once the finished drawings were made. One for the saloon at Sudbrook (*c.* 1715) shows the way he developed the architectural framework and merely indicated areas for further decorative embellishment (Plate 141). The remaining surviving drawings, numbering in their hundreds, served more specifically formal functions (Plate 286). Carefully centred on the sheet, neatly rendered in brown pen, sometimes with grey wash and shaded to give a dimensional effect, occasionally with pink or yellow washes indicating wall-sections of unbuilt areas, they are a reminder of Gibbs's training in the academic tradition of the Italian Late Baroque. Some were sent to clients for approval.[21] One of a set for remodelling the Jacobean hall at Hartwell, Buckinghamshire (*c.* 1740), for example, is annotated 'This Window side to be as designed by Mr. Gibbs Excepting in the Height of the Wainscot which must be but three feet Seven Inches; by Order of Sr: Thos: Lee [the owner]'. In a letter to the governors of St Bartholomew's Hospital dated 27 July 1730 Ralph Allen, who was supplying Bath Stone for the new buildings, concurred 'that the utmost care shou'd be taken in forming of the Agreement to prevent future misunderstandings ... I cou'd not propose any Method to answer this purpose So wel, as a Larg Plan of each Side of the

11. Elisha Kirkall, after Willem van der Velde, *Seascape with ships*, inscribed 'Ex Collectione Jacobi Gibbs Architecti', undated, green mezzotint (Bodleian Library, Oxford)

12. John C. Borlach, *Designs of Architecture, for Arches or Gates*, undated, engraving (Massachusetts Institute of Technology Libraries, Institute Archives and Special Collections, Bulfinch Collection)

building wch: is to be Erected, drawn by Mr Gibbs on the same Scale which the Ornaments
that you Lately sent me was made by, and this Plan to be fix'd to the Articles for our
guide, and if the drawings shou'd in any instance be defective, Let that defect be Supply'd
by an explanation in writing on the Plan its self.'[22] However, few such working drawings
survive. For major commissions requiring more than casual sketches, full sets were presented to the client and these were undoubtedly also used by the builders during construction.
It was sometimes Gibbs's practice to provide alternative designs on attached flaps, as at
St Martin-in-the-Fields, Hampstead Marshall and the Radcliffe Library. In a commission
from the Myddletons for a new library at Chirk Castle, Denbighshire, he was provided
with a plan from which it was hoped he 'will design something handsome' without having
to visit the site at all. Nearly two dozen finished and bound drawings for the new building
of Hampstead Marshall in Berkshire, dated 1739 (Plate 156), include before and after
plans showing those seventeenth-century features of the burnt-out house which were to
be retained rendered in lighter wash, as well as alternative treatments of the entrance
bays and attic and some tentative pencil amendments (not necessarily contributed by
Gibbs). At Catton Hall in Derbyshire, a commission snatched away in 1741 by another
architect and perhaps of only peripheral interest to Gibbs, who was then preoccupied
with supervising the building of the Radcliffe Library, he adopted a shortcut by providing
one drawing for the entrance front which was to serve for two otherwise separate, alternative designs. His method of offering variant solutions for the treatment of the main interiors
of houses is demonstrated in a comprehensive set of drawings for Kelmarsh Hall in
Northamptonshire (Plate 127), which until recently remained in the house. At Milton
in Northamptonshire in 1726, where he competed with a local architect named Robert
Wright, whose ideas were similar to his own,[23] Gibbs bombarded the client with eight
carefully rendered alternative designs, two of which are illustrated in *A Book of Architecture*
accompanied by unusually long descriptions (Plate 129).

The vestrymen of St George's, Hanover Square, in London, hoping for a design for
their new church, reported in 1720 that Gibbs 'will be diligent to the Last degree, for
our satisfaction, as well as his own Creditt to performe this affaire wth: all possible care'.[24]
How then did he organize the work of his major commissions? Early in his career, between
1713 and 1715, he gained much practical experience as one of the surveyors to the Commission for Building Fifty New Churches. Either independently or in collaboration with his
co-surveyor Nicholas Hawksmoor, Gibbs reported on a number of potential church sites,
sometimes making surveys or site plans and charging 14s. to 19s.6d. for this service. For
the Pardon churchyard site in St James's parish, Clerkenwell, he made 'a Plan, Specifying
how much of the said Ground will be Sufficient to build a Church, and Ministers House',
while the soil at the Three Cups Inn, St Andrew's parish, Holborn, was found to be a
solid bed of gravel 10 feet from the surface, capable of carrying any weight. The two
architects were ordered to stake out the ground for the church to be erected at Stockwell
in 1715 and in the same year Gibbs, Hawksmoor and Wren signed a report relating to
ground in Lower Wapping. The co-surveyors also dealt with building operations. In 1714
they drew up the workmens' bills for the new churches at Greenwich, Deptford and Wapping and recommended the vaulting at St Alphege as 'Extreamly Beautifull as well as
Convenient . . . for keeping the pavement drye, for preservation of the Pews, for Security
of the fabrick' and added that 'If it is not vaulted the Paving will never lye even . . .
the pews will always be in a Rotten and Damp Condition, the Walls will be undermined
wth. Sepulture . . . The difference of the Expence in fitting it up with earth, and vaulting
it is not more than—£200'. In June 1714 they noted that the plastering of Greenwich

church should properly be done 'during the best of the Summer that the Worke may be thoroughly Dry before any frost take it' and stonework at St John's should rise only eight feet so 'that the Mortar may have time to Set and the Walls harden, to Avoid bracks and Settling'. Gibbs and Hawksmoor were especially concerned with the quality of brick-work, for example reporting that those used for the East End churches were 'Common place Bricks, mixt with Sea Cole Ash—After the Infamous way of the City of London'. In 1717, after losing the surveyorship to John James, Gibbs nevertheless remained among the 'divers Eminant Surveyors' consulted on the purported imminent danger of the collapse of St George's Chapel in Ormond Street 'through some Weakness and irregularity of the Walls and Roof (whereby many persons have been terrifi'd and still continue Exceedingly discouraged from coming to the publick Worship)'; both Gibbs and James 'proposed several Remedies for these Evils'.[25]

Gibbs's manifold responsibilities at St Mary-le-Strand and St Martin-in-the-Fields included designing not only the churches but most of their details and furnishings. Many individual drawings were prepared for the building committees' approbation, but few survive, perhaps because they then passed into the hands of specialist craftsmen for execution. However, the wooden models made in 1714 and 1721 to provide the Commissioners with a more realistic idea of the completed churches' appearances, and subsequently used as vehicles for altering and perfecting the designs during their construction, remained in Gibbs's possession during building operations (Plates 15, 40). He also surveyed sites, approved building materials, vetted craftsmen's work, checked estimates and bills, advised on matters of construction and generally supervised the daily progress of the work.

Gibbs maintained a close relationship with his craftsmen, many of whom subscribed to *A Book of Architecture* and were employed by him elsewhere. He was thanked for his great services performed at St Bartholomew's Hospital, which included 'Drawing several plans and designs of the new Building; and by his readiness at all times to advise and assist the Committee, in making Contracts with the several Workmen'.[26] This included, for example, advising Ralph Allen in 1736 to inform the committee of his choice of workmen so 'Gibbs and he may Consult together of means for the Building to go on that one may not wait . . . or be hindered'.[27] Gibbs evidently felt the success of the great enterprise of building the Radcliffe Library was partly due to the superior performance of his craftsmen, and uncommon in the architectural literature of the time he lists them in *Bibliotheca Radcliviana*, 1747, and thanks the Trustees on behalf of 'all Persons employed by you [who] do honour you for your punctual Payments, and great Diligence in seeing every Part put in Execution, with the nicest Oeconomy and Equity'. The work of these craftsmen were often interdependent. For example, the St Martin's joiner Charles Griffith, who made the pew fronts to Gibbs's 'good liking', also supplied a walnut-tree wood pattern for the altar rail which was wrought by the smith Thomas Goff.[28] At St Mary-le-Strand the carver made proposals for the ornaments executed by the joiner, while the joiner made patterns for the hinges and bolts of the altar rail and pulpit for the smith's use; the carpenter made several patterns for the stone *œils-de-bœuf* over the east window, while the masons drew flowers on the ceiling as a pattern for the plasterers. These artisans, in turn, were obliged to submit detailed specification agreeing to use 'good Stuff well turned up and wrought in the best manner, and finishd with a good coat of white haird Stuff'. Proposals for St Mary-le-Strand were submitted in 1717 by James Ellis, who had worked at the Greenwich and Deptford churches, and Chrysostom Wilkins, a more experienced craftsmen employed at St Paul's Cathedral and later at St Martin's, who got the Strand job because he was the cheapest (in 1718 he received £3,178.7.8 for the completed plaster work).[29] At St Martin's in 1724 Gibbs laid before the Commissioners 'Two Designs for the Frett Work for the Ceiling . . . marked with the Letters A and B . . . the Board Approved and Agreed That . . . B being the richest Work should be the Design'. Isaac Mansfield estimated £471.12.0 for the plain plaster work, Wilkins £415.9.6 with an additional £257.10.0 for the ornamental work, but a lower quote of £250 submitted by Giovanni Bagutti was accepted. Bagutti was a Swiss *stuccatore* in partnership with Giuseppe Artari, whom Gibbs regarded as 'the best Fret-workers that ever came into *England*' and 'the most proper person to be Employed' (Plates 52–3).[30] Bagutti also agreed in 1722 to execute the ornamental work in the Marylebone Chapel 'in good workmanlike manner . . . performed to the satisfaction of James Gibbs' (Plate 60).[31] Unlike his other craftsmen, Gibbs permitted the *stuccatori* more freedom of interpretation.[32] William and John Townesend, who contracted at St Mary's 'to find all Masons Materials, as workmanship, Sawing Labor, also all manner of Carriage, Scaffolding, Tools and Tackle, together with Working, raising and setting', were in charge of a large work force. They complained in 1715 that several of their men had threatened to leave because of the lack of space to store a sufficient quantity of stone to keep them in work through the winter, 'when Shipps Cannot come,' and in 1717 the Commissioners, hearing that these men were too rowdy in celebrating the completion of the steeple, reprimanded Townesend and ordered him 'to Endeavour, to prevent all such Disorders for the future'.[33]

   With the Strand church Gibbs gained the necessary technical skills, as an incident he related to the Commissioners in 1722 makes clear: 'I was this Afternoon inspecting the Brickwork of the Church . . . and upon finding the materialls and worke insufficient have putt a Stop to the Work.' This resulted in the removal of six defective layers at the bricklayers' own expense and the dismissal of the Clerk of the Works; it was also agreed that 'the Brickwork forthwith be inspected by Mr. Surveyour'.[34] The sensible approach of his detailed report on the condition of Lincoln Minster in 1725, where he noted damage to the west towers, and his remedy of filling in the westernmost bays 'to hinder the weight of the . . . towers from squeezing the peers further', was later complimented by James Essex the younger, who agreed that the walls Gibbs inserted under the towers had succeeded in relieving a great part of their lateral pressure.[35]

   Gibbs sometimes collaborated with other architects. In 1719 the Duke of Chandos, thanking Lord Bingley for advice on the designs for Cannons House, commented that 'Mr. Gibbs was certainly very much in the right to apply himself to your Lordship, whose judgement, he knows very well, I have the greatest opinion of & to whose good taste I shall always readily submit my own'.[36] Francis and William Smith, who in 1707 had been regarded as pretending 'to no great Skill in designing, being plain countery workmen, yet having built very many houses',[37] had by the 1720s risen to become the leading architects in the Midlands and worked as Gibbs's contractors at Ditchley and Derby, while Francis's son William joined him at the Radcliffe Library. At Magdalen College, Oxford, Gibbs was associated with Francis Smith and the amateur architect Edward Holdsworth; also with William Baker at Patshull, Lancelot Brown at Stowe, Roger Morris at Whitton and James Essex the elder at Cambridge. In 1725 Gibbs wrote the Vice-Chancellor of the University regarding Essex that 'the customary way [to pay craftsmen] is to imprest money from tyme to tyme, as they doe in the fifty Churches and other publick buildings, and that his worke be inspected from tyme to tyme according to the money payd him, for it's not to be expected that every man has the same command of money or the same credit, so I think if he has 200 or 300£ at first to enable him to buy his wainscot at the best hand and 100£ some tymes as he is found to goe forward'.[38] The carpenter's bill for work in the Fellows Building at King's College in 1730 is countersigned by Essex and James Horne. The latter, a London joiner, collaborated with Gibbs at King's College, Cambridge, and at St Bartholomew's Hospital, and his drawings for St Mary's at Ealing and Christ Church, Surrey (1735–41), not only incorporate many Gibbsian features, but the draughtsmanship is close enough to Gibbs to suggest Horne may once have been a pupil or assistant.[39]

In another letter to the Vice-Chancellor of Cambridge University in 1730 Gibbs explained 'how I am generally payed. I have at London five per Cnt of the total expence of the Building whither great or small, and if ther are any exterordinary drawings made they are payed for. And if I goe to the Countray I am allowed my Coach hire.'[40] This practice is confirmed in his testimony at the lawsuit between Benjamin Styles of Moor Park and his architect Sir James Thornhill in 1730, which is mentioned in a letter from Nicholas Hawksmoor's widow to Lord Carlisle of Castle Howard: 'Mr Gibbs for designing and Surveying St. Martins Church had 5£ p Cent on near 40,000£ which amounts to 2000£', although Gibbs claimed he received only £550 for this commission, which took six years to complete (1721–7).[41] In 1738 the Radcliffe Trustees agreed Gibbs should be paid £100 annually for designing and supervising the building of the Radcliffe Library and 'drawing all plans that shall be necessary for Compleating that work & Corresponding wh the Builders & going down four times in Every year to see the Building . . . & all other Demands & to Continue for so many years as the Trustees shall think proper to Employ him'. Ten years later, when the major building operations were completed, he had received £1,292 from a total cost of £43,226.6.3.[42]

Gibbs's standard charge for single or small sets of drawings ranged from 5 to 10 guineas; the accounts for Wimpole (1719–21) list payments from one guinea each for drawings for the chapel altarpiece, an urn, a bridge and an obelisk to 3 guineas for stables and summer houses, 10 guineas for the house elevations 'more carefully drawn' (Plates 111–12) and £21 for the Newcastle monument in Westminster Abbey and for enlarging the drawing for the terracotta model. The Kirtlington Park accounts (1741) show he was paid £30 for a set of about a dozen plans and elevations. As one of the New Churches surveyors his salary was fixed in 1713 at £200 per annum and he received an additional £121.19.0 for seeing to the making of the wooden models.[43] He charged £300 for drawings and supervising the construction of the Fellows Building at King's (1724–9),[44] while in his consultative role at Magdalen in 1728 the College authorities did not consider it 'proper to offer him less [than 20 guineas as] a handsome Gratuity . . . for his advice and assistance', Edward Holdsworth adding 'I have not yet pd Him [but] will do it as soon as I think He has deserv'd it'.[45] In the domestic field the Duke of Chandos paid Gibbs £5,500 between 1716 and 1719 for designing and supervising work at Cannons House. Nothing is known of what he was paid for work at Ditchley, but his contractor there, Francis Smith, notified the owner, Lord Lichfield, that between 1723 and 1725 he had distributed approximately £7,850 to workmen 'without any profit to myself. I hope Yor: Lordship will not think much to allow me five pounds for every Hundrd. I have paid, & for my own Trouble, Journeys, proffit out of my workmen, & measuring the Work.'[46] The Dowager Duchess of Norfolk agreed in 1734 to pay Gibbs £300 to inspect the new house in Arlington Street being built according to his plans, and for surveying the building until completion. As architect of St Bartholomew's Hospital for twenty-six years he offered his services gratis, but even so Vertue could report from London in 1746 that Gibbs 'has fortund very well here, by his industry and great business of publick & private works'.[47]

Only the episode concerning payment for work at the London Mansion House proved

unamicable. The City Lands Committee had invited Gibbs to prepare designs as early
as 1728, but after much discussion he lost the commission in 1737 to George Dance the
elder. Acquainting the Committee early in the following year of having taken a great
deal of trouble in drawing plans for two sites, he considered he could not ask less than
200 guineas; yet they voted him only half that amount.[48] How had Gibbs managed to
lose this important commission to an incontestably lesser talent? It is true that his building
estimate of £30,000 was higher than Dance's, but there is also evidence of anti-Catholic
feeling among the City aldermen, which a Captain De Berlain took advantage of in recommending his own design for the Mansion House as 'a perpetual Monument to posterity,
for the happy Revolution, & for the delivrance, of Popery'.[49] Moreover, a story circulated
widely at the time relates how Burlington had offered for the same competition 'an original
design of *Palladio*' which was rejected because it was 'notorious' that the Italian was neither
a Protestant nor a Freeman of the City.[50]

But more significant than such incidents were the tensions which had grown between
the metropolitan-based architects with national reputations and those architects and
builders working more or less exclusively for the City of London. The writer André
Rouquet condemned the City's indiscriminate preference for their own men and saw the
Common Council as consisting 'entirely of people in trade: their choice [of Dance] fresh
proof of the little analogy between the spirit of commerce and a taste for the arts'.[51] The
breach intensified during 1733 and 1734 around the publication of James Ralph's *A Critical
Review of the Publick Buildings, Statues and Ornaments In, and about London and Westminster*.
Championing the work of Lord Burlington, his circle and architects on its fringe, including
Gibbs, it remarked in the Dedication that 'Folly in building is one of the most lasting
reflections on a man's character, because 'tis not only universally known in his own time,
but is often perpetuated thro' many generations. It is incumbent, therefore, on every man
of quality and fortune, to weigh very seriously every undertaking of this nature, and not
precipitate himself into an expence, that neither convenience, or grandeur can justify.'
Ralph was attacked in a series of twenty-eight articles published by Batty Langley in
*The Grub-street Journal* between May 1734 and July 1735. 'It is somewhat hard', he
observed, 'that a noble-man or gentleman cannot lay out six or eight thousand pounds
of his own upon a house for himself, and in laying it out, execute two or three of his
own whims, (which tho' they may not be strictly agreeable to true taste, yet hit his own)
but some critic must immediately stigmatize him in print for it.'[52] Langley thought that
the 'architects by whom most of our buildings were designed [Jones, Wren, Hawksmoor,
Campbell, James and Gibbs] have always been esteemed by the best judges to have been
equal to any who lived before them: and these gentlemen had very carefully considered
the beauties and defects, in the general orders of the Greek, Roman, and Gothic architecture'; nevertheless, Langley condemned Gibbs's work for its failure to conform to what
he considered accepted interpretations of classical vocabulary. In particular he attacked
his use of 'small black rustics [in] a low mince-pye taste', the so-called Gibbs-surround
motif based on Palladio's Palazzo Thiene and first applied to the steeple of St Clement
Danes (Plate 20). At St Martin-in-the-Fields (Plate 27) this breaking of the 'architraves
and freezes . . . by the key stones, is a most terrible absurdity [since it] interrupted . . .
two of the finest ranges of pillasters and columns yet erected, either by ancients or moderns
[and] extreamly diminish the solemn grandeur of this edifice'. Langley also thought the
cupola of St Clement Danes's steeple 'a most intolerable clumsy performance' and the
profile of St Mary-le-Strand 'much the worst of any in or about London . . . The many
breakings of the entablatures, and the different pediments over the upper windows may

please the ignorant: but a judge would have been glad to see the entablature entire' (Plate 17).[53] In *The Builder's Jewel*, 1741, Langley developed this particular criticism by observing that 'we may daily see open Pediments placed without-side . . . But, surely, nothing can be so absurd, unless 'tis the placing of an entire Pediment within-side a Building, where no Rain can fall; as done by Mr. *Gibbs*'[54] in the Strand church (Plate 21).

The controversy did not stop there. William Stukeley, the antiquarian, ridiculed those 'modern *London* builders, who carve every moulding and crown every ornament, which they borrow out of books'.[55] In turn, in *The Builder's Director, or Bench-Mate*, 1751, Langley censured *The Architecture of A. Palladio, as* revised and published by Giacomo Leoni in four volumes between 1715 and 1720, because it 'consists chiefly of Designs of Palaces, Bridges, and Temples, which to Workmen are of little Use; and as those Books are of large Prices, beyond the Reach of many Workmen, and too large for Use at Work; I have therefore, for the common Good, extraced . . . all that is useful to the Workmen [and] made fully as plain and intelligible, as they have done in their large Folio's, and at so easy a Rate, as to be purchased by any common Labourer'.[56] Langley would certainly not have approved of *A Book of Architecture*, which, as stated in the Introduction, aimed at

such Gentlemen as might be concerned in Building, especially in the remote parts of the Country, where little or no assistance for Designs can be procured. Such may be here furnished with Draughts of useful and convenient Buildings and proper Ornaments; which may be executed by any Workman who understands Lines, either as here Design'd, or with some Alterations, which may be easily made by a person of Judgment; without which a Variation in Draught, once well digested, frequently proves a Detriment to the Building, as well as a Disparagement to the person that gives them. I mention this to cautious Gentlemen from suffering any material Change to be made in their Designs, by the Forwardness of unskilful Workmen, or the Caprice of ignorant, assuming Pretenders. SOME, for want of better Helps, have unfortunately put into the hands of common workmen, the management of Building of considerable expence; which when finished, they have had the mortification to find condemned by persons of Tast, to that degree that sometimes they have been pull'd down, at least alter'd to a greater charge than would have procur'd better advice from an able Artist; or if they had stood, they have remained lasting Monuments of the Ignorance or Parsimoniousness of the Owners, or (it may be) of a wrong-judged Profuseness.

Nor were Langley and his fellow practitioners likely to have been sympathetic to Robert Morris's homage to Gibbs as the author of one of the most successful books on architectural instruction.

> Why should the few, the Rules which I impart,
> Be construed ill, be Scandal to the Art?
> When GIBBS, so copious, so enrich'd has been,
> No Part's obscure, but all are useful seen.
>
> Learn of PALLADIO, how to deck a Space;
> Of JONES you'll learn Magnificence, and Grace:
> CAMPBELL will teach, the Beauty they impart;
> And GIBBS, the Rules and Modus of the Art[57]

Morris is referring to *Rules for Drawing The several Parts of Architecture*, published in 1732 and again in 1738 and 1753, which contains designs for triumphal arches, doors, windows, chimneypieces, ceilings, balconies and decorative details (Plate 306). But its primary value was in presenting the vocabulary of classical architecture in a 'More exact and easy manner than has been heretofore practiced, by which all FRACTIONS, in dividing the principal MEMBERS and their Parts, are avoided'. This system derived from Claude Perrault's *Ordonnance des cinq especes de colonnes selon la méthode des anciens*, 1683.[58] Some of the plates were taken from Palladio's *I Quattro Libri d'Architettura* (Gibbs owned both the 1601 and Leoni editions); and in the text he acknowledges the great architect's method of 'dividing and adjusting his Order [as having] excelled the rest, [and] whom I have therefore followed'. Palladio as well as Antoine Desgodetz's *Les Edifices Antiques de Rome dessinés et mesurés tres exactement*, 1695, are frequently cited by Gibbs as his authorities in descriptions of Roman architecture in the 'Short Cursory Remarks', and an important part of his library was devoted to the standard books by Alberti, Blondel, Cataneo, Daviler, Franchini, Fréart, Perrault, Scamozzi and Vignola; he also subscribed to *A Treatise of Architecture*, 1723, Ephraim Chambers's translation of Sebastian Le Clerc.

The idea of *Rules for Drawing* may already have been in his mind by 1728 when William Stukeley, tracing the invention of architecture to Egypt, observed that 'Vitruvius himself was as farr to seek in the origin of the corinthian capitall, and other matters of that sort, as a Campbell or Gibbs would be'.[59] The new book was advertised in the *Monthly Catalogue* for May 1732 as available from the author's Marylebone residence at £1.11.6, and similar announcements appeared in the press.[60] Gibbs devoted 'great Labour and Expence' on its production; there were no subscribers, but the 64 plates were sponsored by Edward Harley, to whom he dedicated the book as a way of 'publickly testifying my Regard to so generous and universal a Patron [whose] extensive Knowledge and good Taste command the Esteem of all that profess or love the Liberal Arts and Sciences'. A Royal Privilege and Licence issued on 19 May 1732 and bound in the book allowed the author sole printing and publishing rights for a term of fourteen years and strictly forbade 'all our Subjects . . . to reprint or abridge . . . or to import, buy, vend, utter, or distribute any Copies . . . reprinted beyond the Seas . . . without [Gibbs's] Consent or Approbation'.[61] Nevertheless, he hoped his 'Method . . . will be acknowledged by proper Judges to be the most exact, as well as the easiest, that hath as yet been published [and] will be found so beneficial to workmen in drawing any part at large . . . that when they are once accustomed to it, they will never follow any other'. The book was 'very much esteemd [in] great demand [and] taught in most of the drawing Schools in London'.[62] Inevitably it attracted plagiarists. In *Ancient Masonry, both in the Theory and Practise, Demonstrating the Useful Rules of Arithmetick, Geometry, and Architecture, in the Proportions and Orders of the Most Eminent Masters of All Nations*, 1734–6, Langley acknowledges this debt to Gibbs, but in *The City and Country Builder's and Workman's Treasury of Designs* (first published in 1740), which also derives in part from Gibbs, he could not resist remarking in the Introduction that in the instructions on interpreting the Orders, the 'Designs of *Inigo Jones*, Mr. *Gibbs*, and all other Masters of this Time, are defective in, and consequently are of no more Use to Workmen, than so many Pictures to gaze at' (Gibbs's name, however, was removed from the 1750 edition). Edward Oakley's *The Magazine of Architecture, Perspective and Sculpture*, 1730–3, and Edward Hoppus's *The Gentleman's and Builder's Repository*, 1737, also reproduced without acknowledgement some plates from *Rules for Drawing*. Perhaps because of this Gibbs published a second edition in 1738, priced at one guinea, with loose sets issued in twenty-one weekly numbers at one shilling each 'for the Convenience of those who don't chuse to purchase the Whole together'.[63] With Hawksmoor and John James, Gibbs also recommended Francis Price's *The British Carpenter*, 1733, as 'a very Usefull and Instructive Piece', and *The Builder's Dictionary: or Gentleman and Architect's Companion . . . Faithfully Digested from the most Approved Writers on these Subjects*, 1734, as containing 'a great deal of useful Knowledge in the Building Business'. An advertisement for the second volume of the dictionary refers to Hawksmoor, James and Gibbs as 'Gentlemen whose Abilities and long Practice in the directing and surveying of numberless Publick and Private Buildings, have rendered them unexceptionable Judges'.[64] Pope wrote:

> Must bishops, lawyers, statesmen, have the skill
> To build, to plant, judge paintings, what you will?
> Then why not Kent as well our treaties draw,
> Bridgeman explain the gospel, Gibbs the law?[65]

Robert Morris further praised Gibbs as an accomplished arbiter in building disputes.

> He that intends an *Architect* to be,
> Must seriously deliberate, like me;
> Must see the *Situation, Mode* and *Form,*
> Of every *Structure*, which they would adorn:
> All Parts *External*, and *Internal*, view;
> Before they aim to raise, a something new.
>     Ask *G——s*, or *F——tc——t*, to correct your Plan,
> They'll freely, when you err, instruct the Man,
> In what's amiss, with Judgment, and with Care,
> Where needfull *add*; and where profusive; *spare*.[66]

In a letter of 1731 from Ralph Allen concerning additional stonework not itemized in his contact with the governors of St Bartholomew's Hospital, he says he was told that the customary method of adjusting matters of this nature was for each of the parties to choose an experienced person as arbitrator, and therefore 'what Mr Gibbs or any other Gentn: of knowledge in Building . . . Shall Judge this Extra Work to be worth I wil be Satisfied with'.[67] Gibbs became involved in this business early in his career. Although one of his clients commented in 1719 that 'Architects will be modest when they Canvass the performances of those of their own trade',[68] in that same year he was among a group of architects and builders who signed a report by Benjamin Jackson, Master Mason in the Office of Works, concerning the inadequate repairs recently made to the House of Lords; this resulted in what proved to be the chief architectural scandal of the day, the dismissal on grounds of incompetence of William Benson as Surveyor-General and Colen Campbell as his Deputy and Chief Clerk.[69] Between 1720 and 1728, with Nicholas Dubois, Thomas Barlow, Benjamin Timbrell and on one occasion Campbell, Gibbs adjudicated a number of disputes arising from building agreements on the newly created Grosvenor Estate in Mayfair, although there is no evidence that he supplied designs.[70] In a contract witnessed on 5 June 1723 between Edward Harley's steward William Thomas and Henry Elkins for 'All the Brickwork of One House in Henrietta Street [built] according to a Design . . . made by James Gibbs . . . all the work [was] to be pformed to the Satisfaccion of . . . Mr. G. who is to determine all disputes that may arise'.[71] Three years later Gibbs and a Mr Scaplehorne were appointed to reckon a fair payment to the carpenter and bricklayer for rebuilding St Bartholomew's out-hospital at Kingsland, Hackney.[72] In 1732, the year *Rules for Drawing* first appeared, Gibbs was appointed with a group of local carpenters, joiners and masons to advise on repairing the Marylebone burial ground, one of several such parochial responsibilities.[73]

Then, during the early 1730s, he was involved in a series of unsavoury City of London disputes which contributed to his disastrous rejection by the Mansion House building committee in 1737. The City Lands Committee had in 1723 rejected a modest scheme (costing £353.15.0) for repairing the venerable medieval Bishopsgate, one of the principal entries along the City's northern boundary, in favour of erecting a new structure designed by the Clerk of the Works 'consistant with the Dignity and Grandeur of this great City'. Groups of local builders submitted estimates ranging from £648 to £1,000, and the lowest one, offered by a Westminster carpenter named Edward Smith, was approved. But when in March 1733 the contract came to be signed, Smith alleged the design had not been drawn up according to his proposal and that he would not build according to the said plan, for if he did he would be a very great looser. In the following month Gibbs arbitrated in favour of the Clerk of the Works's design, which he considered would 'last for ffive hundred Years and more'. Smith still refused to honour the contract and was dismissed (he subsequently fought and won a lawsuit against the City). Meanwhile, a mason named Christopher Horsenaile agreed to build the official design for £950, and the episode would probably have passed without further notice had not the new, partly constructed gate begun to collapse in October 1733. Gibbs now had a change of heart and, with a number of other architects called in to arbitrate, including John Price, George Sampson, Edward Shepherd, John James, John Townesend and George Dance, regarded the disaster as due to the Clerk's faulty design. He was dismissed and the exonerated Horsenaile was charged with repairing the Gate, which finally opened in 1735.[74] This affair upset both London builders and politicians. There was suspicion of favouritism and mismanaged funds, and in an electioneering pamphlet entitled *City Corruption and Mal-Administration Display'd*, 1738, Smith's friends exposed certain Aldermen and Common Councilmen for practising 'the wicked Arts of Deceipt, Misrepresentation and Falsehood . . . in order . . . to uphold themselves in that Power they have so shamefully abused, to the great Dishonour of the City'. It cited particularly those occasions when 'the most exorbitant Sums have been demanded, and receiv'd for any Work, and no Opposition been given to the Undertakers'. The members of this apparently dubious fraternity included Christopher Horsenaile and John Townesend, both of whom had worked for Gibbs on other occasions, as well as some dozen prominent members of St Bartholomew's Hospital, five of whom served on the City Lands or Mansion House committees or both and some of whom had subscribed to *A Book of Architecture*![75] The pamphlet, therefore, is largely an indictment of their misdemeanours connected with the Mansion House, but it provided a ready vehicle for exposing other instances where 'all the meanest Tricks, Evasions, and Artifices have been used to make a good Job [for them and] to exclude every other Citizen from having any chance for the same Work'. Gibbs was involved in three of the most controversial of these, which the pamphlet enumerated in detail. Of Bishopsgate it concluded that 'so shamefully and abominably ill is this Work performed, notwithstanding the monstrous Expence to which the City has been put [£1,730.5.5 instead of £648], that in the Judgment of all experienced Workmen, it cannot possibly be of long Duration, because this Edifice is really a perfect Cripple, and propp'd up, since its first Failure, only by Sleight of Art, not upheld by solid, honourable and skilful Workmanship'. (The Gate was sold for £141 and demolished in 1760.) Of a proposal in 1733 for filling-in the Fleet Channel, a matter of some public concern, Gibbs favoured a solution costing £4,000 submitted, it was claimed, by 'a Person, wholly unacquainted with Workmanship of this Nature'. And, in the affair of the Moorfields railings in 1732–3, although this modest improvement was to have cost £628, the builder delivered a bill for £1,100.12.0, *City Corruption* commenting that

This Procedure meeting Encouragement, instead of Condemnation from your Rulers, rouz'd a just Spirit of Resentment amidst the disinterested Part. However, the Artificer's Friends, who constituted the Committee of City Lands, in order to screen their good Ally and Associate, very artfully proposed to leave the whole to Arbitration . . . Accordingly Mr. G— is proposed by the Committee; a Person wholly unskilled in Business of this Nature, and easily wrought upon to allow whatever should be insinuated as just. This *Gentleman* formally pretends to measure the Work, and brought in his Account [to the] Sum of 1100*l.* 12*s.* Iniquity being suspected in this Matter, the Opposition prevailed that Mess. *James* and *Dance* should remeasure the Work [their estimate came to £638.15.0] . . . Workmen of the greatest Ability and Integrity have declared, that this Work is perform'd in a very ill manner, both with Regard to Execution and Contrivance.[76]

Although Gibbs arbitrated for the City on two further occasions, in 1740–1 in connection with the disputed estimate of £972.15.4 submitted by the carpenter for making the great wooden model of Dance's Mansion House, and two years later with regard to conflicting estimates for rebuilding a warehouse for the Fishmongers' Company, both of which were resolved amicably,[77] his estrangement from the London building world was inevitable.

Gibbs continued, however, to be involved in similar arbitrations in the country. In 1741 William King of Oxford wrote to the Bristol Exchange building committee criticizing John Wood the elder's winning design for the vagueness of its masonry specification and for the lack of a wooden model, for only with one 'nither you nor the Workmen can be deceived'. He suggested 'before it is too late [to] ask advice of some Man that is a Judge of designes and work such as Lord Penbrook or Burlinton Mr. James or Mr. Gibbs all now in being and I am sure would be glad to give their opinion on it'.[78] During the following two years Gibbs was involved in the complicated dispute surrounding the dilapidated medieval parish church at Tetbury in Gloucestershire. Early in the 1740s William Smith, one of the masons employed at the Radcliffe Library, and George Tully, a Bristol architect, inspected the repairs recently made to the fabric but disagreed about the word 'workman-like' used in the recognizance. On 28 July 1742 Tully recommended either Gibbs, James or a Mr Barrat to serve as 'Umpire'; Gibbs was 'pitch'd upon'. He came down in September with John Townesend and John Phillips, both then employed at the Radcliffe, but 'went away, without declaring any Opinion . . . and without giving . . . Tully a sufficient Opportunity of talking with him . . . and answering the several Objections wch . . . Smith might have made . . . and even refusing . . . to send his thoughts of the Matter . . . that they might have the Opportunity of . . . rectifying any Mistakes, or Misapprehensions'. Gibbs eventually reported on 25 October that he had examined every part of the church and recommended that it

had been better pulled down and new built than repaired the Walls in some Places being much out of an Upright and in many Places cracked and decayed and having ordered several Places of the Walls to be opened . . . to view the several Cracks . . . found the same filled up with small Stones and Mortar and Whitened over to deceive the Eye and tho' the new Walls . . . appeared . . . to be of Substance enough Yet [he] could not observe that there were any Bond Stones to tie the Outside and Inside together Nor are the Scantlings of the Timbers of the several Roofs so strong as they ought to be Nor properly framed for the Support of the Slate Covering.

Subsequently, Henry Flitcroft made further minor repairs and the church was finally rebuilt by Francis Hiorn in 1771–81 in the Gothic style.[79]

Although Gibbs too occasionally designed in that style, it was hardly his penchant, and Robert Morris, in *The Art of Architecture*, placed him firmly in the forefront of the classical revival.

> *R-y*, in *Rustick* heavy Buildings still,
> Attempts in vain to please, or shew his Skill;
> How far he strays from the pure *Roman* Stile,
> And labours on in DULNESS all the while!
> With *M—s, F—ft, G—s, L—i, W—e*,
> Let ADMIRALTY, or CUSTOM-HOUSE compare.[80]

Gibbs's training was unusual for more than its foreign locale. His teacher, Carlo Fontana, was not only the leading Roman Baroque architect at that time, but also had a strong interest in classicism and the Antique, a dicotomy which is reflected in his pupil.[81] Little of Gibbs's juvenilia survives, but his interests as a student in Rome are made clear in the 'Short Cursory Remarks' of 1707. He looked primarily at contemporary buildings and the work of Fontana's immediate predecessors. Their influence is particularly felt in St Mary-le-Strand, which combines features from the Palazzi Nari, Falconieri and Barberini (Plates 17–19), the internal vaults of the Gesù, which Gibbs thought extraordinarily fine, and those of S. Nicola da Tolentino, 'one of the finest Churches in Rome for it's bigness',[82] and Fontana's apse in SS. Apostoli.[83] The idea of introducing a royal statue over the portico of the Strand church (Plate 17), which was considered briefly in 1714, may have been inspired by Fontana's temporary decoration for the facade of S. Antonio de' Portoghesi erected on the occasion of the memorial service to King Pedro II in 1707.[84] Borromini's west wall in S. Giovanni in Laterano and the shell-headed niches in S. Carlo alle Quattro Fontane are sources used in the chapels at Cannons and Wimpole, and in the Cambridge Senate House (Plates 26, 57, 254).[85] Although the rejected designs for a 'Round Church' for St Martin-in-the-Fields (Plates 28, 50) derive ultimately from the Roman Pantheon—Gibbs made copies of Fontana's reconstructions illustrated in *Il Tempio Vaticano*, 1694 (Plate 30)—he was also aware of its recent progeny, including the twin churches in Piazza del Popolo, the church of the Collège des Quatre Nations in Paris and probably the Superga near Turin (1717–31), designed by Filippo Juvarra, who was Gibbs's fellow-student in Fontana's office and had visited London late in 1720.[86] Gibbs owned a copy of Juvarra's *Raccolta Di Targhe*, 1722, and a collection of his original drawings for cartouches, which were the inspiration for the sixty-two designs for 'Compartments for Monumental Inscriptions' published in *A Book of Architecture*.[87] The companion designs for vases, described as being in the Antique manner but largely Baroque in appearance, derive from Fontana's *Utilissimo Trattato Dell'Acque Conventi Diviso*, 1696, L. F. Rossi's *Raccolta di Vasi Diversi*, 1713, and other such engraved books.[88]

Gibbs expressed a desire to visit Paris and Versailles during 1717–18,[89] and his interest in the French Baroque at this time is evident in the proposals for Alloa and Dupplin Castle (Plates 97–9) and in the improvements at Burlington House (Plates 226–9) and Cannons (Plate 107). He also made a copy of the plan of Hardouin-Mansart's Pavillion du Roi at Marly,[90] and with a characteristic feeling for Gallic convenience he adapted this arrangement to the 'Passage of communication betwixt the Hall and Withdrawing-Room [so the] Octagonal Room may be private or publick at pleasure' in a villa dated 1720 in *A Book of Architecture* (Plate 297). The curious foliated bases of the vault of the saloon at Sudbrook (Plate 142) were inspired by an illustration of an 'Ordre Attique' from Lavergne's *Livre Nouveau De L'Art D'Architecture*, bound in a volume owned by Gibbs which also includes a set of designs entitled *Trophées Inventez et gravez par Pierrets le Jeune*, 1666, which are the source for the decorative panels of the saloon doorcases (Plate 144). The doorcases themselves come from the Palazzo Altieri in Rome (Plate 143).

Italian and French Baroque sources became less important for Gibbs after the early 1720s, except in his church monuments (discussed in Chapter V). However, he maintained contact with current architectural activities in Rome throughout his life, commenting, for example, on the Trevi Fountain (1732–62) and the new facade of S. Giovanni in Laterano (1733–6).[91] This helps to explain the apparently anachronistic appearance of Baroque ideas late in Gibbs's career, as in the ceiling of Witley chapel (Plate 73),[92] or the Radcliffe Library porch vaults (Plate 281), which come from Borromini's S. Carlo alle Quattro Fontane, and the reading room dome (Plate 276), which owes something to Bernini's S. Andrea al Quirinale.[93]

Giuliano di Baccio's campinale of the Church of the Madonna di S. Biago at Montepulchiano was the model for the steeple of St Martin-in-the-Fields and for the Kirkleatham Mausoleum (Plates 39–41, 268) and Gibbs may have consulted Bramante's upper court of the Belvedere in the Vatican in composing the side elevations of the 'Wide' design for St Mary-le-Strand (Plate 16). He admired Brunelleschi's dome of Florence Cathedral as the boldest piece of architecture in Italy, and in Venice studied the work of Sansovino, 'which shews him to have ben one of the greatest Artists in his time', as well as Scamozzi and Palladio.[94] Except for his use of Palladio's domestic designs, however, Renaissance themes do not appear in Gibbs's work with any consistency and his interest in classicism, what Morris called 'the pure *Roman* Stile', centered around the Antique.

Especially important for his progress towards classicism were Fontana's improvements of Antique and Early Christian buildings in Rome, notably the colonnaded portico of S. Maria in Trastevere (1701), and the work of his son Francesco, who was in charge of the reconstruction of the Temple of Neptune as the Dogana di Terre (1694–1705) and of raising the colossal Antique column of Antoninus Pius—the subject of P. S. Bartoli's *Stylobates Columnae Antoninae*, 1708, which was in Gibbs's library.[95]

Gibbs also owned a drawing from the Fontana circle for the projected facade of S. Giovanni in Laterano (Plate 13) which demonstrates the use even within the extremes of High Baroque of a series of colossal single *free-standing* columns recalling the heroic grandeur of Imperial Rome.[96] Here is one of the hallmarks of the resurgence of early eighteenth-century classicism, so much so that a French visitor to England in 1728 observed that 'present [architects] are obsessed with a mania for columns, and use them everywhere'.[97] This is particularly true of Gibbs. Through Fontana's example he embraced classicism during his student days, and a substantial section of the 'Short Cursory Remarks' is devoted to 'Roman Antiquitys' prefaced with the observation that the 'Authors who have wrote on the Magnificence of the Antient Roman buildings have carried the fame of them all the world over, to the Admiration of all who have read them; they wer so noble and great, that their very ruins shew what Rome was once, when these statlely fabricks wer intire. Its surprising to see the vast remains . . . The magnificent Triumphal Arches, Historical Columns, Mausoleums . . . Prodigious Massive Obelisques . . . and large Pillars.' This is followed by brief 'Remarks on the rebuilding of Rome and of its having layen in Rubbish many hundreds of years'. Antoine Desgodetz's *Les Edifices Antiques de Rome*, 1695, and Palladio's *I Quattro Libri d'Architettura*, 1601, are often cited as authorities. Gibbs notes the practice of refurbishing ancient buildings as churches, such as the Temple of Antoninus and Faustina, which was converted into S. Lorenzo in Miranda and given a 'new Roofe [and] very handsome front to the body of the Temple, within the ancient

38

13. Circle of Carlo Fontana, Design for San Giovanni in Laterano, Rome, 1699–1708, west elevation, pen and wash (Ashmolean Museum, Oxford, Gibbs Collection III.32)

portico'. He also endorsed the progressive idea of adapting classical temple forms for modern Christian use, as in his designs for a London church of 1713 (Plate 31), or his first scheme for St Mary-le-Strand (Plate 32), which is modelled on the church of S. Maria Egiziaca, the former Temple of Fortuna Virilis, 'the finest antient Ionick building in Rome' (Plate 33).[98] A full hexastyle temple portico proposed around 1717 as the chief improvement for the Elizabethan mansion at Witham Park was based on the Portico of Septimius Severus as reconstructed by Desgodetz (Plates 101–103), and the temple-form was finally transformed into a highly individual structure at St Martin-in-the-Fields (Plate III).

In his domestic architecture after 1720, Gibbs most often turned to Palladio. While it has generally been assumed he followed the lead offered by his British contemporaries, particularly Colen Campbell and Lord Burlington, as a student Gibbs had visited numerous villas and palazzi in the Vincentine by Palladio, whom he called 'the great Restorer of Architectur.'[99]

In Gibbs's library were several editions of Palladio, Scamozzi and Vitruvius, Robert Castell's *The Villas of the Ancients Illustrated*, 1728, and Francesco Bianchini's *Del Palazzo De Cesari*, 1738, devoted to reconstructions of ancient Roman palaces; there were books illustrating other classical buildings, among them Alexander Gordon's translation of Count Maffei's *A Compleat History Of the Ancient Ampitheatres*, 1730, Jacob Lauri's *Antiquae Urbis Splendor*, 1612, Montfaucon's seven volume *L'Antiquité Explique*, 1719, Bonaventura van Overbeke's *Les Restes de L'Ancienne Rome*, 1709 and Peter Schenk's *Roma Aeterna*, 1705. Their influence is widely evident in his country houses and college buildings.

Gibbs's approach to classicism was first expounded in writing in *A Book of Architecture*. Perhaps cautioned by Colen Campbell's harangue in *Vitruvius Britannicus* against '*the Productions of the last* Century [the] *affected and licentious . . . Works of* Bernini *and* Fontana [the] *wildly Extravagant . . . Designs of* Boromini, *who has endeavoured to debauch Mankind with his odd and chimerical Beauties, where the Parts are without Proportion, Solids without their true Bearing, Heaps of Materials without Strength, excessive Ornaments without Grace, and the Whole without Symmetry'*, Gibbs firmly rooted his own manifesto in the tradition of classical teaching. He wrote in the Introduction

> In order to prevent . . . Abuses and Absurdities . . . I have taken the utmost care that these Designs should be done in the best Tast I could form upon the Instructions of the greatest Masters in *Italy*, as well as my own Observations upon the ancient Buildings there, during many Years application to these Studies: For a cursory View of those August Remains can no more qualify the Spectator, or Admirer, than the Air of the Country can inspire him with knowledge of Architecture . . . WHAT heaps of Stone, and even Marble, are daily seen in Monuments, Chimneys, and other Ornamental pieces of Architecture, without the least Symmetry or Order? When the same or fewer Materials, under the conduct of a skilful Surveyor, would, in less room and with much less charge, have been equally (if not more) useful, and by Justness of Proportion have had a grand Appearance, and consequently have better answered the Intention of the Expence. For it is not the Bulk of a Fabrick, the Richness and Quality of the Materials, the Multiplicity of Lines, nor the Gaudiness of the Finishing, that give the Grace or Beauty and Grandeur to a Building; but the Proportion of the Parts to one another and to the Whole, whether entirely plain, or enriched with a few Ornaments properly disposed.

By the time his book appeared in 1728, Gibbs had assembled a repertory of classical and Palladian types rivalled only by its two great recent predecessors, William Kent's *The Designs of Inigo Jones*, 1727, to which he subscribed, and *Vitruvius Britannicus*, 1715–25. But if *A Book of Architecture* was a reaction to the injuries suffered through professional rivalry (Campbell illustrated his designs for Burlington House and Witham Park without acknowledgement), it was even more an expression of the reputation Gibbs had recently established as a serious advocate of classical ideas—it will be recalled that later Dr King was to praise his 'knowledge of all Antiquity'—and of his links with institutions of classical learning in London. In 1726 he was admitted to the Society of Antiquaries, which had been founded nine years earlier 'to collect and print all Accounts of antient Monuments . . . and whatever may properly belong to the History of Bryttish Antiquitys'.[100] A fellow member, the Scottish historian Alexander Gordon, expressed these new ideas in the Preface to *Itinerarium Septentrionale: or, A Journey Thro' most of the Counties of Scotland, And Those in the North of England*, 1726, to which Gibbs subscribed:

> Where could our Modern Artists have recovered (after so many Centuries of Ignorance and Darkness) the noble Rules of Symmetry and Proportion in Architecture, were not the august Remains of so many Monuments of Grecian and Roman Buildings, still to be seen in pompous Ruin? And had we not, as yet, the stately Remains of the Colloseum of Titus Vespasian, his, and other Triumphal Arches, together with so many elegant Temples, yet standing in the Forum Romanum; would ever Posterity have seen . . . those of Palladio at Venice, the Banquetting-House by the great Inigo Jones, and many other magnificent Buildings, executed with such Symmetry and Taste? . . . Nor is it improbable, that if this fine Humour for Architecture subsist in the Nation, and such Buildings as the great Artist Mr. Gibbs has adorn'd London with, continues to be carried on, very few Cities in Europe (Rome excepted) will contend with it for Magnificence.

# III

## 'HIS FAIR DAUGHTER IN THE STRAND'

'I DOUBT NOT . . . her proving the most complete little damsel in town and doing honour to the parent', wrote Lord Mar in 1716. The damsel in question was Gibbs's 'fair daughter in the Strand',[1] the church which its architect claimed was 'the first publick Building I was employed in after my arrival from *Italy*'[2] and which shows his unusually self-assured handling of contemporary Italian Baroque ideas but belies the struggles and uncertainties he experienced during the designing and building stages (Plate 20).

St Mary-le-Strand was among the first to be considered by the Commission for Building Fifty New Churches, which was established by an Act of Parliament in 1711 for the purpose of building churches in London, Westminster and their suburbs. The Commissioners, who included Sir Christopher Wren, Sir John Vanbrugh and Thomas Archer, were prompted in the case of the Strand by the parishioners' petition to Queen Anne in November 1711 drawing attention to their present chapel in the Savoy which 'hath but one Isle, and that . . . in a very sad condition'.[3] No more was done until late in 1713 when several proposals were made by the Commissioners' surveyors Nicholas Hawksmoor and William Dickinson.[4] Gibbs's first design reached the model stage by February 1714 (Plate 32), but an independent scheme by Archer was approved on 29 April. Known only in a rough plan, its most interesting feature, the semicircular west portico, recalls his contemporary church at Deptford.[5] Gibbs was soon to take up a similar theme (Plate 17); possibly all three essays were related to the original unique example of S. Maria della Pace in Rome.

The variety of designs for St Mary-le-Strand considered during 1713–14 indicates the prominence accorded this building, which came to symbolize the achievement of the whole New Churches enterprise. Taking their cue from Vanbrugh, who conceived the churches as 'Monuments to Posterity of [the Queen's] Piety & Grandeur',[6] the Commissioners resolved in midsummer of 1713 that 'a Statue of her Majesty [to be made by Grinling Gibbons and Francis Bird] be set up in the most conspicuous & convenient part of each of the 50 New intended Churches'. However, the idea of multiple figures proved too ambitious and by April 1714 was replaced by a scheme for 'one Statue of her Maty in Mettal'. This was to be made by a celebrated sculptor in Florence so that, according to John Talman, who supervised the work, 'Strangers may not say of us [the English] . . . that we only think of eating & drinking; or as Erasmus hinted, that we only dispute about Religion, I wou'd have the world admire us for Polite people in Arts [so as not] to be out done in state by other Nations, when we have mony & opportunity to shew the World, that when we please, we can be as magnificent as any other country whatever'. The job went to Giovanni Battista Foggini, and by autumn 1714 Talman was able to

I. James Gibbs, Design for St Mary-le-Strand, Westminster, London, 1714, east end and steeple, pen and wash (Victoria and Albert Museum, London)

DANGER
MEN WORKING
OVERHEAD

report that the ten-foot-high gilt-bronze statue, costing £800, was the 'finest figure in Europe'.[7]

From the beginning this statue was to be associated closely with Archer's Strand church; and on 29 April 1714, the day his design was approved, the Commissioners also resolved that 'a Steeple in the Form of a pillar be built at the West End of the Church . . . wth: the Queens Statue on the Top of it, wth: Bases capable of Inscriptions, to perpetuate the memory of the building [of] the 50 New Churches'.[8] The wording seems to suggest a pillar-shaped steeple, as Hawksmoor and James were later to build at St John, Horsely-down (1727–33). Then on 1 July the Commissioners considered introducing an independent column at a point west of the Strand church approximately parallel to the entrance to old Somerset House and a week later approved Gibbs's wooden model (subsequently lost) for a 15-foot-diameter, 250-foot-high 'corinthian pillar' crowned by the Queen's statue and with lions at the corners of the base. This model was presented to the Queen, an event which Gibbs seems to depict in the pedestal relief of an alternative design for a colossal Doric column embellished with trophies and concentric bands of reliefs probably narrating episodes from Stuart history (Plate 14). Gibbs had much to say about the celebrated columns of ancient Rome, particularly Trajan's, 'one of the finest peeces of Architectur . . . now extant in the World . . . the beauty and grandeur of it appeared to the spectators like a wonder', noting the '*Bassorielevo* . . . history of the Dacian warr, finely expressed in beautifull figures', the 'Stair case . . . lighted by 43. small lights' and the fact that the original crowning figure was of the emperor 'holding a globe of Gold . . . in which wer his Ashes'.[9] Gibbs therefore found himself in the awkward position of having to build his Pillar as a complement to Archer's church, but the Queen's unexpected death on 1 August 1714 changed the character of the scheme radically and turned the tide of Gibbs's fortune. Work on the Pillar foundation, which had begun in mid-July, was halted on 5 August and a week later the Commissioners, now uncertain about the form the church should ultimately take, met to consider an alternative solution.

It must have been about this time Gibbs offered a new design (Plate 16), later published in *A Book of Architecture*, in which the elevations are divided into two nearly equal stories; each bay is separated by paired Ionic or Composite pilasters. At the west end a double-storey tetrastyle portico projects slightly from the body and is surmounted by 'a small *Campanile*, or Turret for a Bell' rather than a full steeple, so overpowering was the idea of the colossal Pillar. By this time the foundation of Archer's church, 48 by 116 feet, had been constructed, the surveyors reporting on 30 September 1714 that it had reached ground level and was 'redy to receive such Sort of fabrick as this Honorable board shall think fit to order for it'. Gibbs's proposed design, which measured 63 by 123 feet, was too large and so was rejected; the problem of resolving the building's form was further compounded because, despite the Queen's demise, the Pillar had not yet been abandoned. On 2 November both Gibbs and Vanbrugh delivered new proposals for the church, and finally two days later Gibbs's was judged 'most proper for the Scituation'. A wooden model corresponding in most details to the executed building was made at a cost of £32.10.0 (Plates 15, 18).

Gibbs's final solution amalgamated features from Archer's partly built but now abandoned design and his own now equally inappropriate wide design; yet in both cases the differences are as significant. Whereas Archer interpolated steps between each of the portico columns, using them to screen a drum-shaped vestibule from which rose the pillar-like steeple crowned by its royal effigy, Gibbs gave his portico a more classical appearance by raising the columns on an uninterrupted staircase-platform and crowning them with

14. James Gibbs, Design for the Pillar to Queen Anne, The Strand, Westminster, London, 1714, elevation, pen and wash (British Museum, London)

II. (facing page) James Gibbs, St Mary-le-Strand, Westminster, London, 1714–24, detail of south elevation

a saucer dome. This solution seems to have been dictated by the continuing vicissitudes of the Queen's statue. In September 1714, when John Talman reported to the Commissioners from Italy that Foggini's 'grand model for . . . casting the brass [bronze] Statue is almost complete, the brass is likewise in a great measure bought up', he was apparently aware of the uncertain future of the Pillar and suggested, 'Now that the Queen is dead & that it is not the custom in Brittain (in particular) to erect tombs to our Souvregns, what if [the statue] shou'd be so managed as to serve as a sort of a Honorary Monument or Mausoleum? . . . which woud render the town so beautifull, that it wou'd be worth a Travellers while to come to London on purpose to see them.' Talman himself later (in May 1715) offered a design in which the statue formed the centrepiece of an elaborate fountain attended by life-size bronze figures of the Virtues of Religion, Justice, Victory and Fame, which he visualized situated in the middle of Lincoln's Inn Fields; but an official document of March 1715 refers to the statue as 'intended to be fixed on Some conspicuous part of the New Church erecting . . . in the Strand' (Plate 17). Gibbs shows the Queen in a surprisingly unconventional position crowning the single-storey portico, a sort of modified pillar; the effect would have been as if the monarch herself, holding

15. (facing page) James Gibbs, St Mary-le-Strand, Westminster, London, 1714, view of west and north elevations of model, boxwood (Royal Institute of British Architects Drawings Collection, London, lent by the Marquess of Exeter)

16. James Gibbs, 'Wide Church' design for St Mary-le-Strand, Westminster, London, 1714, west front, Plate 23 in *A Book of Architecture*, 1728

17. James Gibbs, St Mary-le-Strand, Westminster, London, 1714–21, view of west and south elevations, Plate 21 in *A Book of Architecture*, 1728

18. James Gibbs, St Mary-le-Strand, Westminster, London, 1714, south elevation of model, boxwood (Royal Institute of British Architects Drawings Collection, London, lent by the Marquess of Exeter)

19. Francesco Borromini, Palazzo Barberini, Rome, 1634–41, detail of façade, engraving, Plate 39 in D. De 'Rossi, *Studio D'Architettura Civile . . . di Roma*, 1702

the sceptre and orb, had just emerged from the temple-like passage behind. He was familiar with this idea as it had been developed in the Italian Baroque and he would have known Carlo Fontana's early designs (1696) for the monument in St Peter's to Queen Christina of Sweden, where her majestic, full-length figure stands over a sarcophagus in a vaulted recess framed by engaged columns.[10] In the Strand model (Plate 18) Gibbs introduced a series of statues in the tabernacles on the north and south elevations, giving the church the appearance of an Antique sarcophagus and reinforcing Talman's notion of using the Queen's statue as part of 'a Honorary Monument or Mausoleum'. This sculpture programme again proved too ambitious: the side figures were never executed and the Queen's statue, of little significance to the new Whig-dominated Commission appointed in December 1715, was quietly replaced on both the model and the church itself by a flaming urn (Plate 20). These vicissitudes had a further notable effect: on abandoning the Pillar and concentrating the royal statue above the portico, Gibbs says he 'was ordered to erect a [loftier] Steeple instead of the *Campanile* first propos'd. [But the] Building being then advanced 20 feet above ground [to the top of the ground-storey windows], and therefore admitting of no alteration from the East to West, which was only 14 feet [the width of the westernmost bay] was obliged to spread [the steeple] from South to North, which makes the Plan oblong',[11] so creating the 'High and Bold Structure' recommended by Vanbrugh and giving a dramatic slab-like emphasis to the portico and statue, which would have been seen from a considerable distance along the Strand.[12]

It appears that as Gibbs gained confidence both in the special significance which this church seems to have taken on and in his own increasingly personal contribution to its design, he felt less obliged to conform to some of the Commissioners' recommendations. He followed Vanbrugh's notions that the church 'be so plac'd, [as] to be fairly View'd at such proper distances, as is necessary to shew their Exterior Form, to the best Advantage, as at the ends of Large and Strait Streets' and be 'Adorn'd with Portico's; [since] no part in Publick Edifices being of greater use, nor no production in Architecture so solemnly

20. (facing page) James Gibbs, St Mary-le-Strand, Westminster, London, 1714–24, looking towards St Clement Danes (steeple by Gibbs, 1719–20)

Magnificent'. But he rejected the idea that 'one general design, or Forme be agreed upon for all the fifty New . . . Churches were the Scites will admit . . . Towers excepted'[13] and Vanbrugh's insistence on 'a plain, but Just and Noble Stile, without running into those many Divisions and Breaks which other buildings for Variety of uses may require; or such Gayety of Ornament as may be proper to a Luxurious Palace'. Gibbs's handling of surfaces and ornament became increasingly more complex as he assimilated the New Churches requirements into his own, recent Roman experiences.

The Strand church is divided into two equal storeys, as in his earlier wide design, but with a more complicated surface pattern of various planes and recesses. Gibbs explains that the windows were concentrated in the upper storey, with the lower walls 'adorned with Niches [but made] solid to keep out Noises from the Street';[14] a foreigners' guide to London, however, soon reported that the church was 'too much exposed to the rattling of Coaches, which hinders the hearing of Divine Service plain enough therein'.[15] The overall decorativeness of the exterior (Plates I and II), so antithetic to the contemporary churches of Hawksmoor and Archer, was attacked immediately by some critics. Colen Campbell's design for a church in the 'Vitruvian Stile' (based on the Temple of Fortuna Virilis in Rome), which he published in *Vitruvius Britannicus* in 1717, was intended to demonstrate the abstention from 'any Ornaments between the Columns, which would only serve to enflame the Expence and clog the Building'. It was a rebuff to those 'trifling, licentious, and insignificant Ornaments, so much affected by some of our Moderns', and although not naming the Strand church, it is surely this building he had in mind when observing further the wholly unclassical practice of superimposing Orders on the outside of temples and of dividing the walls 'into little Parts'; 'whereas the Ancients were contented with one continued Pediment from the Portico to the Pastico, we have now no less than three in one Side where the Ancients never admitted any. This Practice must be imputed either to an entire Ignorance of Antiquity, or a Vanity to expose their absurd Novelties, so contrary to those excellent Precepts in *Vitruvius*, and so repugnant to those admirable Remains the Ancients have left us.'[16] James Ralph, a persuasive Burlingtonian voice against Baroque, was more explicit in condemning St Mary's as 'one of the strongest instances in the world, that 'tis not expence and decoration that are alone productive of harmony and taste . . . this church will always please the *ignorant*, for the very same reason that it is sure to displease the *judge*'.[17] Batty Langley, writing in *The Grub-street Journal*, was usually opposed to Ralph's opinions; but in this case he was equally contemptuous and regarded the church as 'much the worst of any in or about London . . . the whole is a mere groupe of absurdities'.[18] Many later writers agreed that the church was 'loaded with a redundancy of ornament' and 'cut up into littlenesses'.[19]

Because of the then unusually narrow, island site the Strand church interior, uniquely among its contemporaries, is a *single* chamber of only 38 by 64 feet, to which is appended the semicircular chancel (Plate 22). This enabled Gibbs to consider the space as an uninterrupted whole (Plate 21) in which uniform architectural components could be repeated along the walls as a means of achieving a simple homogeneity rather than the dramatic contrasts of space and light which preoccupied Hawksmoor and Archer. Langley criticized what he saw as the disparity between the absence of internal galleries (which is also unique among the New Churches) and the superimposed orders of the exterior.[20] Yet he apparently failed to notice that this tight, multi-layered articulation was translated on the internal north and south walls into a pattern of paired fluted Corinthian pilasters on *two* levels, the lower raised on a panelled dado, the upper resting on ornamented bases, with the pilasters repeated in the jambs to form modified Venetian windows corresponding

21. James Gibbs, St Mary-le-Strand, Westminster, London, 1714–24, interior towards chancel

to those on the outside. Furthermore, just as the portico and vestibule with its adjuncts echo the semicircular chancel and its flanking domed vestries, so the superimposed stories of engaged columns lying behind the portico and (as originally conceived) the royal statue, each with a rosetted barrel-vaulted passage, is duplicated as a two-tiered triumphal arch framing the chancel and carrying the royal arms. This close relationship between the west front and the chancel was worked out carefully, with adjustments made during construction: in 1717–18 John Townesend was paid for making models for the east end and the portico and for adapting the masonry at the west end to that of the portico upon its being advanced further than first designed. Again Langley ridiculed the chancel arch by observing in *The Builder's Jewel*, 1741, that 'As the entire Pediment by its reclining Surfaces carries off and discharges the Rains at its Extreams, therefore none but entire Pediments should be employed abroad . . . But, surely, nothing can be so absurd, (unless 'tis the placing of an entire Pediment within-side a Building, where no Rain can fall; as done by Mr. *Gibbs*').[21] Nor did Langley appreciate the vaulting (Plate 23), which he criticized as 'something curved, but not enough; much too near the eye, and much too full of ornaments', although Gibbs was careful to explain that he designed the Strand with squares and rhomboids because he considered this has a 'very good effect'.[22] These parallel bands of coffering framed by moulded and embellished ribs spring across the vault to bind the north and south walls. No other of the New Churches exhibits such a profusion of brilliant ornament, and in 1718 the surveyors warned that a 'Stop should be put to the extravagt. Carvings within' (Plate 24).[23] Undoubtedly the more flagrant effects of the Roman Baroque were mitigated by the original sombre colouring, which appears from the specifications to have consisted of white ceilings, a combination of white and an undesignated colour on the walls, and 'plain Colour on the Stone work & Carving over the Altar', further tempered by clear glazing in all the windows. Nevertheless, the writer of *A Tour Thro' the Whole Island of Great Britain*, 1761, who lauded London churches for

22. James Gibbs, St Mary-le-Strand, Westminster, London, 1714–24, plans, Plate 16 in *A Book of Architecture*, 1728

23. James Gibbs, St Mary-le-Strand, Westminster, London, 1714–24, nave vault

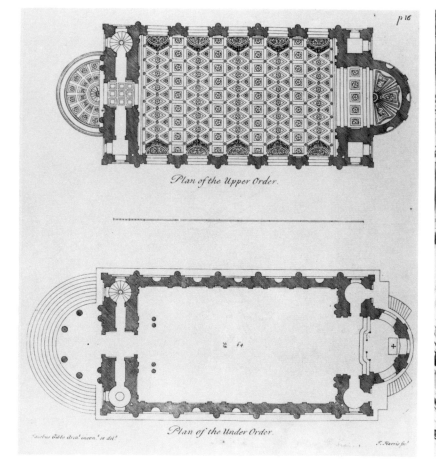

*Plan of the Upper Order.*

*Plan of the Under Order.*

their abstention from 'Pomp and Pageantry, as in *Popish* Countries; but, like the true Protestant Plainness, have very little Ornament either within or without', would have found little to admire here.[24] St Mary's blatantly Roman associations were probably the fundamental cause of Gibbs's dismissal as surveyor to the New Churches in the first week of January 1716, following closely on the appointment of a new, predominantly Whig commission in the previous month. On 13 January he wrote them an embittered yet optimistic letter:

> Having had a Summons . . . to appear before you this day, I must aquant you that I am sorcy I have not the honor to serve you as Surveyor . . . However I hope you will not be against my proceeding with the Church in the Strand, since I have caryed it up so farr to the intire satisfaction of every body, the Building can not be too fine for the situation, since it's so much in vive [view], and I will ingage it will answer the estimat, you yourselves shall state the prices of the workmen, your surveyours [now Hawksmoor and James] shall measur and inspect the work to save you from being cheated . . . this is so reasonable that I belive you would have condecended to have done, if I had not ask'd it.

Gibbs hoped that the church would 'gain me a reputation to recommend me to other business'.[25] The Commissioners acquiesced, and during the next eight years he controlled the building operations.

By August 1716 Gibbs was receiving payments from James Brydges, Earl of Caernarvon

24. James Gibbs, St Mary-le-Strand, Westminster, London, 1714–24, detail of chancel

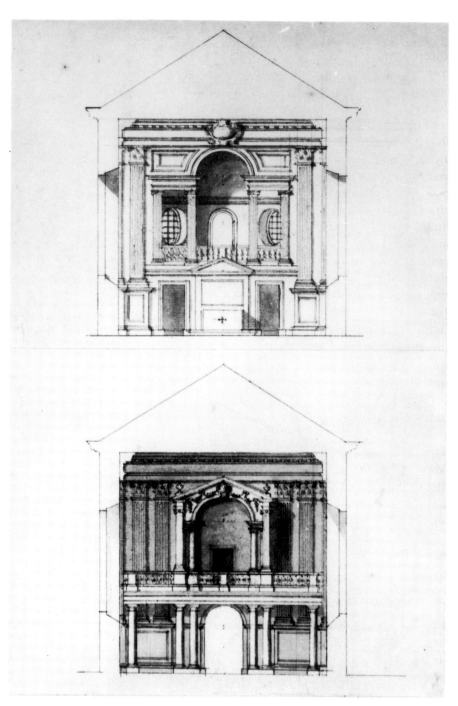

25. James Gibbs, Design for the chapel, Cannons House, Middlesex, 1716–20, plan, pen and wash (Greater London Record Office)

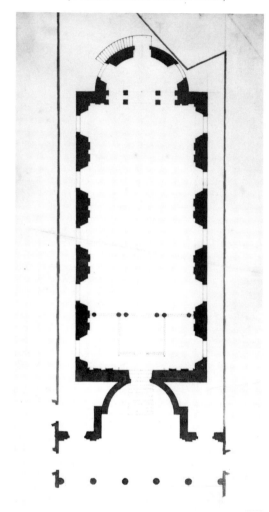

26. (right) James Gibbs, Design for the chapel, Cannons House, Middlesex, 1716–20, sections towards east and west, pen and wash (Greater London Record Office)

(later 1st Duke of Chandos), for remodelling Cannons House in Middlesex, including the addition of a private chapel which Daniel Defoe thought 'a singularity, not only in its building, and the beauty of its workmanship, but in . . . that the duke maintains there a full choir, and has the worship perform'd . . . with the best musick [Handel serving as *Kapellmeister*], after the manner of the chappel royal, which is not done in any other noble man's chappel in Britain'.[26] In 1715 Brydges completed rebuilding St Lawrence at Whitchurch on the southern edge of the estate, but his complaint to the architect John James, 'I fear it is not design'd so well as it ought to have been', may have precipitated Gibbs's appearance the following year.[27] He received regular payments until May 1719 and the chapel was open for worship on 29 August 1720, Vertue pronouncing it 'a fine compleat peice . . . extreamly rich'.[28] Unfortunately it survived only twenty-seven years before disappearing in the general demolition which overtook the mansion after Chandos's death in 1744. Surprisingly, because of its apparently unrivalled splendour among country-house chapels, no views are recorded, but Gibbs's working drawings (Plates 25–6) show that it was a single, aisleless space, like St Mary-le-Strand, and of a similar size, 25 by 70 feet. A colonnaded apse at one corner of the house provided an imposing entrance, and a private overhead corridor linked the Duke's dressing room to a canopied family pew raised on six marble Doric columns. This is echoed at the east end where the semi-circular vestry was screened by a reredos surmounted by a grand Venetian opening of fluted Ionic piers framing the organ. Visitors' reports and the sales catalogues of 1747 mention the canopy, communion table and pulpit adorned with crimson velvet embroidered with gold.[29] There was a pair of carved and gilt armchairs similarly uphol-stered and an elaborate carved and gilt chandelier. The ten windows on both long eleva-tions contained coloured glass depicting episodes from the Old Testament painted by Joshua Price of York, supposedly after Sebastiano Ricci's cartoons. The ceiling contained richly coloured paintings of the Nativity, Crucifixion and Ascension flanked by putti hold-ing emblems of the Passion by the Venetian Antonio Bellucci, with ornamental plasterwork surrounds by Gibbs's favourite *stuccatori*, Artari and Bagutti, treated so robustly that some parts required metal armatures. This extraordinary opulence overlaid a strong architec-tural framework of paired Corinthian giant pilasters raised on tall bases, a new feature in Gibbs's ecclesiastical interiors, anticipating St Martin-in-the-Fields.

But before embarking on this great building in 1720 he re-established his eminence as a leading church architect by completing Wren's St Clement Danes (Plate 20). In May 1719 the Vestry resolved to let John Townesend build on to the unfinished tower of the 1682 church an 'ornamentall Steeple' designed by Gibbs; the cost was £1,650. Langley had much to say of the results, mocking the 'small block rustics' of the first-stage windows for their 'low mince-pye taste' and while he thought the 'three heights of columns . . . are of tolerable good taste . . . the small cupola . . . placed to finish the whole, is a most intolerable clumsy performance; and . . . should be removed to make way for a pyramis . . . of easy diminution, like that on the top of St. *Bride's*'.[30] Another observer, however, paired this steeple with St Martin-in-the-Fields as holding up their 'Heads with Grandeur and Magnificence',[31] and Gibbs's sympathetic use of elements from the London City Churches was clearly intended to honour the eighty-seven year old Wren. Gibbs next turned to St Clement's interior. In June 1720 he recommended repairs to the roof, its 'Rafters haveing Sprung from the King posts wch. must be secured wth. plates of Iron bolted', leading the Vestry to recommend that the church 'wants to be new beautifyed'. They discussed whether to have the columns fluted and the capitals gilt but decided instead to replace the old chancel furnishings with a porphyry table with two steps for candlesticks on a frame of gilt wrought-iron, and matching rails. In 1721 William Kent was commis-sioned to paint 'the Glory' over the altar.[32] Much of this disappeared in the 1941 bombings.

# IV

## ST MARTIN-IN-THE-FIELDS

PENSIVE, I view'd a *sacred pile*, of late
Which *falls*, like *man*, to rise, in *nobler* state[1]

THE NEW ST MARTIN'S was the most significant ecclesiastical building in the English-speaking world of the eighteenth century (Plate III).[2] The decision to demolish the medieval fabric had been made in 1710 when a survey revealed that the decayed walls had 'spread out by the Weight of the Roof' and the fabric could not be 'supported by repairing but must be rebuilt'. It was therefore included on the Commissioners for Building Fifty New Churches' list of 1715, but since no further progress was made the Vestry petitioned Parliament independently in 1717 and an Act for rebuilding 'at the charge of the inhabitants of the parish' was passed in that year. This provided for the establishment of a separate Commission with wide-ranging responsibilities, like those of the New Churches. The Commissioners' Minutes and the Treasurer's Accounts reveal that between June 1720 and May 1721 a surveyor was appointed, designs were submitted and approved and teams of craftsmen and workmen were hired; between June 1721 and March 1722 the old church was demolished, the new foundations were dug and important changes were made to the approved design; between April 1722 and January 1723 the church was under construction and further changes were made to bring the design more-or-less to its present appearance, while the fabric was completed between February 1723 and its consecration on 20 October 1726. The Commission first met on 23 June 1720, when it called for plans and estimates, and six days later Nicholas Dubois, George Sampson, John James, Sir James Thornhill and Gibbs each delivered designs.[3] Gibbs's was chosen on 14 September and he was recommended 'as the properest Person to be Employed as Surveyor', although his election was postponed until 24 November and his design was not finally approved for another six months.

Gibbs's original scheme delivered on 29 June 1720, although not specifically identified in the Minutes, very likely is represented by the 'several Plans of different Forms' mentioned in *A Book of Architecture*; that is, the series for a large church in the shape of a domed rotunda entered through a prostyle temple portico out of which rises the lofty steeple, a form he chose because it was most 'capacious and convenient' to accommodate a large congregation able to view the communion table and pulpit with equal ease (Plate 28)[4]. Although rare in English church architecture—the closest parallel is Wren's Great Model of 1673 for St Paul's Cathedral (Plate 29)—the form was very much in Gibbs's mind at this time, for on 27 July, less than a month after delivering his first designs for St Martin's, he had been invited to participate in the project for the new Radcliffe Library,

P 8

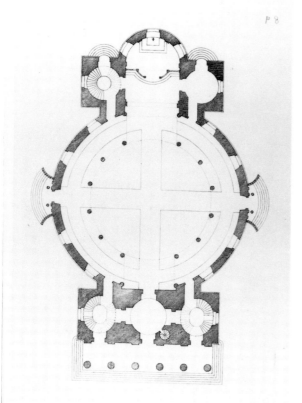

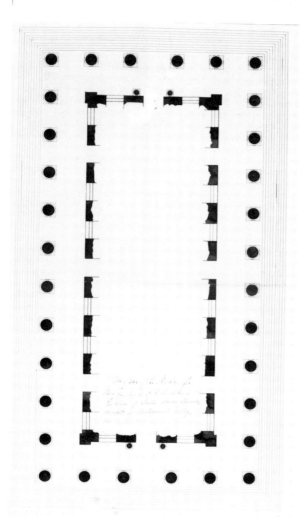

C. Front of the portico made by Marcus Agrippa.

D. The Antient Pediment, appearing above that of Agrippas

E. The Timpan of the pediment made by Marcus Agrippa
Adorned with some history but now demolished.

for which Nicholas Hawksmoor had already prepared several schemes for rotundas.[5] But undoubtedly Gibbs's model was the celebrated Roman Pantheon, long in use as a church, which he described and drew in the 'Short Cursory Remarks' both in its original form and with the monumental portico (Plate 31).[6]

Gibbs later claimed that these round designs were rejected on 'account of the expensiveness of executing them'[7] but the documents suggest a more important reason, which also explains the Commissioners' irresoluteness during the eleven months between July 1720 and May 1721. The available ground within the old churchyard was an irregular rectangle approximately 145 by 180 feet but with intrusions of private properties along the south side which reduced the width there to less than 100 feet. The building published as plates 8 to 12 in *A Book of Architecture* (the only one of the round designs with measurements) would have been 165 feet long and 90 feet from north to south in the centre of the rotunda and, therefore, could be accommodated only by acquiring additional land.[8]

However, the Commissioners were obliged under the 1717 Act to erect a tabernacle to house furnishings removed from the medieval church and also to provide a place of worship during the interval between the demolition of that fabric and the construction of the new one which had to be built on the same site. At their first meeting on 23 June 1720 designs for this temporary structure were also requested, and the problem of locating a site was a recurrent issue of subsequent meetings. In July and August the Commissioners considered requisitioning a nearby private house; in September the King was petitioned without success to grant part of the Green Mews, and the Tennis Court in James Street was also considered. In November Gibbs visited the possible sites, none of which proved acceptable, and finally between 10 and 31 January 1721 a wedge of vacant ground between St Martin's churchyard and Lancaster Court to the south was chosen. Gibbs submitted a design on 7 February and the tabernacle, shown in plate 1 in *A Book of Architecture* sandwiched between houses and the south-east corner of the church, was built during the next months. The round designs, of course, were now obsolete, and sometime between January and May 1721 Gibbs shifted to the idea of a smaller rectangular structure. This was a radical change, yet far from a lamentable one, since it forced him to reconsider the rectangle's inherently more classical temple form, with its giant Order as the principal unifying agent. It was, in fact, towards this end that his earliest church designs had been striving, and in order to understand what happened subsequently at St Martin's we must first return to those fledgling ventures.

On 14 May 1713, some months before gaining the New Churches surveyorship, Gibbs offered the Commissioners 'Several Draughts for Churches' which, although unsolicited, were sufficiently interesting for peartree-wood models to have been made. The first of these, delivered on 9 June (subsequently lost, but recorded in a later plan, Plate 30), was in the form of a classical temple raised on a stepped platform with the *cella* encompassed by thirty-two free-standing Ionic columns presumably supporting full pediments on the short elevations. Apparently the only non-classical feature was a full steeple rising from the west end of the roof. The tremendous size of the projected church, 88 by 188 feet, led Professor Donaldson in the mid-nineteenth century to proclaim it 'a splendour of architecture which has never been realized for churches in this country and which . . . would in point of date have given us priority over the Madeleine at Paris'[9]

Although remarkably advanced for its date, even in a European context, the design to a great extent subscribed to the Commissioners' proposals of 1712 that the New Churches should have 'the Appearance & reality of strength' to give them the 'Reverend look of a Temple' and that 'Such Fronts as shall happen to lie most open in View should

28. (top left) James Gibbs, 'Round Church' design for St Martin-in-the-Fields, Westminster, London, 1720, plan, Plate 8 in *A Book of Architecture*, 1728

29. (top right) Sir Christopher Wren, The Great Model for St Paul's Cathedral, London, 1673–4, oak, pear-wood and plaster (Courtesy of the Dean and Chapter of St Paul's Cathedral)

30. (bottom left) James Gibbs, Design for a church with an Ionic Order, London, 1713, plan by T. L. Donaldson of the lost wooden model, pen and wash (Royal Institute of British Architects Drawings Collection, London)

31 (bottom right) James Gibbs, after Carlo Fontana, Reconstruction of the Pantheon, Rome (from *Il Tempio Vaticano*, 1694), entrance elevation, pen and wash, in *A Manuscri by Mr. Gibbs Memorandums, &c.* (The Trustees of Sir John Soane's Museum, London)

be adorned with Porticos, both for Beauty and Convenience . . . no part of Publick Edifices being of greater use, nor no production in Architecture so solemnly Magnificent . . . together with handsome Spires . . . rising in good Proportion above the neighbouring Houses . . . High and Bold Structures . . . so form'd . . . that nothing but Time, and scarce that, shou'd destroy them'.[10] Gibbs developed the temple theme further than any of his contemporaries, endorsing particularly the use of classical forms for modern Christian churches and even, as we have noted, the notion of refurbishing ancient temples. In this respect his second design, of 14 May 1713, offered as a model on 24 June and intended as the largest of the New Churches (92 by 192 feet), is less adventurous in its rich groups of giant pilasters, niches and doors on the long elevations, with columns screening a west porch *in antis* and towers at each corner of the building.

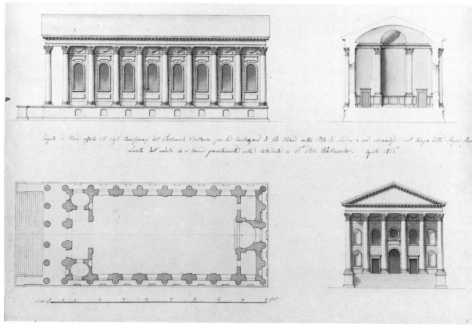

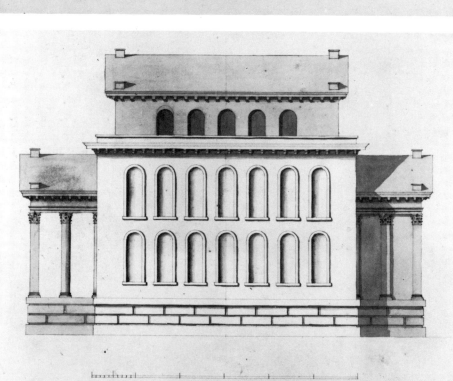

32. (left) James Gibbs, First design for St Mary-le-Strand, Westminster, London, 1714, plan, elevations and section (drawn in 1826) of the lost wooden model, pen and wash (Victoria and Albert Museum, London)

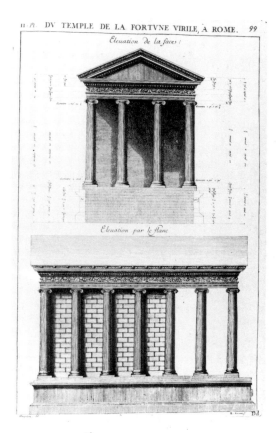

33. Architect unknown, Temple of Fortuna Virilis, Rome *c.* 100 BC, elevations, Plate II in A. Desgodetz, *Les Edifices Antiques de Rome*, 1682, p. 99

34. (left) Nicholas Hawksmoor, Design for St Mary-le-Strand, Westminster, London, *c.* 1714, south elevation, pen and wash (Westminster Public Library, Archives Department, London)

In his first design for St Mary-le-Strand, requested on 9 December 1713 and delivered as a model on 4 February 1714 (Plate 32), Gibbs returned to the classical precedents of either the Maison Carrée at Nimes or the Temple of Fortuna Virilis at Rome (Plate 33), by then converted to the church of S. Maria Egiziaca.[11] He adapted the latter's delicate frieze to the bands of decoration below the architrave but added large windows to the intercolumnation, reducing the portico to the function of a screen in order to gain additional internal space. He made concessions to the Protestant liturgy by raising the semicircular chancel three steps above the nave and flanking it with vestry rooms.[12] He also introduced a steeple, which had vanished by the time the model was recorded in 1826, but presumably it rose from the west end of the roof. When compared to Hawksmoor's contemporary offering for the Strand church (Plate 34), a hexastyle temple-like structure interrupted by broad projecting blocks on the north and south elevations and surmounted by a pedimented attic,[13] Gibbs's greater commitment to the Antique form is all too evident. Both designs, as we have seen, were usurped by Archer's in April 1714, and when a few months later Gibbs regained the commission his ideas had moved irrevocably towards the Baroque (Plate 17). His initial experiments with temple forms reawakened only with the decision in the spring of 1721 to replan St Martin-in-the-Fields as a rectangle.

The problem which had obviously troubled him most with the round design was how best to integrate in such a complex composition the disparate elements of portico, vestibule, body and steeple. In his presentation drawings of June 1720 (Plate 35) the giant order of the portico is repeated only in solitary pairs flanking doors on the north and south curves of the rotunda, while the steeple rises independently from the portico roof with its rear wall plunging into an awkward cavity linking the vestibule and rotunda. The debt to Wren's Great Model for St Paul's (Plate 29) is obvious but without observing the niceties of its masterfully integrated parts. Such timidity is partly resolved in the two alternative designs published as plates 8 to 15 in *A Book of Architecture* (Plate 292) by manipulating the roof shapes and treating the giant Order more consistently throughout the building; but it is evident Gibbs remained uncertain how to harmonize all these elements. Nor was this problem exclusive to the rotunda designs. In October 1720, while the St Martin's Commissioners debated the various entries for their new church, Gibbs prepared several schemes for St George's, Hanover Square. One lacked a vestibule and seems to have incorporated the structurally dubious idea of supporting the steeple directly on a portico composed of piers rather than columns placed close to the west wall. This must have worried Gibbs, because he prepared a more conventional alternative (Plate 36) in which the steeple (surmounted appropriately by the royal crown) rises from a firm base immediately behind the tetrastyle portico. Yet when approached from the north,[14] the relationship between the steeple and the bay directly below it is unresolved. For unspecified reasons a design by John James was preferred (built 1721–5), which played safe by shouldering the steeple on an attic placed atop the temple portico roof.[15]

Meanwhile, the site for St Martin's tabernacle having been fixed in January 1721, Gibbs now prepared at least three alternative designs for the new church which revived the idea of the pseudoperipteral rectangular form of 1713 but introduced a monumental projecting hexastyle temple portico across the entire west front (Plates 37). This allowed for an unbroken continuity from its outer columns to the evenly spaced giant pilasters of the north and south elevations, held rigidly within the continuous horizontals of the foundation platform and the crowning balustrade (Plate 38). A narrow moulding running behind the Order separates the windows corresponding to the internal aisles and galleries.

IV. William Hogarth, *The Wedding of Stephen Beckingham and Mary Cox*, 1729–30, oil on canvas (Philadelphia Museum of Art)

The most significant innovation is the prominence given the giant pilasters in the western-most bay of the side elevations, suggesting for the first time an alliance between the portico, body and steeple—the miniature distyle porches repeat elements in the second stage of the steeple— and it is now possible to visualize the steeple base (the vestibule, in fact) anchored within the body and therefore structurally equipped to support the steeple as it rises unhindered from the roof. These elements are embodied in a further design which was submitted and approved on 23 May 1721 (Plate 39); from this a pine and mahogany model with a detachable roof and steeple and furnished interiors, was produced with the intention of using it as a guide for the Commissioners and, as we shall see, a vehicle for adjusting details while the fabric was under construction (Plate 40). At this critical stage

36. (right) James Gibbs, Design for St George's, Hanover Square, Westminster, London, 1720, north elevation, pen and wash (Ashmolean Museum, Oxford, Gibbs Collection VII.14)

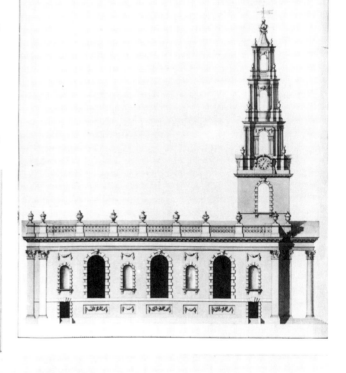

35. James Gibbs, 'Round Church' design for St Martin-in-the-Fields, Westminster, London, 1720, south elevation, pen and wash (Ashmolean Museum, Oxford, Gibbs Collection VII.4)

37. (facing page top left) James Gibbs, Rectangular design for St Martin-in-the-Fields, Westminster, London, 1721, west elevation, pen and wash (Ashmolean Museum, Oxford, Gibbs Collection III.96)

38. (facing page top right) James Gibbs, Rectangular design for St Martin-in-the-Fields, Westminster, London, 1721, south elevation, pen and wash (Ashmolean Museum, Oxford, Gibbs Collection VII.10)

39. (facing page bottom) James Gibbs, 'Approved' design for St Martin-in-the-Fields, Westminster, London, 1721, west and south elevations, pen and wash (Ashmolean Museum, Oxford, Gibbs Collection VII.1)

41. Antonio da Sangallo the elder and Giuliano di Baccio, Church of the Madonna di S. Biagio, Montepulciano, Italy, 1518–64, exterior

Gibbs made two radical but interdependent adjustments to the earlier rectangular studies. First, the hexastyle portico was reduced in width from 85 to 65 feet (with the intercolumnation 9 rather than 11 feet) in order to expose a vertical section of wall between the outer columns and the corners of the body. At the points where the now narrowed portico roof meets its wider main section, the crowning balustrade turns abruptly inwards to meet the front of the steeple as it breaks suddenly through the roof. Furthermore, in each of the slightly wider western most bays of the north and south elevations the main wall was recessed five feet from the line of pilasters and interpolated with pairs of giant free-standing columns which embrace small doors leading to the galleries. This motif was inspired by the bottom stage of the tower of S. Biagio at Montepulciano (Plate 41), the pinnacle of which was the source of the steeple of this (and no other) St Martin's design.

The next and most dramatic improvement, considered during the winter of 1722 while the Portland stone substructure was under construction and unanimously approved by the Commissioners on 4 January 1723, involved increasing the 'breadth of the portico ... more then expressed in the Originall Modell' (Plates 40, 27). This meant advancing the portico's foundation, which purposefully had not yet been laid, from 21 to 33 feet, bringing the steps to the edge of St Martin's Lane. In so doing an additional column could be placed between the west wall and both outer columns of the portico, thereby transforming it from a mere screen to a porch in the manner of the Roman Pantheon (Plate 30).[16]

These changes must have been on Gibbs's mind for some time because in order for the steeple as seen from the ground not to appear stunted in relation to the enlarged

40. (facing page) James Gibbs, St Martin-in-the-Fields, Westminster, London, 1721, west and south elevations of model, pine and mahogany (Royal Institute of British Architects Drawings Collection, London, lent by the Vestry of St Martin-in-the-Fields)

portico, it had already been resolved in October 1721 to raise its first stage higher than expressed in the model, with the happy result that the height of the steeple from foundation to pinnacle (170 feet, excluding the ball and vane) now equalled the full length of the church. No single feature of St Martin's interested Gibbs more than the steeple, for which he prepared over a dozen variations, some shown on flaps attached to his drawings, others published in *A Book of Architecture* (Plate 315). He explained with reference to the Strand church that 'Steeples are . . . of a Gothick Extraction; but they have their Beauties, when their Parts are well dispos'd, and when the Plans of the several Degrees and Orders of which they are compos'd gradually diminish, and pass from one Form to another without confusion, and where every Part has the appearance of a proper Bearing'.[17] Nevertheless at St Martin's the forms derive from the City Churches with additional Italian embellishments. Some of the more vigorous motifs used in the preliminary studies were abandoned in the executed steeple as a result of the design Gibbs submitted in April 1724, shortly after the brick carcass was completed, 'for the Alteration of the intended Steeple . . . Varying from the Originall Modell, whereby a Considerable Charge might be saved'.

The crucial element of all these alterations is the column *in antis* bays of the side elevations, one of Gibbs's most original architectural ideas (Plate 42). Until the formation of Trafalgar Square and its surrounding streets in the nineteenth century, which exposed the west and south elevations to uninterrupted but unintended vistas, it was only the front section of the church which could be seen from St Martin's Lane, and at that only

42. James Gibbs, St Martin-in-the-Fields, Westminster, London, 1721, north elevation of model, pine and mahogany (Royal Institute of British Architects Drawings Collection, London, lent by the Vestry of St Martin-in-the-Fields)

from obtuse angles, since the Lane was a narrow thoroughfare running north and south
enclosed on both sides by two and three-storey dwellings (Plate 43). An early visitor found
it 'much to be regretted that this fine Edifice is almost shut up, except its west front,
which looks into St Martin's lane, where you are greatly too near to view it to advantage'.[18]
(In 1766 John Gwynn proposed transforming the Royal Mews to the west of the Lane
into King's Square, opening an avenue the 'width of the Portico [to give] a noble view
of the front' of the church and throwing back the line of houses on the east side to expose
the portico, for 'at present the expence bestowed on the exterior . . . answers very little
purpose, there being no point from whence it can possibly be seen to advantage, which
is greatly to be lamented'.)[19] James Ralph, too, advocated an expanded western vista,
for he knew not 'one of the modern buildings about town which better deserves such an
advantage', but recognized the vital unifying function of the 'round columns, at each
angle of the church, [which] are very well conceiv'd, and have a very fine effect in the
profile of the building'.[20] In effect they serve as bold external expressions of the steeple's
sequestered base and provide the necessary visual support for the lofty steeple itself.[21]

But the columns *in antis* also suggest that the portico has penetrated the west end of
the body as a prelude to re-emerging inside as rows of giant columns flanking the nave,
which in turn echo exactly the giant pilasters on the side elevations (Plate 44); a temple
within the temple, which Gibbs demonstrates in an unusual manner in an engraving of
the ceilings (Plate 45). Unlike Wren and Hawksmoor, Gibbs envisaged his building as

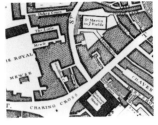

43. John Rocque, The parish of St Martin-in-the-Fields, (detail), engraving in *A Plan of the Cities of London and Westminster*, 1747

44. James Gibbs, St Martin-in-the-Fields, Westminster, London, 1720–7, ground plan, Plate 2 in *A Book of Architecture*, 1728

45. James Gibbs, St Martin-in-the-Fields, Westminster, London, 1720–7, ceiling, Plate 6 in *A Book of Architecture*, 1728

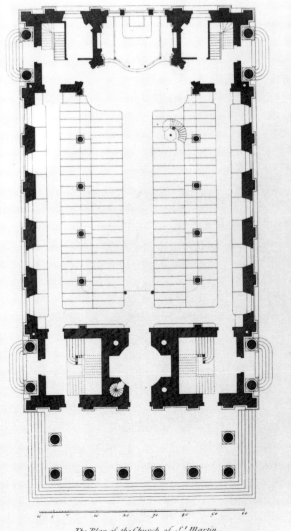

The Plan of the Church of St Martin.

The Ceiling of the New Church of St Martin.

46. James Gibbs, 'The inside of St. Martin's in the Fields', Westminster, London, 1720–6, engraving by G. Bickham, after T. Malton, undated (author's collection)

47. Vitruvius, Basilica at Fano, Italy, *c.* 27 BC, engraving, reconstruction of interior, Plate XL in C. Perrault, *Les Dix Livres D'Architecture de Vitruve,* Livre V, 1684

consisting of a single unified form composed of few but bold architectonic elements. Rather than the common arrangement of columns-on-piers, he favoured *giant* columns carrying the galleries (Plate 46). Wren had introduced this pattern in St Augustine, Watling Street (1680–3), but in adopting it to the larger and more regular internal space of St Martin's Gibbs clearly intended to conjure up the heroic appearance associated with the public buildings of classical antiquity, such as Vitruvius's celebrated basilica at Fano (*c.* 27 B.C.). Although long since destroyed it was the subject of a theoretical reconstruction published in an architectural treatise by Claude Perrault which was in Gibbs's library (Plate 47).[22] The interior had ranges of giant columns rising to the vault with shorter pilasters attached behind to support the beams carrying the galleries. At St Martin's, however, Gibbs abandoned the pilasters and in a bold stroke attached the gallery fronts directly to the sides of the column shafts. He further enhanced the integrity of each of the isolated columns by freeing the arches supporting the vault from a continuous entablature and springing them directly from short sections of cornice. The motif may have been borrowed from the relatively rare example of Brunelleschi's S. Spirito in Florence, which in itself seems again to have been an interpretation of Vitruvius.[23] In St Martin's it opened vistas from the nave into the upper area of the galleries and allowed all the sections of the ceiling to be treated as an uninterrupted surface. Gibbs found its elliptical shape 'by Experience to be much better for the Voice than the Semicircular, tho' not so beautiful'[24] and this also allowed the ceiling to be brought physically closer to the congregation; not surprisingly in a preliminary design the entire nave ceiling is covered with pictorial panels in the manner of contemporary Roman churches (Plate 48). But in the final, more Protestant solution (Plate 45) the arches merge gently into the simpler ornamental panels of the nave's outer row of compartments, while the rosettes in the centre are repeated in the galleries' saucer domes and also on a smaller scale at the intersections of the guilloched ribs which tie together the rows of evenly spaced giant columns. Gibbs regarded this solution as having a good effect,[25] and he anticipated the composition in the portico ceiling, just as the portico itself heralds the internal arrangement of columns.

One other important change was made to the approved design. In June 1721, before the model was begun, the Commissioners decided that the vestry room originally placed under the chancel should be resited on its flanks at ground level. In the earlier rectangular designs these areas had been reserved for gallery staircases; but now by tucking smaller stairs in the corners he released the spaces above for use as royal pews. These are given special significance in the penultimate east bay of the nave (Plate 49) by transforming the columns into giant pilasters supporting an unbroken entablature attached to sections of wall which curve inward on both flanks to meet the narrower rectangular chancel, as if Gibbs was resurrecting a segment of the abandoned round design (Plates 28, 50). Richly plastered and painted royal arms appear strategically in the centre of the corresponding canopied bay of the ceiling, mirroring those in the portico pediment. These special pews are served by private entrances in the recessed bays at the east end of the church, whose columns *in antis* are echoed in the giant pilasters of the concave bays inside. The pair of large upper openings provided unobstructed views of the communion table, reading desk and pulpit, while allowing the congregation to see the royal family as if they were appearing in boxes on either side of the proscenium arch of a theatre. This theatricality is evident in Hogarth's painting of *The Wedding of Stephen Beckingham and Mary Cox* (1729–30, Plate IV).[26] The idea may have derived from engravings of Andrea Pozzo's designs for the elaborately scenographic temporary architecture devised for the chancel of the Gesù on the occasions of the *quarantore* performances held in 1685 and 1695 (Plate 51).[27]

Nor was this the only way Gibbs moderated St Martin's rigid temple appearance. At the same meeting in June 1721 which decided to resite the vestry, he was ordered to prepare each side of the model with different sorts of windows (Plates 40, 42), and in October the south elevation with the 'Rusticated Windows on a plain Ground' was chosen; the composition was subsequently refined by slipping a string-course between the tiers of

48. James Gibbs, Design for St Martin-in-the-Fields, Westminster, London, *c.* 1720–1, ceiling, pen and wash (Ashmolean Museum, Oxford, Gibbs Collection VI.31)

49. James Gibbs, St Martin-in-the-Fields, Westminster, London, 1721, interior of model towards chancel, pine and mahogany (Royal Institute of British Architects Drawings Collection, London, lent by the Vestry of St Martin-in-the-Fields)

50. James Gibbs, 'Round Church' design for St Martin-in-the-Fields, Westminster, London, 1720, section, Plate 12 in *A Book of Architecture*, 1728

51. Andrea Pozzo, Design for the scenic altar arrangement for the Church of the Gesù, Rome, 1695, Figura 47 in *Perspectiva Pictorum et Architectorum*, 1700, Vol. II, p. 73

windows to create the more subtle effect of a continuous wall running just behind the pilasters.[28] Yet no other eighteenth-century church was so deeply committed to the Antique temple form, as the vicar of St Martin's, Dr Pearce, evidently recognized, for he appended to the published version of his consecration sermon delivered on 20 October 1726 *AN ESSAY on the Origin and Progress of TEMPLES*, in which he conjectured that Solomon's Temple at Jerusalem was the first to be 'covered entirely with Roofs' and only then were 'Porticos . . . built on the Outside of the temple'.[29] The similarities to St Martin's are obvious and help to explain why a variant of Gibbs's church formed the centrepiece of the Rev. William Stukeley's extraordinary 1751 reconstruction of Solomon's Temple.[30]

Long before the details of the final design were resolved, the church was under construction. The dedication stone was laid on 19 March 1721 by Sir Thomas Hewett, Surveyor-General of the King's Works, and the Bishop of Salisbury, deputising for the King, gave the stone 'two or three Knocks with a Mallet, upon which the Trumpets sounded; and a vast Multitude made Loud Acclamations of Joy, when his Lordship laid upon the Stone a purse of One Hundred Guineas, as a Present from His Majesty for the use of the Craftsmen'. The church's progress is recorded fully in the Commissioners' Minutes and Accounts for 1720 to 1727. A series of bills submitted by the mason Christopher Cass show that by July 1722 work had reached 'from the Beginning of the Foundation to the Under Side of the portland Bases of the Three foot 4 Inch Corinthian order' on all four elevations, by February 1723 to 'the Top of the Facia In height 16ft.4In. containing the Outside periphery and all the Inside Work . . . Excepting the pillars on the outside from their Bases and the Inside Columns' and by October to the crowning balustrates and the east pediment including carving '2 pieces of Leather Work . . . palm Branches . . . Musk Head with Scrolls . . . Flowers [and] Laurell Leaves' in its circular window (Plate 324). In March 1724 Cass estimated that the steeple would cost £2,760 to complete (he was paid for work to the top of the spire on 8 December and it received finishing touches in the winter of 1726) and the portico £1,623 (which was started May 1725, and in June 1726 he delivered a bill for 'Raiseing & Striking the Scaffold at the Front of the Portico In Order for Cutting the Letters in Frieze').

By the spring of 1724, then, the brick and Portland stone carcass was finished and the carpenters, joiners, smiths, plumbers, plasterers, painters and glaziers submitted proposals. The cost of the bold cast-iron railings surrounding the churchyard, for which Gibbs prepared a drawing and the joiner Charles Griffith carved a pattern, was estimated at

£1,000, and an equal amount was to be spent on the internal plasterwork. Chrysostom Wilkins, who had worked at St Mary-le-Strand, was responsible for the plain work and Giovanni Bagutti, who was considered 'the most proper person to be Employed to Do the Frett Work [and] Gilding', demanded £320; their work was completed by the autumn of 1726 (Plates 52–3). Gibbs supplied detailed drawings for the internal decoration and furnishings, of which those for the pulpit and brass chandeliers survive (Plate 54). Griffith charged £80 for making the 'Pullpet in Right Wainscott'; Thomas Bridgewater carved the decorative work.[31] The carpenters Benjamin Timbrell and Thomas Phillips made the Venetian window frame in the chancel to a design by Gibbs, for which he charged £10.14.6 in June 1725; the ornamental painting on glass was done by James and William Price, who charged £130 in September 1726. Another member of this celebrated family had already executed the ten pictorial windows for Gibbs's chapel at Cannons in 1719–21 (now at Witley, Worcestershire). Those in St Martin's, which were destroyed in the nineteenth century but recorded in early views, consisted of a complex geometric pattern of enframed circles, probably vibrantly coloured in the manner of William Price's other windows.[32] Unfortunately, even less is known about the original colour scheme of the interior. The painters' bill for 1726 itemizes oil work on both wood and stone surfaces but mentions no colours; however, some of the ornamental plasterwork was gilded.[33]

In April 1722 Gibbs delivered an 'Estimate of the Generall Charge of the Severall Works necessary for rebuilding', including £11,227 for masonry, £2,548 for bricklaying, £2,616 for carpentry, £2,106 for joinery, £1,245 for smithing, £1,465 for plumbing, £520 for

54. James Gibbs, Design for St Martin-in-the-Fields, Westminster, London, 1724–6, chandelier, plan and elevation, pen and wash (Ashmolean Museum, Oxford, Gibbs Collection IV. 28)

55. James Gibbs, St Giles, Shipbourne, Kent, 1722–3, west and south elevations, from a photograph taken prior to demolition in 1880

56. James Gibbs, Design for the chapel at Arundel Castle, Sussex, c. 1730, tabernacle, pen and wash (Victoria and Albert Museum, London)

plastering and so forth, totaling £22,497. At the end of operations in June 1727 the final bill had reached £29,056.10.6. To celebrate the church's completion Thomas Cadman, 'the Italian Flyer', descended on his belly head-first down a rope stretched from the top of the steeple into the Royal Mews.[34]

St Martin's greatly enhanced Gibbs's prestige as a church designer. In *The Honour and Vertue of Building, Repairing, and Adorning, Churches: And the Sacredness of them, when Built, and Consecrated. A Sermon Preached At Shipburn in Kent, Upon the Opening of the New Church There; Entirely rebuilt at the sole Expense Of the Right Honourable The Lord and Lady Barnard,* 1723, the Rev. Joseph Trapp (who preached at St Martin-in-the-Fields 'now Rebuilding . . . by the Skill of . . . Mr. Gibbs . . . the same excellent Architect whom Your Lordship employ'd') goes some way to explain Gibbs's approach to this building type. The more conservative elements of the Anglican Church had long pressed for a simple treatment for country churches. Trapp observed that it had been 'objected by Some, that Parish-Churches, at least in obscure Country-Villages, should not be fine, and splendid. But They seem not to consider, that the Almighty Author of our Being is no less the God of the Country as well as of the City, than of the Valleys as well as of the Hills [paraphrasing I Kings 20:23].' Referring to Gibbs's new church at Shipbourne, which he calls a 'beautiful Fabrick', he exclaims 'How delightful is it to see a beauteous sacred Edifice encompass'd with Fields, Trees, and Meadows; The Artificial Gilding of That and the Natural Verdure of These casting a mutual Lustre upon Each other, and Both upon the great Creator! This Contraste is thought proper, when Houses are built for Men: And why should it not be so, when they are built for God?' His attempt to exonerate what by ordinary parochial standards must have seemed a lavish building is elaborated in the sermon's central theme,

that in the Building, Finishing, and Preserving of . . . Places for the Publick Worship of God . . . *Decency* at least is necessary; and even *Magnificence* highly commendable', adding 'sensible Images and Representations may be of great Use to us, even in the most refin'd and spiritual of our Performances. The same Observation may be apply'd to the distinguishing Habits of Those who minister in holy Things, the sacred Utensils, Church-Musick, Paintings, Gildings, Carvings, and all Ornaments whatsoever. In all which, the Medium should be kept between too much Plainness and Simplicity on the one Extreme; and too much Lightness, Gayety, and Gaudiness on the other. Much more should the Middle be maintain'd between no Ornament, Beauty, nor even Decency at all, the Extreme of some Protestants in our Country; and extravagant, immoderate Ornaments, superstitious Foppery, and gross Idolatry, the Extreme of the Papists in all Countries, where their most corrupt Religion prevails ... if Some will be so perverse as not to distinguish between *Decoration* and *Adoration*; we are sorry for it, but cannot help it.[35]

Unfortunately, little is known about Shipbourne church, which was demolished in 1880. The exterior (Plate 55) was a simple rectangle with round-headed windows on the north and south elevations, pedimented east and west ends, a rusticated west door and a square tower rising directly from the pitched roof, embellished with an open octagon surrounded by urns. Trapp may have associated this modest treatment with the 'primitive Simplicity' of Abraham's Temple ('This great Prince did not build, but plant a Temple; a vegetable Sanctuary; rooted not founded; and far more the Work of Nature than of Art'); but of his hints at Shipbourne's internal splendour, which he links to the 'Carving and Images in the Temple built by *Solomon* ... the most glorious Structure that ever the World saw, built, and adorn'd with inconceivable Beauty, and Magnificence',[36] nothing remains in the present church except Gibbs's lavishly carved marble monument to the Barnards (Plate 83). Of this type of rich ecclesiastical furnishings there is, however, the ormolu tabernacle enshrining an emblematic figure of the Lamb of God and supporting a crucifix, which the German goldsmith Charles Frederick Kandler made around 1730 to Gibbs's design (Plate 56) for the premier Catholic Duke of Norfolk's chapel at Arundel Castle and now in the Cathedral.

Trapp's sermon was an exhortation to others to adopt more liberal attitudes towards church improvement, for he concluded 'If such be the *Use, Necessity*, and Holiness of Churches; How great must be the *Virtue* and *Honour* of Those who build them? In which Number must be included Those who *rebuild* them ... And the like is to be said, in *Proportion*, of Those who *repair, enlarge*, and *beautify* them ... Few, but the *Great*, and the *Noble*, are *singly* enabled to perform such Work; so They are never more Great and Noble, than *when* They perform them.'[37] Among the enlightened were Lady Barnard's niece Henrietta, Countess of Oxford, and her husband Edward Harley (whose father had helped Gibbs secure the New Churches surveyorship in 1713), for whom he had already designed chapels at Wimpole Hall and in Vere Street, Marylebone.

The remodelling of the seventeenth-century house at Wimpole was in progress by 1713 and early designs incorporate a family chapel in the five-bay wing attached to its south-east corner (Plate 110). Gibbs's preliminary idea for the interior, represented in a drawing (Plate 57), perhaps one of those for which he was paid 10 guineas in July 1719, shows that the rich treatment of paired Ionic pilasters raised on panelled dados and supporting broad bands of rosetted coffers depended closely on St Mary-le-Strand (Plate 21), while at the west end the Doric columns and pedimented door leading to the ante-chapel, formed from an existing room in the house, is reminiscent of Cannons chapel (Plate 26). The reredos, less heroic than at Cannons, echoes a motif Gibbs intended incorporating in the centrepiece of the remodelled house (Plate 111). Subsequently, the need for windows on the north side was abandoned in favour of a solid wall treated with feigned architecture

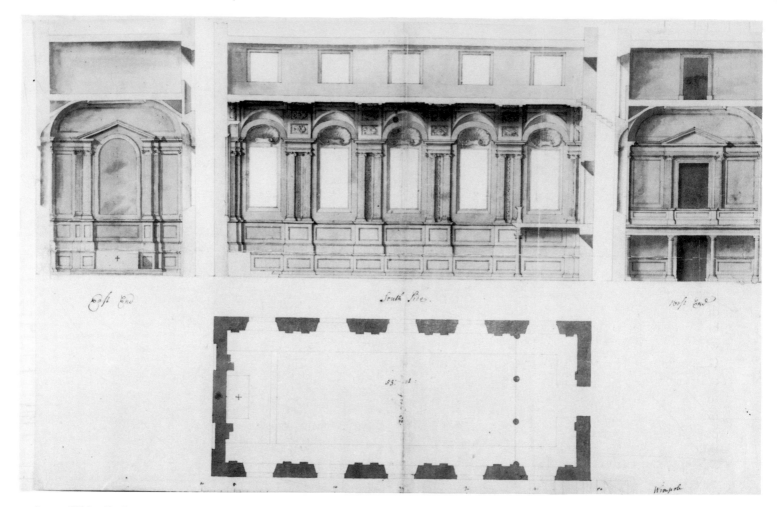

57. James Gibbs, Design for the chapel, Wimpole Hall, Cambridgeshire, 1713–24, plan and elevations of interior, pen and wash (The Trustees of Sir John Soane's Museum, London)

58. Sir James Thornhill, Study for painted decoration in the chapel, Wimpole Hall, Cambridgeshire, c. 1721, pen and wash (The Trustees of the Cecil Higgins Art Gallery, Bedford)

and sculpture. Sir James Thornhill, a member of Harley's Virtuosi, was involved by March 1721, when he speculated with Gibbs on the scheme,[38] transforming his sedate Protestant room into a glorious, colourful reminder of the Venetian Baroque (Plate VII). On the east wall an *Adoration of the Magi* is dramatically revealed to the congregation by putti drawing aside a certain. The painted architecture, a *trompe-l'œil* version of the Venetian opening in Cannons chapel (Plate 26), might be supposed, from payments to Gibbs in May 1721 for drawings for the 'altar', to have been his idea. Certainly he continued to be responsible for the general design, since much of the painted architecture relates to his earlier scheme. But the painted niches with statues of the Four Doctors of the Church on the north wall follow closely Thornhill's sketches (Plate 58). He enlivened the architecture with putti surmounting each pair of engaged columns, and the ceiling is covered entirely in feigned rosetted coffers painted in stone colour and luminous blue heightened with gilt. Thornhill signed and dated the paintings in 1724 and was paid £1,350.

Harley must have been pleased with the room because in 1721 he commissioned Gibbs to design the proprietory chapel (Plates 59–60, 312) for his newly created estate in Marylebone, having rejected a design proposed two years earlier by his surveyor, John Prince.[39] The contract with Benjamin Timbrell and Thomas Phillips, the carpenters at St Martin-in-the-Fields, to build the chapel according to Gibbs's design in a 'Workmanlike manner with Sound and Substantial Materials of all sorts & kinds . . . according to [his] Directions & . . . Satisfaction' for £3,000 specifies the use of red and grey stock bricks with Portland stone quoins, doorcases and other dressings, a wooden cornice 'to go all round the Eaves', blue slate roofing, stone or metal urns with gilded flames and a gilt brass vane. The general appearance resembles Shipbourne but with more sophisticated details; the belfry is closer to alternative designs for St Mary-le-Strand and there is a bold, single-storey Doric temple portico of Portland stone on the west front embellished with urns and the Oxford arms. The contract is dated 8 August 1721, a few months after Gibbs delivered his 'approved' design for St Martin's, and the two interiors not unexpectedly are similar, in particular the provision for the nave columns to 'go up to the Cieling to support the Roof'. The flat ceiling suggested on the contract drawing was, with the hindsight of St Martin's, abandoned in favour of a barrel vault divided into larger elegant polylobed compartments. The contract called for the ceiling over the altar to be 'Distinguished with Frettwork', and a separate agreement of 1722 with Giovanni Bagutti again specified a 'good workmanlike manner perform[ed] & finish[ed] . . . to the satisfaction

59. James Gibbs, Marylebone or Oxford Chapel, St Marylebone, London, 1721–4, west and north elevations

60. James Gibbs, Marylebone or Oxford Chapel, St Marylebone, London, 1721–4, interior towards west

of James Gibbs', for which the plasterer received £70. Christopher Shrider, a well-known organ-maker of St Margaret's, Westminster parish, agreed to supply 'One good & Compleat Organ with a case [of] good Right Wainscott . . . to be Wrought & Carved according to a Design [lost] Signed by the sd. Parties [with] so much of the Ornaments as shall be Directed by . . . Gibbs . . . to be Guilt, & the Carving, Guilding & Workmanship to be performed to his Satisfaction'. The case survived until 1852. The carpenters also supplied pews carved with beadwork and raised panels and a handsome pulpit and altarpiece to his specifications (destroyed 1881). A contemporary guidebook called the chapel 'a Jewel of its Kind.'[40]

The total cost of building, including Harley's gift of plate in 1724, was £4,296.4.8½. About the same amount was available for rebuilding Derby parish church, although because funds had to be raised by public subscription and the hotly disputed sale of pews, the work was completed only by an arduous and somewhat unlawful procedure on the part of its determined vicar, Dr Michael Hutchinson. Because of the decrepit condition of the medieval fabric 'several of the Parishioners absented themselves from divine Service, and others who were assembled, were so much frightned at every crack of Wind (which shook the whole Fabrick) as to run out of the Church for their Security'.[41] In 1719 the Vestry approved a design for rebuilding offered by William or Francis Smith, and in 1722 another design by the Yorkshire architect Ralph Tunnicliffe was considered; but on 20 August of that year it was agreed to have 'a Modell or plan in wood . . . made after the manner . . . drawn by Mr Smith' at a cost not to exceed ten guineas. Unfortunately, none of these projects can be traced. The situation shifted again in February 1723 when a new design was approved, this time by Gibbs, who had perhaps been called in to resolve differences between the Vestry and the Smiths, who were henceforth relegated to the role of contractors.[42] This final design was more ambitious, requiring additional building funds, so Dr Hutchinson launched a nationwide subscription which attracted the Duke of Devonshire, Sir Robert Walpole, Edward Harley and numerous local landowners. Benefactions were encouraged by issuing a print of Gibbs's scheme (Plate 61). Heinrich Hulsberg was paid £12.17.8 for engraving the copper plate and striking 300 cuts, which were later reused in *A Book of Architecture*; £4,162.13.6 was raised among some 150 subscribers.[43] But Hutchinson's troubles were hardly begun. Derby Corporation held the view 'that a Wall run up against the Chancel, at about a Hundred Pounds charge, would have secured [the old church] for a great many Years [and] *catechiz'd* [the vicar] *how he dar'd to lay out above 3000l.* [the sum solicited by subscriptions] *in rebuilding*'. He retorted by asking if they would have preferred him to build '*a paltry Church at that Price, and . . . put the rest into his own Pocket?*'[44] Still the Corporation dallied and Hutchinson resolved the issue in the pre-dawn of 18 February 1723 by secretly ordering workmen to demolish the fabric so that, according to the astonished Mayor, 'there was no Way left, but for every one to lend his helping Hand' towards building a new church.[45]

Only the glorious Perpendicular west tower was preserved. The new body was to be plain because, Gibbs says, this 'makes it less expensive, and renders it more suitable to the old Steeple'.[46] The body has no medievalisms although the series of single windows supported on a continuous string-course and the slightly projecting paired Doric pilasters crowned by urns seem intentionally to echo the fenestration and buttresses of the former structure.[47] In the interior (Plate 62), the resemblance to St Martin-in-the-Fields and the Marylebone Chapel is greatly diminished by the use of unobstructed giant Doric columns, a solution Gibbs regarded as 'the more beautiful' because galleries as well as pews 'clog up and spoil the Inside of Churches, and take away from that right Proportion which

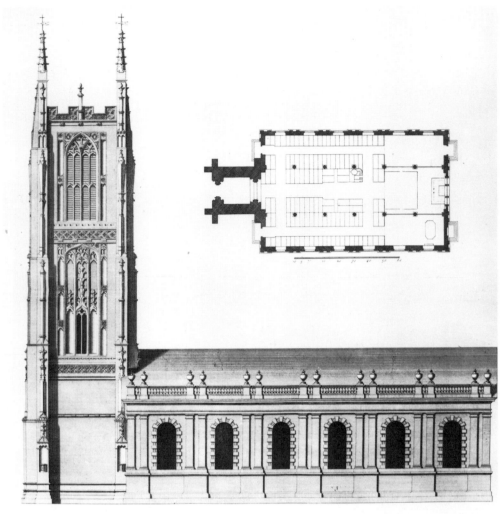

*Australe latus Ecclesiæ Omnium Sanctorum apud Derbienses, mox ab imis instaurandæ una cum Sepulchrali Monumento insignis adeoque Venerabilis Decani Præsepæ conduntur. Stante adhuc Turri magnificâ, quæ ad 178 pedes caput sublime attollit. Minister & Paro chiani ejusdem Ecclesiæ Præi Decrevensis. Viri memores integræ mentibus quam splendidis. Vitalitys illustri humillime dedicant.*

*Delineavit Ja. Gibbs. Sculp. H. Hulsbergh.*

61. James Gibbs, All Saints (now the Cathedral), Derby, Derbyshire, 1723–6, plan and south elevation, Plate 26 in *A Book of Architecture*, 1728

62. James Gibbs, All Saints (now the Cathedral), Derby, Derbyshire, 1723–6, interior towards chancel prior to remodelling between 1954 and 1972

they otherwise would have, and are only justifiable as they are necessary'.[48] Hutchinson, however, was dissatisfied. Deprived of the additional seating which was to be a vital source of building revenue—'Several of the best of the Parishioners who had before contributed handsomly towards rebuilding the Church, propos'd to advance a great deal more, in case they might have Seats appropriated to themselves and their Families . . . This raised a mighty Clamour and Noise [and] a Spirit of Faction broke out in the Parish'; so 'New Measures were concerted, between Doctor *H.* and the Undertakers, to make the Work neater and better than was originally design'd'.[49] In 1726 Gibbs was asked to supply a design for a west gallery having sufficient room for an organ, and a handsome entrance to the church through the steeple; but apparently he declined, for the reasons later expressed in *A Book of Architecture*, since the one erected in 1731–2 was designed by Francis Smith. An even more virulent controversy surrounded the chancel.[50] The joint responsibility of the Vestry and Derby Corporation (which contributed £210 towards the rebuilding), it had to accommodate the liturgical heart of the interior, with its communion table and altarpiece, as well as the vestry room and space for occasional Corporation business such as Mayoral elections. Finding himself in the awkward position of serving two clients with divided responsibilities, and mistrustful of each other's intentions, Gibbs discarded the idea of a deep chancel with flanking rooms, which had been an important feature of his earlier churches. He returned to a medieval parish church plan and consolidated all these functions *within* the rectangular body, appropriating exactly one-third of its length, and enclosing them in exquisite wrought and cast-iron screens, the masterpiece of the great Derby smith Robert Bakewell.[51] (Unfortunately, the dazzling effects of silhouette have been ruined by the recent rearrangement of the east end when the fine Venetian window was replaced by a chancel and baldachin.) Despite these quarrels the new fabric was reported in 1725 as 'commended by all that saw it'.[52] By 1725, then, Gibbs had emerged as one of the leading church architects both in the country and in London. His early successes were developed further in his subsequent schemes which, although more modest and not always fulfilled, are nevertheless interesting.

At St Giles-in-the-Fields, London, after several unsuccessful petitions to Parliament,

63. James Gibbs, Design for St Giles-in-the-Fields, Holborn, London (?), 1731, north elevation, pen and wash (Ashmolean Museum, Oxford, Gibbs Collection III.67)

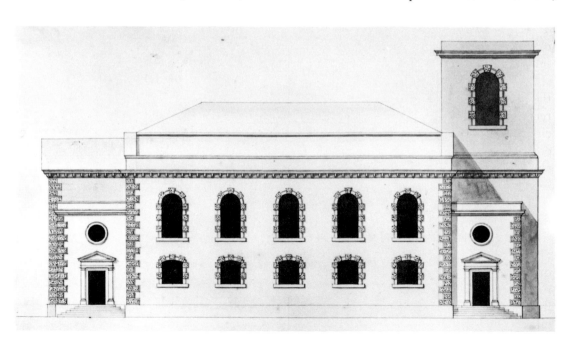

64. James Gibbs, Sir
William Turner's Hospital
Chapel, Kirkleatham,
Cleveland, 1741–7,
interior towards chancel

65. James Gibbs, Sir
William Turner's Hospital
Chapel, Kirkleatham,
Cleveland, 1741–7, west
elevation

the rejection of two dramatic designs by Hawksmoor and a report by the rector that the fabric was 'very Ruinous and out of Repair . . . the ffloors . . . very Damp and Unholsome',[53] the *Daily Post* announced on 4 February 1731 that 'Mr. Gibbs, Mr. [Edward] Shepherd, and Mr. [Henry] Flitcryft, three famous Architects, are Candidates for rebuilding the Parish Church'. Gibbs proposed a scheme (Plate 63) with vermiculated window surrounds and internal giant Doric columns supporting the galleries, their sectioned-entablatures springing into the barrel-vaulted nave in the manner of St Martin's and the Marylebone Chapel; but, restricted by limited funds (£8,000), he adopted the simpler rectangular plan of St James's, Piccadilly, which Wren recommended as 'the most capacious . . . that hath yet been built [as well as]beautiful and convenient, and as such, the cheapest of any Form I could invent'.[54] The result bears a striking resemblance to the church designed and executed by Flitcroft, the drawings for which are dated in the following month, 29 March 1731, and which also adopted St Martin's steeple (Plate 291).

About ten years later St Martin's themes reappeared in the chapel addition to Sir William Turner's Hospital at Kirkleatham, Yorkshire, originally built in 1676 but comprehensively remodelled during the 1740s and 1750s for the local landowner Cholmley Turner (Plates 64–5). It would have been a simple matter for Gibbs to have supplied drawings on an occasion around 1740 when he was involved in designing the Turner Mausoleum nearby. A local joiner, Robert Corney, received regular payments for work at the Hospital from 1741, the year Turner was returned as M.P. for the county, although work on the chapel itself seems to have been most active towards the end of the decade: a Mr Carpenter was paid £27.2.11 in October 1748 for painting the interior, John Bagnall (who plastered the Great Room of the York Assembly Rooms, 1731–4) received £108.8.4 in November 1748 for similar work in the chapel, and Corney was paid £250.9.11 in the same month. This coincided with Cholmley Turner's purchase of a pair of gilt-wood armchairs suitably embellished with the Duke of Chandos's monogram (entwined *C*'s), a gilt-pine chandelier and perhaps other items from Gibbs's chapel at Cannons (1716–20), which was dismantled in 1747.[55] As in other isolated provincial commissions, when it was difficult to remain on site, Gibbs permitted the craftsmen some interpretative freedom, which helps to explain such idiosyncracies as the delicately carved foliage in the pulvinated frieze and gallery fronts and the treatment of the wood surfaces of the fluted Ionic Order with stone-coloured, sand-textured paint to simulate the more expensive material. The west front of the chapel closely resembles Gibbs's unexecuted 1741 design for Marylebone parish church (Plate 66), although it has a more elaborate ashlar tower detailed from other plates in *A Book of Architecture*.[56] Gibbs used similarly chaste forms in several churches of the 1740s, perhaps chiefly because of inflated building costs irritated by the impending war with France.

66. James Gibbs, Design for St John's, St Marylebone, London, 1741, west elevation, pen and wash (Ashmolean Museum, Oxford, Gibbs Collection IV.17)

When early in 1741 the parishioners of the London village of St Marylebone contemplated rebuilding their dilapidated medieval church (the subject of Hogarth's derisive episode 'Married to an Old Maid' in *The Rake's Progress*, 1735),[57] the Lord of the Manor, Edward Harley, agreed to concur with any reasonable proposal for remedying the situation, with the proviso that 'it be done without over burthening the Inhabitants with any unnecessary Charge; especially at this time when provisions of all kinds bear so high aprice'.[58] The Vestry invited Gibbs, who lived nearby, to view the fabric, which he found in a dangerous condition and unable to be repaired, and he advised that it be taken down. A design for a new church was presented in February 1741 (Plate 66). Nevertheless, an alternative scheme was prepared by two local builders, John Lane and Walter Lee, and when soon after the Vestry decided finally on rebuilding, it was another design by Lane, with an estimate not to exceed £800, which was chosen. But since he was requested to 'Advise with Mr. Gibbs', it is hardly surprising the two proposals are so similar, with Lane minimizing the embellishments and building entirely in stock brick, reserving Portland stone for the sills. He retained the broken pediment rising above the string-course, which is also a feature of Kirkleatham Hospital chapel, but rejected Gibbs's projecting west porch and reduced the tower to a belfry perched on the edge of the roof. The barrel-vaulted nave with galleries supported on Doric columns, a traditional Wren arrangement recommended for its cheapness, was also pared down to a simple proprietory box. Construction began in July 1741, with Lane and Lee as builder and mason respectively. By the winter Benjamin Timbrell and Roger Morris were engaged in measuring and valuing the work, which was completed by February 1742 at a total cost of £1,051.19.0. Gibbs bequeathed £100 in 1754 towards enlarging the fabric, although nothing was done. Several schemes for a grander structure were later suggested by William Chambers and John Woolfe, but it was not until 1813–17 that Thomas Hardwick built the present church. Lane's building was demolished in 1952.[59]

Gibbs again found himself involved with rebuilding a country church when on 14 February 1742 the Bishop's Consistory Court at Lichfield, having considered the case for demolishing the old parish church of Patshull in Staffordshire, which was 'in a very inconvenient Place by reason it lies remote from the Village', granted the patron, Sir John Astley, a faculty to rebuild 'at his own proper Cost and Charge'. Gibbs may have already been building Astley's great mansion, Patshull Hall, which lies on a hill overlooking the village. His design for the new church (Plate 67), attached to the Court citation of 14 February, has a west tower rising to a domed octagonal belfry (rebuilt 1874–8) almost exactly like those at Kirkleatham and Marylebone, a three-bay nave and narrower chancel with simple arched windows and a large Venetian window at the east end. The whole building is ashlar-faced. The tower-base serves as the vestry and has no external door; instead a distyle Tuscan porch is placed in the middle of the south elevation so that one enters in the centre of the starkly geometric nave (Plate 68), opposite a late seventeenth-century monument to the Astleys placed against the north wall, imbuing the church with mausoleum qualities.

Gibbs's use of simple forms in his late work is especially apparent at St Nicholas in Aberdeen. William Adam had reported to the Town Council in 1732 on the extensive repairs required to the decrepit western section of their principal church and in 1740 mentions his intention to send designs, although apparently he did not. Meanwhile, in 1739 Gibbs had been made a burgess of the town,[60] undoubtedly in anticipation of being solicited for a design (the Council perhaps having heard that he had offered his services as architect gratis to St Bartholomew's Hospital in London after being elected a governor). In July 1741 he delivered two alternative designs for the new church, which was estimated to cost not less than £5,000. His first idea entailed a conventional exterior resembling the Marylebone Chapel but introducing at the west end the unusual combination of a rusticated doorcase, reminiscent of the Radcliffe Library (Plate 283), crowned by a Diocletian window, a feature he ordinarily reserved for domestic and college buildings (Plates 146, 258) but which Palladio had used in several Venetian churches.[61] In his alternative design

67. James Gibbs, Design for St Mary's, Patshull, Staffordshire, 1742, plan and south elevation redrawn by W. T. C. Walker from a 1742 survey in Litchfield Joint Record Office

68. James Gibbs, St Mary's, Patshull, Staffordshire, 1742, interior towards chancel

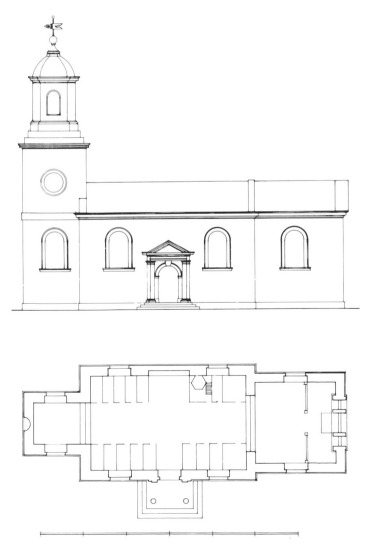

(Plate 69) Gibbs produced a more satisfactory solution based on the interlocking pedimented facades of S. Giorgio Maggiore but stripped of the Order and most embellishment.[62]

What could have accounted for this sudden late recollection of Palladio's churches? The answer may lie in the fact that St Nicholas posed a difficulty Gibbs had not encountered previously. Soon after the Reformation, when the high altar was no longer the focal point of the service, the medieval building was divided by a wall into the east church, refashioned out of the choir, transepts and crossing with its central tower, to which a lofty steeple had been added in 1513, and the west church (the original Norman nave), which had fallen into disrepair and now required rebuilding. Gibbs had to design a west facade which was self-sufficient because it was isolated from the existing tower—the antithesis of that most poignant architectural relationship he had created at St Martin's—and so he seems to have turned for inspiration to Palladio's Venetian churches, with their campanile placed to the rear of the eastern choir. In the interior (Plate 71) the delicate St Martin's trabeation of the first design was replaced by a bolder arcuated system of Tuscan pilasters mounted on piers between tall arches, a treatment more suitable to the harsher environment of northern Scotland.[63] Because of lack of funds, work on the west church was postponed until 1752, when the Edinburgh mason James Wyllie contracted to rebuild according to the plans, elevations and sections drawn by Gibbs, which specified that the 'gallerys [were] to be supported from pillar to pillar by a principal beam [the] roof of the body in the middle part . . . to be an elipsis arch which rises from a large Doric cornice the whole length of the church, all of good lath and plaster, and to be well

69. James Gibbs, Design for St Nicholas West Church, Aberdeen, Aberdeenshire, 1741, west elevation and interior towards west, pen and wash (Ashmolean Museum, Oxford, Gibbs Collection III.131)

70. James Gibbs, Design for St Nicholas West Church, Aberdeen, Aberdeenshire, 1741, pulpit, pen and wash (Victoria and Albert Museum, London)

Section from South to North of ye Church of St Nicolaus

The West Front of ye Church of St Nicholas

Maskall

71. James Gibbs, St Nicholas West Church, Aberdeen, Aberdeenshire, 1741–55, interior towards east

whitened, [with the] pulpit, clerk's seat, raills and sounding boards to be all of good wainscott and finished in a genteel handsome manner according to the Corinthian order with a modelian cornice enriched and plain pavilion roof'. Gibbs also supplied the design for the pulpit (Plate 70). The new church opened on 9 November 1755.[64]

The full extent of his involvement in the chapel built for the Foleys at Witley Court in Worcestershire between 1733 and 1735 remains uncertain. He would have been an obvious choice as architect, since Robert, 1st Earl of Oxford, and his brother Edward 'Auditor' Harley both had married daughters of Thomas, 1st Lord Foley, and other members of the family were associated with the Fifty New Churches and St Bartholomew's Hospital and had subscribed to *A Book of Architecture*.[65] The new chapel was part of a general Palladianizing of the Jacobean mansion begun by the 1st Lord, who died in 1733,

72. James Gibbs, Chapel, Witley Court, Worcestershire, 1733–47, west elevation

73. (below) James Gibbs, Design for the chapel, Witley Court, Worcestershire, 1733–47, walls and ceiling, pen and wash (Victoria and Albert Museum, London)

and continued by his widow and son Thomas, 2nd Lord Foley. Its original appearance, before the nineteenth-century stone refacing, is described by Dr Pococke in 1756 as 'built of brick, with a balustrade at top, window frames, and a Doric open portal, all of free stone [with] the west end . . . well adorn'd . . . with a handsom cupola' (Plate 72).[66] All this is reminiscent of Gibbs. The interior, a single aisleless space with a shallow chancel and transepts and a west vestibule supporting a gallery and organ, must have remained unfinished for some years after 1735. The ten windows richly painted with New Testament subjects by Joshua Price in 1719–21 for Cannons chapel were not acquired by Foley until the Cannons sale in 1747; they had to be adapted to the larger openings at Witley. Gibbs's splendid drawing for decorating the 69-foot-long barrel-vaulted ceiling (Plate 73), which shows the bald carcass of the walls and coving, incorporates frames for the canvases of biblical subjects by Antonio Bellucci originally painted for Cannons chapel. Since these canvases are not listed in the 1747 sale catalogues, Foley may have acquired them privately from the Duke of Chandos's heirs following his death in 1744, and this drawing, therefore, may date to that earlier time. But further links with Cannons seem improbable because the ornamental surrounds, long accepted as Giovanni Bagutti's reinstalled plasterwork from the chapel ceiling, are in fact gilt papier mâché.[67] This was a technique fashionable around mid-century, which Lady Luxborough described to William Shenstone as

> a sort of stucco-paper . . . stamped so deep as to project considerably . . . very thick and strong [with] the ornaments . . . all detached; and put on seperately . . . I am assured that the paper carvings are quite as beautiful, and more durable, than either wood or stucco; and for ceilings infinitely preferable, especially as they may be moved, being only fastened up with tacks. They adorn chimnies and indeed whole rooms with them, and make picture-frames of them. The paper is boiled to mash and pounded a vast while, then it is put into moulds of any form . . . when it is tacked up, you either paint it white, or gild it, as you would do wood . . . Lord Foley has done his Chapel in Worcestershire with it.[68]

The executed ceiling decoration differs in some details from Gibbs's drawing, suggesting that here, as with other similar work, he allowed flexibility among the craftsmen with whom he collaborated. In this case the changes produced a hearty expression of rococo which was nearly without equal at that time in Britain.

Gibbs's concern at Witley with the rehabilitation of flotsam from his earlier commission was, of course, not typical; nor was the opulent rococo character of its decoration. The late churches and chapels do not possess the unity of ideas peculiar to his work of the 1720s, the designing and building of which were closely related: the penultimate proposal for St Martin-in-the-Fields was approved in May 1721 and the contract for the Marylebone Chapel was signed several months later, in August; construction on St Martin's began in January 1722; the Derby design was approved in February 1723 and Shipbourne was consecrated in June of that year; the Marylebone Chapel was finished by March 1724, Derby by November 1725 and finally St Martin's, the compositional anchor of the group, was consecrated late in 1726. Understandably Gibbs was reluctant to stray from this highly successful pattern. After this prosperous decade, as he became less involved in church building, perhaps because of his growing country house practise, nothing so important as the London and Derby churches again came his way.

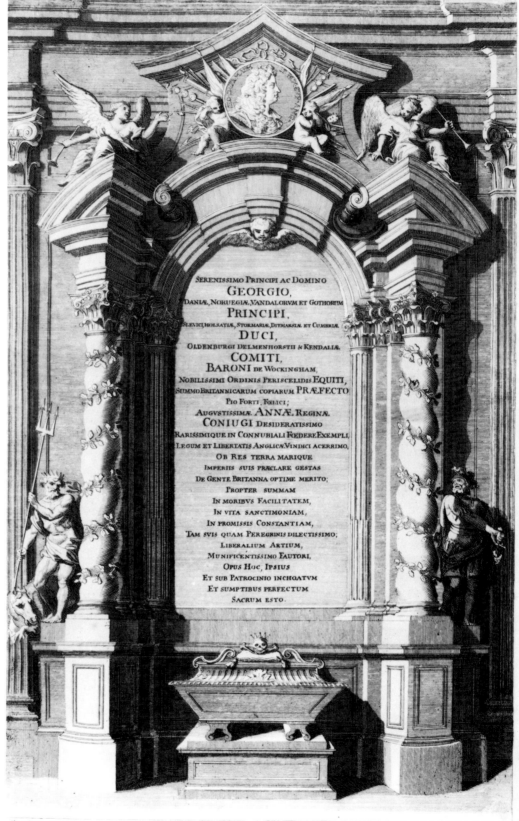

74. James Gibbs,
Dedication page of
J. Flamsteed, *Historiæ
Cœlestis*, 1712, engraving
by L. du Guernier (British
Library, London)

# V

## 'IMMORTAL FAME'

WRITING FROM EXILE at Chillon in 1726 about the proposals for his monument in Alloa church in Scotland, John Erskine, Earl of Mar, gave his son 'liberty to alter [my design] according to your own fancie' but encouraged him to consult those 'who understand and have a right teast of such things, as your acquaintance Mr Gibb'.[1] Gibbs was the first British architect to recognize and make full use of the benefits of designing church monuments, which previously had been almost the exclusive preserve of the sculptor and the master mason.[2]

In Italy, however, this activity had long been a pursuit of the professional architect (Michelangelo, Bernini and Fontana being the most celebrated examples) and Gibbs's enthusiasm for the Baroque tombs and altars which he had first seen as a student in Rome and later had access to in engravings was revealed in one of his earliest works, the engraved dedication page to John Flamsteed's book on stellar observations, *Historiæ Cælestis*, published in London on 5 December 1712 (Plate 74). The Royal Society committee promoting the enterprise included Dr John Arbuthnot, who was soon to recommend Gibbs for the New Churches surveyorship. His composition is based closely on Figure 80 in the second volume of Andrea Pozzo's *Perspectiva Pictorum et Architectorum*, 1702 (Gibbs's engraver Louis du Guernier, a founder member of Kneller's Art Academy in 1711, even imitated the engraving technique of the original plate). Yet, the differences are significant. The pair of putti supporting the portrait medallion of Prince George of Denmark (Queen Anne's husband), the trumpeting angels on the pediment, and the canted sarcophagus derive from Carlo Fontana designs (Plate 75).[3] The transformation of Pozzo's Old Testament figures into Mars and Neptune, alluding to the Prince's role as Lord High Admiral, and other traditional *mementi mori* and resurrection symbols, suggest the engraving was intended as a sort of alternative monument to the Prince, who died in 1708 and was buried without any sculptural commemoration in Westminster Abbey. Certainly Gibbs had this engraving in mind when a few years later he came to design the first and most ambitious of his Abbey tombs. John Holles, 1st Duke of Newcastle, had died in 1711 as the result of a hunting accident, having made no provision in his Will for a monument. His daughter Henrietta first commissioned a design from the Flemish emigré sculptor John Nost, but this slipped away when she married Edward Harley, Lord Oxford, in October 1713, by which time Gibbs had moved into their family circle. One of his early suggestions for the monument (Plate 76) incorporates Newcastle's portrait in a medallion held aloft by a seated angel, again an idea derived from Fontana.[4] The architectural frame is pinnioned by free-standing allegorical statues. The Jacobite Rising in 1715 and Sir Robert Harley's imprisonment on a treason charge during 1716–17 may have interrupted progress on the monument, but in 1721 Gibbs was paid £21 for 'several drawings . . . and inlarging the drawght for the moddel' and £10.10.0 for 'two new drawings . . . carefully done to be adjoynd to the Contractes', which show the monument virtually as erected (Plate 77). A further payment of £40 was received for 'the moddell neatly done in pear tree and the figures done in beard [baked] earth' (a lost terracotta, one of the earliest such preparatory objects in English monumental sculpture). The model was undoubtedly made by Francis Bird (1667–1731). Regarded as 'the most famous Statuary, that this Nation ever bred',[5] Bird had studied on several occasions before 1700 in Rome with one of the leading exponents of the late Baroque, Pierre le Gros the younger. The second visit, in 1698–9, coincided with Le Gros's preoccupation with his masterpiece, the Altar of St Louis Gonzaga in S. Ignazio, executed to Andrea Pozzo's design, about which Gibbs was to write so enthusiastically a few years later: 'an exterordinary fine [and] noble Composition of different sorts of curious Marbles, very rich and magnificent [the] columns support a cornice having a broken pediment over it, and above that an Antick upon which ther is a very fine shield . . . and the pediment of the Attick is adorned with figures of Angles . . . in the middle parte [is] the figure of this holy person as big as the life, exquisitely well cut in white marble . . . and so are all the figures of this Altar peece . . . allowed to be one of the finest . . . in Rome'.[6] Bird, therefore, could bring an Italianate fluency to the execution of Gibbs's unprecedentedly ambitious monument, then as now the largest in the Abbey; and he offered the added attraction of having had 'great dealings in Italy for Marbles'[7] which are an essential ingredient of the design. Gibbs's source was Carlo Rainaldi's polychromatic altar in the Gesù e Maria (Plate 78), while the flanking figures are based on the Wisdom and Charity in Domenico Guidi's monument to Gaspare Thiene (1678) in S. Andrea della Valle.[8] Gibbs's confident handling of the most sophisticated Roman Baroque vocabulary was a strikingly new feature in the Abbey. The entire convex structure is hinged to the piers of the easternmost bays of the north transept so that Newcastle's figure, dressed in modern armour and flanked by Wisdom and Charity, as well as the attic group of angels and putti, swell towards the spectator. Although Gibbs commended the figures as 'well perform'd', some critics disapproved. James Ralph thought the ducal figure 'full of absurdities: it neither sits nor lies, is employed in no action, has no expression, no dignity, and abounds with manifest, open disproportions; the two statues on each side are equally tame and unmeaning, and have no more relation to the principal, than if the were still in the statuary's yard: I am as much displeased with the two brace of angels that incumber the upper part of this pile', and he believed the monument to be 'only the admiration of the vulgar [since] magnificence has been consulted only, and not beauty'.[9] And George Vertue, who considered the Newcastle monument a work of 'great . . . nobleness as the immagination of men of Art and Skill coud invent and Contrive', could not refrain from recounting how the sculptor Peter Scheemakers, that 'little animal', told Edward Harley 'to his Face that in that magnificent monument . . . there was such figures that disgracd it, that to do it right, his Lordship shoud take them away—upon which [Harley] turnd about & said nothing but walkt away'.[10] He employed Bird and Gibbs again in 1727–8 on the monument to members of the Cavendishe family, including Henrietta Harley's mother, at Bolsover church in Derbyshire (Plate 79). This is a huge Corinthian aedicule offering full play to the sculptor's stock of multi-coloured marbles, with only a pair of reclining allegorical figures. These, unlike the architecture, are poorly carved and exiled to the gloomiest reaches of the vault.[11]

Gibbs seems to have been more alert than some of his clients to Bird's technical disabili-

75. Carlo Fontana, Queen Christina of Sweden's monument, St Peter's, Rome, 1697–1702, engraving, Plate 36 in D. De' Rossi, *Studio D'Architettura Civile . . . di Roma*, II, 1711

76. James Gibbs, Design for monument to John Holles, 1st Duke of Newcastle, Westminster Abbey, London, 1721–3, pen and wash (The Trustees of Sir John Soane's Museum, London)

77. James Gibbs and Francis Bird, Monument to John Holles, 1st Duke of Newcastle, Westminster Abbey, London, 1721–2, Plate 111 in *A Book of Architecture*, 1728

78. Carlo Rainaldi, Altar in the Church of the Gesù e Maria, Rome, 1671–80, engraving, Plate 48 in G. J. De' Rossi, *Disegni di Vari Altari e Cappelle nelle Chiesa di Roma*, 1713

79. James Gibbs and
Francis Bird, Monument
to Cavendishe Family, St
Mary's, Bolsover,
Derbyshire, 1727–8

ties because even before the Newcastle monument was finished in 1723 he had approached
Michael Rysbrack (1694–1770), who had recently arrived from Antwerp. Vertue reported
in October 1720 on having seen his 'very excellent' clay models which showed him to
be 'a great Master *tho' young*' and mentioned 'he was recommended to Mr. Gibbs . . .
who from the time of his first comeing . . . has much imployd him'. Three years later
Vertue hinted that Gibbs patronized the sculptor only 'for his own advantage not for
Encouragement' and recorded a conversation with 'poor' Rysbrack who 'told me of
[Gibbs's] extravagant exactions on his labour that he coud not possibly live had not other
business come in to help him of more proffit', concluding that this was 'an unreasonable
gripeing usage to a most Ingenious Artist. in his way [having] far more merrit than Gibbs
ever will be M[aste]r of'.[12] Nevertheless, both men remained friends, bound further by
their interest in collecting works of art and their adherence to Roman Catholicism. In
1725, when Rysbrack was carving the marble busts of Gibbs (Frontispiece) and one of
Pope also commissioned by the architect (Plate 10), they each took up residence in terrace
houses on either side of the Marylebone Chapel, where they carried on their respective
businesses and lived in considerable splendour. They later appeared together in Gawen
Hamilton's conversation pictures of 1730 and 1735 (Plate 8). Rysbrack was employed
on nearly all Gibbs's important commissions up to 1730 and is praised for the beauty
of his carving on several occasions in *A Book of Architecture*, to which he subscribed. His

81. Pierre-Étienne Monnot, Monument to John Cecil, 5th Earl of Exeter, St Martin's, Stamford, Lincolnshire, 1703–4, pen and wash, drawing by John Michael Rysbrack, *c.* 1721 (Plymouth Art Gallery)

80. (left) James Gibbs, Design for monument to John Sheffield, Duke of Buckingham. Westminster Abbey, London, 1721–2, Plate 116 in *A Book of Architecture*, 1728

considerable accomplishments as a draughtsman also seem to have been useful to Gibbs, who rendered figures awkwardly, and in some of his drawings these features may have been improved by Rysbrack's livelier hand.[13]

His immediate effect is apparent in Gibbs's design of 1721 for the monument to John Sheffield, Duke of Buckingham (Plate 80). The Duke had died on 24 February 1721 and was laid in state in his London house 'in a very magnificent Manner . . . in a Room . . . hung with Velvet, within an Alcove, and a Canopy, with Feathers, the Coronet, Cap, and Cushion, and all the Trophies of Honour fix'd round him'.[14] Gibbs offered a similarly flamboyant design for his Abbey tomb. Abandoning the rigid architectural frame of the Newcastle monument, although retaining the poses and positions of the statues of Wisdom and Charity, the ducal effigy is tilted forward and attended by additional allegorical figures. This new, relaxed approach owes something to French taste,[15] although the composition obviously derives from Pierre-Étienne Monnot's monument to John Cecil, 5th Earl of Exeter, and his wife. Gibbs, remarking favourably on other work by the same sculptor in the Gesù,[16] may have seen the monument being carved in Rome in 1703, but a sketch of it by Rysbrack after its installation in St Martin's church at Stamford, Lincolnshire, in 1704 (Plate 81), suggests he may have been employed to record the work specifically for reuse in the Buckingham commission and, furthermore, that this was one of Gibbs's methods of building-up his repertory of forms.[17] Unfortunately, Buckingham died before work began and his widow transferred the commission to the Belgian sculptors Denis Plumière, Laurent Delvaux and Peter Scheemakers; their sumptuous monument was erected in 1722.

In the following year, however, Gibbs reasserted his position. Two new monuments, to John Smith and the Marchioness of Annandale (together with that to the Duke of Newcastle, also completed in 1723), representing the most advanced examples of the new trend, were described and illustrated in John Dart's important book *Westmonasterium, or The history and Antiquities of The Abbey Church of St. Peters Westminster*, 1723. Dart considered the monument to John Smith (Plate 85), a Commissioner of the Excise (paid for by his son-in-law Sir Edward Desbouverie of Longford Castle and Gibbs's fellow-governor at St Bartholomew's Hospital), as 'one of the justest and most beautiful in this Church', while Ralph though it 'much in taste . . . in a stile most harmonious and agreeable', admiring particularly Rysbrack's 'fine bust . . . supported on a weeping figure, representing his daughter, both [of] which are designed and executed with great judgment and spirit', although he drew attention to the awkwardness of the unsupported shoulder.[18] The monument set up by the Scotsman James Johnstone, 2nd Marquess of Annandale (described in 1723 as 'a hopeful Nobleman, just returned from his Travels' in Italy),[19] to the memory of his mother the Marchioness Sophia (Plate 82) is placed carefully within one of the Gothic bays of the south aisle but is entirely classical in character. This unassuming, exclusively architectural design of subtly contrasting white, pink, light and dark grey variegated marbles was radically new, simpler and more elegant than any of its earlier neighbours. Gibbs and some of his clients regarded such luxurious Abbey monuments as equally appropriate for rural churches. The Rev. Joseph Trapp, in his pamphlet *The Honour and Vertue of Building, Repairing, and Adorning Churches*, 1723, mentions that the patrons of the new church at Shipbourne in Kent, Lord and Lady Barnard, 'by a Christian Contempt of Death' also commissioned their own 'noble Monument' of marble with 'August Statues, and other Decorations' (Plate 83). The monument is unsigned, but the fine carving and sympathetic treatment of the figures point to Rysbrack.

By the middle of the 1720s Gibbs's reputation as a daring monument designer had spread outside London, although there he did not always collaborate with Rysbrack. In the monument to Montague and Jane Drake at Amersham, Buckinghamshire (Plate 84), a less proficient sculptor was chosen because the client, Montague Garrard Drake, wished to spend only £180. His contract of 1725 with the French-born Andrew Carpenter, a sculptor of St Martin-in-the-Fields parish who specialized in lead garden figures, specified the portrait medallions 'to be of the best Statuary Marble, And the Shields, either of Marble or mettal Bronsed as required, And the medalls to have fframes round them of black and yellow marble'. These expensive-looking materials as well as the composition itself reflect Fontana's celebrated monument to Queen Christina of Sweden in St Peter's, completed in 1702, just before Gibbs arrived in Rome (Plate 75).[20] But the carving on the Drake monument is poor and the architecture uninspired; the family were clearly disappointed, because Montague's own monument, commissioned by his widow in 1730, was designed and carved at a cost of £600 by a more able sculptor, Peter Scheemakers.[21] At Aston near Birmingham Gibbs provided a wall tablet for Sir John and Lady Bridgeman in 1726 which developed a composition represented by Camillo Rusconi's tomb to Raffaele Fabretti (c. 1700) in S. Maria sopra Minerva, Rome.[22]

Gibbs's most important sculpture achievement in the provinces is the splendid monument to Edward Colston in All Saints at Bristol (Plate 86) commissioned towards the end of the 1720s by his kinsmen, who were associated with Gibbs at St Bartholomew's

82. (facing page top left) James Gibbs, Monument to Sophia Fairholm, Marchioness of Annandale, Westminster Abbey, London, 1723, pen and wash (Ashmolean Museum, Oxford, Gibbs Collection I.41)

83. (facing page top middle) James Gibbs, Monument to Christopher Vane, Lord Barnard, Lady Barnard and Elizabeth Vane, St Giles, Shipbourne, Kent, 1723

84. (facing page top right) James Gibbs, Monument to Montague and Jane Drake, St Mary's, Amersham, Buckinghamshire, 1725, Plate 121 in *A Book of Architecture*, 1728

85. (facing page bottom) James Gibbs and John Michael Rysbrack, Monument to John Smith, Westminster Abbey, London, c. 1723

The Publick Charities and Benefactions Given and Founded by EDWARD COLSTON, Esq.

In BRISTOL, on St. Michael's Hill.

An Alms-House for 12 Men and 12 Women, the Chief Brother to receive 6s. the others 3s. per Week, besides Coal, &c.—To a Chaplain 10l. per Ann.—The whole to be paid by Fee-Farm Rents on Estates in Northumberland, Cumberland, and Durham, and by some Houses and Lands near the House.—The Charge about 8500l.

In King-Street.

Six Sailors to be maintain'd in the Merchants Alms-House, by a Farm in Congersbury, Somerset.—The Charge 600l.

In Temple-Street.

A School for 40 Boys, to be Cloath'd and Taught, endow'd with an Annuity out of the Manour of Tomarleaze, Somerset; and a House and Garden for the Master.—The Charge 3000l.

In the College-Green.

To the Re-building the Boys Hospital, and for 6 Boys to be Cloath'd, Maintain'd, Instructed, and Apprentic'd, a Farm of 70l. per Ann. in Congersbury.—The Charge 1500l.

In St. Peter's Parish.

To St. Peter's Hospital 200l.
And for Placing Out Poor Children 200l.

On St. Augustin's Back.

An Hospital for a Master, two Ushers and a Cate-chist, and for One Hundred Boys to be Instructed, Cloath'd, Maintain'd, and Apprentic'd.—The Charge about 40000l.
For 12 Years after his Death 100l. per Ann. to such as were Apprentic'd from this or Temple School
To the several Charity Schools, each 10l. per Ann. given for many Years whilst he lived, and continued 12 Years after his Death.

To the Repair and Beautifying Churches.

| | £ | | | £ |
|---|---|---|---|---|
| All Saints | 250 | | St. Michael | 50 |
| Cathedral | 260 | | St. Stephen | 50 |
| Clifton | 50 | | Temple | 100 |
| St. James | 100 | | St. Thomas | 50 |
| St. Mary Redcliff | 100 | | St. Werburgh | 160 |

For Reading Prayers at All-Saints every Monday and Tuesday Morning, 7l. per Ann. 140l.
For 12 Sermons at Newgate, 6l. per Ann. 120l.
For 14 Sermons in Lent 20s. per Ann. 400l.

In LONDON.

To St. Bartholomew's Hospital 2500l.
To Christ-Church Hospital 2000l.
To St. Thomas's Hospital 500l.
To Bethlehem Hospital 500l.
To the New Workhouse without Bishops Gate 200l.
To the Society for propagating the Gospel 500l.
To the Company of Mercers 100l.
6100l.

At Sheen in Surry.

An Alms-House for 6 Poor Men, built and endowed.

At MORTLAKE.

For the Education and Cloathing of 12 Boys and 12 Girls, 45l. per Ann. 900l.
To 85 Poor People at his Death, 20s. each 85l.

In DEVONSHIRE.

Towards Building a Church at Tiverton 50l.

In LANCASHIRE.

Towards Building a Church at Manchester 20l.

To 18 Charity-Schools in several Parts of England for many Years of his Life, and continued 12 Years after his Death, 90l. per Ann.

To the Augmentation of 60 Small Livings 6000l.

This Great and Pious Benefactor was known to have done many other excellent Charities; and what he did in Secret, is believ'd not to be inferior to what he did in Publick.

Edward, the Son of William Colston, Esq. (and Sarah his Wife) was Born in BRISTOL Novemb. 2, 1636. Died at Mortlake in SURRY Octob. 11, 1721. and lies Interr'd in All-Saints Church, BRISTOL.

THE MONUMENT OF THE LATEWORTHY, GREAT, GOOD, PIOUS, AND CHARITABLE Edward Colston Esq.

Printed and Publish'd according to Act of Parliament 1751.

Hospital. Colston (died 1721), the great Bristol philanthropist, is shown in everyday clothes reclining on a tomb chest, his hand pressed gently to his breast (Plate 87). Rysbrack was the executor of this handsome figure. Although Lady Luxborough disliked the use of 'dress and full-bottomed wig on a tomb',[23] the lack of pomposity in the figure was clearly intentional, for a popular engraving of the time shows two groups of figures representing Charity and the succoured poor paying homage to Colston's considerable beneficences, which are listed on the pair of tablets. The beautifully detailed architecture was carved and presumably also erected in 1729 by Michael Sidnell, a local mason who subscribed to *A Book of Architecture*, in which Colston's monument is illustrated. On 11 July 1728, a few months after its publication, Rysbrack and Walter Lee, a Marylebone mason, agreed for £500 to execute Gibbs's design for Sir Edward Seymour's tomb in Maiden Bradley church in Wiltshire (Plate 88). The effigy is posed like Colson's but surrounded by a more complex architecture, compounding elements from earlier Gibbs designs. It is executed in festive multi-coloured variegated marbles perhaps intended to recall the deceased himself, who according to the epitaph was a 'man of such Endowments as added Lustre to his noble Ancestry, Commanded Reverence from his Contempories, and stands the fairest pattern to Posterity'. *The Grub-street Journal* called it a 'beautiful Monument' in 1731.[24]

86. (facing page) James Gibbs, Monument to Edward Colston, All Saints, Bristol, Avon, 1728–9, engraving by G. Scotin, 1751 (City of Bristol Museum and Art Gallery)

87. James Gibbs, John Michael Rysbrack and Michael Sidnell, Monument to Edward Colston, All Saints, Bristol, Avon, 1728–9

90. (facing page) James Gibbs and John Michael Rysbrack, Monument to Katherine Bovey, Westminster Abbey, London, 1727–8, figure of Wisdom

88. James Gibbs and John Michael Rysbrack, Monument to Sir Edward Seymour, All Saints, Maiden Bradley, Wiltshire, 1728–30

89. James Gibbs and John Michael Rysbrack, Monument to Katharine Bovey, Westminster Abbey, London, 1727–8

The Baroque tendencies in these works reached a climax towards the end of the 1720s in London. The most remarkable example, perhaps Gibbs's Abbey masterpiece, is the monument to Katherine Bovey of 1727 (Plate 89). Its most striking feature, representing a new theatrical departure in English sculpture, is the pair of allegorical figures perched on the corners of a sarcophagus, Wisdom leaning towards the profile portrait of Mrs Bovey (Plate 90), Faith glancing upward to read the laudatory inscription. The 'lively and free' carving by Rysbrack[25] shows greater skill than the figures on the Shipbourne monument of a few years earlier (Plate 83). The composition was developed from Giovanni Battista Foggini's tomb to Francesco Feroni (1691–3) in SS. Annunziatta at Florence, and a group of celebrated papal tombs, particularly Le Gros's to Gregory XV and Cardinal Ludovisi (completed 1713) in S. Ignazio, which Gibbs may have seen in its early stages before leaving Rome in 1708.[26] Roman late Baroque elements also appear in an unusual scenic design

ory,

91. James Gibbs, Design
for a monument to 'a
Noble Lord and Lady',
undated, Plate 118 in *A
Book of Architecture*, 1728

92. James Gibbs,
Monument to John
Dryden, Westminster
Abbey, London, 1720–1,
engraving, Plate IX in J.
Dart, *Westmonasterium*, I,
1723

(Plate 91) where flying putti undrape a baldachin to reveal the profile portraits of 'a Noble Lord and Lady' mounted on an obelisk with attendant figures of Justice and Wisdom. Gibbs here seems to have recollected the temporary decoration Fontana created for the memorial services held in Rome in 1705 for Emperor Leopold I at S. Maria dell'Anima and for King Pedro II of Portugal at S. Antonio dei Portoghesi two years later.[27] Gibbs described his design in 1728 as 'executed with some variation', probably meaning the more modest wall tablet at Mitcham, Surrey, erected to the London philanthropist Sir Ambrose Crowley and his wife, which incorporates almost identical profile portraits and vestigial curtains in relief.

By the end of the decade the majority of Gibbs's monuments were still strongly Roman Baroque in appearance, yet his buildings had moved irrevocably towards the new classicism. This stylistic schizophrenia seems to have been caused by the fact that most of the monument commissions came from either conservative Scots or Tories uncommitted to more progressive English artistic trends; some were governors of St Bartholomew's Hospital, a Jacobite stronghold, and others were staunch Jacobite Catholics with attachments to Rome. Nevertheless, in a few examples in Westminster Abbey Gibbs introduced

93. James Gibbs, Design for monument to Ben Jonson, Westminster Abbey, London, *c.* 1723, pen and wash (Ashmolean Museum, Oxford, Gibbs Collection III.104)

94. (right) James Gibbs, Monument to Matthew Prior, Westminster Abbey, London, 1721–3, Plate 112 in *A Book of Architecture*, 1728

some important classical innovations. He favoured particularly the classical portrait bust and in the otherwise Baroque monument to the celebrated Bart's physician Dr John Freind, set up in Westminster Abbey in 1730–1, the bust was praised for its 'plainness and simplicity'.[28] But the tomb bust *à l'antique* was associated especially with literary figures.

> See where the tombs of poets round us rise,
> Where the bright ruin of *Parnassus* lies.
> GAY, PRIOR, DRYDEN, those bright sons of fame,
> Those shining honours of the *British* name[29]

It is significant that the monument to John Dryden (Plate 92), the first that Gibbs completed in the Abbey (commissioned in 1720 and on public view in January of the following year) and also one of the first Georgian incursions into Poets' Corner, was praised for being 'very neat . . . the more Beautiful for its Plainness' and for having a 'Plain, majestick, and just [appearance], equal to the . . . Merits of the Poet',[30] who was a Jacobite Catholic, like Gibbs, obliged to maintain a low public profile with regard to personal beliefs. Gibbs

devised an unpretentious architectural composition, devoid of epitaph, allegory and politically suspect imagery. Notwithstanding, so new was the idea of burying venerated poets
around Chaucer's tomb in the south transept still in 1720 that the Dean of Westminster
requested Alexander Pope (who was involved in the commission and had been campaign-
ing for a more rigorous continuance of this observance begun by the Elizabethans) to
maintain a modest propriety by erecting a smooth free-stone wall behind Dryden's monument which would screen St Benedict's chapel in the south ambulatory and 'remove the
Eysore there would otherwise be to those who go into that Chappel to see the Tombs'.[31]
Dryden's was acceptable because, like its predecessors, the monuments to Michael Drayton
and Thomas Shadwell, it was dominated by the poet's laurel-crowned bust. A contemporary poem linked this portrait with Homer.[32] The sculptor is unrecorded and around 1731
the bust was replaced by one carved by Peter Scheemakers;[33] later the architectural frame
was also removed so that nothing now remains of the original concept.

The initial success of Dryden's monument was of great importance to Gibbs. He
repeated some of its elements in the famous wall tablet erected by 1723 to Ben Jonson,
probably using Rysbrack as sculptor (Plate 93). The delicate relief masks of Comedy,
Tragedy and Sophocles allude to Jonson as 'the first who regulated the *English* Stage,
after the manner of the Ancients'.[34] Ralph thought it 'executed with great happiness,
and looks with abundance of life and spirit', the tablet 'beautiful, and the decorations
few, proper, and elegant'.[35]

The formula of the Antique bust for Poets' Corner was firmly established in 1721 in
a special and unexpected way. On 18 September Matthew Prior died at Wimpole. A
week later his remains were interred near the tomb of Edmund Spenser, and by this time
Gibbs, who was one of the official mourners, had prepared a design (Plate 94) under
the stimulus of a provision of £500 in the poet's Will, which he refers to as his 'last piece
of *human Vanity*'.[36]

> As Doctors give Physic by way of prevention,
> MATT alive and in health of his Tomb-stone took care;
> For delays are unsafe, and his Pious Intention
> May haply be never fulfill'd by his Heir.[37]

Its commanding feature is Prior's marble bust *en négligé*, which is more than an expression
of the Poets' Corner tradition:

> Philips and Laurell'd Dryden seem's to Smile,
> To see great Prior bury'd in this Isle;
> Greatly rejoic'd each venerable Bust,
> To see Him mingl'd with Poetic Dust.[38]

It is also an exceptional portrait by the greatest French sculptor of the time, Antoine
Coysevox, carved some years earlier in Paris.[39] The flanking figures of Poetry and History
were Rysbrack's responsibility, the payment for which had caused the rift reported by
Vertue in 1723, for Gibbs was unwilling to give 'more than 35 pounds for each statue
to be cut in Marble. when others have above a hundred pounds, & [he himself] is to
have . . . upwards of a hundred pounds for each'.[40] Ralph condemned them because they
'hurt' the bust and recommended an alternative design incorporating 'a simple urn, with
the head on a pedestal over it, [which] would have had a finer effect, and better deserve
our admiration'.[41] Nevertheless, Gibbs's composition, which was without precedence in
English sculpture, was generally admired and led one commentator to rhapsodize:

While Gibbs displays his elegant Design
And Rysbracks Art does in the Sculpture shine
With due composure. & proportion just
adding new lustre to the finish't Bust
Each Artist here, perpetuates his Name
And shares with Prior, an Immortal Fame.[42]

Yet this portrait occupies an even more significant place in English sculpture history. A few months after Prior's death his former secretary Adrian Drift reported to Edward Harley having seen in the studio of Richard Dickenson, a Piccadilly 'figure-maker . . . a fine Copy of the Buste of Mr: Prior, bespoke by Mr: Gibbs, and done after his own Fancy, the head is the same, but the other part is less, and in lieu of the Cap, Mr Dickenson has put short hair a la romaine, which has this Effect as to show a greater likeness of Mr: Prior's face, and is more in the manner of the Ancient Busto's'.[43] This is surely an indication of the architect's rejection of a fashion which a few other artists and critics were also just beginning to regard as outmoded. While Ralph 'justly esteemed' Coysevox's bust as 'one of the best things in *England*', he agreed that 'if a little *French* embroidery on the cap, and drapery, were spared . . . it would be far from a disadvantage to it, because it would be then more a-kin to the chastity and purity of the Antique'.[44] Gibbs seems to be offering the bust of Prior 'done after his own Fancy' (unfortunately lost) as a new solution, for it is not another example of a modern imitation of the Antique but a consciously radical physical transformation of a celebrated Baroque bust and for its time

95. James Gibbs, Design for monument to James Craggs, Westminster Abbey, London, 1724–7, pen and wash (Victoria and Albert Museum, London)

96. James Gibbs, Design for monument to William Shakespeare, Westminster Abbey, London, undated, pen and wash (Ashmolean Museum, Oxford, Gibbs Collection III.101)

appears to have been a unique phenomenon in British sculpture. In this context Rysbrack's undraped, wigless and seemingly unflattering bust of Gibbs, 1723–6 (now in the Radcliffe Library, Oxford) makes sense.

The architect's full commitment to this new classical mode is best seen, however, in his most revolutionary monument, that to James Craggs, one of the Secretaries of State for Scotland, who died in 1721 (Plate 95). Commissioned three years later, it is an elegant concept, with the life-size figure of young Craggs standing cross-legged and free of the pedimented frame, his arm supported on an urn. Although the pose was not unique in English sculpture, it was the first in the eighteenth century to drive directly from classical Roman sources, examples of which were shown in Montfaucon's *L'Antiquité Expliquée*, 1719.[45] Ralph considered there was 'much judgment in setting his statue upright, because it fills the vista [terminating the west end of the south aisle], with great harmony, and looks advantageously even at the greatest distance; the attitude of it is delicate and fine; the thought of resting it on an urn, pathetique and judicious ... the architecture is alike plain, and the embellishments few, and well chosen. In a word, many tombs have more beauties, none fewer faults.' He felt only that 'if the face and head had been more finish'd, the whole [would have] been without blemish'.[46] Pope, who composed the epitaph and supervised the progress of the carving, too, was worried about the likeness, which was based on a painting or engraving, although by the time the terracotta model was being prepared in July 1724 he felt that it had been brought 'to a greater degree of resemblance than I could have thought'.[47] The sculptor was Giovanni Battista Guelfi who, although less talented than Rysbrack, was Burlington's protégé and, therefore, regarded as better equipped to interpret the Antique character of the design. Nevertheless, the treatment of drapery, which follows closely Gibbs's drawing, looks more like the flamboyant Baroque of Guelfi's master, Camillo Rusconi, and indicates one aspect of the teething troubles experienced by the emergence of the classical style in English sculpture.[48]

Pope was convinced the monument 'will make the finest figure ... in the place' and Gibbs returned to the theme in his monument at Kirkleatham, Yorkshire (1739–41), to Marwood William Turner, who, like Craggs, had died young. Yet Gibbs seems to have hesitated about the appropriateness of the pose and decided on a seated figure, which is shown in his presentation drawing for the mausoleum which was to house the monument (Plate 271). Nevertheless, in 1741 the job went to Peter Scheemakers, who returned to the standing cross-legged pose which he and William Kent were using contemporaneously in the famous Abbey monument to Shakespeare.

Gibbs's own proposal for the Bard (Plate 96), which may date as early as 1726 when John Rich, manager of Covent Garden Theatre, launched the idea of erecting a national monument, is merely a blending of familiar features from the Prior and Bovey designs. His executed monuments after 1730 are all unambitious wall tablets with no figurative work. He seems to have had nothing new to contribute to this branch of business and devoted less and less time to it. The end came when one of his most prestigious patrons, John Campbell, 2nd Duke of Argyll and Greenwich, died in 1743 and the commission for designing and carving his splendid Westminster Abbey monument went to the French emigré Louis François Roubiliac, who demonstrated here 'the greatness of his Genius in his invention design & execution in Every part equal, if not superior to any others. this monument now out shines for noblenes & skill all those before done, by the best sculptors, this fifty years past'.[49]

# VI

## Country Houses

### Early Houses

GIBBS RETURNED FROM ITALY in 1708 to find domestic architecture in Britain undergoing a radical change. Castle Howard, Blenheim, Heythrop, Stainborough and a host of other great Baroque houses were under construction. Most country house owners still looked to modern Italy and France for inspiration, and Lord Harrold, the younger son of the Duke of Kent, was not alone in his desire to travel abroad 'to get what printed plans he can of the best houses he meets with and to endeavour to be Informed of the best Architects In severall places of Italy'.[1] But soon after 1708, at Wilbury House in Wiltshire, William Benson reintroduced a new classical pattern based on the Renaissance villa, while Colen Campbell and Giacomo Leoni began preparing to launch a virulent condemnation of Baroque, which they published in 1715 in the first volume of *Vitruvius Britannicus* and *The Architecture of A. Palladio*.[2] These were years of indecision and transition, and it was Gibbs's special contribution to demonstrate how such apparently irreconcilable stylistic attitudes as Baroque and Classical might be combined into a workable architectural design.

The scheme for Dupplin Castle in Perthshire for Thomas Hay, 6th Earl of Kinnoull, illustrates the nature of his initial commitment to the Continental trends. Kinnoull had considered improving the family seat at least since 1707, yet little was done until the early 1720s when the Edinburgh architect James Smith built a new house for the 7th Earl. Some time between those dates Gibbs offered a design of such daring and splendid eccentricity that it is difficult to imagine how seriously it could have been taken (Plate 97). Two hundred and twenty-five feet long, slightly shorter than the garden front of Castle Howard, its central domed rotunda, seventy feet in both diameter and height, was bisected by four obtusely angled wings to form an immense symbolic Cross of St Andrew, a sort of Baroque equivalent to the medieval Scottish fortified keep. French sources provided many ideas for the planning and detailing.[3] With Kinnoull's arrest for complicity in the abortive Jacobite rising in late 1715, Gibbs's design became superfluous, as were also his suggested improvements to Alloa in Clackmannanshire for Hay's son-in-law John Erskine, 11th Earl of Mar, a former Secretary of State for Scotland, who led the rising in the North. In 1709 Mar had secured his protégé an officer's post at Stirling Castle, which was merely a sinecure to allow him to participate in the extensive programme of remodelling the Earl's estate a few miles away. An engraved plan of the property issued in the following year (Plate 99) shows the medieval tower-house on the edge of the town as the nucleus of a vast Versailles-like layout of formal gardens, plantations and tree-lined avenues des-

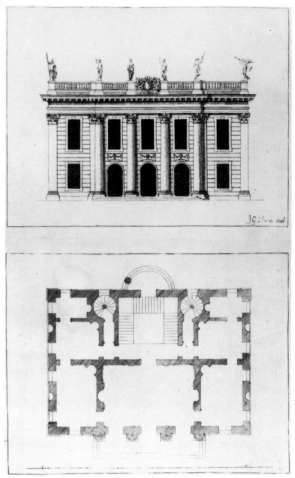

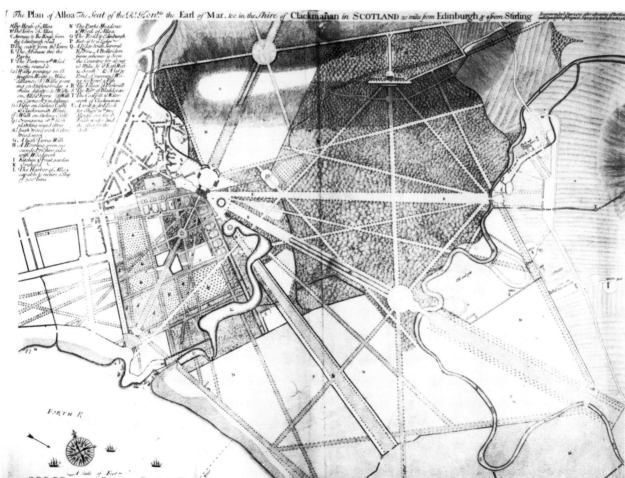

The Plan of Alloa The Seat of the R.t Hon.ble the Earl of Mar, &c. in the Shire of Clackmanan in SCOTLAND 20 miles from Edinburgh & 4 from Stirling

FORTH R.

A Scale of Feet

cribed in 1723 as far exceeding Hampton Court or Kensington. It contained a 'Parterre, spacious and finely adorn'd with Statues and Vases; and from this Parterre to the River *Forth*, runs a fine Terras ... from whence ... you have Thirty Two different Vistoes, each ending on some remarkable Seat or Mountain ... The Avenue to the *East*, through the Wood, is prodigiously long and large, and between each Visto, from the Parterre, are Wildernesses of Trees for Birds, and little *Grottoes*.'[4] Little of this now survives, leaving Gibbs's contribution uncertain, but he had proposed the 'Lodge with Several Rooms, A Bellvidere from whence is Seen the Country for about 16 Miles' on a terrace aptly named Comley Bank, which is shown on the 1710 plan in the north-east section of the park. The composition of the lodge (Plate 98), as might be expected from a young and untried architect, was an amalgamation of well-known Continental buildings he had seen as a student.[5] Because of the sudden fall of land which allowed for the addition of a base-ment on the terrace side, Gibbs was able to create an unusually compact plan. The ground floor is occupied by an entrance hall, four small living rooms and a large staircase leading to the first floor; an additional pair of spiral stairs descend to further quarters which have access to the terrace. Mar's ostentatious proposals for Alloa were abandoned when he fled into exile in 1715.

Unfortunately little is known about Gibbs's movements during these early years, but his interest in French architecture is suggested by this small group of designs and his inten-tion to visit Paris in 1717.[6] Although later in date, the position of French sources in the conflict between the old and the new in British architecture is well shown in work associated with Gibbs at Houghton Hall, the Norfolk mansion of the Prime Minister Sir Robert Walpole (Plate 100). The new residence, designed by Campbell and begun in 1722, exem-plified Palladian principles on a palatial scale and expressed the owner's political and

97. (facing page top left) James Gibbs, Design for Dupplin Castle, Perthshire, undated, plan and elevation, engraving (George Clarke Collection, Worcester College, Oxford)

98. (facing page top right) James Gibbs, Design for Comley Bank Lodge, Alloa, Clackmannanshire, *c.* 1710, plan and entrance elevation, engraving (George Clarke Collection, Worcester College, Oxford)

99. (facing page bottom) J. Sturt, 'The Plan of Alloa', Clackmannanshire, 1710, engraving (The Earl of Mar and Kelly Papers, Scottish Record Office, Edinburgh)

100. Colen Campbell and James Gibbs, Houghton Hall, Norfolk, 1722–35, west elevation

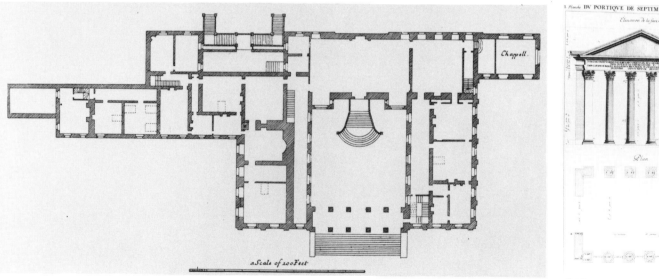

102. (bottom left) James Gibbs, Design for Witham Park, Somerset, *c.* 1717, plan, engraving, Plate 91 in C. Campbell, *Vitruvius Britannicus*, 1717

103. (bottom right) Portico of Septimius Severus, Rome, plan and elevation, engraving in A. Desgodetz, *Les Edifices Antique de Rome*, 1682, p. 165, Plate I

dynastic ambitions; for the foundation stone reads 'God grant, That after its Master, to a mature Old-age, shall have long enjoyed it in Perfection, his latest Descendents may safely possess it, in an unimpaired Condition, to the End of Time'[7]. Yet the new classicism was not adopted wholeheartedly, and as the fabric rose its design was radically altered. In place of Campbell's square 'Wilton' towers at each of the four corners Walpole now favoured large panelled domes with lanterns of Portland stone; these were constructed by 1735. No doubt the intention was to enliven the huge static Palladian bulk of the house set in its stark landscape, for Lord Hervey told the Prince of Wales in 1731 that 'the country and situation are not what [Walpole] would have chosen ... The soil is not fruitful, there is little wood, and no water: absolutely none for ornament, and all that is necessary for use forced up by art. These are disadvantages he had to struggle with.' The four domes, he adds, 'were obstinately raised by the master, and covered with stones in defiance of all the virtuosi who ever gave their opinions about it'.[8] Edward Harley, on a visit in the following year (reporting that the house 'has made a great deal of noise, but I think it is not deserving of it . . . it is neither magnificent nor beautiful, there is a very great expense without either judgment or taste. [The] hall, as well as the plan of the house, are exhibited in that ignorant rascal's book called "Vitruvius Britannicus"'), noted that the alterations were 'by Mr. Gibbs from the first design. The house as it is now is a composition of the greatest blockheads and most ignorant fellows in architecture that are. I think Gibbs was to blame to alter any of their designs or mend their blunders.'[9] Since Walpole was a generous benefactor in 1724–5 to the building programmes at both King's College and the Public Building at Cambridge,[10] Gibbs's presence at Houghton is understandable; but was he really responsible for this lapse of discipline? Although Walpole is purported to have said that he himself had taken the idea of the towers from Osterley Park,[11] domes of this distinctive form and position, with œil-de-bœuf windows breaking above the balustrade, are French in character.[12] It may be that this Gallic amendment was suggested by Robert's brother Horatio, 1st Baron Walpole, who was English ambassador to France between 1723 and 1730 (and also one of the commissioners for rebuilding St Martin-in-the-Fields).[13]

Gibbs's early failures in Scotland, largely due to political uncertainties, were at first compounded by professional jealousies in England, where he turned to the more lucrative business of country house remodelling. In *Vitruvius Britannicus* Colen Campbell neglected to credit him as architect of the important new improvements (both suggested and executed) at Burlington House in Piccadilly (1715–16), Lowther Hall in Westmorland and Witham Friary in Somerset (both *c.*1717). In the last case, Campbell had attempted without success to attract the owner Sir William Wyndham's attention by alluding to the 'Decorations that sufficiently express the Magnificence of the generous Patron'.[14] Gibbs had probably met Wyndham, a former Secretary of State for War and Chancellor of the Exchequer, in London in 1714 and then, having lost the New Churches surveyorship in January 1716, felt a special kinship with Wyndham, who was forced into retirement in July of that year for leading the Jacobites in the south-west. But political exile had the one salutary effect of providing him with time for improving Witham.[15] The medieval house (Plate 102) had a central courtyard surrounded on three sides by a hall and various apartments. Gibbs proposed forming a new approach (Plate 101) by screening the open end of this court with a pair of monumental hexastyle temple porticos, one placed directly behind the other, with the outer portico given greater importance by the addition of a cupola and a richer treatment of the flanking bays; these bays continue across the adjacent elevation. In an earlier scheme (around 1702) William Talman had introduced the idea of a doubled hexastyle screen, but his surviving plan suggests that only the middle bay, with its additional forward columns, was pedimented. In Talman's second design (which Campbell originally intended publishing before finally choosing Gibbs's) the screen is replaced by an arcade embellished with engaged Ionic columns in the manner of Hardouin Mansart's Grand Trianon at Versailles. Furthermore, Hawksmoor, Thornhill and George Clarke of Oxford suggested conventional unpedimented prostyle porticos with solid back walls. Only Gibbs pursued the more heroic idea of a doubled 'transparent' temple portico,

101. (facing page top) James Gibbs, Design for Witham Park, Somerset, *c.* 1717, entrance elevation, pen and wash (Ashmolean Museum, Oxford, Gibbs Collection IV.22)

which derives from reconstructions of the ancient Portico of Septimius Severus in Rome (Plate 103). For some unknown reason none of these schemes was realized.

Little more success was achieved at Lowther Hall in remote Westmorland (Plate 104). Gibbs was again faced with the problem of remodelling a U-shaped house of medieval origins which had already been 'butified' on three occasions between 1630 and 1656. A pair of large stable blocks flanking an outer courtyard with statues, gates and lodges, possibly based on designs supplied by Robert Hooke, William Talman and the inventor Sir Samuel Morland, were added between 1678 and 1694. When Ralph Thoresby passed by in the latter year he found Sir John Lowther, 1st Viscount Lonsdale, had built 'such a palace-like fabric, as bears the bell away from all'.[16] This was the complex of buildings Gibbs examined in August 1717, and the result of his visit was a proposal (Plates 105–6) to refashion the central block and rebuild completely the inner wings, presumably in an attempt to rival Castle Howard, the greatest mansion in the North.[17] Gibbs suggested adding a double flight of steps to the central block and a solid parapet with blind *œil-de-bœuf* windows above the main cornice to camouflage the irregular roofscape. The existing entrance bays, condemned because the pilasters were of bad proportion, were improved by the addition of a pedimented attic, while the flanking wings, which obscured the corners of the central block, were to be entirely rebuilt.[18] The open arcades in the rusticated basement serve both as vestibules to transversely placed rooms—on one side is the family chapel—and as passages connecting the house to the outer arcades and the pair of Stuart stable blocks, which Defoe described as the largest and finest that any nobleman in Britain was master of;[19] these were to be retained unaltered. A new pair of quadrant carriage drives link the two courtyard levels, and careful consideration was given to the gradually sloping site which opens on a 'a prospect . . . not surpassed in any other part of the British dominions'.[20] The whole group of buildings covered an area 590 by 410 feet and lay close to the ground, a particular requirement Lonsdale inherited from his father, who observed, 'Some object that [the house] tis too lowe, But when tis considered that this is Westmerland not Italie or ffrance, and that nothing is handsome but what is convenient, perhaps it will not be thought an Objection'. At the same time he condemned those who built lofty piles to be tossed and battered by the storms just because such houses were frequently built in the warmer countries; he added, 'The greatest part off our Lives is spent in our houses, and therefore ought to be made most pleasant and Easie . . . I have consulted Strength as well as Ornament, Suitable to the coldness off our Climate, and Necessare to defend us ffrom the Rigour off the Winter'.[21] These requisites were sensitively interpreted by Gibbs as austere and largely unembellished elevations, and his set of presentation drawings suggest that Lonsdale had considered the scheme seriously before all prospects of remodelling had to be abandoned in 1718 when fire ravaged the central block and east inner wing.

Much more was achieved in the remodelling of the legendary Duke of Chandos's Elizabethan mansion at Cannons near Edgware in Middlesex, where

> O'er all the Waste, a blooming Change prevails,
> A Desart rising to a grand *Versailles*[22]

In 1722 John Macky visited a residence 'inferior to few Royal Palaces in *Europe*'.[23] James Brydges, Earl of Caernarvon and 1st Duke of Chandos, who had made a fortune as Paymaster-General of the forces abroad, acquired the estate in May 1713 and three months later married his cousin Cassandra Willoughby, who brought a dowry of some £33,000. William Talman immediately prepared designs for new outbuildings near the house, which

104. (facing page top left) Lowther Hall, Westmorland, bird's-eye view, engraving, Plate 41 in J. Kip, *Britannia Illustrata*, 1707

105. (facing page top right) James Gibbs, Design for Lowther Hall, Westmorland, *c.* 1717, plan, pen and wash (Royal Institute of British Architects Drawings Collection, London)

106. (facing page bottom) James Gibbs, Design for Lowther Hall, Westmorland, *c.* 1717, courtyard elevations and sections, pen and wash (Royal Institute of British Architects Drawings Collection, London)

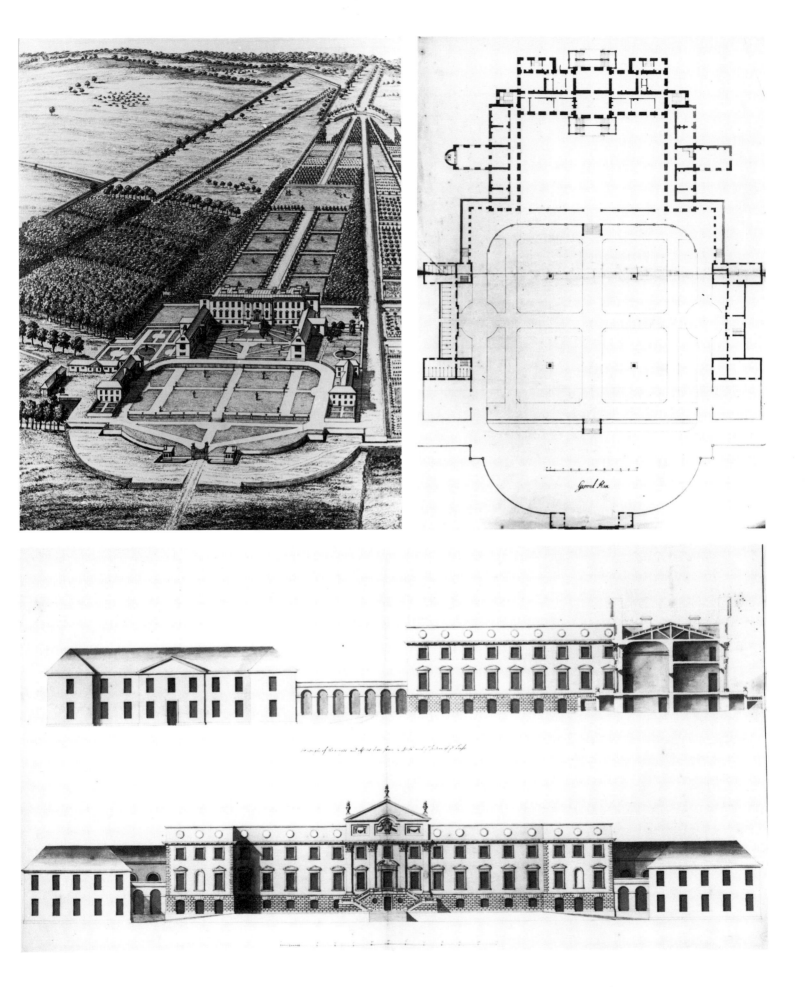

Ground Plan

Cannons in the County of MIDDLESEX One of the Seats of His Grace James Duke of Chandois &c

To most Humbly Dedicated To His Graces most obedient humble Serv.ts Geo. Sefser John Milner & Hen.ry Chappelle 1739

were built at a cost of £1,600, but Brydges complained that 'so little care was taken of what the workmen did . . . I would willingly give £500 . . . that the offices had never been built'.[24] Talman was replaced by John James in November 1713 and during the next two years he remodelled the north front with its corresponding apartments and rebuilt the parish church of St Lawrence at Whitchurch, making use in both of the same giant Doric pilasters, thus suggesting that his concept was of a grand, unifed architecture throughout the estate. But the south front design which Brydges had requested from him in September 1714 never materialized, and he expressed misgivings to John Vanbrugh about James's use of giant pilasters which 'I now plainly see to be a great misfortune, in regard they enforce a necessity to making all the fronts in some measure correspond to them'.[25]

Early in 1716 Gibbs was called in to bring order to these piecemeal improvements and also to build the new family chapel (Plates 25–6). The job was not without competition, for in January 1717 Thornhill prepared a design for the east front. But unfortunately it is now almost impossible to determine the appearance of this fabulous mansion which was demolished in 1747 without adequate pictorial record.[26] Gibbs's solution for the 148-foot-long south front (Plate 107) was to repeat the giant Order (but using the Composite rather than the Doric) between each bay, with the centre as an engaged tetrastyle temple portico. Portland stone was to be used throughout, in contrast to the brick of the adjacent fronts. The effect was considered splendid. Charles Gildon's *Canons: or, The Vision.*, 1717, had already praised 'CANONS Noble Pile, whose Fame shall ever live',[27] and Samuel Humphreys enthused on how the

Magnificent o'er all the Fabrick shin'd
The rich Profusion of a Royal Mind.[28]

These monarchical allusions are more than literary ones, for Gibbs's design (and to an extent the fronts as revised and erected after 1719) owe much to the Pavillion du Roi at Marly on the fringe of Versailles, even to the use of that unifying device of identically composed elevations. Both Macky and Defoe reported that the main south and east fronts were exposed fully to view by the divisions of the grounds 'made by Ballustrades of Iron, and not by Walls', so that on approaching along the main south-east avenue 'the two fronts [totalling twenty-two bays appear] join'd as it were in one, the distance not admitting you to see the angle, which is in the centre; so you are agreeably drawn in, to think the front of the house almost twice as large as it really is'.[29] Gibbs's bold vision, foreshadowing St Martin-in-the-Fields and the Cambridge Public Building (Plates 27, 253), was greatly weakened in the final revisions (Plate 108). On 3 September 1719 Brydges (recently created 1st Duke of Chandos) wrote thanking the amateur architect Robert Benson, Lord Bingley, for 'the obliging concern you are pleasd to express for my success in what I am doing at Canons', adding,

Mr. Gibb was certainly very much in the right to apply himself to your Lordship, whose judgement . . . I have the greatest opinion of & to whose good taste I shall always readily submit my own: accordingly I have agreed to alter the design I had form'd &, instead of breaking the entablature [over the centre and end bays], I propose to carry it streight, & make it project over the middle part of the house, where the pillars are. These too (instead of making them semi collums) I intend to make almost entire collumns.[30]

Comparing Gibbs's design with the south front as it appeared in 1739, it is easy to see how the main architectural elements could have been reorganized, presumably by John

107. James Gibbs, Design for Cannons House, Middlesex, 1716–9, south elevation, pen and wash (Ashmolean Museum, Oxford, Gibbs Collection I.27)

108. James Gibbs and John Price (?), Cannons House, Middlesex, 1719–24, south elevation, engraving, Plates 24–5 in J. Badeslade and J. Rocque, *Vitruvius Britannicus*, 1739

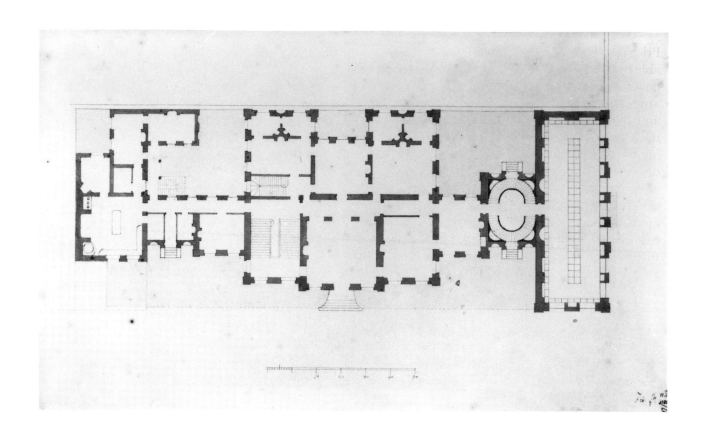

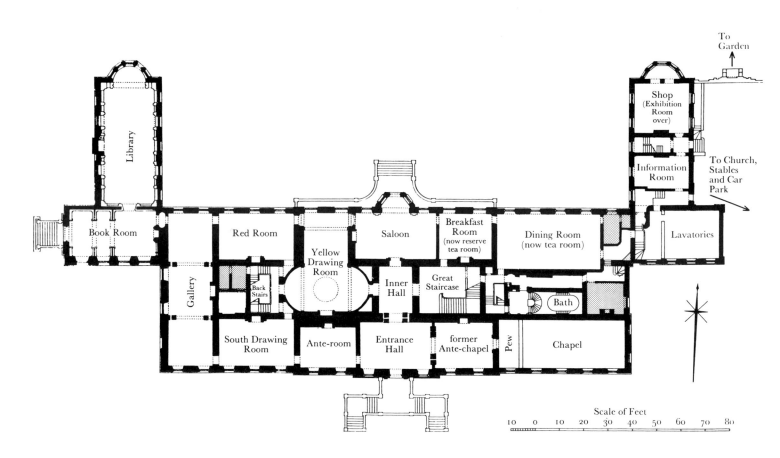

To
Garden

Library

Book Room

Gallery

Back
Stairs

South Drawing
Room

Red Room

Yellow
Drawing
Room

Ante-room

Saloon

Inner
Hall

Entrance
Hall

Great
Staircase

Breakfast
Room
(now reserve
tea room)

former
Ante-chapel

Pew

Bath

Chapel

Dining Room
(now tea room)

Shop
(Exhibition
Room
over)

Information
Room

Lavatories

To Church,
Stables
and Car
Park

Scale of Feet

10    0    10    20    30    40    50    60    70    80

Price the elder, who supervised the last stage of building after Gibbs's sudden and inexplicable departure in 1719. The Order was changed from Composite to Ionic and the temple portico expanded one bay on each side to form a hexastyle screen with a Witham-like attic replacing the pediment and balustrade; the arched windows with enriched spandrels and panelled under-sills were repeated on the lower storey but confined to the area of the 'former' portico. In an effort to integrate the new screen with the outer bays the flanking windows were made rectangular, lengthened into the basement, as in the published design for Witham, and the giant pilasters were omitted except at the corners where, of course, they were obligatory. The fronts, with their deliberate archaisms, now more closely resembled Wren's work at Hampton Court.[31] Nothing is known about the interiors apart from general descriptions and the materials and furnishings listed in the 1747 sale catalogues. Most writers agreed the rooms were exceptionally lavish: 'the whole Structure', commented *The Foreigner's Guide* of 1729, 'is built with such a Profusion of Expence, and finished with such a Brightness of Fancy, and Delicacy of Judgment, that many sovereign Prince's Palaces abroad do not equal it',[32] while a French visitor in 1728 described the main apartments as 'panelled in marble, and all the door-cases also are either made of marble, or of walnut, or are inlaid. The locks and door-handles are of silver, and most of the chimney-pieces are fitted with silver fire-backs and grates. There is silver everywhere . . . The outlay has been immense, but carried out in the worst taste in the world . . . It appears that the only aim has been to spend, without the least trouble being given to exercising any intelligence.'[33] Part of the difficulty lay in adapting the Elizabethan carcass to grander Baroque rooms, for another visitor in the same year remarked that the hall 'so much talkd of is finely finish'd . . . but so low, that tis no Room. the Chimneys fine, with Stucco & Marble but too big for the height'.[34]

This same French visitor found more to admire in the newly remodelled Wimpole Hall near Cambridge, where the 'rooms are large and well furnished, with velvet and crimson damask hangings, fringed with gold'.[35] Begun by Gibbs in 1713 and still unfinished twenty years later, it is the most complete of his surviving early houses. The estate came to Edward Harley on his marriage to the Newcastle heiress Henrietta Cavendishe Holles, which took place in the old drawing room at Wimpole in October 1713. By this time Gibbs had already prepared his first designs (Plate 109). Two plans dated 4 February 1713, unfortunately without their corresponding elevations, show he initially intended retaining the seven-bay brick nucleus of the seventeenth-century house, offering alternative rearrangements of the main staircase and additional rooms at the rear. The most important improvements were concentrated in a new wing which was to be dominated by a remarkably ambitious library, intended to contain Harley's collection of what eventually grew to comprise 350,000 pamphlets, 50,000 printed books, including 900 devoted to the Arts, 41,000 prints and 8,000 volumes of manuscripts (part of which went to the British Museum after his death in 1741).

In November 1714 Gibbs informed Harley that his 'house goes one very forward',[36] but during this period of incessant family lawsuits and the imprisonment (1715–16) in the Tower of his father Robert Harley, little more than repair work to the house is likely to have been done. Thomas Warren was paid £48.13.11 in 1716 for iron rails for the top of the house and for the stairs into the garden, and quantities of furniture were supplied. But in August 1718 Dr Covel of Christ's College, Cambridge, reported on Harley's 'most noble and magnificent design of building and furnishing a Vatican at Wimpole'.[37] From May 1720 visitors were admitted to the temporary library, probably the suite of three rooms in the new west wing (Plate 110).[38]

109. James Gibbs, Design for Wimpole Hall, Cambridgeshire, 1713, plan, pen and wash (The Trustees of Sir John Soane's Museum, London)

110. Wimpole Hall, Cambridgeshire, plan of house today, with Gibbs's chapel, great staircase, library and east bay of book-room (The National Trust)

Gibbs began receiving payments for work in June 1719; in July he was paid 34 guineas for various drawings for library doors, the chapel, summer houses and urns, and in May 1721 for the main fronts and stables (Plate 111–12). His idea now was to refashion the Caroline house, keeping the form of the single-bay frontispiece on the south front towards the basecourt, but adding a Doric porch surmounted by a pedimented window resembling the upper section of the slightly later Prior monument (Plate 94), and an attic containing a coat of arms. For the north front he offered two contrasting solutions, one unusually austere, the other monumentalized by a giant engaged temple portico which shows the influence of his recent improvements at Cannons. This nucleus was to be extended by two-storey wings, with the chapel in the south-east section and a suite of new apartments to the west linking the house to the seventeenth-century greenhouse and eventually to

111. James Gibbs, Designs for Wimpole Hall, Cambridgeshire, 1713–21, south elevation, pen and wash (The National Trust and the Trustees of Sir John Soane's Museum, London)

the new library. One of the drawings shows an arcaded wing connecting the east side
of the house to the old stables; and a site-plan by the gardener Charles Bridgeman, who
was involved on the estate at least from January 1721, offers an alternative idea for form-
alizing the basecourt with paired quadrants and outbuildings. However, only the main
wings were built (Plate 113), the old house remaining unreformed during Harley's lifetime
and provoking the criticisms that 'not withstanding the Cost bestowed upon it [the] Buildings are ... in a very bad Taste' and the 'house does not appear to be very modern on
the outside [although] the rooms within are very handsome'.[39] The interiors were being
renovated at least from 1719: green mohair-covered window cornices were supplied for
Harley's dressing room, and curtains, vallances and cornices of the same material for the
little parlour and press rooms next to the library.[40] But much of what Gibbs may have

112. James Gibbs, Designs
for Wimpole Hall,
Cambridgeshire, 1713–21,
north elevation, pen and
wash (The National Trust
and the Trustees of Sir
John Soane's Museum,
London)

113. (above) James Gibbs
and Henry Flitcroft,
Wimpole Hall,
Cambridgeshire, 1713–
c. 1750, south elevation

114. James Gibbs,
Wimpole Hall,
Cambridgeshire, 1713–32,
staircase

contributed disappeared in subsequent work by Flitcroft for the Earl of Hardwicke after
1741 and further changes in the nineteenth century; Gibbs's chapel (1719–24) remains
the least altered room (Plate VII). The main staircase (Plate 114) with its rich Baroque
plasterwork and very large paintings representing buffalo, bear and stag hunting by
Snyders[41] is described in 1728 by Sir Matthew Decker, who also found the new library
'wonderffull magnificent . . . adorned with many anticq bustoes of great value . . . curi-
ositys of immages, and other things more fitt to be admired by virtuosos than by us'.[42]
Existing presses were being moved into the new rooms during 1727–8 but they could
not then have been finished, for a plan by our French visitor in 1728 still shows the new
west wing detached from the greenhouse and as yet no library extension northward. Workmen were still being paid in April 1732, including £31.18.0 to William Rattford for framing the timber work of the roof and floor of the new library. In the summer of 1730,
however, Pope wrote Harley of his impatience to stand 'on the Stone-Steps at the Great
door . . . to follow you to the New-roof'd Library, & see what fine new lodgings the Ancients
are to have . . . I salute the Little Gods & antiquities in my way in the Anti-room, wishing
them joy of the New Temples they are to be Inshrined in'.[43] The library (Plate 115) has
altered greatly since that time, although the plasterwork ceiling, and the one in the ante-
room, remain intact and are almost certainly the work of Giovanni Bagutti and Isaac
Mansfield (who were responsible for similar work in Gibbs's Senate House at Cambridge,

115. James Gibbs,
Wimpole Hall,
Cambridgeshire, 1713–32,
library

Plate 254). The west wall was originally entirely shelved (two bays were made into windows in the present century), while the east wall contained windows and the short north wall opposite the entrance (now with a bay added after 1742) apparently contained a chimneypiece.[44]

Both the number and variety of alternative designs required for Wimpole, few of which were realized, and a process of haphazard remodelling over a long period undoubtedly in part accounts for its unsatisfactory appearance; perhaps these difficulties highlighted the often unviable nature of country house improvement, and so Gibbs began to move in new directions.

## Mature Houses and Villas

Early in the 1720s Gibbs developed a new type of house with a strong classical character which, nevertheless, was unlike in appearance the contemporary work of the Burlington circle. To take two modest but significant details: his windows invariably rested on bracketed sills rather than string-courses and on occasions when the Order was not used the corners of his elevations were quoined rather than plain (Plate 116). Moreover, it would be wrong to imagine that at this time the Palladians alone advocated the characteristically new architectural simplicity. Lord Harrold of Wrest observed in 1715 that the best architects at present in Italy (referring among others to Filippo Juvarra, Gibbs's fellow pupil in Fontana's office) are against making many breaks in the composition of facades and advocate a plainness in the building; he further noted that in 'a great many buildings . . . Churches [as well] as houses [I] found the greatest beauty in those that were the plainest and the Least Loaded with ornaments, wherein the Roman Architecture is much distinguished from that of Venice, where Statues & are everywhere crowded upon one another, except some that were built by Palladio'.[45]

The most important of Gibbs's early classical residences, which demonstrates most clearly his move away from Baroque and his changing ideas on the treatment of the large country house, is Ditchley in Oxfordshire. This is a wholly new house designed for a virgin site. George Henry Lee, 2nd Earl of Lichfield, a Catholic, who succeeded to the title and estate on the death of his father in 1716, almost immediately demolished the old timber-frame house and prepared to build afresh a quarter of a mile away. A Mr Tinley offered a curious scheme which the Warwick architect Francis Smith, who was acting as mason-contractor, condemned as impractical in a letter of 4 May 1720. 'If your Lordship builds according to this designe the timber for over the Hall [already ordered] must be still longer then by the other Draught'. He added that 'alterations in the Draught may cause some alterations in the scantlings [measurements] of the Stone therefore the Sooner Your Lordship fixes upon a Draught the better upon all accounts'. Smith had submitted his own design (untraced) and estimate of £2,187.5.0 for building the carcass. Gibbs, however, had submitted a plan, probably the 'other Draught' mentioned by Smith, with an estimate of £1,975. Of his two surviving studies, both show imposing central rectangles with service wings flanking the entrance court. One (Plate 117) has engaged tetrastyle temple porticos on both fronts and short convex colonnades linking the wings; the garden front is extended on either side by long, pavilioned wings which contain a greenhouse, chapel and library. This 350-foot elevation, complemented by a 700-foot terrace, effectively screening the service courts to the sides of the house, is reminiscent of Castle Howard, although the vocabulary is no longer Baroque. The other scheme, representing the house as built (Plate

116. (above) James Gibbs,
Ditchley House,
Oxfordshire, 1720–7,
entrance elevation

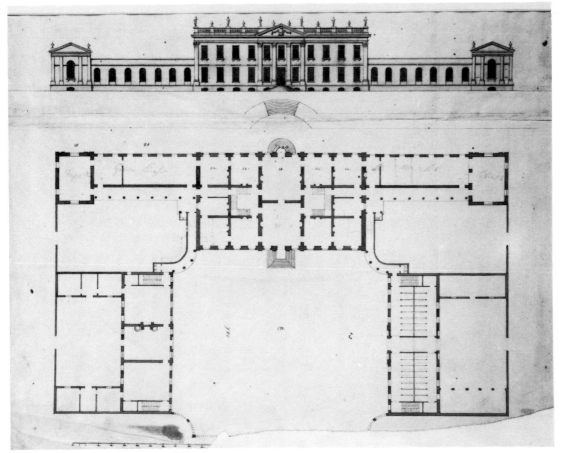

117. James Gibbs, Design
for Ditchley House,
Oxfordshire, 1720, plan
and garden elevation,
pen and wash (Victoria
and Albert Museum)

116), using a combination of fine local stones, included a hall slightly narrower than Tinley's. Gibbs's planning is now more compact, both the screen-wings and giant pilasters are abandoned, including those placed awkwardly at the corners, and the end bays project to form a stunted *H*. The service blocks, now attached to Doric quadrants, are reoriented with their long elevations parallel to the house, spreading laterally to form a shallower court offering a more expansive view of the main front. Such additional embellishments as a central pediment above the attic, octagonal cupolas crowning the corner bays and small pedimented attics with Diocletian windows on the wings shown in another design were rejected. In the executed building, apart from the Gibbs-surround doors, a set of vases and the pretty bell towers on the stable, the only external decoration is a pair of lead figures over the attic supplied by Andrew Carpenter in 1722–3. An early visitor found the house 'handsome, tho' plain' while another commented that in 'the making of the Stair-Case they have well avoided the grand schemes on the one hand and the pitiful new-fashioned Italian Stair-cases on the other; this is not wide or grand at all, but wondrous neat and pleasing, particularly for that it takes up the least Room that I ever saw, though it reaches to the top of the house, where a Window from the Leads affords it a sufficient Light'.[46] The sixth edition of Defoe's *Tour Thro' the Whole Island of Great Britain*, 1761, proclaimed it 'a Piece of Architecture . . . inferior to none for the Justness of its Proportions, and the convenient Disposition of its Apartments . . . finished with Taste rather than with Splendor; and adorned with that Elegance which results from Simplicity'.[47] This combination of convenience and simplicity at once separates Ditchley from Gibbs's earlier country houses.

A 'rich, though chaste, style'[48] was also chosen for the hall (Plate 118), a near-cube room of $31\frac{1}{2}$ by 35 by 34 feet high, which Gibbs decorated in the new Palladian manner of isolated, symmetrically arranged features on flat walls. A unique preliminary study

118. James Gibbs, Ditchley House, Oxfordshire, 1720–7, hall (National Monuments Record)

for the north wall (Plate 119) indicates the pair of William Kent paintings, which were paid for and probably installed by 1731. But, while certain ornamental details, such as the paintings' carved wood frames, correspond to those as executed, the swagged drapery, the bracketed and enframed bust and the profile portrait medallions do not follow the scheme carried out between 1722 and 1727 by Gibbs's team of talented *stuccatori*, Adalbertus and Giuseppi Artari, Francesco Serena and Francesco Vassalli. They charged £26.5.0 for the bas-reliefs and the beast's heads with flowers in the four corners of the ceiling, 26 guineas for nine busts of classical poets with festoons underneath, £21 for the six reclining figures on the door pediments, representing Geometry, Sculpture, Poetry, Music, Geography and Astronomy, and 4 guineas for four eagles (later replaced by the lions' heads and lanterns). The temple-like entrance to the saloon, with its reclining figures and garlanded mask, imitates the magnificent doorcase in Inigo Jones's dining room at Wilton, which was considered 'one of the noblest [apartments] Architecture has yet produced'.[49] The classical character is continued in the pair of large historical pieces from the Aeneid painted by William Kent, who also contributed the Assembly of the Gods in the central oval of the ceiling; the buffet-niche on the side wall (Plate 120) once held a life-size copy of the Venus de' Medici. Across the hall, over the chimneypiece carved by the partnership of Holborn masons Edward Stanton and Christopher Horsenaile, is a portrait of the owner. Horace Walpole admired the hall but condemned the adjacent saloon (Plate 121) as 'too small, [with] bad carved figures', which apparently was not helped by being painted olive green.[50] Paired and fluted Corinthian pilasters cocooning the room help counteract the ornamental exuberance of the plasterwork but even so the walls between them have almost life-size figures in relief of Minerva and Diana framed in panels crowned by paired *amorini* perched on segmented pediments; there is also an overmantel with a medallion supported by putti, a buffet-niche with caryatids, and overdoors embellished

119. James Gibbs, Design for Ditchley House, Oxfordshire, 1720, north wall of hall, pen and wash (Ashmolean Museum, Oxford)

120. James Gibbs, Ditchley House, Oxfordshire, 1720–7, hall buffet

with voluptuous female figures, masks and family coats of arms. Gibbs was clearly responsible for the design, since the ceiling (Plate 122), with its central panel depicting Flora and Zephyrus, resembles his drawings for Gubbins and a ceiling that once existed at Tring, where he was working in the mid-1720s, but the details are sufficiently indebted to North Italian Baroque plasterwork[51] to conclude that he permitted a considerable freedom of interpretation to his *stuccatori*, who were paid £105 for completing the saloon.

The saloon at Ditchley is certainly the most luxurious of Gibbs's early grand domestic rooms. Some of the ideas were used in other interiors of the same years but of these only a few survive. The finest is the Great Room at Fairlawne in Kent, added to the east side of the seventeenth-century house shortly before the death of the owner, Christopher Vane, 1st Baron Barnard, in October 1723. Gibbs had also rebuilt the nearby church at Shipbourne and erected the family monument inside, and proposed improvements to Barnard's Durham estate at Raby Castle, for which he received substantial payments between April 1722 and May 1723. The work at Fairlawne is mentioned in June 1723 in connection with 'the Character of a Great Man [Barnard], who delights more in being Good, than in being Great; Who takes more Pleasure in providing Subsistence for the Poor, Churches for the Commonalty, and Both for the Glory of God, than Magnificent Houses for Himself; tho' in the Last too He is sufficiently magnificent'.[52] Gibbs's new room, only 20 by 30 feet, is treated heroically; its pedimented distyle door has splendid fluted Ionic half-columns and oak leaf bolection mouldings similar to Ditchley but with a carved-wood overdoor of naturalistic flowers. The tall rectangular windows are flanked by mirror-sconces attached to the wall, a feature found nowhere else in Gibbs's *œuvre* but carefully delineated in his preliminary drawing. The carver's name is not recorded, but the work recalls that in the Cambridge Senate House (executed 1724–30 by Thomas Phillips and Benjamin Timbrell). The fine fretwork and painted ceiling incorporating medallion heads which may represent family portraits was destroyed in the late nineteenth century.

Gibbs equipped a similarly sized and shaped room in the house at Roehampton, Surrey, shared by the London Turkey merchant Bartholomew Clarke and his brother-in-law Hitch Young (Plate 123). Its windows, Gibbs tells us, looked on 'a fine prospect of the River Thames and the villages round it, and the Hills towards the North'. Clarke purchased the estate in May 1724, and it may not have been coincidental that his relative Sir Edward Desbouvrie, a fellow Turkey merchant, was elected a governor of St Bartholomew's in February of the following year.[53] The new room, destroyed by fire around 1788, was particularly opulent. Gibbs's preparatory drawings show the walls divided by fluted pilasters; the large frames held paintings (of unrecorded subjects) by the Venetian artist Giacomo Amigoni, who was working in England between 1729 and 1739. Gibbs considered several alternatives for the marble chimneypiece, which was carved by Michael Rysbrack.[54] Another room apparently of this type once existed at Acton Place in Suffolk, built for Robert Jennens in 1725 but left incomplete at his death early in the following year and finally demolished in 1825.

One other surviving room of the early 1720s is worth considering. Thomas Wentworth, 1st Lord Strafford, who owed some of his political success to Robert Harley, employed Gibbs at Stainborough (later renamed Wentworth Castle) in Yorkshire to complete the great east wing designed around 1710 by the Prussian court architect Johann von Bodt. Bodt's scheme incorporated a thirteen-bay gallery running the full 180 feet of the two upper floors of the new wing (Plate 124). In 1714 Strafford asked the British Consul at Leghorn to forward the bronze statues ordered from the Florentine sculptor Massimiliano

121. James Gibbs, Ditchley House, Oxfordshire, 1720–7, saloon

122. James Gibbs, Ditchley House, Oxfordshire, 1720–7, detail of saloon ceiling

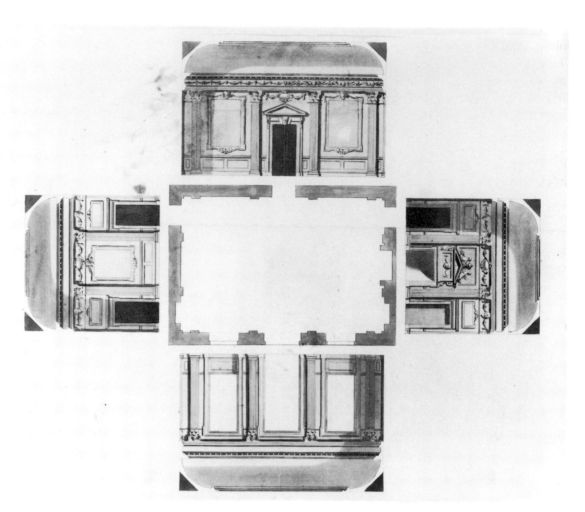

123. (above) James Gibbs, Design for Bartholomew Clarke and Hitch Young house, Roehampton, Surrey, c. 1724–9, room, plan and elevations, pen and wash (Ashmolean Museum, Oxford, Gibbs Collection II.49)

124. James Gibbs, Stainborough Hall (now Wentworth Castle), South Yorkshire, 1724–5, Long Gallery photographed in 1924

Soldani and also to supply marble columns, pilasters and pedestals for his 'large gallery'. The Consul replied in September that 'the Brazen statues [will] injoy the passage of the first man of war that comes' and that he had 'ordered the four Colones, bassis & Capitals, the four Piedestalls for statues & the four Pilasters of a fine white marble with a darke blew vein, which is the best & prettyest this country affords, The Dementions & order shall be observed according to the model in the exactest manner possible, But I should be desirous to know whether you would have them intirely finished & pollished here, or the Feuillages etc. markt out in a rough manner to be finished in England.'[55] A plan of the gallery consisting of a long central rectangle with square pavilion ends screened by pairs of columns, in which 'the noble Patron is preparing a curious Collection of Painting, Sculpture, and other excellent Decorations', was published in *Vitruvius Britannicus* in 1715.[56] But little more was done until 1720 when the York carver Daniel Harvey agreed to carve eight Corinthian capitals in Roche Abbey stone for the imported marble columns and pilasters. The York architect and carpenter William Thornton was consulted about the marble pedestals but died the following year, although his assistant Jonathan Godier carried on by agreeing to lay the wooden floor. Perhaps at this moment Gibbs and his team of craftsmen were brought in. In 1723 Richard Huss of Derby received £50 in part payment for plain plastering and on 28 July 1724 Charles Griffith, the joiner at St Martin-in-the-Fields and Johnston's Octagon at Twickenham, agreed to wainscot the gallery designed by Gibbs.

> [The] middle part of the Gallery [was] to be wainscouted to the foot of the Architrave, behind all the Pictures to be Lined with Deal, the Pavillions att each end . . . wainscouted Surbass high & thence upward to the foot of the Architrave only . . . framing to be wrought with a Double moulding, Pannels Raised & a bead Stuck on . . . Deal architraves round the windows & Dores, wallworke opposite to the 3 Compass [round-headed] windows [in the centre] to answer the front . . . Saffeters [soffits] & windo boards to be of Right wainscout the 15 frount windows to have the Jamms linned with Ditto & to appear as window shutters [the Venetian] windows att Each End the Gall, to have Real Shutters . . . their are to be twenty Pillasters in the whole worke.

The entire job was to be executed in London. By September 1724 work was 'very forward' and Griffith enquired if the 'pitture [frame] of the 3 Kings is [to be] the same size as the Chimneypiece att Secretary Johnsons' (Plate 169) and whether the pilasters should be similarly fluted since the 870 yards of deal worked at 6 shillings a yard would include 'compass worke and mouldings at the same price'.[57] In the same month a visitor found the gallery finished and hung with paintings[58] and by 1725 Lord Bathurst proclaimed it 'a very magnificent room now the pillars are up'.[59]

Encouraged by the favourable reception accorded at Ditchley, Gibbs began to tackle more systematically the problems of designing entirely new houses. The most notable of these are Kelmarsh and Milton in Northamptonshire and Lowther in Westmorland. Like Lord Lichfield, William Hanbury demolished his Stuart house at Kelmarsh, which a visitor in May 1728 reported was 'a miserable old house just going to be pulled down',[60] and abandoned the site for one more advantageous a mile away overlooking the valley of the Ise Brook. Gibbs's published design (Plate 125), while influenced by Ditchley, has the attic windows contained within the *piano nobile* and a variety of window treatments enlivening the facade. And instead of Ditchley's spacious hall there is a narrow windowless lobby flanked by twin staircases, which accounts for the uneven rhythm of the openings on the facade. The main rooms are distributed on the garden side. Hanbury evidently

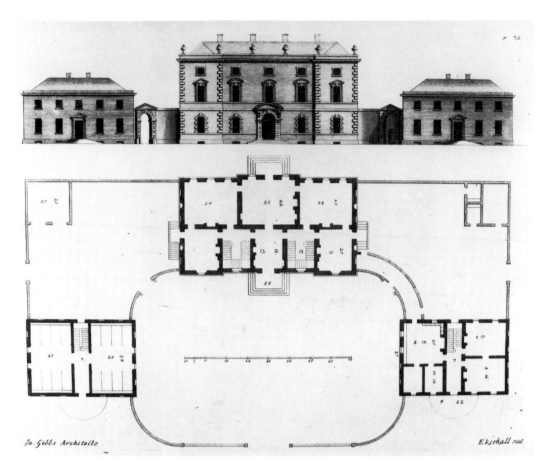

125. James Gibbs, Design for
Kelmarsh Hall,
Northamptonshire, 1728, plan
and entrance elevation, Plate 38
in *A Book of Architecture*, 1728

126. (below) James Gibbs,
Kelmarsh Hall,
Northamptonshire, 1728–32,
garden elevation

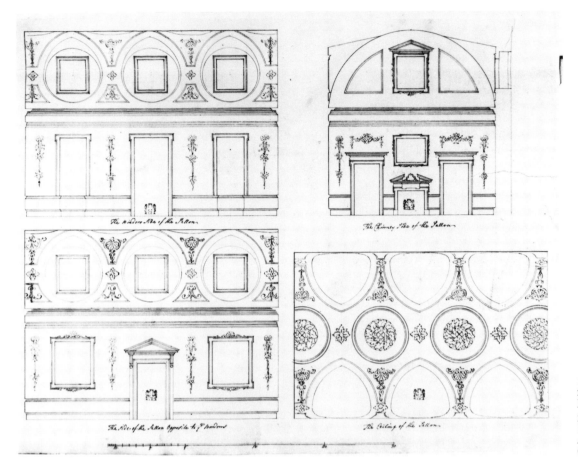

The window Side of the Saloon.

The Chimney Side of the Saloon.

The Side of the Saloon Opposite to y.e windows.

The Ceiling of the Saloon.

127. James Gibbs, Design for Kelmarsh Hall, Northamptonshire, 1728–32, saloon, pen and wash (Royal Institute of British Architects Drawings Collection, London)

thought this arrangement unsatisfactory because, although the house is described in *A Book of Architecture* as 'now building', it was, in fact, a quite different design which was then under construction (Plate 126). Represented by an unusually comprehensive group of thirty-one working drawings which remained until recently in the house and was used by the various craftsmen employed there, it is more deeply committed than Gibbs's earlier houses to the Anglo-Palladian ideals of simple balanced and uniform tripartite facades repeated on both the entrance and garden fronts. Considerable thought was given to the form and decoration of the saloon. In one drawing the upper part of the walls has large rectangular and circular windows above which rise spandreled arches framing a flat ceiling; in an alternative (Plate 127) he offered a splendid space lit by square windows incorporated into blind *œils-de-bœuf* which penetrate deeply into the surface of the barrel-vault. The other main rooms have since been altered and only the main staircase survives more or less intact. Some of these themes reappear in an unidentified design published as plate 37 in *A Book of Architecture*, described as a house 'for a Person of Quality in *Somersetshire* . . . The principal Front commands a fine Prospect of the *Severne*, and the Garden-Front a beautiful view of the Park'.[61] The influence of this important type can be seen in the stable block built at Compton Verney in Warwickshire (Plate 128).

The remodelling of Milton House near Peterborough had been in the air since the 1680s, when the 1st Earl Fitzwilliam attached an imposing office block to the north front; other improvements were made in 1715. His son the 2nd Earl contemplated further additions including a wing 'to be joyned to the great House on the East side of the Great Garden' proposed in 1725 by a local master-carpenter-cum-architect named Robert Wright. Two

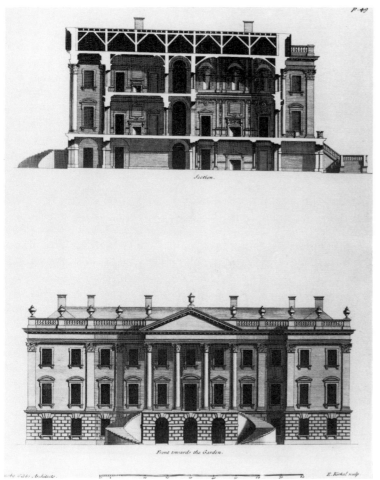

Section.

Front towards the Garden.

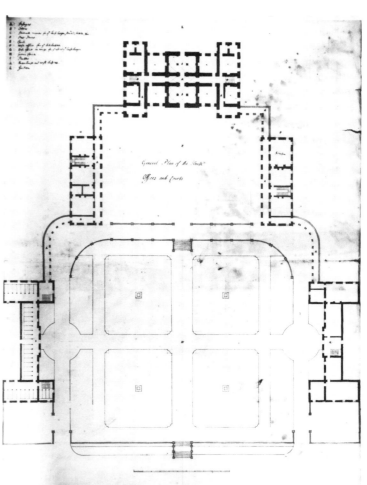

General Plan of the House

Offices and Courts

P. 49

years earlier Wright had submitted a more explicitly Palladian design for an entirely new house. Although the Earl rejected it, he seemed determined to rebuild. In 1726 Gibbs submitted eight different designs, two of which were subsequently published in *A Book of Architecture* (Plate 129) for a mansion of eleven to thirteen bays, 140 to 168 feet long, with impressive service blocks and connecting quadrants. In one group a large temple portico on the garden front has inner columns standing just free of the carcass; in others the entire portico is moved progressively closer to the wall, first as a screen, then as attached quarter-columns. The great number and variety of the designs may have been dictated by Fitzwilliam himself, who took a personal interest in the scheme and in 1723 had considered Wright's eleven-bay proposal but thought that without projections seven windows in width would be sufficient.[62]

Gibbs's comprehensive programme for the 'noble Apartments' at Milton gives an idea of the requirements of a great Georgian country house. In the basement, below the richly decorated hall and saloon, is a characteristic Palladian arrangement of a common room divided with columns, to give a communication from the front door under the stone stairs to the great staircases. Apart from numerous bed and dressing chambers, a library and a chapel lit by a Venetian window, there was a large billiard-room and a saloon or great dining room towards the garden; below stairs there was an assortment of service quarters ranging from the butler's and steward's pantries, housekeeper's room, servants' hall, nursery, waiting room and parlour or common dining room to a vine cellar, strong beer cellar and confectionary. Had any one of these designs been realized Milton would have ranked among the most imposing Palladian houses in Britain, but the project was abandoned with the Earl's death in 1728.

Gibbs fared no better at Lowther. After the fire in 1718, which was reported to have destroyed entirely the Stuart house with all its contents, although in fact only the central block and east inner wing were gutted, Viscount Lonsdale converted one of the huge stable blocks into a temporary residence. This released the ruined nucleus for demolition, including the inner wings which in any case had been condemned for 'eclipsing' part of the front,[63] so that the new house could be built as an independent structure. This is demonstrated by a comparison between Gibbs's pre- and post-fire designs (Plates 105, 130). Some time between 1725 and 1729 both Gibbs and Campbell prepared schemes, each with self-contained central blocks flanked by new wings linked by various corridor forms. Their respective solutions reveal the individual approaches of two leading Palladian architects. Campbell presented a variety of designs drawn from explicit but loosely reassembled Palladian models, concentrating on the favoured villas at Fanzolo and Montagnana but relating the new house only tentatively to the outer wings and making no allowance for the gradually rising ground. Gibbs's offering is more conservative (Plates 131–2), hardly differing in plan or elevations from the published Milton design; yet he considered the site more carefully and attempted to blend the new and old by omitting ornamentation and giant pilasters. He retained the pre-fire idea of arcaded passages and quadrants spreading outward towards the old office blocks. The sparse treatment of the buildings seems particularly appropriate for the Cumbrian climate, recalling the older Lonsdale's advice to remember that this was Westmorland, not Italy or France.[64] Nevertheless, the organization of the buildings is based on one of Palladio's largest houses, the Villa Trissini at Meledo, where, not unlike Lowther, the 'situation is very fine, being on a hill . . . in the midst of a spacious Plain . . . And because every front . . . has a very fine prospect, there are . . . four portico's of the *Corinthian* order'.[65] Lonsdale subscribed to *A Book of Architecture* but also to Kent's *Designs of Inigo Jones*, 1727, and the third volume

128. (facing page top) James Gibbs, Compton Verney, Warwickshire, by 1740, stables

129. (facing page bottom left) James Gibbs, Design for Milton House, Northamptonshire, 1726–8, garden elevation and section, Plate 49 in *A Book of Architecture*, 1728

130. (facing page bottom right) James Gibbs, Design for Lowther Hall, Westmorland, after 1728, plan, pen and wash (Royal Institute of British Architects Drawings Collection, London)

of *Vitruvius Britannicus*, 1725, and he seems to have preferred one of Campbell's designs for the house, although in fact none of the schemes was initiated.

Another group of country house designs of the 1720s—Sacombe, Kedleston and Kirkleatham, none of which was executed—took up the unusual variant on a Palladian theme of the giant engaged temple portico. Campbell had developed this in a 'New Design of my Invention' (*c.* 1717) dedicated to Sir Robert Walpole, which 'endeavoured to introduce the *Temple* Beauties in a private Building [giving] the Appearance of a large and magnificent Structure, when in Effect it is of a moderate Bigness'.[66] Gibbs first applied this idea to Sacombe Park in Hertfordshire (Plate 326) some time around June 1719 when, having succeeded Nicholas Dubois, Alessandro Galilei, John Price and Vanbrugh, he was paid £14.8.0, probably for drawings. Compared to Vanbrugh's huge scheme—the kitchen garden walls alone were 'so strongly built . . . as if they were to defend a City'[67]—Gibbs offered a villa-like house, only 136 by 72 feet, with its Ionic temple portico gently laid against an unvaried front. The design seems to have been tailored to suit the forthcoming events of 1720 surrounding the South Sea Bubble, in which the owner, Edward Rolt, found himself ensnarled.[68] The commission ended abruptly with his death in December 1722. A larger and more majestic version of this composition was proposed for Kedleston in Derbyshire but again failed because of the owner's death in 1727 (Plate 133). Sir John Curzon had subscribed £50 in 1723 towards rebuilding All Saints at Derby and must have been impressed enough with the results to consider altering his own house, which had only recently been completed by Francis Smith. On 14 September 1726, about a

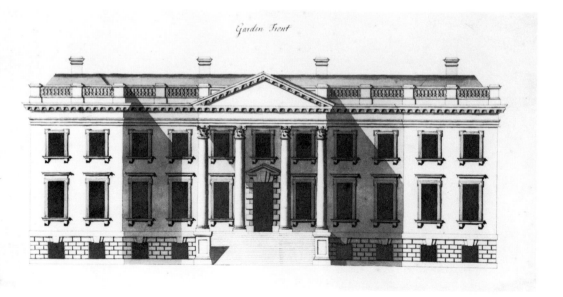

*Garden Front*

year after the church's consecration, Gibbs received ten guineas from Curzon probably for drawings for a new house and garden buildings. The former was to be 157 feet long, raised on a low, rusticated basement with a pedimented cartouche recalling the east end of St Martin's (which was completed by October the same year). The third and most fully developed design in this group, described in *A Book of Architecture* as 'a large House for a Gentleman in the County of *York*', can be identified with Kirkleatham Hall near Middlesbrough, the seat of Cholmley Turner (Plate 328). The commission seems to have originated in an earlier association, for in 1723 Thomas Clarke, Headmaster of Kirkleatham School (which Turner had built in 1708–9), perhaps acting for his patron, subscribed five guineas towards the new Public Building at Cambridge.[69] In 1727 Turner was returned as M.P. for Yorkshire, which may have provided the incentive to rebuild his Jacobean house. Gibbs's first idea is interesting as an attempt, not entirely successful, to amalgamate a stately 186-foot-long front of repetitive Gibbs-surround windows with the rusticated three-bay centrepiece which he normally reserved for villas and small houses. Then he changed his mind and the published design, with an even longer front (230 feet), has monumental temple porticos on both elevations, the one towards the garden being supported on a terrace rather than a conventional perron. The internal planning is just as ambitious. On the entrance side is a columned hall of 36 feet square flanked by suites of rooms, a longitudinal passage links the great and back stairs at each end of the block, a chapel and a library lie in the middle of the flanks; in the centre of the block is a saloon lit by side courts and beyond, facing the garden, a 102-foot-long gallery overlooking a raised terrace. Later remodellings of the house and its demolition without adequate record in 1954–6 make an assessment of Gibbs's involvement virtually impossible. Yet the contact proved fruitful, for he returned to the estate in the early 1740s to build the remarkable family mausoleum (Plate 269) and the hospital chapel (Plates 64–5).

Gibbs also introduced features normally associated with the more modest villa type in a group of large country houses datable to the early years of the 1720s. The house described as 'intended to have been built at *Greenwich* . . . on a beautiful Situation' in 1720 (Plate 134) can be associated with a property on the north side of the Park inherited by the immensely wealthy Sir Gregory Page, 2nd Baronet, on the death of his father on 15 May 1720. Here Gibbs introduced a giant temple portico *in antis* on the entrance front

133. James Gibbs, Design for Kedleston Hall, Derbyshire, 1726, entrance elevation, pen and wash (Kedleston archives, courtesy of the Earl of Scarsdale)

134. (top left) James Gibbs, Design for Sir Gregory Page's house, Park Terrace, Greenwich, London, 1720, plan, Plate 46 in *A Book of Architecture*, 1728

135. (top right) James Gibbs, Design for a house for 'a Gentleman in the Country', undated, plan and elevation, Plate 57 in *A Book of Architecture*, 1728

136. (bottom left) James Gibbs and John Moyle, Antony House, Cornwall, 1718–24, bird's-eye view by an unknown artist, oil on canvas (The National Trust)

137. (bottom right) James Gibbs, Antony House, Cornwall, 1720–4, service wing

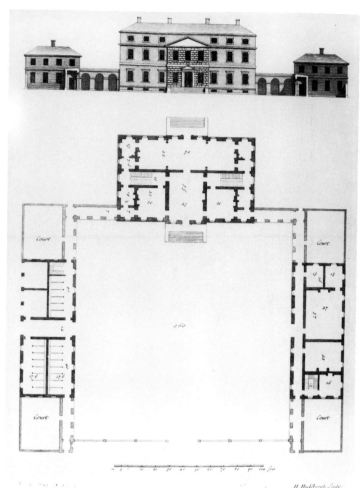

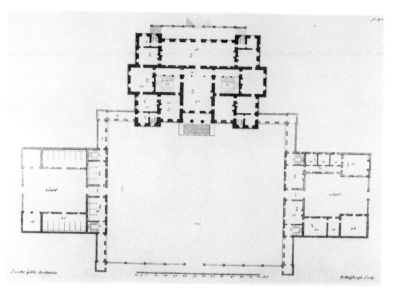

so as to offer dazzling prospects of the Thames. This was based on one of his favourites among Palladio's villas, Thiene at Cicogna (Plate 140). At the same time Gibbs transformed Vanbrugh's idea of the Baroque arcades and pavilions at Eastbury in Dorset (begun 1718) into a powerful classical feature which probably was based on Pliny's description of the Peristyle preceding the Praetorium (the arcaded forecourt of the master's house) of the Villa Rustica.[70]

Gibbs had intended the Greenwich house to have been built with Portland stone and finished in a very expensive manner, but the commission was abandoned during the final months of 1720 in the panic caused by the fall in South Sea Company stocks, in which Page was heavily involved. By 1723, however, he had recovered and purchased the Wricklemarsh estate nearby at Blackheath, and John James, Clerk of the Works at Greenwich Hospital, built a mansion of strikingly similar appearance, which the press hailed as possessing a 'princely magnificence [surpassing] everything in point of grandeur that had been exhibited by a citizen of London since the days of the munificent . . . Gresham and almost equall to the Italian merchants of the ducal house of Medici'.[71]

The experience of Greenwich, however, was not lost. Probably in the same year, 1720, Gibbs improved Sir William Carew's lovely small house of silvery Pentewen stone at Antony, lying on the banks of the Tiddy estuary beyond Plymouth Sound (Plate 136). He is unlikely to have been responsible for the house itself, which the Exeter master-builder John Moyle was constructing in 1718 (completing the carcass in 1721); Moyle himself may have been the designer. However, Gibbs seems to have considered remodelling the entrance front by facing the three centre bays with rusticated stonework (Plate 135). The corners are unembellished and a substantial attic replaces the dormered roof. His forecourt wings penetrated by arcades and pavilions recall Greenwich. Carew, like Page, was involved in the confusing events surrounding the South Sea Bubble in 1720, which may account for his failure to take up Gibbs's proposal for the central block, while the stately arcades and wings (Plate 137) were executed in less expensive red brick, with eccentric lead domes over the outer pavilions. Another possible casualty of the Bubble was the scheme for new houses at Cannam Heath and Abbotstone in Hampshire for Charles Pawlett, 3rd Duke of Bolton, whose father had lost heavily in the Third Money Subscription in the winter of 1720.[72]

The Palladian experiments of the 1720s were not restricted to country houses. Gibbs also designed a number of smaller suburban residences and villas which represented a new domestic type in Britain he helped to pioneer. The beginnings of this type in a national context have still to be charted in detail, but Gibbs's fledgling efforts show one way it was developed. His earliest examples are to be found in the Thames Valley villages around Twickenham. 'The Genius of the inhabitants inclines not towards Commerce', Mrs Pye observed, 'Architecture seems their chief Delight; in which if any one doubts their exceling, let him sail up the River and view their lovely Villas beautifying its Banks; Lovers of true Society, they despise Ceremony, & no Place can boast more Examples of domestic Happiness [than] this Earthly *Elesium*'.[73] In the lush countryside above Richmond, which was known as the 'Frascati of England', Gibbs built one of the first and most remarkable of these residences, Sudbrook (1715–19), which he specifically described as a 'Villa' (Plates 138, 140). While by no means the first English reference to this building type, it is an early application of the term to describe a particular-shaped house with special social functions: a small compactly planned suburban seat used as a convenient place of temporary retirement. Sudbrook was built for John Campbell, 2nd Duke of Argyll and Greenwich. Colen Campbell, supposing his kinsman amenable to the new Whig architecture, dedicated to him a house 'of my own Invention in the Style of Inigo Jones' (actually Palladio's Palazzo Thiene) which he published as Plates 19–20, with the date 1714, in *Vitruvius Britannicus* in the following year. But Gibbs had already captured Argyll's patronage and he later dedicated *A Book of Architecture* to him because of the 'early Encouragement I received from Your Grace, in my Profession upon my Return from *Italy*, and the Honour of Your Protection every since'. Work at Sudbrook began late in 1715, within days of the Duke

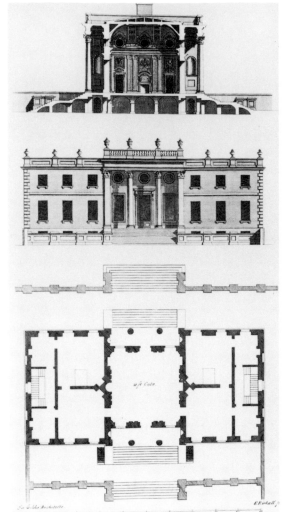

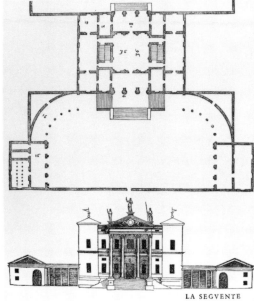

138. James Gibbs,
Sudbrook House,
Petersham, Surrey, 1715–
19, plan, elevation and
section, Plate 40 in *A Book
of Architecture*, 1728

139. (far right) Andrea
Palladio, Villa Thiene,
Cigogna, 1554–6, plan and
elevation, engraving in A.
Palladio, *I Quattro Libri
dell'Architettura*, 1570, II,
p. 62.

140. (below) James Gibbs,
Sudbrook House,
Petersham, Surrey, 1715–
19, entrance elevation

LA SEGVENTE

purchasing the estate near his birthplace at Ham House and, ironically, on the eve of the Jacobite Rising in which Argyll and Lord Mar, then Gibbs's chief patron, were to confront each other at the decisive battle at Sheriffmuir. Argyll's London banker George Middleton reported on 19 November that he had informed 'Mr Gibbs I have £600 to pay the people att Sudbrook and that they shall have £800 more att Christmass which he says will please them very well. In a Day or two he goes there to Direct every bodys particular share of this £600.'[74] Enough progress had been made by April 1716 for the exiled Mar to have received news at Avignon that Gibbs had 'work enough upon [his] hands . . . at Richmond' and in July we hear that Argyll intended spending most of the summer at Sudbrook.[75] In February and March John Townesend was paid £700 for masonry work, which must have included carving the marble chimneypiece in the Cube Room (Plate 142) since it is detailed similarly to his chancel ornaments in St Mary-le-Strand, executed in the same year (Plate 24). Another Strand craftsman, John Reynolds, was painter at Sudbrook, and the bricklayer Thomas Churchill was also there in 1717. There is good reason to believe, therefore, that the plan and elevation of the villa sketched by William Dickinson on 26 February 1718 is an accurate record of the fabric nearing the end of construction. Gibbs received payments until late in 1719.

Although it resembles Comley Bank Lodge at Alloa (Plate 98), Gibbs introduced important new ideas specifically associated with the concept of the villa. He described Sudbrook as a 'pleasant retraite from bussiness . . . being but twelve miles from London'.[76] Possibly the precedent he had in mind was Pliny's Laurentinum, a 'Villa Urbana, or Country House of Retirement' which lay in beautiful country near the coast only seventeen miles from Rome 'so that, having finished the Business of the City, one may reach it with Ease and Safety by the Close of the Day' and which contained a winter dining room called the Praeterea Coenatio, 'placed in the highest Part of the House [so] as to over-look the Garden [and] could on both sides command a large Prospect'.[77] Similarly, Sudbrook was built 'upon a plesent situation' and, occupying only 104 square feet, included among its five small main apartments a handsomely decorated cube room lit by two raised porticos. This composition seems never to have found favour previously in England; it is noticeably absent from *Vitruvius Britannicus*. Gibbs's models, particularly for the single central room approached directly through porticos *in antis* in the middle of *both* fronts, were Palladio's villas at Lisiera and Cicogna (Plate 139), while the idea of straight balustrades rather than pediments over the porticos may have come from the Villa Nani Mocenigo near Rovigo.[78] Gibbs's growing awareness of Sudbrook's special villa character is evident in his changing attitude towards the window treatment. As built (Plate 140), they are segmental-headed, embellished with typical late Stuart rubbed-brick aprons, while the engraving published in *A Book of Architecture* in 1728 (Plate 138) has been 'corrected' by squaring the form, reducing their height and substituting modest bracketed sills in the Italian manner. Gone too are the broad corner quoins favoured by Gibbs in the middle of the previous decade.

The Cube Room is his earliest intact domestic interior (Plate 142). The shape allowed him to treat all four walls uniformly with pairs of fluted Composite pilasters rising to a boldly coved ceiling compartmented by broad coffered ribs of a type he was shortly to suggest for Wimpole chapel (Plate 57). Between each of the ribs is an *œil de bœuf*, which in an early sketch (Plate 141) frames a portrait bust (this idea was abandoned here but used in James Johnston's Octagon across the Thames at Twickenham). As the design developed, the decoration became increasingly ornate. The doorcases received Roman Baroque inverted 'ears' based on details in the Palazzo Altieri (Plate 143), and other

141. James Gibbs, Design for Sudbrook House, Petersham, Surrey, 1715–19, saloon, pen and wash (Ashmolean Museum, Oxford, Gibbs Collection III.97)

142. (below) James Gibbs, Sudbrook House, Petersham, Surrey, 1715–19, saloon

143. G. A. De' Rossi, Palazzo Altieri, Rome, 1670–6, doorcase to a *piano nobile* room, engraving, Plate 122 in D.De' Rossi, *Studio D'Architettura Civile . . . di Roma*, 1702

144. *Trophées Inventez et gravez par Pierrets le Jeune*, 1666, title page, engraving (author's collection)

features such as the overdoor trophies come from Continental engravings owned by Gibbs (Plate 144). This sumptuous ornament was intended as a reminder of the Duke's military achievements, which Colen Campbell saw as the basis of his own design for the same patron, since his dedication in *Vitruvius Britannicus* is to 'this illustrious Name, whose great Actions have filled the World with Surprize and Admiration; *Ramellies* and *Tanniers* are immortal'.[79]

Gibbs repeated the Sudbrook form, perhaps as late as 1740, in a design for the Duke's Oxfordshire residence at Adderbury, and earlier at his brother's house at Whitton near Twickenham; in both cases he added a pediment to the portico *in antis* in the manner of Palladio's Villa Emo. At Adderbury the choice seems inappropriate because the new 'villa' was to be attached to the front of a large irregular Jacobean building which Argyll purchased in 1717. The house was described by Horace Walpole in 1768 as 'very inconvenient [and] built at several times . . . The Architect was Campbell I believe or Gibbs, the taste as bad as Vanbrugh's'.[80] It appears to have been a piecemeal remodelling by Roger Morris (1731–40) and perhaps William Smith, who are mentioned in the Duke's bank account in 1744.

At Whitton, however, where Archibald Campbell, Earl of Ilay, was creating a remarkable new garden in the ancient Roman manner the villa pattern was ideally suited (Plate 170). Colen Campbell had published as Plates 53–4 in *Vitruvius Britannicus*, 1715, a 'new Design of my Invention' for a house modelled on Palladio's Palazzo Iseppo de' Porti, with windows proportioned and dressed in the Palladian style, dedicated to the Earl, but again he failed to attract the family's patronage. Gibbs appeared around 1725, presumably

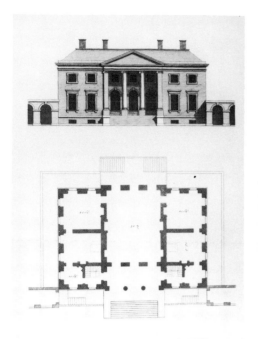

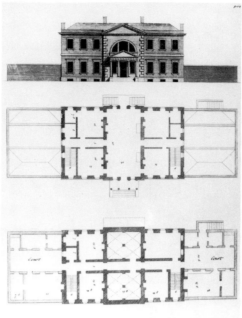

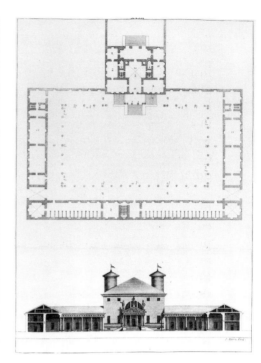

145. James Gibbs, Design for Whitton Place, Middlesex, 1725–8, plan and entrance elevation, Plate 59 in *A Book of Architecture*, 1728

146. James Gibbs, Design for Whitton Place, Middlesex, 1725–8, plan and entrance elevation, Plate 62 in *A Book of Architecture*, 1728

147. Andrea Palladio, Villa Pisani, Bagnolo, 1561–9, plan and court elevation, engraving, Plate XXXII in G. Leoni, *The Architecture of A. Palladio*, II, 1715

on Argyll's recommendation, and offered two alternative designs, both inspired by Palladio's villas. One (Plate 145), like Emo, has a portico *in antis* raised on a broad flight of steps with the block flanked by low arcades, a feature Palladio cites as 'one of the most considerable conveniencies that ought to be desir'd in a Country-house'. This relationship is strengthened by the similarities of the situation, for he also relates that behind Emo 'is a square garden . . . in the midst of which runs a little river'. Furthermore, Whitton's orchards recall those at the Villa Angarano 'celebrated for . . . the fruits that grow there' and perhaps not coincidentally Gibbs also considered its plan for Whitton, where the portico is flanked by internal stairs and leads to a two-storey Great Room supported on a vaulted basement.[81] This villa air was to be further enhanced by Gibbs's choice of materials: 'The Portico, Windows, Fascia's, Entablature, and all the projecting parts . . . to be of Stone, and the rest of Brick finish'd over with [painted] Stucco'.[82] His other design is for a smaller residence (Plate 146) with a miniature temple portico surmounted by a Diocletian window (repeated on the garden front as an engaged feature) taken from Villa Pisani at Bagnolo (Plate 147). 'You ascend five Steps into a Portico', Gibbs tells us, 'and thence go into an arch'd Salon of 20 feet by 40, and 25 feet high, lighted from the Fore and Back-Fronts, by Semi-circular Lights, and two Windows on each side of the Door. There are four Rooms with Closets off the Salon, and four more over them, with two Staircases. The Offices [are] underground . . . as also the Kitchin and Servants Hall, which are in Courts without-doors'; the latter is a partly subterranean area screened by walls in the manner of Palladio's Villa Foscari at Malcontenta.[83] Whitton's starkness was perhaps the client's choice since he was then involved in building Marble Hill at Twickenham, the Anglo-Palladian villa *par excellence* designed by the Earl of Pembroke and Roger Morris; it was Morris whom Ilay eventually chose as architect of the villa at Whitton (Plate 170).

With the rapid growth of Palladianism as a fashionable style in the 1720s Gibbs sought to confirm his pioneering position in the evolution of the English villa. His most important contribution, Sudbrook, largely constructed by 1719, predates Campbell's earliest comparable essay, Newby Park in Yorkshire (1720); as we have seen, Gibbs modified his original composition to make it more acceptably classical for inclusion in *A Book of Architecture* in 1728 (Plates 138, 140). Furthermore, three anonymous and unexecuted designs (Plates 286, 297, 299) published in the book as Plates 43, 44 and 54, each incorporating distinctive features derived from Palladio, Scamozzi or Vignola,[84] are given preferential treatment in the text by being dated to 1720 (Gibbs rarely signified his published designs in this way), presumably to demonstrate that they anticipated ideas used by his rivals. What of his other early villas: do they also reveal as decisive a commitment to Palladian and other classical Renaissance sources?

Despite an abundant literature, unfortunately too little is known about the building history and early appearance of the villa he designed in 1719 for Alexander Pope at Twickenham (later altered and then demolished in the nineteenth century). Pope leased the property on the bank of the Thames towards the end of 1718 and by February of the next year was 'pursuing very innocent pleasures, building, planting, and gardening'. Some time in the spring of 1719 Gibbs wrote inviting him 'to call att my house . . . the designes shall be ready for you to aprove or disaprove of according as you shall finde them to your purpose', adding, 'I should always be proud of the honor of spending my tyme so aggreeably'. Work progressed quickly, because the poet reported on 1 May 1720, 'My Building rises high enough to attract the eye and curiosity of the Passenger from the River, where, upon beholding a Mixture of Beauty and Ruin, he enquires what House is falling, or what Church is rising? . . . what I am building . . . will afford me a few pleasant Rooms for . . . a Friend . . . or a cool situation for an hour or two.'[85] The earliest view, painted by Peter Tillemans about 1730 (Plate 148), shows a modest five-bay front towards the

148. James Gibbs, Alexander Pope's Villa, Twickenham, Middlesex, 1719–20, view of river elevation by P. Tillemans, c. 1730, oil on canvas (Marble Hill House, Twickenham)

river with an attic over the middle section, stone quoins and ochre-coloured stucco walls. A simple door raised on a double flight of steps frames the entrance to the celebrated grotto, which was formed by 1722.[86] These features are conventional enough and have little to do with contemporary ideas on the classical villa. However, in 1720 Pope invited a friend to visit 'My Tusculum' (a reference to Pliny's villa in Tuscany) and in his May letter alludes to 'my *Tuscan* Porticos, or *Ionic* Pilasters', which is perhaps a reference to the superimposed porticos on the side elevation vaguely indicated in Tilleman's painting and more clearly in later views. A common Palladian feature, it may here have functioned like the Zotheca at Pliny's Laurentinum where 'you have a Prospect of the Sea, from its back that of neighbouring Villas . . . and the Woods, so many Windows offering so many Prospects'. There can be no doubt the poet had these Antique references in mind, for the Laurentinum dining room with its 'Folding-Doors and Windows [offering] beautiful natural Prospects, which [Pliny] seemed to prefer to those of Art'[87] finds a precise formal equivalent in a sketch plan for a villa among Pope's draft translations of 1716–23 for the *Iliad* and *Odyssey*.[88]

Gibbs's inaugural improvements at Twickenham attracted some of Pope's neighbours. Nearby he built a riverside villa for Barnaby Backwell, a London banker, and added a fine room to the house of Sir Chaloner Ogle, Admiral of the Fleet; similar work was done to the Dowager Duchess of Norfolk's villa at Chiswick. He built a small hunting lodge (demolished *c.* 1794) near the River Wey at Byfleet in Surrey for Colonel Henry Cornwall, a neighbour of Pope's literary friend Joseph Spence. Little more is known about these commissions.

A few miles away from Twickenham Gibbs also remodelled Dawley, the house of Henry St John, 1st Viscount Bolingbroke, between 1725 and 1728. Antique rather than Palladian

149. James Gibbs, Design for Down Hall, Essex, 1720, plan and entrance elevation, pen and wash (Bodleian Library, Oxford)

150. James Gibbs, Design for Down Hall, Essex, 1720–1, plan and entrance elevation, Plate 55 in *A Book of Architecture*, 1728

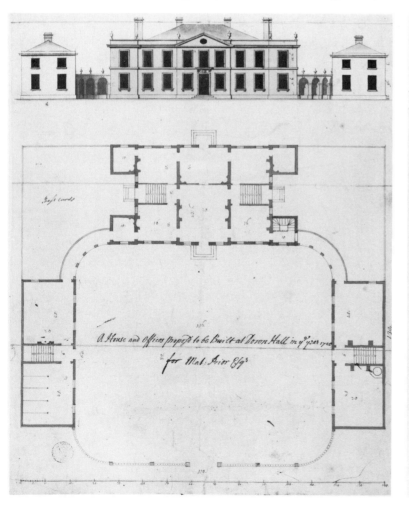

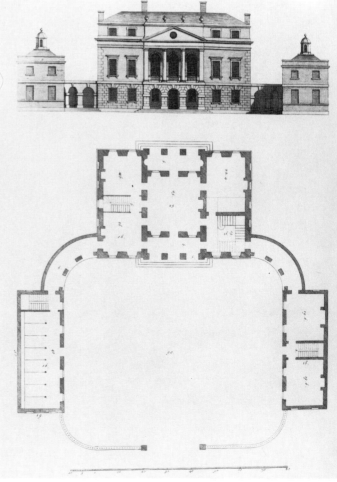

in its classicism, in many ways it epitomized the new villa residences of the Tory clique. Bolingbroke had risen to political eminence with Robert Harley in 1710 but fled to France because of his Jacobite associations; returning in 1723 he purchased 'Dawley Farm' two years later. Lady Luxborough, Bolingbroke's half-sister, remarked that he had transformed it into 'a Ferme ornée' although 'its environs were not ornamented, nor its prospects good [and] the house was much to fine and large to be called a Farm'.[89] Demolished after 1770, little is known about its appearance, but it undoubtedly possessed villa characteristics. In June 1728 Pope reported overhearing Bolingbroke agree to have the 'country-hall [painted] with Trophies of Rakes, spades, prongs, &c. and other ornaments merely to countenance his calling this place a Farm' and later in the year refers to 'all the Insignia and Instruments of Husbandry painted . . . in the Hall, that one could wish to see in the fields of the most industrious Farmer in Christendome'.[90] These were rendered 'in black crayons only: so that one cannot avoid calling to mind . . . the figures so often seen scratched with charcoal upon the kitchen-walls of farm-houses. And, to heighten the same taste, we read over the door . . . this motto: *Satis beatus ruris honoribus*.'[91] *Dawley FARM*, an anonymous poem published in 1731, explains the meanings of this decoration:

> See! emblem of himself, his *Villa* stand!
> Politely finish'd, regularly grand!
> Frugal of ornament, but that the best,
> And all with curious negligence express'd,
> No gaudy colours stain the rural hall,
> Blank light and shade discriminate the wall
>
> Here the proud trophies and the spoils of war
> Yield to the scythe, the harrow, & the car;
> To whate'er implement the rustic weilds,
> Whate'er manures the gardens or the fields.
>
> Sees on the figur'd wall the stacks of corn,
> With beauty more than theirs the room adorn,
> Young winged *Cupids* smiling guide the plow,
> And peasants elegantly reap and sow.[92]

Here then was Bolingbroke's rural retreat, with the minimum of formal planting and the fields uncommonly close to the house. The *General Evening Post* of 1738 linked it with '*Stow's* pure air',[93] but the resemblance to Pliny's description of the 'Villa Rustica' or 'Farm House' is stronger. This, according to *The Villas of the Ancients Illustrated*, Robert Castell's English translation of 1728, 'was always join'd to the Master's House, or but very little remov'd from it [where] Men, Cattle, and Fruit were under one common roof'.[94]

Gibbs's most mature villa design, Down Hall in Essex, was commissioned by the poet Matthew Prior in 1720 but abandoned at his death the following year. Like Pope he was an outstanding representative of a new phenomenon in English social life, that of the writer who achieved the status of a gentleman by imitating his pursuits of collecting and building. 'Among these Arts of a Mechanical Consideration', Prior wrote, 'I reckon Architecture, Sculpture, Painting, Gardening &ca . . . These Arts . . . Instruct and amuse, help Men that have Estates to employ them agreably . . . For there is no Man that does any thing of this kind but is pleased to show it . . . besides the Company wch the Exercise of these Arts bring a Man into is as well Honorable as agreable'.[95] Something of this is revealed in the development of Down. The estate was acquired in 1719 with the proceeds of the sale of *Poems on Several Occasions*, 1718, a gift of £4,000 from his patron Edward Harley and help from his Essex agent John Morley. In *Down-Hall; A Ballad*, written in 1721, Prior sang

> . . . of Exploits that have lately been done
> By two BRITISH Heroes, call'd MATTHEW and JOHN;
> And how they rid friendly from fair LONDON Town,
> Fair ESSEX to see, and a Place they call DOWN.

What they found was an old decrepit house:

> Oh! now a low, ruin'd, white Shed I discern,
> Until'd, and unglaz'd, I believe 'tis a Barn,
> A Barn!—Why you rave—'Tis a House for a Squire,
> A Justice of Peace, or a Knight of our Shire.
>
> A House shou'd be built, or with Brick, or with Stone.
> Why 'tis Plaister, and Lath, and I think that's all one;
> And such as it is, it has stood with great Fame,
> Been call'd a Hall, and has given its Name
>      To DOWN, DOWN, hey derry DOWN.
>
> Oh! MORLEY, Oh! MORLEY, if that be a Hall,
> The Fame with the Building will suddenly fall.
> With your Friend JEMMY GIBBS about Building agree;
> My Business is Land, and it matters not Me.[96]

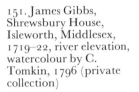

151. James Gibbs, Shrewsbury House, Isleworth, Middlesex, 1719–22, river elevation, watercolour by C. Tomkin, 1796 (private collection)

152. James Gibbs, Gumley House, Isleworth, Middlesex, before 1730, courtyard

On 16 June 1720 Prior told Harley he had 'invited the *virtuosi* t'other day [although] Gibbs . . . could not come' and a few days later he took Robert Benson, Lord Bingley (himself an amateur architect then building a house on Harley's Marylebone estate), to Down and reported that he 'exclaims against me for thinking of building anything at Down, and then talks of a saloon of thirty feet upon thirty, and an ante-chamber and bed-chamber'.[97] Prior, however, was determined to rebuild.

> GREAT MOTHER, let me Once be able
> To have a Garden, House, and Stable;
> That I may Read, and Ride, and Plant,
> Superior to Desire, or Want.[98]

153. James Gibbs, Design for a sconce, undated, pen and wash (Ashmolean Museum, Oxford, Gibbs Collection II.21)

154. James Gibbs, Designs for mantle clocks, undated, pen and wash (Ashmolean Museum, Oxford, Gibbs Collection III.107)

In July 1720 he reported having 'surveyed the estate . . . It is impossible to tell you how beautiful a situation Down is . . . but for the house, as all the cross unmathematical devils on earth first put it together, all the thought and contrivance of man cannot make a window to be looked out of, or a door to be shut, in case it were made otherwise habitable: so sooner or later I forsee *destruit domum*' and shortly after speaks of 'hortification and edification, but nothing more than projection upon paper'. On 13 September he told Harley, 'I am to go to sup with Dhayl, Wooten and Gibbs . . . to talk of buildings . . . Gibbs has built me a house.'[99] He proposed a modest tripartite group (Plate 149) resembling the Earl of Albemarle's Dutch residence De Voorst (by Jacob Roman, 1695–1700) which Prior, of course, could have seen during his secretaryship to the English ambassador at The Hague in 1697–8.[100] This may not, however, have been the chosen design. Prior had proclaimed his love of Down 'more than Tully did his Tusculum, or Horace his Sabine fields',[101] and Gibbs prepared an alternative which seems closer to this idea of the Antique (Plate 150). Here the central block is taller, its middle bays on both fronts accommodating temple porticos *in antis* raised on rustic-arched porches. These led to a low hall of 25 foot square above which is a 25-foot cube room 'lighted on two sides from [the] two Portico's', a plan similar to Sudbrook but with the porticos raised to greater prominence.[102] Building materials were gathered towards the end of 1720 and Prior expressed hope that the work 'may be effected in eighteen months, for I have already lopped the tree that is to make the plank that is to saw the timber, that is to floor the room'.[103] But on 18 September,

> *All is Vain.* Alas! the Poet's Dead;
> The Wonder-working Muses too are Fled,
> And the Old tott'ring house nods down its mournful Head[104]

Gibbs's special feeling for the Down design, nevertheless, found expression in other, anonymous schemes published in *A Book of Architecture* and in a proposal for Trewithen House in Cornwall around 1730, which was subsequently built to another design by a Greenwich architect named Thomas Edwards.

Unfortunately, few of Gibbs's villa designs were realized. A small Thames residence at Isleworth which the 14th Earl of Shrewsbury inherited in 1718 already 'finely Furnished' was remodelled by 1722 (Plate 151), when the entrance and river fronts were refaced in brick with stone dressings; it was demolished early in the next century. Nearby, at the residence of John Gumley, a noted mirror manufacturer, Gibbs added a pair of Doric colonnades flanking the entrance court (Plate 152). It may not be coincidental that he also designed a small number of mirror-frames and sconces (Plate 153) as well as some movable furniture (Plate 154).[105] At East Barnet in Hertfordshire, where there are 'some pleasant Houses . . . which stand amongst the Hills, and so near the *Chase*, that they are enough in the Country, though in less than ten Miles [north] of *London*',[106] the residence of John Cotton, a gentleman of Middle Temple, called New Place was built some time between 1719 and 1725 (and demolished *c.* 1927). The link arcades recall Plate 57 in *A Book of Architecture*, while the tall flat-arched windows look back to Sudbrook.

## LATE HOUSES

As architect to the Radcliffe Library for the last seventeen years of his life, during which time he also continued to be involved in the rebuilding of St Bartholomew's Hospital, Gibbs seems to have devoted less time to his country house practice and consequently accepted fewer commissions. The group of designs for Kirtlington Park in Oxfordshire of 1741, which are merely variations on Ditchley, Down, Sacombe and a rejected scheme for the London Mansion House, suggests he had little new to contribute to this aspect of the business. He even seems on this occasion to have miscalculated the client's interests, for Sir James Dashwood, 2nd Baronet, was to prove an ideal patron. He had spent four years, 1732–6, on the Grand Tour, followed by his appointment as High Sheriff of Oxfordshire in 1738, marriage to an heiress (the sister of the Duchess of Hamilton) and eventually the spending of £32,388 on his new house at Kirtlington (1742–8), which was designed by William Smith (the contracting mason at the Radcliffe Library) and John Sanderson. It is also true Gibbs's late houses tended to be too conservative and in their plain and

155. James Gibbs, Balveny House, Banffshire, 1724–6, entrance elevation, engraving, Plate 91 in W. Adam, *Vitruvius Scoticus*, 1812

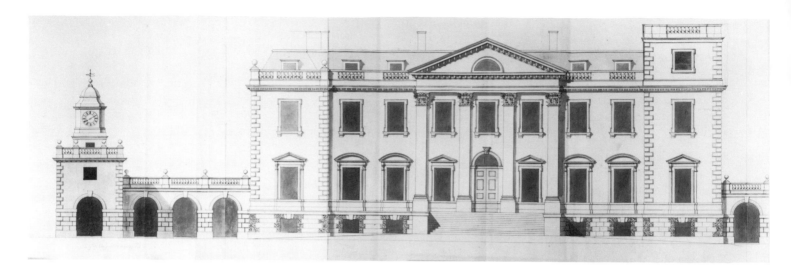

156. James Gibbs, Design for Hampstead Marshall, Berkshire, 1739, entrance elevation, pen and wash (Ashmolean Museum, Oxford, Gibbs Collection V.3)

undramatic treatment went against the tide of national taste. This trend was already evident in the 1720s. Balveny in Banffshire (Plate 155), built between 1724 and 1726 for William Duff of Braco, which later suffered the tribulations of serving as a distillery and was almost entirely demolished in 1929, had a reticence peculiarly suited to the bleak climate of northern Scotland. Another northern residence of this plain type was Park House at Gateshead near Newcastle-upon-Tyne (recently demolished).

Gibbs fared less well in the larger country house commissions which came his way during these final decades. Nevertheless, these houses are not without interest. For William, 3rd Earl of Craven, he prepared a set of twenty-five drawings, some with alternative ideas mounted on hinged flaps, for a new house at Hampstead Marshall in Berkshire (Plate 156) to replace the mansion built by Sir Balthazar Gerbier and William Winde between 1662 and 1688 and destroyed by fire in 1718. Although Craven had met Gibbs by 1726, when he was elected a governor of St Bartholomew's Hospital,[107] and in the next year subscribed to *A Book of Architecture*, it was not until 1739 that work on repairing the house began. Two schemes were offered, both suggesting Gibbs may have intended incorporating some of the surviving Caroline gate-piers and garden walls. In his first scheme the central block is flanked by quadrant walls and service wings screened on the garden side by a pair of long, terraced greenhouses. The last general plan agreed on, however, is more inventive, with the same nucleus flanked by a pair of short, *L*-shaped arcades each terminating in a pavilion crowned by a domed cupola. The arrangement is reminiscent of Sir Gregory Page's Greenwich house and its progeny, but the boldness of the elements and the use of rusticated piers is closer to his abortive scheme for a royal palace in London. Not only does Gibbs offer the now familiar giant engaged temple portico but also a temple-like centrepiece of superimposed Doric and Ionic pilasters, while another design has rusticated walls in place of the lower Order with a group of three Venetian windows above. The pavilioned end-bays could be heightened by the addition of square 'Wilton Towers'; in some drawings the basement windows have vermiculated Gibbs-surrounds, in others they are segmental or square-headed and set against rusticated walls. The foundation-stone of the new house, with an engraved copper plate proclaiming 'Jacobo Gibbs Architecto', was laid in 1739, and in the same year he had carried up the walls a considerable height when Lord Craven died and work was abandoned.

His scheme of 1741 for Catton Hall near Burton-on-Trent designed for Christopher Horton, a friend of Sir Walter Wagstaffe Bagot, one of the Radcliffe trustees, was also abortive. In this case the client seemed reluctant to spend the necessary amount of money; it should be remembered that the impending war with France increased construction costs

157. James Gibbs, Design for Catton Hall, Derbyshire, 1741, entrance elevation, pen and wash (Hatherton Collection, Staffordshire County Record Office)

and this in turn inhibited building generally. A lengthy 'Estimate of all Charges finding all Materials & Workmanship for finishing the inside of a new house designed by Mr. Gibbs' (Plate 157), which still remains in the house and was probably supplied by the Staffordshire mason Richard Trubshaw (who had worked for Bagot at nearby Blithfield Hall in 1738), stipulates the reuse of old wainscoting and chimneypieces from the earlier house (since demolished). Nevertheless, this was to be done 'in a handsome strong Workmanlike manner with the best of all Materials'. The 'Mouldinges [were] to be Stucco or woud as Mr Horton pleases . . . [the] Sides of the Hall to be finished in plain Stucco the Architrave Frize & Cornice . . . in the Dorick Order to be run all round the room . . . The Chimney peice . . . of Hollington Stone [or marble] . . . worked accordin to Mr. Gibbs design'. The best parlour chimneypiece was to be statuary marble decorated with an Apollo's head, the rest white and veined, and the woodwork of the main rooms painted stone colour. Trubshaw estimated 95 loads of stone, 135 of lime and 600,000 bricks. The outside work was to be finished by October 1741, the inside by the following January, at a total cost of £3,535, with the 'Timber in the Old House to be reckon'd into the £100 that Mr Horton is to allow' him, the client providing carriage. However, in January 1742 Horton signed a contract for building the house to a similar design supplied by William Smith. An equally stern four-square house was planned for Sir Robert Fagg at Wiston in Sussex but never built.

Gibbs's interest in such uncomplicated Palladian compositions, often combining red brick and modest stone dressings in a manner reminiscent of William Talman's houses of the late Stuart period,[108] must have been greatly reinforced by the commission he received in 1741 from Edward Harley's nephew Thomas Osborne, 4th Duke of Leeds. This was largely concerned with embellishing the garden at Kiveton in Yorkshire, but some modernization to the house built between 1698 ind 1704 was also required. Gibbs's set of carefully rendered plans, elevations and sections recording the Stuart fabric (Plate 158) shows it was uncommonly sedate for its time and contained many classical features. The elevations were to remain unaltered except for amending the form of the quoins, as he had also suggested at Antony House (Plate 136). The stables were to be converted into offices, a great stable court and chapel added to the north and one room in the house remodelled into a library. None of this was apparently executed, although the total demolition of the house in 1811 leaves the question of Gibbs's contribution unresolved. In the early 1740s he was also involved with the great Elizabethan mansion at Longleat in Wiltshire. Thomas Thynne, 2nd Viscount Weymouth, had inherited in 1714 at the age of four but only in 1733, following his Grand Tour, did he begin making improvements.

*The Principall Front of Kiveton House towards the Court.*

Payments for stonework are recorded in 1739 and in 1742–3 Gibbs received £42 for 'survey works', but the nature of his involvement is unspecified.

After Gibbs returned from Aix in the autumn of 1749 recuperated but not cured of 'stone & gravel' he was sixty-seven years old, with few remaining responsibilities at St Bartholomew's or the Radcliffe. In a final spurt of creativity he built and improved three important country houses: Ragley Hall in Warwickshire, Patshull Hall in Staffordshire and Bank Hall at Warrington in Lancashire. Bank (Plate 159) seems to have been started just before his visit to Aix, for the owner Thomas Patten was preparing to build in March 1749 and when Dr Pococke passed through on 8 June 1750 he noted that 'Mr Paten is building a grand house at the end of the town of brick, with window cases, &c., of hewn stone'. Patten's cousin reported on 5 September that the nearly completed fabric presented 'as elegant a house as any in the County, where there are a great many fine Houses', adding that the front 'is one of the most elegant I have anywhere seen, & is looked upon by Gibbs, who is its architect, as the masterpiece of all his Designs in this way'.[109] He showed particular sensitivity towards this client, who was not a member of the landed gentry but a successful local ironmaster whose father had made the nearby Mersey navigable to enable the transport of copper from Cornwall and Ireland directly to his smelting works at Bank Quay. The new residence had to be imposing but unpretentious, a suburban rather than a country house. He therefore used simple red brick with stone dressings, large blocks of recycled copper slag for the foundation and window frames of copper and iron, materials of the emerging Industrial Revolution. A surprising feature is the position of the flanking stable and office blocks (Plate 160); they lie parallel to

158. (facing page top) William Talman or Daniel Brand, Kiveton House, South Yorkshire, 1698–1704, entrance elevation, pen and wash, drawing by James Gibbs, 1741 (Ashmolean Museum, Oxford, Gibbs Collection VIII.5)

159. (facing page bottom) James Gibbs, Bank Hall, Warrington, Lancashire, 1749–50, entrance elevation

160. James Gibbs, Bank Hall, Warrington, Lancashire, 1749–50, service block

the sides of the house rather than forward of it, enclosed by quadrant walls forming the service-yards, an arrangement unique in Gibbs's *œuvre* and recalling Villa Godi at Lonedo, described by Palladio as having 'a very fine prospect, near a river' and incorporating on 'each side of the house great yards with coverts, serving for country use'.[110] The internal planning is in the manner of Ditchley but with the bedrooms separated by a lateral corridor linking the pair of stairs on the upper floor. Although the house's use as the Town Hall since 1870 has led to inevitable alterations, many rooms have original chimneypieces and rococo plasterwork.

At Patshull, Sir John Astley demolished the old residence and rebuilt on higher ground. The new approach by a long, formal, tree-lined avenue through the middle of a large forecourt and gatehouse into a smaller court dominated by the main house with its flanking service wings, all built of red sandstone, is spectacular. Gibbs was, however, responsible only for the nucleus of the complex, which towards the inner court (Plate 161) appears modest, only four storeys with a mezzanine of windows and inset panels of relief garlands (now partly obscured by taller pavilions and a Victorian porch), but towards the garden (Plate 162) is unusually deep, with large, undecorated elevations overlooking a panorama already in 1759 regarded as 'the most beautiful place in the county'.[111] Of the interior the entrance hall is probably his, and the cornice in the adjoining saloon, a bold composition of alternating scrolled-brackets and rosettes above an egg and dart moulding, is close to the 'great Modilion Cornice over the Arches' in the reading room of the Radcliffe Library (Plate 272). The flamboyance and occasional awkwardness of the remaining decoration points to the provincial hand of the Cheshire architect William Baker, who was already involved there in 1749, when he received a large sum for undesignated work. In 1754 he laid the foundation of the parlour and library in the new west wing, which was completed in the following year; in 1757–8 he received payments for drawing plans for the stables in the inner court and the chapel in the east wing. Baker was certainly responsible for the ungainly assimilated pavilions flanking the entrance front of Gibbs's house as well as all the outbuildings.

At Ragley, too, Gibbs contributed towards constructing a grand house at great expense which was left unfinished at his death (Plate 163). Originally built in 1679–80 for the 1st Earl of Conway, work proceeded slowly after 1683, and the view published in 1707 of a large *H*-shaped block of fifteen bays, the three middle ones pedimented and framed by giant half-columns, probably incorporates many proposed rather than executed features. Indeed, a visitor in 1743 saw 'upon an eminence commanding a most noble prospect . . . a shell, built . . . but never finished, in which state it has continued ever since. It has nine windows in front, & consists of 2 noble large storys & garretts. you ascend to the Hall, by a double flight of stairs, which is indeed a noble room; but has nothing but bare walls . . . Behind this grand house is a small old irregular building [of 1591, subsequently demolished], which is the present mansion house of Ld Conway; but he talks of putting this Grand house in repair.'[112] Gibbs's 'directions for the repairs of Ragly', made perhaps on the occasion of Francis Conway's elevation to the earldom of Hertford in August 1750, therefore, presumably included building three-bay pavilions on to each side of the original nine-bay shell, introducing an imposing double return flight of stairs on the east front (remodelled by James Wyatt between 1779 and 1797, when the temple portico was added) and completing the corresponding hall and saloon and their flanking rooms. The Kiveton commission provides ample evidence of Gibbs's sympathetic approach in dealing with seventeenth-century houses. The hall at Ragley originally had been intended to be very magnificent with Corinthian pillars supporting

161. (above) James Gibbs, Patshull Hall, Staffordshire, 1742–54, entrance elevation

162. James Gibbs, Patshull Hall, Staffordshire, 1742–54, garden elevation

163. Robert Hooke, James
Gibbs and James Wyatt,
Ragley Hall,
Warwickshire, 1679–1768,
entrance elevation

the galleries between which would be 'niches which may serve to Receive Statues, Busts, vases or the like, according to the most noble way of the Antients & some of our better sort of modern buildings'.[113] Gibbs's first idea was to introduce a column-screen at the inner end of the room to support a gallery and to relieve the bare walls with single widely spaced half-columns. But the result was clearly inadequate for what Horace Walpole called 'this leviathan hall'[114] (71 bv 42 by 50 feet high), and so in the executed room (Plate 164) Gibbs returned to the experience of his earlier interiors. The ungainly impression of too great a height is resolved by introducing bold features in a separate upper section of the walls in the form of decorated spandrels supported on broad bases. This solution was particularly recommended for galleries in *Rules for Drawing*, since flat ceilings were to be reserved for 'the common Buildings in *England*, [where] we are forced to give Rooms a lower proportion in regard to the coldness of the Climate and the expence of building'.[115] Ranged along the lower section of the walls are paired, fluted Composite pilasters supporting a continuous richly carved entablature. First used as early as 1715 at Sudbrook (Plate 142) and in the scheme (before 1724) for remodelling the medieval high hall at Raby Castle, the County Durham seat of Christopher Vane, 1st Baron Barnard, the hall at

164. (facing page) James
Gibbs, Ragley Hall,
Warwickshire, 1750–4,
hall

Ragley is a far more splendid affair. The architectural grid had already been worked out in drawings for the saloon at Hampstead Marshall (Plate 165), but in place of the monument-like tablets in the upper walls are now Antique busts and urns on brackets. A military theme is introduced in the plasterwork figures symbolizing War and Peace in panels above the chimneypieces (Plate 166), and battle trophies fill the spandrels in place of the traditional heraldic banners featured in earlier Great Halls.[116] The ceiling has a large central tableau depicting Britannia riding in a chariot drawn by winged lions while Jupiter and his emblematic eagle hover in the clouds. Gibbs's control over the plaster and carved-wood decoration was apparently less than it had been in previous commissions. When Horace Walpole visited in July 1751 the houe was 'just covered in' and the family had 'begun to inhabit the naked walls of the attic story' although the hall was 'unfloored and unceiled'. In 1756, two years after Gibbs's death, it was 'just new modelled and embellished with ornaments in stucco'; Giuseppe Artari was still working there in 1759–60, which probably accounts for the excessively rococo appearance of the plasterwork in this and many other of the State rooms. Walpole remarked that he was 'going to pump Mr. [Richard] Bentley for designs'.[117] The hall is unmatched in grandeur by any other English room of the decade, a triumph of the decorator's art but also of the practical requirements imposed on remote country house living, for this abundance of plasterwork had the advantage of being 'a great prevention to the progress of Fire if any shou'd happen and we see it frequently does happen, to great houses of Noble Men, haveing their Rooms so stuffed with Deal Wainscot, that Burning is Unavoydable'.[118]

The hall at Ragley remains largely Gibbs's conception and is the most comprehensive statement of his final thoughts on the treatment of domestic interiors. It contains no hint of the budding neoclassicism which was to become popular a few years later following the return of Robert Adam and William Chambers from Italy. Nor does it show the single-mindedness and pioneer spirit of the Burlington circle's adoption of Palladian themes. Gibbs's late houses generally belong to neither school and seem closest to the conservative designs of contemporary middle-of-the-road architects such as John Carr, Robert Taylor and some of the men—William Baker, William and David Hiorn and William Smith among them—who had been working with him.

165. James Gibbs, Design for Hampstead Marshall, Berkshire, 1739, section of hall and saloon, pen and wash (Ashmolean Museum, Oxford, Gibbs Collection V.8)

166. James Gibbs, Ragley Hall, Warwickshire, 1750–4, hall

# VII

## 'The Wonder of our Days'

In September 1726 Gibbs journeyed to Stowe in Buckinghamshire to assume responsibility as architect to Richard Temple, Viscount Cobham, in place of Sir John Vanbrugh, who had died the previous March. Although far from finished the house and gardens had already 'gaind the reputation of being the finest Seat in England'.[1] Gibbs stayed for six days, discussing work which, although he did not know it then, was to last for twenty-two years and on this first foray he was accompanied by Charles Bridgeman, the Royal Gardener. Their collaboration was to prove remarkably fruitful particularly as Gibbs's few independent designs for garden layouts show little originality and have an uncompromisingly formal approach oblivious of current trends in landscaping.[2] So he came to rely on Bridgeman's initial contact with clients to promote this side of his now lucrative country house practice.[3] But although they had collaborated as early as 1720 Gibbs continued for several years after that to work by himself.

His first venture, as we have seen, was for Lord Mar at Alloa around 1710, and while the position of Comley Bank Lodge was carefully considered within the formal planting there is no evidence of Gibbs's more direct involvement in the garden layout itself (Plates 98–9). The same is true of the commission for Mar's neighbour at Twickenham. The house of James Johnston (Plate 167), a former Secretary of State for Scotland, had been designed in 1710 by John James and the owner probably laid out the garden himself, for he was regarded as 'the greatest master [of this business] now in England'.[4] A letter of 1716 from Mar to Gibbs mentioning 'your acquaintance of last year for whom the convener [Mar] made you a sketch with a round room in the middle and that I believe you are executing since with some improvements of your own',[5] fits no other known work of this time better than the octagonal pavilion and its flanking wings built adjacent to Johnston's house (Plates 168 and V). This was certainly completed by October 1721 and the connecting greenhouse shown in later views was presumably built as a result of the fire in November of the following year which destroyed offices and outbuildings but left the octagon and house untouched. Early descriptions of these buildings emphasize their close relationship to carefully planned views. One from the hall of the house 'fronting the Pleasure-Garden' and the 'Parlour fronting the Parterre provided a delicious Prospect of the whole . . . when the Doors are open'[6] and 'the Eye is entertain'd with a Thousand Beauties, not to be conceived but from this Situation.'[7] Daniel Defoe reported in 1725 that 'the king [George I] was pleased to dine . . . in a pleasant [octagonal] room which Mr. Johnson built, joyning to the green house; from whence is a prospect every way into the most delicious gardens'.[8] The royal family and members of the court dined there again

V. James Gibbs, James Johnston's pavilion, Twickenham, Middlesex, *c.* 1716–21, exterior

VI. (left) James Gibbs,
James Johnston's pavilion,
Twickenham, Middlesex,
c. 1716–21, ceiling

167. John James and
James Gibbs, James
Johnston's house and
pavilion, Twickenham,
Middlesex, 1710–21, view

from the river Thames,
engraving after A. Heckel,
1744 (Richmond-upon-
Thames Libraries
Department)

168. James Gibbs, James
Johnston's pavilion,
Twickenham, Middlesex,
c. 1716–21, plan, elevation
and section, Plate 71 in *A
Book of Architecture*, 1728

in 1729 (by which time the king, now George II, had built the nearby villa at Marble Hill for his mistress the Countess of Suffolk). On this occasion the party was seated round a *U*-shaped table from which could be glimpsed views through the tall windows into the gardens and the river beyond.[9] Gibbs's choice of shape, therefore, was dictated by both function and site, rendering unconvincing John Macky's criticism in 1722 that the octagon was 'too nigh his House, and . . . very much spoils the Symmetry of it. It would have stood better, and seem'd more rural, either at his Grotto, at the West End of his Parterre, in his Wilderness, or at his Mount at the West End of his Pleasure-Garden.'[10] During the brief year or so between the pavilion's completion and the addition of the greenhouse, five of the eight sides had large windows surmounted by *œils-de-bœuf*. Two other sides connected to service wings have internal distyle doors *in antis* (Plate 169), a feature also found in the contemporary final designs for St Martin-in-the-Fields (Plate 38). The remaining wall with its chimneypiece is echoed by a window which originally opened to provide access directly into the garden so that the main axis of the pavilion lay obliquely to the river front of the house. Its unembellished geometry and the invigorating contrasts between Portland stone and red and rubbed vermilion brick, combined with an heroic use of Gibbs-surround windows, give a sense of monumentality to a building only 30 feet in diameter and 34 feet in height. This left Defoe on his first visit unprepared for the 'exquisitely finish'd' room inside (Plate VI),[11] a remarkable forecast of the English taste for rococo which was hardly in vogue until the following decade.[12] Gibbs would have been familiar with the new French vocabulary from published sources like Jean Berain's *Ornamens Inventez*, 1711, and Giles Demortain's *Les Plan, Profils, et Elevations, des Ville, et Château de Versailles, avec les Bosquets, et Fontaines*, 1716, which were in his library. Nor would this new mode have been misunderstood by the King and Queen (whose portraits appear in the overdoors), who had been brought up in the Gallicized courts of Hanover and Brandenburg-Anspach. The joyous French atmosphere of the room, with Artari and Bagutti's gilded plasterwork, so different from the sombre Roman treatment of the contemporary octagonal saloon in Plate 44 in *A Book of Architecture* (Plate 297), nevertheless is rooted in a firmly architectonic framework of fluted pilasters which mirror those on the exterior.

Soon after Johnston's octagon was finished Archibald Campbell, Earl of Ilay, the Duke of Argyll's younger brother who was involved in the formation of Marble Hill, began redeveloping fifty-five acres of unpromising waste ground at Whitton, a few miles away on the edge of Hounslow Heath (Plate 170). When Sir John Clerk of Penicuik, a country gentleman with architectural interests, and William Adam visited on 9 April 1727 they already found 'a small spot of ground well air'd & water'd but no house' (the villa by Roger Morris in the eastern section was built in 1731–9), with Ilay living temporarily in Gibbs's newly erected 'Green house built of Brick & finish'd with stuco [incorporating] a dinning Room & . . . 3 other chambers not yet finish'd'.[13] This building (demolished *c.* 1935) consisted of two independent units placed back-to-back of a party wall and further separated outside by yards and fruit-walls. Each front therefore is treated differently. On the north, approached through a court with ornamental iron gates and stove-walls for the cultivation of orange trees, the pedimented entrance to the living quarters is flanked by wings. An alternative design shows the court filled by a colonnaded hall with the door in the form of a large Venetian opening (Plate 171). On the south, facing the garden, is a rusticated arcade with glazed sashes which Gibbs likened to Covent Garden Piazza.[14] According to a description of 1765 the walls were painted stucco and the internal wainscot stairs with turned banisters were lighted by side windows; on the first floor 'two genteel bed rooms' had marble chimneypieces, carved wood friezes and walls ornamented with

169. James Gibbs, James Johnston's pavilion, Twickenham, Middlesex, *c.* 1716–21, interior

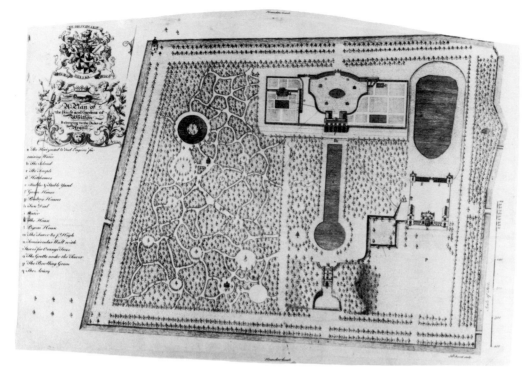

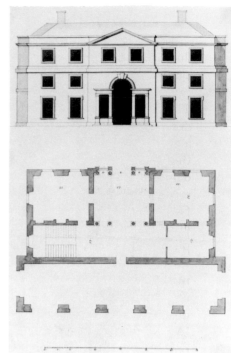

170. (above) James Gibbs and Roger Morris, Whitton Place, Middlesex, 1725–40, bird's-eye view, engraving by J. Dorret (Hounslow Public Library)

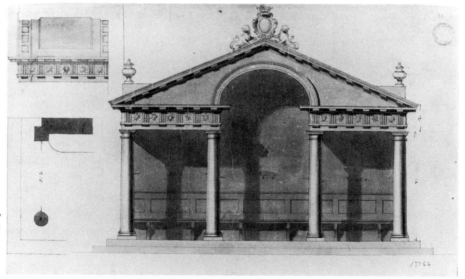

171. (above) James Gibbs, Design for the greenhouse, Whitton Place, Middlesex, 1725–7, plan and courtyard elevation, pen and wash (Ashmolean Museum, Oxford, Gibbs Collection III.88)

172. (right) James Gibbs, Design for a garden pavilion, Adderbury House, Oxfordshire, 1734–40, plan, elevation and section, pen and wash (Buccleuch MS, Scottish Record Office, Edinburgh)

173. (right) James Gibbs, Design for a triumphal arch, Ditchley House, Oxfordshire (?), 1720–6, plan and elevation, pen and wash (Victoria and Albert Museum, London)

fluted Corinthian pilasters.[15] Clerk was 'regal'd with a sight of [Ilay's] china' and advised against painting the carving 'with oyle colours [because] by this sort of daubing the small cavities wou'd be fill'd up & wou'd not receive a 2d or 3d coat but to great disadvantage'. The greenhouse was at the northern end of a 370-foot-long canal, opposite to what Clerk described in 1727 and again on a second visit in May 1733 as 'an artificial mount with a grotto & above a Round Temple supported by two rowes of pillars'.[16] This was perhaps the Vollery mentioned in 1725 and almost certainly designed by Gibbs, which was either demolished or incorporated into the fabric of the 80-foot-high triangular prospect tower erected not later than January 1748 when William Adam's son John sketched it. Both Gibbs and Morris, who was also Ilay's architect of the Gothic Revival Inveraray Castle (1745–60), were capable of designing such a medieval style building. But the issue is complicated by a presentation plan and elevation drawn by William Adam which might relate to Ilay's decision in 1736 to 'having A Carpenter or joyner from Scotland to live with me at Whitton to do A thousand little things I have to do there in the way of that Trade & one who would not think it below him to put his hand to any other work I have to do there'.[17] Nevertheless Gibbs was surely responsible for other features at Whitton: the 'Aviary in an Octagon Form', an 'Octagon Temple. Supported by pillars' and the sundial on the greenhouse terrace which is like those in Plates 148–9 in *A Book of Architecture*. His design for 'a little House . . . proposed to be of Brick, plaister'd over, and all the projecting parts to be of Stone' with the kitchen and servants' hall on the flanks screened by a 10 foot high wall was probably not built, although the 1765 sale catalogue mentions 'a garden house' near the 'Chinese temple situated on a mount, surrounded by a fosse brick wall, with a bridge to go over'. A group of cenotaphs ornamented with marble portrait medallions of Michelangelo, Bernini, Wren and Gibbs was a reminder of his presence there. Altogether Whitton was 'Delightfully laid out in a grand taste with gravel, grass and serpentine walks'[18] in the manner advocated in *New Principles of Gardening* by the Twickenham-born gardener Batty Langley, and in Robert Castell's reconstruction of Pliny's estate at Laurentinum in *The Villas of the Ancients Illustrated*, both published in 1728. Nothing at all now remains. Gibbs also designed several garden features for the Duke of Argyll at Adderbury in Oxfordshire, including a Doric seat with an interrupted pediment (Plate 172) probably inspired by the Renaissance Tempietto at Bomarzo.[19] However, although the house stood 'upon an Eminence in a green Field, from whence there is an extensive View [and] a pleasant Grove on the Declivity of the Hill, at the Bottom [of which] is a fine Piece of Water', there was no garden[20] and Gibbs's designs were not carried out.

An unexecuted proposal of 1726 to complete Ditchley, a few miles from Adderbury, called for 'temples [and] Triumphal Arches for the Formation of the three long Vistas, cut through the wood'. The arrangement of wide tree-lined avenues radiating from a broad, grassed amphitheatre in front of the house, shown in a plan of that year plotted by Edward Grantham, is reminiscent of Bridgeman's layout at Wimpole, although the Royal Gardener is not known to have been employed at Ditchley. There are no identifiable drawings for the temples, but several for triumphal arches might be associated with this scheme (Plate 173). A remark by a visitor in 1735 that the central vista provided 'a fine Prospect of Blenheim, the Park & Obelisk [four miles away]. A most agreable View certainly to an English Peer, which puts him in Mind of the Glorious Day, to which we owe our Lives, Liberties, & present happy Establishment', suggests that the owner, Lord Lichfield, conceived the parkland and its buildings as a symbol of the English liberties safeguarded at Ramilles.[21] In this case Gibbs's triumphal arches, based on those of Titus, Constantine and Septimius Severus in Rome, take on a special meaning.

A classical, more precisely a Renaissance, character also pervades the garden at Hack-wood in Hampshire laid out by the 1st Earl of Bathurst for the owner, Charles Pawlett, 3rd Duke of Bolton.[22] By 1728 Gibbs had built a Menagerie or Pheasant House, which remains intact, and two temples there. One of Greek-cross plan (demolished) had the unusual asymmetrical arrangement of a rusticated front, facing a canal, and an adjacent facade, overlooking 'a beautiful Parterre', with a large Venetian opening (Plate 174). This latter motif, used again at Whitton and Kedleston (Plates 171, 189), can be traced to Vignola's twin garden pavilions known as the Rooms of the Muses at Villa Lante.[23] In the same way Sanmicheli's rotunda in the Lazzarette of S. Pancrazio at Verona[24] was possibly the model for the domed rotunda with a Doric peristyle (Plate 175), still surviving in a ruined condition, placed in the centre of a *rond-point* 'back'd with high Trees that render the Prospect . . . very agreeable' at the convergence of eight yew-hedge avenues in the area called Spring Wood to the south-east of the house.

The classical character of these gardens, which are attempts at recreating the celebrated examples of Antiquity where temples 'were dispersed among the *Groves* and *Woods*, which Art or Nature had made, with Vistas to them',[25] was cultivated by Gibbs even in the most modest and functional buildings. An icehouse (Plate 176) designed around 1743 for Thomas Thynne, 2nd Viscount Weymouth, for his grounds at Old Windsor (which rose 'in an easy ascent from the banks of the river [Thames], to an ornamented upland [from which] unfolded a prospect of great variety, beauty, and interest')[26] is based on Vitruvius's description of a hut (Plate 177) built by the Phrygians who 'select a natural hillock, run a trench through the middle of it . . . build a pyramidal roof of logs fastened together, and this they cover with reeds and brushwood [which made] their winters very warm and their summers very cool'.[27] In the same manner Gibbs's delightful design for a pigeon-cote (Plate 178) was inspired by Columella's advice, published in *The Villas of the Ancients Illustrated*: 'Pidgeons ought to be fed within an House [where] The Walls [are] fill'd with continued Nests, or if this cannot be done, let Boards be put upon Post's driven into the Ground to receive the Lockers or earthern Pidgeon-holes [with] Perches being placed before them . . . the whole . . . smoothed over with white Plaister, because Pigeons take a particular Delight in that Colour.'[28]

The large number of both published and unpublished designs for summerhouses, seats, bridges, columns, obelisks and gates, mainly anonymous and unbuilt, testify to Gibbs's feeling for such building types. Perhaps the most interesting is the group for domed pavilions (Plate 179).[29] A similar structure once existed in Burlington's garden at Chiswick. Work there began in 1715 and within four years at least two buildings had been constructed: the Earl's own Bagnio and the pavilion at the end of the central *allée* (Plate 180), which on stylistic grounds is unlikely to be his work or that of either Colen Campbell or Henry Flitcroft, who were associated with the estate by 1719. While the evidence favouring Gibbs is circumstantial, his authorship is strengthened by the similarities to Plate 83 in *A Book of Architecture* as well as details at St Mary-le-Strand and Witham Park (Plates 18, 101). An entry in Burlington's accounts on 15 September 1719 records a payment of 9 guineas to Sam Gunn 'being in full a bill for measuring the masons and other [brick-layers'] work as by a bill of particulars signed. by Mr Gibbs', which is likely to refer to this building.[30]

Gibbs and Bridgeman probably first worked together at Wimpole. In 1719 and 1721 Gibbs was paid for drawings for summerhouses, a bridge and an obelisk, while Bridgeman received frequent payments from January 1721 until June 1726. Eyewitness accounts tell us of two pavilions, both painted internally by James Thornhill, located in the bowling

174. (facing page top) James Gibbs, Pavilion, Hackwood Park, Hampshire, *c.* 1728, elevations, Plate 73 in *A Book of Architecture*, 1728

175. (facing page middle) James Gibbs, A 'circular Building in form of a Temple', Hackwood Park, Hampshire, *c.* 1728, plan, elevation and section, Plate 72 in *A Book of Architecture*, 1728

176. (facing page bottom left) James Gibbs, Design for an icehouse, Old Windsor, Berkshire, *c.* 1743, plan and section, pen and wash (Ashmolean Museum, Oxford, Gibbs Collection II.25)

177. (facing page bottom middle) Phrygian hut, engraving, Plate V, Figure II in C. Perrault, *Les Dix Livres D'Architecture de Vitruve*, 1684, Livre, p. 33

178. (facing page bottom right) James Gibbs, Design for a pigeon-cote, undated, plan and elevation, pen and wash (Ashmolean Museum, Oxford, Gibbs Collection IV.57)

Jacobo Gibbs Architecto

E. Kirkall sculp

10  5  7  10        20        30        40        50

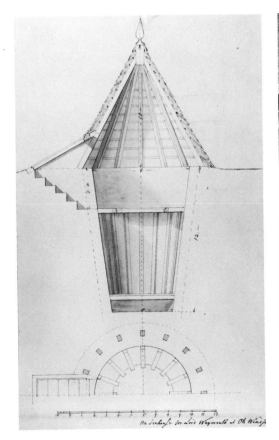

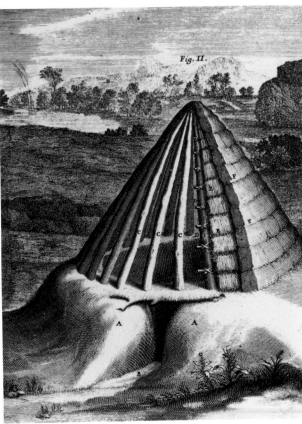

Fig. II.

green (demolished), and a group of magnificent Portland stone vases (Plate 181) originally 'set upon two large Peers on each side of the principal Walk' now surround the basecourt (Plate 113). Gibbs was paid 10 guineas for drawings, and Andrew Carpenter, whom he subsequently employed at Ditchley and Amersham, carved twelve vases at £7 each and twenty-four baskets at £1.10.0, for which he received a total of £85.10.0 during 1719–20. A similar set of vases were supplied for Gibbs's gate piers to Governor Richard Phillips's house at Stanwell, Middlesex, the only features now surviving of that estate.

While collaborating at Wimpole, Gibbs and Bridgeman were also talking with Matthew Prior 'of nothing but canals, parades and vistas' for Down Hall, the modest Essex property which Edward Harley purchased for his favourite poet in the spring of 1720. 'It is impossible to tell you', he wrote to his mentor in July, 'how beautiful a situation Down is, and how fine the wood may be made'. By December Bridgeman, whom Prior described as his *virtuoso grand jardinier*, had 'laid out squares, rounds and diagonals, and planted quincunxes' on paper.[31]

> Pleas'd with the Place, Poetick-Plans you drew
> Of Houses, Gardens, Walks in Paper View[32]

These plans (Plate 182) combined formal lawns and avenues with serpentine walks intended, like Gibbs's proposed villa at Down (Plate 150), to evoke a specific classical ambience, for Prior told Harley 'Down in itself considered I love more than Tully did his Tusculum, or Horace his Sabine field'.[33] No garden buildings are indicated in these designs and it is doubtful if much at all was realized before Prior's death in September 1721.

> For *Vain* indeed, by Fate's severe Decree,
> Thy plans of Pleasure prov'd, *Great Man*, to THEE;
> Since THOU art call'd in haste away to tread

179. James Gibbs, Design for a seat 'for the ends of Walks', plan and elevation, Plate 83 in *A Book of Architecture*, 1728

180. James Gibbs (?), 'Pavillon au bout de la Grande Allée', Chiswick House, Middlesex, *c.* 1719, engraving in J. Rocque, *Plan du Jardin & Vuë des Maisons de Chiswick*, 1736 (author's collection)

Jacobo Gibbs Architecto.                                                    E. Kirkall sculp.

181. (above) James Gibbs, Designs for vases, Wimpole Hall,
Cambridgeshire, 1719–20, Plate 138 in *A Book of Architecture*, 1728

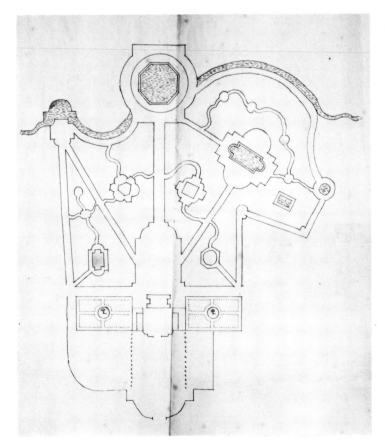

182. James Gibbs and Charles Bridgeman, Down Hall, Essex,
1720, 'First Plan' for the garden, pen (Portland Papers,
Department of Manuscripts, British Museum)

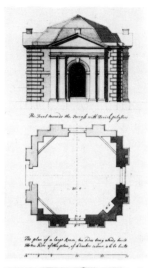

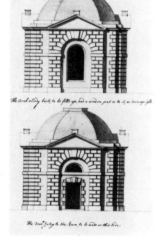

garden front, the drawings for which are still preserved in the house and shed important new light on the part Gibbs played in its architectural history. One drawing (Plate 191) indicates that he considered refashioning and pruning the number of windows in the outer bays of the central block and introducing a monumental pediment to unify the middle section. The front as eventually remodelled (Plate 192) has a more elaborate double-superimposed pediment flanked by a pair of domed octagons. It is not altogether clear if these final modifications were made by Gibbs or one of the other architects associated with the estate, who included William Kent and Francis Smith, the contractor at Ditchley. However, with Bridgeman's help Gibbs succeeded in partly realizing an heroic ceremonial sequence of buildings fanning out from the house towards the broad formal avenues of the parkland, which is shown in a contemporary perspective drawing (Plate 191). To link the house firmly to the landscape low passages were extended laterally from either side of the north front to a pair of monumental gates, which were to provide access from the carriage drive on the perimeter of the great lawn into the series of courts flanking the house. Gibbs's first ideas were for conventional domed pavilions (Plate 193) but according to the accompanying annotation on his drawing these structures were already partly built when it was decided that in one the arch was to be filled in and a window added. Evidently this solution proved no more satisfactory because subsequently both pavilions were demolished or perhaps encased within the present gates with their distinctive blocked engaged columns and attic storeys, for which Gibbs also supplied the design. The perspective also shows that a pair of obelisks were to be introduced along the drive, and further out among Bridgeman's softly curving ridges of trees are a pair of large temples (Plate 194) inspired by Palladio's Villa Almerico (Rotunda) near Vicenza, although with Gibbs's characteristic Pantheon-like domes and a more complex arrangement of columns and piers encompassing the entire building. Just as Palladio grouped this design in *I Quattro Libri* among palazzi rather than villas because of its proximity to the town and yet remarked that it enjoyed 'the advantage of fine prospects on all sides, some confin'd, some more remote, and some farther than the sight can reach',[46] so Gibbs's temples were to be tied formally to and within sight of the house yet could also take advantage of the views '12 wayes down to the parishes and grounds beyond all thro' glides or vistos of trees'.[47] Neither the temples nor the obelisks were realized.

193. (above) James Gibbs, Design for pavilions, Badminton House, Gloucestershire, by 1745, plan and elevations, pen and wash (Badminton House archive, by gracious permission of the late Duke of Beaufort)

194. James Gibbs, Design for a pair of temples, Badminton House, Gloucestershire, by 1745, plan, elevation and section, pen and wash (Badminton House archive, by gracious permission of the late Duke of Beaufort)

VII. (facing page) James Gibbs and Sir James Thornhill, Wimpole Hall chapel, Cambridgeshire, 1719–24, interior toward east (The National Trust)

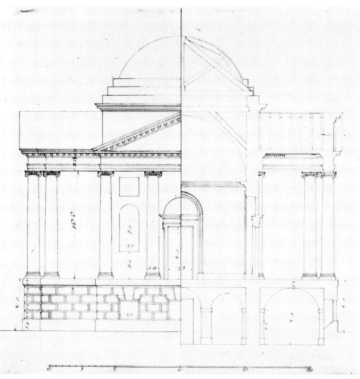

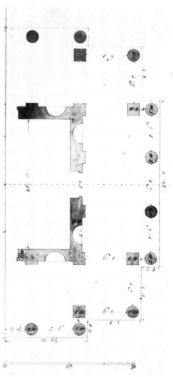

VIII. (facing page) James Gibbs, Palladian Bridge, Stowe, Buckinghamshire, 1738–42

Gubbins in Hertfordshire presents an even more complete picture of the mature Gibbs–Bridgeman garden (Plate 195). Almost entirely destroyed in the nineteenth century but well recorded in prints and descriptions, it was a carefully integrated ensemble of ornamental buildings and plantings on a large scale, more varied and more casual than their earlier commissions. Formed some time after 1728 for Sir Jeremiah Sambrooke, there were already 'fine Gardens [and] Water Works' there when Queen Caroline visited in 1732.[48] Ten years later the beauty of its gardens, as well as the house (which Gibbs remodelled), was 'one of the most remarkable Curiosities in *England*'[49] and a French guidebook recommended it as 'un des plus agréables séjours des environs de la capitale'.[50] In 1774 *The Ambulator; or, The Stranger's Companion in a Tour around London* published a route which must describe much of the original layout. Upon entering through

a charming wood [with a walk] irregularly cut through the underwood [the visitor] came suddenly [to] a perfect rotunda, of about the same diameter with the ring in Hyde-Park . . . On one side is a large alcove. Opposite to the place of our entrance . . . is another avenue, which brought us to a large alcove, situate at the end of an oblong piece of water, on each side of whose banks are fine gravel-walks, lined with rows of trees. The pond is so formed, that a part of it is deep, and therefore the bottom not easily seen, but the other part is shallow . . . The grass at the bottom, when covered with water, hath a fine effect. From the alcove we have a view over the water to a fine large figure of Time . . . holding a large sun-dial . . . beyond whom, through a vista, the eye is led to an obelisk at a considerable distance beyond the gardens. Leaving this spot . . . we were conducted through a most superb and elegant walk, which terminated at a summer house, built of wood, in the lattice manner, and painted green. We

195. Gubbins, Hertfordshire, by 1732 (?), author's reconstruction based on J. B. Chatelaine's engravings of 1748 and the 1838 sale catalogue, drawn by W. T. C. Walker, 1984

196. James Gibbs, Design for a pigeonhouse, Gubbins, Hertfordshire, by 1732 (?), plan and elevation, pen and wash (Ashmolean Museum, Oxford, Gibbs Collection III.87)

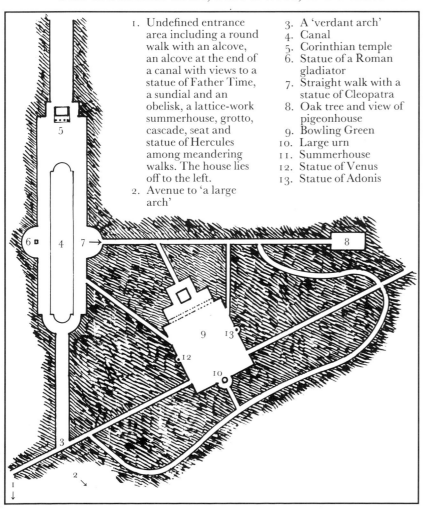

1. Undefined entrance area including a round walk with an alcove, an alcove at the end of a canal with views to a statue of Father Time, a sundial and an obelisk, a lattice-work summerhouse, grotto, cascade, seat and statue of Hercules among meandering walks. The house lies off to the left.
2. Avenue to 'a large arch'
3. A 'verdant arch'
4. Canal
5. Corinthian temple
6. Statue of a Roman gladiator
7. Straight walk with a statue of Cleopatra
8. Oak tree and view of pigeonhouse
9. Bowling Green
10. Large urn
11. Summerhouse
12. Statue of Venus
13. Statue of Adonis

then turned to the left through meandering walks . . . to a grotto, which having passed a large arch presents itself across the walk, and through it we behold a cascade. Continuing onward, we turned to the right . . . to a seat where the cascade has a more distant sound. This is a very contemplative situation. From this seat a walk brought us to a good statue of Hercules . . . from whence, through a verdant arch, appears a beautiful canal [Plate 197], at the end of which is a handsome temple, whose front is supported by four pillars. In this temple are two bustos of Miss Sambrookes . . . On one side [of] this canal is a Roman gladiator. . . . Leaving the canal we ascended a straight walk, which brought us on the left to a Cleopatra, as stung with an asp . . . and on our right appears a very large and beautiful urn. The top of our walk terminated at a large oak, from whence there is a view, over the canal . . . to the gladiator, and from thence through a grove to a lofty pigeon-house [Plate 196]. Turning to the right we came to a neat and retired bowling-green [Plate 198], at one end of which is the urn . . . at the other a summer-house full of orange and lemon trees. On one side of the green is a statue of Venus, and on the other one of Adonis.[51]

Significantly, the earliest printed description of Gubbins appears as an appendix to *Les Charmes de Stow: ou Description de La belle Maison de Plaisance de Mylord Cobham par J.d.C. à Londres*, 1748, which George Bickham incorporated into *The Beauties of Stow* published two years later.

Imagine to youself a vast Hill, shaded all over with a Forest of Oaks, through which have been cut an infinite Number of Alleys covered with the finest Gravel . . . a large Square, embellished with Orange-trees and Statues, and with a beautiful Summer-house, whose Windows present on every Side a most delicious Prospect . . . a magnificent Bason, adorned with green Pyramids, Orange-trees, Statues, and surrounded with wide-extending Alleys; and then you see a kind of verdant Circle, all covered with the Trees of the Forest, but illumined with so much Art and Taste, as to fill the Eye with Raptures. In short, the Beauty of the Alleys, whose verdant Hedges are of a surprising Height, the pleasing Variety of the Prospects, the Richness of the Ornaments, the singular Taste that prevails through the Whole Distribution, and the Choice of the different Parts of this charming Place, form all together almost the only Garden in its kind.

It deserved 'a Traveller's Admiration' and had 'a sensible Resemblance in Miniature to *Stow* [yet] not withstanding all the surprising Greatness of *Gubbins*, still it must submit to *Stow*'.[52]

Here was the most celebrated and influential of the new landscape gardens. When Gibbs appeared at Stowe in September 1726 Bridgeman had been working there for a decade and Vanbrugh had designed over a dozen buildings and other features in the nucleus of the garden lying south and west of the house (Plate 199). His last work, the Pyramid, was hardly begun in 1726, and this may have been among Gibbs's first responsibilities as Viscount Cobham's new architect;[53] his subsequent interest in the form at Tring, Hartwell and Kiveton bears this out. His drawing proposing to reface in ashlar blocks Vanbrugh's Brick Temple (later renamed the Temple of Bacchus) suggests that he not only completed unfinished work but was asked to improve some existing buildings. A payment of £21 in 1727 may relate to the four new designs for pavilions published in *A Book of Architecture* in the following year.

The pair of Boycott Pavilions (Plate 200) at the west entrance to the estate, named after the nearby lost hamlet of Boicot, are described in Gilbert West's poem, *Stowe, The Gardens*, 1732.

197. James Gibbs and Charles Bridgeman, 'A perspective View of the Canal at Gubbins in Hertfordshire', engraving by J. B. Chatelaine 1748 (Bodleian Library, Oxford)

198. James Gibbs and Charles Bridgeman, 'A perspective View of the Bowling Green . . . at Gubbins in Hertfordshire', engraving by J. B. Chatelaine, 1748 (Bodleian Library, Oxford)

scrolled brackets was abandoned for a lighter, less virile character. Pedestalled busts of Bacon, Hampden, Locke, Milton, Newton, Shakespeare, Queen Elizabeth and William III carved by Michael Rysbrack surrounded the pavilion. This is the earliest expression of the liberty theme which was to dominate Gibbs's later architecture at Stowe.

> Around thy Building, *Gibbs*, a sacred Band
> Of Princes, Patriots, Bards, and Sages stand:
> Men, who by Merit purchas'd lasting Praise,
> Worthy each *British* Poet's noblest Lays:
> Or bold in Arms for Liberty they stood,
> And greatly perish'd for their Country's Good:
> Or nobly warm'd with more than mortal Fire,
> Equal'd to *Rome* or *Greece* the *British* Lyre:
> Or Human Life by useful Arts refin'd
> Acknowledg'd Benefactors of Mankind.[57]

Placed at the outer perimeter of the garden, on a small mount above an icehouse, this building offered views of 'the different Vista's that terminate there, through a Thousand charming Alleys . . . It is designed like a Glass of Bitters before Dinner, to quicken your Appetite for the elegant Entertainment that is to follow', wrote George Bickham. 'I find it a very great Relief to my Eye, to take it from those grand Objects, and cast it for a few Minutes upon such a rural Scene as this.'[58] Looking across Home Park the visitor could see the huge south front of Stowe House, where Gibbs made additions to the late seventeenth-century fabric, now utterly lost in later remodellings. Bridgeman's bird's-eye view of the estate drawn around 1719 shows Vanbrugh's proposal for a colossal temple portico flanked by colonnades, pedimented corner towers and pavilions. Certainly he was responsible for refacing the north front, but the earliest topographical record of the south front, a drawing of 1733–4 by Jacques Rigaud (Plate 203), shows quite different wings and superimposed porticos in the centre of the brick block. This must have been constructed between 1731 and 1735, a period when Gibbs was still active at Stowe, for a tourist in June 1735 noted that the front 'towards the gardens has a double-story Portico in the middle the lower supported by 4 Dorick, & the upper by four Ionick Corinthian Pillars', while in the same year another visitor remarked that the house had been 'improved since I was here' on 20 May 1731, and mentions the 'double Colonnade, one over the other [which has] a very good effect [although not] the four blunt Turrets, one at each corner, which is also a late addition.[59] The outer pavilions with their attached temple porticos recall the street elevations of the Cambridge Public Building (Plate 250). Bickham regarded the architecture as 'Italian'; indeed Palladio, Serlio and Scamozzi had published villas with such features. Furthermore, Pliny's Laurentinum had a winter dining room 'placed in the highest Part of the House . . . purely for the sake of Prospect [so] as to over-look the Garden'.[60] So the upper portico at Stowe House, like Gibbs's Building, served as a belvedere from which to view the estate. This became increasingly necessary in the 1730s as the gardens expanded eastward of Bridgeman's original layout into William Kent's Elysian Fields and beyond into Hawkwell Field, which Gibbs began furnishing around 1739. Before turning to this major enterprise, which occupied his attention for almost a decade, it is worth looking at what he was doing a dozen miles away in another Buckinghamshire garden.

The owner of Hartwell near Aylesbury, Sir Thomas Lee, was probably introduced to Gibbs by his kinsman and neighbour, the 2nd Earl of Lichfield, of Quarrendon House

202. James Gibbs, 'View of Gibbs's Building': or Belvedere, Stowe, Buckinghamshire, 1726–9, engraving by J. Rigaud in S. Bridgeman, *Views of Stowe*, 1739

203. John Vanbrugh and James Gibbs, 'View of the House from the Parterre', Stowe, Buckinghamshire, 1719–34, pen and wash by J. Rigaud, 1733–4 (Harris Brisbane Dick Fund, Metropolitan Museum of Art, New York)

representation of Genius writing history among the classical ruins of Antiquity, was copied from Thornhill's engraved frontispiece to the second volume of *Remarks on Several Parts of Italy* in *The Works of the Right Honourable Joseph Addison*, 1721 (Lee subscribed to the fourth volume and presumably owned the set). Gibbs's suggested improvements to the house and the buildings he added to the garden were unusual in the 1730s for their sombre geometry and use of the Doric and Ionic Orders exclusively; there was neither rococo embellishment nor extravagant building types (apart from the Gothic tower), and except for the 'wilderness' the layout was uncompromisingly formal. When Madame Du Boccage visited in 1750 she remarked that the 'place is fine, and well situated [but] if a *Frenchman* had the same revenue of 70000 livre a year, he would make much greater show than the master of this place'.[63]

During the 1740s Gibbs was also involved with other country-house gardens. The most interesting was Kiveton in Yorkshire, the seat of Thomas Osborne, 4th Duke of Leeds. The grounds, described in 1724 as having a 'very large . . . Parterre . . . adornd with many statues & large vases, [with] a wilderness & beyond it a bowling Green [which] commands a fine prospect & answers many avenues of length in the Park',[64] originally had no garden buildings. Gibbs proposed adding to the existing pattern of planting, for he was now without Bridgeman's assistance (he had died in 1738), a variety of classical buildings including lodges and bridges, a triumphal arch, a Bowling Green House recalling the Canal Temple at Gubbins, a domed octagon to be placed in the upper part of the park near the White Gates which terminate the Chestnut Walk, and a bathhouse placed over St Nicolaus's Well (Plate 212) with facilities like those recommended in descriptions of Laurentinum.[65] There was also a remarkable pyramid reminiscent of the one at Tring but more closely associated with the Antique prototype, the Pyramid of Cestius, because it was proposed to be erected upon the spot where Roman bones were buried. Unfortunately nothing of this scheme was realized. Nor was the irregular octagonal pavilion, similar to one for the Chestnut Walk at Kiveton, suggested for Wynnstay astride the Dee Valley in Denbighshire. Its more architectonic treatment, with pilasters and rusticated walls, may have resulted from the activities of the owner, Sir Watkin Williams Wynn, as a Radcliffe Trustee from 1741. At Wrest Park in Bedfordshire Henry Grey, 1st Duke of Kent, had commissioned Archer, Hawksmoor, Kent, Leoni, Batty Langley and Filippo Juvarra to embellish the formal gardens, and by 1735 they were considered 'undoubtedly some of the finest in England'.[66] The Duke subscribed to *A Book of Architecture*, but Gibbs may not have appeared until after Jemima, Marchioness Grey, his daughter, inherited in 1740; in the same year she married Philip Yorke, who was soon to acquire Wimpole. In 1748 she visited Stowe, 'a Place as well worth passing a few Hours in, [which] both exceeded my Expectation & disappointed It'. She admired particularly Gibbs's recent buildings in Hawkwell Field: the Temple of Friendship 'is reckoned the Best, but that to Female Friendship is the best Room [and] The Gothic Building . . . is the most Uncommon . . . in its Way'.[67] Not surprisingly the Imperial Closet on the edge of the Field (Plate 216) and the Belvedere (Plate 202) in the earlier garden reappear in Gibbs's unexecuted designs for Wrest (Plate 213). The ties between the two estates were reaffirmed by an inscription on the Marchioness's Hermitage: 'Thou count'st, as thine, the Good of all Mankind, Then, welcome, share the friendly Groves of *Wrest*',[68] which imitates the couplet

> All great, all perfect Works from *Genius* flow,
> The *British Iliad* hence, and hence the Groves of *Stowe*[69]

In two decades this celebrated garden had grown from the original twenty-eight acres

211. James Gibbs,
Hartwell House,
Buckinghamshire, 1740,
hall chimneypiece

On the exterior was the motto *Amicitiae S.*—Sacred to Friendship. The central room was originally adorned with ten marble busts by Rysbrack and Peter Scheemakers of Cobham and members of a circle supporting Frederick, Prince of Wales, who was also represented, in his struggle against the King and Sir Robert Walpole, which led the latter's son Horace to equate the building with 'the Temple of Janus, sometimes open to war, and sometimes shut up in factious cabals'.[73] Francesco Sleter painted the walls with emblems of Friendship, Justice and Liberty, and on the ceiling Britannia was flanked by 'the Glory of her Annals on Cartoons, whereon these Words are written, *The Reigns of Queen* Elizabeth *and* Edward III. and on the other is offered the Reign of ——, which she frowns upon, and puts by. The Name is artfully covered with Britannia's Hand; but it is an easy Matter to guess what Reign is meant.'[74] The political theme was continued nearby in the Imperial Closet (Plate 216). Such a building had been planned by 1728, when a design was included among the 'square Pavilion for . . . *Cobham* and others' in plate 78 in *A Book of Architecture*. As executed, the pyramid roof was replaced by a straight cornice crowned by a Palladian ball, like the rusticated arch at Hartwell. The interior was painted by Sleter with life-size figures of Titus, Trajan and Marcus Aurelius standing in pedimented aedicule, as if they were Roman funerary stele. In William Gilpin's *A Dialogue upon the Gardens at Stow*, 1748,

Polypth wished that Calloph 'could persuade all the Kings in *Europe* to take them as Patterns. But, God knows, public Spirit is now at a low Ebb amongst us.'[75]

Gibbs next worked northward up the funnel-shaped Field, where a spur of Bridgeman's Octagon Lake had to be forded. By 1738 a magnificent bridge was being built (Plate VIII), which then consisted of 'one large Arch, with a Smaller one each side of it; The Piers and Butments are Rustick . . . & from thence the Work is carryd up with Windows, Balconies, &c. ornamented with Festoons, and other Peices of Carved Work and the whole is roof'd . . . so that This Peice of Architecture not only carrys you over the Water, but if a Sudden Shower interrupts your Walk you here find a Shelter . . . The Scaffolds and Men employ'd on this Work prevent a perfect View of it.'[76] Finished by 1742, it was described as the Palladian bridge, referring to 'un ponte di pietra di mia inventione' in the third book of Palladio's *I Quattro Libri*, of which a new English translation by Isaac Ware had appeared in 1738; it was also recognized as a copy of Lord Pembroke's bridge at Wilton (1736–7).[77] Differences were noted, however, particularly the substitution of the rear range of columns for a large stone relief (removed in 1762) carved by Scheemakers depicting the four quarters of the world bringing various products to Britannia. This dramatically screened-off one of the main eastern vistas of the garden and was considered 'a proper Ornament for a Bridge, which, like Commerce, unites divided Lands'.[78] Sleter again frescoed the end pavilions with portraits of Raleigh and William Penn holding respectively a map of Virginia and the laws of Pennsylvania which 'keep the honest inoffensive People there in extreme good Order'. Bickham added that 'Our Sailors mention his Colony as a very happy Set of People; they live intirely at Peace amongst themselves [and] are able to preserve the most sociable Terms with their Neighbours'.[79] Cobham's manly Temple of Friendship was complemented on the northern slope of Hawkwell Field by the Lady's Temple (1744–8, rebuilt by 1773) 'where every thing ravishes the Eye, particularly the extreme Elegancy and Beauty of the Ornaments' which depicted 'Ladies employing themselves in Needle and Shell-work . . . diverting themselves with Painting and Music [and] other Embellishments represent all manner of Exercises suitable to the Fair Sex'; these too were painted by Sleter.[80] The architecture was adapted from Gibbs's abortive design for Lord Oxford's Bowling Green House at Down (Plate 183) but without a dome and using the rustic arcades of the basement as a viewing point for prospects both southward towards Friendship and northwards into the newly planned Grecian Fields and the 115-foot-high Cobham Column. Lady Newdigate reported in 1748 that Lady Cobham was building this on the model of Trajan's Column at Rome although neither the eccentric fluted octagonal shaft nor the circular temple surmounting the entablature has Antique antecedents.[81] Nor apparently was this Gibbs's contribution, for although work began in 1747, during the period he was still likely to have been associated with Stowe, a letter of 1750 written by Capability Brown makes it certain that he was the designer.[82]

The focal point of these buildings, indeed, the climax of the eastern garden and Gibbs's most original contribution to Stowe, is the Temple of Liberty (1741–8), its rusty-orange Northamptonshire ironstone set against the lush landscape (Plate IX). The triangular shape (Plate 218) encloses a galleried and domed rotunda with polygonal towers, one rising seventy feet, the whole standing on a bastion located about halfway up the eastern edge of the Field. It was ideally suited to the site which 'makes a good Point of View, & has the finest Prospect over the Garden & Country of Any' of the buildings.[83] Some mistook the Temple as 'half Church half Tower'[84] and Horace Walpole, who found little to appreciate in Gibbs's medievalism—on one occasion he was pleasantly surprised that

Oxford still 'charms me [of] what remains of the true Gothic *un-Gibbs'd*'—nevertheless confessed that 'in the heretical corner of my heart I adore the Gothic building, which by some unusual inspiration Gibbs has made pure and beautiful and venerable' (Plates 217–19). He thought the windows filled with coloured glass (since destroyed) and the internal dome painted with family armorial bearings and imitation gold mosaics (Plate X) had 'a propensity to the Venetian or mosque Gothic',[85] although Gibbs seems to have turned to more accessible sources. The main fronts, with their picturesque enrichment of colonnettes, blind arcading and domed lanterns, which do not appear in Gibbs's drawing but existed by 1750, are features found at Westminster Abbey and King's College Chapel, Cambridge (Plate 258), while the unusual internal structure of the dome (Plate X) was probably inspired by the octagonal ribbed timber roof of the great kitchen (1485) at Stanton Harcourt Manor, a few miles outside Oxford, which Pope regarded as 'the true picture . . . of a genuine Ancient Country Seat', the epitome of 'an ancient majestic piece of Gothic architecture . . . more strong and more solemn' than that of the classical style.[86]

By the 1740s Gothic garden buildings were no longer a rarity; Batty Langley's *Ancient Architecture Restored and Improved by a Great Variety of Grand and Useful Designs entirely new in the Gothick Mode for the ornamenting of Buildings and Gardens* had appeared in 1742, but the Temple of Liberty is an uncommonly ambitious and serious example from the pre-Strawberry Hill era. What is also unusual is the association between the Gothic style and the theme of liberty. Samuel Boyse's poem *The Triumphs of Nature*, 1742, not only describes

> High on a summit all below commands,
> Fair *Liberty* thy destin'd *temple* stands

but glimpsing '*freedom's shrine*' from Kent's Temple of British Worthies in the Elysian Fields where the series of portrait busts, including those transferred in 1735 from Gibbs's Building, symbolize British emancipation from the shackles of foreign tyranny.[87] This theme was reinforced around 1743 by the decision to encircle the Temple of Liberty with Rysbrack's statues of the seven pagan deities removed from the Saxon Temple in the Vanbrugh–Bridgeman garden, where Gilbert West saw them in 1732 as

> Gods, of a Nation, valient, wise, and free,
> Who conquer'd to establish *Liberty*!
> To whose auspicious Care *Britannia* owes
> Those Laws, on which she stands, by which she rose.[88]

For Cobham, Saxon and Gothic were bound together with the Whig ideal. A 'real *Whig*', Viscount Molesworth observed in the preface to the 1721 edition of *Franco-Gallia: or, an Account of the Ancient Free State of France, and Most other Parts of Europe; before the Loss of their Liberties. Written Originally in Latin by the Famous Civilian Francis Hotoman, In the year 1574*, 'is one who is exactly for keeping up to the Strictness of the true old *Gothick Constitution* . . . A true *Whig* is of Opinion, that the *Executive* Power has as just a Title to the *Allegiance* and Obedience of the Subject, according to the *Rules of known Laws enacted by the Legislative*, as the *Subject* has to *Protection, Liberty* and *Property*.' Molesworth hoped 'to dye with the Comfort of Believing, that Old *England* will continue to be a free Country . . . Our Ancestors under *Boadicia* made that noble Effort for Liberty, which shook the Old *Roman* Dominion among us. Queen *Elizabeth* freed us from the double Tyranny of New *Rome* and *Spain* . . . Certain it is . . . other Nations have never flourish'd more, in good Laws, Wealth and Conquests, than under the Administration of Women.'[89] These ideas help to explain not only the motto associated with the Temple of Liberty: 'Je rends grace aux Dieux de n'estre pas Romain'—I thank God for not being a Roman[90]—but its proximity to the Lady's Temple. These associations between early medieval history and a renewed nationalism based on Whig precepts of constitutional democracy marked the ideological climax of Cobham's programme at Stowe. He seems to have turned a blind eye to Gibbs's Catholicism and Toryism perhaps because he admired the architect's intellectual approach to Gothic.

Gibbs moved in a circle of distinguished scholars, which included William Stukeley, author of *Stonehenge A Temple Restor'd To The British Druids*, 1740, William Maitland, who wrote a celebrated history of London, Humfrey Wanley, the librarian at Wimpole, George Vertue and others, who were members of the Society of Antiquaries in London. This had been founded in 1717 for the purpose of studying 'the venerable remains of our Ancestors . . . to the end the knowledge of them may become more universal, be preserv'd and transmitted to futuity'. Members agreed to collect and publish 'all Accounts of ancient Monuments that come to their hands whether Ecclesiastic or Civil . . . and whatever may properly belong to the History of Bryttish Antiquitys'.[91]

Gibbs's serious interest in medieval architecture does not seem to predate his election to the Society in 1726. As a student he did not go out of his way to examine this period: Milan Cathedral he regarded as 'a very grand noble gothick Fabrick in it's kinde, and much admired by some, but I only take notice of the modern buildings'; and the stylistic parallel he employed to describe Borromini's niches in the nave of S. Giovanni in Laterano as 'a particular Architectur, and beautifull in their kinde, altho a little bordering upon the gothick' seems the same as Campbell's derision of that architect's 'odd and chimerical Beauties'.[92] In a letter to Lord Mar of 1716 regarding 'Our brothers of the brush [Jacobites who] go on in the same style of building as formerly', Gibbs wished 'some of them would travel to improve their knowledge in that science, for it is but Gothick at best, but they will go on in this way rather than run upon new whims as they call it, although this Gothick style costs them ten times more'.[93] Gibbs did not approach Gothic with the same uncritical enthusiasm as some of his contemporaries. He expressed unqualified admiration only for King's College Chapel, 'a beautiful Building of the Gothick Tast . . . the finest I ever saw' (Plate 258), and the magnificent Perpendicular tower of Derby church (Plate 61).[94] He believed that church steeples were 'of a Gothick Extraction' but turned to them for inspiration not as repositories of ornament but because of their 'Beauties, when their parts are well dispos'd, and when the Plans of the several Degrees of Orders of which they are compos'd gradually diminish, and pass from one Form to another without confusion, and when every Part has the appearance of a proper Bearing'.[95] For this reason in his own churches he preferred Wren's type to the more heroic monoliths of Hawksmoor. There is also the important evidence of Lincoln Minster. When Edward Harley visited there in April 1725 he found 'a most magnificent pile, but . . . in a very poor condition, and has all the tokens of entire ruin approaching' but added that 'Mr. Gibbs had been lately there to view it in order to think of some method of securing it against an utter desolation'.[96] Gibbs's survey of the previous month recommended £10,000 worth of improvements to the roof, external walls, windows, battlements, gutters and so on, some of which 'should be taken away, being only a place to harbour nastiness'. Essential repairs were concentrated on the fifteenth-century west towers which 'have damaged very much the arches and split the peers below them . . .and unless five of these arches are fill'd up . . . with a stone wall to hinder the weight of the said towers from squeezing the peers further I believe them very much in danger'. John James, called in as a co-surveyor, con-

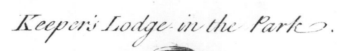

Keeper's Lodge in the Park.

Plan and Upright of a building in imitation of ye Gothick to be placed over the Rocks

curred but suggested 'making the heads of all the apertures . . . with the pointed angular arch . . . after the Gothick manner in which the whole Church is built [rather] than the semicircular arch as drawn by Mr. Gibbs, and consequently the ornaments about them of the same style'; but he added that 'this is of no consequence to the fabrick whether one way or another'.[97] The simple solution of inserting tall round-headed doors (the Gothic colonnettes were added in 1776) surmounted by oculi in the new structural walls at the west end (Plate 221) may have been Gibbs's way of solving the problem of integrating his work with the geometric recesses and round windows of the Norman west front, to which this space now formed the internal vestibule.[98] When the Archbishop of Canterbury's sanction of the repairs was made public on 20 September 1726 the local people rioted; the Mayor was severely reprimanded and the disturbance only suppressed 'when it was known that care had been taken to have this necessary work directed by Mr. Gibbs and Mr. James, two of the greatest architects in the kingdom'. But the controversy centred not on the internal repairs but Gibbs's proposed replacement of the wooden spires of the west towers by what were described as octangular lanterns of stone at each corner. These he felt 'would ease the towers very much, and be more graceful than the present spires [which] makes but a very indifferent figure'; and 'So I think the better and cheaper way will be, to raise small cupelettes of stone covered with lead with fains'; the same solution was recommended for the corners of the crossing tower. James, then Surveyor to the Dean and Chapter of Westminster Abbey, also favoured removing the spires but thought Gibbs's embellishment would not 'add any beauty, [and] may do great mischief', and he suggested 'thin peramidal acroteria [in the corners], after the Gothick manner'.[99]

Gibbs's other excursions into Gothic should be seen within this pioneering and perhaps as yet still stylistically naive framework. His remodelling of medieval buildings never included the use of period motifs, as we have seen at Lincoln and Derby, and the suggested improvements to the upper hall at Raby Castle (by 1723) were entirely Palladian in character. At Hartwell House (c. 1740) little regard was paid to the existing mullion windows. But in Hartwell's 'wilderness' a sophisticated sort of medievalism was introduced by 1738 in the castellated tower, with its pointed and quatrefoil openings and an internal dome supported on crudely modelled corbels (Plates 210, 220). This work offers the possibilities of Gibbs having designed similar buildings with less securely documented histories. The ironstone Keeper's Lodge at Stowe (Plate 222) was under construction in 1741–2 by the carpenter John Smallbones, who was then also working at the Temple of Liberty. A few years earlier in date is the Castle (1738) far to the east of Hawkwell Field built as a farmhouse disguised by a rough castellated wall 'but on account of its being seated on the Side of a rising Hill, makes a beautiful Appearance'.[100] Similar features are found on the castellated brick arch at Gubbins (Plate 223), the only building now surviving in that garden, which may be identified with the 'large arch' mentioned in *The Ambulator* in 1774 but the date of construction of which is unknown.

Gibbs's Gothic became progressively more serious, that is, more archaeological. When in 1740 he added the Turner Mausoleum to the medieval parish church at Kirkleatham, the door-frame leading from the chancel into the new structure was designed, as his presentation drawing indicates, 'in the gothick manner'. More revealing of his approach is the 'building in Imitation of ye Gothick to be placed over the Rocks' at Kiveton (Plate 224), which can be dated precisely to 1741, the year the Temple of Liberty was begun. Intended as an eye-catcher it is one of the most original creations of the early Gothic revival, more sombre than Kent's or Langley's essays yet more truely picturesque.

# VIII

## LONDON TOWN HOUSES

GIBBS'S EARLIEST DATED COMMISSION was to divide into 'two distinct Habitations' a large residence in the Privy Gardens at Whitehall, just behind Inigo Jones's Banqueting House, used by the Secretaries of State for Scotland, the Earls of Mar and Loudoun. The building was demolished in the early nineteenth century and little is known about its appearance, but letters from the architect to Loudoun in 1710 suggest that the project was modest and of a type which could have been undertaken by any competent mason or carpenter. On 10 October he refers to 'working at the wanscoting as fast as eight men can worke. We have lathed and plastered your garets [as well as] the party partition that divides your lordships servants lobie from my lord Mars'. On 14 October Gibbs enclosed 'a few scraches' indicating suggested alterations to 'a passage betuixt your dining roome below stairs which if you think fitt may serve for a little buffet and have your clostule [close stool] besides' and also reported having 'gott upp all your back staires [and] just now about furring . . . your floors'. The piers supporting the great stairs had to be shorn-up to install a toplight, an operation Gibbs found very difficult, and on 2 November he apologized that the house would not be habitable for another two months because heavy rains had dampened the partitions and plastering, but eventually the fabric was made wind and water tight. However, Gibbs also dealt with equipping out the interiors, asking Loudoun if he 'will have a looking glass done in that false dore that is to be made above staires, as likewise what sorte of framed glasses you will have over your new chimneys, if you will have them gilded or black plain frames'.[1] The conversion cost £5,509.

No further comparable work in London was received for several years, while Gibbs concentrated on his job as the New Churches surveyor and on building up his country house practice. Then in 1715, across Green Park, he launched an adventurous scheme for remodelling the great Stuart mansion in Piccadilly of Richard Boyle, 3rd Earl of Burlington (Plate 225). Why he attracted Burlington, a prominent Whig, is unclear, for they moved in different artistic and political circles. Yet it is understandable that the Earl, returning from his Grand Tour in May 1715 (a month after coming of age but several years before becoming an architect himself) and wishing to continue the remodelling begun a few years earlier by his mother, should have turned to this young erudite architect for professional assistance. Gibbs's additions of wings and colonnades to the forecourt must date after the Earl's return to London since they would surely otherwise have been reported in the first volume of *Vitruvius Britannicus*, 1715, which illustrates only the unreformed mansion. Some progress was made by April 1716 when Mar in a letter to Gibbs refers to the 'work . . . upon your hands in Piccadilly'.[2] The undramatic treatment

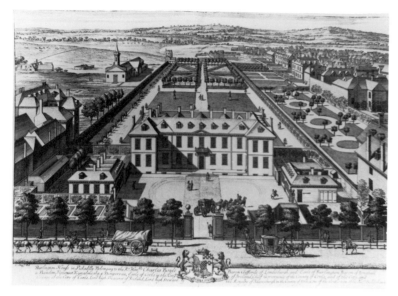

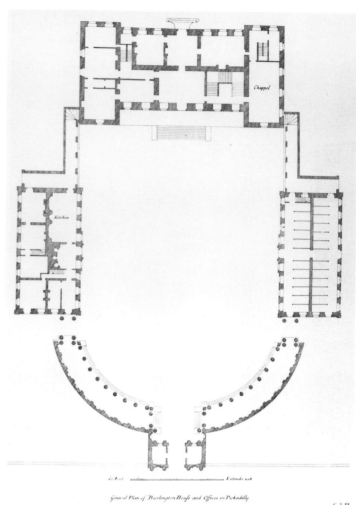

225. Burlington House, Piccadilly, London, 1665–8, bird's-eye view, engraving, Plate 29 in J. Kip, *Britannia Illustrata*, 1707

226. Pierre Delisle-Mansart, Hôtel de Souvré, Paris, 1667, bird's-eye view, engraving, Plate in *Le Grand œuvre d'architecture de Jean Marot*

227. James Gibbs and Colen Campbell, Burlington House, Piccadilly, London, 1715–19, plan, engraving, Plate 22 in C. Campbell, *Vitruvius Britannicus*, 1725

228. (facing page top) James Gibbs and Colen Campbell, Burlington House, Piccadilly, London, 1715–19, courtyard, photographed before demolition in 1868 (Royal Academy, London)

229. (facing page bottom) James Gibbs and Colen Campbell, Burlington House, Piccadilly, London, 1715–19, courtyard, watercolour by J. Buckler, 1828 (Department of Prints and Drawings, British Museum, London)

of the pair of service wings (Plate 226) recalls Hardouin-Mansart's Trianon sous Bois at Versailles, which has similar chamfer-jointed quoins and simple moulded window-frames; the doorcase is a type appearing frequently in French seventeenth-century pattern books.[3] French too is the pair of Doric quadrants sweeping funnel-like towards the carriage gate (Plates 227–9), which was probably inspired by the *cour d'honneur* of the now demolished Hôte de Souvré (1667) in the rue de Temple, Paris (Plate 226), which is illustrated in *Le grand œuvre d'architecture de Jean Marot* (despite John Macky's recollection of Bernini's colonnade at St Peter's 'from whence his Lordship, I suppose, took the Model, when he was there').[4] These additions (demolished 1868), therefore, complemented the French character of the Stuart house (which disappeared in 1717–20 under Colen Campbell's Palladian refacing). They established the new ensemble as the byword in fashionable Anglo-Gallic taste, which is what Burlington's agent Richard Graham must have meant when he wrote in 1716: 'I congratulate my *Countrey-men*, upon the happy Prospect they have, of saving them-selves the Trouble and Expence of a Journey to *Rome* or *Paris*, for the Study of those *Arts*, which they may find in their utmost Perfection at BURLINGTON-HOUSE.'[5] Although in 1716 John Gay also admired '*Burlington's* fair Palace [where] Beauty within, without Proportion reigns',[6] the forecourt then still had an unsatisfactory appearance, for the site was particularly awkward. The Piccadilly screen-wall changed axis slightly at the junction with the carriage-gate and was not parallel to the front of the house. The quadrants, therefore, while functioning as covered passages, also had to disguise this irregular alignment. James Ralph praised the theatricality of

The Colonnade and Gateway of Burlington House

231. James Gibbs, 9–11
Henrietta Street, St
Marylebone, London,
1723–7, exteriors

named John Prince, took ninety-nine year leases on various properties. In September the *Weekly Medly* announced the layout of 'a very spacious and noble Square, and many streets that are to form avenues to it'. A plan indicating sites for the estate chapel and market house was engraved in 1719 to help promote the enterprise (Plate 230). By 1726 'large, well-built Brick houses, well wainscotted, and fitted up with Marble Chimney pieces [situated] in a very pleasant Air' were advertised in the press.[11] *A New Guide to London: Or, Directions to Strangers; Shewing the Chief Things of Curiosity and Note In the City and Suburbs* announced in 1726 that in Cavendish Square 'you will see very fine Buildings, not yet finish'd [but] enough to satisfy your Curiosity, both with respect to the Largeness, Beauty, Magnificence and Regularity of the Houses, even the smallest of them. Every Street deserves to be seen.'[12] What of this was Gibbs's contribution?

It would not be unreasonable to suppose that he was involved with the brick market house of 1726–37 (demolished 1882) in Marylebone Place[13] and the Court House of 1729 (demolished in 1803) in Marylebone Lane although no architects are mentioned in the documents and no accurate views survive. However, he made a design for Harley's coat of arms, which Michael Rysbrack carved in Portland stone in 1733 for over the Court House door.

Much more is known about Gibbs's involvement in the domestic development of the estate. It is true he was not always consulted by those of his country house clients who owned properties in and around Cavendish Square: William Gore of Tring had a design

from John Prince and the Duke of Chandos first turned to John Price, Edward Wilcox, Edward Shepherd and the Florentine Alessandro Galilei and only in 1733 consulted Gibbs. The architects Henry Flitcroft, John James, Roger Morris and John Wood (later practising in Bath) as well as many local craftsmen who worked with Gibbs, John Lane, Walter Lee, Isaac Mansfield, George Mercer, Thomas Phillips, Alexander Rouchead and Benjamin Timbrell, were also building or leasing terrace houses on the estate.[14] But Gibbs too recognized the advantages of speculative building. Between 1725 and 1727 he took long leases on three houses, Nos. 9 to 11 Henrietta Street, opposite the Marylebone Chapel; and in the same year he was rated for a house in Cavendish Square, which is probably the one described in a Hand-in-Hand Insurance Company policy as 'the 3d house West from Prince's Street' on the south side, consisting of four storeys, with a stable and coach house in the back, assessed at £1,450.[15] A fourth residence in Henrietta Street was leased in 1731.[16] Five years later Gibbs, Morris and Phillips agreed to build on ground in Westminster belonging to John Campbell, Duke of Argyll, 'one New Street of dwelling Houses to be called Argyll Street', and in 1740 Gibbs took sixty-six year leases on Nos. 4 and 29. By 1754, as his Will shows, he owned six properties in Marylebone, including his own house at the corner of Henrietta and Wimpole Streets, and one in Westminster, bringing an annual rent of £525.[17]

Little more is known about the Argyll Street enterprise or what Gibbs achieved at the houses of William Hanbury in Mortimer Street, Edward Harley in Dover Street and the

208

234. James Gibbs, Design for 16 Arlington Street, Westminster, London, 1734–40, elevation and section, pen and wash, (Ashmolean Museum, Oxford, Gibbs Collection II.134)

235. James Gibbs, Design for 16 Arlington Street, Westminster, London, 1734–40, room, plan and section, pen and wash (Ashmolean Museum, Oxford, Gibbs Collection III.58)

236. James Gibbs, 16 Arlington Street, Westminster, London, 1734–40, dining room

Duke of Chandos in Cavendish Square, or what alterations he made for Thomas Coke, 1st Earl of Leicester, at Thanet House in Great Russell Street, or of the repairs to Viscount Weymouth's residence in Hanover Square, Sir Thomas Hanmer's in Grosvenor Street or Sir George Savile's in Leicester Square, all demolished. Clearly from the new house built for Sir Phillip Parker Long on the east side of this square (1733–4, demolished after 1830) Gibbs did not vary their compositions significantly and made little distinction in the design of facades for large townhouses or speculative terraces. Both types were constructed in brick with stone dressings and never monumentalized with the giant pilasters favoured by the Burlingtonians.

Of work on the Marylebone estate, however, much more has survived.[18] A contract of 5 June 1723 with the bricklayer Henry Elkins for work on a house of red and grey bricks with a 25-foot frontage in Henrietta Street designed by Gibbs (Plate 231), apart from incidental details, conforms to a standard design described in a 1724 lease as consisting of a 'uniform and continued Building . . . with straight or Compass Arches & the Returns or Jambs of the Windows to be Rubbed Brick or Stone The Parapett Walls to be Coped with Stone & other proper Ornaments'.[19] A drawing room (Plate 232) from the now demolished Henrietta Street group, re-erected in the Victoria and Albert Museum, although modest in size has unusually splendid wood-carving in the overmantel (the marble chimney is not original), and in the frieze Bacchic masks are linked by delicate garlands. The ceiling plasterwork (Plate 233), recalling those at Ditchley and Gubbins, was executed by Gibbs's team of *stuccatori*. It frames an oval canvas depicting *Time unveiling Truth and Love repelling Hatred* surrounded by emblematic figures of the Arts painted in *grisaille*.

This room is now the most complete domestic interior by Gibbs surviving in London, but a more comprehensive idea of his planning and decorating skills can still be seen in the fine Palladian house he built between 1734 and 1740 for Maria, Dowager Duchess of Norfolk, at 16 Arlington Street. This was an important commission, for the residence was in 'one of the most beautiful situations in *Europe*, for health, convenience, and beauty; the front [originally towards Arlington Street] is in the midst of the hurry and splendour of the town, and the back [overlooking Green Park] in the quiet and simplicity of the country'.[20] Work began soon after the Duchess's second marriage to Peregrine Widdrington in 1733. On 12 April the following year Thomas Michener, bricklayer, agreed to erect 'a Messuage or Tenemen together with Severall Outhouses and Offices . . . with all convenient speed Digg . . . out the Foundation . . . begin carry on and finish all the Brick work . . . in a good Substantial and workmanlike manner with good Materialls the two fronts being of the best grey stock bricks according to the plan or Elevation . . . Drawn Designed and Agreed on by James Gibbs'.[21] He in turn was paid £300 for designs and surveying (Plate 234). The house was approached through a vermiculated-arched lodge into a forecourt. This was apparently an uncommon feature because *The Grub-street Journal* commented in 1734, presumably of this very residence, that 'If between the front of every gentleman's houses, and the street it stands in, court-yards could be made; as are before the two new houses lately built in *Arlington-street* . . . they would be found very convenient, and the buildings more retired and quiet'.[22] The street front (now obliterated by an extension of 1937) was a simple three-bay composition (repeating with variations a theme used for Parker Long's house) that originally led into the vestibule beyond which, screened by Ionic columns, is the great staircase rising through two storeys to a deeply coved ceiling with a glazed lantern. The ironwork panels of the stair, a delightful rococo foil to the sedate Palladian architecture, were wrought by Thomas Wagg in 1737 for £179.10.0. William Wilton, father of the celebrated sculptor, was responsible for the decorative plas-

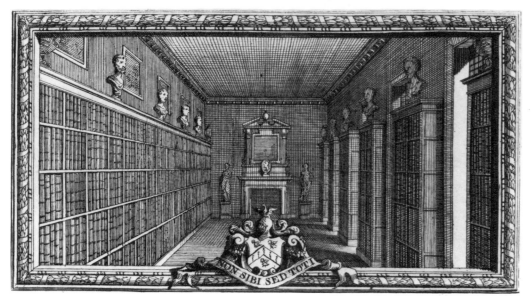

237. James Gibbs, 49 Great Ormond Street, Holborn, London, by 1734, library, engraved frontispiece to M. Maty, *Authentic Memoirs of the Life of Richard Mead, M.D.,* 1755 (British Library, London)

238. Edward Feline, Silver cup and cover, 1726, presented by Dr Richard Mead to James Gibbs, 1734 (courtesy of the Earl of Mar and Kellie)

ter. Several rooms on the first floor have carved woodwork, for which a number of working drawings exist (Plates 235–6).

Equally splendid improvements were made about this time to the Great Ormond Street house of Dr Richard Mead, the King's physician-in-ordinary. Gibbs transformed it 'into a Temple of Nature, and a Repository of Time' to display an art collection 'equalled by nothing in the Kingdome in the hands of a private man',[23] which Mead opened to artists and members of the public. When he wrote to Edward Harley in 1731 about the recent fire at Ashburnham House that had destroyed half the manuscripts of the Cotton Library[24] his own library must have been uppermost in his mind. It was probably already under construction by 1732 when the satirical poem *Of Taste* refers to 'a vast and valuable Library, stor'd with all Sorts of Books'.[25] An early view (Plate 237) shows simple stacks ranged on both long walls crowned by urns and busts. At the far end is a chimneypiece and overmantel embellished with a profile portrait medallion. The completion of this work in 1734 was marked by the doctor's presentation of a fine silver cup inscribed to his 'outstanding architect' (Plate 238).[26]

XI. (facing page) James Gibbs, Turner Mausoleum, Kirkleatham, Cleveland, 1740, exterior

# IX

## 'Augusta Triumphans'

In 1723, just as Gibbs was securing his reputation in London with the achievements of St Mary-le-Strand and St Martin-in-the-Fields and was beginning to attract the attention of influential City men, he was chosen as one of the governors of St Bartholomew's Hospital at Smithfield. He was not the only architect associated with this famous medieval hospital: Lord Burlington and George Dance the elder were also governors, while Nicholas Hawksmoor and the master-mason John Townesend were members of a committee formed in that year to look into the proposal 'that some part of this House be imediately rebuilt and that the whole in process of time will fall under the same necessity'.[1] Yet clearly Gibbs was invited with the specific intention of serving as the Hospital's architect, although work on the new buildings was delayed for five years. During the interval, however, he was able to attract some independent commissions from fellow governors.

In 1722 a group of physicians and surgeons had asked the authorities to consider building a Dissecting Room according to a plan proposed by a former governor, Dr John Radcliffe, which he had been willing to erect at his own expense because of the governors' reluctance to finance such facilities for doctors who taught on hospital premises for private gain. The scheme had foundered with Radcliffe's death in 1714, but it was now revived with the suggestion that building funds might come from the residue of the doctor's estate. However, the Radcliffe Trustees were already involved in the complex business of building the Library at Oxford and nothing further was done. Out of this idea may have grown Gibbs's series of schemes (Plate 239) for Dr John Freind, the eminent physician and medical historian, externally looking like his designs for domed garden buildings but inside with tiers of seats around the walls focusing on a central demonstration arena illuminated by large high-level windows. Not surprisingly these designs recall Inigo Jones's anatomical theatres built at the College of Physicians and the Barber Surgeons.[2] It was probably Freind's death in 1728 that prevented the scheme from going ahead, although Gibbs designed his Westminster Abbey monument.

On 1 August of that year the governors of St Bartholomew's original resolution to rebuild was reaffirmed and the committee was requested to prepare a design 'So that what future Buildings shall be entered upon for the benefitt of this Hospitall may be conformable to one Design and the whole in process of time become Regular and more usefull'. The emphasis on regularity resulted from frequent criticisms of previous remodellings which had made the complex 'so irregular that there is scarce any Communication between the several pts. of it & the whole has hardly so much as the outward appearance of an hospital And by the Erecting of buildings intermixed with those of the hospital soon after

XII. James Gibbs, Senate House, Cambridge, 1721–30, exterior

the Fire of London for the accommodation of the Cittizens who suffered in that great Calamity the free Course of the Air for the benefitt of the poor hath been much obstructed'.[3]

Gibbs's scheme (Plate 240) consisted of four nearly identical rectangular blocks each occupying one side of a quadrangle 200 by 160 feet. The block nearest Smithfield, with its rusticated tripartite coach-passage and slightly projecting end bays, was to contain the counting house and clerk's residence, a room for governors and another for in- and out-patients; most of the first floor was to be occupied by a court room used for governors' meetings and approached by a grand staircase. The other three buildings were to contain wards, twelve to each block, which would accommodate a total of 504 patients, with nurses' rooms and staircases on the ends. All four blocks were to be unembellished except for the introduction of Gibbs-surround windows on the ground storeys and vases crowning the cornices. The traditional arrangement in both Continental and British hospitals up to this time of a single block with attached wings was discarded in favour of four independent buildings; this Gibbs explains was to prevent the spread of fire.[4] *The London and Westminster Guide, Through the Cities and Suburbs*, 1768, thought 'Upon the whole, it forms a very elegant . . . Continuation of Edifices; because the Sides that form the quadrangle, are not, as is usual, joined at the Angles, but by four intermediate Walls, each having a large Gate of Admission . . . for People or Carriages'.[5]

Gibbs submitted his design for the administration block, with an estimate of £8,500, on 12 September 1728 and was ordered to prepare a plan of the whole proposal. On 1 May 1729 four hundred impressions of this general design were ordered to be printed on the finest paper; on 24 July it was unanimously approved and a building subscription launched. The principal sources of revenue were investments in South Sea Company annuities, rent from properties owned by the Hospital and the private benefactions of governors; as funds diminished, new, wealthy governors were elected. Gibbs offered his services free and left the Hospital £100 in his Will.[6]

239. James Gibbs, Design for Dr Freind's Anatomical Demonstration Theatre, by 1728, plan and elevation, pen and wash (Ashmolean Museum, Oxford, Gibbs Collection III.108)

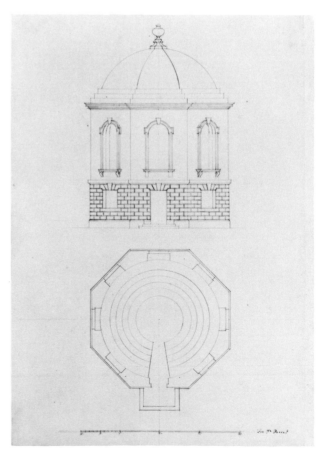

Shortly after the foundation-stone was laid on 9 June 1730 the appearance of the new buildings was changed radically. As they would be confined and largely unseen within the older group, the original proposal recommended a modest construction of brick, with the ornaments of Portland stone. But maybe now the imposing character of Gibbs's design encouraged the governors to think in more grandiose terms; and on 25 June they began to negotiate with Ralph Allen of Bath for the sale of stone from his quarries. Having tried unsuccessfully to introduce this material into the London building trade at Greenwich Hospital in 1728, Allen assured the governors that 'their highest expectations shall be fully answer'd by the Exactest performance'. He was furnished with 'The Geometrical Elevation of the Several Ornaments [of the administration block] to be according to Mr Gibbs's Larg Draughts' and Allen submitted an estimate of £1,700, but in July 1730, after examining these drawings, he reported that they were 'either alter'd or . . . the Person who made my Estimate mistook Some of the dimentions . . . which makes Savings in Some articles & exceedings in others . . . However Since the Governs: have acted in So obliging a manner by me as to Shew So Strong an inclination to cause a Publique introduction of my Stone into London, I wil out of the Seventeen hundred pounds make a Complimt: of one hundred to the Hospital.' Gibbs supplied Allen with further detailed drawings for each part of the building and the stone blocks were shipped by sea from Bristol and cut 'in the Strickest Manner . . . wth. the Utmost Exactness' on site by Allen's own workmen.[7] Construction progressed through 1730 and 1731; four hundred tons of stone were shipped from Bristol, but the Clerk reported that 'the Masons Work is obstructed by the great dillitaryness of the Carpenters in Laying the Floors pray Quicken that Work'.[8] By August 1732 the building was advanced enough for two of the rooms to be 'Furnished with Tables Chaires and Benches for discharging & taking in of Patients'.[9]

The south block of 'Wards for the Use of the poor Patients only' was launched in 1735 with a new subscription encouraged by an anonymous gift of £2,000. This was to be of the same height and to have the same ornaments on the outside but with no projecting

240. James Gibbs, St Bartholomew's Hospital, London, 1728–68, view of courtyard, engraving by T. Jefferys, 1752 (Department of Prints and Drawings, British Museum, London)

ends and a partially blind centrepiece screening a narrow corridor which divides the wards. The foundation was laid in August 1736 and two years later *A Tour Thro' the Whole Island of Great Britain* reported on 'several vast Additions . . . still making . . . which when finished will be a noble Work indeed'.[10] The masonry was completed by March 1739 and during that year the building was furnished.

The west block proved more troublesome. Begun in March 1743 with another subscription, it is shown outlined but still unbuilt in John Rocque's *Plan of the Cities of London and Westminster, and Borough of Southward* published in 1746. By July 1743 Allen was preparing to deliver 'a Sufficient quantity of Stone against the time 'twil be wanted', reaffirming his desire to 'Cause the New Work to be Executed in the best manner however Expensive it may prove to me'. But in January 1744 he reported his failure to secure vessels to carry the stone because of the Navy's needs, though he bought 'part of a Larg Ship . . . which wil Enable me to Send a Sufficient quantity to Build the first Story . . . before the end of the next Summer, & to finish that Building by the end of the Summer that follows [1745]'. However, eight months later he wrote more apprehensively that 'this French War wil I fear render it Impracticable for me to do it within five Years, and if then it must be at an Exorbitant Expense'. Anticipating a possible decision to use more accessible materials he offered the governors a gift of £500 as 'the Last proof' of his desire to 'Incourage their Laudable design'.[11] The governors, wishing to continue building with Bath stone, were prepared to await the return of peace, so Allen ceased deliveries and the foundation was covered with straw in December 1745. Gibbs, working with Christopher Horsenaile and the bricklayer William Cooper, made a design in April 1747 for a laboratory for the Apothecary Shop on a site behind the west block; but the scheme was abandoned.

Then in January 1748 the governors decided to recommence construction and asked Allen to deliver 'with all Convenient Speed . . . a Sufficient Quantity of Bath Stone . . . to Compleat the Building'. He generously offered a gift of one thousand tons, 'all the Stone which they shall want for this third Pile' if transport could be arranged to London. The governors replied in June that 'the price of freight at Bristol was not as yett affected by the signing of the Preliminaries [of the Treaty of Aix-la-Chapelle] but remained as extravagant as in time of War' and therefore resolved 'not to proceed in the Building till . . . March next [1749]'. That month Allen sent his manager William Biggs to London to 'Wait on Mr Gibbs' with 'a proper Number of hands to prepare Stone', and the third block was finally finished in 1753. But some time before that date Gibbs, suffering from kidney stones, had ceased participating in the enterprise. Although he attended a meeting on 7 September 1749,[12] his responsibilities as architect had been delegated in the previous month to a London carpenter, William Robinson, who supervised the building of the east block between 1758 and 1768 according to the original design.

No sooner had the carcass of the administration block been completed than it came under criticism. Ralph thought the building 'tho' beautiful in itself and erected at prodigious expence [was] stifled with the circumjacent houses'.[13] Batty Langley, writing in *The Grub-street Journal*, agreed that this was 'undoubtedly a very great injury, to the nobleness of the design' and suggested opening the front towards Smithfield 'to receive quadrangular colonades on each side, with an open pallissade of iron, extending from one to the other',[14] which would have resulted in the demolition of a handsome Baroque gate and the Hospital's medieval church. But generally the new buildings were well received, described in popular guidebooks and, like other institutions of this type, visited by members of the upper classes and foreign tourists. One governor reported that com-

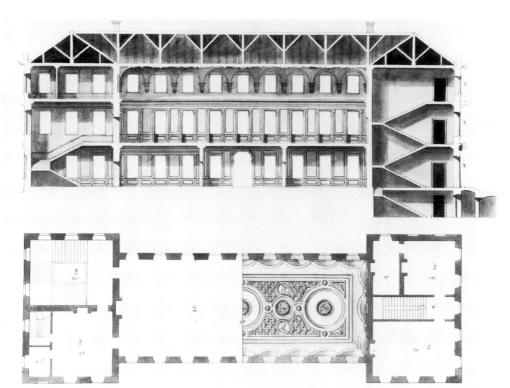

241. James Gibbs, Design for St Bartholomew's Hospital, London, 1728–38, Administration Block, plan and section, pen and wash (Ashmolean Museum, Oxford, Gibbs Collection II.66)

242. (below) James Gibbs and William Hogarth, St Bartholomew's Hospital, London, 1728–38, staircase

plaints had been received 'that wet Linnen is frequently hung upon lines in the Great Court Room . . . to the detriment of the Hall and discredit of the Hospital and the great displeasure of Persons coming to see the Room and paintings'.[15]

The hospital in eighteenth-century England, therefore, was more than a functional building dedicated to the care of the sick. It was also an institution where all sections of society could act together for the relief of the poor, 'the most miserable of our Species', and in this way benefit the prosperity of the nation.[16] This Christian spirit of justice and charity is reflected in the large number of hospitals built in London and in the provinces during the first half of the eighteenth century and also in the reporting of such activity in the popular press.[17] In 1744, for example, the *Gentleman's Magazine* printed this verse occasioned by the proposal to erect the Berkshire County Hospital:

> Thou sure *Asylum!* for the poor distress'd,
> At once by sickness and by want oppress'd.
> When chronical distempers fill the heart,
> And the whole human frame with in ward smart,
> Or fractur'd limbs augment their present grief,
> Here they may hope to find a sure relief.[18]

St Bartholomew's, one of the oldest London hospitals, expresses the philanthropic ideals of the time in the organization of the new buildings and the iconography of paintings and other works of art embellishing the interior of the administration block. It seems likely that visitors would follow a carefully arranged circuit from building to building during which both the history and the function of the Hospital would be revealed. The main entrance from Smithfield was (and remains) a triumphal arch built between 1701 and 1703 incorporating a life-size marble statue of Henry VIII, who had granted the Hospital its royal charter in 1542.[19] Passing through this gate, with Little St Bartholomew's on the left, the vista is closed by Gibbs's administration block, with a marble tablet placed high up on the imposing facade carrying an inscription recording that the Hospital 'was Rebuilt at the Sole Expence & by the voluntary Subscriptions & Donations of many of the Worthy Governors & other Charitable persons' and naming Gibbs as architect.[20] Below this is a second triumphal arch-like entrance leading through the atrium of the block into the quadrangle, where the visitor first sees the full extent of the new work (Plate 240) and then turns left and passes through a door at the south-east corner of the administration block into a spectacular staircase hall (Plates 241–2). Its ornamental ceiling is the work of an obscure but talented plasterer named John Baptist St Michele, but the chief glory of the hall is the great wall paintings depicting the Hospital's ancient history and charitable works. The commission for these was originally to have gone to Giacomo Amiconi, a Venetian painter whom Gibbs had employed a few years earlier at Roehampton; but he was usurped by William Hogarth who, like Gibbs, offered his services free and was elected a governor in 1734[21]. Hogarth was, of course, familiar with the royal iconography of his father-in-law Sir James Thornhill's great cycle of paintings in the dining room of the naval hospital at Greenwich, but for St Bartholomew's he chose subjects which the governors proudly described as 'Characters (taken from Sacred History) wch. illustrate the Charity extended to the Poor Sick & Lame'.[22] One canvas, completed in 1736, covering the east wall opposite the entrance and having over life-size figures, illustrates the episode at the Pool of Bethesda where Christ, surrounded by the emaciated and maimed, extends his hand to a half-naked cripple and 'said unto him, Rise, take up thy bed, and walk', with this passage from John 5:2–8 inscribed on a small painted cartouche immediately

below. The cripple recalls Hogarth's figure of the insane Rake in Bethlem madhouse in
the final episode of *The Rake's Progress* (1723, engraved 1735) but is transformed here
into an image of miraculous salvation. This biblical story was popularly associated with
hospitals, and was no doubt encouraged by the reputation of the St Bartholomew paintings: a verse published in 1741 'On the DEVON *and* EXETER *Hospital*' stressed

> Revive, ye *poor*, nor drop a silent tear,
> Your ills shall find a new *Bethesda* here

and another of 1748, referring to the Northampton Infirmary,

> Shewing the poor, deficient, ailing soul
> *Bethesda's* sacred type and healing pool![23]

The second canvas, on the adjacent wall, completed in 1737, illustrates the story of the
Good Samaritan and again with the text from Luke 10:30–4 appearing in a pendant
cartouche. Hogarth enriched both narratives with smaller vignettes painted in terracotta-
coloured grisaille to imitate relief sculpture illustrating the vision of the Hospital's founder,
Canon Rahere, upon recovering from an illness while visiting the Roman Temple of
Aesculapius, which had been converted into a church dedicated to St Bartholomew; a
companion panel shows monks tending the sick.[24]

243. James Gibbs, St
Bartholomew's Hospital,
London, 1728–38, court
room

The walls at the top of the staircase are painted by a Mr Richards, who was probably a scene-painter at Covent Garden Theatre, with baskets of medicinal flowers and herbs, while medallions with profile portraits of Galen and Hippocrates appear over the doors.

Beyond the Galen door is the immense space of the governors' court room, 35 by 90 feet and 30 feet high (Plate 243), dominated by a single unsupported ceiling decorated with fretwork designed by Gibbs and made by St Michele in 1733-4. The series of rectangular compartments framing rosettes, foliage, oak wreaths, palm branches and the Hospital's initials, was described in 1738 as exceedingly fine and painted in a scheme of three different (but unspecified) colours, although the whole is now white. The original background colour of the walls was olive.[25] Gibbs, Hogarth and Richards collaborated in the decoration where the major events in the history of the Hospital and its many philanthropic acts, already suggested on the entrance gate and the staircase walls, are ultimately reaffirmed. The ancient foundation in 1123 is celebrated by a plaster bust of Rahere copied from his monument in Great St Bartholomew's church and placed on the chimneypiece in the centre of the long north wall in 1738.[26] Then in 1743 a painted-glass picture depicting Henry VIII delivering the Hospital's charter to the governors in 1542 was installed in the middle window opposite, so that the two principal historic events complement each other across the broad space of the room.[27] Five years earlier the King's life-size portrait, a seventeenth-century copy after Holbein, was moved from the counting house to the end wall of the court room, opposite the Galen door, and Gibbs and Hogarth were 'desired to see [it] properly framed and fixed with decent & respectfull Ornaments', which consisted of scrolls and swags of carved wood.[28] Surrounding this portrait and covering most of the wall surface of the room are carved wood tablets, swags, coats of arms and painted shields, installed in 1737-8 by Richards under Gibbs's supervision, recording in gilt Roman letters on a dark porphyry ground the names of governors and benefactors who contributed to the rebuilding. Apart from the court room of the Foundling Hospital, which was decorated between 1742 and 1752 by Hogarth and his fellow artists,[29] few British hospitals of the eighteenth century celebrated their achievement in a more noble and artistic fashion, nor contributed more resolutely to Daniel Defoe's idea of *Augusta Triumphans*, the theme of which was 'The Way to Make London the Most flourishing City of the Universe'.

Gibbs's association with St Bartholomew's earned him great respect in London, and many of his ideas concerning the design of hospitals and civic buildings were affected by what he did there. In December 1734 he answered the call first published in the *Daily Advertiser* for a design for the proposed new St George's Hospital at Hyde Park Corner, a commission he may have hoped to gain through his friendship with two of the governors, Edward Harley and Dr Richard Mead.[30] The Minutes record only Gibbs's offer to 'Present . . . a Plann if this Board would inform him what conveniencys would be wanting', which resulted in his being asked to view the site, but no designs are mentioned. Other architects were also consulted, including Nicholas Dubois, Henry Flitcroft and Thomas Archer; but in 1735 Isaac Ware's design was preferred and subsequently built.

Gibbs fared little better in promoting his design for a royal palace, presumably for a London site (Plates 244-5). This was to have had a domed gate leading to a forecourt surrounded by the main buildings containing a sequence of State apartments, including a large chapel patterned on the interior of the royal parish church of St Martin-in-the-Fields, and culminating in the throne room where the King's chair was to be framed by an elaborately draped canopy. Schemes of this sort were discussed frequently during the first half of the eighteenth century, for there was need for new accommodation. A

244. James Gibbs, Design for a royal palace, undated, entrance elevation, pen and wash (Royal Institute of British Architects Drawings Collection, London)

245. James Gibbs, Design for a royal palace, undated, section, pen and wash (Royal Institute of British Architects Drawings Collection, London)

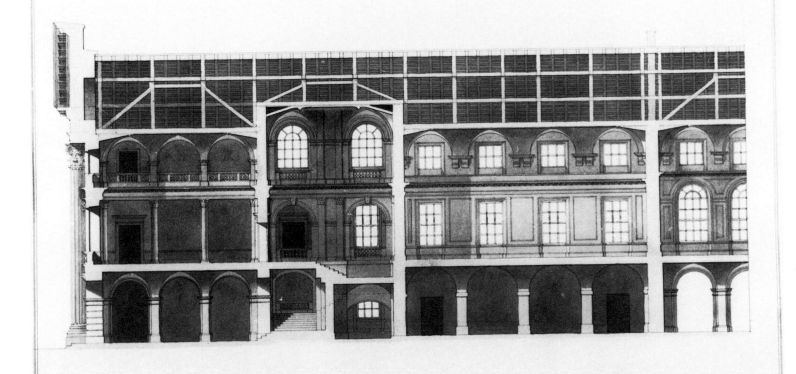

contributor to the *Daily Post* in 1736 complained that the 'Stately Palaces I have seen abroad made me often blush to think of the hovels in which we lodge our Monarchs'; but he added 'judge then the Pleasure it was to me to read . . . that Her Majesty has ordered a plan to be laid before her for building a Royal Palace in St James's Park . . . Britain, in half a Century, would bring in all the expence by the Daily Concourse of Foreigners to see it'; Versailles and Marly are cited as models.[31] Nor did Gibbs realize his stately Palladian design for a new Town Hall at Hertford to replace the decrepit Elizabethan fabric (Plate 246). The council chamber and municipal offices on the upper floors, approached by a grand staircase, were to be supported on twenty-eight internal columns enwrapped by a uniform Covent Garden-like arcade of the sort he also introduced at Whitton greenhouse (Plate 170).

Yet an even more serious disappointment was the loss of the commission for a new Mansion House for the Lord Mayor of London, one of the most coveted civic enterprises offered by the City at any time during the eighteenth century. Some of the St Bartholomew's governors were also Aldermen serving on the City Lands Committee which dealt with such work and on 2 July 1728, only a month before Gibbs was asked to prepare a general design for the Hospital, the newly formed Mansion House sub-committee invited him to draw a plan for them. A design for the Stocks Market site, lying between the Royal Exchange and Walbrook, was ready within a week, but the project remained unresolved into the next year, when Gibbs was asked to prepare a second design for an alternative site at Leadenhall Market. The merits of both sites were discussed in June 1729, but little more was accomplished until March 1735 when a new sub-committee was elected to proceed further with the scheme. On 18 March Gibbs, Giacomo Leoni and John James were invited to prepare designs for the Stocks Market site. On the previous day Batty Langley announced that he would shortly offer a design which would be 'a Just representation of the Magnificency, Granduer, Riches, Trade &c of London (the Most famous Metropolitan in the world)' and which he hoped the Court of Aldermen 'like the noble and virtuous old Romans, will impartially consider'.[32] The three official competitors delivered their designs on 8 May and were asked to survey the Stocks and Leadenhall Markets as well as the Gresham College site: the last was rejected almost immediately as too difficult to be procured, while Leadenhall, although having the problem of the additional cost of demolishing and rebuilding the market elsewhere, remained a candidate; but the Stocks Market was favoured because it was 'the most free from Buildings . . . would Add much to the Regularity of the ground and Beauty of the Building

247. James Gibbs, Design for the Mansion House (Leadenhall Market site), London, 1735, entrance elevation, pen and wash (Ashmolean Museum, Oxford, Gibbs Collection II.124)

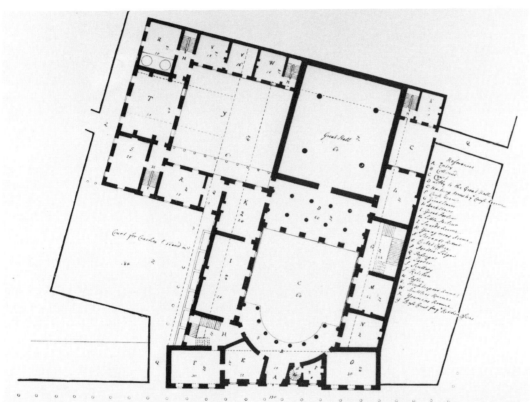

248. James Gibbs, Design for the Mansion House (Leadenhall Market site), London, 1735, plan, pen and wash (Corporation of London Records Office)

249. James Gibbs, Designs for the Mansion House (Stocks Market site), London, 1735, plan and elevations, pen and wash (Ashmolean Museum, Oxford, Gibbs Collection II.122)

[and express] the Honour of the City, and the Dignity of its Chief Magistrate'.[33] Two other architects now appeared on the scene, George Dance the elder, recently appointed the City's Clerk of the Works, and a Captain De Berlain, who described himself as a mathematician, engineer and architect. The latter's design incorporated the Doric, Corinthian and 'Britanick, or Protestant' Orders and was claimed as excelling 'in beauty, rigularty, & Simetrie, any Building in the World, for its bigness'.[34] But the committee, perhaps fortunately, refused to consider it.

Gibbs's first proposals, of 1728–9, are untraced. The set of drawings submitted on 8 May 1735 for the Stocks Market, with a main elevation of 94 feet, incorporates many features reminiscent of the ward blocks at St Bartholomew's (the south block was inaugurated in February 1735); but because of its more conspicuous site it has been enriched with a giant tetrastyle temple portico. A small central door leads into a colonnaded vestibule with the main staircase to the right flanked by reception rooms; at the rear is a large two-storey hall screened by columns at its entrance end and with a gallery around three sides approached by corner stairs. A huge Venetian window on the rear wall at gallery level would have overlooked Wren's domed church of St Stephen Walbrook. The unadventurousness of the planning was due partly to a restricted site; but in the Leadenhall design (Plates 247–8), which was requested on 17 July and presented on 19 November 1735, the larger ground, 130 by 228 by 120 feet, allowed Gibbs to develop a more expansive and dramatic building. The main elevation has slightly projecting engaged temple porticos at both ends, while the central bay with its Venetian window crowned by the City's arms is only slightly wider than its flanks. This unusual failure to emphasize the middle bays was done to camouflage the sudden shift of axis from Leadenhall Street caused by the irregularity of the site. An inconspicuous entrance leads through a short passage which accommodates the changing axis into a large courtyard with two-storeyed semicircular colonnades at the entrance end, in the manner of Vignola's Villa Giulia at Rome.[35] (Gibbs had used a similar solution to overcome the same difficulty at Burlington House.) Beyond this is a colonnaded lobby supporting a 'Publick Room' on the first floor, which leads to a grand hall lying at the rear of the building, two storeys high with a perimeter gallery supported on columns. The Assembly Rooms surround a second inner court lying to the left, with the service quarters below. The Lord Mayor's residence is on the first floor overlooking Leadenhall Street with access from both a private staircase and the upper storey of the semicircular colonnade, which communicates directly with the Dancing Room. Only Isaac Ware's later plans for the same site (6 July 1737) introduced such varied and complicated room arrangements. The site, however, proved impracticable and in another Stocks Market design (Plate 249) Gibbs returned to a more conventional solution of domestic character in which one elevation is reminiscent of Down Hall and the other is a standard Palladian type which had already been used by the unrecorded architect of the York Mansion House (1725).[36]

It was Dance's report of December 1735, pointing out that the rebuilding of Leadenhall Market alone would cost as much as £3,040, which led finally to the decision to build at the Stocks Market. The site was officially approved in March 1736. The final designs and estimates were submitted in the following year and on 6 July the Court of Common Councilmen voted in favour of Dance (his scheme was built between 1739 and 1753); Gibbs received half as many votes, and Leoni, James and Ware none at all. Gibbs never attracted further important City patronage, and it was instead at the universities, where he was able to establish an unrivalled position, that his talent as a designer of public buildings found its most fruitful expression.

# X

# OXFORD AND CAMBRIDGE

'WE HEAR FROM CAMBRIDGE', reported the *Public Advertiser* in 1753, 'that great improvements are made in the Buildings . . . There seems to be a public Spirit prevailing in the several colleges, to make everything neat & decent.'[1] This new spirit had been evident at the two universities for several decades. Many of the improvements had been done by local builders, but the more spectacular achievements were the work of London architects. In particular, 'Gibbs seems to have engross'd all the business . . . and to do him justice, a better & more skilfull Architect could not have been found for planning out and directing the nice execution of designes'.[2] He made his debut at Oxford and Cambridge almost simultaneously. In November 1719, following a reception at St John's, Cambridge, for Edward and Henrietta Harley, who lived nearby at Wimpole and were regarded as potential benefactors of a scheme to rebuild the deteriorating College chapel, John Newcombe, a Fellow, wrote to the Harleys' poet Matthew Prior about 'promoting our new Chapel, which is so much wanted. [One] much wider and longer, might be made magnificent and convenient . . . for about ten thousand pounds . . . We have some hopes that Mr. Gibbs will survey the ground and calculate the expense'; he added 'but if the project cools, it dies abortive',[3] and that is what happened.

Eight months later, in July 1720, Gibbs was among a group of 'the ablest architects' (including Wren, Vanbrugh, Hawksmoor, Archer, James and Thornhill) which the Trustees considered inviting to prepare designs for the new Radcliffe Library at Oxford. Gibbs had to wait seventeen years to capture this most important of university commissions. But at Cambridge early in 1722 he became involved in the prestigious enterprise of designing the Public Building, the new heart of the University consolidating previously scattered scholastic, administrative and ceremonial functions. Attempts had been made since the early seventeenth century to establish such a nucleus, but little was done until George I's gift in 1715 of Bishop Moore of Ely's 30,000 volume library reawakened interest and Nicholas Hawksmoor prepared a grand scheme for a University Forum.[4] By 1719 a Syndicate of members of the University, among them John Newcombe, was appointed to deal with the site and raise funds for the new building and in the following year the first benefactions were received, encouraged by a donation of £2,000 from the King.[5] On 11 December 1721 Edward Lany, one of the Syndics, thanked Edward Harley for sending 'Mr. Gibbs's design for our building. I design to offer it to the Syndics as soon as they meet . . . I have not skill enough myself to judge of it, but . . . we have already a design very near the same from Mr. [James] Burroughs, only his is upon rustic pillars, not unlike those that support Lincoln's Inn Chapel.' Burrough, also a Syndic and a Fellow of Gonville and Caius, was soon to be involved in the construction of the Public Building and he played an increasingly important part in its design, but his contribution during this formative stage remains unclear. The apparent archaism of his design, which reminded Lany of the undercroft of Lincoln's Inn Chapel (1619–23) with its engaged Tuscan columns supporting a Gothic rib-vault, seems to have little to do with what was finally achieved.[6] Nevertheless, when Gibbs gave 'his advice about a Plan' on 27 February 1722 and a few days later was 'imploy'd & retain'd to supervise & conduct the said work', he was also asked to 'take up wth him to London Mr Burrough's Plan . . . & make what improvements he shall think necessary'. To add to the confusion John James and William Dickinson also made proposals some time before 1724.[7] All these designs are lost.

The one sent by Harley in December 1721, which was subsequently translated into a topographical perspective, shows Gibbs had immediately established the essential ingredients (Plate 250). Three similarly composed attached blocks—the Senate or Commencement House on the north, the Royal Library on the west, the Consistory and Register Office on the south—are arranged round a courtyard, with the complex bounded by King's College to the south, Gonville and Caius to the north, the Schools to the west and Trumpington Street with Great St Mary's, the University parish church, to the east. This arrangement in itself was not innovative.[8] Yet, because the Public Building was associated with no particular college but represented the equivalent of a civic centre (such as Michelangelo's Campidoglio at Rome, which Gibbs regarded as a perfect piece of architecture of its kind),[9] it was treated more heroically, with engaged temple porticos and a repeated giant Order enveloping the five main facades. The north and south blocks are identical and the west block is differentiated only by a slightly wider portico and the introduction of recessed panels in the ground-storey spandrels. This was a motif Gibbs favoured in contemporary designs for St Martin's and the south front of Cannons (Plates 38, 108), the seat of the Duke of Chandos, who was one of the first benefactors of the Cambridge Building. The Library is supported on an internal colonnade, an idea undoubtedly inspired by Wren's Trinity College Library.[10] The perspective was prepared for engraving by Heinrich Hulsbergh, who was paid 8 guineas for a copper plate on 2 July 1722, and a few weeks later 1,000 prints were issued to attract further benefactions.

A second design, perhaps resulting from Gibbs's visit to Cambridge in February 1722, calls for a larger building with a deeper courtyard (189 by 118 rather than 173 by 106 feet). The Library block at first was merely a screen-wall to the older Schools, where Bishop Moore's books were being stored temporarily, with a narrow vestibule in place of North School Street. This curious arrangement was presumably imposed by economic considerations, but the Syndics had second thoughts because on 18 March 1723 they agreed to remove the wall at the west end of the new building in order to enlarge the enclosed colonnade below the Library, which was subseqently reinstated in a second engraving (Plate 251) differing from the preparatory drawing only in minor details; 524 prints of this new design were issued between April and July 1723. Three important new ideas had appeared by this time. The Library, lengthened by ten feet, is made more prominent by the change from a tetrastyle to a hexastyle temple portico, with both the panelled soffits and string-course abandoned. Engaged porticos are introduced in place of single doors on the courtyard elevations of the Senate House and Consistory, echoing those facing Trumpington Street, so that each of the five main facades is now dominated by a temple portico. There is also a move towards greater simplicity in the change from varied window and door shapes to consistently round-headed ones and from rusticated walls against which the giant Order contrasts prominently to smooth unembellished surfaces. An almost iden-

250. (above) James Gibbs, Design
for the Public Building,
Cambridge, 1721, courtyard and
street elevations, pen and wash
(Ashmolean Museum, Gibbs
Collection III.113)

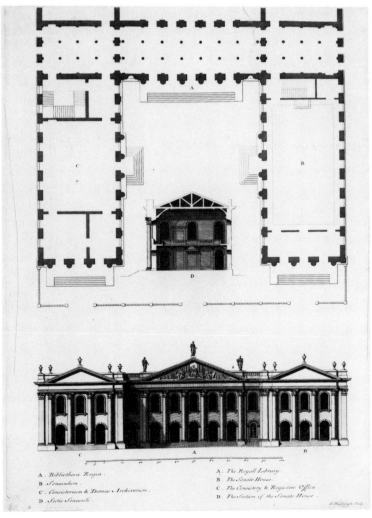

A. *Bibliotheca Regia*.
B. *Senaculum*.
C. *Consistorium & Domus Archivorum*.
D. *Sectio Senaculi*.

A. *The Royall Library*.
B. *The Senate House*.
C. *The Consistory & Register Office*.
D. *The Section of the Senate House*.

251. James Gibbs, Design for the
Public Building, Cambridge, 1723,
plan, section and elevations,
engraving (King's Maps, British
Museum, London)

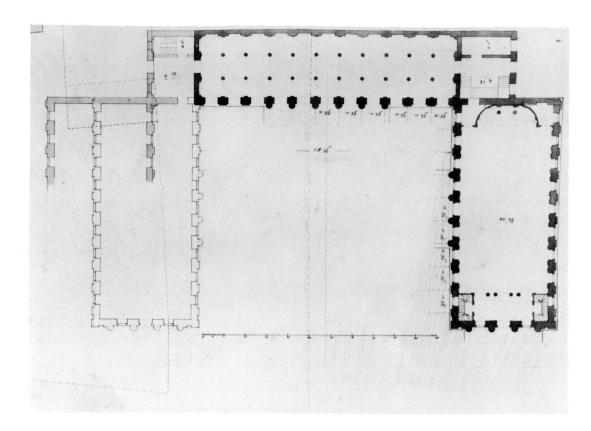

252. James Gibbs, Design for the Public Building, Cambridge, 1724, plan, pen and wash (Ashmolean Museum, Oxford, Gibbs Collection IV.13)

tical procedure had taken place some months before at St Martin-in-the-Fields, between May 1721, when the wooden model of the penultimate design was ordered to be made with 'each side [prepared] with severall sorts of Windows' (one with moulded frames against rusticated walls, the other with Gibbs-surrounds on plain walls), and October 1721, when the latter combination was chosen. By the spring of 1723, therefore, it would seem only a short step to realizing the final design at Cambridge, yet that is not what happened.

The original intention had been to house the Royal Library in a remodelled part of the Schools to allow construction on the new Public Building to begin with the Senate House. By 27 February 1722, the day Gibbs was summoned from London to discuss his first proposal, the Syndics had already ordered workmen to prepare the foundation for this block and by November this had been laid and the carcass started, despite the fact that neither the final form of the building nor its exact relationship to the surrounding blocks had yet been resolved.[11] An Act of Parliament passed in 1720 had enabled the University to purchase the necessary College land to realize the entire scheme and make 'the Approach . . . more commodious and beautifull'.[12] Nevertheless, the negotiations proved difficult, and one plan shows the access to St Mary's Lane, which separated the proposed Building from King's College, camouflaged by a false entrance through the end bay of the Consistory. The subsequent engraving (Plate 251) tidied this up by broadening the whole block and reinstating the covered colonnade of the Library, now much extended on its flanks and with its rear wall pierced by openings leading directly into the Schools. A more serious problem was the relationship between the Building and Great St Mary's. On 22 October 1724 the Syndics enquired about purchasing land belonging to King's 'as will enable Us to bring the West end of [the church] into the Centre-Line of the Regent-Walk', which was planned as the central axis to the new Library.[13] Plate 252 shows Gibbs struggling to adjust the two buildings along this axis. He also considered an alternative site for the Consistory somewhat further south and almost abutting the corner of King's Chapel. This presupposed the acquisition of College property, but here the Syndics were not successful. In May 1727, after the foundation trench for the Library block had been dug, the Master of Caius refused to grant the use of land to the west of the Senate House and condemned what was called 'the attaching Scheme' on the grounds that the 'chief Place in our Thoughts and Care' should be to use the available money to finish the Senate House and fit up rooms in the Schools as a library and not 'to execute a Scheme for which I do in my Conscience believe the whole World will condemn Us; a Scheme that will so effectually shut out all View of that noble fabrick Kings-Chapell, that I wonder how the University or that College can bear it; and a Scheme so injurious to Caius College, that I am fully resolv'd not to bear it'. A few months later he reaffirmed that should Gibbs's scheme go forward 'for all Time to come . . . the commodious View and Passage [the College] now enjoy, as likewise the Health of the Members . . . is like to be greatly injured'; moreover, 'many Persons of the best Understanding in Architecture do affirm that the said Buildings may be better carry'd on in another Way'.[14] Gibbs defended his 'attached' scheme in a letter of 1728 by pointing out the 'Conveniency of passing dry from one part of the Building to the other' and of having 'one united Building [which] will appear more Beautifull in it self [and] will skreen the Inferior Building of Cajus', although he pressed for the retention of the Schools. Moreover, a detached scheme would

253. James Gibbs, Senate House, Cambridge, 1721–30, exterior

prove 'impracticable' since the alignment of St Mary's steeple and the middle bay of the
new Library block would shift the Consistory to within eighteen feet of King's Chapel
'which I believe that College will not suffer'. (Gibbs was then also acting as its architect.)
But most especially he felt the very great difference in cost between 'an Insular or Detach'd
[and] a continued and attach'd Building ... deserves ... consideration where money
comes in so slowly that the Building is already at a stand for want of a Supply. If the
Building may be joyned the back parts may be plain, and the Expence will be only layd
out on the Ornaments of the Principal Fronts'.[15] Although a court judgement delivered
in 1730 favoured the attached proposal, Gibbs's design was not pursued, and when in
the following September he came to settle his expenses he mentions 'other drawings that
wer made upon account of unhappy differences'.[16]

Nevertheless, by 1730 the Senate House had been built at a cost of £13,000 (Plate
253). Since it was to fulfil, and still does, a unique function at the University—a single
spacious room used for the conferring of degrees—for which few architectural precedents
then existed, Gibbs amalgamated the forms of two more familiar classical building types:
the basilica and the temple. A simple rectangle of 50 by 110 feet, the courtyard and street

elevations together recall the pseudo-peripteral temple form towards which St Martin-in-the-Fields was also moving during these same years (Plate 39); this association seems to have been in Gibbs's mind because a visitor to Cambridge in 1724 remarked on the 'very rich Corinthian Pillars & Pillasters . . . taken from a fragment of Jupiter Stator Temple in Rome'[17] (Plate XII), which he also used on the church. The Senate House's classical appearance is further enhanced by the choice of white Portland stone, which was then uncommon at the University.[18]

Like Jones's Banqueting House at Whitehall, which was then regarded as 'without Dispute, the first Room in the World',[19] the street entrance of the Senate block is screened internally by paired columns and the two tiers of windows along the north and south walls are separated by narrow galleries supported on scrolled brackets (Plates 254–5). The Doric frieze and underside of these galleries, echoing the Antique source of the exterior (the Temple of Jupiter), as well as the pairs of fluted Doric pilasters between the lower windows and other exquisitely carved woodwork in '*Norway* Oak, of the Colour of Cedar',[20] is by Thomas Phillips and Benjamin Timbrell. The west end of the room has a panelled apse with a tetrastyle temple portico (Plate 256), like the entrance to Marylebone Chapel (Plate 59), canopying the Vice-Chancellor's 'Large strong Wallnuttree Chair . . . cover'd with the best Blew Turkey Leather Done . . . with Guilt Nails'[21]; on either side are chairs for the Heads, Doctors, Regents, Non-regents and noblemen of the University, an arrangement in the manner of the ancient Roman basilica. The wall above is decorated with plaster niches flanked by elaborately framed panels which are repeated on the long walls. An early proposal for coving the huge unsupported ceiling was rejected in favour of a flat expanse with the grid of enriched square and rectangular compartments corresponding to both the internal and external Order in a formal relationship which was then also concerning Gibbs at St Martin's (Plate 45). The ceiling was executed by Isaac Mansfield and the partnership of Artari and Bagutti.

The finished work was thought 'one of the most elegant Rooms in the Kingdom',[22] yet it is showier and lacks the simple Palladian balance and unity of Jones's masterpiece. One early visitor faulted it not only because the audience 'cannot hear in it' but for the 'wonderfully too narrow' entrance doors which had to be fitted into the unvaried widths of the porticos' intercolumnation.[23] Perhaps this constriction would have been less apparent had Gibbs succeeded in building the whole scheme, but he disappeared from the scene in 1730; other architects completed the west elevation of the Senate House (James Essex, 1766–8) and designed and built the Library (Stephen Wright, 1754–8); the Consistory block was never realized.

Early in 1724 the Provost and Fellows of King's College decided to improve their medieval fabric and Gibbs received 50 guineas for his journeys from London to Cambridge, designing and drawing plans, surveying and laying out the ground. The sequence of events was remarkably like that at the Public Building. Improvements had been the subject of discussions since the fifteenth century but with little accomplished until 1713 when Hawksmoor offered drawings and wooden models (Plate 257). But it was Gibbs's 'handsom plain Manner' that was preferred,[24] although again only part of the scheme was realized (Plate 258). Like Hawksmoor, Gibbs intended grouping his three blocks—the Hall and a pair of Fellows' Buildings—around a quadrangle of 240 by 282 feet to the south of the Chapel in accordance with the specifications in Henry VI's Will of 1448.[25] It had been noted as early as 1719 that the 'chargeableness of building at Cambridge . . . is greater than in most parts of England',[26] and the College authorities found it difficult to raise funds. So in the following year they were advised 'to make preparations for the building against

257. Nicholas Hawksmoor, Fellows' Building, King's College, Cambridge, 1713, wooden model (King's College, Cambridge)

258. James Gibbs, 'The East Prospect of King's College in Cambridge, as intended to be finish'd', bird's-eye view, engraving by James Essex, Jr, 1741 (author's collection)

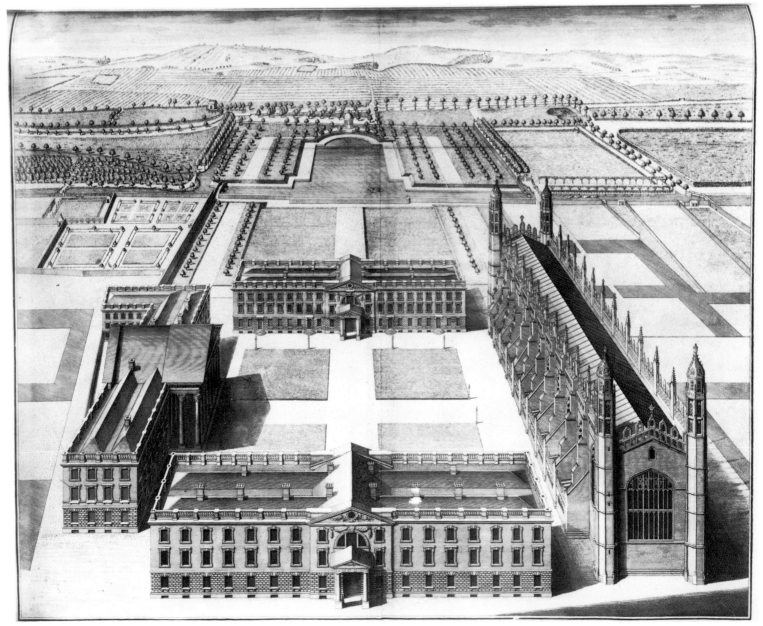

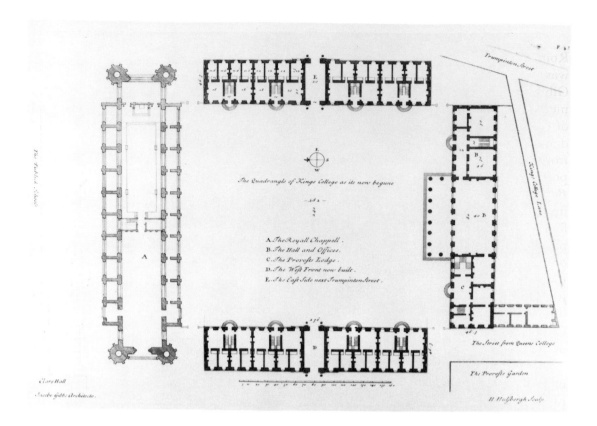

The Quadrangle of Kings College as its now begune

A. The Royall Chappell.
B. The Hall and Offices.
C. The Provofts Lodge.
D. The Weft Front now built.
E. The Eaft Side next Trumpinton Street.

259. James Gibbs, Design
for King's College,
Cambridge, 1723–31,
plan, Plate 32 in *A Book of
Architecture*, 1728

next spring, that the world may be convinced, you are in earnest, and then . . . you will
find a great many freinds very ready to assist you with their contribution'.[27] By the time
the foundation-stone was laid on 25 March 1724 about £4,000 had been donated.[28] The
University Press published the sermon preached on that occasion, which encouraged
'Assistance not to an airy Scheme, but to a real Work, actually begun, and prosecuted
with Earnestness and Vigour . . . pursuant to a PLAN design'd by Mr. *Gibbs*'. An engraving
of this design was included, which was later reused in *A Book of Architecture* (Plate 259).
Various attempts at raising money—the sale of timber and South Sea annuities—did not
alleviate the debts incurred during construction, and in 1727 the builders, Cass, Phillips
and Timbrell, offered two years' credit free of interest on condition that the College proceed with the work.[29] It was hoped the cost, which eventually reached £11,539, would
be met by the legacy of John Hungerford, but this did not become available until 1742,
and in 1734 the College was forced to sell their old bells 'for as good a price as can be
got for them . . . The money . . . to be applied towards the Discharge of the building
Debts'.[30] Gibbs waited another eight years to receive the balance of £154.10.0 owed him.[31]

The grand design first published in 1724 shows three blocks of nearly the same
dimensions—the Fellows' Buildings of 236 feet long, the Hall, Provost's Lodge and offices
240 feet, all 53 feet high—with straight elevations of carefully tiered storeys in contrasting
plain and rusticated Portland ashlar. Answering the Provost's request for 'plainness
[where] all Ornaments might be avoided' in accordance with Henry VI's specification
for a 'substantiall setting apart [of] superfluity',[32] variety is introduced only in the middle
bays. Gibbs had been developing a suitably utilitarian style during this decade—a popular
guidebook noted that the Fellows' Building was 'much in the Taste' of St Bartholomew's
Hospital[33]—and he had directed the authorities' interest in this by encouraging them to
subscribe, first in 1725 to Alexander Gordon's *Itinerarium Septentrionale*, which deals with

Romano-British antiquities, and then in 1727 to his own *A Book of Architecture*.[34] 'Plainness' was stressed partly so that the new buildings would be 'answerable' to the Chapel, which Gibbs admired as 'one of the finest gothick Buildings that can be seen anywher'.[35] His method of uniting these stylistically disparate elements without succumbing to the use of Gothic vocabulary (as, for example, Hawksmoor had done at All Souls, Oxford) is demonstrated in the Hall block, which underwent a transformation similar to the west front of St Martin-in-the-Fields. In the 1724 subscription engraving a hexastyle temple portico is placed close to the main wall, but in the design revised for publication in *A Book of Architecture* it was enlarged to an octastyle with additional single columns on the inside of each end. By increasing the number of columns while preserving the overall 90-foot length, the greater vertical stress of the portico combined with the tall windows and panelled recesses of the main wall seem to echo the rhythm of buttresses and windows on the corresponding south elevation of the Chapel. A further indication of Gibbs's attitude towards preserving the character of the Chapel without recourse to reviving an earlier style is his proposal (1724–7) for replacing the Stuart reredos (Plate 260). This was clearly intended to complement the celebrated Renaissance choir-screen across the centre of the Chapel, but the project was shelved in 1727 when funds were re-routed for the construction of the Fellows' Buildings.

Here Gibbs departed from the earlier schemes in one important respect. Perhaps aware of the Provost's objections to Hawksmoor's cramped design (Plate 257) which had prompted the suggestion in 1713 to 'set more backward [the west block] to give a full view

260. James Gibbs, Design for King's College Chapel, Cambridge, 1724–7, altarpiece, plan and elevation, pen and wash (Victoria and Albert Museum, London)

of the Chappel', Gibbs entirely detached his pair of Fellows' blocks from the edges of the great Gothic structure. This was done because, as we have seen, he recognized in it 'a different kind of Building'; and on a practical level such an arrangement would help 'prevent damage by any accident of Fire'.[36] Hawksmoor's design had been further criticized for the 'jetting out of the [numerous] Pillars of the Portal'.[37] Gibbs's solution was to introduce a large simple distyle door crowned by a Diocletian window in the central bay of both main elevations. This monumentalizing of familiar *domestic* motifs (Plates 146) must have seemed appropriate because the blocks were intended as the Fellows' residences. In considering its 'one great fault . . . that the arch is too narrow for its height'[38] the Bishop of Waterford failed to appreciate not only an essential domestic requirement of providing the maximum living space but the primary function of the arches themselves, which was to draw the eye along an axis across the centre of the new quadrangle. As early as September 1724 Lord Perceval mentioned that 'One side [the east block] is to open to [Trumpington] Street, from whence there will be a view through their garden three miles into the Country'.[39] On 20 December Charles Bridgeman was invited 'to Lay out the Ground from the west side of the new Building to the Road; and to draw two or three Schemes of different Designs'.[40] These drawings are lost, but the idea is reflected in James Essex's engraving of 1741 of the College as intended to be finished (Plate 258), showing the River Cam between King's and Clare bridges formalized into a *T*-shaped canal with the central axis terminating in a small rotunda. *Cantabrigia Depicta*, 1763, thought 'no Place is capable of greater Improvement, by cutting Vista's through the Grove, and laying out the waste Ground about it into regular Walks and Canals; all which is designed to be done (when the remaining Part of the great Square is finished)'.[41] The College's failure to realize this scheme was unfortunate because the expectation of its formal expanse had contributed in a significant way to Gibbs's concept of the whole architectural composition. In plan (Plate 259) each of the three floors of the pair of Fellows' Buildings has eight apartments, four on each side of the central arch; these are further grouped in pairs divided by a party wall but sharing a common staircase and the space behind it. Therefore, in each individual apartment the study and bedrooms are slightly wider than the sitting room facing the quadrangle[42]. As a result the two fronts towards the quadrangle, with their confined views, have twenty-one bays with densely packed four-foot-wide windows placed at six-foot intervals. In contrast the river front of the west block (Plate 261) has the unique advantage of being seen from a far greater distance (much less so in the case of the Trumpington Street front of the identical east block, which in any case was not constructed). Here the solid wall is widened by three feet, which in turn reduced the number of bays from twenty-one to seventeen. In this way the elevations have been subtly adjusted to the pecularities of the site, which Bridgeman's layout, had it been carried out, would have greatly enhanced.

Four days after Gibbs's grand design was approved, on 14 January 1724, the College resolved to begin immediately constructing the Fellows' Building on the west side of the quadrangle, facing the river. The foundation-stone was laid on 25 March and by May Christopher Cass, who was working at the same time for Gibbs at the Senate House, began receiving large quantities of stone shipped from Portland to King's Lynn and then overland to Cambridge. By October 1725 the brick and Portland stone carcass had reached the top of the first-storey windows and the central arches with their decorative carvings were completed; by December of the following year the masonry work had reached the top cornice. In April 1729 the floors, sashes and staircases were in hand and in the following month a visitor reported that the carcass was nearly finished.[43] By February 1730 Cass's bill for masonry had reached £6,054.15.5. Isaac Mansfield, another member of the Senate

261. James Gibbs, Fellows' Building, King's College, Cambridge, 1724–31, river elevation

262. James Gibbs, Fellows' Building, King's College, Cambridge, 1724–31, sitting room

House team, and John Mines began plastering the interior in that year. Phillips and Timbrell, Gibbs's London carpenters, and the Cambridge joiner James Essex were wainscotting the rooms in 1731 (Plate 262). In the same year Thomas Wiseman began painting
the interiors: the ceilings and chimneypieces were white, the walls and woodwork variations of 'Blew' and 'olive', 'Brim Stone & Olive', 'Olive and Chocolate', 'pearle and
olive' and 'pearle and Olive and Chocolate'. Some of the doors and shutters were made
of mahogany.

Although the twenty-four apartments were described as 'exceeding grand and commodious'[44], William Cole wrote in 1750 that 'ever since I inhabited the New Buildings
now about 16 years, not half of the Rooms had been let . . . the Fellows chose rather
to inhabit the *old* Building, where they pay nothing for their Chambers, and are near
the *Hall* . . . the distance from which makes the New Building very inconvenient; besides
the new Apartments are so sumptuous and grand that it requires more than the narrow
Appointment of a Fellow of the College to fit up in such a manner as would become
them'; he suggested that if a 'less magnificent Building had been erected . . . there [would
have] been a greater *probability* of seeing the whole Quadrangle *compleated*; which, as the
case now stands, there seems to be a small Prospect of'.[45] Had Gibbs succeeded in realizing
his comprehensive schemes for both King's and the Public Building, the northern end
of Trumpington Street, the University's main thoroughfare, would have been dominated
by a sequence of Portland stone buildings of truly Roman grandeur contrasted with the
picturesque Gothic of King's Chapel and Great St Mary's. Nevertheless, many of his unexecuted ideas for these commissions proved useful in other university improvements.

Magdalen College at Oxford, for example, was described as 'so decriped that Repairing
any part (except the hall and Chappell) signify's but Little, so that the whole must . . .

263. William Townesend
(?), Design for Magdalen
College, Oxford, elevations
of the quadrangle
buildings, engraving by W.
H. Toms in W. Williams,
*Oxonia Depicta*, 1732
(British Library, London)

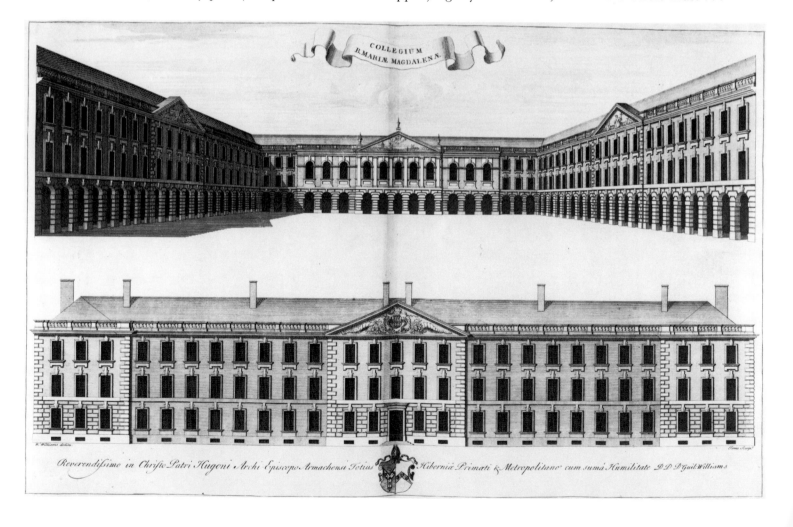

be new'.[46] Hawksmoor, Francis Smith, William Townesend and the amateur architects Lord Digby, George Clarke and Edward Holdsworth were involved in various schemes for rebuilding. Holdsworth, a member of the College who seems to have been its principal architect at this time, was a Non-Juror with strong attachments to Italy, which helps to explain why he sought Gibbs's professional assistance. On 13 January 1728 he wrote from London to the President, Dr Edward Butler,

> I fear you imagine that I have thought very little of the new College since I have been in town, but I assure you I have not neglected it ... Mr Gibbs ... has deliver'd me all the Plans, wch I have shewn to Mr Williams [William Williams, author of *Oxonia Depicta*, 1732–3], but as they are still very incorrect, & want many alterations, I cou'd not put them into his hands ... Mr Williams tells me that you and the Society seem to approve of my new scheme for placing the Library out of the Quadrangle, if so, be pleas'd to signify your sentiments by letter, that I may have time to prepare a draught accordingly.

In May 1728 Holdsworth reported that he again 'laid the Plan before Mr Gibbs, And He has undertaken to revise it, and has promis'd ... to give us his best assistance and to draw the whole design himself in order to settle the Proportions very nicely'. The scheme was considered for some time because a year later Holdsworth mentions leaving 'all the Plans, wch [Gibbs] has promis'd to have drawn fair, that I may revise them before I go abroad', and in August 1729 he went to 'see wt progresss is made ... Some mistakes have been committed in my absence, but those will soon be rectified, And I hope to see the College entirely built in paper before I leave England wch I propose to do in about 3 weeks.'[47]

Very few of these drawings, some of which Holdsworth took abroad, can be traced. But three prepared by Gibbs's draughtsman John Borlach were issued in 1731–2 as prints (Plate 263)[48]. They show that Holdsworth proposed reorienting the entire College by creating a grand approach from Long Wall Street on an axis of new buildings to the north of and unobstructed by the venerable medieval chapel and tower. A drive led to the entrance courtyard surround on three sides by the Library and the President's Lodgings. A cloister cut through the ground floor of the Library block to the new quadrangle of a nearly identical arcaded range, which was to be built on the site of the partially demolished medieval cloister. However, the correspondence make it clear that other solutions were being considered at the same time. Townesend requested Butler to 'pleas explain to me, whether you intend the inside of the Library next the College & the outside ... next the Grove, or asection of the Library ... of wch there are three differant' schemes corresponding to 'Borlacks Drawings'.[49] There are also in the College papers the elevations for the north and south sides of the quadrangle with the Corinthian Order raised on a rustic 'cloister'. Holdsworth mentions this design in letters of 1743–4 from Italy in which he proposed building a library with a portico like that at St Martin-in-the-Fields; but realizing it might prove too expensive he offered an alternative which was still 'only in Idea' and required borrowing 'some hints from any of the Palaces I see in Rome. A door or windowcase from hence may perhaps give a good air to a building'.[50] Meanwhile, in 1734 Hawksmoor had reappeared on the scene with a revision of Holdsworth's published designs. He suggested making the Gothic tower stand alone, adding a long terrace on the east front next to the river and finishing the 'Turrets' of the Library 'as Mr Inigo Jones has done [in] such sort of facades' in order to achieve 'beauty ... Conveniency [and] Duration ... which are the 3 principall qualifications in a publick (or in a private

Fabrick)'. He also pressed for a more regular design to show the Hall and Chapel more beautifully to visitors approaching the city, and he deplored the extensive remodelling suggested by other architects because not only did it defame the 'Memory of the Founder [but it] is an affront to History to Race out the Monuments and Fabricks of former times'.[51] In the event only the New Building on the north range of the quadrangle was constructed as an independent block (begun 1733), probably to a design by William Townesend, with the authorities agreeing to consult Gibbs and Smith on matters of construction. The main elevations resemble the King's College building in their sparseness and lack of the Order.

By the early 1730s, then, Gibbs had established his reputation at Oxford as a dependable assessor in those controversial and unmanageable cases relating to remodelling old colleges. Two minor commissions brought him into contact with the even more lucrative business of new building. All Souls College consulted him about completing the bookshelves in the Codrington Library left unfinished by Hawksmoor's death in 1736. Gibbs replied on 18 April 1740,

> Since you asked my opinion about the design of your Presses . . . I think them Carried too high, And if the Attick story was taken intirely away . . . they would looke lighter and better, And if ther was a Modilion Cornich with its Architrave and Frize made according to the Ionick Order, with a handsome Pedestall over it, for Bustos, Vases, or Balls, in place of the Attick and its gallery, it would give a better proportion to the Room . . . and lighten the heavy appearance of the Presses . . . and if it wer mine I should rather chuse to pay for the work allrady done, tho not put up, than have the attick upon any account what ever.[52]

The alterations were finally carried out in 1748–9, and in the following year the London sculptor John Cheere supplied twenty-four busts in bronzed-plaster of notable Fellows and twenty-five companion vases. Gibbs also replaced the Jacobean screen in the Hall of St John's College with a simple yet bold Ionic design executed in Portland stone in 1743 (Plate 264). By this year he was already deeply involved in building the Radcliffe Library, his major achievement at Oxford.

Dr John Radcliffe, Queen Anne's physician, had died in 1714 leaving £40,000 for the project.[53] Extravagant claims were made for the proposed building, which 'will far exceed that of the *Vatican* at *Rome*, or that at *Paris*'.[54] Some of the early proposals submitted by Nicholas Hawksmoor show a domed rotunda attached to the old Bodleian Library, but an Act of Parliament passed in 1720 enabled the authorities to purchase land in the

264. James Gibbs, St John's College, Oxford, 1743, Hall screen

undeveloped ground between there and St Mary's church and so release the building to develop as an independent structure. At this crucial moment Gibbs made his first tentative appearance as one of seven of the ablest architects practising in England whom the Radcliffe Trustees considered inviting to make designs for this new site. He subsequently offered three alternatives, each rectangular in plan, in the tradition of Wren's Trinity College Library at Cambridge (Plate 265). Gibbs's surface treatment is more austere, with stronger Palladian contrasts between smooth and rusticated areas; the unambiguous relationship between the exterior and the interior—in this proposal specifically the repetition of the engaged Corinthian Order on the two long fronts as a double row of free-standing columns supporting the vault of the central longitudinal aisle of the reading room—also removes these designs from the Baroque. The financial losses sustained when the South Sea Bubble burst in the autumn of 1720 brought this phase of the enterprise to an unsuccessful end.

When fourteen years later the Trustees returned to the project, Hawksmoor, who had remained the official architect, was still considering his original idea of a domed rotunda but one which was now to be free-standing in the middle of the ground (Plate 266). It was believed that the building would stand with the architect's other works as a monument 'of his great Capacity inexhaustible Fancy. and Solid Judgement'.[55] But he died after a long illness on 26 March 1736, leaving Gibbs in full control.

In May of the previous year Gibbs had already charged the Trustees £42 for plans. These may be associated with a set of drawings in which he returned to Hawksmoor's concept of the Library as a domed rotunda although now closely based on the Roman Pantheon. But when Gibbs and the masons William Townesend and Francis Smith attended the Trustees in 1737 yet another design was being considered, for Townesend delivered two estimates, one for £15,087.10.11½ supposing 'the Body . . . is to be adorned with Columns' and the other for £14,932.15.2¼ if 'the Columns are reduced to Pilasters' (Plate 267). The Trustees ordered the latter design engraved and this was distributed for the approval of the Heads of the colleges and the undergraduate nobility in a limited number of sets of five engravings dated 1737 stitched in paper wrappers entitled *Bibliotheca Radcliffiana*. One of the plans appears in Williams's portrait of Gibbs, which was presumably painted to commemorate his appointment as architect (Plate 5). His approach to the concept of a domed rotunda differs significantly from Hawksmoor's. The rectangular podium of Hawksmoor's model, a vestige of his earlier attached design but with the corners now boldly concaved, is abandoned in favour of a basement described as 'a regular Polygon of sixteen Sides'[56] in which the surfaces are modulated so subtly with projections and

265. James Gibbs, Design for the Radcliffe Library, Oxford, 1720–37, elevation, pen and wash (Ashmolean Museum, Oxford, Gibbs Collection I.124)

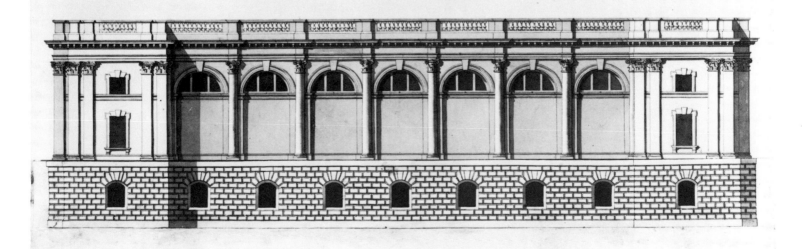

recessions that the overall appearance is nearly circular. It was Gibbs, then, who made the radical change to the full rotunda form, and although one observer considered this 'improper for the use to which [the Library] is destined',[57] the form, with its many viewpoints, satisfied the problem of accommodating such a huge building on an awkward site.[58]

The rotunda is also a suitable architectural expression of the building's encyclopaedic function (in the eighteenth-century sense of the term), and although this shape was uncommon for libraries Gibbs would have known Wren's rejected designs for Trinity College.[59] More to the point it appears to have been generally regarded in the eighteenth century that the Radcliffe was modelled on the famous circular library at Wolfenbüttel (1705–10) in Lower Saxony, where Leibniz served as librarian.[60] There was also a feeling that Dr Radcliffe's benefaction should be associated with the great achievements of the ancient world: Dr William King compared the new building to 'the magnificent *Alexandrian* Library . . . the first publick Library among the *Romans*'.[61] Moreover, Thomas Salmon commented in 1748 that 'whatever the Doctor designed or expended from his laying out 40,000*l.* in building one Room, I find a great many People of Opinion, that he intended to perpetuate his Memory by it; and therefore give it the Name of *Radcliff's Mausoleum*'.[62] The idea of an Antique-inspired cenotaphic building of rotunda form may, therefore, have been in Gibbs's mind as the final adjustments to the design were being made between 1738 and 1741. By coincidence during these years he had a further opportunity to develop these associations.

A former client Cholmley Turner of Kirkleatham in Yorkshire commissioned him to design a mausoleum for his only son Marwood, who died in October 1739 at the age of twenty-two at Lyons while on the Grand Tour (Plate XI). By the following year Gibbs had prepared a design (Plate 268) for a 63-foot-high octagonal monolith raised on a vermi-

*The Upright of the Building intended for the Radcliffe Library as it is seen on all sides.*

This Mausoleum was erected to the memory of Marwood William Turner Esq.r the best of sons. 1740.

268. James Gibbs, Design for the Turner Mausoleum, Kirkleatham, Cleveland, 1740, elevation, pen and wash (North Yorkshire County Record Office)

*Mausoleum der Arthemisia, welches sie hat erbauen laßen.* *Mausolée qu' Arthemise, fit bâtir à Halicarnasse entre*
*ihrem Ehegemahl dem König Maußolo. Zu Halicarnasso in Caren.* *le Temple de Vénus et le Palais Roïal en memoire du*
*Zwischen dem Tempel Venus und den Königlichen Pallast.* *Roÿ Maußole son epouce*

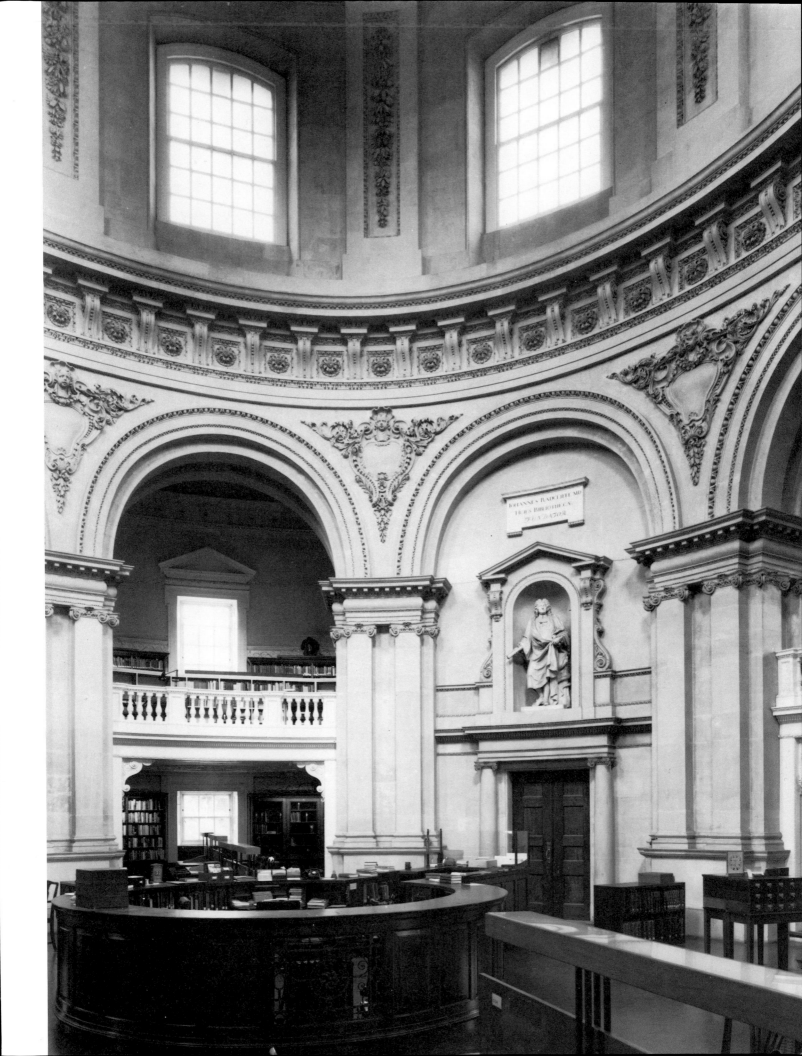

*Previous page*

272. James Gibbs, Radcliffe
Library, Oxford, 1737–47,
reading room with J. M.
Rysbrack's statue of Dr John
Radcliffe

273. James Gibbs, Design
for the Radcliffe Library,
Oxford, 1737, section,
engraving, Plate V in
*Bibliotheca Radcliffiana*, 1737
(author's collection)

274. James Gibbs, Design
for the Radcliffe Library,
Oxford, 1737–40,
elevation, engraving, Plate
IV in *Bibliotheca
Radcliffiana MDCCXL*,
1740 (author's collection)

culated rockwork podium with two sides attached to the chancel end of what was still then the medieval parish church (rebuilt *c.* 1760–3 in the Palladian style). The main structure (Plate 269) recalls the top stage of the steeple of the approved design for St Martin-in-the-Fields, in turn derived from the Renaissance campanile of S. Biago at Montepulciano (Plates 39–41); but is now enriched by alternating bands of smooth and vermiculated stonework, scroll-topped buttresses and blind niches tied together by a narrow band inscribed 'THIS MAUSOLEUM WAS ERECTED 1740 TO THE MEMORY OF MARWOOD WILLIAM TURNER, ESQUIRE THE BEST OF SONS'. The octagonal roof crowned by a flaming urn and embellished originally with family coats of arms has a boldly concave base, a motif already used on the Boycott Pavilions at Stowe (Plate 200). At Kirkleatham these features combine to resemble Fischer von Erlach's reconstruction of the Mausoleum at Halicarnassus published in *Entwürff Einer Historischen Architectur*, 1721, which Gibbs owned (Plate 270). The text relates that Artemisia, King Mausoleus's sister and wife, 'Not contented with having made herself a living Tomb for the Ashes of her Husband, which she swallow'd ... was thoughtfull of a *Monument* to his Memory, which should outbrave *even Death* & *Time* ... It was of the most exquisite Marble, and of such Magnificence, that all *Tombs*, whose Structures are more than common, do yet borrow the name of *Mausoleum* from it.' Artemisia's building incorporated a statue of the King.[63] Similarly, within the domed rotunda of Turner's mausoleum Gibbs proposed placing a life-size marble figure of Marwood (Plate 271). Meanwhile, and not unrelated to this, Michael Rysbrack was commissioned to carve a six-foot marble statue of Dr Radcliffe according to Gibbs's model for the niche over the entrance to the Library reading room (Plate 272). Its focal position was noted by visitors who found it 'most advantageously viewed from the Point opposite ... in the ... Gallery'.[64]

*Sectio sive Orthographia interior Bibliotheca Radcliffiana.*

*Elevatio sive Orthographia exterior Bibliotheca Radcliffiana.*

Let us return to the Library building itself. In the first set of engravings issued in 1737 (Plates 267, 273) the rustication of the basement encircles a cross vaulted stone porch, its seven arched-entrances hung with ironwork grilles, three serving as gates which could be locked at sunset in order, as Gibbs explains, to 'preserve [the building] from being a lurking Place for Rogues in the Night-time, or any other ill Use'.[65] His preoccupation with regular unambiguous relationships between the exterior and the interior is demonstrated by the way the paired giant pilasters enwrapping the main external cylinder (perhaps inspired by 'the fine peristylium or colonad . . . which went round the costly Monument of the Emperor Hadrian' in Rome)[66] are echoed on a smaller scale on the piers of the gallery surrounding the reading room. (Again this recalls the arrangement at St Martin-in-the-Fields.) Two stages of windows light the desks and presses, which are placed within the areas of solid wall created by the alternating bays of external blind niches. The cone of the room, a cylinder within a cylinder, is illuminated from above by eight large windows in the drum, while the dome has a glazed lantern.

The set of 1737 engravings was distributed throughout the University, but the design was received with some apprehension. One recipient thought the building would be 'a decoration, if not of much use'.[67] Nevertheless, the foundation-stone was laid on 17 May 1737, the press reporting the event and reproducing the copperplate inscription fixed to the stone identifying 'Jacobo Gibbs Architecto'. But, as in the case of St Martin's, he continued to modify the design, referring to 'unforseen Accidents, which occasioned a few Alterations'.[68] One of these occurred by February 1738 when he received £105 'for drawing further plans and for Journeys to Oxford' probably in connection with the decision formalized on 21 April to 'have three quarter collumns according to Mr Gibbs's last plan' (the more expensive alternative first mooted in the previous year). Only now did

275. James Gibbs, Design for the Radcliffe Library, Oxford, 1737–40, section, drawing for Plate V in *Bibliotheca Radcliffiana MDCCXL*, 1740, pen and wash (Ashmolean Museum, Oxford, Gibbs Collection III.76)

276. James Gibbs, Radcliffe Library, Oxford, 1737–47, section, engraving, Plate IX in J. Gibbs, *Bibliotheca Radcliviana*, 1747

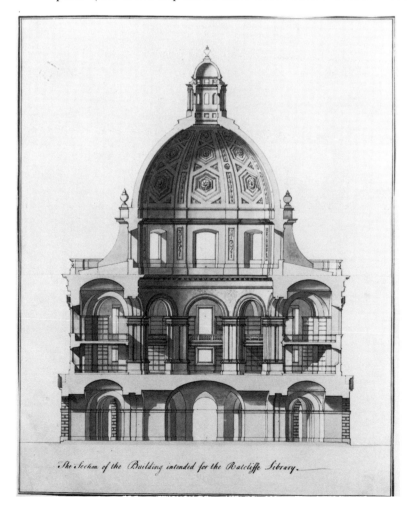

*The Section of the Building intended for the Radcliffe Library.*

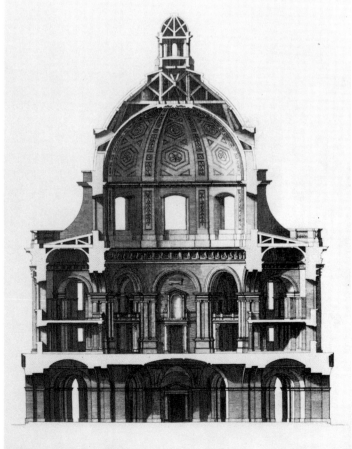

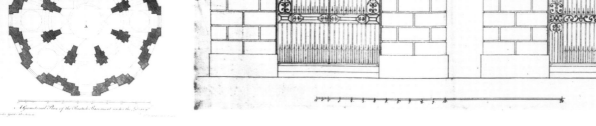

the Trustees enter into contract with Gibbs to draw 'all plans that shall be necessary for Compleating that work & Corresponding wh the Builders & going down four times in Every year to see the Building . . . & to Continue for so many years as the Trustees shall think proper to Employ him', for which he received an annual salary of £100.[69] On 8 March 1740 Gibbs was asked if he intended making further alterations and was pressed not to do so, and a second set of five engravings by George Vertue dated 1737 and 1740 was issued under the title *Bibliotheca Radcliffiana MDCCXL* (Plates 274–5). Here a number of important changes were made. The blind niches in the rusticated basement were reinforced by projecting bases, and the crowning balustrade was opened above each bay. Most significantly, the drum was reduced in height while the dome and lantern were increased (the overall dimensions, therefore, remaining more-or-less the same); in turn their structural ribs and columnation became both more elaborate and closer to the rhythms of the rotunda itself. Gibbs's debt to Michelangelo's St Peter's is obvious: he claimed for that 'Magnificent Church [the] first place . . . Amongst the Modern Buildings' in Rome.[70]

Internally Gibbs vaulted the porch with circular concave compartments and subsequently enriched them with various geometric divisions he called '*Mosaic* Work' (Plate 280).[71] The ground floor of the reading room remained unaltered, but in the gallery he first suggested modelling the balustrade of each bay as a bold concave. It is unclear why he introduced this uncomfortable feature, which would have reduced the gallery's floor space and interrupted the smooth geometry of the central rotunda; perhaps it had something to do with the way the balustrade cut into the piers, which was not universally admired.[72] But this first solution was rejected and a more successful one using scrolled-brackets abutting against the giant pilasters to support the floor of the gallery was offered (Plate 277). Finally, the tranquil pattern of diminishing octagons and diamonds in the 1737 dome was replaced by more dynamic hexagons and triangles framed by foliated ribs which drop into the drum and emphasize the increased height of the structure.

By the time the second set of engravings was issued for general approbation in 1740 the Library had nearly achieved its final form. The construction of the carcass, crisply cut in local Burford and Headington stones (Plate XIV), had already reached the top of the balustrade crowning the rotunda, and the masons Townesend and Smith had submitted an estimate for work to the base of the lantern. But on 10 February 1741 the Trustees

280. James Gibbs, Radcliffe Library, Oxford, 1737–47, interior of porch

277. (facing page top) James Gibbs, Radcliffe Library, Oxford, 1737–47, detail of reading room

278. (facing page bottom left) James Gibbs, Radcliffe Library, Oxford, 1737–47, plans, engraving, Plate III in J. Gibbs, *Bibliotheca Radcliviana*, 1747

279. (facing page bottom right) James Gibbs, Radcliffe Library, Oxford, 1737–47, alternatives for ironwork gates, pen and wash (Badminton House archive, by gracious permission of the late Duke of Beaufort)

ordered them not to proceed with any part of the building until further directed, and on 4 March they were asked to submit an account of work done on the dome and the interior work proposed to be done that summer. The problem revolved around the uncertainties of attempting an entirely masonry structure, for no stone dome of such size had been built in England. On 20 April Gibbs suggested it would be more advisable to finish it with wood and lead, which is what was done. He described the construction as 'all of Heart of Oak, being an excellent Piece of Carpentry well considered, and executed in the best Manner, the Ends of the Timbers being fixed in Shoes of Metal, to preserve them from any Damp that might affect them from the Stone' (Plate 276).[73]

The design was fully resolved by 1741 and construction proceeded without further incident, indeed with such vigour in an attempt to complete the job on schedule that in 1745 the workmen were forbidden to labour by candlelight in the darkness of winter mornings and evenings for fear of fire.[74] John Phillips's proposal for carpentry in the dome 'agreeable to the Second Modell' delivered in March 1742 carried an assurance that the work would be completed within twelve months and by February 1743 he and Jeremiah Franklin had erected scaffolds around the dome for the plumber and installed a staircase from the gallery to the lantern. Proposals for executing the ornamental plasterwork were delivered on 18 March 1743 and Giuseppe Artari was chosen, having offered the lowest estimate, £61.14.9. In the same month the masons estimated they had £1,203.1.6¾ worth of work still to do, mainly ornamental details such as the exquisite carving of balustrades, vases, doorcases and the 'great Geometrical Stair Case'; they gave alternative estimates for paving in Portland stone at £229.12.0 or in 'the best Black and best White Vein'd Marble' at £631.8.0. The basement pavement was 'all laid regularly in Courses drawn from the Centre of the Building [in] a hard Sort of Stone', while the reading room floor mixed Portland with red Swedish and Bremen stones, Gibbs having rejected marble as 'improper for the Place, because of the air condensing upon it, occasioned by its Hardness (which commonly, though improperly is called sweating) makes the Place damp, especially when no Fire is kept, and is fitter for Churches, Portico's, Common Halls, and Passages, than a Library'.[75] On 29 February 1744 Robert Bakewell's proposal was approved for executing to Gibbs's design the seven external gates using the best Swedish iron (Plate 279). On the same occasion the Trustees approved John Phillips's scheme for joinery work on the book presses 'according to the design, with the dryest and best right Wainscott, well match't, and wrought in the neatest manner, and Circular according to the form of the building, all the uprights to be Groved very thick, that the Shelves may be moved as occasion requires'. On 18 February 1745 Charles Stanley in partnership with a local plasterer, Thomas Roberts, delivered their bill for the rococo ornament under the reading room gallery and on the ceiling of the circular staircase again 'according to a drawing made by Mr Gibbs' (Plate XV). On 13 March 1746 the architect presented an estimate for outstanding work, and during the next ten months much of the remaining internal details were executed. The vocabulary of William Linnell's bill of 1746 for carving evokes some idea of the careful segregation of the architectural parts: the window cornices are 'inriched with Egg & Anchor', the architraves with 'Raffle leaf and tongue bead husk OG & Tongue & Ribbon & Steek', the doors with 'bubbles & split Tongues', 'Water leaf & Tongue & Egg & Anchor' on the caps and a rich cornice of 'Raffle leaf & upright Tongue 5 leav'd Grass bubbles & split Tongues & flowers & band', and so on.[76] In 1746 Phillips also made the doorcases, the desks and presses in the reading room and the polished mahogany handrail of the circular staircase. Thomas Wagg, who had worked for Gibbs at 16 Arlington Street, London, agreed to make the balustrade according to his design,

281. James Gibbs,
Radcliffe Library, Oxford,
1737–47, porch vault

282. James Gibbs,
Radcliffe Library, Oxford,
1737–47, staircase

283. James Gibbs,
Radcliffe Library, Oxford,
1737–47, view of the
exterior, coloured
engraving in R.
Ackermann, *A History of
The University of Oxford*, II,
1814

a particularly splendid piece of architectural ironwork (Plate 282). In 1747 *The Gentleman and Lady's Pocket Companion for Oxford* announced that 'the most magnificent Structure in Oxford is the new public Library',[77] and in the same year Gibbs issued an unusually elaborate advertisement of his achievement under the title *Bibliotheca Radcliviana: or, A Short Description of the Radcliffe Library, at Oxford*. This contains twenty-three copperplate engravings by Pierre Fourdrinier of plans, elevations, sections and ornamental details, with an 'EXPLANATION', printed for the author and dedicated to the Trustees. A portrait of Gibbs (Plate 6) engraved by Bernard Baron after a drawing by Hogarth and another of Dr Radcliffe engraved by Fourdrinier after Baron's copy of a Kneller original, both with elaborate frames designed by the architect, were included. The plates were ready for distribution to the Colleges in May 1748. On 29 March 1748 Gibbs was paid 'in full of all accounts and demands as architect' and although the Library, which eventually cost more than £43,000 (of which Gibbs received £1,292), was now finished, the opening planned for August 1748 was postponed until April the following year. Gibbs continued to be involved in small ways. In 1750 he offered a scheme for increasing the area of the Library towards St Mary's; in 1752 he was present at a meeting when John Townesend was paid for erecting twenty obelisks and lamps around the outside of the Library. In 1753 he provided a design for fitting up a room for storing title deeds and in March of the following year, a few months before his death, he was consulted about glasses for the obelisks and asked to make patterns for seats for the use of the Library. Gibbs had begun his association with this great work thirty-four years earlier and was sole architect during the last seventeen years of his life. It is a powerful statement of his final thoughts on architecture and reveals him during this period as a designer of undiminished vitality and imagination (Plate 283 and Plate XIII). A later biographer, Allan Cunningham, rightly thought the Library 'the grandest feature in the grandest of all English architectural landscapes'.[78]

XIII. James Gibbs,
Radcliffe Library, Oxford,
1737–47, exterior

*Following pages*

XIV. James Gibbs,
Radcliffe Library, Oxford,
1737–47, detail of exterior

XV. James Gibbs,
Radcliffe Library, Oxford,
1737–47, staircase

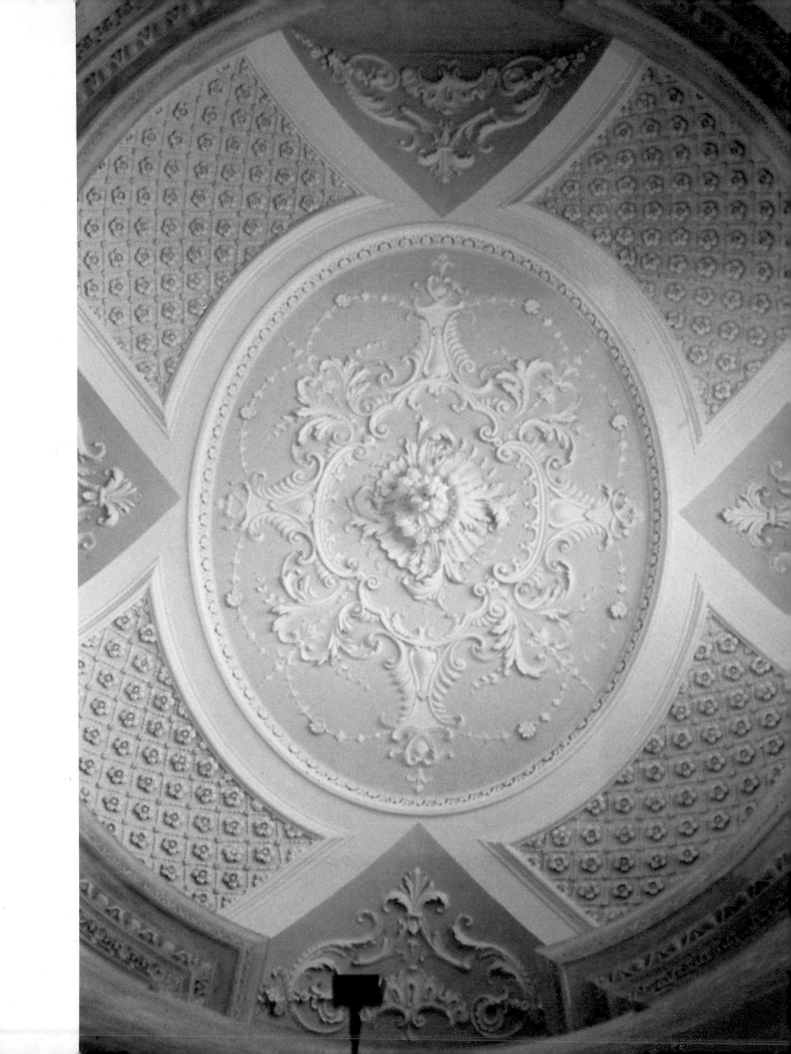

# XI

## 'OF USE TO GENTLEMEN CONCERNED IN BUILDING'

IN HIS INTRODUCTION to *A Book of Architecture* Gibbs defined the nature of the publication and the clientele to which it was directed. The collection of designs was 'undertaken at the instance of several Persons of Quality [who] were of opinion, that such a Work . . . would be of use to such Gentlemen as might be concerned in Building, especially in the remote parts of the Country, where little or no assistance for Designs can be procured. Such may be here furnished with Draughts of useful and convenient Buildings and proper Ornaments; which may be executed by any Workman who understands Lines, either as here Design'd, or with some Alteration, which may be easily made by a person of Judgment.' So an examination of Gibbs's enormous influence both at home and abroad should begin with a history of this book.

Contemplating issuing a collection of his own designs as early as 1713, Gibbs wrote to Robert Harley:

> I would willingly be doing something to establish my reputation here, by showing the world by demonstration that I know something of what I pretend I have learned while I was abroad, and by making this as advantageous as I can . . . In order to [do] this I have a mind to publish a book of architecture, which indeed is a science that everybody criticises here, and in all the countries that ever I was in, never did I see worse performers . . . this is my design, which I think to go about this summer if your Lordship will encourage me by accepting the dedication, and being at the expense of the plates, for I am so far from being able to pay the charge myself, that I am fifty pounds in debt.[1]

A unique pair of proof engravings of designs for Comley Bank Lodge and Dupplin Castle (Plates 97–8) may relate to this early initiative, but for some unknown reason the scheme was postponed and then complicated by Harley's fall from political favour in July 1714, his imprisonment in the following year, and Gibbs's own dismissal from the New Churches surveyorship in January 1716. Anticipating the possibility of a bleak future as a church architect he begged the Commissioners 'to give to no body the designes of the Church in the Strand nor suffer the same to be copied, in order to have them printed, becaus I am now about graving them my self at my own proper Charge in order to publish them', referring to the view later included in *A Book of Architecture* (Plate 17).[2]

Another sponsor, however, soon came forward, John Campbell, 2nd Duke of Argyll and Greenwich, for whom Gibbs had designed Sudbrook in 1715 and to whom the book

XVI. Asher Benjamin and Ithiel Town, First Congregational Church, New Haven, Connecticut, 1812–4, exterior

is dedicated. No previous British architectural publication had been so single-minded, with one architect's *œuvre* represented by some 380 different designs on 150 finely engraved plates and, therefore, unlike its closest rivals, Colen Campbell's *Vitruvius Britannicus* and William Kent's *Designs of Inigo Jones*, which included contributions by various architects. Gibbs was inspired by Continental models, above all Palladio's *I Quattro Libri Dell' Architettura*, 1601. While a student in Italy he had praised this 'great Restorer of Architectur' and noted 'numbers of fine palaces and Villas … which never wer published, and it's strange no person of fortune who was a lover of Architectur has not employed some proper draughtsman to take the plans and uprights of them, in order to have them ingraved and published for the good of the Publick such a work would turn to very good accompt if they wer done exactly. For ther are many of his fine buildings there, which never wer printed, nor mentioned in his books of Architectur.'[3] Gibbs's own book was finally in hand by the middle of the 1720s, for the plate of the Newcastle monument in Westminster Abbey was engraved by George Vertue in 1725 (Plate 77). On 15 March 1727 Gibbs issued

PROPOSALS
FOR PRINTING by
SUBSCRIPTION,

PLANS, Uprights, Sections and Perspectives of Buildings; as, the Churches of St. *Martin in the Fields*, St. *Mary le Strand, All-Hallows* in *Derby*, and *Shipburn* in Kent; the Steeple of St. *Clement's Danes*, and other Designs for Steeples; the Duke of *Chandos's* Chapell at *Canons*, and the Earl of *Oxford's* at *Marybone*; the Publick Building and *King's College* at *Cambridge*; Buildings for Decoration of Gardens in the form of Temples, &c. Columns, Obelisques, Peers and other Ornaments for the temination of Walks and Visto's; Various Designs of Gates, Doors, Windows and Niches, with their Proportions and Ornaments; the Monuments of the Duke of *Newcastle*, Mr. *Prior, Ben. Johnson*, Mr. *Smith* and others in *Westminster-Abbey* and elsewhere; Urns, Sarcophagus's and Vases; Cartels, Shields and Compartments for Monumental Inscriptions; Chimney-pieces, Cisterns, Fonts, Tables and Pedestals for Dyals, &c.

By James Gibbs.

THE Work will consist of 140 Plates, engraved by the best Hands, and printed on Imperial Paper, with Descriptions in *English* and *French*. The Price to Subscribers will be Four Guineas; half to be paid at the time of Subscribing, and the remainder on the delivery of a Book in Sheets. The Whole will be finished by *Michaelmas* next, most of the Plates being already graved; Proofs of which may be seen at the Author's House in *Henrietta-Street Marybone*, at Mr. *Strahan's* in *Cornhill*, at Messieurs *Woodman*

and *Lyon's* in *Russel-Street Covent-Garden*; at Mr.
*Prevost's* over against *Southampton-Street* in the
*Strand*, and at Mr. *Stagg's* in *Westminster-Hall*; at
all which Places Subscriptions are taken.

According to advertisements in the *Monthly Catalogue* for April 1727 ninety plates had
already been engraved under the proposed title of 'Designs of Buildings and Ornaments'.[4]
The bi-lingual format was intended not only to capture the French market but also to
rival *Vitruvius Britannicus*, which also sold at 4 guineas. But a second proposal issued 1 May
1727 shows that Gibbs changed his mind. The French translation as well as the designs
for Shipbourne church and the chapel at Cannons were abandoned. The number of plates
was increased to 150 (yet nevertheless such major works as Burlington House, Cannons
House, Kedleston, Lowther, Wimpole, Witham and the Westminster Abbey monument
to James Craggs were not to be included).[5] This meant, according to the May *Proposal*,
the book 'cannot be finished before *Christmas* next, though most of the Plates first proposed
by already graved'.[6]

Subscriptions were also being gathered during these months, for Edward Holdsworth
reported to the President of Magdalen College that he had been 'several times at [Gibbs's]
house, but He has always been in the country . . . As a convincing proof that I have been
[there] I have herewith sent you Proposals he gave me for Printing by Subscription a
Volume of Architecture.'[7] In the Introduction Gibbs' paid homage to 'the Zeal of my
Friends in encouraging and promoting the Publication', and although it attracted no
members of the Royal Family and fewer from the peerage than *Vitruvius Britannicus*, it
did include powerful men: the Principal Secretary of War, the Lord President of the
Council and the Lord Steward of the Household, the Duke of Chandos, the Earl of Oxford
and Viscount Cobham. Moreover, the social milieu was wide and included academics,
professionals and merchants, a substantial number of whom were drawn from St Martin-
in-the-Fields parishioners, subscribers to the rebuilding of All Saints at Derby, governors
of St Bartholomew's Hospital and Gibbs's fellow-members of the Society of Antiquaries
as well as no fewer than sixty architects, painters, engravers, sculptors and assorted craftsmen. By 1728 he had gathered 481 subscribers, each paying 4 guineas. Copper plates
and royal paper had to be paid for as well as work by six engravers, but costs were kept
down because Gibbs published the book himself in sheets, leaving the binding to individual
subscribers.[8] Heneage Legge, son of the 1st Earl of Dartmouth, for example, wrote to
his brother-in-law Sir Walter Wagstaff Bagot, one of the subscribers, on 2 July 1728 that
he had had a copy of 'the Gibbean Architecture' for some time but 'as you seem'd to
desire It should be nicely Bound, have waited ever since in order to Inform Myself where
It should be most likely to gett it so done'.[9] Gibbs told Vertue he made £1,500 profit
on sales.[10] In May 1728 he announced that the book 'is ready to be delivered to the Subscribers at his House [in Henrietta Street] . . . upon Delivery of the Receipts, and Payment
of two Guineas, which is the Second Payment. The Subscribers are desired to send for
their Books between 7 and 11 of of the Clock in the Morning; and between 4 and 7 in
the Afternoon'.[11]

Compared to similar English publications of this decade *A Book of Architecture* offered
a greater variety of building and decorative types, from churches, chapels, tombs,
sarcophagi and coats of arms, university buildings and country houses, to chimneypieces,
windows, doorcases, niches and balusters, pavilions, obelisks, columns, gates, vases,
cisterns, tables, dials and pedestals for gardens. It was enormously successful and a second

284. (above) John Clark, after James Gibbs, *Thirty Three Shields*, 1731, title page and Plate I, engraving (Department of Prints and Drawings, British Museum, London)

285. William Etty, Holy Trinity, Leeds, West Yorkshire, 1722–7, exterior; steeple by R. D. Chantrell, 1839

venture seems to have been contemplated, for a number of finished drawings for anonymous country houses with the same format of elevation and plan survive among Gibbs's drawings in the Ashmolean Museum.[12] But nothing came of this and by 1738 the copper plates of the first edition were sold for £400 to the consortium of London booksellers W. Innys, R. Manby, J. and P. Knapton and C. Hitch. They sold off the remaining stock at 3 guineas, advertising in the provincial press in the same year that the price was 'a Guinea less than formerly sold', and in 1739 issued a second edition under their own imprint, in every way identical but without the subscription list.[13] Thereafter both editions sold for as little as £1.5.0[14] and occasionally were available for loan: for example, one of the original subscribers named Leake of Bath, 'who keeps one of the finest Booksellers Shops in *Europe* [promoted] a Subscription, which is but Five Shillings the Season, for taking Home what Book you please'.[15]

Some of the designs in *A Book of Architecture* were also available in more modest publications. One in which Gibbs may have been involved, *THIRTY THREE Shields & Compartments FOR Monumental Inscriptions, Coats of Arms, &c. Of Great Use to Artists & Others, Neatly Engrav'd from the Designs of that Curious Architect, MR. JAM: GIBBS*, was issued in 1731 in an unbound set of ten plates, priced one shilling, by a Gray's Inn engraver and bookseller named John Clark, who recut plates 128 to 135 on a smaller format (Plate 284). He added a title page with a cartouche taken from a detail in the *Galerie de Girardon*, 1715.[16] But more often designs were pilfered without acknowledgment. Edward Hoppus not only used the Gibbs original but also Clark's collection for vignettes in *The Gentleman's and Builder's Repository*, first published in 1737 as a 'New Magazine [which would] prove, upon the Perusal, to be the most copious and compleat, as well as the cheapest, Performance of the like Nature hitherto extant'. So also did Edward Oakley in *The Magazine of Architecture, Perspective, & Sculpture*, 1730. More blatant cases of plagiarism are found in Batty Langley's *The City and Country Builder's and Workman's Treasury of Designs*, first published in 1740 at sixteen shillings in sheets and thereafter in many editions. *A Book of Architecture* was

286. James Gibbs, Design for a house for 'a Person of Quality', 1720, plan and elevation, pen and wash drawing for Plate 54 in *A Book of Architecture*, 1728 (Ashmolean Museum, Oxford, Gibbs Collection I.29)

287. William Etty (?), Mansion House, York, 1725–6, exterior

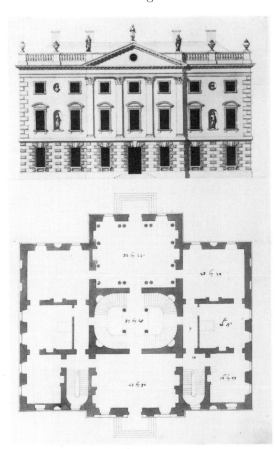

288. William Adam, The Town House, Dundee, 1732–4, elevation, engraving, Plate 104 in W. Adam, *Vitruvius Scoticus*, 1812

advertised in Langley's *The Builder's Director, or Bench-Mate*, 1751, and in other inexpensive manuals Gibbs's designs were widely disseminated.

How and to what extent were they used in Britain? A good many isolated examples can be found, such as the pedestal in Plate 148 which appears in a slightly more embellished form on the tradecard of the Bath carver Joseph Greenway;[17] Thomas Greenway, a member of the same family, had executed a vase and pedestal (1725) at Cliveden to Gibbs's design and may also have worked for him at Stanwell House, Middlesex. Occasionally Gibbsian features appear in such variety in a single building, such as Leyburn Hall, Yorkshire (*c.* 1750), that there is little doubt that either the owner or his architect had access to *A Book of Architecture*.[18]

William Etty of York, one of the dozens of architects and builders who subscribed to the publication, was apparently already familiar with Gibbs's work by 1723 when he sent his friend Ralph Thoresby a drawing of his wooden model for Holy Trinity, Leeds (Plate 285), which combines Strand-like windows with giant pilasters and Gibbs-surround doors reminiscent of St Martin-in-the-Fields (the Gibbsian steeple is an addition of 1839).[19] Etty visited London in 1725 'in Hopes to see something that might be newer fashioned',[20] when he may have met Gibbs and been shown some of the designs prepared for publication (Plate 286); in this context there is a strong probability that in the same year he designed York Mansion House (Plate 287).[21]

Another visitor to London, this time in 1727, who took 'an opportunity of being introduced to many people of genius and taste and of seeing various buildings' was the Edinburgh architect William Adam. With Sir John Clerk of Penicuik he visited James Johnston's Octagon at Twickenham, the garden buildings at Whitton, St Martin-in-the-Fields and St Mary-le-Strand, as well as Wimpole Hall.[22] Both Adam and Clerk subscribed to *A Book of Architecture*, and the former had already decided by 1726 to publish engravings of Scottish buildings in the manner of *Vitruvius Britannicus*. This collection, called *Vitruvius Scoticus*, begun in 1730 but not issued until 1812, was eventually to contain Gibbs's Balveny House (Plate 155) and a preponderance of Adam's own work, some of which was inspired by *A Book of Architecture* or made great use of its vocabulary (Plate 288). The temple 'to be built in the Centre of a Belvidere att Eglintoune', Ayrshire (*c.* 1738), published as Plate 123, is a close copy of the circular temple at Hackwood (Plate 175). William was not

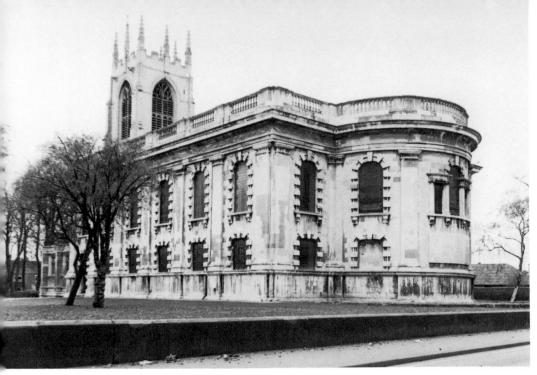

289. Francis Smith, All Saints, Gainsborough, Lincolnshire, 1734–44, exterior

290. Allan Dreghorn, St Andrew's, Glasgow, Strathclyde, 1740–56, exterior

the only member of the Adam clan to show such interest. On a 'Jaunt into England' in 1759 his son John examined Gibbs's buildings at Cambridge and Stowe. His younger brother James, who possessed a copy of *A Book of Architecture*, still thought enough of Gibbs as late as 1768–71 to reuse elements of his rejected design for Hertford Town Hall (Plate 246) for the Shire Hall built on the same site.[23] Similarly, James Essex, who completed the west elevation of the Senate House at Cambridge (his father had been the joiner there as well as *A Book of Architecture* subscriber), turned to Gibbs's grand design (Plate 250) for his unexecuted scheme for additions to Corpus Christi College (1748).[24] One of William Townesend's designs for Magdalen College, Oxford (Plate 263), is clearly based on the grand scheme for King's (Plate 258). Benjamin Timbrell and Thomas Phillips, two other subscribers, offered a variation of the Marylebone Chapel for the Grosvenor Chapel (1730) on the adjacent Mayfair estate.[25] There were even closer associations between Gibbs and Francis Smith of Warwick who, although not a subscriber, collaborated during the 1720s at Ditchley, Calke Abbey and All Saints, Derby, the first of Gibbs's churches to have been built a considerable distance from London. In 1734–5 Smith and Francis Bickerton of York, 'two . . . Professed Surveyors of Buildings, of unquestionable Credit', examined the 'decayed & shaken' medieval church of All Saints at Gainsborough, Lincolnshire. Smith recommended retaining the tower but rebuilding the nave and chancel (Plate 289) for £3,000 in what the Vestry described as 'a different Manner' and which obviously derived from Derby (Plate 61), for they had troubled to examine 'sevl. Schemes, & enquired into the Methods that had been taken in other Places'.[26]

Of all Gibbs's churches St Martin-in-the-Fields, 'indisputably the most magnificent Parochial Church in *London*', exerted the greatest influence.[27] Yet neither in Britain nor abroad did architects demonstrate that they understood the innovational character of the original design (Plate 27). Features such as the temple portico, the multi-tiered steeple, the Gibbs-surround doors and windows and the treatment of the internal columns were inevitably used only in isolation. Early neoclassicists' condemnation of the steeple because it 'appears to stand upon the roof of the church', which seems to have been ignited by John Gwynn in 1766, was the basis of Horace Walpole's criticism of Mereworth church in Kent (1744–6, perhaps by Roger Morris), where the steeple, copied from Plate 30 in *A Book of Architecture* (Plate 315), 'is so tall that the poor church curtseys under it'.[28] An equally awkward adaptation is St Andrew's, Glasgow (Plate 290), by Allan Dreghorn (1740–56), where a disproportionately thin steeple is isolated on the roof of a body copied carefully from plates in the *Book* but avoiding the essential binding motifs of bays *in antis* and modelled balustrades; however, the interior and many of its details are closely based on St Martin's.[29] Stephen Riou's solution, illustrated in *The Grecian Orders of Architecture*, 1768, was to place a wholly detached steeple and base to the east of a St Martin's-like church 'after the Manner of an ANTIQUE TEMPLE'.[30]

Nevertheless, by the 1730s St Martin's had been accepted as the most compelling Protestant church form. In 1731 Henry Flitcroft altered his first proposal for the steeple of St Giles-in-the-Fields in favour of this prototype, despite its diminutive Order being unrelated to the simple Palladian character of the body (Plate 291).[31] Flitcroft was also concerned with the rebuilding of St John's, Hampstead, offering in 1744 a plan and estimate *gratis* on condition that he had no competition from other architects (for a design had also been submitted by James Horne). The Vestry refused to comply and instead chose a scheme which closely follows St Martin's interior submitted by John Sanderson, a local architect who appeared on the scene suddenly in November 1744.[32] Another church built along the same lines, St John's at Wolverhampton (1756–9), was designed by William Baker, who had been associated with Gibbs at nearby Patshull Hall.[33] In a late and splendid adaptation of St Martin's interior, the parish church of Badminton (1785), Thomas Wright introduced an up-to-date neoclassical vocabulary.[34]

By that time progressive church architecture had been redirected towards a more advanced European solution utterly different from Gibbs's. Nevertheless, during a brief period between 1770 and 1800, the rejected round designs for St Martin's (Plate 292) found favour among some neoclassicists. Perhaps the earliest was William Chambers, whose unexecuted design for St Marylebone parish church is mentioned in the London press in 1771 as exceeding St Martin's in size and taking the form of 'a rotunda, from

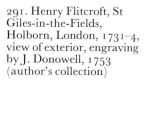

291. Henry Flitcroft, St Giles-in-the-Fields, Holborn, London, 1731–4, view of exterior, engraving by J. Donowell, 1753 (author's collection)

a curious design in Italy', although the plan clearly derives from Gibbs.[35] Then followed
Andrew Frazer and William Sibbald's delicate Adamesque St Andrew's, Edinburgh
(1781–7), David Stephenson's All Saints, Newcastle-upon-Tyne (1786–9), George
Steuart's St Chad's, Shrewsbury (1790–2), and S. P. Cockerell's church at Banbury
(1792–7). By 1818 the pattern had reached the British colony in India (Plate 293)[36]. In
Denmark, beyond British spheres of influence but where its architecture was admired,
Vincents Lerche, who owned a copy of *A Book of Architecture*, and Laurids de Thurah
proposed versions of the St Mary-le-Strand and St Martin-in-the-Fields steeples as additions during the 1740s to the Frue Kirkes, the cathedral church of Copenhagen, and the
Frelsers Kirkes at Christianshavn, the designs for which were published in the first volume
of Thurah's *Den Danske Vitruvius*, 1746, while the Strand steeple (Plate 17) appeared again
in a design for the new Fridenchs Kirkes (Plate 294).[37]

Occasionally individual St Martin's features were utilized in secular buildings (Plate
288). A variant of the executed steeple crowns Berwick-on-Tweed Town Hall (1750–5)
by the London builders Samuel and John Worrall, while in the 1760s the amateur Scottish
architect Sir James Clerk, whose father had admired the church on a visit in 1727, introduced another version on the stables at Penicuik, Midlothian. Sir Robert Taylor, who owned
the second edition of *A Book of Architecture*, adapted the entire St Martin's nave to the
Transfer Office of the Bank of England in London (1766–88).[38]

Although *The Antiquities of St. Peter's, or, the Abbey-church of Westminster ... Adorned with
Draughts of the Tombs* appeared in 1722 and in the following year John Dart's sumptuously
illustrated two volume *Westmonasterium*, Gibbs was the first British architect to publish
a large number of his own designs for monuments in a book directed to both artists and
laymen. His more ambitious examples attracted few imitations, yet the Bristol architect
Thomas Paty turned to Prior's monument (Plate 94) for his own to William Hilliard in
the Lord Mayor's Chapel (*c.* 1750) and the unpublished but much admired figure of James
Craggs (Plate 95) had a considerable progeny, not least of all Kent's celebrated monument
to Shakespeare (1740).[39] Another substantial design, Plate 117 in *A Book of Architecture*,
which Gibbs reused for John Freind in 1728, was with some minor changes again favoured
for the monument to Sir Charles Gouter Nicholl (d. 1732) at Racton, Sussex. The designer
and carver are unrecorded, but it may not be coincidental that at nearby Cuckfield
Thomas Adye adapted the John Smith monument (Plate 82) for Charles Sergison

*South Side.*

292. James Gibbs, 'Round
Church' design for St
Martin-in-the-Fields,
Westminster, London,
1720, south elevation,
Plate 15 in *A Book of
Architecture*, 1728

293. Thomas De
Havilland, St Andrew's,
Madras, India, 1818–20,
view of exterior,
watercolour by J. Gantz
(India Office Library and
Records, London)

(d. 1732).[40] Andrew Carpenter, Gibbs's carver at Amersham, based his tomb to the Earl and Countess of Warrington (1734) at Bowden in Cheshire on the Bovey monument (Plate 89).[41] But presumably because they were easier to interpret and also occupied less space in churches which were becoming increasingly cramped with furnishings, Gibbs's wall monuments embellished with busts, putti or urns were more frequently copied, especially in the years immediately following 1728 when *A Book of Architecture* was still without rivals. We find Rysbrack, who subscribed to the book, and a number of unrecorded sculptors often turning to the left-hand design in Plate 123 (Plate 296). After 1730 Rysbrack went his own way as an independent designer but continued to be inspired by Gibbsian motifs.[42] Charles Easton, a London city mason, incorporated what may be a contemporary bust of the Elizabethan philanthropist Richard Watts in a marble wall monument at Rochester (Plate 295) which he agreed to carve in 1736, based on the centre and right-hand designs in Plate 123.[43] Robert Singleton and George Bottomley used the centre design in Plate 126 for the monument to Thomas Batcheler (d. 1729) in Norwich Cathedral, and the pattern again appears in Charity Newburgh's (d. 1745) monument in Dublin, while the right-hand design of the same plate was copied with only minor differences for the monument to Sarah Ballidon (d. 1736) at All Saints, Derby. Dr William Phipps's (d. 1727) monument at Kenilworth is a blend of two designs from Plate 124.[44] In all latter three examples the sculptors are unknown. The frequency of their application suggests these engravings were widely available, presumably even as single unbound plates,[45] but it should be noted that some of Gibbs's monument designs were plagiarized by Batty Langley for *The City and Country Builder's and Workman's Treasury of Designs*, first published in 1740.

A group of Gibbs's early domestic proposals which hint at his pioneering contribution to the Palladian revival also attracted attention. The saloon at Sudbrook (Plate 142), his first villa, reappeared in a similar form at Oulton Park, Cheshire, a mysterious house said to have been built in 1715. If this was the case the unknown architect was apparently familiar with Sudbrook before its inaugural publication in *A Book of Architecture*.[46] A design dated 1720 (Plate 297), a variant of Palladio's Villa Rotunda modified by restricting access to two sides and introducing an octagonal saloon lighted by semicircular windows in the manner of Scamozzi's Villa Molin near Padua (features which do not appear in comparable pioneer villas by Colen Campbell) is an important precursor of Burlington's Villa at Chiswick (Plate 298).[47] One of the 'uncommon' fronts of 'a House made for a Gentleman', also dated 1720 (Plate 299), was used by the exiled Earl of Mar in a design for the Marquis de Tessé's house at Chatou (which also incorporates an octagonal hall with angle niches) dated May 1728, the same month *A Book of Architecture* appeared (Plate 300). Although the evidence is circumstantial Mar seems to have been both Gibbs's patron and his pupil. Gibbs called him 'a great Lover of Architecture' and the Earl acknowledged that he was 'infected with the disease of building and gardening'. Their correspondence during the years following the Jacobite rising reveal that in 1716 Gibbs had taken 'all his drawings into . . . custody', some of which he sent to the Earl at Avignon. In 1718 Gibbs expressed the wish 'to be with you to see the progress you have made in your studies', although he was dissuaded from making this politically perilous visit.[48] The influence of Plate 55, Matthew Prior's villa at Down, is more problematic because its date is uncertain. Gibbs's first design (Plate 149) is a conventional Palladian composition and excluded the loggia *in antis* raised on rustic arches shown in the published version (Plate 150); but if this too dates before the poet's death in 1721 then it may have anticipated Campbell's first use of this feature at Pembroke House, Whitehall (1723).[49]

The new entrance front of Creech Grange in Dorset (1738–41) designed by the West

294. (facing page top left) Laurids de Thurah, Design for the Fridenchs Kirkes, Christianshavn, Denmark, before 1755, west elevation, pen and wash, prepared for the unpublished third volume of *Den Dansk Vitruvius*

295. (facing page top right) Charles Easton, Monument to Richard Watts, Rochester Cathedral, Kent, 1736

296. (facing page bottom) James Gibbs, Designs for church monuments, Plate 123 in *A Book of Architecture*, 1728

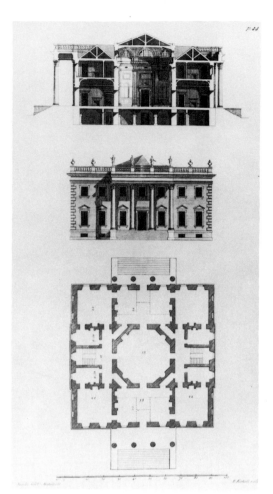

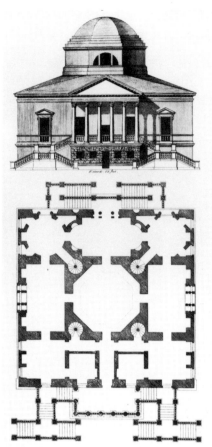

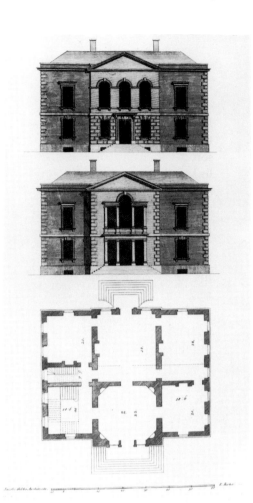

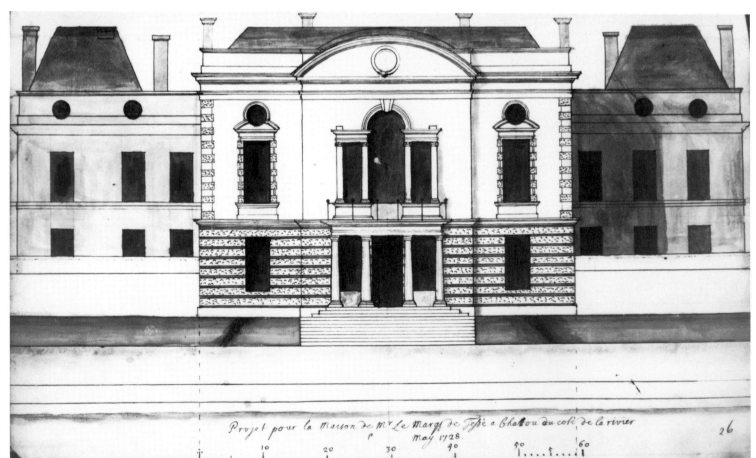

*Projet pour la Maison de M.r Le Marq.s de Teßé a Chatou du coté de la rivier*
*May 1728.*

10    20    30    40    50    60

26

Country architect Francis Cartwright in the spirit of *A Book of Architecture*, Plate 66 (described as 'a House for a single Gentleman'), is likely to have been the choice of the owner Dennis Bond, who subscribed to Gibbs's book.[50] Another subscriber, Charles Jennens, the librettist of the *Messiah*, probably also dictated the Gibbsian motifs which appear in some of the garden buildings on his Leicestershire estate at Gopsall (*c.* 1747–70). Close links existed between his architects William and David Hiorn and their fellow Warwick architects Francis and William Smith, who worked for Gibbs (David Hiorn was also associated with both Gibbs and the Smiths at Tetbury in 1742).[51] Nevertheless, none of these provincial designers is known to have owned the publication.

*A Book of Architecture* was not, however, the only available source of Gibbs designs. It is unfortunate so little is known about his relations with other architects or to what extent his unpublished designs may have been used by them. The majority of his drawings remained in his possession until they passed to the Radcliffe Library in 1754, but some are likely to have been accessible before then.[52] A group for an unidentified interior, for example, bears a striking resemblance to the hall at Barnsley Park, Gloucestershire, designed (perhaps 1720–31) by an unknown architect for Henry Perrot, a relative of the Duke of Chandos.[53] Gibbs's presentation drawings made in 1726 for a new mansion at Milton (unexecuted), until recently kept in an album in the house, were copied by an unknown architect concerned with the same commission, and another group of various designs, now in the Victoria and Albert Museum, passed perhaps still during Gibbs's lifetime into the hands of an obscure bricklayer named Nicholas Maskall, who resided in Stanhope Street, St Clement Danes parish, from 1730 (see the introduction to Catalogue of Works). It is unclear why he should have possessed them, but some link such as this might help to enlighten the undocumented and problematic history of High Head Castle in Cumberland, for which the identities of both designer and builder remain a mystery (Plate 301). This unusually sophisticated house (gutted by fire in 1956 and now a shell), was probably built soon after 1744 for Henry Richmond Brougham. Buck's engraved view of 26 March 1739, made just before Brougham inherited, still shows only the medieval castle on the site. The new house has many Gibbsian motifs, including centrepieces to the main and side facades like those in Plates 43 and 57 in *A Book of Architecture* (Plates 136, 299) and a Doric hall-screen reminiscent of the Cambridge Senate House.[54]

By the middle of the eighteenth century a number of Gibbs's buildings were also known through popular descriptions and prints in guidebooks and histories, such as the view of Antony House in William Borlace's *The Natural History of Cornwall*, 1758.[55] Illustrations in the early Stowe guides, the first being George Bickham's *The Beauties of Stow*, 1750, of the Palladian Bridge and Temple of Liberty must account for the appearance of similar buildings in the now-destroyed park at Dogmersfield, Hampshire.[56] The Temple of Liberty (Plate 217) was also one of the models for the Arlington Street townhouse Sanderson Miller built during 1757–60 for the Gothophile Countess of Pomfret (Plate 302) who, on an earlier visit to Stowe, had found Gibbs's building 'full of imagination'.[57] An engraving of St Martin-in-the-Fields based on Plate 1 in *A Book of Architecture* was issued as early as 1739 in Robert West's *Perspective Views of All The Ancient Churches, and Other Buildings, In the Cities of London, and Westminster*, to which Gibbs subscribed. Gibbs himself probably prepared the drawing of the interior of the church for Boydell's engraving of 1751,[58] and 'A Representation of the COMET that Appear'd on Janry: ye 26. &c. &c. 1743/4 in the Evening. Taken near St. Martin's-Church in the Strand' (Plate 303) was published on 11 February 1744, priced 3*d*. By 1775 *Sayer and Bennett's Enlarged Catalogue of New and Valuable Prints* was offering cheap engravings of his London churches as well as Stowe, Ditchley

POMFRET Caſtle, *Arlington street, built by Lady Pomfret. A.º 1760.*

301. Architect unknown,
High Head Castle,
Cumbria, *c.* 1744, exterior

302. Sanderson Miller,
Pomfret Castle, Arlington
Street, Westminster,
London, 1757–60, bird's-
eye view, pen and wash by
W. Stukeley, 1760
(Bodleian Library,
Oxford)

and the Radcliffe Library. A number of these items were directed towards the foreign market. They had, like the many popular guidebooks published in London, both English and Continental texts (this was, it will be recalled, Gibbs's intention for *A Book of Architecture*); some views were plagiarized by Continental engravers (Plate 304), others were re-engraved for architectural treatises and pattern-books. George Louis Le Rouge's *Détails Des Nouveaux Jardins à la Mode*, 1776–87, illustrates the house and temples at Stowe, Christian Cayus Lorenz Hirschfeld's *Théorie de L'Art des Jardins*, published in Leipzig between 1779 and 1785, copied buildings from not only *A Book of Architecture* but the Stowe guides, while other plates found their way into C. L. Stieglitz's *Plans et dessins tirés de la belle architecture*, Paris, 1801.[59] A fine view of St. Bartholomew's Hospital, with English and French captions, was engraved by Thomas Jefferys in 1752 (Plate 240) and the buildings were illustrated in J.-B. Barjaud and C. P. Landon's *Description De Londres et De Ses Édifices*, Paris, 1810–11.[60] Views of the Radcliffe Library, largely based on *Bibliotheca Radcliviana*, 1747, appeared in the *Gentleman's Magazine* in April 1749, the *University Almanacks* for 1751 and 1752 (Plate 1), the *Oxford Magazine* in April 1769 and elsewhere. The detailed description in Francesco Milizia's *Le Vite de' piu celebri Architetti*, Rome, 1768, in which he proclaims the exterior 'nobile e corretto . . . ad esempio anche in ciò de' buoni Architetti antichi, imitazione che giovrebbe parimenti ai moderni', is a reminder of contemporary Italian interest in this most Italian-looking of Gibbs's buildings.[61]

303. James Gibbs, St Martin-in-the-Fields, Westminster, London, 1720–6, steeple, engraving of 'A Representation of the Comet', 1744 (author's collection)

304. (below) James Gibbs, St Martin-in-the-Fields, Westminster, London, inscribed 'The Inside of St MARTINS Church in the Fields. Vuë du dedans de l'Eglise de St. MARTIN á Londre', 1720–6, interior towards west, engraving issued for the English and French markets for use in Optical Viewing Machines, c. 1750 (author's collection)

But of all his work Continental visitors and writers, particularly the French, most admired St Martin-in-the-Fields.[62] In *L'Etat des Arts, en Angletérre*, 1755, André Rouquet suggested that the portico was 'borrowed from a Greek temple without any alteration', by which he meant its monumental prostyle form, and that by 'this choice, the architect had shewn the elegance of his taste, and the solidity of his judgment',[63] a poignant analogy in the decade in which the design of Sainte-Geneviève (now the Panthéon) in Paris was evolving. But St Martin's distinctive allure abroad was its series of internal giant columns each with an isolated section of entablature supporting the springs of the vaults (Plate 304). French neoclassicists seem to have associated Gibbs's application of this system with their own concurrent rediscovery of its use (which the Abbé de Cordemoy called 'le dégagement') in Gothic cathedrals. By the mid-eighteenth century St Martin's was well known in numerous Continental copies of the interior perspectives issued by the London print impresario John Bowles and others (Plate 46).[64]

St Martin's found its most irresistible following in the American colonies. But it would be erroneous to imagine that Gibbs's influence lay in this great church alone, for long before it was first imitated there his name and reputation were known along the eastern seaboard.[65]

In 1727 the engraver Peter Pelham, Gibbs's Gerrard Street neighbour, emigrated to Boston, taking with him the mezzotint portraits on which he hoped to re-establish his career, undoubtedly including one of Gibbs issued by 1723 (Plate 3). In 1748 Pelham married the widowed mother of the young painter John Singleton Copley, who owned a copy of *A Book of Architecture*, perhaps inherited from his stepfather.[66] Pelham's sometime collaborator, the Scottish portrait painter John Smibert, who had included Gibbs in a

305, John Smibert, Faneuil Hall, Boston, Massachusetts, 1740–2, exterior, engraving by S. Hill in the *Massachusetts Magazine*, 1789 (The Henry Francis du Pont Winterthur Museum Libraries, Pennsylvania)

306. James Gibbs, 'Arches over Arches', engraving, Plate XXXVI in J. Gibbs, *Rules for Drawing The several Parts of Architecture*, 1732

conversation picture of 'The Eminent Artificers of this Nation' in 1724 and was a fellow-member of the Society of Antiquaries in London, followed Pelham to Boston in 1728–9.[67] There he later designed Faneuil Hall (1740–2), one of the first examples of Palladianism in New England (Plate 305). Although this building is unrelated to a specific Gibbs design, it may be seen as a demonstration of 'the Arcades and Intercolumnations of each Order' and the 'Rule for placing Orders above Orders' illustrated in *Rules for Drawing The several Parts of Architecture* published in 1732 and 1738 (Plate 306).[68] The earliest references to this publication in the colonies appears in a Philadelphia bookseller's catalogue of 1754,[69] but copies were undoubtedly available earlier, and in Smibert's case his friendship with George Berkeley, in whose entourage he had made the journey from England, may have been important. Berkeley was a persuasive advocate of the new classicism. He wrote as early as 1718 to his friend Sir John Perceval, Gibbs's mentor, that 'I pretend to an uncommon skill in architecture, as you will easily imagine when I assure your Lordship there is not any one modern building in Rome that pleases me, except the wings of the capitol . . . and the colonnade . . . before St. Peter's . . . This gusto of mine is formed on the remains of antiquity that I have met with in my travels, particularly in Sicily, which convince me that the old Romans were inferior to the Greeks, and that the moderns fall infinitely short of both in the grandeur and simplicity of taste.'[70] A few years later he remarked on the 'noble' art of architecture which has 'an influence on the Minds and Manners of Men, filling them with great Ideas, and spiriting them up to an Emulation of worthy Actions. For this Cause [it was] cultivated and encouraged by the *Greek* Cities, who vied with each other in building and adorning their Temples, Theaters, Portico's and the like Public Works.'[71] It should be added that Perceval, who was also committed to the new style, enjoyed links with other such colonists including his co-founder in 1732 of Georgia, General James Oglethorpe, who subscribed to Robert Castell's *The Villas of the Antients Illustrated*, 1728.[72]

Eyewitness reports of Gibbs's buildings also reached the colonies through travellers such as Norborne Berkeley, Governor of Virginia, who moved in the Beaufort circle (centred at Badminton House) and received an honorary degree from Oxford on the occasion of the opening of the Radcliffe Library in 1749.[73] The portrait painter Cosmo Alexander, who had inherited Gibbs's Marylebone house in 1754 (and then sold its contents two years later), spent 1765 to 1771 travelling between Philadelphia and Newport.[74] Between 1785 and 1787 the young Boston architect Charles Bulfinch visited family friends in different parts of England, and in London he must have studied St Martin-in-the-Fields; at that time he probably purchased J. C. Borlach's *Designs of Architecture, for Arches or Gates* (Plates 12), thereby introducing the work of a second generation Gibbsian to New England.[75]

In 1786 Thomas Jefferson and John Adams, both destined to the United States Presidency, toured English country houses and gardens including Pope's Villa at Twickenham, and Stowe, where Adams admired the Temple of Friendship for being 'in a higher Taste' than Vanbrugh's pavilions.[76] Jefferson's interest in buildings, which by 1771 had included the acquisition of *A Book of Architecture* and *Rules for Drawing*,[77] may have been nurtured by his friendship with Francis Fauquier, the English Governor of Virginia during the ten years from 1758. He had previously leased one of Gibbs's London houses and was a beneficiary under his Will, and may even have been related through the architect's stepmother Isabel Farquhar.[78] Jefferson used Gibbsian patterns more unconventionally than his colleagues. Unlike any colonial house up to that time, Monticello (Plate 307), his villa near Charlottesville begun in 1767, incorporates canted bays and an octagonal dome on drum, ideas amalgamated from garden temples illustrated as Plates 67 and 69 in *A Book of Architecture* (Plate 308). He sketched both these plans and commented on 'the attic serving as a background for the pediment', the 'circular lights in the Attic' and 'the wings [with] pediments in flank'. From Plate 77 came the distinctive motif of a stepped roof for the nearby icehouse. Other ideas were adopted from *Rules for Drawing*.[79]

Yet Jefferson's reliance on these publications, however precocious, was by no means unique. Copies were widely available throughout America during the whole of the eighteenth century. The New York and Philadelphia booksellers Rivington and Brown, who offered 'a constant Supply of Books, with all the new Articles as they are published in Europe; and from whence all Orders directed to them from the Country, whether in a wholesale or retail Way, will be punctually complied with', advertised copies in their 1760 and 1762 catalogues, as did a Boston bookseller in 1771; others were registered to the Incorporated Charlestown Library Society in 1770, the Library Company of Philadelphia in 1774 and 1789 and the New York Society Library in 1793.[80] This cannot, of course, presuppose their automatic use. The buildings of even an ambitious provincial master-joiner like Isaac Fitch of Lebanon, Connecticut, who claimed to be well acquainted with architectural publications and whose copy of *A Book of Architecture* was assessed at £1.16.6 after his death in 1791, show none of its influence.[81] Likewise, the entrance doorcase of Lady Pepperrell House (1760) at Kittery Point, Maine, may just as easily have derived from the plate plagerized from *A Book of Architecture* (Plate 331, the left-hand design) published in Batty Langley's *A City and Country Builder's and Workman's Treasury of Designs*, one of the most popular English pattern-books in the colonies.[82] Moreover, some plates in both Gibbs books were reused in colonial publications, notably *The Town and Country*

307. Thomas Jefferson, Monticello, Charlottesville, Virginia, 1767–1809, garden elevation

308, James Gibbs, Design for 'a Building of the Dorick Order in form of a Temple, made for a Person of Quality', plan, elevation and section, Plate 67 in *A Book of Architecture*, 1728

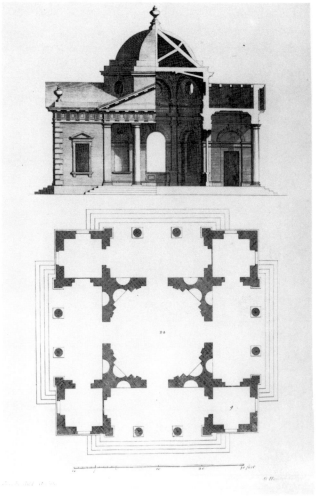

309. Architect unknown,
Apthorpe Mansion, New
York City, c. 1764,
exterior, photographed
before demolition in 1892
(Ware Memorial Library,
Columbia University
School of Architecture,
New York City)

310. Architect unknown,
Mount Pleasant,
Philadelphia,
Pennsylvania, 1761–2,
entrance elevation

311. Peter Harrison,
King's Chapel, Boston,
Massachusetts, 1749–54,
interior towards chancel

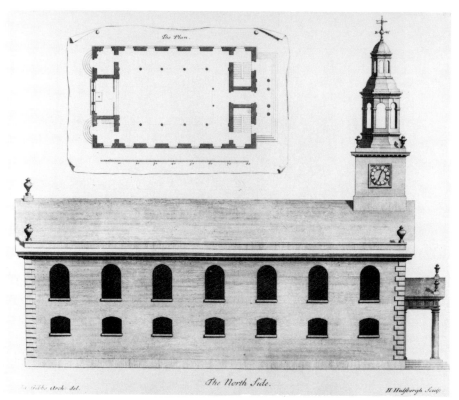

312. James Gibbs,
Marylebone or Oxford
Chapel, St Marylebone,
London, 1721–4, plan and
north elevation, Plate 24 in
*A Book of Architecture*, 1728

313. James Gibbs (?), St
Paul's, Halifax, Nova
Scotia, 1749–51, view of
exterior, engraving by J.
Fougeron, after D. Serres,
1764

*Builder's Assistant: Absolutely Necessary to be Understood, By Builders and Workmen in General
. . . By a Lover of Architecture* issued in Boston by J. Norman,[83] and the *Articles of the Carpenters
Company of Philadelphia: and Their Rules for Measuring and Valuing House-Carpenters Work*,
both of which appeared in 1786.[84]

Nevertheless, the preponderance of copies of *A Book of Architecture* in Philadelphia and
New York in the early 1760s helps account for the appearance of Gibbsian features in
three notable local houses of that decade. Apthorpe in New York City (Plate 309) by
an unknown architect was unprecedented for its ambitious and convincing classical temple
form, built entirely in ashlar, which seems to have derived from the Cambridge Senate
House (Plate 253).[85] At Mount Pleasant in Philadelphia (Plate 310), again the work of
an unknown architect, the use of Venetian windows to light the upper hall, an idea which
was to become increasingly fashionable in the colonies, is Gibbsian in origin (Plate 299),as
at Cliveden in Germantown near Philadelphia (1763–7), designed by the owner Benjamin
Chew, is the use of stock Palladian patterns for the main elevation.[86] The familiar Gibbs-
surround doors and windows are found along the whole seaboard.

Besides these isolated and often tentative yet persistent borrowings the debt to Gibbs
can best be seen in the careers of some leading colonial architects. Perhaps the first English
emigré to employ his idiom critically and on more than one occasion was Peter Harrison
(born in York in 1716), who settled in Rhode Island in 1740 and by the time he died
in 1775 owned several dozen English Palladian architectural books, one of the most comprehensive collections in the colonies, including *A Book of Architecture* and *Rules for Drawing*.
Gibbsian details appear in the Touro Synagogue (1759–63) and in a summerhouse for
Abraham Redwood, both at Newport. Harrison's early interest in Gibbs may have been
encouraged through his friendship with John Smibert's nephew Thomas Moffat, and very
likely he would have known Bishop Berkeley's *Proposal For the better Supplying of Churches
in our Foreign Plantations, and for Converting the Savage Americans to Christianity*, published in
London in 1724, and perhaps the Rev. Trapp's *The Honour and Vertue of Building, Repairing,
and Adorning Churches*, a sermon delivered at the consecration of Gibbs's new church at
Shipbourne, Kent, and published in 1723; these are part of a considerable early Georgian
literature advocating church improvements. One of Harrison's first commissions, King's
Chapel at Boston, the design for which the Vestry requested on 5 April 1749, shows him
amalgamating the body of Marylebone Chapel (Plate 312), here using local granite
(Ralph Allen offered to supply Bath stone but nothing came of this), and a St Martin's-like
steeple (unexecuted but known from a contemporary description of Harrison's lost set
of drawings presented to the Vestry on 15 September 1749). He transformed Gibbs's
characteristic treatment of the internal Order into a bolder solution by pairing the columns
(Plate 311). In his more modest Christ Church at Cambridge, Massachusetts (1759–61),
the Ionic columns are detailed from *Rules for Drawing*.[87] The Boston chapel particularly
demonstrates Harrison's emphatic pioneer break with the Wren tradition of church building in America, but it was not alone in achieving this. During these *same* months in 1749
the wooden structure for St Paul's Church in the newly founded British garrison town
of Halifax in Nova Scotia was 'framing at Boston' (Plate 313). The site was announced
in April and in November the first rector, William Tutty, who had arrived from England
the previous summer, communicated to the Venerable Society for the Propagation of the
Gospel in Foreign Parts in London that the new church, estimated at a cost of £1,000,
would be 'capable of holding 900 persons'. On 17 March 1750 he reported that 'as soon
as the frost is quite gone the foundation will be laid and I hope finished for the church
[frame] by the time it can arrive from Boston'. The cornerstone was laid on 13 July and

who perhaps owned a copy of *A Book of Architecture*. Their further collaboration at Christ Church (1727–54), the principal Philadelphia church, shows they were also aware of St Martin-in-the-Fields.[91] St Paul's Chapel on Broadway (Plates 314, 316), which Médéric Louis Elie Moreau de Saint-Méry considered 'la plus belle' of the twenty-two houses of workship in New York City in 1794 and which survives today virtually intact,[92] amalgamates features from Marylebone Chapel, St Martin-in-the-Fields and Gibbs's various published designs for steeples (Plate 315). The latter engraving was a presentation ideally suited to occasions like this one when the colonial builder was faced with making additions to an unfinished fabric.[93] The rectangular body of St Paul's was erected in 1763–6 by an obscure Scottish emigré architect named Thomas McBean, purported without foundation to have been Gibbs's pupil. The steeple and perhaps also the portico were added around 1794 by James Crommelin Laurence who, in partnership with a builder named T. Colbourne, apparently had previously worked in London.[94]

St Paul's was by no means the first colonial church to feature a monumental temple portico. St Philip's at Charleston (1727, rebuilt 1835–8) had tetrastyle Doric porticos on three fronts. The architect is unrecorded, but the church was illustrated and described as 'one of the most regular and complete structures of the kind in America' in the *Gentleman's Magazine* in 1753.[95] By this time St Michael's (1752–62) was also under construction in Charleston (Plate 317). This is an inordinately heroic version of St Martin's, with a giant Doric portico, a steeple of diminishing octagons and a liberal use of giant pilasters and Gibbs-surround windows. Again the architect is unrecorded, but no doubt he consulted *A Book of Architecture*, since the *South-Carolina Gazette* announced in 1752 that 'This Church will be built on the Plan of one of Mr. Gibson's Designs; and 'tis tho't, will exhibit a fine Piece of Architecture when compleated'.[96]

Few communities could have afforded such luxurious structures, and one advantage offered by the alternative pattern of Marylebone Chapel was that it allowed the colonial architect to reject the costly and pretentious features of St Martin's yet retain the essential character of a classical front. This was frequently combined with a St Martin's-like steeple rising from an exposed vestibule rather than directly from the roof. This is the solution adopted in 1775 for the First Baptist Meetinghouse (Plate 318) by the Providence architect Joseph Brown. He was sent by the building committee to examine churches in Boston, and his design, not unexpectedly, incorporates some characteristic colonial features: the west front, for example, suggests he may have known St Paul's, New York (Plate 314).[97] Nevertheless, many features originate in *A Book of Architecture*. The interior is a simple and beautiful version of Marylebone Chapel, the arched recess over the west porch comes from the centrepiece of the Fellows' Building at King's (Plate 258), the side entrance from Plate 100. The *Providence Gazette* reported on 10 June 1775 that the steeple derived from the middle design in Plate 30 of Gibbs's book (Plate 315), a sure indication of the continuing popularity of his publication well into the century. Brown's own copy of *A Book of Architecture* passed to Caleb Ormesbee, another local architect (whose First Congregational Church, 1795, shows a debt to Gibbs), then to the builders John Truman and Silvanus and Samuel Tingley. A copy once owned by a leading contemporary Boston architect named Thomas Dawes has 'Providence' inscribed over Plate 30.[98]

The First Baptist Meetinghouse exemplifies the direction followed by a large number of American churches subscribing to the Gibbsian formulas. Many were imitations through the intermediary patterns in Asher Benjamin's *The Country Builder's Assistant*, published in Boston in 1797, sometimes blended with regional venacular or even Gothic, and often the links with the prototype lay only in the disposition of the general parts.

Occasionally an original idea was produced. In the case of the Anglican Cathedral in Quebec the choice in 1800 of the royal parish church as a model was linked with Bishop Mountain's petition to the King for funds towards building 'a proper Church' which would be 'exclusively appropriate to our Worship [and] give weight & consequence' to Anglicanism in the province. The architect, Major William Robe, quoted various erudite classical sources for his design, notably St Martin-in-the-Fields, but he explained that the limited materials and workmanship then available in Canada had obliged him to modify the prototype to a 'plain design'. In particular, the Pointe-aux-Trembles stone could not without enormous expense be quarried in large enough blocks, so that the giant Ionic Order of the temple portico had to be flattened into pilasters set against a solid wall articulated by shallow arches.[99]

At the First Congregational Church on New Haven Green, Connecticut (Plate XVI)

317. Architect unknown, St Michael, Charleston, South Carolina, 1752–62, north and west elevations

318. Joseph Brown, First Baptist Meeting House, Providence, Rhode Island, 1775, west and south elevations

built between 1812 and 1814 by Asher Benjamin and Ithiel Town, the exposed steeple
base, serving also as the vestibule, fills the centre bay of an otherwise fully formed prostyle
temple portico, while the normally disregarded monumentality of the side elevations is
here achieved by introducing bold, blind arcades in place of a continuous giant Order
supporting the cornice and balustrade.[100] The Corinthian prostyle portico of John and
Isaac McComb's St John's Chapel, New York (Plate 319), was, like St Martin-in-the-
Fields, narrower than the full width of the west front; unusually, a tall steeple rose
unhindered from the roof and a giant pier articulated each of the corners of the building,
giving it a monumental and noble appearance.[101] After 1800 the combination of prostyle
portico and steeple was also adapted unselfconsciously to civic buildings, and, of course,
it proved ideal as a model for the Greek Revival because the isolated porticos could be
developed along stylistically independent and archaeological lines. As early as 1814 at
the New South Church, Boston (Plate 320), Charles Bulfinch attached to the domed octagonal body a sleek granite Doric temple portico and St Martin's steeple, which a contemporary described as 'an attempt . . . to unite the massive simplicity of the Grecian temple
with the conveniences of the Christian church'. This was the only American example
inspired by Gibbs's rejected round church (Plate 292), and although Bulfinch's library
did not include *A Book of Architecture*, he had access to the copy owned by his mentor
Thomas Dawes and had visited London between 1785 and 1787.[102] Other Greek versions,

319. John and Isaac
McComb, St John's
Chapel, New York City,
1803–7, west and south
elevations, photographed
before demolition in 1918

320. Charles Bulfinch,
New South Church,
Boston, Massachusetts,
1814, west elevation,
photographed before
demolition in 1868 (The
Bostonian Society)

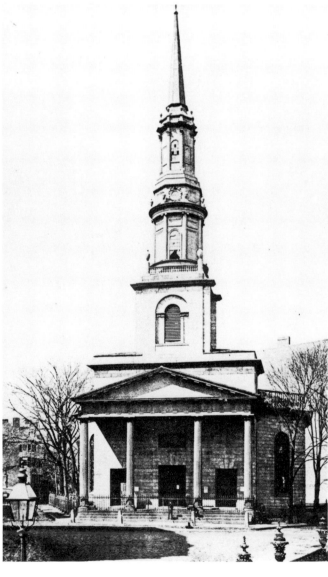

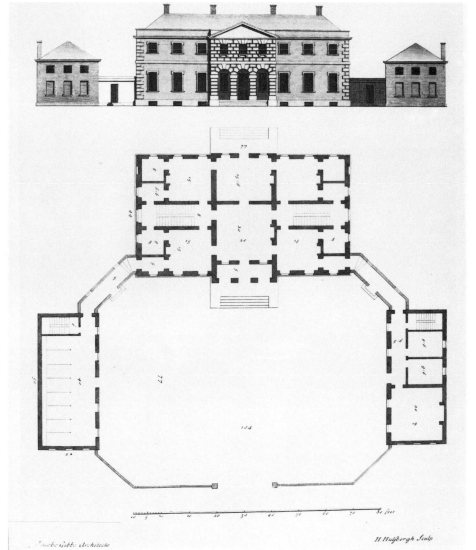

321. (above) John Ariss,
Mount Airy, Virginia,
1758–62, south elevation

322. James Gibbs, Design
for a house for 'a
Gentleman in *Dorsetshire*',
undated, plan and
elevation, Plate 58 in *A
Book of Architecture*, 1728

Cross Deep House, *see* Middlesex, Twickenham

Dawley Farm, *see* Middlesex

## DENBIGHSHIRE

### Chirk Castle NE

JOHN MYDDLETON OR MIDDLETON (d. 1747)*

Robert Myddleton wrote his brother John from London on 27 November (year unrecorded) about the latter 'preparing the scheme of your Library the plan sent was by Mr Gibbs . . . that which came after was as plain as I could make it from instructions', and on 4 December: 'The exact draft or plan of the intended Library came to hand. & I have shewed it to Mr Gibbs . . . who will design something handsome' (National Library of Wales, Chirk Castle Collection E 3975 and E 126); references in these letters to 'Gibbs who built the new Church in the Strand' suggest a date around 1720. Myddleton succeeded to the estate in January 1717 and immediately began making improvements (I. Edwards, *Davies Brothers Gatesmiths*, 1977, pp. 33–5; *Markham*, pp. 154–5).

### Wynnstay by 1749, NE

SIR WATKIN WILLIAMS-WYNN, 3RD BARONET (1692–1749)*

*ASH* III.42–44: 'the irregular Octogonal Room. for Sr Wat: By James Gibbs Arch:' (P. Howell and T. W. Pritchard, 'Wynnstay', *CL*, 23 March 1972, p. 687, fig. 6) are proposals for additions to an estate where Francis and William Smith worked between 1736 and 1739 (*Bodleian* MS Eng. misc., f. 556, p. 21; *Colvin*, p. 751).

## DERBYSHIRE

Bolsover, St Mary
### Monument to Henry Cavendishe, 2nd Duke of Newcastle (1631–91), and others E 1727–8

EDWARD HARLEY, 2ND EARL OF OXFORD (1689–1741),*
AND HENRIETTA, COUNTESS OF OXFORD (1693–1755)*

Recorded in *ABA*, p. xxiii, pl. 114 (*ASH* I.22), the monument, which also commemorates Margaret Holles, Henrietta Harley's mother, was commissioned in 1727 (on the inscription) and signed 'F: Bird. Fecit. 1728'; Francis Bird received £81 on 22 April 1727 (*BL Portland Papers Loan* 29/387). *ASH* III.104 is the contract drawing inscribed 'For Ld Oxford at Bolsover' with various marbles indicated: 'A. Black B. white & veind C. Statuary D. purple E. Black & yealow F. Motteld'. *SAL* MS 263, f. 33, is a schematic drawing without pediment figures or urn.

### Calke Abbey E 1727–9, D 1806

SIR JOHN HARPUR, BARONET (d. 1741)*

Harpur, who subscribed to the All Saints, Derby, rebuilding in 1723 (*Cox*, p. 77), in the same year paid Ralph Tunnicliffe 10s. 6d. for a 'draft' of new steps at Calke (*Colvin*, p. 843) but

in 1727 Gibbs received 2 guineas towards *ABA* subscription and 5 guineas 'for severall Drafts for Caulk steps' (lost), for which Francis Smith 'the Builder for the stone steps in the [south] frount' was paid £100.14.0 (Calke archives: 'Sir John Harpur's account book, 1716–33'; *Colvin*, p. 751). Although later removed, their appearance is recorded in J. Harris, *The Artist and the Country House*, 1979, p. 137, pls. 144, IX; H. Colvin, 'Calke Abbey', *CL*, 20 October 1983, pp. 1063–4, figs. 5–6.

### Catton Hall 1741, NE

CHRISTOPHER HORTON (1700–64)

Staffordshire *CRO* Hatherton Collection D260/M/E 379–81, 383–8, 390–5, 397, and *ASH* II.4 are related to a lengthy 'Estimate of all Charge finding all Materials & Workmanship for finishing the inside of a new house designed by Mr. Gibbs to be built by Mr. Horton of Katton', which included 'The [hall] Chimney peice to be worked accordin to Mr. Gibbs design'; this estimate of £3,530, submitted by Richard Trubshaw (*Colvin*, pp. 841–2), specified the work should be finished between October 1741 and January 1742 (Mr D. W. H. Neilson's possession; A. Gomme, 'Catton Hall', in H. Colvin and J. Harris, eds., *The Country Seat*, 1970, pp. 157–63, pls. 101–3). The present house was designed (in 1742) and built by William Smith (D260/M/E 389, 396, 398, and signed drawings at Catton shown in Gomme, *op. cit.*, pls. 99–100; A. Oswald, 'Catton Hall', *CL*, 17–24 March 1960, pp. 566–9, 624–7; R. Ussher, *An Historical Sketch of the Parish of Croxall, in the County of Derby*, 1881, p. 178).

### Derby, All Saints (the Cathedral) E 1723–6

DR MICHAEL HUTCHINSON AND THE VESTRY

Craftsmen: Robert Bakewell, smith; William Hall, carver; ? Mannings, joiner; William and Francis Smith, contractors (Derby Cathedral archives: Churchwarden's Account Book, I, pp. 137v–45v, 'An account of moneys paid by Dr. Hutchinson to Mr. Smiths the undertakers and others for the use of the Church of All Ste. from May 16.1723', reprinted in *Cox*, pp. 79–80).

Gibbs 'built the great Church at Derby . . . to the great old gothick Tower' (*Gibbs MS*, p. 96). Hutchinson and the Vestry committee approved a design (lost) by 'Mr Smith of Warwick' on 16 November 1719 (Cathedral archives: Parish Order Book, II and III, p. 7), paid 'Mr Tunnecliff' (probably Ralph Tunnicliffe) 3 guineas 'for Drawing a Draughts of the Church' (lost) in 1722 (Account Book, I, p. 128v; *Colvin*, p. 843) and ordered 'a modell or plan in wood after the manner and order of the plan drawn by Mr Smith' (lost) on 20 August 1722 (Order Book, III, pp. 4, 6; Account Book, I, p. 128v). However, they 'accepted for the Modell . . . a plan . . . Contributed by Mr Gibbs' (*ABA*, p. viii, pls. 26–7; *ASH* II.39 in T. Friedman, *James Gibbs as a Church Designer*, 1972, no. 46 illus.) and the Smiths were ordered on 12 February 1723 'to give in an Estimate of the Charge [for] the materialls and workmanshipe' (Order Book, III, p. 11). Their respective contributions are discussed in *Doctor H—— Vindicated, or the Case Relating to the Differences about All-Saints Church in Derby, Truly Stated. By a Lover of Peace, and an Inhabitant of the Borough of Derby*, 1725(?), p. 4 (*DLSL*: Derbyshire Pamphlet 5316). In 1723 £4,162.13.6 was

329.
Jr, ar
Man
the C
York
sectio
(The
Histo

330. J
Desig
'a Ger
Coun
sectio
*Book o*
1728

331. J
Desig
Plate
*Archite*

raised (*The Subscriptions obtain'd by the Revd. Dr. Hutchinson for new Re-building our parish Church of All-Saints in Derby are enter'd into this Book which will be a lasting Monument of the Drs Zeal for doing Good and his being a most worthy Benefactor to our said Parish*, reprinted in *Cox*, pp. 77–9) and H. Hulsberg's engraving (*ABA*, pl. 26) was issued to 150 subscribers ('An account of moneys paid by Dr. Hutchinson', under 14 December 1725). Payments made between May 1723 and 1725 include £25 to Gibbs, £181 to Bakewell and £3,572.7.12 to the Smiths. The first sermon was preached in the new building on 21 November 1725. Further work occurred between 1726 and 1733 (Order Book, III, pp. 68–9, 71, 74–5, 90–1; Account Book, I, pp. 137v–45v; *BL* Add. MS 5842, f. 134) including a proposal of 9 November 1726 to build 'a Gallery at the West end . . . according to such Draught as shall be drawn by Mr Gibbs' (lost) although it was Francis Smith's design that was erected in 1731–2 by Thomas Eboral (Order Book, III, pp. 75, 155, 163). The building history is described in *Cox*, Chapter IV, and M. A. Mallender, *The Great Church*, 1977, pp. 18–27. Gibbs's east end (*ABA*, pl. 27; *ASH* I.9) was removed and rebuilt to another design in 1967–72 ('The Restoration of Derby Cathedral', *Derbyshire Life and Countryside*, May 1972, pp. 48–51, which illustrates the monument to Sarah Ballidon, *c.* 1736, based on *ABA*, pl. 126 right).

## Kedleston 1726, NE

SIR JOHN CURZON (1674–1727)*

Curzon subscribed to the rebuilding of All Saints, Derby, in 1723 (*Cox*, p. 77) and 'Paid Mr Gibbs 10:10:0' on 14 September 1726 (Kedleston archieves: Day Book, 1718–1750, p. 66) probably for drawings for a new house (in the album entitled 'Plans & Uprights of Kedleston') to replace a fabric of only slightly earlier date (H. M. Colvin, 'Francis Smith of Warwick, 1672–1738', *Warwickshire History*, 1972–3, II, No. 2, p. 9; the Day Book, 1718–1750, p. 48, records a £54.1.0 payment to Smith in 1724). Gibbs also proposed a pair of pavilions 'to have been built opposite to one another' as well as 'an Obelisque upon a Hill . . . the execution of which was prevented by [Curzon's] Death' (*ABA*, pp. xviii–xix, pl. 70; *ASH* I.48). The latter were designed in collaboration with Charles Bridgeman (Kedleston archives: 1758 survey plan) who received £116.1.0 between 1722 and 1726 (Day Book, 1718–1750, pp. 31, 66; Hoare's Bank, London: Curzon's account, 10 November 1722).

Ditchley House, *see* Oxfordshire

Down Hall, *see* Essex

Dulwich College Chapel, *see* London

Dupplin Castle, *see* Perthshire

## COUNTY DURHAM

Gateshead
**Park House,** E 1730, gutted 1890s, D 1970s

HENRY ELLISON

Ellison acquired the property on his marriage to Hannah Cotesworth, whose brother Robert subscribed to *A Book of Architecture*. An early scheme for the new house was regarded by his uncle Colonel George Liddell as inadequate, according to a letter of 16 March 1730 addressed from London: 'I have looked into yor. plans, but cannot get them to please my Fancy, & yet I cannot find how to mend them. [I] have a great Objection to the Irregularity of comeing in on one Side . . . To me it would be much better to come in directly forward into a Hall or Salloon, in wch. on the left hand to have yor. Staircase . . . If I can get a Clever Architect, I will trye what he and I can make of it.' On 24 April 1730 Liddell reported: 'Since writing I recd. Mr. Gibbs's plans for yor. Alterations which for want of knowing the Ground he has drawn to advance 8 foot further South than the present front, wch. I doubt cannot be done wthout moving your Garden walls. However . . . I think his design is good & may put you . . . on some New thought.' In a final letter of 20 May 1730 he added: 'I do not think Mr. Gibbs's Scheme can be any great Addition to yor. Expence, & it (wth some little Variation) will be of great Convence, as well as Ornament: I think £200 would do it' (Gateshead Central Library: Ellison MS; E. Hughes, *North Country Life in the Eighteenth Century: The North-East, 1700–1750*, 1952, pp. 25–32). The new front and internal staircase are recorded in drawings of 1889 by W. H. Knowles (Gateshead Central Library). The site is now occupied by Messrs Clarke, Chapman-John Thompson Ltd.

## Raby Castle by 1723, NE

CHRISTOPHER VANE, 1ST BARON BARNARD (1653–1723)

*ASH* II.48, 50, 62 and Raby Castle archives: Vol. A, pp. 8–9 (A. Rowan, 'Gothick Restorations at Raby', *AH*, 1972, XV, pp. 38–9, figs. 5–6), relate to repairs to the high hall initiated after Barnard was forced by the Chancery Court to refurbish the medieval castle he had begun to demolish in 1714; the dimensions indicated on the drawings for a room 36 by 36 by 72 ft. correspond closely to the space before William Burn's 1843–7 remodelling (Rowan, *op. cit.*, p. 24, n. 4, fig. 2, and A. Rowan, 'Raby Castle', *CL*, 22 January 1970, p. 188, fig. 8; *BL* Add. MS 15540, ff. 39–40). For payments to Gibbs presumably partly related to Raby, see SHIPBOURNE.

East Barnet (NewPlace), *see* Hertfordshire

## ESSEX

## Down Hall partly E 1720–1, D 1868–73

MATTHEW PRIOR (1664–1721)

*ASH* I.32; *ABA*, p. xv, pl. 55: 'for *Matthew Prior*, Esq; to have been built at *Down-Hall* [with the] Cube-Room . . . lighted on two sides from two Portico's . . . Mr. *Prior's* Death prevented the building of this House', replaced a more conservative design (for remodelling the old fabric which Prior purchased in 1718–19) represented by 'A plan proposed for Down Hall . . . 1720' (*BL Portland Papers Loan* 29/357) and 'A House and Offices proposd to be Built at Down Hall in ye year 1720' (*Bodleian* Gough Maps 46, nos. 260–4; H. M. Colvin, *Architectural Drawings in the Bodleian Library*, 1952, p. 6, pl. 17). Prior refers to the commission in *Down-Hall; A Ballad*, 1721: 'With your Friend JEMMY GIBBS about Building agree' (H. Bunker Wright and M. K. Spears, *The Literary Works of Matthew Prior*, 1959, I, pp. 550–7). Building accounts (*BL Portland Papers Loan* 29/316–17) and letters from the poet to Edward Harley of 1719–21 record Gibbs's involvement between June and September 1720 (*HMC Bath* III, pp. 482–4, 487–90) including surveying the site and discussing 'edification'; a note on 13 September mentions that 'Gibbs has built me a house' on paper (p. 488). Gibbs, Prior and Charles Bridgeman also planned a garden (*Bodleian* Gough Maps 46, no. 262; *BL Portland Papers Loan* 29/357; *Willis*, pp. 73–5, pl. 67) for which some work was carried out (29/317, ff. 79v–81v, 175v). Prior hoped in June 1721 that work 'may be effected in eighteen months' (*HMC Bath* III, p. 504), but he died on 18 September 1721.

## Down Hall 1721–6, NE

EDWARD HARLEY, 2ND EARL OF OXFORD (1689–1741)*

On Prior's death Down reverted to Harley (*BL Portland Papers Loan* 29/317, f. 6v) and subsequently work continued on the old house (29/316, ff. 11, 18v, 39v; 29/317, f. 145v; 29/387 under 29 January 1726) but largely concentrated on the garden and its buildings. Gibbs's designs include a 'Bowling-Green [with] the Middle part to be open, for shelter [and] two Venetian Windows to the great Room' (*ABA*, p. xviii, pl. 68; *ASH* I.53; *Willis*, pl. 68). Alternative schemes for the interior of this building are shown in *ASH* II.57–8, IV.24, the latter inscribed 'For Mr Baguti att More Parke near Rikmonworth in Hertfordshire' referring to the design being sent to Gibbs's *stuccatore* Giovanni Bagutti probably in order to obtain an estimate of cost (T. P. Hudson, 'Moor Park, Leoni and Sir James Thornhill', *Burl Mag*, November 1971, p. 661, n. 27). In addition 'two other Pavillions propos'd for the same place' (*ABA*, p. xviii, pl. 69; *ASH* I.48; *Bodleian* Gough Maps 46, no. 270; *Willis*, pl. 69), a pavilion or perhaps mausoleum (Gough Maps 46, nos. 274, 276) and 'Dyals of Lord Oxford at Down Hall' (*ASH* I.30, IV.33; *ABA*, p. xxv, pl. 148; J. A. Rush, *Seats in Essex, c.* 1897, p. 66).

Fairlawne, *see* Kent, Shipbourne

Gateshead, *see* County Durham

Glasgow (House in Dry Gate), *see* Strathclyde

## GLOUCESTERSHIRE

## Badminton House partly E by 1745

HENRY SOMERSET, 3RD DUKE OF BEAUFORT (1707–45)*

The remodelling of the Stuart mansion has a complicated history. Gibbs's grand scheme for the north front (perhaps replacing an elaborate Baroque proposal by an unidentified Italian architect represented by a set of drawings in the Badminton archives) was presented in his perspective view, inscribed 'Bridgman's Design for Badminton', which was drawn no later than *c.* 1732 since it was probably used for John Wootton's painting *The Beaufort Hunt* of that date (*Willis*, p. 88,

pls. 86–7; Hoare's Bank, London: Beaufort's account, Ledger L, f. 160). The perspective shows the central block of the house crowned by a pediment and the wings terminated by twin pavilions, for which Gibbs's separate working drawings also survive in the archives and *ASH* II.1; flanking the house and further out in the landscape are a pair of obelisks and Villa Rotunda-like temples, for which independent studies also exist in the archives, although these features were not carried out. Gibbs also supplied an alternative, unexecuted design for the central block of the house without a crowning pediment (archives) as well as a group of drawings for the terminal pavilions with distinctive rusticated blocked columns, inscribed 'the evidence [muniments] room', which proves that he rather than William Kent was the architect of these features as built. Gibbs's other drawings in the archives include a domed pavilion inscribed 'a large Room, tuo sides being alrady built [the sections] of a darker colour, is to be built ... The Arch alrady built to be filld up, and a window put in to it' (H. Colvin, 'Georgian Architects at Badminton', *CL*, 4 April 1968, pp. 800–4, figs. 4–11). Kent was apparently responsible for introducing the tiered pediment and twin corner cupolas on the north front of the house, as it appeared in the 1740s and remains today (C. Hussey, *English Country Houses: Early Georgian*, 1955, pp. 161–6). Payments to Francis and William Smith and various craftsmen are recorded between 1730 and 1760 (Beaufort's account, Ledger N, f. 257ff; *Bodleian* MS Eng. misc., f. 556, pp. 5–6, 10–16).

Greenwich (House, Park Terrace), *see* Kent

Gubbins, *see* Hertfordshire

Gumley House, *see* Middlesex, Isleworth

Hackwood Park, *see* Hampshire

## HAMPSHIRE

## Abbotstone House after 1721, NE

CHARLES PAWLETT, 3RD DUKE OF BOLTON (1685–1754)*

Gibbs 'made ... a large design for a building to be erected at Abots stone ... but the finances failing ther was neither of them [see CANNAM HEATH HOUSE] executed' (*Gibbs MS*, p. 89). *ASH* IV.25: 'For ye Duke of Bolton' is perhaps Gibbs's offering or his record of the *c.* 1685 house (D *c.* 1760) described in 1719 as 'a large noble Brick house edged with stone built ... for a convenient Hawking Seat [in the] Italian manner [with] above 100 Rooms [but] little regarded & left unfinished' (*BL* Add. MS 14296, f. 62). *ASH* II.28: 'The Plan & Upright of a New De[sign] A House for his Grace the Duke at Abbotstone. by Talman' and *Bodleian* Gough Maps 10, f. 37: 'The Plan of the Scituation of His Grace the Duke of Boltons Seat at Abbotstone on ye Rising Ground Opposite to ye Front of the Old House' seems to be the design of another architect for the 2nd Duke, who died in 1722 (*Colvin*, p. 807; J. Harris, *William Talman, Maverick Architect*, 1982, p. 22). Galilei also worked for the same client before 1720 (I. Toesca, 'Alessandro Galilei en Angleterre', *English Miscellany*, 1952, No. 3, p. 201).

**Cannam Heath House** after 1721, NE

CHARLES PAWLETT, 3RD DUKE OF BOLTON (1685–1754)*

Of the 'great many drawings for a new . . . House for [Bolton] at Cannam Heath . . . but the finances failing ther was neither of them [see ABBOTSTONE] executed' (*Gibbs MS*, p. 89) there is no trace. The earlier house was D 1805.

**Hackwood Park** E *c.* 1728–40, partly D

CHARLES PAWLETT, 3RD DUKE OF BOLTON (1685–1754)*

In 1740 *Vertue* (V, p. 127) noted 'a new stone. portico. next the Gardens. designd by Mr. Gibbs'. This is perhaps an addition to the otherwise unrecorded 'much newer [south or] back front' (S. Shaw, *A Tour to the West of England in 1788*, 1789, p. 592) of the 1683–8 house (J. Harris, *William Talman, Maverick Architect*, 1982, pp. 22–3) to which later additions were also made by John Vardy, 1761–3, and S. and L. Wyatt, 1807–13 (*BL* Add. MS 15776, f. 224; *Colvin*, pp. 804, 855, 953, 958; Hampshire *CRO*: 11.M.49; J. Harris, 'C. R. Cockerell's "Ichnographica Domestica"', *AH*, 1971, XIV, p. 16, fig. 13a; J. P. Neale, *Seats*, 1819, II). Gibbs had already 'built a great many Temples and Ornamental Buildings for the Duke of Bolton at Hackwood' (*Gibbs MS*, p. 89). These included: 'A circular Building in form of a Temple . . . erected . . . at *Hackwood*, upon the upper ground of an Amphiteatre, back'd with high Trees' (*ABA*, p. xix, pl. 72; *ASH* III.111; *VAM* E. 3617–1913; H. A. Tipping, *English Homes*, 1929, Period IV, Vol. I, fig. 299), a 'Pavillion built at *Hackwood* [with a] Rustick Front' (*ABA*, p. xix, pls. 73–4; *ASH* I.53) and 'the Menagery at *Hackwood* . . . That with the Columns is built' (*ABA*, p. xx, pl. 84; *ASH* I.49). The garden layout by Allen, 1st Earl of Bathurst (Shaw, *op. cit.*, pp. 594–5), had a 'Lawn on both sides the great Walk . . . Wood with waks . . . Spring Wood [and] Fezon House' (*Bodleian* Gough Maps, 10, f. 52). The overmantel design for Bolton's townhouse attributed to Gibbs (J. Harris, *A Catalogue of British Drawings for Architecture, Decoration, Sculpture and Landscape Gardening, 1550–1900, in American Collections* (1971) p. 105, pl. 71) is by John Vardy.

Hampstead Marshall, *see* Berkshire

Hartwell, *see* Buckinghamshire

HERTFORDSHIRE

East Barnet
**New Place** E *c.* 1717–25, D *c.* 1927

JOHN COTTON (1671–1736)*

Gibbs 'built . . . Mr Cottons House at East Barnet' (*Gibbs MS*, p. 90) sometime between its purchase around 1717, when it was called Little Grove, and 1725, when J. Schynvoet's engraving *The West Prospect of New-Place in East Barnet . . . The Seat of John Cotton Esqr.* (*Bodleian* Gough Maps 11, f. 38B) was issued by John Warburton, probably as part of his proposed but unpublished 'New Map of *London, Middlesex, Essex, and Hertfordshire*', in which the 'Seats [are] all explained by familiar Characters and References', advertised on 28 January 1725

(Chetham Library, Manchester: ho 575 (51)). The property was sold in 1733 (F. C. Cass, *East Barnet*, 1885–92, p. 88; D. Lysons, *Environs of London Counties of Hertfordshire, Essex and Kent*, 1796, IV, pp. 9–11; *VCH, Hertfordshire*, 1908, II, pp. 338–9).

**Gubbins** E by 1732?, D after 1838

SIR JEREMIAH SAMBROOKE (d. 1754)*

The 'addition of a large Room to Mr Sambrooks house, at Gubbons in Hartfordshire' (*Gibbs MS*, p. 91) may have been the library which had a 'Chimney Piece supported by finely sculptured Carriatides . . . Book recesses, niches for Busts, panelled wainscotting divided into compartments, by handsome fluted corinthian Pilaters [and a] beautifully ornamented Ceiling, in bold Relief' (Hertfordshire *CRO*: 34418, *Particulars Of that celebrated Mansion and Domain of Gobions*, 1838) for which the design is *ASH* IV.40: 'Ceiling for Mr Sambrooks at Gubbins' (*Beard 1981*, pl. 64). Gibbs also 'built . . . some Ornamental Temples and did other buildings for that gentleman' (*Gibbs MS*, p. 91) in collaboration with Charles Bridgeman. A visit by the Queen to the gardens is mentioned in *GM*, 19 July 1732, p. 874. A plan of the garden with some architectural features was published in the 1838 *Particulars*. Les Charmes de Stow, 1748, p. 6 (*Stowe Papers*); *Bickham*, pp. 66–7; *The Ambulator*, 1774, pp. 72–3 (reprinted in *Londres et ses Environs . . . par M.D.S.D.L.*, 1788, pp. 122–5) and J.-B. Barjaud and C. P. Landon, *Description De Londres et ses Édifices*, 1811, pp. 216–17, describe a number of features, including a domed rotunda, obelisk, lattice-work summerhouse, icehouse, grotto, Lion's Den and urn, which were perhaps designed by Gibbs. He was certainly responsible for the Canal and Bowling Green temples (shown in *Bodleian* Gough Maps 11, ff. 37B–8; *Willis*, pp. 18, 86–7, pl. 84) and a pigeon-house (*ASH* III.87: 'For Mr Sambrooke at Gubbins'; *Willis*, pl. 83 right); the Gothic Arch, the only surviving feature in the garden, is not necessarily part of Gibbs's contribution (Hertfordshire *CRO*: J. C. Buckler, *Views of Hertfordshire*, 1840, IV, following p. 448; N. Pevsner, *The Buildings of England: Hertfordshire*, 1953, pp. 96–7, pl. 50b). The anonymous view ascribed to 'Gobions' (Gough Maps 11, f. 37B) in fact is of Hagley (*AH*, 1982, XXV, pl. 12C).

**Hertford Town Hall** NE

THE MAYOR AND ALDERMEN

'A Town house for Harford' (*ASH* IV.19–21; *Little*, fig. 28) may relate to a reference of 5 December 1737 (mentioned in *Little*, p. 150, as among the Mayor's and aldermens' records but now untraced) concerning an anonymous gift of £100 made in March 1737 towards rebuilding the dilapidated Elizabethan fabric (shown in *BL* Add. MS 32350, Vol. III, f. 43). The aldermen included Thomas Saunders-Seabright, Ralph Freeman and Charles Caesar, all *ABA* subscribers; moreover, the mayor in 1726 and 1733 was a cousin of Charles Bridgeman, the Royal Gardener (R. Clutterbuck, *The History and Antiquity of the County of Hertford*, 1815; *Willis*, pp. 148–9, 156).

**Sacombe Park** 1719–22, NE

EDWARD ROLT (d. 1722)

*ABA*, p. xiv, pls. 52–3, are designs 'for a House intended to have been built in *Seacomb-Park* . . . but the Execution of it was prevented by [Rolt's] Death' on 22 December 1722 (R. Clutterbuck, *The History and Antiquity of the County of Hertford*, 1821, pp. 426–7). *ASH* II.91, a 13-bay variant, may be related to the £14.8.0 paid to 'Mr. Gibbs' on 24 June 1719 (Hoare's Bank, London: Rolt's account, Ledger 20, f. 436). Gibbs, perhaps in collaboration with Charles Bridgeman (*Willis*, pp. 60, 182, pls. 46a–b), succeeded John Price, Nicholas Dubois and John Vanbrugh who had worked there in 1716–18 (Ledgers 18, f. 266; 20, ff. 6, 436; 21, f. 10; K. Downes, *Vanbrugh*, 1977, p. 278). An undescribed house existed there in 1745 (*Daily Advertiser*, 7 March 1745, in *Burney* 407b; N. Salmon, *The History of Hertfordshire*, 1728, p. 225; *VCH, Hertfordshire*, 1912, III, p. 137).

## Tring Park E *c.* 1724–39, partly D

WILLIAM GORE (d. 1739)*

The 'several Ornamental Buildings . . . built . . . in Tring park' (*Gibbs MS*, p. 91) as part of Charles Bridgeman's garden (*Willis*, pp. 60, 183–4, pl. 45) include a greenhouse, mentioned in 1724 (*YAS* MS 328, p. 10), a seat, a pyramid and various pavilions as shown in *VB*, 1739, pls. 104–5, and Hertfordshire *CRO* Clutterbuck Hertfordshire Illustrated, IV, following p. 500, all of which are demolished. Gibbs's contribution also probably included the surviving Ionic temple (R. Strong, M. Binney and J. Harris, *The Destruction of the Country House*, 1974, nos. 344–5) and Nell Gwynn's Monument, an obelisk similar to *ABA*, pls. 85–6. The house of *c.* 1670, D 1890 (*Colvin*, p. 925), contained in 1724 richly decorated rooms with 'carv'd Cielings' (*YAS* MS 328, p. 10) including one in the boudoir (*NMR* DD58/83) which is similar to ceilings designed by Gibbs at DITCHLEY and GUBBINS.

Heythrop Hall, *see* Oxfordshire

Houghton Hall, *see* Norfolk

Isleworth, *see* Middlesex

Johnston's Octagon, *see* Middlesex, Twickenham

Kedleston, *see* Derbyshire

Kelmarsh Hall, *see* Northamptonshire

# KENT

Greenwich
## House, Park Terrace 1720, NE

SIR GREGORY PAGE, 2ND BARONET (1687–1775)*

'A House intended to have been built at *Greenwich* in 1720. on a beautiful Situation . . . with *Portland* Stone, and finish'd in a very expensive manner' (*ABA*, p. xiii, pls. 46–7; *ASH* I.36) is probably an unexecuted scheme for the Park Terrace property on Maze Hill (D 1821) Page inherited on his father's death on 15 May 1720. He subsequently built *c.* 1725 a similar house

nearby called Wricklemarsh designed by John James (A. Alister, 'Page of Greenwich', *Transactions of the Greenwich and Lewisham Antiquarian Society*, 1971, VII, No. 5, pp. 256–7, 259, pls. III–IV; *Colvin*, p. 454).

## Mount Morris E?, D after 1839

MORRIS DRAKE MORRIS

The attribution of the 'large square brick house by Gibbs' (J. C. Loudon, *An Encyclopedia of Gardening*, 1827, I, Part IV, p. 1070) cannot be confirmed by documents or views (J. Harris, *History of Kent*, 1719, I, p. 156; E. Hasted, *The History and Topographical Survey of the County of Kent*, 1799, VIII, pp. 55–6), although Matthew Robinson, husband of Elizabeth Drake of Mount Morris, appears with Gibbs in Hamilton's painting *A Conversation of Virtuosi*, 1734–5 (H. F. Finberg, 'Gawen Hamilton: An Unknown Scottish Portrait Painter', *Walpole Society*, 1918, VI, pp. 51–8).

Shipbourne

## Fairlawne E *c.* 1723

CHRISTOPHER VANE, 1ST BARON BARNARD (1653–1723)

Gibbs 'built . . . for . . . Lord Barnard . . . an addition . . . at Fairelawn, wher ther is a handsome Room 20 by 30 with a fine fretwork Ceiling' (*Gibbs MS*, p. 96). Payments to Gibbs totalling £2,628.10.0 (Hoare's Bank, London: Barnard's account 11 April 1722–18 May 1723, Ledger G, ff. 46, 116, 235) relate to work at RABY CASTLE, SHIPBOURNE church and this house. The drawings are *ASH* II.68, 71, IV.41: 'Ceiling of ye New Room at Fairlaw in Kent ye Seat of Ld Vane' (T. Friedman, 'Gibbs's Designs for Domestic Furniture', *Leeds Arts Calendar*, 1972, No. 71, pp. 20–1, figs. 2–3; C. Hussey, 'Fairlawne', *CL*, 30 October 1958, pp. 998–1001, figs. 6–9; D. Sherborn, 'Room by Gibbs at Fairlawne', *CL*, 27 November 1958, p. 1247, illustrating Gibbs's plaster and painted ceiling, later destroyed). This is mentioned in J. Trapp, *The Honour and Vertue of Building, Repairing, and Adorning, Churches: And the Sacredness of them, when Built, and Consecrated. A Sermon Preached At Shipburn in Kent*, 29 June 1723. Hussey, *op. cit.*, p. 999, suggests Gibbs rebuilt the belfry, although the house underwent several later alterations and fires are recorded in 1739 and 1742 (E. Hasted, *The History and Topographical Survey of the County of Kent*, 1798, V, p. 24). William Lord Vane* succeeded to the estate in 1723.

## St Giles E 1722–3, D 1880

CHRISTOPHER VANE, 1ST BARON BARNARD (1653–1723)

Gibbs 'built the Parish Church of Fairelawn in Kent for the Right Honble the Lord Barnard, and his fine Monument there' (*Gibbs MS*, p. 96). Trapp (see above) mentions 'Mr. Gibbs [the] excellent Architect whom [Barnard] employ'd' and the work is listed among his commissions in the 15 March 1727 Proposal for *ABA* (Chetham Library, Manchester: Proposals and Prospectuses folder III, no. 866). For payments to Gibbs related to the church, see the previous entry. Consecrated on 29 June 1723, only its exterior is recorded in a watercolour (M. Whiffen, *Stuart and Georgian Churches*, 1948, p. 39, pl. 52) and a photograph (in the present church) taken shortly before demolition and rebuilding in 1880–1. A pair of vases from the tower is said to survive nearby (*Little*, pp. 80–1).

St Giles
**Monument to Christopher Vane, 1st Baron Barnard (1653–1723), Elizabeth, Lady Barnard (d. 1725) and Elizabeth Vane (d. 1688)** E by 1723

CHRISTOPHER VANE, 1ST BARON BARNARD

Trapp (see above) mentions this monument on 29 June 1723 as already installed. The substantial changes made between the preliminary design (*ASH* III.86: 'Monument for Lord and Lady Vane') and the executed work (re-erected in the present church in 1881) may have been the contribution of the sculptor, probably Michael Rysbrack (C. Hussey, 'A Gibbs-Rysbrack Monument', *CL*, 13 November 1958, p. 112). *ABA*, p. xxiii, pl. 119; 'a Monument for a Person of Quality' has a similar architectural frame and may represent either a rejected design for this commission or the monument erected at Acton, Suffolk, to Robert Jennens (d. 1726), for whom Gibbs built ACTON PLACE, by his wife and son William, both *ABA* subscribers (W. Harrison and G. Willis, *The Great Jennens Case*, 1879, pp. 103–7).

Kirkleatham, *see* Cleveland

Kirtlington Park, *see* Oxfordshire

Kiveton Park, *see* South Yorkshire

LANCASHIRE

Warrington
**Bank Hall** (now Warrington Town Hall) E 1749–50

THOMAS PATTEN (1690–1772)

Gibbs 'built a very good Countary seat for Thomas Pattin Esqr near Warrington . . . having tuo Courtyards of offices all the building is done with good Brickwork . . . it is a plain good use-full building with which it's Master is very well pleased' (*Gibbs MS*, p. 97). Preparations were in hand by 11 March 1749 (Winmarleigh Estate Office, Warrington: Patten Deeds, bundle 30); *ASH* II.29 are alternative designs for the entrance centrepiece. The house was under construction by 8 June 1750 (J. J. Cartwright, ed., *The Travels Through England of Dr. Richard Pococke . . . during 1750, 1751, and Later Years* (Camden Society, NS, XLII), 1888, p. 9) and 'almost finished' by 5 September 1750 according to a letter of that date from Patten's cousin to Thomas Hall (Hampshire *CRO* Herriard Collection, 44 M69/E83); rainwater-heads are dated 1750. J. Harris, 'The Prideaux Collection of Topographical Drawings', *AH*, 1964, VII, p. 38, pl. 107, and Warrington Public Library: W.9105, show the completed ensemble. Many internal features survive (C. Amery, ed., *Three Centuries of Architectural Craftsmanship*, 1977, pls. 93–5; P. Fleetwood-Hesketh, *Murray's Lancashire Architectural Guide*, 1955, pp. 66–7; E. F. Massey, 'The Town Hall, Warrington', *AR*, July 1928, pp. 30–1; J. R. Harris, *The*

*Pattens of Warrington: The Copper Industry*, 1964; Warrington Public Library: MS 1358). The extended basement story and the low corner pavilions were added by 1772 (Warrington Public Library: dated map). Two drawings for service blocks attributed to Gibbs (Yale Center for British Art, New Haven: B 1975.2.224–225) perhaps relate to Bank Hall.

The attribution to Gibbs of Holy Trinity, Warrington (W. Beamont, *Annals of the Lords of Warrington and Bewsey*, 1873, p. xviii), is without foundation.

Leighton Buzzard (Leighton House), *see* Bedfordshire

Leighton House, *see* Bedfordshire, Leighton Buzzard

LINCOLNSHIRE

**Lincoln Minster** partly E 1725–6

THE BISHOP AND DEAN

Edward Harley reported in April 1725 that 'Gibbs had been lately' to Lincoln to examine the fabric and recommend repairs (*HMC Portland*, VI, p. 84). Gibbs's report of 16–18 March 1725 discusses the west and crossing towers as well as minor repairs and refers to 'copies of the surveys' and drawings (lost) sent to the Archbishop of Canterbury (*PRO* State Papers Domestic, George I, Vol. LXIII, no. 51(3)). This document, John James's survey of 29–30 April 1725 and subsequent events are quoted in J. W. F. Hill, 'The Western Spires of Lincoln Minster and their Threatened Removal in 1726', *Lincolnshire Architectural Society's Report*, 1954, NS, V(ii), pp. 101–7. Gibbs's 'new Arches rais'd' under the west towers are mentioned by John Loveday (*Diary of a Tour in 1732*, 1890, p. 205) and Philip Yorke noted in 1744 'A few years ago the west end of the nave was falling; and Mr. Gibbs, in order to support it built a wall intersected by an arch' (*Godber*, p. 133). James Essex's 1776 report on his survey of Gibbs's repairs (Archives of Dean and Chapter: A.4.13, Miscellaneous Letters and Papers) is discussed in *BL* Add. MS 5842, ff. 164–9v; T. H. Cocke, 'James Essex, Cathedral Restorer', *AH*, 1975, XVIII, pp. 16–20; T. H. Cocke, 'Tact with Medieval Architecture', *CL*, 8 December 1977, pp. 1724–5).

LONDON

**Designs for unnamed churches** 1713–15, NE

COMMISSIONERS FOR BUILDING FIFTY NEW CHURCHES

**Church with an Ionic Order** 1713, NE

One of the peartree wood 'Modells' commissioned from the 'Several Draughts for Churches' delivered on 14 May 1713 (*LPL* 2690, p. 87) is described in 'Mr James Gibbs's bill for Modells' under 9 June 1713 as 'a Church with a Colonad round it of Ionick Order Steeple and inside finishing Complete' costing £25 (2708, f. 7) and in 1733 as 'with a peristilium by Mr Gibbs' (2724, f. 4). T. L Donaldson ('Some Account of the Models of Churches Preserved in Henry V's Chantry, Westminster Abbey', *The Architect*,

*Engineer and Surveyor*, 1 December 1843, IV, p. 351, no. 9) noted that this model measured 22 × 47 in., or 88 × 188 ft. if built (on a scale of ¼ in. to 1 ft.) and described it as 'an imitation of a hexastyle peripteral Ionic temple [with] a lofty steeple, rising over the pediment of the front portico at a short distance from the front'. The model and drawings are lost, although Donaldson prepared a plan in 1843 (*RIBA* OS5/9(9)). This and the following model, which he described as having 'architectural features made out with considerable care, and the whole of the internal fittings, even to the font . . . accurately modelled [and] easily seen, as the roofs are fitted with hinges', are mentioned in *LPL* 2690, pp. 132, 242, 244; 2706, f. 81; 2707, ff. 14, 97; 2726, ff. 69–70, 75–6; *HMC Portland*, X, p. 301; *Bill*, pp. xvii–xix.

## Church with a Corinthian Order 1713, NE

The second of the 'Modells' made from 'Several Draughts of Churches' submitted on 14 May 1713 (*LPL* 2690, p. 87) is described in 'Mr James Gibbs's bill for Modells' under 24 June 1713 as 'a Church Ornamtd. with pillasters of the Corinthian Ordr: the Inside finished wth: Corinthian pillars Supporting the Roof all Complete' costing £28 (2708, f. 7) and by Donaldson (*op. cit.*, p. 351, no. 12), who made a plan (*RIBA* OS5/9(12)), as 'a very large model, of the Corinthian order . . . The front represents a tetrastyle . . . disposition, with coupled columns, having a pediment over them, and a tower at each of the four angles . . . One side of the flanks . . . plain, but the other . . . enriched' and measuring 23 × 48 in. or 92 × 192 ft. if built. The original model and drawings are lost, although ASH III.102 may represent a scheme showing alternative treatments for the side elevations.

## Church for Lady Russell's ground (Bloomsbury) 1714, NE

Gibbs made a survey and 'ground plat of a Church to be Erected thereon' between 24 February and 3 March 1714, charging 14*s*. 6*d*. (LPL 2690, pp. 143, 144a; 2708, f. 7), perhaps the plans (2750, nos. 20–1).

## Church for Bastwick Johnson's ground (Lower Wapping) 1715, NE

Wren, Hawksmoor, Gibbs and Henry Box reported on the site on 31 May 1715. Gibbs made a survey for 15*s*. and was ordered on 28 June 1715 to submit 'a plan of a Church the most Convenient that can Stand East and West upon the Ground already purchasd . . . and another as it will Stand Supposeing the Additionl Ground should be purchas'd', both lost (LPL 2690, p. 223; 2708, f. 7; 2714, f. 138); the site is shown in 2750, no. 19.

## Church for Thomas White's ground (St Giles Cripplegate) 1715, NE

Gibbs reported on 16 March 1715 as having viewed this ground, which he found 'capatious enough for a Church & Ministers House [but] cannot Recommend [the foundation because of] black Mudd & water' (*LPL* 2690, p. 206; 2714, f. 248). His charge of £1.2.0 for 'trying the Foundacion' (2708, f. 7) suggests he prepared a plan, perhaps 2750,

no. 31, showing a church 70 × 90 ft. with a projecting tetrastyle portico raised on a staircased platform.

## Church for Sir John Thornicroft's ground (Stockwell) 1715, NE

Gibbs and Hawksmoor each surveyed this site and made 'a plan of a Church to be Erected' there (lost) between 23 March and 5 August 1715, for which Gibbs charged 18*s*. 6*d*. (*LPL* 2690, pp. 209, 229; 2708, f. 7).

## Houses in Argyll Street (Westminster) E 1736–40, D

ARCHIBALD CAMPBELL, EARL OF ILAY (1682–1761)*

Gibbs, Thomas Phillips and Roger Morris contracted on 6 March 1736 'to build . . . one New Street of dwelling Houses to be called Argyll Street', receiving jointly £81.9.6 on 1 May 1740 (Coutts Bank, London: Lord Ilay's account, Ledger 1738–40, f. 284). An individual payment to Gibbs of £64.14.9 on 3 June 1740 (Ledger 17, f. 2) may relate to this commission. He leased Nos. 4 and 29 on 3 April 1740, but his responsibilities as designer remain unclear (M. Cosh, 'Lord Ilay's Eccentric Building Schemes', *CL*, 20 July 1972, pp. 142–3; *S of L*, 1963, XXXI, Part II, pp. 286–91).

## 16 Arlington Street (now Over-Seas House, Westminster) E 1734–40

MARIA SHIREBURN, DOWAGER DUCHESS OF NORFOLK (d. 1754)

Craftsmen: George Mercer, mason; Thomas Michener, bricklayer; Thomas Phillips, carpenter; Thomas Wagg, smith; William Wilton, plasterer.

Gibbs 'built the Dutchess dowger of Norfolks house in Arlington Street . . . a very usefull convenient building' (*Gibbs MS*, p. 97). *ASH* II.73, 79, 134, 141–2, 144; III.58; IV.46, 48 (T. Friedman, 'James Gibbs's Designs for Domestic Furniture', *Leeds Arts Calendar*, 1972, No. 71, p. 23, fig. 5) relate to the request to Gibbs on 4 May 1734 'to inspect a new building in Arlington Street erecting by My order . . . according to plans designd by him, & approv'd on' by the Dowager Duchess who agreed to pay £300 for 'plans [and] surveying the said building's till they shall be compleated'. Michener agreed 'To Erect and Build a Messuage or Tenemen together with Severall Outhouses and Offices . . . according to the plan and Elevation hereof Drawn Designed and Agreed on by James Gibbs'; proposals from Phillips and Mercer are dated 9–10 May 1734, the latter witnessed by the architect (Lancashire *CRO* Weld (Shireburne) of Stonyhurst Papers DD St). Wagg received £179.10.0 'To making Ironwork to the Great Stairs & fixg do.' and 10*s*. 4*d*. for 'Iron work to 12 Chimneys wth: Grates' as well as railings and lamps between November 1736 and July 1740 (*PRO* Chancery Masters Exhibits C.109 25, Daybooks and Ledgers of Thomas Wagg, 1727–48, Part I; III, 24 February 1739; V, p. 47; VII, October 1737, which also mentions Wilton). For the Green Park elevation (S. Houfe, 'A Taste for the Gothick', *CL*, 24 March 1977, p. 728, fig. 3), the carriage gate (D. Cruickshank and P. Wyld, *London: The Art of Georgian Building*, 1975, p. 58, pl. 20) and interiors (D. R. Sherborn, *Over-Seas House London*, n.d.).

**Burlington House, Piccadilly** (Westminster) E 1715–16, D 1868–93

RICHARD BOYLE, 3RD EARL OF BURLINGTON (1694–1753)

'Burlington had him to build and adorn his house and offices in piccadilly, they are all built of solid portland stone, as is likewise the fine circular colonad fronting the house' (Gibbs MS, p. 90). Athough the scheme was published in VB, 1725, p. 7, pl. 22, and Colen Campbell (working there 1717–20) remarked that the 'Stables were built by another Architect . . . which obliged me to make the Offices opposite, conformable to them', no designs were included in ABA, to which Burlington did not subscribe. A James Gibbs was rated for a house in nearby Burlington Street in 1714 (S of L, 1963, XXXII, Part II, p. 398) and Lord Mar remarked to Gibbs on 16 April 1716 that he had 'work enough upon your hands in Piccadilly' (HMC Stuart, II, p. 93). The problems of attribution are discussed fully in S of L, 1963, XXXII, Part II, pp. 390–425, pls. 43–7, 50–3.

**Chandos House, Cavendish Square** (St Marylebone) 1735, NE

JAMES BRYDGES, 1ST DUKE OF CHANDOS (1674–1744)*

For an unspecified addition to this house Gibbs provided an estimate on 25 November 1735 of £1,500, which Chandos considered too expensive (Baker, pp. 282, 287–8).

**House in Dover Street** (Westminster) by 1737, NE?

EDWARD HARLEY, 2ND EARL OF OXFORD (1689–1741)*

The lost 'Draughts for the Front of Dover Street-House, by Mr. Gibbs' of 1737 (BL Add. MS 18240, f. 36) may relate to the various repairs made to 'My Lord's House' during 1733–6 by the carpenters Walter Lee and Robert Wanmer (18243, ff. 33v–5). An agreement of 1741 with John Lane refers to 'Brick work . . . performed in the same manner as Lord Oxford's new Library in Marylebone was done last year' (MLHC Vestry Proceedings, 1729–40, p. 338; Vertue, VI, p. 63).

**Dulwich College Chapel** (Dulwich) E 1729

THE REV. JAMES HUME

In September 1729 Hume 'agreed with Mr. Van Spanger [Richard Vanspangen*] to make me a Font of the Dimensions and form of the Draught [lost] made by Mr. Gibbs Architect. The Bason and pedestal to be of the best white vein'd marble. The Plint of black marble vein'd with Gold, and the step of Portland stone. The whole to be perforated, with a brass stopcock to carry off the water into a cistern below, and to be set up in Dul. College Chapel'; the executed font is dated 1729 (D. H. Allport, 'Fonts with Palindrome', Notes and Queries, 13 March 1943, pp. 173–4; Gunnis, p. 408).

**49 Great Ormond Street** (Holborn) E by 1734, D 1872–6

DR RICHARD MEAD (1673–1754)*

Gibbs 'built . . . Dr Meads Library in town' (Gibbs MS, p. 90),

incorporating a chimneypiece similar to ASH II.79, as shown in the frontispiece engraving to M. Maty, Authentic Memoirs of the Life of Richard Mead, M.D., 1755 (M. Webster, 'Taste of an Augustan Collector', CL, 24 September 1970, p. 765, fig. 1). Work was completed by 1734 when Mead presented Gibbs with a silver cup and cover made by Edward Feline hallmarked 1726 and inscribed 'IACOBO GIBBS eximio architecto ob operam in aedificanda bibliotheca Sua Feliciter positam hoc poculum dono dedit Richardus Mead med-reg MDCCXXXIV' (The Earl of Mar and Kellie collection). The house became the London Hospital for Sick Children in 1851 (T. T. Higgins, Great Ormond Street, 1852–1952, 1952, pp. 14–21; H. Phillips, Mid-Georgian London, 1964, p. 207).

**52 Grosvenor Street** (Westminster) E 1727, D

SIR THOMAS HANMER (1677–1746)*

A bill for £20 dated 4 January 1727: 'To Mich: Rysbrack by the hand of Mr Gibbes for carving in my two large Chimneypieces' (Suffolk CRO Bunbury Papers E 18/660.2) suggests Gibbs supplied the designs. A 'Library Chimney' for Hanmer is mentioned in the context of a James Thornhill drawing (R. R. Wark, Early British Drawings in the Huntington Collection, 1600–1750, 1969, p. 50). The house had been built by Benjamin Timbrell in 1720–3, employing Giovanni Bagutti as plasterer, and was sold to Hanmer unfinished in 1721. Gibbs is mentioned again in the client's private account book on 17 January 1729 in respect of a subscription payment for ABA (S of L, 1977, XXXIX, p. 104, pl. 8c; 1980, XL, p. 49).

**House in Hanover Square** (Westminster) E 1740, D

THOMAS THYNNE, 2ND VISCOUNT WEYMOUTH (1710–51)

Gibbs 'made additions . . . to Lord Weymouths at Old Windsor, besides other things for his Lordship' (Gibbs MS, p. 88) including unspecified work in 'Hanover Square' for which he received £31.10.0 in 1740 (Longleat archieves: Account Book).

**9–11 Henrietta Street** (St Marylebone) E 1723–7, D 1956

JAMES GIBBS

Henry Elkins contracted on 5 June 1723 to undertake 'All the Brickwork for One House in Henrietta Street . . . according to a Design . . . made by James Gibbs' (BL Add. MS 18238, ff. 40–1). The street facade of this and the adjacent terrace houses are recorded in NMR photographs (J. Summerson, 'Henrietta Place, Marylebone, and its Associations with James Gibbs', London Topographical Record, 1958, XXI, pp. 26–36, figs. 1–3). The drawing room of No. 11, for which ABA, p. xxi, pl. 91 right, and VAM E.3633-1913 are designs for the chimneypiece and overmantle, was re-erected in an incomplete state in the Victoria and Albert Museum (W5-1960, Woodwork Department Register 1960–2). The plasterwork here is attributed to Giuseppe Artari (Beard 1981, p. 243) and the ceiling paintings to Antonio Bellucci (see references under WITLEY COURT).

**25 Leicester Square** (Westminster) E 1733–4, D after 1830

SIR PHILLIP PARKER LONG, 3RD BARONET (1683–1741)

306

CATALOGUE OF WORKS

Gibbs 'built Sr Phillip Parker Longs house in Lichster fields' (*Gibbs MS*, p. 97), having demolished (1733) the residence occupied until 1731 by the portrait-painter William Aikman (*S of L*, 1966, XXXIV, p. 491). The new house, perhaps represented by the plans in *ASH* IV.56, is shown in *Crace*, XVIII, nos. 14–17; J. B. Papworth, *Select Views of London*, 1816, p. 52, pl. 25; H. Phillips, *Mid-Georgian London*, 1964, pp. 86–7, 288–9, fig. 102.

### Lincoln's Inn Hall (Holborn) E 1720, D 1924–8

THE HONOURABLE SOCIETY OF LINCOLN'S INN

'Mr Gibbs' was paid £330 'for work in the Hall', as recorded in the 'Accounts of Francis Wilkinson, Esq. the Treasurer, from Jan. 23rd, 1719, to Jan. 23rd, 1720' (W. P. Baildon, ed., *The Black Books: The Records of the Honourable Society of Lincoln's Inn*, 1899, III, p. 258). Sir John Summerson, to whom I am indebted for this reference, has suggested (*Transactions of the Ancient Monuments Society*, 1984) that Gibbs may have gained the commission through the association of Robert Harley, 1st Earl of Oxford, with Lincoln's Inn and, moreover, that the architect's improvements to the 1489–92 Hall consisted of constructing below the five-bay, arch-braced wooden roof a new elliptical barrel vault in plaster of classical design, with consoles of a type used at ALL SAINTS, DERBY. The vault, destroyed in 1924–8, is shown in R. Ackermann, *The Microcosm of London*, 1808, I, opposite p. 193; *London Interiors*, 1841–4, opposite p. 49; and in a photograph in the *Royal Commission on Historical Monuments (England): West London*, 1925, II, pp. 46, 50–1, pl. 78.

### The Mansion House (City of London) 1728–38, NE

MANSION HOUSE COMMITTEE

Following the Committee's decision in 1722 to consider 'a proper & Convenient place ... to Erect a manion house for the mayor' (*CLRO* Misc. MS 319.7(1), p. 1) and on 24 May 1728 'to find out a proper place for Ericting it and procure plannns' (*CLRO CCJ*, p. 181), Gibbs was invited on 2 July 1728 'to Draw a plan of such a House as will be fit for the accomoadating of a mayr'. The Stocks Market site design was delivered on 9 July, while others (also lost) were considered on 16 and 23 July 1728 and 4 March 1729 (*CLRO 113B*, I, Folder 1728). Gibbs was again ordered on 26 May 1729 to make Stocks and Leadenhall Market sites designs (*113B*, Folder 1729). Further discussions took place during 1729–30, followed by the appointment of a new Committee on 5 March 1735 (*CCJ*, pp. 183–4, 208, 338; *113C*, p. 1). Gibbs was asked to attend the Committee (with Giacomo Leoni and John James) on 13 March and on 18 March 'desired to prepare a Design' for the Stocks Market (*113C*, pp. 4–5; *113B*, Folder 18 March–8 May 1735). *ASH* II.119–23 and *VAM* D.1161–'98 (*Perks*, Plans 41–4) were delivered on 8 May (*113C*, p. 6). Stocks and Leadenhall Market and Gresham College sites were surveyed in May–June (*113B*, Folder 5–26 June; *113C*, pp. 6, 8–11, 13–15) and considered between 26 June and 9 July (*CCJ*, pp. 361–3; *113C*, pp. 16–26), when Gibbs was ordered to 'prepare Plans' for the Leadenhall site: *ASH* II.124 (*113B*, Folio 3–24 July, 19 November 1735; *113C*, pp. 25–6, 29–30; *Perks*, Plans 45–7). The Stocks Market was chosen on 15–18 December (*CCJ*, pp. 373–v, 379–83; *113C*,

pp. 31–43). Gibbs submitted an estimate on 17 June 1737 for 'about £30000, to finish it Handsomely' (*113B*, Folder 1736–7; *113C*, pp. 89–90). However, George Dance the elder's design was approved as 'the most Eligible' on 6 July 1737 (*113B*, Folder 1736–7; *113C*, p. 92; *Perks*, Plans 50–8). Events from 1734–7 are summarized in *113C*, pp. 95–7. Gibbs wrote on 16 February 1738 concerning payment for 'making several Drawings for different Places' and received 100 guineas (*113B*, Folder January–March 1737–8; *113C*, pp. 117–18, 121). The 'several plans ... drawn by Experienced Architects' (*CCJ*, pp. 361–3): Leoni, Captain De Berlain (both lost), Isaac Ware, Batty Langley and John James are discussed in *Perks*, pp. 164–70, Plans 33–40, 48–9; F. Barker and R. Hyde, *London As it might have been*, 1982, pp. 198–9.

### Marylebone Court House (St Marylebone) E 1729–33, D 1803–4, 1935

EDWARD HARLEY, 2ND EARL OF OXFORD (1689–1741)*

*ASH* III.83 and *VAM* D.1160–'98 relate to a bill for £16 dated 31 March 1733 'To Mr. Michael Rysbrack for My Lord and Lady's Arms & Supporters &c. Carved in Portland Stone set over the Court house-Door, including Stone' (*BL* Add. MS 18243, f. 26v). The Court House in Marylebone Lane was erected in 1729 by George Mercer and William Gunn; the arms were resited over the entrance of the new building of 1803–4 (shown in *Architect and Building News*, 1 February 1935, Supplement No. 37) but disappeared after that building, in turn, was demolished in 1935 (E. B. Ashford, *Tyburn Village and Stratford Place*, 1969, St Marylebone Society Publication No. 10, pp. 14–16; F. H. W. Sheppard, *Local Government in St. Marylebone, 1688–1835*, 1958, pp. 25–7).

### Marylebone or Oxford Chapel (now St Peter, Vere Street, St Marylebone) E 1721–4

EDWARD HARLEY, 2ND EARL OF OXFORD (1689–1741)*

Craftsmen: Giuseppe Artari and Giovanni Bagutti, ornamental plasterers; David Audsley, plain plasterer; Henry Elkins, bricklayer; Thomas Johnson, smith; John Mist, pavoir; William Pickering, painter; Christopher Shrider, organ builder; Thomas Phillips, Benjamin Timbrell and John Williams, carpenters (*BL* Loan 29/42 (accounts 1724–46); Add. MS 18238, ff. 37–40; 18240, f. 48).

'Oxford employed him to build his handsom Chaple near Cavendish Sqr' (*Gibbs MS* p. 91) 'for the Accommodation of the Inhabitants of the new Buildings in *Marybone* Fields. It is a plain Brick Building, except the Portico, Coines, Door-cases and the *Venetian* Window. The Cieling is handsomely adorned with Fret-work by Signori *Artari* and *Bagutti*' (*ABA*, p. vii, pls. 24–5; *ASH* I.12, 60; *VAM* E.3601–1913). The site was being discussed in June 1720 (*HMC Portland*, V, pp. 598–9). Timbrell and Phillips signed a contract on 8 August 1721 'for building Marybone Chapell ... according to a Plan & Upright ... Designed by James Gibbs' for £3,000 (18238, ff. 37v–8; *ASH* I.12 is annotated 'Our hands this eight day of August 1721. Witnesses Ja: Gibbs: Wm: Thomas Edward Harley Benj: Timbrell Thos: Phillips'). Bagutti agreed in 1722 to undertake 'the Stucco Work ... according to a Design [lost] Signed by the sd. parties' for which he received £70 (18238,

f. 37). Shrider agreed on 20 February 1723 to supply the organ with a case 'Wrought & Carved according to a Design [lost] Signed by the sd. Parties . . . so much of the Ornaments as shall be Directed by James Gibbs . . . to be Guilt, & the Carving & Workmanship to be performed to his Satisfaction' (18238, ff. 39–40); rebuilt in 1852, the original case is shown in a set of drawings of 1820 by T. Leverton and T. Chawners (*MLHC* Ashbridge 241 (495–8)). Mist received £333.5.10½ for paving (18240, f. 48). The cost of 'Building & Furnishing' by 4 July 1726 including plate was £4,296.4.8½ (18240, f. 43). William Wilton repaired and cleaned the plasterwork in 1730 and 1740 (29/42). The arms on the portico were removed in 1832 when the chapel was reconsecrated as St Peter's (T. Smith, *A Topographical and Historical Account of the Parish of St. Mary-le-Bone*, 1833, p. 123) and the interior was altered and refurbished between 1871 and 1892 (*West London Gazette*, 12 December 1908 in Ashbridge 2189(241)) and again in 1979–80 with disastrous results.

## House in Mortimer Street (St Marylebone) E c. 1735–40, D

WILLIAM HANBURY (d. 1768)*

Between October 1735 and March 1740 the Marylebone smith Thomas Wagg executed unspecified work for Hanbury 'in the Country' (Gibbs's KELMARSH HALL) and in town (*PRO* Chancery Masters Exhibits C.109 25, The Daybooks and Ledgers of Thomas Wagg, 1727–1748, III, 30 June 1739; V, p. 109; VI, p. 207; XVIII, 20 March 1740). The latter was probably in connection with Gibbs's work for the client represented only by the drawing of 'The Ground plan of Mr. Hanbury's house in Mortimer Street' in the Kelmarsh album (*RIBA* K3/6), about which nothing more is recorded (*Friedman 1973*, p. 22).

## Oxford Market House (St Marylebone) E 1726–37, D 1880–2

EDWARD HARLEY, 2ND EARL OF OXFORD (1689–1741)*

Craftsmen: Thomas Johnson, smith; George Mercer, mason; Joseph Pattison, smith; Robert Wanmer, carpenter; William Wilton, plasterer (*BL* Add. MS 18243, ff. 27–v, 34).

No architect is mentioned in connection with this building and its history is unclear, but Gibbs is a likely candidate (*Colvin*, p. 339). John Prince's 1719 estate plan shows a proposed Market House in Marylebone Place (*Willis*, pl. 15a). On 21 June 1720 Harley wrote 'I have taken upon me to direct immediately the building [of] the market house' (*HMC Portland*, V, p. 599). A Mr Grantham offered a scheme on 5 September 1720 (18240, f. 28) but the structure as built (*Crace*, XXIX, nos. 30, 69–70; *MLHC* Ashbridge 431 (1449); G. Bush, *Old London*, 1975, p. 85, pl. 60; H. Hobhouse, *Lost London*, 1971, p. 182; H. Phillips, *Mid-Georgian London*, 1964, figs. 324–5) is related to a 4 July 1726 estimate 'To Building the Markethouse, Colonnade & Vaults' for £1,875.17.9 (18240, f. 42v) which by 25 July 1727 'his Lordship has already, at a very great Expence built' (18239, ff. 28v, 30). Payments for construction are recorded until 1737 (18239, f. 23v; 18240, ff. 36, 48; 18243, f. 27v). *ASH* II.50–1 (*Little*, pl. 23), based on Henry Bell's Tuesday Market Cross at King's Lynn, 1707–10 (*Colvin*, p. 105), may be associated with this project.

## Houses in the Privy Gardens, Whitehall (Westminster) E 1710–11, D after 1807

JOHN ERSKINE, 11TH EARL OF MAR (1675–1732), AND HUGH CAMPBELL, 3RD EARL OF LOUDOUN (d. 1731)*

Craftsmen: John Chaplin and Thomas Highmore, painters; Francis Nost, mason (National Register of Archives (Scotland): Marquis of Bute (Loudoun Papers), NRA (S) survey 631, Bundles A243 and A251).

Gibbs reported to Loudoun on 10 October 1710 that 'Your house . . . is going on appace', mentioning 'plastering . . . the party partition that divides your lordships servants lobie from my lord Mars', while on 14 October that he had 'express'd' the improvements 'in a few scraches here incloas'd' (plans of the ground floor of the house and dining room, since lost) so that 'now the house is wind and water tight'. On 2 November Gibbs apologized that the house would not be ready for another two months and that he was working on the forestairs and renewing the rotten foundation. On 22 October 1711 the builders sent a representation for payment of about £3,000, and Nost was paid on 29 December 1711 (Bundles A243, A251). A Lords Commissioners of His Majesty's Treasury reported on 29 July 1715 regarding workmen's bills totalling £5509.16.8 for 'repairing the house in the Privy Garden, now in the Possession of the Earls of Marr and Lowdon', which included 'altering the disposition of the first Fabrick, which was then all in One House, with an Office for the Secretary's of Scotland's Clerks in part of it, But is now made into two distinct Habitations, wth severall new Walls from the Ground, addicionall Closets Built on the Outside, and A new Stair Case, with severall other conveniencys within, besides what was done in the Alteracons and Repairacons of the Building first Erected, together with severall Works without Doors in Steps, Paving, filling up the Fountain and makeing it a Court inclosed with a Pallasadoe and posting'; the report concluded that the bills were 'not unreasonable as they now stand, after Sr. Christopher Wren's Abatements, wch were very considerable, and We have the Affidavid of Mr Gibbs who was the Person concern'd in surveying the said Building' (*PRO* Works 6/6, pp. 78–9). Views of the house (*Crace*, XVI; H. Phillips, *Mid-Georgian London*, 1964, pp. 30–2) give little indication of the nature of this work.

## Queen Anne's Pillar, The Strand (Westminster) 1714–15, NE

COMMISSIONERS FOR BUILDING FIFTY NEW CHURCHES

A 'Modell of a Pillar to be Erected in the Strand' ordered on 1 July 1714 (*LPL* 2690, p. 174) resulted in a design (lost) by Thomas Archer (2724, f. 4) and another by Nicholas Hawksmoor (*Downes*, p. 277, pl. 79b) which were rejected on 6 July, as was Gibbs's first design (*BM* Department of Prints and Drawings 1913-12-16-9 and 10). The favoured design was an alternative by Gibbs described as 'a corinthian pillar . . . fifteen foot [in] Diameter' (2693, p. 75) and in 'Mr James Gibbs's bill for Modells' under 1 July as 'a Monument being a Corinthian pillar flooted, with a Geometrical Stairs within it Standing on a pedestall with the figure of the Queen on the top & four Lyons on the four Corners of the pedestall' costing £11.1.6 (2708, f. 7; 2726, ff. 75–6). Its appearance is uncertain, as the model subsequently disappeared: it is described as being from 200 to 250 feet high and 12 feet in diameter (*Gibbs MS*, pp. 85–6; *ABA*, p. vii). This was approved by the Queen, the foundation was laid by Samuel Tuffnell and Edward Strong (2690, pp. 175, 177, 180) and although still under consideration in October 1714 (2724, f. 35) it was virtually abandoned as a result of the Queen's death on 1 August (2690, p. 184). T. Friedman, 'Foggini's Statue of Queen Anne', in K. Lankheit, ed., *Kunst des Barock in der Toskana*, 1976, pp. 39–56, charts the complex history of the royal figure, which was being made in Florence under John Talman's supervision between 1714 and 1717, with additional references in L. Monaci, *Disegni Di Giovan Battista Foggini*, 1977, Gabinetto Disegni e Stampe degli Uffizi, XLVIII, nos. 85–6, 88, figs. 70–2, and *LPL* 2690, pp. 205, 231, 344; 2705, f. 79v; 2707, f. 228v; 2724, ff. 69–70.

## St Bartholomew's Hospital (Holborn) E 1728–68, South Block D 1937

THE GOVERNORS

Principal craftsmen: William Biggs, manager of Ralph Allen's stoneworks; William Chapman and John Phillips, carpenters; ? Harris and Thomas Williams, smiths; William Hogarth and ? Richards, decorative painters; Thomas Marriott, Clerk of the Works; Tobias Preist, joiner; John Baptist St Michele, plasterer; Robert Taylor, mason (*Bart's Journal* Ha 1/10–12; 19/1–6); Philip Hardwick's alterations of 1845 are reported in 1/19, pp. 349–53.

Gibbs 'gave the plans and directed the building of St Batholomeus Hospital ... consiting of four large buildings ... detached from each other to prevent fire, and only appear to be joyned by iron gates ... All the four sides ... are built uniforme with bath stone ... He gave all his drawings, time, and attendance gratis ... out of Charity for ye poor' (*Gibbs MS*, pp. 98–9; Ha 1/12, pp. 141–2). The Hospital archives contain *Journals*, 1708–57 (1/9–1/12), cash and receipt books, bills, agreements (19/1–35). The building history is further described in V. C. Medvei and J. L. Thornton, *The Royal Hospital of Saint Bartholomew, 1123–1973*, 1974; N. Moore, *The History of St Bartholomew's Hospital*, 1918; A. Oswald, 'Gibbs's Great Hall at Bart's', *CL*, 25 May 1961, pp. 1198–1200; D'A. Power, *A Short History*, 1935. Gibbs was chosen a governor in April 1723 (Ha 1/10, p. 83) and appointed on 25 July to the committee dealing with rebuilding the ancient fabric in Smithfield to 'a General Plan ... for the whole' (1/10, p. 93). A 'Plan ... conformable to one Designe' called on 1 August 1728 (1/10, pp. 182–v) is shown in 'A Perspective View of St: Bartholomew's Hospital' by R. West and in 'The General plan of the New Building' by B. Cole (*Crace*, XXVI, nos. 44, 48). A cardboard model of the hospital, probably of nineteenth century date, is in the Department of Sculpture, Victoria and Albert Museum.

### North Block E 1728–38

Ha 19/40 and *ASH* II.66 are Gibbs's design for 'one part of the square ... thought proper to be first rebuilt' at a cost not exceeding £8,500 submitted on 12 September 1728, when he was ordered 'to prepare a Plann of the whole intended building & Cause the same to be Engraved' (Ha 1/10, pp. 184v–6); the print was prepared by May 1729 (1/10, p. 192v; 19/29/12; G. Whitteridge and V. Stokes, *A Brief*

*History*, 1961, illus. opp. p. 34; Guildhall Library, London: Prints 51/BAR) and approved on 24 July with the order 'that all future Buildings ... be regulated & done in all respects agreeable to ye same Plann' (1/10, pp. 196v–8). In September 1729 the committee authorized this to be erected 'with all convenient speed' (1/10, p. 202). The foundation-stone was laid on 9 June 1730 (19/3). Ralph Allen agreed on 25 June 1730 to supply Bath stone, received 'the draughts' on 11 July and proposed 'Errecting & finishing the outside of the Principal Pile ... according to Mr Gibbs's Larg Draughts' (lost) for £11,700 (19/25/5; 19/29/1–2; 19/31/22); further discussions and a donation of £100 were considered on 18 and 27 June 1730 (19/29/3, 6); the agreement is dated 14 August (19/10). Allen and Gibbs discussed designs and materials during November–December (19/29/7–8), Allen reckoning on 19 January 1732 that the 'whole of my work wil be finished by ... this week' (19/29/16, 18, 21). Hogarth painted the main staircase during 1734–7 (1/11, p. 128; 1/12, pp. 282, 462; *Croft-Murray 1970*, pp. 33–4, 223, pls. 53, 55; E. Croft-Murray, 'Hogarth's Staircase at Bart's', *CL*, 18 August 1960, pp. 324–5; R. Paulson, *Hogarth: His Life, and Times*, 1971, I, pp. 353, 378–88, pls. 140–3). The Great Hall was decorated 1733–7 (1/11, pp. 134–5) including St Michele's ceiling, as based on *ASH* III.89, at a cost of £192.16.0 (19/1, pp. 2–3; 19/5/1). Gibbs advised alterations to the wall decoration between 8 September 1737 and 27 April 1738 (1/11, pp. 134–5, 141, 149) and on 19 December 1738 supervised the installation of Henry VIII's portrait with 'decent & respectfull Ornaments' (1/11, p. 173; *Markham*, p. 528).

### South Block E 1735–40, D 1937

A £2,000 gift and subscriptions for 'Building a second Wing' launched this block on 31 July 1735 (Ha 1/11, p. 42; 19/1, p. 10). It consisted of 'Wards for the poor Patients ... agreable to the Plan prepared' which was approved on 21 April 1736 (1/11, pp. 63–4; 19/30/5). The foundation-stone laying was reported on 17 August (19/31/1); the stone work was finished by 15 March 1739 (1/11, pp. 180, 183); the upper wards were 'finishing [under] Mr. Gibbs Directions' by 12 April 1739 (1/11, p. 190) and furnished by 1740 (1/11, p. 201).

### West Block E 1743–53

On 24 March 1743 the governors resolved that 'another new pile ... of wards ... be forthwith built' by subscription (Ha 1/11, p. 308). The ground was cleared in June–July (1/11, pp. 315, 317; 19/31/2; J. Rocque, *A Plan of the Cities of London and Westminster, and Borough of Southwark*, 1746, D1). Allen agreed on 30 July 1743 to deliver stone 'however Expensive it may prove' (19/31/3–4). Although construction was delayed by the War of the Austrian Succession in 1744 (1/11, p. 445; 19/3; 19/31/5–12), it was resolved on 31 January 1748 'to carry on the Building with all Expedition' (19/30/7; 19/31/10, 16). Biggs arrived in London in the winter of 1749 to supervise the stonework (19/31/18). William Robinson was appointed surveyor on 7 March 1749 and on 6 July Gibbs was thanked formally for his contribution (1/12, pp. 120–1, 134, 141–2). The block was finished by October 1752 and occupied by May 1753 (1/12, pp. 339, 375, 406; 19/3).

## Apothecary Shop Laboratory E 1747

On 19 March 1747 'Gibbs, Mr. Christopher Horsenaile, and Mr. William Cooper [were ordered] to assist in giving proper Directions [for] a Laboratory' (Ha 1/11, pp. 537–8, 543). Gibbs was asked to 'prepare a Plann' on 10 April (1/11, p. 547) which he delivered on 28 April, but the decision to incorporate this unit into the existing block resulted in Gibbs drawing 'another Plan' (1/11, pp. 548–9), both lost. This second design was approved on 12 May and built by Cooper (1/11, pp. 554–5, 565, 597–8; Hc 19/2/2, *Plan Book 2*, no. 35).

## East Block E 1758–68

This was built according to Gibbs's design under Robinson's supervision (Ha 1/13, pp. 26–7; 19/2; 19/31/19–47; Hc 19/8 plan and elevation dated 1761).

## St Clement Danes (Westminster) E 1719–21, partly D 1941

THE VESTRY

The Vestry Minutes for 1716–25 (*WPL* B1063) record a resolution on 26 May 1719 that 'the Tower shall be raised [by] an ornamentall Steeple'; this was executed to Gibbs's design (*Gibbs MS*, p. 86) for £1,650 by the mason John Townesend, who was commissioned on 29 May (B1063). The new steeple is shown in Kip's engraving (*Crace*, XVII, no. 136); *ASH* I.11; *ABA*, p. viii, pl. 28. As part of the scheme discussed on 9 June 1720 to make the church 'new beautifyed', roof repairs were initiated on 21 June and the 'Representation of Mr James Gibbs Surveyor' recommending remedial work was received by 30 June. *ASH* III.95 inscribed 'St Clements Church', showing the redecorated chancel, is related to a 2 March 1721 resolution 'that the Glory wch is to be over the Alter ... be painted ... by Mr. Kent'. Other relevant references are under 10 June and 1 October 1719, 18 April, 5 May, 4 August and 3 November 1720, 17 and 22 May 1721, and 27 June 1723. Christ Church, Oxford: Inv. 1139 is an interior view looking east attributed to Gibbs. The church was gutted in 1941 and restored in 1957–8 (E. Beresford Chancellor, *The Annals of The Strand, Topographical and Historical*, 1912, pp. 229–49; B. F. L. Clarke, *Parish Churches of London*, 1966, pp. 176–7).

## St George, Hanover Square (Westminster) 1720, NE

COMMISSIONERS FOR BUILDING FIFTY NEW CHURCHES

*ASH* II.5 and 38, inscribed 'We whose names are here unto subscribed doe approve of this Plan for the intended Church in great George street near Hannover square', are related to General William Steuart's letter to the Commissioners of 13 October 1720 about their 'desiring I wou'd send Mr: Gibbs to wait upon the Board wth. a designe wh. hee had prepared, for a new Church, near Hanover Square, wch: was don. accordingly, and as hee informed mee [that the Commissioners] were satisfied wth: the Draught ... and desired to know, if I wou'd [inform] the Board that the Draught produced was approved off by the persons Cheifley concerned to have [the] Church built ... the Cheif persons of quallity & others liveing in, and near the Square, and as many as were then in Towne signed their aprobation of the Draught, and desired ... that Mr:

Gibbs (of whose performance they have a very good Oppinion) might bee recomended ... to have the direction of so good a Worke, wch: they are affared hee will do, to all their satisfactions ... wee hope the Board will fix this matter So, as that Mr: Gibbs wth: out further loss of time ... may ... begin to prepare all things in order to go on Early in the Spring ... that hee will finish this good worke in about 18 Months ... we all know that Mr: Gibbs will bee diligent to the Last degree, for our satisfaction, as well as his own Creditt to performe this affaire wth: all possible care and diligence, and will give undeniable Security for Effecting the same ... if this matter is aproved of there will bee a Sufficient Security given that Mr Gibbs will not Exceed Ten thousand Pounds' (*LPL* 2714, f. 15). *ASH* II.37 and VII.14–18 are variant designs, perhaps those submitted on 23 November 1720 (2691, pp. 126–7). Although Steuart 'cou'd never get a Compleate Draught from either Mr: Hawnmore [Nicholas Hawksmoor] nor Mr. [John] James ... the first being much afflicted wth: the Gout, and the other Living out of Towne' (2714, f. 15), both architects prepared designs in 1720 and James's was approved on 14 December (2691, pp. 121, 125, 128–9); his church cost £19,078.16.3 (2711, f. 55) and was consecrated in 1725 (B. F. L. Clarke, *Parish Churches of London*, 1966, p. 180).

## St George's Hospital (Westminster) 1734–5, NE

THE GOVERNORS

Following the governors' resolution of 19 October 1733 to 'fitt up and furnish ... the Infirmary now Erecting at Lanesborough House', Hyde Park Corner, a notice was ordered on 15 May 1734 to be placed in the *Daily Advertiser* announcing their intention 'to enlarge their House by some Additionall Wards' and calling for 'Proposalls [from] Any person ... who shall be willing to Undertake the same' to be delivered by 29 October. On 11 December 'Mr. Gibbs the Architect offered to Present ... a Plann ... of a New Building ... if this Board would inform him what conveniencys would be wanting' and was invited on 7 February 1735 'to View the Ground for the Planns [he] offered to make' (St George's Hospital archives: Minute Book 19 Oct 1733 to 31 Decbr 1735, pp. 6–8, 111, 211, 224, 245). These activities perhaps brought forth the series of designs in *ASH* II.125–6, 128–32. Nicholas Dubois, Henry Flitcroft, Thomas Archer and Isaac Ware were also involved and the latter's design, perhaps based on one by Burlington, who was a governor (*RIBA* Boy 27/2–3), was chosen on 5 June 1735 (Minute Book, pp. 10, 13, 116, 119, 211, 224, 245, 316). This building (*Crace*, X, nos. 29, 31) was rebuilt in 1828–9.

## St Giles-in-the-Fields (Holborn) 1731, NE

THE VESTRY

The *Daily Post* reported on 4 February 1731 (No. 3551, p. 1; *Burney* 286b) that 'Mr. Gibbs, Mr. Shepherd, and Mr. Flitcryft, three famous Architects, are Candidates for rebuilding ... St. Gile's in the Fields'. Only designs by Flitcroft (*Colvin*, p. 310; J. Harris, *The Palladians*, 1981, pp. 86–7) and Gibbs (*ASH* III.67–70) survive, both for buildings measuring between 115 and 118 feet long. Flitcroft's executed design is dated 29 March 1731; the new church was opened on 14 April 1734 (B. F. L. Clarke, *Parish Churches of London*, 1966, p. 122;

*Defoe 1738*, I, p. 144; J. Parton, *Some Account of the Hospital and Parish of St. Giles in the Fields, Middlesex*, 1822, pp. 207–14; *S of L*, 1914, V, Part II, pp. 130–2, pls. 43–51).

## St John's (St Marylebone) 1741, NE

### THE VESTRY

Although John Prince submitted 'Draughts for rebuilding Marybone Church' in 1724 (*BL* Add. MS 18240, ff. 30-v), it was not until 1741 that further progress was made. Gibbs was asked to view the old parish church (*MLHC VP* 1740–52, p. 3): 'A South East View of St Mary le bone Church near London' (*MLHC* Ashbridge 221 (431), in J. Summerson, *St Marylebone Old Church An Appreciation*, 1951, p. 6, seems to be his record of this building). John Lane and Walter Lee were asked on 2 February to survey and 'make such Designs as they think proper for the Effectual reparation ... & Advise with Mr. Gibbs or such others as they think fit'. On 12 February Lee delivered his 'repairing' design, which was 'layd before Mr. Gibbs for his perusal & [ordered] that an Estimate of the Charge of Executing ... be made when Mr. Gibbs shall have settled the same'. Gibbs presented 'Designs for a new Church [*ASH* IV.17]; and also other Designs ... by Mr. Lee' on 24 February. Lane's proposal was estimated to cost £800 on 31 March and the Vestry decided to rebuild according to it. The contract on 2 June 1741 mentions Lane, Lee and John Deschamps as building according to the 'plan ... Annext [and] approved by James Gibbs'. All but Gibbs's design are lost. Construction began in July, Benjamin Timbrell and Roger Morris were measuring during the winter and work was more-or-less completed by February 1742 at a cost of £1,051.19.0, although construction continued into 1743 (*VP* 1729–40, pp. 329, 335–8; 1740–52, pp. 5–15, 17–53, 69, 71, 99–100). The new church is shown in J. B. Chatelain, *Views in the vicinity of London, c.* 1750, no. 28; Guildhall Library, London: Prints M/MAR; and measured drawings and photographs in *NMR*. Gibbs left £100 'towards enlarging' the church in 1754, but nothing was done (*VP* 1752–68, p. 41; P. C. C. 288 Pinfold). The building was closed in 1926 and demolished *c.* 1952; the pulpit survives in St Barnabas, Finsbury (*St. Marylebone Society Newsheet*, 7 February 1956, No. 75; B. F. L. Clarke, *Parish Churches of London*, 1966, p. 125; T. Smith, *A Topographical and Historical Account of the Parish of St. Mary-le-Bone*, 1833, p. 62; F. H. W. Sheppard, *Local Government in St. Marylebone, 1688–1835*, 1958, pp. 28–32).

## St John's (St Marylebone)
## Monument to James Gibbs (1682–1754) E *c.* 1754

### JAMES GIBBS

Gibbs requested in his Will of 9 August 1754 to 'be buried within the parish church of Saint Mary le Bon and [with] a small Monument of Marble wth I have ordered to be made by Mr. Walter Lee Mason ... with a short Inscription upon it as shall be thought fit by my Executors' (P. C. C. 228 Pinfold). This simple pedimented wall tablet, its inscription (quoted on p. 20) repainted in 1816, survives in the present parish church (D. Lysons, *Environs of London*, 1811, II, p. 554).

## St Margaret's (Westminster)
## Monument to Robert Stuart (d. 1714) E by 1728 (north aisle)

### ELIZABETH STUART

Gibbs 'made ... Mr Stuarts monument in St Margrat's' (*Gibbs MS*, p. 91) inscribed 'Et in Memoriam Conjugis Clarissimi hoc Monumentum Posuit Elizabetha Vidua' (St Margaret's: MS Vestry Records on monuments), as illustrated in *ABA*, p. xxiv, pl. 127 centre.

## St Martin-in-the-Fields (Westminster) E 1720–7

### THE VESTRY

Principal craftsmen and total payments: Giovanni Bagutti (£419.6.0) and Chrysostom Wilkins (£593.4.4), plasterers; Thomas Bridgewater, carver (£107.5.0); Christopher Cass, mason (£15,147.1.4); Nicholas Courtney (£1,757.19.11½) and Thomas Goff (£120.3.8¼), smiths; Charles Griffith, joiner (£2,012.14.8¼); Thomas Phillips and Benjamin Timbrell, carpenters (£5,615.6.3¼); Thomas Sledge (£1,213.19.½) and John Witt (£2,181.19.11), bricklayers; James and William Price, glass-painters (£130) (*SMIF* 419/309–311, 'An Account of all the Bills' on back page of 419/311; T. A. M. Bishop, *A Catalogue of Parish Records in the Archives of the City of Westminster*, F6033, F6035–6; *Colvin*, p. 600). Petitions for the post of Clerk of the Works were received on 25 August 1721 from Thomas Hinton, John Woodward and Edward Oakley, the first named being appointed although subsequently replaced by James Browne (309, pp. 78, 80). On 28 April 1722 Gibbs delivered an estimate of £22,497 for a 'Generall Charge of the Severall Works necessary for rebuilding' (309, p. 128). At the end of building operations the total cost reached £29,056.10.6. Gibbs received £632.4.6: £550 for 'his Trouble as Surveyor ... for six years', £71.10.0 for the wooden model of the church and £10.14.6 for the (lost) 'plann for the East Window' (311, p. 122 and back page).

*Gibbs MS*, pp. 92–3, and *ABA*, pp. iv–v, describe at length the history from 1720 of the rebuilding of the medieval church as recorded in George Vertue's engraving (*S of L*, 1940, XX, pls. 8–9) based on Gibbs's perspective drawing (*ASH* IV.26). The 1710 survey of the fabric and 'Act of Parliament for Rebuilding' are discussed in J. McMasters, *A Short History of the Royal Parish Church of St. Martin-in-the-Fields*, 1916, p. 71, and *S of L*, 1940, XX, p. 24. Useful studies are also in Anon., 'St Martin's Church and its Architect', *Builder*, 23 October 1858, pp. 710–11; B. F. L. Clarke, *Parish Churches of London*, 1966, pp. 181–2; K. A. Esdaile, *St Martin in the Fields, Old and New*, 1944; W. Maitland, *The History of London*, 1739, pp. 731–7; *S of L*, 1940, XX, Chapter 3; J. Summerson, *Architecture in Britain, 1530 to 1830*, 1970, pp. 350–5; J. Summerson, *Georgian London*, 1945, pp. 70–2. Many engraved views are in *Crace*, XVIII; Guildhall Library, London: WZ/MAR; *WPL* F131 and St Martin's Boxes 1–4; a pen and ink interior perspective perhaps drawn by Gibbs is at Christ Church, Oxford: Inv. 1138.

1720: Plans and estimates for the new church were requested on 23 June, delivered on 29 June and viewed by the Vestry between 6 July and 31 August (309, pp. 2–3, 5–13). These presumably include Gibbs's designs for the so-called Round Church (*ASH* I.13–15, II.5, III.94, VII.3–6; *ABA*, pp. iv–vi, pls. 8–15). Contemporary contributions from Nicholas Dubois (lost) and James Thornhill (J. Harris, *The Palladians*, 1981, pl. IX) were withdrawn by September (309, pp. 6, 21). An unidentified design by Gibbs was approved on 14 September, when he was recommended for the post of surveyor (309, p. 16). George Sampson's design (lost) was withdrawn on 11 November (309, p. 25). Gibbs was elected in favour of John James on 24 November (309, pp. 26–7).

1721: A series of alternative rectangular designs were prepared during the spring (*ASH* III.96, VII.7–13) and although the composition was still unresolved the dedication-stone was laid on 19 March (McMaster, *op. cit.*, p. 75; *SAL* Minute Book, I, p. 59). Another design was approved on 23 May (*ASH* VII.1–2, signed by members of the Vestry), when a wooden model to cost £71.10.0 was ordered (309, p. 52; J. Wilton-Ely, 'The Architectural Model', *AR*, July 1967, pp. 30–1). On 12 June the Vestry requested alternative elevation treatments to be indicated on the model and they ordered the resiting of the vestry room from the basement to the chancel flanks (309, p. 53; *Friedman 1973*, pp. 24–5, fig. 24). The south elevation treatment was approved and the steeple was ordered heightened on 31 October (309, p. 94). Gibbs supplied various steeple designs (*ABA*, p. viii, pls. 29–30; J. Harris, *A Catalogue of British Drawings for Architecture, Decoration, Sculpture and Landscape Gardening, 1550–1900, in American Collections*, 1971, p. 105, pl. 72).

1722: The substructure was prepared between 4 January and 9 March, the stone platform and lower section of wall were constructed by July (309, pp. 111–38). Alterations to the internal east end were considered on 28 August and, together with improvements to the west end, were approved on 9 October (309, pp. 144, 147). Alterations to the portico were also approved but a decision to delay their implementation was made on 3 November (309, p. 150).

1723: Alterations to the breadth of the portico were approved on 4 January (309, p. 157) and the building now achieved more-or-less its final and present form (*ABA*, pp. iv–v, pls. 1–7; *ASH* I.1–6; *VAM* E.3599-1913). On 29 January Gibbs approved the 'Modell of a Truss for the Roofe . . . differing in some parts from [the carpenters'] Originall proposall' (309, p. 158). Construction of the 'outside periphery and all the Inside Work' reached 16 feet by 6 February (311, p. 2) and the balustrades on the north, south and east elevations by 7 October (311, pp. 3–7), by which time the east pediment cartouche had been carved (*ABA*, p. xxii, pl. 110; *ASH* III.125, IV.30; *VAM* E.3637 and 3638-1913). Gibbs reported on 25 October that it 'will be proper to remove the Masons Capstall out from the Middle of the Church . . . that the turning of the Arches for the Vaults may not be obstructed' (309, p. 183). The portico foundation was considered on 16 November (309, p. 186).

1724: Craftsmen's estimates including that for making the cast-iron churchyard railings to Gibbs's design (*ASH* II.45) were delivered on 9 March (309, pp. 193–5). Gibbs submitted 'Designs for the Alteration of the intended Steeple' (perhaps *WS*, 1935, XII, pl. XXXV) and 'Two Designs for the Frett Work' (309, pp. 198–9; perhaps *ASH* IV.31: 'Ceiling for ye new Church of St Martin', in L. Turner, *Decorative Plasterwork in Great Britain*, 1927, fig. 308C), the execution of which Bagutti, Wilkins and Isaac Mansfield competed between 16 March and

18 April (309, pp. 195–202). The carpenters' bill of 4 July refers to 'Making a Modell for Branches' or chandeliers (311, p. 39, with all subsequent references 419/311) based on Gibbs's design (*ASH* IV.28–9: 'For St Marti' and 'Branches for St Martins Church') for which the 'Machine to hang' them was installed by 15 August (pp. 39–40). Another bill of 19 September mentions 'Making the Window at East End' (p. 41). The mason's bill for work 'to the Top of the Spire' is dated 8 December (p. 6).

1725: The portico foundation was begun by 7 May (p. 52). Among many references to bills are Gibbs's for 21 June for a 'plann for the East Window' for £10.14.6 (p. 122), Griffith's of 7 July for the pulpit (p. 65) based on Gibbs's design (*ASH* II.83, IV.34–7), the carpenters' of 24 October for 'making a Scaffold for Mr Bagutty to Work the Ornamt. on Earth Side of Organ' (p. 49) and Cass's through December (pp. 59–60). The portico columns were carved by 22 December (pp. 8–9).

1726: Bills include one dated 18 January for 'Underpinning Cornice of Portico' (p. 56) and another for painting (pp. 72, 126), in February–March for 'Carrying Rubbish to Levell the Ground to lay the Purbeck Paveing' and 'out of Gallerys for Plaisterers and Joyners to go to Work' (pp. 57, 61), the joiner's of 28 May for a 'pattern for the Iron Ballusters', of 3 June for a 'Walnut Tree pattern for the Altar Rail' of the chancel (p. 68) and 18 June for scaffolding 'to Gild Over the Altar' (p. 71); also in August for 1,801 feet of 'Crown Glass' at £90.1.0 (p. 105) and for plain plasterwork (pp. 94–5). By September scaffolding used on the steeple and portico, including that for 'Cutting the Letters in Frieze', was struck (pp. 61–2). On 26 September William and James Price received £130 for 'Painting the Glass of the East Window' (p. 104). The new church was consecrated on 20 October. The total cost of building was £33,661.16.7¾ (back page).

## Tabernacle

Plans and estimates for the temporary structure shown in *ABA*, pl. 1, abutting the south-east corner of the church were requested on 23 June 1720 (309, p. 2). Various sites were considered and properties requisitioned during July–September and part of the churchyard was chosen on 31 January 1721 (309, p. 35). On 7 February Gibbs's design was approved and workmen's estimates based on a 'plann [which] may be seen at Mr: Gibbs' were called (309, p. 36). Phillips and Timbrell's 'Draught of the Articles' is dated 28 February (309, p. 39). The gallery fronts were ready for painting by 11 July 1721 (309, p. 66).

## St Mary-le-Strand (Westminster) E 1713–24

COMMISSIONERS FOR BUILDING FIFTY NEW CHURCHES

Principal craftsmen: John Grove, Robert Jelfe and John James, carpenters; Henry Hester and Francis Withers, bricklayers; John Simmons, joiner; John and William Townesend, masons; Chrysostom Wilkins, plasterer (payments recorded in E. G. W. Bill, *The Queen Anne Churches: A Catalogue of the Papers in Lambeth Palace Library of the Commission for Building Fifty New Churches in London and Westminster, 1711–1759*, 1979, pp. 235–7 and under individual names). James replaced Gibbs as surveyor on 5 January 1716 (*LPL* 2690, pp. 237, 239). The history of the

Commission is described in *ABA*, pp. vi–vii; H. Colvin's introduction in *Bill*; J. Field, 'The Sources of James Gibbs' Architecture and his Connection with the Commissioners' Churches of 1711', 1958 (MA London University); J. Field, 'Early Unknown Gibbs', *AR*, May 1962, pp. 315–19.

'Mr Gibbs [was ordered] to make some elegant designs for [a church] near the May pole in the Strand . . . which was done . . . and laid befor [the Commissioners] and they made choice of Mr Gibbs's as the most ornamental, and propperist for that situation' (*Gibbs MS*, pp. 85–6). The site was approved in November 1711 (2690, p. 418).

First Design: Gibbs was ordered on 9 December 1713 to 'draw Designes' (2690, p. 132), which resulted in the wooden model submitted on 4 February 1714 described in 'Mr James Gibbs's bill for Modells' as 'a Church 3 Quartr Columns of the Corinthian Order Steeple and inside finishing' costing £15.13.0 (2708, f. 7; 2724, ff. 16–23) and recorded in a drawing of 1826 (*VAM* E.3024-1909) before disappearing. Other designs were also considered (2690, p. 152); Thomas Archer's (*WS*, 1933, X, pl. 13 top, overplan) was approved on 29 April 1714 (2690, p. 157; 2717, f. 100) and construction began.

Second Design: *ABA*, p. vii, pls. 22–3, 31, was produced as a result of meetings on 15 July and 28 October 1714 (2690, pp. 177, 186, 190) but subsequently abandoned because of a width too great to be accommodated by the existing foundation (*c.* 1714 site plan in 2750, f. 64).

Executed Design: Designs were submitted by John Vanbrugh (lost) and Gibbs by 2 November 1714 (2693, p. 76). Gibbs's scheme (*ABA*, pls. 16–21) was chosen on 4 November (2690, p. 192) and two wooden models (both now in *RIBA*) were made: (1) as described in Gibbs's models bill (above) as 'a Church of two Orders of Columns, Vizt. the Ionick and Corinthian being the Church of the Strand as now building wth. Inside finishing & Steeple all Complete' costing £32.10.0 (2708, f. 7; 2724, f. 16), which survives but incomplete and much damaged, and (2) a contemporary replica showing the church as published in *ABA* (*Friedman 1973*, p. 25, fig. 25; J. Wilton-Ely, 'The Architectural Model', *Apollo*, October 1968, pp. 256–9; *AR*, July 1967, pp. 26–7). *ASH* III.98 ('Vases for ye new Church in ye Strand') is perhaps related to a payment for a drawing of 'Three urns of the Strand Church 03.03.0' in Harley's accounts of 24 July 1719 (*WS*, 1940, XVII, p. 10). *ASH* III.112 is the perspective mentioned in 1716 (2726, ff. 77–8), subsequently used in David Lockley's print of 1719 (T. Friedman, *James Gibbs Architect, 1682–1754: 'a man of great Fame'*, 1982, no. 23, illus.) and in *ABA*, pl. 21. *ASH* I.5, 11 and *VAM* E.3600-1913 are preparatory drawings for *ABA* pls. 18, 20, 31.

Construction: The foundation of Archer's church (above) reached ground level by September 1714 (2724, f. 37). Building materials were stockpiled by June 1715 (2716, f. 48). Masonry work reached the 'pedestall above the first Order [and] all the Free Stone in the Inside' of Gibbs's church by December 1715 (2697, ff. 425–8). The upper storey was partly completed by March 1716 (2711, f. 14). A model for the roof was delivered in July 1716 (2690, p. 294; 2697, f. 437). Masonry work reached the crowning balustrade by December 1716 (2697, ff. 441–6). Pewing and plastering proposals were approved during May–June 1717 (2690, p. 333; 2703, ff. 80–1; 2716, ff. 58, 62). The steeple was completed by September 1717 (2690,

p. 358). The portico, west pediment and vases and the ornament over the altar was carved by December 1717 (2697, ff. 451–64; 2721, ff. 108–16). A 'Modell for the East End and an other for the portico [and] Altering the Section of the Portico' were prepared during 1717–18 (2697, ff. 459–60; 2721, ff. 108–10). By 1718 'the Steeple and Portico . . . are in a manner finished' and 'The Carvers are finishing the inside Ornamts. of Stone over the Altar' (2724, ff. 60–2, 64–5v, 67–8). 'Alterations in the Lunetts over the Windows by Mr. Gibbses order' in 1718 (2721, f. 131); 'Additions & Alterations of the Design by the Surveyor' are noted in 1719 (2697, f. 478). By October 1721 the building 'wants only the Paving & Pulpit to be Finished' (2724, f. 85v); unfinished work was reported in November 1722 (2716, f. 90). Simmons received 6 guineas for 'Making A Model of the Tower as agreed wth Mr. Gibbs' during 1722–4 (2698, f. 13). The church was consecrated on 1 January 1724 (2711, f. 79). *Vertue*, III, p. 30, gives the cost of building as £17,000; *LPL* 2711, f. 55, as £20,106.8.7. The interior was refitted by R. J. Withers between 1861 and 1878 (E. Beresford Chancellor, *The Annals of The Strand Topographical and Historical*, 1912, p. 228). Views are in the *Architects' and Builders' Journal*, 4 February 1914; *Crace*, XVII; *WPL* G131; Guildhall Library, London: W2/MAR4.

## Savile House, 6 Leicester Square (Westminster) E 1733, D 1865

SIR GEORGE SAVILE, 7TH BARONET (d. 1743)

John Packer, a Marylebone joiner, was employed in 1733 to alter the late seventeenth-century house, including adding a third storey and refurbishing the drawing, dining and dressing rooms for £1,337 'according to the Draughts made by Mr. James Gibbs Surveyor' now lost (Nottinghamshire *CRO* DDSR 215/59). The house was sacked in the Gordon Riots in 1780 and subsequently altered (*S of L*, 1966, XXXIV, pp. 459–64, pls. 46b, 48a; H. Phillips, *Mid-Georgian London*, 1964, p. 289, figs. 102, 104).

## Thanet House, Great Russell Street (Holborn) E 1719, D

THOMAS COKE, 1ST EARL OF LEICESTER (1697–1759)

'To Mr. Gibs Architect for his design in the Alteration of the house his trouble and Attendance in giving directs to the Workmen &c: and likewise his Examination of the Workmens Bills for the making of the proper Abatements' £21 on 23 February 1719 (Holkham Archives: Domestic Accounts HDA 4,II,72 'An Accompt of the Disbursements made by Jno. Casey for his Master . . . Thomas Coke . . . containing the Charge of Repairs & Alterations of his House in London . . . from Michmas: 1718 to the 25 March 1719'). £1,554.2.0 was spent on repairs and alterations, £651.11.6 on decoration (J. Lees-Milne, *Earls of Creation*, 1962, p. 235; L. Schmidt, *Holkham Hall, Studien zur Architektur und Ausstattung*, 1982 (Phil. Diss., Freiburg), pp. 112 (no. 221), 141). Coke owned Gibbs's preliminary drawing for *ABA*, pl. 63 (Sir John Soane's Museum: 4D, f. 50; L. Schmidt, *Thomas Coke, 1st Earl of Leicester: An Eighteenth Century Amateur Architect*, 1980, p. 8, no. 21).

Westminster Abbey

## Monument to Sophia Fairholm, Marchioness of Annandale (1667–1716), William Johnstone, Lord Annandale (1695–1721), and James Johnstone, 2nd Marquess of Annandale (1688–1730) E 1723 (south aisle)

JAMES JOHNSTONE, 2ND MARQUESS OF ANNANDALE

Gibbs 'made the Marquess of Annandals monument in the Abbey' (*Gibbs MS*, p. 91), which is signed on the inscription panel 'IA: GIBBS ARCHI:' and illustrated in *ABA*, p. xxiii, pl. 120; *ASH* I.41; *VAM* E.3639-1913; the sculptor is unrecorded. The gilt arms over the pediment (*ASH* III.106) are the client's. The monument was erected in 1723 (*Dart*, II, p. 72, pl. 99).

## Monument to Katherine Bovey (1670–1727) E 1727–8 (south aisle)

MARY POPE

Gibbs 'made the . . . monument in the Abby [to] Mrs Boves' (*Gibbs MS*, p. 91), signed 'JACOBO GIBBS ARCHITECTO', with figures 'very well handled by Mr. *Rysbrack*' (*ABA*, p. xxiii, pl. 115; *ASH* I.22). Bovey died on 21 January 1727; permission was granted on 20 February to Mary Pope to erect the monument (according to the inscription) 'upon the payment of Twenty Guineas', which was received in 1728 (Westminster Abbey Chapter Book 8, Treasurer's Accounts, 1728, NO. 33760).

## Monument to John Sheffield, Duke of Buckingham (1648–1721) 1721–2, NE

JOHN SHEFFIELD AND KATHERINE, DUCHESS OF BUCKINGHAM

According to his published Will dated 9 August 1716 Buckingham expressed the wish that should his wife 'think fit to have any Monument bestowed on my Grave . . . I positively forbid it should cost above 500 *l*. besides and over and above the Charge of my Funeral, which I also forbid to be any Thing extraordinary', and he also composed the epitaph (*Remarks and Collections of Thomas Hearne* (Oxford Historical Society, VII), 1906, p. 226). Gibbs prepared a design (*ABA*, p. xxiii, pl. 116), but the Duke died in 1721 before work began and his widow approved another design, by Denis Plumière, which he executed with Laurent Delvaux and Peter Scheemakers by 1722 (*Dart*, I, pp. 161–4, pl. XLII; C. Avery, 'Laurent Delvaux's Sculpture in England', *National Trust Studies 1980*, 1980, pp. 150–70).

## Monument to James Craggs (1686–1721) E 1724–7 (south aisle, partly D and resited south-west transept)

ANN NEWSHAM AND ALEXANDER POPE (1688–1744)

Mrs Newsham, Craggs's sister, asked Pope early in 1724 to oversee the execution of the monument (*ASH* II.13; *VAM* E.3641-1913, in J. Physick, *Designs for English Sculpture, 1680–1860*, 1969, pp. 69–71, figs. 40–1; *Sherburn*, II, pp. 217–18). This was carved by Guelfi (*Vertue*, III, p. 74; M. Whinney, *Sculpture in Britain, 1530 to 1830*, 1964, pp. 80–1; K.

Esdaile, 'Signor Guelfi, an Italian', *Burl Mag*, November 1948, pp. 317–21; M. I. Webb, 'Giovanni Battista Guelfi: An Italian Sculptor working in England' and 'The Craggs Monument in Westminster Abbey', *Burl Mag*, May 1955, pp. 139–45, August 1955, p. 261). On 9 July 1724 Pope says Guelfi 'has not yet finished his clay model [but] has brought it to a greater degree of resemblance than I could have thought' (*Sherburn*, II, pp. 242–3); the model is in Sir John Soane's Museum (M. Brownell, *Alexander Pope & the Arts of Georgian England*, 1978, pp. 347–50, pls. 80–3). On 8 August Pope was satisfied that Guelfi should 'proceed upon the Statue forthwith' and by 13 October marble had been acquired (*Sherburn*, II, pp. 246, 266). On 22 February 1725 30 guineas was 'demanded . . . for leave to put up' the monument, on 6 February 1726 work was stopped 'till the Inscription be laid before the Dean' and on 16 February 'Mr Stanton the College Mason' was ordered to estimate costs to 'repair the Damage done to the Wall . . . by the Workmen imployed to put up' the monument; £31.10 was received in 1727 (Westminster Abbey Chapter Book 7 and Treasurer's Accounts, 1727, No. 33759). *Mist's Weekly Journal*, 17 December 1726, p. 2, reported the monument's progress (*Burney* 249b). On 20 October 1727 Pope reported that, with Francis Bird assisting, the 'statue is boxed up' and that 'it will make the finest figure . . . in the place' (*Sherburn*, II, pp. 456–7). The *Evening Journal*, 14 December 1727, announced that a 'fine white Marble Monument [was] now opened', although detailed work continued until 1728 (*Sherburn*, II, p. 484). Its original state and site are shown in R. Ackermann, *The History of the Abbey Church of St. Peter's Westminster, Its Antiquities and Monuments*, 1812, II, pp. 30–1, pl. 16; K. Esdaile, *English Monumental Sculpture since the Renaissance*, 1927, p. 160, pl. XXXIII.

## Monument to John Dryden (1632–1700) E 1720–1 (Poets' Corner), D from 1731

JOHN SHEFFIELD, DUKE OF BUCKINGHAM (1648–1721), ALEXANDER POPE (1688–1744) AND FRANCIS ADDERBURY

Gibbs 'made the . . . monument in the Abby [to] Mr Drydon' (*Gibbs MS*, p. 91). Adderbury, who supplied alternative epitaphs, asked Pope in August 1720 to 'hasten the Execution of the Design' and in September refers to 'fixing Dryden's Name only below, and his Busto above' (*Sherburn*, II, pp. 51–2, 55). The monument was on public view on 23 January 1721 (M. Brownell, *Alexander Pope & the Arts of Georgian England*, 1978, pp. 341–2, pl. 77) and in December 1721 Vertue presented the Society of Antiquaries with an engraving of the design (*SAL* Minute Book, I, p. 51), presumably the proof for either *The Antiquities of St. Peter's, or, The Abbey Church of Westminster*, 1722, II, p. 29, or *Dart*, I, pp. 90, 164, pl. IX. The sculptor is unrecorded. The original bust (lost) was replaced in 1731 by one by Peter Scheemakers (K. A. Esdaile, *English Church Monuments, 1510 to 1840*, 1946, p. 116) and the architecture was subsequently demolished.

## Monument to Dr John Freind (1675–1728) E 1730–1 (south aisle)

ROBERT FREIND*

Gibbs 'made the monument in the Abby [to] Dr Freinds' (*Gibbs MS*, p. 91), who died on 26 July 1728, which is signed on the tomb chest 'Jac: Gibbs Architecto' and 'M. Rysbrack Fecit'. Permission was granted on 7 November 1730 to install the monument 'on the East side of Mr Congreves, in the Nitch adjoining & of the like Size' for a fee of 15 guineas, which was paid in 1731 (Westminster Abbey Chapter Book 8 and Treasurer's Accounts, 1731, No. 33763). The epitaph is recorded in W. Maitland, *The History of London*, 1739, p. 1703. *ABA*, p. xxiii, pl. 117, is a similar design for a 'Monument for a Gentleman in the Country'.

### Monument to Ben Jonson (1574–1637) E *c.* 1723 (Poets' Corner)

EDWARD HARLEY, 2ND EARL OF OXFORD (1689–1741)*

Gibbs 'made the . . . monument in the Abby [to] Ben Johnson the Poet' (*Gibbs MS*, p. 91), which, signed 'J.G. ARCHI:', was 'erected at the charge of the . . . Earl of *Oxford*' and immediately illustrated in *Dart*, II, p. 61, pl. 93, later in *ABA*, p. xxiv, pl. 124 middle (*ASH* III.104; *BM* Department of Prints and Drawings 1913-12-16-11). The sculptor, although unrecorded, is generally accepted as being Michael Rysbrack (M. Whinney, *Sculpture in Britain, 1530 to 1830*, 1964, p. 256).

### Monument to John Holles, 1st Duke of Newcastle (1662–1711) E 1721–3 (north transept)

EDWARD HARLEY, 2ND EARL OF OXFORD (1689–1741),* AND HENRIETTA, COUNTESS OF OXFORD (1693–1755)*

'The Earl of Oxford employed him to build . . . the Costly and Magnificent Monument to the Late Duke of Newcastle in Westminster Abbey, which his Lordship was obliged to do, by the Dukes will' (*Gibbs MS*, p. 91). 'The Design is very grand, and executed at a great expence; the Marbles are rich, and the Figures well perform'd. This Draught was pitched upon amongst many others . . . and was executed by Mr. *Francis Bird*' (*ABA*, p. xxii, pl. 111; *ASH* I.16), who received £50 on 16 May 1721 (*BL Portland Papers Loan* 29/387: Harley's Account Book 1719–31; *Vertue*, VI, p. 64). The monument was illustrated in *Dart*, II, p. 125, pl. 142, and engraved in 1725 for *ABA*. 'My Lord Harley's accompt' for 17 May 1721 (*WS*, 1940, XVII, p. 11) lists: 'two new drawings for the monument carefully done to be adjoynd to the Contractes' £10.10.0 (*SAL* Harley Collection, VI, f. 18: 'Design for John Holles Duke of Newcastles monument executed and put up in Westr Abbey'; *WS*, 1935, XII, pl. XXXIII), 'the moddell neatly done in pear tree and the figures done in beard earth' £40 (lost) and 'several drawings for a monument and inlarging the drawght for the moddel' £21 (perhaps the preliminary studies in Sir John Soane's Museum: box titled 'Wren', folio II, no. 59, and Welbeck Abbey in *WS*, 1935, XII, pl. XXXIII; 1940, XVII, p. 11, pl. XIII top). This design replaced John Nost's proposal (J. Physick, *Designs for English Sculpture, 1680–1860*, 1969, pp. 60–1, fig. 33). The tomb chest inscription, signed 'Jacobo Gibbs Architeco', records its erection in 1723 (J. L. Chester, *The Marriage, Baptismal, and Burial Registers of the Collegiate Church or Abbey of St. Peter, Westminster*, 1876, p. 272; *GM*, October

1755, p. 440; M. Whinney, *Sculpture in Britain, 1530 to 1830*, 1964, pp. 77–8).

### Monument to Matthew Prior (1664–1721) E 1721–3 (Poets' Corner)

EDWARD HARLEY, 2ND EARL OF OXFORD (1689–1741),* AND MATTHEW PRIOR

'Mr. Prior . . . ordered by his Will 500lb to be laid out upon a Monument for him self . . . which he used to call his last peece of vanity, and desired Mr Gibbs to make a drawing . . . but he dyed soone after and never saw it, yet the Earl of Oxford, ordered the Monument to be made' (*Gibbs MS*, p. 91). 'The Marbles are very good . . . The Figures . . . are very well perform'd by Mr. *Rysbrack*, an excellent Sculptor. Mr. *Prior*'s Busto was done at *Paris* by M. *Coizivaux*' (*ABA*, pp. xxii–iii, pl. 112; *ASH* III.110). Antoine Coysevox's bust is listed in a 1721 inventory as 'done at Paris 1714' (*BL Portland Papers Loan* 29/317, f. 17) and not 1700 as given in F. Souchal, *French Sculptors of the 17th and 18th Centuries: The Reign of Louis XIV*, 1977, A–F, p. 209, no. 73; for the bust's progeny see T. Friedman and T. Clifford, *The Man at Hyde Park Corner: The Sculpture of John Cheere, 1709–1787*, 1974, nos. 57–9. The monument is signed 'Jacobo Gibbs Architecto' and 'M. RYSBRACK.F.'. Prior died on 18 September 1721, having made provision for a tomb in his Will (29/317, ff. 6–v). Hearne reported on 25 September 'there will be a stately Monument erected in the . . . Abbey . . . to which will be fixed a Bust' (*Remarks and Collections of Thomas Hearne* (Oxford Historical Society, VII), 1906, p. 283). The work is illustrated in *Dart*, I, pl. 61, and mentioned in 1723 by *Vertue* (III, p. 17; VI, p. 19).

### Monument to William Shakespeare (1564–1616) NE

Although the site of *ASH* III.101 ('For ye Monument of Shak') and *VAM* E.3640-1913 is undesignated the design was undoubtedly intended for Poets' Corner and may relate to John Rich's inauguration in 1726 of the idea for a national monument (D. Piper, '*O Sweet Mr. Shakespeare I'll have his picture*', 1964, p. 20). Nothing further was done (*Ralph*, p. 80; *GM*, May 1734, p. 246) until the promotion in 1741 by Rich, Burlington, Pope and Dr Mead which resulted in William Kent's design being executed by Peter Scheemakers (N. Ault and J. Butt, ed., *Alexander Pope: Minor Poems*, 1954, pp. 395–6; M. Whinney, *Sculpture in Britain, 1530 to 1830*, 1964, pp. 96–7, pl. 75). Gibbs owned J. Maurer's 1742 engraving of this monument (*ASH Prints* no. 58).

### Monument to John Smith (d. 1718) E 1723? (south aisle)

SIR EDWARD* AND LADY MARY DESBOUVERIE

Gibbs 'made the . . . monument in the Abby [to] Mr Smiths' (*Gibbs MS*, p. 91) with the 'Figure and Medal done by Mr. *Rysbrack*' (*ABA*, p. xxiv, pl. 22 centre; *ASH* I.47) inscribed 'in Sepulchro prope Longford Famaliae de Bouverie sacro conduntur Reliquiae' (his daughter and son-in-law) and signed on the tomb-chest 'I:G:ARCH.'. The monument was erected in time to be engraved in *Dart*, II, p. 94, pl. 114

(1723) according to a slightly different design (*ASH* III.105). *SAL* MS 263, f. 71, is perhaps another alternative.

Longleat House, *see* Wiltshire

Lowther Hall, *see* Westmorland

Maiden Bradley, All Saints, *see* Wiltshire

Marbury Hall, *see* Cheshire

## MIDDLESEX

### Cannons House E 1716–19, D 1747

JAMES BRYDGES, EARL OF CAERNARVON AND 1ST DUKE OF CHANDOS (1674–1744)*

'Chandos Ordered Mr Gibbs to rebuild his House and Chapel at Cannons, which was done at a vast Expense, the Appartments highly finished, the Chapel was reckoned the finest in England, both as to its design and Ornaments' (*Gibbs MS*, p. 87). The layout of the estate and house is recorded in a 1728 plan (*VAM* MS 86NN2, p. 139) and in I. Dunlop, 'Cannons, Middlesex: A Conjectural Reconstruction', *CL*, 30 December 1949, pp. 1950–4.

### House

The complicated rebuilding history of the Elizabethan mansion near Edgware under William Talman, John James, John Vanbrugh, James Thornhill (east front drawing dated 15 January 1717, in *Colvin*, p. 825), Gibbs and others from 1713 is described in *Baker*, pp. 114–29, 140–9, and in A. W. Ball, *The Countryside Lies Sleeping: Paintings Prints and Drawings of Pinner, Stanmore and other Former Villages now in the London Borough of Harrow, 1685–1950*, 1981, pp. 192–225. Gibbs received £5,500 between 17 August 1716 and 27 May 1719. His designs for the west and south fronts (*ASH* I.27-v, IV.12), which appear to have been modified in September 1719 on the advice of Lord Bingley, were executed during 1720–4 under John Price's supervision (*Baker*, pp. 140–3). This is the house engraved in 1720, 1731, 1736 and 1739 (*Baker*, opp. pp. 117, 124; *VB*, 1739, pls. 24–7; *BM* Maps George III Coll.XXX25b and 6.11.324.1881).

### Chapel

A plan and sections looking east and west (Greater London Record Office, Middlesex Records: Stowe Collection ACC 262/50/60–61) may relate to the material intended for *ABA* mentioned in Gibbs's 15 March 1727 'Proposal' but rejected by 1 May 1727 (Chetham Library, Manchester: Proposals and Prospectuses folder, III, nos. 866–7); *Baker*, opp. p. 125, is another plan. The opening 'on Monday last' was reported in *Mist's Weekly Journal*, 3 September 1720. The painted-glass windows and ceiling paintings were reinstalled by Gibbs in his church at WITLEY COURT after 1744; other items survive in his chapel at KIRKLEATHAM, and in Fawley church (*Colvin*, pp. 323, 341). The house and chapel were demolished in 1747 (*A Catalogue of all the Genuine Household Furniture, &c*, beginning 1 June 1747, and *A Catalogue of all the Materials of the Dwelling-House, Out-*

*Houses, &c. Of His Grace James Duke of Chandos, Deceas'd, At his late Seat call'd Cannons*, beginning 16 June 1747, in Middlesex Records: ACC 262/13).

## Chiswick

### Burlington's Villa E 1719, D after 1739

RICHARD BOYLE, 3RD EARL OF BURLINGTON (1694–1753)

Burlington's building accounts record payments of £9.9.0 to Sam Gunn 'for measuring the bricklayers and mason work' and 'in full a bill for measuring the masons and other work as by a bill of particular signed. by Mr Gibbs' (Chatsworth archives, Messers Graham and Collier Joynt Accounts, 23 June 1719 and 26 July 1722, pp. 2–4). Gibbs received £39.7.0 on 1 December 1724 and £38.18.0 on 1 July 1725 (Hoare's Bank, London: Collier's account, Ledger H, ff. 198, 354). That these references may relate to Gibbs's work at BURLINGTON HOUSE in London *c.* 1716 remains a possibility. However, J. Harris (*The Palladians*, 1981, pp. 18, 75) and C. M. Sicca ('Lord Burlington at Chiswick: Architecture and Landscape', *Garden History*, spring 1982, X, No. 1, p. 38) associate these payments with the 'Pavillion au bout de la Grande Allée', which was 'covered with lead' by 22 October 1719 (Chatsworth archives, Graham Correspondence, 154.1) and recorded in a 1728 estate plan (*VAM* MS86NN2, pp. 137–8), *VB*, 1739, pls. 82–3, a contemporary painting (J. Harris, *The Artist and the Country House*, 1979, p. 158, pls. 187f, 189) and G. L. Le Rouge, *Nouveaux jardins à la mode*, 1776, cahier I (D. Wiebenson, *The Picturesque Garden in France*, 1978, pl. 87).

### Duchess of Norfolk's Villa E after 1746, D 1832

MARIA SHIREBURN, DOWAGER DUCHESS OF NORFOLK (d. 1754)

Gibbs 'repaired and made additions to her Villa at Cheswick upon the Thames' (*Gibbs MS*, p. 97), a Jacobean fabric, later called Corney House (J. Hayes, *Catalogue of the Oil Paintings in the London Museum*, 1970, pp. 116–17, pl. 61), which passed from Peregrine Widdrington to his widow the Dowager Duchess in 1747 (T. Faulkner, *The History and Antiquities of Brentford, Ealing, & Chiswick*, 1845, pp. 368–70; W. P. W. Phillimore and W. H. Whitear, *Historical Collections Relating to Chiswick*, 1897, pp. 29, 244). There is no pictorial record of these improvements.

### Dawley Farm E 1725–8, D *c.* 1770

HENRY ST JOHN, 1ST VISCOUNT BOLINGBROKE (1678–1751)*

Gibbs 'new models Dawley for Lord Bolingbrooke, and made large additions . . . He made it a most delightfull place, and laid out a great deal of money upon it. He [Bolingbroke] used to call it his Farme and inded it is one of the finest Farme houses in England, But his Lordship being obliged to go to France, sold it for a great deal less money than it cost the building' (*Gibbs MS*, p. 89). In 1725 Bolingbroke purchased the estate shown in *Britannia Illustrata*, 1707, pl. 48, and internal redecoration of the house was carried out by 1728 (*Sherburn*, II, pp. 290, 503, 525; H. T. Dickinson, *Bolingbroke*, 1970, pp. 173–8). J.

Rocque, *Carte Topographique de la comte de Middlesex*, 1754, shows a tripartite plan of house and service blocks round a circular court, like *ABA*, pl. 64. *ASH* III.90 is a 'Bridge for Lord Bolingbrooke' with the 'Level of ye Bridg 14ft above the door of ye House' estimated at £400 'all included'. The estate was sold in 1738–9 for £26,000 (*Sherburn*, IV, p. 177) and by 1802 there was not 'a vestige left' (*GM*, August 1802, II, pp. 724–5; D. Jacques, 'The Art and Sense of the Scriblerus Club in England, 1715–35', *Garden History*, 1976, IV, No. 1, pp. 45–8; W. Walford, *Greater London*, 1894, I, pp. 201–3).

## Isleworth

### Gumley House (now the Convent of the Faithful Companions of Jesus) E BY 1729

JOHN GUMLEY (d. 1729)*

Gibbs 'made Additions to Mr Gumleys ... at Isleworth' (*Gibbs MS*, p. 88), presumably the Twickenham Road piers and screen-wall and the pair of Doric colonnades flanking the entrance courtyard (M. Jourdain and R. Edwards, *Georgian Cabinet-Makers*, 1944, pp. 20–2, fig. 9; *VCH Middlesex*, 1962, III, pp. 91–2, 130, 135).

### Shrewsbury House E 1718–22, D c. 1810

GEORGE TALBOT, 14TH EARL OF SHREWSBURY (d. 1733)

Gibbs 'built at Isleworth upon the Bank of the Thames a Villa for the Earl of Shrewsbury, a very convenient habitation' (*Gibbs MS*, p. 89). The building recorded in C. Tomkin's views of 1795–6 (Guildhall Library, London: Wakefield Collection; *A House in the Country*, 1971, Sabine Gallery, no. 94) was a remodelling of the fabric inherited in 1718 (*The Life and Character of Charles Duke of Shrewsbury. In a Letter to a Noble Lord. By a Gentleman*, 1718, pp. 35–6). This was described soon after as a 'little Seat, finely adorn'd with the Tapestry, and other Ornaments, brought by the late Duke [of Shrewsbury], during his Embassy in *France*' (*Macky 1722*, I, p. 72). Its later history is mentioned in *VCH Middlesex*, 1962, III, pp. 91, 130, and Hounslow Public Library: 942.114/VF/ISL.180.

### Somerset House D 1803

SIR JOHN CHESHIRE

Gibbs 'made Additions to ... Sr John-Chesters house at Isleworth' (*Gibbs MS*, p. 88). Cheshire was a resident of Somerset House mentioned in local records from 1719 (Hounslow Public Library), but of the building's appearance nothing is known.

### Stanwell House E by 1750, partly D

RICHARD PHILLIPS (1661–1750)*

Gibbs 'made additions to Governor Phillips seat at Stanwell' (*Gibbs MS*, p. 88), of which only a group of spectacular gate piers and carved stone vases survive; these resemble vases advertised by the Bath carver Joseph Greenway (T. Friedman, 'A Decorative Sculptor's Trade Card', *Leeds Arts Calendar*, 1974, No. 75, pp. 29–32, fig. 1) whose family worked for Gibbs at CLIVEDEN. Phillips was governor of Nova Scotia in 1717–49 but resided in England from 1722 (F.-J. Audet, 'Lieutenant Governors and Administrators of Nova Scotia, 1604–1932', MS, Library of the Public Archives of Nova Scotia).

## Twickenham

### Cross Deep House E

BARNABY BACKWELL

Gibbs 'new moddled Mr Backwells the Bankers house' (*Gibbs MS*, p. 88), described as a 'good house [with an] extensive, beautiful, and picturesque' view (*Miscellaneous Antiquities, (in Continuation of the Bibliotheca Topographia Britannia,) No VI. Containing Mr. Ironside's History of Twickenham*, 1797, p. 86) and frequently engraved (M. Brownell and J. Simon, *Alexander Pope's Villa*, 1980, cat. nos. 2, 18). The flanking canted bays are similar to *ASH* III.48. Backwell was elected a governor of St Bartholomew's Hospital in 1745 (*Bart's Journal Ha* 1/11, p. 416).

### Johnston's Octagon (now Orleans House Gallery) E c. 1716–21

JAMES JOHNSTON (1655–1737)*

Craftsmen: Giuseppe Artari and Giovanni Bagutti, plasterers; Charles Griffith, joiner (*ABA*, p. xix; *Beard 1981*, pp. 243–4, 262).

Gibbs 'built ... Secretary Johnstons fine Room at Twickenham [in] 1720 ... the fine fretwork done by the Italian plasterers, the Ornaments all gilt, it is plesantly situated upon the River Thames, and has fine prospects from it, he designd it for an intertaineing Room, his house being too small for that purpose' (*Gibbs MS*, p. 88). The design (*ABA*, p. xix, pl. 71; *ASH* I.40; *VAM* E.3615 and 3620-1913, in T. Friedman, *James Gibbs, 1682–1754: 'a man of great Fame'*, 1982, pp. 33–5, illus.; C. Hussey, *English Country Houses: Early Georgian*, 1955, pl. 35) seems to have been prepared by 1716 (*HMC Stuart*, II, p. 93). The pavilion, still detached from the house, is shown in Mar's October 1721 estate plan (*SRO* Mar and Kellie deposit, RHP 13256, no. 89) and described by *Macky 1722*, I, pp. 63–4, and *Defoe 1725*, II, pp. 12–13. Gibbs may also have designed the greenhouse, perhaps as a result of a fire 'which burnt done some Out-houses and Offices' (*Weekly Journal or Saturday Post*, 17 November 1722, p. 1241). In 1737 the estate contained the house (D 1926–7), offices, stables, dovehouses, a coach house, a 'commodious Icehouse' and 'a large Octogon, with two small Rooms adjoining A large Kitchen, A Scullery, A Laudry, A Room for Fruit, And three or four pretty good Bedchambers, Vaults under the Octogon' (Dorset *CRO* D 396/T813). C. Musgrave, 'The Octagon', *Connoisseur*, October 1956, pp. 80–1; J. Walker, 'The Thames through 18th-Century Eyes', *CL*, 3 July 1969, pp. 24–7.

**House** E by 1750, D

SIR CHALONER OGLE (d. 1750)

Gibbs 'repared the house and built a fine Room for Sr Chaloner Ogle' (*Gibbs MS*, p. 88), the residence later called Chapel House and Holyrood House on the north side of Montpellier Row (R. S. Cobbett, *Memorials of Twickenham: Parochial and Topographical*, 1872, p. 376).

**Pope's Villa** E 1719–20, D 1807–8

ALEXANDER POPE (1688–1744)

Gibbs 'made additions to Mr Popes Villa at Twickenham' (*Gibbs MS*, p. 88) which is mentioned in his letter to the poet of spring 1719: 'the designes shall be ready for you to aprove or disaprove' and in another from Pope dated 1 May 1720: 'My Building rises high enough to attract the eye' (*Sherburn*, II, pp. 4, 44). This is presumably the small house painted by Peter Tillemans *c.* 1730, before Burlington's(?) portico addition (*Sherburn*, III, p. 356) shown in subsequent views (M. Brownell and J. Simon, *Alexander Pope's Villa*, 1980; M. Mack, *The Garden and the City*, 1969). For Gibbs's other associations with the poet, see M. R. Brownell, *Alexander Pope & the Arts of Georgian England*, 1978.

Whitchurch, St Lawrence

**New Monument Room** E 1735–6

JAMES BRYDGES, 1ST DUKE OF CHANDOS (1674–1744)*

Benjamin Timbrell estimated the cost of the addition to rehouse the family monuments at £170 based on a plan by the Duke's secretary James Farquharson, which Gibbs may have improved; he also supplied his own design (lost) and superintended construction (*Baker*, pp. 414–17). This interior was painted by G. Brunetti *c.* 1736 (*Croft-Murray*, II, p. 177).

**Whitton Place** E 1725–31, D by 1935

ARCHIBALD CAMPBELL, EARL OF ILAY (1682–1761)*

Designs for the '*Villa at Whitton* . . . propos'd to be of Stone, and . . . Brick finish'd over with Stucco', one with 'Offices under-ground [and] the Kitchin and Servants Hall . . . in Courts without-doors' (*ABA*, pp. xvi–ii, pls. 59–60, 62; *ASH* I.35–6; *VAM* E.3612-1913: a five bay variation) were rejected in favour of Roger Morris's design of 1731–2 (*Colvin*, p. 561; Coutt's Bank, London: Ilay's account, Ledgers 1729–31, ff. 101–2, 137; 1736–8, f. 128). Work on the garden apparently began in 1723 (J. Kalm, *Kalm's Account of his Visit to England on his way to America in 1748*, 1892, pp. 57–8); *Willis*, pp. 77–8, suggests Charles Bridgeman was involved. Of the buildings illustrated on the estate plans (*BL* King's Maps K.XXX, 21-a; Hounslow Public Library: MS 942, 114/VF/WP.1) and noted in D. Croft, *A Particular of the Noble Large House, Gardens, the Tower, Temples, and other Buildings and Erections, of The Late Duke of Argyll, Situate at Whitton*, 17 July 1756, accompanied by a plan (*Bodleian* Gough Maps 18, f. 5r; Guildhall Library, London: Fo.Pam 1330) Gibbs perhaps designed the 'Vollery' mentioned on 10 June 1725 (National Library of

Scotland: Saltoun Papers, letters) and the 'Round Temple supported by two rowes of pillars' mentioned on 20 May 1733 (*SRO* Clerk of Penicuik Papers GD 18/2110, p. 18). He also designed the 'little House' (*ABA*, p. xvi, pl. 61; *ASH* I.39) and the Greenhouse (*ASH* III.88–90: 'Lord Ilay'), for 'Islay ordered him to build his green house at Whitten, with several Rooms behind it for offices, and lodging Rooms over it . . . built with Rustick Arches, like to Covent Garden, the Arches are fitted with strong shafhes and the front . . . being exposed to the south side gives a great heat to the exotic plants' (*Gibbs MS*, p. 88), which is mentioned on 6 March 1725 (Saltoun Papers, letters) and on 9 April 1727 (*SRO* GD 18/2107, pp. 17–18) but was later remodelled (1768, D *c.* 1935). The adjacent sundial shown in W. Woollett's 'A View of the Canal and the Gothic Tower' (1757) must also be by Gibbs (M. Cosh, 'Lord Ilay's Eccentric Schemes', *CL*, 20 July 1972, pp. 142–5, figs. 3–7; P. Foster and D. H. Simpson, *Whitton Park and Whitton Place*, 1979; B. Gascoigne and J. Ditchburn, *Images of Twickenham with Hampton and Teddington*, 1981, pp. 86–7, 243–4; *The Practical Examplar of Architecture*, 3rd series, n.d., pl. 93).

Milton House, *see* Northamptonshire

Mitcham, SS. Peter and Paul, *see* Surrey

Mount Morris, *see* Kent

Netheravon House, *see* Wiltshire

New Place, East Barnet, *see* Hertfordshire

NORFOLK

**Houghton Hall** E *c.* 1727–35

SIR ROBERT WALPOLE, 1ST EARL OF ORFORD (1675–1745)*

The change from Campbell's original idea of corner 'Wilton' towers (*VB*, 1725, pls. 29–30) in favour of domes (I. Ware, *The Plans, Elevations and Sections of Houghton in Norfolk*, 1735; J. Harris, *Catalogue of the Drawings Collection of the Royal Institute of British Architects: Colen Campbell*, 1973, pp. 10–11, nos. 12–13, figs. 33–5) was made, according to Edward Harley writing in 1732, 'by Mr. Gibbs from the first design. The house as it is now is a composition of the greatest blockheads and most ignorant fellows in architecture that are. I think Gibbs was to blame to alter any of their designs or mend their blunders' (*HMC Portland*, VI, p. 160). The south-east dome has a wind-vane dated 1727 (J. Harris, 'The Prideaux Collection of Topographical Drawings', *AH*, 1964, VII, pp. 29–30, fig. 50); *The Muse's Commission To the Right Honourable Sir Robert Walpole, At Houghton-Hall*, 1732 (*BL* C.116.i.4(13)) refers to 'his *Dome*, With the hugh *Lanthorn*', while a 1735 visitor noted 'a round turret at each corner' (*BL* Add. MS 15776, ff. 61–6).

NORTH YORKSHIRE (formerly North Riding of
Yorkshire)

Nunnington, All Saints and St James
**Monument to William, 4th Lord Widdrington (1678–
1743)** E *c.* 1743

KATHERINE, LADY WIDDRINGTON

The monument, a simple wall tablet crowned by a broken pediment signed 'IACOBO GIBBS ARCHI:', has an inscription recording
its erection by the deceased's second wife. The carver is unrecorded. The monument to William's brother Peregrine Widdrington (1692–1749) at Great Mitton, West Yorkshire, set up
by his wife Maria, Dowager Duchess of Norfolk (see LONDON,
16 ARLINGTON STREET), is based on *ABA*, pl. 123 left.


NORTHAMPTONSHIRE


**Kelmarsh Hall** E 1728–32

WILLIAM HANBURY (d. 1768)*

Gibbs 'built... Mr Hanberys House near Northampton' (*Gibbs
MS*, p. 90), describing it in 1728 as 'now building' (*ABA*, p. x)
although not following the design shown in the accompanying
pl. 38 (*ASH* I.10) but rather in *RIBA*: K3/12, 5–35 (an album
of plans, elevations and sections formerly deposited in the
house, *Friedman 1973*, pp. 21–2, figs. 18–19). This includes views
of the old and new houses used for engravings by J. Mynde
later published in J. Bridges, *The History and Antiquities of
Northamptonshire*, 1791, II, opp. p. 40. The carcass was finished
by 1732 (dated rainwater-head). Only Gibbs's hall and staircase survived James Wyatt's *c.* 1778 internal alterations (A.
Oswald, 'Kelmarsh Hall', *CL*, 25 February 1933, pp. 198–203;
*Colvin*, pp. 407, 947).


**Milton House** 1726, NE

JOHN, 2ND EARL OF FITZWILLIAM (*c.* 1685–1728)*

Gibbs 'made a great many drawings for Lord Fitzwilliams
House near Peterburough, but that Nobleman dying [8 August
1728] they wer not executed' (*Gibbs MS*, p. 90). These included
*ABA*, pp. xiii–xiv, pls. 48–51; *ASH* I.18–9, 27, II.21; Northamptonshire *CRO* Fitzwilliam Papers, Milton, plans 59–77 in
an album titled 'Plans & Elevations for a House Earl Fitzwilliam 1726', which together represent at least eight different
schemes. *ASH* II.21 is for gatepiers perhaps related to work by
the smiths James Montigny and Thomas Johnson (both *ABA*
subscribers) carried out in 1725–7 (Fitzwilliam Papers, letters
1710–44, drawings 43–4, 52–4, 85; C. Hussey, 'Milton', *CL*,
18 May 1916, p. 1150, fig. 6). For earlier schemes for the house
(*Colvin*, pp. 797–8, 805, 932) including work by Robert Wright,
1723–5, and an unidentified imitator of Gibbs's published
designs, see letters 1710–44, drawings 58, 78–9, 135, 150, 155–6,
map 1966.


Nunnington, All Saints and St James, *see* North Yorkshire

Old Windsor, *see* Berkshire


OXFORDSHIRE

**Adderbury House** 1734–40, NE

JOHN CAMPBELL, 2ND DUKE OF ARGYLL AND GREENWICH
(1680–1743)*

Although Horace Walpole was uncertain if the 'large but very
inconvenient House' was by Campbell or Gibbs (*Toynbee*,
p. 66)—it appears to have been designed by Roger Morris,
working with Edward Shepherd, Benjamin Timbrell, and John
and William Townesend during 1731–44 (*Colvin*, p. 561;
Coutts Bank, London: Argyll's account, Ledgers 16, f. 2; 17,
f. 1; 1740–2, f. 151; 18, f. 1; 1744–5)—references to 'Ja: Gibb's
bill on John Rashleigh' for £300 on 19 October 1734 and a
payment of £64.14.9 on 13 June 1740 (Letter Book 19, f. 581;
Ledger 17, f. 2) suggests Gibbs was involved in some capacity,
perhaps in connection with his schemes for an addition to the
old fabric and for new garden features (*SRO* Buccleuch MS,
RHP 13766–8, 13772; M. Cosh, 'Two Dukes and their Houses',
*CL*, 13 July 1972, p. 80, fig. 5). The house, described in 1740
as 'a new thing' with a 'very high-finished' gallery but 'no grand
Stair-case' (*Markham*, p. 334), was much remodelled in the
nineteenth century (*Colvin*, p. 207; G. Nares, 'Adderbury', *CL*,
7 January 1949, pp. 30–2).


**Ditchley House** E 1720–7

GEORGE HENRY LEE, 2ND EARL OF LICHFIELD (1691–1742)*

Craftsmen: Giuseppe and Adalbertus Artari, Francesco Serena
and Francesco Vassali, ornamental plasterers; William Baker,
joiner; Andrew Carpenter, sculptor; John Hiron, Christopher
Horsenaile and Edward Stanton, masons; William Kent,
decorative painter; ?Morrise, carpenter; Joshua Needham,
plain plasterer; Francis Smith, mason-contractor (*DIL* I/p/1h,
I/p/5; *Beard 1981*, pp. 22, 81, 102 and Part III; *Croft-Murray*,
II, p. 233; *Colvin*, pp. 419, 750; *Gunnis*, p. 210).

Gibbs 'built ... Ditchly ... with its' Offices, which proves a
very Convenient, and usefull building' (*Gibbs MS*, p. 96). Lichfield succeeded to the estate in 1716 and had demolished the
old house by 1718 (G. Green, *Lord Rochester's Monkey*, 1976,
p. 15). A design by Tinley(?) of 1720 for the new house (*Colvin*,
p. 828) was discarded in favour of one by Gibbs (*VAM* E.3605-
1913), which he subsequently altered to the composition as
built (*ASH* I.10; *VAM* E.3603-1913; *ABA*, pp. x–xi, pl. 39). In
turn a modification of this scheme represented by an untraced
plan and elevation incorporating domed corner cupolas (A.
Oswald, 'Ditchley', *CL*, 9 June 1934, p. 592, figs. 5, 7) seems
to be that referred to in Smith's letters of 4 May 1720 and 19
December 1721: 'a Schetch of the office buildings which I hope
you will deliver to him [Lichfield] assoon as you can ... if it
be to his Lordships liking I shall be very Glad And if not Ile
endeavour assoon as I can ... to make what alterations he shall
think most proper' (I/p/1a and c). An estimate of £2,187.5.0
'for the Building the Carcase of a house ... at Ditchly ...
according to a draught given in by ffrancis Smith' (I/p/1d) was
outflanked by one 'according to a Draught given in by Mr
Gibbs' for £1,975 (I/p/1e). The finished carcass (rainwater-
head dated 1722) received Carpenter's pair of lead figures on
the roof in 1722–3 (I/p/4x). Smith acted as contractor (I/p/1l).

A drawing by Gibbs for the north wall of the hall, with a partial plan (Ashmolean Museum, Oxford: Miscellaneous 18th century English Architecture, bought Christie's, 2 April 1943, lot 42) shows a variant decorative treatment which incorporates some features as executed. Gibbs also designed the saloon, and the plasterwork ceiling of the Tapestry Room (*ASH* II.14). Payments for building and decorating the main apartments are recorded to Smith and Hiron (I/p/1c, e, h, l, n, q), Stanton and Horsenaile (I/p/3bg), 'The Italian Plaisterer's Account, for worke Done by them, in severall room's att Ditchley' totalling £201.12.0 (I/p/3g, h i-iii,n, r) and Kent 'for the middle picture in his great Hall' (I/p/4an). In 1734 'one half the house below Stairs [was] not yet fitted up' (*Markham*, p. 173). William Smith and Henry Flitcroft decorated further rooms between 1736 and 1760 (I/p/1t, x; I/p/3f). Gibbs 'gave likewise several [unidentified] drawings for temples, for the woods in the park, as also Triumphal Arches for the Termination of the three long Vistas, cut through the woods, seen from the House' (*Gibbs MS*, p. 96). The layout is indicated on an estate plan of 1726 'Surveyed and Plotted by Edw. Grantham' (I/i/2a–b; G. Jellicoe, 'Ronald Tree and the Gardens at Ditchley Park: The Human Face of History', *Garden History*, spring 1982, X, No. 1, pp. 80–90), and workmen were paid in 1729 for 'moving the Rubill & Laying of Hils' (I/p/8). Drawings for triumphal arches perhaps related to this unexecuted scheme are *ASH* II.88, III.41; *VAM* D.1162-'98, E.3626-1913. In 1734 there were 'no Gardens ... but a very pretty Terrace is almost finished to a back-front' (*Markham*, p. 173). Anon., 'Description of Ditchley', *Oxford Magazine*, September 1772, IX, pp. 101–3, illus.; Anon., *The New Oxford Guide*, 1759, pp. 108–14; C. Hussey, *English Country Houses: Early Georgian*, 1955, pp. 66–71; T. Martyn, *The English Connoisseur*, 1767, I, pp. 30–4; A. Oswald, 'Ditchley', *CL*, 9 and 16 June 1934, pp. 590–5, 622–8; G. W. Whiteman, *Some Famous English Country Houses*, 1951, pp. 121–30.

## Heythrop Hall E after 1718, gutted 1831, remodelled 1870

CHARLES TALBOT, 14TH EARL OF SHREWSBURY (d. 1733)

The house, which the client inherited in 1718 (*The Life and Character of Charles Duke of Somerset. In a Letter to a Noble Lord. By a Gentleman*, 1718, pp. 35–6), had been built in 1707 by Thomas Archer and Francis Smith (*BL* Add. MS 40776, ff. 55v–6, 61, 63) but was still being decorated in 1722 (the 'great Stair-case and Apartments above, were not quite finished when I was there' wrote *Macky 1722*, II, pp. 119–21) and as late as 1735 (*BL* Add. MS 5842, f. 130v; 47030, ff. 83–v). Gibbs 'finished the inside of his House in Oxford shire' (*Gibbs MS*, p. 89). However, the illustrations in *VB*, 1771, pls. 82–3, and descriptions prior to the fire in 1831 which gutted the interior (*Markham*, pp. 174–5; E. J. Climenson, *Passages from the Diary of Mrs. Philip Lybbe Powys*, 1899, pp. 199–200, visiting in 1778) give no precise clues to the character of Gibbs's contribution.

## Kirtlington Park 1741, NE

SIR JAMES DASHWOOD, 2ND BARONET (1715–79)

'Mr: Gibbs, Architect' received £30 for a set of drawings, including a group labelled 'Plans of a House by Gibbs', on 25 September 1741; on the same day Daniel Garrett was paid £26.6.0 ('A Generall Account of Money Expended on my New-house, and the outworks about it, begun 12th: September 1741', in private collection). William Smith also submitted a design and on 29 April 1742 received £210 towards building the house in collaboration with William Hiorn and John Sanderson, 1742–59; the total cost was £32,388.8.0 (*Colvin*, pp. 333, 716, 763; C. Hussey, *English Country Houses: Early Georgian*, 1955, pp. 170–4; P. Remington, 'A Mid-Georgian Interior from Kirtlington Park', *Metropolitan Museum of Art Bulletin*, March 1956, pp. 157–69; J. Townsend, *The Oxfordshire Dashwoods*, 1922, pp. 22–6).

Oxford

### All Souls College
## Codrington Library E 1740–50

THE PRINCIPAL AND FELLOWS

On 18 April 1740 Gibbs advised on remodelling the bookshelves left unfinished by Nicholas Hawksmoor in 1736 (*Downes*, pp. 141–3, pl. 49a) by replacing his idea of an attic with 'a Modilion Cornich [of] the Ionick Order, with a handsome Pedestall over it, for Bustos, Vases, and Balls ... something like the Rough Sketch here below' (College Archives: All Souls MS D.D.c.256, no. 79). The scheme was approved on 4 November 1741 and executed under Richard Tawney's contract of 9 December 1748. In 1749–50 John Cheere supplied 25 vases and 24 busts in bronzed plaster for the cornice (All Souls MS 401 (b), ff. 179r–80v, 185v; *VCH Oxfordshire*, 1965, III, p. 191; T. Friedman and T. Clifford, *The Man at Hyde Park Corner: Sculpture by John Cheere, 1709–1787*, 1974, no. 22, App. B). H. Walpole, *Anecdotes of Painting in England*, 1771, p. 46, and A. à Wood, *The History and Antiquities of the University of Oxford*, 1796, II, Part 2, p. 976, may have had the above commission in mind when attributing All Souls to Gibbs rather than to Nicholas Hawksmoor.

## Magdalen College 1728–32, NE

THE PRESIDENT AND FELLOWS

According to the College archives (*MCL* correspondence, accounts and plans relating to the New Buildings, *c.* 1720–40) Edward Holdsworth, an amateur architect associated with Magdalen (J. Dallaway, *Anecdotes of the Arts in England*, 1800, p. 114), reported from London on 13 January 1728 that he had shown his 'very incorrect' designs for the new College buildings to Gibbs, but noted on 15 March that they would not be ready until 'next winter'. On 21 April he mentions 'laying the plan before Mr Gibbs' and paying 20 guineas 'for his advice and assistance', and on 7 May the features 'approv'd of by ... Mr Gibbs [who has] undertaken to revise' the design. Holdsworth noted on 19 August 1729 'Some mistakes ... committed in my absence [which] will soon be rectified' and on 8 September having to 'inspect the fair Drawings ... almost evry day [by] Berlow' (Gibbs's draughtsman John Borlach) and leaving them 'in such forwardness ... to prepare the work for the Engraver'. A plan and bird's-eye view mentioned in *MCL* (letters of 15 August and 27 November 1731, 19 April 1732, 1 March 1735) were published in the *University Almanacks* for 1730–1

(H. M. Petter, *The Oxford Almanacks*, 1974, pp. 57–8) and in W. Williams, *Oxonia Depicta*, 1732; a separate scheme by an unknown architect also appeared in the latter (H. Colvin, *Unbuilt Oxford*, 1983, figs. 85–7, 90). These seem to have been issued under Holdsworth's direction, since '6 Drawings of the whole College to send abroad', where he went in 1729, are mentioned in Speakman's bill of 18 October 1729 and in letters of 27 October 1743 and 31 January 1744 from Rome (*MCL* 906 iii–iv). This information casts doubt on George Clarke's authorship of the scheme as suggested in *VCH The University of Oxford*, 1954, III, p. 206, and H. M. Colvin, *A Catalogue of Architectural Drawings of the 18th and 19th Centuries in the Library of Worcester College, Oxford*, 1964, pp. xxi–ii, nos. 86, 146–8, pls. 91–3, although revised in his *Unbuilt Oxford*, 1983, pp. 78–86, as a result of newly discovered documents. Of this grand project only the New Buildings were erected. A 'Plan of the New building . . . contracted according to the Scheme deliv'd in by Mr Townshend' on 8 November 1730 was approved 1 February 1731, William Townesend being ordered on 28 July to 'consult Mr Gibbs & Mr [Francis] Smith' (*MCL* Order Book 1708–86; *Colvin*, p. 835). Gibbs discussed the 'Estimat of intended Building according to Mr Townsends Proposals' on 11 February 1733 (*MCL*). The foundation-stone was laid on 27 September. For Nicholas Hawksmoor's involvement from 1724, see H. Colvin, *Unbuilt Oxford*, 1983, pp. 78–85, figs. 84, 88–9; *Downes*, pp. 154–5, fig. 31, pl. 51a; *MCL* 906 i–ii, letters of 25 March and 11 April 1734.

### Radcliffe Library E 1720–54

RADCLIFFE TRUSTEES

Principal craftsmen: Joseph (Giuseppe) Artari, Thomas Roberts, Charles Stanley, ornamental plasterers; Robert Bakewell and Thomas Wagg, smiths; Thomas Brockley, locksmith; Jeremiah Franklin and John Phillips, carpenters; William and John Green, painters; Thomas Jersey and George Shakespeare, clerks of the works; William Linnell, carver; Michael Rysbrack, sculptor; Francis and William Smith, John and William Townesend, masons (*BR*, p. 5; *Gillam*, pp. 1–112, 181; Hoare's Bank, London: Radcliffe trustees' account Ledger R, ff. 278–9). The trustees are listed in *BR*, p. 5.

Gibbs 'designd and erected this Library, being a beautyfull Building' (*Gibbs MS*, pp. 99–100, which quotes the foundation-stone inscription ending 'Jacobo Gibbs Architecto'). *Gillam* reprints the building contracts for 1737–59 and relevant extracts from the trustees' Minute Books for 1720–54 (pp. 1–112, 180) together with a catalogue of drawings (pp. 147–79), which is summarized here.

Rectangular designs: *ASH* I.117–32 (*Gillam*, pp. 162–6, pls. 18–27) consisting of three alternative designs for a large rectangular building are perhaps related to the trustees' suggestion on 27 July 1720 to invite Gibbs, one of 'the ablest architects [to] be apply'd too, for draughts' (*Gillam*, p. 99), although H. Colvin, *Unbuilt Oxford*, 1983, pp. 69–73, prefers a date of 1734–5 for this group.

Pantheon design: *ASH* II.101–3 (*Little*, pl. 25) and a variant plan in *ASH* III.36 (*Gillam*, pp. 161–2, pl. 16b) represents

a Pantheon-like building perhaps related to a payment to Gibbs of £42 on 29 May 1735 for 'drawing plans' (*Gillam*, pp. 100, 180).

Final designs: Gibbs took over as architect after Nicholas Hawksmoor's death on 25 March 1736 and subsequently prepared a series of alternative designs on the rotunda theme. Those published by Gibbs in *Bibliotheca Radcliffiana*, 1737, and *Bibliotheca Radcliffiana MDCCXL* as well as *ASH* III.71–6, 78–80; *BL* Add. MS 31323 JJJ and KKK; *Bodleian* MS Don.a.7, f. 12, and the stone model of the dome now at St Giles' House, Oxford (*Gillam*, pp. 166–75, pls. 28–33, 36, 37b–8), relate to a payment to Gibbs of £40 on 4 May 1737 ('altering Drafts and making new plans') and £105 on 10 February 1738 ('drawing further plans and for Journeys to Oxford'), for which George Vertue prepared engravings between March 1737 and February 1741 (*Gillam*, pp. 100–3, 180), and to Townesend's estimate on 12 March 1737 of £15087.10.11½ 'on a Supposition that the Body of the Building is to be adorned with Columns' and £14932.15.2½ 'If the Columns are reduced to Pilasters' (*Gillam*, pp. 1, 100). The former 'three quarter collumns according to Mr Gibbs's last plan' was approved on 21 April 1738 (*Gillam*, p. 101). An agreement of 14 July 1738 stated that 'Mr Gibbs shall have one Hundred pounds a year for [designing] & supervising the Building . . . & drawing all plans . . . & Corresponding wh the Builders & going down four times in Every year to see the Building . . . & to Continue for so many years as the Trustees shall think proper to Employ him' (*Bodleian* MS Autog.c.9, f. 107, c. 19, ff. 1–3; Hoare's Bank, London: trustees' account Ledger R, f. 278). Gibbs, Francis Smith and William Townesend discussed the construction on 4 March 1737 (*Gillam*, p. 100). The foundation-stone was laid on 16 June (*BR*, p. 6). Final alterations to the design were agreed on 8 March 1740 although the dome changed its form between February and April 1741 (*Gillam*, pp. 103–4). The progress of construction is reported in *Gillam*, pp. xiv–xxi, 1–112. The finished building is shown in *Bibliotheca Radcliviana: or, A Short Description of the Radcliffe Library, at Oxford*, 1747; *ASH* I.106–16, III.38, 77, 81 (*Gillam* pp. 109, 175–9, pls. 34–5, 37a, 39–47) and Badminton House archives (alternative design for gates).

*ASH* I.111 and III.82 relate to Rysbrack's contract of 21 March 1745 to 'make a figure . . . in Statuary Marble Six foot high . . . finished according to the model agreed on', which was completed by spring 1746 (*BR*, p. 10, pl. XII; Hoare's Bank, London: trustees' account Ledger R, f. 279; *Gillam*, pp. xviii, 62–3, 68, pls. 51, 59). The Library opened in April 1749 (*Gillam*, pp. xxi–iii; H. M. Petter, *The Oxford Almanacks*, 1974, pp. 66–7; S. G. Gillam, 'The Radcliffe Library', *VCH The University of Oxford*, 1954, pp. 55–6; S. Lang, 'By Hawksmoor Out of Gibbs', *AR*, April 1949, pp. 183–90).

St John's College
### Hall screen E 1743

THE PRESIDENT AND FELLOWS

Gibbs received £5.5.0 in 1743 'for Plans [lost] of the Hall Screen' which divided the Hall and Buttery and was erected by John Townesend (d. 1746) for £144.19.3. Thomas(?)

Stevens was paid £30.14.6 on 10 September 'for the Hall Gate, & Carriage' (College archives: Computus Annuus, 1743, ff. 45, 47, Bills and Receipts). Described as being 'in the modern Taste, with great Elegance' (*Defoe 1761*, II, p. 245), it replaced the 1616 screen (*CL*, 2 November 1929, p. 610, fig. 8).

Patshull Hall, *see* Staffordshire

Patshull, St Mary, *see* Staffordshire

## PERTHSHIRE

**Dupplin Castle** by 1719, NE

THOMAS HAY, 6TH EARL OF KINNOULL (d. 1719)

A proof engraving, perhaps for a rejected plate in *ABA*, in the George Clarke Collection YC 20, 5 (H. M. Colvin, *A Catalogue of Architectural Drawings of the 18th and 19th Centuries in the Library of Worcester College, Oxford*, 1964, p. xxv, pl. 116), inscribed 'J. G. delin et scul:' and with a reference to the client, presumably represents an unexecuted design for Dupplin Castle, which was rebuilt *c.* 1720–5 by James Smith (*Colvin*, p. 758). The engraved design may conceivably have been for George Hay, 7th Earl of Kinnoull's English estate at Brodsworth, Yorkshire, where Gibbs visited him in 1718 (*HMC Stuart*, V, p. 378) but where as late as 1757 there was still 'neither house nor garden [only] the sweetest Woods imaginable' (Leeds City Archives Department, Vyner Papers 13634).

Petersham (Sudbrook House), *see* Surrey

Pope's Villa, *see* Middlesex, Twickenham

Quarrel House, *see* Stirlingshire

Raby Castle, *see* County Durham

Ragley Hall, *see* Warwickshire

Roehampton (House for Bartholomew Clarke and Hitch Young), *see* Surrey

Sacombe Park, *see* Hertfordshire

Shipbourne (Fairlawne), *see* Kent

Shrewsbury House, *see* Middlesex, Isleworth

## SOMERSET

**Witham Park** *c.* 1717, NE

SIR WILLIAM WYNDHAM, BARONET (1687–1740)*

William Talman (J. Harris, 'The Transparent Portico', *AR*, February 1958, pp. 108–9, fig. 11; *RIBA* volume of drawings for *VB*, 1717), George Clarke, Nicholas Hawksmoor and James Thornhill (H. M. Colvin, *A Catalogue of Architectural Drawings*

*of the 18th and 19th Centuries in the Library of Worcester College, Oxford*, 1964, cat. nos. 318–20, pls. 119–21) each proposed solutions for remodelling the main front of the medieval house at Witham Friary (J. Collinson, *The History and Antiquities of the County of Somerset*, 1791, II, p. 234). Gibbs's contribution is *ASH* IV.22 (J. Harris, *Colen Campbell: Catalogue of the Drawings Collection of the Royal Institute of British Architects*, 1973, fig. 126). This design was reworked with alternative window treatments in a drawing inscribed 'Jacob. Gibs' (Harris, *op. cit.*, p. 16, cat. no. 32.2, fig. 125) but perhaps by Campbell since it is the preparatory drawing for the elevation dated 1717 published in *VB*, 1717, p. 5, pls. 91–2. Campbell also made a variant design closer in spirit to Wanstead (Harris, *op. cit.*, p. 6, cat. no. 32.1, fig. 124). All these schemes date *c.* 1717 when illustrations for volume II of *VB* were being compiled (T. P. Connor, 'The Making of "Vitruvius Britannicus"', *AH*, 1970, XX, pp. 20–1). *VB*, 1717, p. 5, mentions 'when the whole Design is finished', but there is no evidence that construction took place, and the medieval house was demolished without record before 1762 (T. P. Connor, 'A Study of Colen Campbell's Vitruvius Britannicus' (Ph.D. Oxford University), 1977, pp. 344–9; *Friedman 1973*, p. 24).

Somerset House, *see* Middlesex, Isleworth

Soulbury, All Saints, *see* Buckinghamshire

SOUTH YORKSHIRE (formerly West Riding of Yorkshire)

**Kiveton Park** 1741, NE

THOMAS OSBORNE, 4TH DUKE OF LEEDS (1713–89)

*ASH* VIII, bound in original boards inscribed 'A Book of Drawings of Kiveton in Yorkshire. The Seat of His Grace The Duke of Leeds By James Gibbs Architect. 1741', comprises a record of the 1698–1704 house 'is it now stands' (*VB*, 1739, pls. 11–18; *Colvin*, pp. 309, 806) with proposed alterations and additions including a chapel (nos. 1–16) and the following new garden features, none of which appears to have been built: Keeper's Lodge (17), Bowling Green House (18–19 and *ASH* II.33–4, 36), 'Bath Called St Nicolaus's Well' (20–2), lodge (23–4), triumphal arches 'betwixt ye Woods' (25–6), pyramid 'wher ye Romans bones are buried' (27–8 and *ASH* II.69), pavilion for 'the Chastnut Walk' (29), bridges 'over the Hollow way' (30–1), Gothic arcade 'to be placed over the Rocks' (32). The estate was abandoned in 1811, and the house subsequently disappeared (E. Prinz, 'The Building of Kiveton Park' (B.A. Leeds University), 1976).

**Stainborough Hall** (now Wentworth Castle) E 1724–5

THOMAS WENTWORTH, LORD RABY, 1ST EARL OF STRAFFORD (1672–1739)*

Craftsmen: ?Addinell, painter; Jonathan Godier, carpenter; Charles Griffith, joiner; Daniel Harvey, carver; Richard Huss, plain plasterer (*Beard 1981*, pp. 261–3, 266).

In a contract dated 28 July 1724 Griffith agreed 'to wainscout the Gallery att Staineborough as Desined by Mr. Gibbs' (*BL* Strafford Papers Add. MS 22239, f. 128), thus resolving the decoration of the space as first conceived by Johann von Bodt *c.* 1710 (*VB*, 1715, pp. 6–7, pl. 92; *Colvin*, pp. 108, 120–1; J. Lees-Milne, *English Country Houses: Baroque, 1685–1715*, 1970, pp. 236–42; J. Harris, 'Bodt and Stainborough', *AR*, July 1961, pp. 34–5). Between 1713 and 1720 Thomas Archer, William Thornton and Robert Benson, Lord Bingley, had also been consulted (*BL* Add. MS 22239, ff. 88, 90; 22241, f. 85; M. Whiffen, *Thomas Archer*, 1973, pp. 15–7; Sheffield City Libraries: L1121 (184–5)). A 26 November 1721 letter reported that the 'Carpenter has ceil'd Gallery [and] Goodyear . . . will lay . . . Floor' and by 8 January 1723 he was 'coving the Gallery'. In 1723 Huss received £50 for plastering, in 1724 Harvey negotiated for carving work and Addinell received £97.9.6 on 16 September 1727 'for painting the Gallery' (*BL* Add. MS 22239, ff. 120–v, 136v; 22241, ff. 28v–9; LD1121, pp. 5v, 7v, 10).

Gibbs's association with Wentworth Woodhouse, the nearby seat of Thomas Watson-Wentworth, later Earl of Rockingham, as suggested by W. Ison ('A Plan for Wentworth Woodhouse', in H. Colvin and J. Harris, eds., *The Country Seat*, 1970, pp. 106–9) and by the present author (*Friedman 1973*, pp. 23–4) now seems unlikely (M. Binney, 'Wentworth Woodhouse Revisited', *CL*, 17 March 1983, pp. 624–7).


## STAFFORDSHIRE

### Patshull, St Mary E 1742

SIR JOHN ASTLEY, 2ND BARONET (d. 1771)

Gibbs 'built . . . a new parish Church not far from the house [PATSHULL HALL] which is very handsom' (*Gibbs MS*, p. 96). Astley gained permission on 9 February 1742 to demolish the old church and erect 'at his own proper Cost . . . a New Church . . . which lies nearer and more comodious to the . . . Village . . . agreeable with a Plan Scheme or Modell . . . to be ammended to the . . . faculty' (Lichfield Joint Record Office: Court Books B/c/2/101, p. 345). A Citation of 14 February (B/c/5) is attached to surveys of the old and new churchyards with a plan and south elevation of 'the New Church intended to be built at Patshulle' drawn by Gibbs or based on a lost drawing supplied by him. S. Shaw, *The History and Antiquities of Staffordshire*, 1801, II, part I, p. 286, pl. XXXVI, describes the building as 'an elegant Grecian fabrick' and shows quoins throughout and the belfry with urns. W. C. Banks recorded the church before and after making additions in 1873–8, including a new north aisle, porch, vestry and organ loft; he had authority to 'sell and dispose of such of the materials . . . as may not be required in restoring and enlarging', including some furnishings (Citation of 1873, B/c/5). The chancel screen was added in 1893 (M. Whiffen, *Stuart and Georgian Churches*, 1948, pp. 40–1, pl. 119).


### Patshull Hall (now Wolverhampton Area Health Authority Resident Rehabilitation Centre) E 1742–54

SIR JOHN ASTLEY, 2ND BARONET (d. 1771)

Gibbs 'built Sr John Astleys House called Patts Hall . . . wher he had ben at a great expense in firnishing it, and makeing it Convenient, he has built it all with stone, and the Offices are all out of doors' (*Gibbs MS*, p. 96). Gibbs was responsible for the central block of the present house (*ASH* II.19 being a detail of the central bays of the garden front now partly

obscured by a Victorian *porte-cochère*). The wings and outbuildings are probably by Baker, 1749–58 (*Colvin*, p. 84; A. Oswald, 'William Baker of Audlem, Architect', *Collections for a History of Staffordshire* (Staffordshire Records Society, 1950–1), 1954, pp. 117–18), although Francis Smith seems also to have been involved (*Colvin*, p. 749, with later alterations listed pp. 167, 937, 953). Views of the house are in the William Salt Library, Stafford: Patshull Vol. VII.


Stainborough Hall, *see* South Yorkshire

Stanwell House, *see* Middlesex


## STIRLINGSHIRE

### Quarrel House 1734–5, NE

JOHN DRUMMOND*

On 12 December 1734 Drummond expressed the 'opinion still that Mr. Gibs plan has been and is the most reasonable for me to follow [for the] small addition to my house', mentioning carrying 'the new building 2 foot farther forward than Mr. Gibbs dos [and] the ornament of the lowest windows to be as Mr. Gibs had made them'. On 4 January 1735 he refers to 'talking of the addition . . . in the presence of Mr Gib Sir Andrew fountain and other persons of teast . . . if it were no longer then Gibbs draught [lost] both as to room and stare case it will please me as well as any way because it will come out cheaper' (*SRO* GD 24/1/506–7, 520, 527). It is doubtful how far Gibbs's design was adhered to in execution.


Stowe, *see* Buckinghamshire


## STRATHCLYDE

Glasgow
### House in Dry Gate 1718–21, NE

JAMES GRAHAM, 1ST DUKE OF MONTROSE (1682–1742)*

On 26 December 1718 Montrose mentions 'Entertaining a long Conversation wt Mr Gibbs' and sending 'a Skectch [lost] that Mr Gibs made of [the agent's] draught' (*SRO* Montrose Papers GD 220/5/827/10 and 828/4) which is related to renovations proposed and partly executed from 1716 by Alexander McGill* (GD 220/5/820/5 and 19; 823/10; 824/7 and 19; 825/12; 826/8 and 23; 220/6 Vol. 11, including drawings dated 1717 in RH 6285/1–16 (*Colvin*, pp. 530–1). A revised design was also to be considered on the 'advice of Mr Gibbs' (828/8 and 12), who made 'Amendments' to the main front in 1719 (829/12; 982/3), Montrose remarking 'There's no great difference between them and Mr Mc gills, But I doe think Mr Gibbs the handsomest' (829/15). McGill's plans had been sent for Gibbs's 'approbation' by June 1719 (98517 and 19) and returned by January 1720 (830/20; 831/4; 986/2) but cost prohibited their realization (831/9 and 14). In December 1721 Gibbs received 10 guineas 'for drawing draughts [lost] of a house at Glasgow' (220/6/30, p. 496). The building was D *c.* 1855.

Sudbrook House, *see* Surrey, Petersham

Sudbrook Villa, *see* Surrey, Petersham, Sudbrook House

## SUFFOLK

### Acton Place E *c.* 1725–6, D 1825, 1961

ROBERT JENNENS (1672–1726)

'This is a large dwelling house with Offices built for Mr Jenings, near Stow market, some of the Rooms are pretty large and well finished' (*Gibbs MS*, p. 90). The house, under construction in 1725 (dated chimneystack recorded in *BL* Add. MS 19077, f. 52; W. A. Copinger, *The Manors of Suffolk: Notes on Their History and Devolution*, 1905, I, p. 13; N. Pevsner, *The Buildings of England: Suffolk*, 1961, pl. 58a), was noted for 'the grandeur of its hall and the massive elegance of its marble chimney-piece, as well as the beauty and extent of its stables and other offices ... The staircase ... and one entire wing of the house [with] a vast and superb ball-room, were left totally incomplete' on Jennens's death on 25 February 1726 (W. Harrison and G. Willis, *The Great Jennens Case*, 1879, pp. 85, 98–9, 104–5). In 1791 the house 'still exhibited some vestiges of its former splendour [with the hall] adorned with alto relievos; and the ceiling with the paintings from the heathen mythology. At each corner ... a figure of one of its fabled divinities. At the end, and on each side ... paintings of fruit and animals, by Snyders. Some circular recesses also contained six busts of admirable workmanship ... The offices [formed] wings on each side' (T. Cromwell, *Excursions in the County of Suffolk*, 1818, I, pp. 55–6). An 1825 sale of building material (Harrison and Willis, *op. cit.*, pp. 113–14) preceeded partial demolition, the stables followed in 1961 (*NMR* photographs). Jennens's widow and son subscribed to *ABA*.

## SURREY

### Byfleet
### Hunting Box E by 1748, D *c.* 1794

GENERAL HENRY CORNWALL (d. 1756)*

Gibbs 'built a very convenient small Hunting Box for General Cornwell at Byfleet in Sury' (*Gibbs MS*, p. 89) shown in a sketch plan of 1748 (R. W. King, 'Joseph Spence of Byfleet', *Garden History*, winter 1978, p. 53). O. Manning and W. Bray, *The History and Antiquaries of the County of Surrey*, 1814, III, p. 181, describe 'a large house ... on the *Dutch* plan'. A quadrant entrance wall survives (L. R. Stevens, *Byfleet: A Village of England*, 1953, p. 84).

### Mitcham, SS. Peter and Paul
### Monument to Sir Ambrose (1659–1713) and Lady Crowley (1664–1727) E *c.* 1727

*ASH* II.24, 27 and *VAM* E.4910.52 are variations on the executed design (J. Physick, *Designs for English Sculpture, 1680–1860*, 1969, pp. 76–7, figs. 44–5). *ABA*, p. xxiii, pl. 118: 'A Monument for a Noble Lord and Lady, executed with some variation' may represent an earlier idea. Crowley's son John

and three sons-in-law Richard Fleming, Humphrey Parson and Lord St John of Bletshoe subscribed to *ABA*; Parson was elected a governor of St Bartholomew's Hospital in 1727 (*Bart's Journal* Ha 1/10, p. 144).

### Petersham
### Sudbrook House (now Richmond Golf Club) E 1715–19

JOHN CAMPBELL, 2ND DUKE OF ARGYLL AND GREENWICH (1680–1743)*

Craftsmen: Thomas Churchill, bricklayer; John Reynolds, painter; John Townesend, mason (Coutts Bank, London: Argyll's account, Ledger 3, ff. 621, 628, 654, 657; Ledger 4, f. 20; Ledger 1718–19).

'John Duke of Argyle and Greenwich employed him to build his agreeable Villa at Peetersam ... upon a plesent situation adjoining to Richmond park, in this building ther is a beautifull Cube Room of thirty feet, richly adorned with military Tropheys ... the duke has made fine plantations here, and being but twelve miles from London, is a pleasant retraite from bussiness' (*Gibbs MS*, p. 87). *ASH* I.65 and III.97 are early designs related to *ASH* I.7 and *ABA*, p. xi, pl. 40, described as 'A *Villa* built ... at *Sudbrooke* ... of Brick, except the Ornaments, which are *Portland* Stone'. Argyll purchased the estate in November 1715 and Gibbs was involved with workmen by 19 November, when the banker George Middleton informed 'Mr Gibbs I have £600 to pay the people att Sudbrook' (Coutts: Letter Book 9, ff. 88, 112, 115v, 118v, 130, 139). Argyll was in residence by July 1716 (Letter Book 10, f. 15). An elevation and two plans of the villa as built were recorded by William Dickinson on 'Feb 26 1717–8 Duke of Argiles at Petersume near Richmd p Mr. Gibbs' (*Bodleian* Gough London 125, p. 400); see also H. M. Colvin, *A Catalogue of Architectural Drawings of the 18th and 19th Centuries in the Library of Worcester College, Oxford*, 1964, no. 77. Gibbs received £67 on 19 March 1717, £138.15 on 28 August 1718, and £91 on 9 December 1719 (Ledgers 4, f. 20; 1718–19, f. 210; 1719–23, f. 1). Townesend received £1,020 on 25 February 1718 (Ledger 1718–19). Payments cease in the summer of 1720 (Ledger 6). A payment of £157.7.0 to William Townesend on 13 January 1729 (Ledger 10, f. 330) may relate to the existing gate-lodge, which resembles *ASH* VIII.23–4 and is perhaps connected with the purchase of additional land in 1726 (H. M. Cundall, *Sudbrook and Its Occupants*, 1912, pp. 16, 24). The villa was altered *c.* 1767 and is shown in a later watercolour view (T. Friedman, *James Gibbs, Architect, 1682–1754: 'a man of great Fame'*, 1982, no. 78, illus.). A. T. Bolton, 'Sudbrook Park', *CL*, 19 October 1918, pp. 332–7; M. Cosh, 'Two Dukes and Their Houses', *CL*, 13 July 1972, pp. 78–9, fig. 3; J. M. W. Halley, 'Sudbrook Golf House Petersham', *Architectural Record*, December 1912, pp. 309–16; N. Lloyd, *A History of the English House*, 1931, pp. 129–30, figs. 229–30, 798.

### Roehampton
### House for Bartholomew Clarke and Hitch Young
E *c.* 1724–9, D *c.* 1788

BARTHOLOMEW CLARKE (1678–1746)* AND HITCH YOUNG (1688–1759)*

Gibbs 'repaired the Countray Seat of Messrs Clark and young

at Rohampton . . . a most agreeable situation, having a fine
prospect of the River Thames and the villages round it, and
the Hills towards the North . . . ther is here a fine new room
20ft. and 30ft. and 20ft., high, coved, the sides of this Room
is richly adorned with the paintings of Amiconi the famous
Italian painter when he was here, it has likewise a very fine
Chimney peece done by Mr Rysebrack' (*Gibbs MS*, p. 89). The
drawings for the room and its chimneypiece are *ASH* I.63, II.9,
16, 49, III.53; *VAM* E.3631-1913; *ABA*, p. xxi, pl. 92. The
property, later called Elm Grove, was purchased by Clarke in
1724 (Digby Stuart College archives: Court Roll of Admission,
25 May 1724, 4 July 1726). By 1754 it consisted of a 'House
& Garden Stable Yard & Barn' (Wandsworth Public Library:
Putney Poor Rates Assesment Book, 1754–69, I, p. 15) but was
destroyed by fire *c.* 1788 (H. Davidson, *The Story of Elm Grove*,
1967, pp. 2–6).

## SUSSEX

### Arundel Castle by 1732, NE

THOMAS HOWARD, 8TH DUKE OF NORFOLK (1683–1732)*

Gibbs 'made at the desire of . . . Norfolk, a large design [lost]
for Arandale Castle, the Old House being much decayed, he
intended to have pulled it quite down, but his Grace altered
his minde and laid out that money upon his House at Worsop
Mannor' in Nottinghamshire (*Gibbs MS*, p. 90). No documents
associate Gibbs with the remodelled south range at Arundel
Castle of *c.* 1716 or with the Duke's schemes for repairing the
dilapidated apartments or erecting others of 'more modern
appearance' mentioned by the historian M. A. Tierney (*The
History and Antiquities of the Castle and Town of Arundel*, 1834,
p. 79). The only identified work by Gibbs for this Catholic
client is a design for the magnificent ormolu tabernacle (*VAM*
Vol. 93E28, 8934.104), which was made by C. F. Kandler
probably in 1730 for the chapel (later converted into the dining
room) and which survives in Arundel Cathedral (J. M. Robinson, *The Dukes of Norfolk: A Quincentenial History*, 1982, pp. 152–
54, 202). The MS 'Plans, Elevations and Particular Measurements of Arundel Castle in Sussex', *c.* 1786–1801 (reprinted
with an introduction by F. W. Steer, 1976, pp. 20–1), records
that the 'Tabernacle is covered with Gold, adorned with
Emblematical Figures from the 5th. Cap. of St Johns Apo-
calypse ['Worthy is the Lamb. . .'], the Crucifiction of our bles-
sed Saviour &c. neatly ornamented.'

### Wiston Park NE

SIR ROBERT FAGG, BARONET, SENIOR (d. 1736) OR JUNIOR
(d. 1740)

*ASH* VI.1–9 (folio inscribed 'Plans for Wiston House the seat
of Sr Robert Fagg Barronet. by James Gibbs Architect') and
*ASH* II.139 are schemes for replacing the sixteenth-century
house. Some remodelling, apparently not by Gibbs, was completed by 15 April 1747 (according to an inscription stone)
including splendid plasterwork in the hall (*CL*, 27 February
1909, pp. 306–7; *VCH, Sussex*, 1980, VI, Part I, p. 262).

Trewithen House, *see* Cornwall

Tring Park, *see* Hertfordshire

Turner Mausoleum, *see* Cleveland, Kirkleatham

Sir William Turner's Hospital Chapel, *see* Cleveland,
Kirkleatham

Twickenham, *see* Middlesex

Warrington (Bank Hall), *see* Lancashire

## WARWICKSHIRE

### Aston, SS. Peter and Paul
### Monument to Sir John Bridgeman (1630–1710) and Lady Bridgeman (1640–1713) E 1726

CHARLOTTE BRIDGEMAN

Recorded in *ABA*, p. xxiv, pl. 123 centre, and *ASH* II.24, the
white and black veined marble monument is signed 'JACOBO
GIBBS ARCHITECTO'. Bridgeman's daughter 'erected this Monument at her own Expence; Anno Domini 1726' (on the inscription); a son Orlando subscribed to *ABA*.

### Compton Verney E by 1740

JOHN VERNEY

On 27 March 1740 John Loveday refers to the client having
'built the Stables which are very handsome and which above
Stairs contain Lodging-Rooms, and Rooms for other uses',
although this building is not mentioned on a visit in 1735
(*Markham*, pp. 190, 332, 497). *ASH* II.95 is a variant of II.75–6,
the stable block as built; the cupola is a later addition (A. T.
Bolton, 'Compton Verney', *CL*, 18 October 1913, pp. 528–35).

### Ragley Hall E 1751–c. 1760

FRANCIS CONWAY, 1ST EARL OF HERTFORD (1719–94)

Gibbs 'gave directions for the repairs of Ragly Castle the seat
of . . . the Earl of Hartford, as it is said that it will turn out
one of the best houses in England' (*Gibbs MS*, p. 90). A plan
in *BL* Add. MS 31323 WWW: 'The First or Principall Floor
of Ragley House' (A. Oswald, 'Ragley Hall', *CL*, 1 May 1958,
p. 941, fig. 8), represents the penultimate stage in the completion of the house begun in 1677 (*Britannia Illustrata*, 1707, pl. 71;
*Colvin*, pp. 431, 440; P. Leach, 'Ragley Hall Reconsidered',
*Archaeological Journal*, CXXXVI, 1979, pp. 265–68) described
in 1743 as 'a shell' of nine windows in front with a hall of 'bare
walls' (*BL* Add. MS 15776, f. 171). The hall was still 'unfloored
and unceiled' in 1751 but plastered by 1756, probably by
Giuseppe Artari (*Beard 1981*, pl. 79; P. Toynbee, ed., *The Letters
of Horace Walpole*, 1903, III, p. 66). The chapel was still
unfinished in 1758 and although the house then had 'a great
deal done to it since [Walpole] was there last [and had] no
striking faults' he felt it 'wants a few Chute-Bentley-touches'
(Toynbee, *op. cit.*, IV, pp. 174, 199). The pair of hall
chimneypieces appear in houses not associated with Gibbs and
may have been designed or supplied by Thomas Carter the
elder (C. Hussey, *English Country Houses: Mid-Georgian*, 1956,

fig. 241). The fabric was completed by 1768 (*BL* MS 36390, f. 90). James Wyatt described his contribution to the remodelling between 1779 and 1797 as 'extensive [but] of no concern in any decoration' (*BL* Egerton MS 3531, f. 13; *Colvin*, p. 947). Walpole reported in 1758 that unfortunately 'whole rooms full [of family papers] were by the ignorance of a steward consigned to the oven' (Toynbee, *op. cit.*, IV, p. 175).

Wentworth Castle, *see* South Yorkshire, Stainborough Hall

## WESTMORLAND

### Lowther Hall *c.* 1717–28, NE

HENRY LOWTHER, 3RD VISCOUNT LONSDALE (1694–1751)*

Gibbs reported on 11 August 1717 going 'to Lowther . . . at 4 tomorrow morning, but in ten days shall be back' (*HMC Stuart*, IV, p. 568) which presumably resulted in the first scheme (*RIBA* K3/2 (1–4); *VB*, 1725, p. 11, pl. 76) for remodelling the Stuart house (J. Kip, *Britannia Illustrata*, 1707, pl. 41). This supplanted a scheme by an unknown architect shown in *VB*, 1717, p. 4, pls. 78–80. The project was abandoned due to a fire in 1718 which gutted the central block and east inner wing (*HMC Polworth*, I, pp. 462–3; *SRO* GD18/2109, p. 21). After 1728 Gibbs submitted a new design (*RIBA* K3/2 (5–17); J. Harris, *The Palladians*, 1981, p. 70) but another architect was favoured (J. Harris, *Colen Campbell: Catalogue of the Drawings Collection of the Royal Institute of British Architects*, 1973, pp. 13–4, figs. 76–85) although neither was realized. The old house was demolished and rebuilt as Lowther Castle during 1806–10 (H. Colvin, J. Mordaunt Crook and T. Friedman, *Architectural Drawings from Lowther Castle Westmorland*, 1980, pp. 12–13, nos. 4–7, 14–26; T. P. Connor, 'A Study of Colen Campbell's Vitruvius Britannicus (Ph.D. Oxford University), 1977, pp. 254–62; J. Harris, *The Artist and the Country House*, 1979, pl. 168; G. Hedley, *Capability Brown and the Northern Landscape*, 1983, cat. nos. 31–2; *Friedman 1973*, pp. 22–3, figs. 22–3).

Weston Underwood House, *see* Buckinghamshire

Whitchurch, St Lawrence, *see* Middlesex

Whitton Place, *see* Middlesex

## WILTSHIRE

### Longleat House E 1742–3

THOMAS THYNNE, 2ND VISCOUNT WEYMOUTH (1710–51)

Gibbs 'repaired and made additions . . . to Lord Weymouths at Old Windsor, besides other things for his Lordship' (*Gibbs MS*, p. 88) including unspecified work at Longleat which is recorded in two bills, one dated 1742 'To James Gibbs, Esq., Architect in part of his bill for '42 at Longleat' for £21, the other on 12 January 1742 to 'Mr James Gibbs in full for survey work at Longleat and Old Windsor' for £21 (Longleat archives: Account Book 1740). The circumstances surrounding this commission are unrecorded, but the work may well have included repairs following a major fire of unrecorded date which is mentioned in Lord Mar's 1722 proposal for refacing the east front with a colossal engaged temple portico 'in place of that wch was burned down' (*SRO* Mar and Kellie deposit, RHP 13256). In 1738 a visitor reported 'there are but three compleat fronts to the house; another [the north] is much wanting, the Eye demands it' (*Markham*, p. 294). Unspecified stone and carpentry work is also recorded in 1733–4 and 1739 (D. Burnett, *Longleat: The Story of an English Country House*, 1978, p. 103; R. Gunnis, *Dictionary of British Sculptors, 1660–1851*, 1953, p. 311; T. P. Connor, 'A Study of Colen Campbell's Vitruvius Britannicus' (Ph.D. Oxford University), 1977, pp. 251–2).

Maiden Bradley, All Saints
### Monument to Sir Edward Seymour (1633–1708) E
1728–30

FRANCIS SEYMOUR*

The contract of 11 July 1728 between Seymour and Walter Lee specified erecting for £500 a marble tomb 'according to the draught or design [lost] drawn thereof by James Gibbs . . . The Figures and all the rest of the Carving . . . shall be carved and finished by Michael Rysbraelk. Statuary'. Lee received £400 on 9 October 1729 (*PRO* Chancery Masters Exhibits C107/126). *ASH* III.52 is presumably a replica of the contract draught rather than as identified by *Little*, p. 106, pl. 17. The monument was erected in 1730 (K. Eustace, *Michael Rysbrack Sculptor, 1694–1770*, 1982, pp. 20, 80, fig. 33) and mentioned in *GSJ*, 28 January 1731, No. 56, p. 2.

### Netheravon House NE

HENRY SOMERSET, 3RD DUKE OF BEAUFORT (1707–45)*

Gibbs's 'Elevation of a House for Netherhaven' (Badminton House archives) may relate to Francis Smith's work there in 1736, concurrent with Badminton and employing many of the same craftsmen (*Bodleian* MS Eng. misc., f. 556, pp. 1–4). The house was later much altered (*Colvin*, p. 769).

Wimpole Hall, *see* Cambridgeshire

Wiston Park, *see* Sussex

Witham Park, *see* Somerset

Witley Court, *see* Worcestershire

## WORCESTERSHIRE

Witley Court
### Chapel (now St Michael and All Saints) E 1733–47

THOMAS, 2ND LORD FOLEY (d. 1766)

'Lord Fouley bought all the pictures, and everything else which could be moved [from CANNONS CHAPEL], and ordered Mr Gibbs to fitt them to his Chapel at his Seat in Wostershire, called Whitly Court, wher his Lordship has adepted them very properly' (*Gibbs MS*, p. 87). This includes Joshua Price's ten painted-glass windows (*A Catalogue of all the Materials of the Dwelling-House, Out-Houses, &c. Of His Grace James Duke of Chandos, Deceas'd, At his late Seat call'd Cannons*, 22 June 1747, p. 33, lot 68; J. A. Knowles, 'The Price Family of Glass-Painters', *The Antiquaries Journal*, July–October 1953, pp. 184–92) and Antonio Bellucci's ceiling paintings on canvas (*Croft-Murray*, II, pp. 170–1, pl. 10; E. Young, 'Antonio Bellucci in England and Elsewhere', *Apollo*, May 1973, pp. 492–99; P. Cannon-Brookes, 'A Modello by Antonio Bellucci for Canons', *Burl Mag*, April 1975, pp. 238–42) but apparently not the ornamental ceiling, which is made of papier-mâché according to Gibbs's design (*VAM* 2216.34), and probably dates from about 1747 (*Knight*, pp. 223, 236–7). The chapel itself, built by a faculty resulting from Lady Foley's petition to the Bishop of Worcester on 9 November 1733 and consecrated in 1735, may also have been Gibbs's responsibility. The original appearance of the exterior (shown in T. R. Nash, *Collections for the History of Worcestershire*, 1781, II, p. 464; J. Harris, 'C. R. Cockerell's Ichnographica Domestica', *AH*, 1971, XIV, p. 28, figs. 24–5a) was altered in a refacing by Dawkes *c.* 1860 (C. Hussey, 'Witley Court', *CL*, 8 June 1945, pp. 992–5).

Wrest Park, *see* Bedfordshire

Wynnstay, *see* Denbighshire

## LOCATIONS UNKNOWN

**Dr Freind's Anatomical Demonstration Theatre** by 1728, NE

DR JOHN FREIND (1675–1728)*

*VAM* E.3619-1913 and *ASH* III.108–9: 'For Dr Freind', may relate to the proposal presented on 21 July 1722 by a deputation of physicians and surgeons to build a 'Dissecting Room' in the grounds of St Bartholomew's Hospital, London, where Freind served as a governor and Gibbs was soon, from 1723, to act as architect. Another design for such a building by an unknown architect (*Bart's* Ha 19/1/2 Plan Book XVII–XVIII centuries) had been 'taken in the lifetime of Doctor Radcliffe [who] dyed [in 1714] before [it] was put in execution' (*Bart's Journal* Ha 1/10 p. 66v; J. L. Thornton, *The Royal Hospital of Saint Bar-*

*tholomew, 1123–1973*, 1974, pp. 45–7). Gibbs also designed Freind's Westminster Abbey monument, 1728–31.

## Royal Palace NE

*RIBA* K3/3(1–14) and perhaps *ASH* II.140 represent a design for a palace incorporating the English royal arms. The *RIBA* drawings were purchased without provenance at Sotheby's, 20 October 1950 (H. M. Colvin, *Royal Palaces*, 1968, pp. 38–9, fig. 23; *Friedman 1973*, p. 22, figs. 20–1; T. Friedman, 'James Gibbs's Designs for Domestic Furniture', *Leeds Arts Calendar*, 1972, No. 71, p. 21, fig. 1).

## Monument to William Stafford Howard, 2nd Earl of Stafford (d. 1734)* NE

The arms incorporated in *ASH* III.106, a pedimented wall tablet, identify the deceased, a Jacobite Catholic who died in Paris in January 1734 and whose heart was buried in the church of the Blue Nuns there.

## Monument to Humfrey Wanley (1672–1726) NE

Wanley, Edward Harley's librarian at Wimpole, is buried in Marylebone parish church (G. Clinch, *Marylebone and St Pancras: Their History, Celebrities, Buildings, and Institutions*, 1890, p. 24) although commemorated by a monument different from that shown in *ABA*, p. xxiv, pl. 124 left; *ASH* III.85.

## Chimneypieces NE

BOSCAWEN FAMILY

Two designs for chimneypieces with overmantles (*ASH* II.15) annotated on the verso 'to come this Evening to Mrs Boscawens In St James place and inquier for Miss Rice any time before seven o'clo[ck]' may be associated with the new house built for Hugh Boscawen, 2nd Viscount Falmouth, at 2 St James's Square, 1752–4, by the team of Barlow, Spencer and Benjamin Timbrell (a local carpenter working frequently with Gibbs). The house was destroyed in a Second World War air-raid (*S of L, The Parish of St James Westminster*, Part 1, South of Piccadilly, 1960, XXIX, pp. 82–3).

# GIBBS'S FINE ART LIBRARY

IN HIS WILL dated 9 August 1754 (P.C.C. 228 Pinfold) Gibbs bequeathed to the Radcliffe Trustees 'all my printed books, Books of Architecture, books of prints'. These items were delivered to the Radcliffe Library on 7 December (*Gillam*, pp. 85, 112–13, 115) and listed in 'A Catalogue of Mr Gibbs's Books which he has given to the Radcliffe Library at Oxford 1754' (*Bodleian MS Eng. Misc. c.28* and Rad. Science Lib. H.5). Some books were subsequently dispersed and bear the stamp 'Sold by Order of Radcliffe Trustees 1894. H. W. A. Library'; the remainder are now deposited in the Bodleian Library, Oxford, shelfmark *Rad*, many with the architect's bookplate. The following books bear inscriptions recording the names of their former owners:

P. Bertrand, *Livre Nouveau de L'Art D'Architecture des cinq ordres*, n.d., with other treatises and individual engravings: 'Ce proseut livre a partieu a Piere Binart laino eu lanöo 1689' (author's collection)

A. Felibien, *Des Principes de L'Architecture, de la Sculpture, de la Peinture*, 1676: 'P V Baert' (Yale Center for British Art, New Haven)

S. van Noyen, *Thermae Diocletianae*, 1557: 'Chr: Wren' (*Rad.*), listed in *A Catalogue of the Curious and Entire Libraries Of that ingenious Architect Sir Christopher Wren, Knt. and Christopher Wren, Esq; his Son*, Langford, 27 October 1748, p. 19, lot 564 (D. J. Watkin, ed., *Sale Catalogues of Libraries of Eminent Persons*, 1972, IV (Architects) p. 39)

J. J. Sandrart, *Salvator Rosa*, n.d. (*Rad.*): with the arms of Henri-Jacques-Nompar de Caumont, Duc de la Force, 1675–1726 (E. Olivier, G. Hermal and R. de Roton, *Manuel de l'amateur de relivres armoriées françaises*, 1929, pl. 1726, no. 1, fer. 2)

Books devoted to the fine arts represent fewer than half the items listed in the 1754 catalogue of Gibbs's library, which included a wide range of subjects. The volumes in the following list have been re-arranged alphabetically by author and given their full titles, replacing the abbreviated form adopted in the original manuscript catalogue; additional items not included there but known to have been in Gibbs's library (mainly on the evidence of his bookplate), including books to which he subscribed (indicated by an *), are also listed.

Anonymous, *The Builder's Dictionary: or, Gentleman and Architect's Companion*, London, 1734, 2 vols.

Anonymous, *Prodromus, seu Præambulare Lumen Reserati Portentosæ Magnificentiæ Theatri*, Vienna, 1735

Leon Battista Alberti, *De Re Aedificatoria*, Florence, 1550

James Anderson, *Royal Genealogies*, London, 1732*

Pietro Santi Bartoli, *Gli Antichi Sepolcri, ovvero mausolei Romani, ed Etruschi trovati in Roma, ed altri luoghi celebri*, Rome, 1697

Pietro Santi Bartoli, *Le Antiche Lucerne Sepolcrali Figurate*, Rome, 1691

Pietro Santi Bartoli, *Stylobates Columnæ Antoninæ Nuper e Ruderibus Campi Martii*, Rome, 1708

William Bates, *The Works Of the late Reverend and Learned William Bates*, London, 1723*

Giovanni Pietro Bellori, *Le Vite de' pittori, scultori et architetti moderni*, Rome, 1672 (another copy listed as 'Vite di Pictori, Per Bellori')

Jean Berain, *Ornemens Inventez par J. Berain*, Paris, n.d.

Pierre Bertrand, *Livre Nouveau de L'Art D'Architecture des cinq ordres*, Paris, n.d., bound with Antoine Le Pautre, *Plans, et Elevations du Corps de L'Eglise du Pont Royal*, Paris, 1652–3; Pierrets le Jeune, *Trophées Inventez et gravez*, Paris, n.d.; and engravings by Jean Marot, Perelle and Silvestre

Francesco Bianchini, *Del Palazzo De Cesari Opera Postuma De Monsignor Francesco Bianchini Veronese*, Verona, 1738

Frederik Bloemaert, *Oorspronkelyk en Vermaard Konstryk Tekenboek van Abraham Bloemaart*, Amsterdam, 1740

François Blondel, *Cours D'architecture*, Paris, 1698, 2 vols.

Georg Bocklern, *Theatrum Machinarum Novum*, Nuremberg, 1673

Filippo Bonanni, *Numismata summatoum pontificum templi vaticani fabricam indicanti*, Rome, 1715

Abraham Bosse, *Traite des Manieres de dessiner les Ordres de l'Architecture*, Paris, 1664

Louis Bretez, *La Perspective pratique de l'architecture*, Paris, 1706

Colen Campbell, *Vitruvius Britannicus*, London, 1715, 1717, 1725, 3 vols.

Luca Carlevaris, *Le Fabriche, e Vedute Di Venetia Disegnate, Poste in Prospettiva, et Intagliate da Luca Carlevariis*, Venice, 1703

Robert Castell, *The Villas of the Ancients Illustrated*, London, 1728

Pietro Cataneo, *L'Architettura Di Pietro Cataneo Senese*, 1567

Ephraim Chambers, trans., *A Treatise of Architecture, With Remarks and Observations. By that Excellent Master thereof Sebastian Le Clerc . . . Translated by Mr. Chambers*, London, 1723\*

Giovanni Ciampini, *Vetera Monimenta*, Rome, 1690

Jean Cotelle, *Livre de divers Ornamens*, Paris, 1670–1700

Jean Courtonne, *Traité de la Perspective Pratique*, Paris, 1725

Jean Cousin, *Livre de la Perspective*, Paris, 1560

Pierre Danet, *A Complete Dictionary of the Greek and Roman Antiquities*, London, 1700

C. A Daviler, *Cours d'architecture qui comprend les ordres de Vignole*, Paris, 1720, 2 vols.

Paul Decker, *Füerstlicher Baumeister Oder: Architectura Civilis*, Augsburg, 1711–16, 2 vols.

Philibert De L'Orme, *Nouvelles Inventions pour bien bastir et à petits Fraiz*, Paris, 1561

Giles Demortain, *Les Plans, Profils, et Elevations, des Ville, et Château de Versailles, avec les Bosquets, et Fontaines, Tels Quils son a Present; Levez sur les Lieux, Dessinez et Gravez en 1714. et 1715*, Paris, 1716

Antoine Desgodetz, *Les Edifices antiques de Rome. Dessinés et mesurés tres exactement*, Paris, 1695

Wendel Dietterlin, *Architectura*, Nuremberg, 1598

Jacques Androuet du Cerceau, *Quonian apvd veteres alio structuræ genere temple*, Orleans, 1550

William Dugdale, *Antiquities of Warwickshire illustrated*, London, 1656

William Dugdale, *The History of St Paul's Cathedral in London*, London, 1716

John Evelyn, trans., Roland Fréart, Sieur de Chambray, *A Parallel of the Ancient Architecture with the Modern*, London, 1707

Giovanni Battista Falda, *L'acque Romane*, Rome, 1691 (another copy listed as 'Fontane di Romae e Tivoli bound together'), bound with Joseph Emanuel Fischer von Erlach (see below)

André Félibien, *Des Principes de L'Architecture, de la Sculpture, de la Peinture*, Paris, 1676

André Félibien, *Entretiens sur les vies et sur les ouvrages des plus excellens peintres anciens et modernes*, London, 1666–9, 5 vols.

Tobias Fendt, *Monumenta Illustrium vivorum, et elogia*, Amsterdam, 1638

Johann Bernhard Fischer von Erlach, *Entwürff Einer Historischen Architectur*, Vienna, 1721

Joseph Emanuel Fischer von Erlach, *Prospecte und Abrike einiger Gebaüde von Wein*, Vienna, 1715 (see Falda)

Carlo Fontana, *Funerale del Ré di Portogallo*, Rome, 1707

Carlo Fontana, *Il Tempio Vaticano*, Rome, 1694

Carlo Fontana, *L'Anfiteatro Flavio descritto, e delineato*, The Hague, 1725

Domenico Fontana, *Della transportation dell'obelisco Vaticano*, Rome, 1595

Alessandro Franchini, *Livre d'architecture*, Paris, 1631

Roland Fréart, Sieur de Chambray, *Parallele de l'architecture antique et de la moderne*, Paris, 1650 (see also Evelyn)

C. A. Du Fresnoy, *The Art of Painting*, London, 1716

John Gay, *Poems on Several Occassions*, London, 1720\*

James Gibbs, *A Book of Architecture*, London, 1728

James Gibbs, *Rules for Drawing The several Parts of Architecture*, London, 1732, and *Bibliotheca Radcliviana*, London, 1747 ('bound together')

James Gibbs, *Rules for Drawing The several Parts of Architecture*, London, 1753

François Girardon, *Galerie de Girardon*, Paris, 1714 ('bound up together with other Prints')

Alexander Gordon, trans., Francesco Scipione Maffei, *A Compleat History Of the Ancient Ampitheatres*, London, 1730

Alexander Gordon, *Itinerarium Septentrionale: or, A Journey Thro' most of the Counties of Scotland, And Those in the North of England*, London, 1726\*

A. F. Gori, *Museum Florentinum*, Florence, 1734 (see also Norden)

Jean Joseph Granet, *Histoire de L'Hôtel Royal Des Invalides*, Paris, 1736

Walter Harris, *A Description of The King's Royal Palace and Gardens at Loo. Together With a Short Account of Holland*, London, 1699

William Hogarth, 'Hogarth's Prints bound up together in a large Volume'

John James, *The Theory and Practice of Gardening*, London, 1712

John James, *A Treatise of the Five Orders of Columns in Architecture*, London, 1708

Inigo Jones, *The most notable antiquity of Great Britain, vulgarly called Stone-Heng*, London, 1723

Filippo Juvarra, *Raccolta Di Targhe Fatte da Professori Primarj in Roma*, Rome, 1722

Basil Kennet, *Romæ Antiquæ Notitia, or the Antiquities of Rome*. London, 1708

William Kent, *The Designs of Inigo Jones, with some Additional Designs*, London, 1727, 2 vols.\*

Jan Kip, *Nouveau Théâtre de la Grande Bretagne*, London, 1724, 4 vols.

Athanasius Kircher, *Ad Alexandrum VII. Pont. Max. Obelisci Aegyptiaci*, Rome, 1666

Elisha Kirkall, 'Kirkals Collection of Prints Engraved by him, wth. other Prints'

Gerard de Lairesse, *The Art of Painting*, London, 1738

Bernardo Lamy, *De Tabernaculo Fœderis, De Sancta Civitate Jerusalem, et De Templo Ejus. Libri Septem. Autore Bernardo Lamy*, Paris, 1720

Jacob Lauri, *Antiquæ Urbis Splendor*, Rome, 1612

Sebastian Le Clerc, *A Treatise of Architecture*, London, 1723 (see Chambers)

Thomas Lediard, *The History of England. Written originally in French as far as the Revolution, By M. Rapin de Thoyras*, London, 1737, Vol. III\*

Giacomo Leoni, *The Architecture of A. Palladio*, London, 1715

Antoine Le Pautre, *Les Oeuvres D'Architecture*, Paris, 1652

Antoine Le Pautre (see Bertrand)

David Loggan, *Oxonia illustrata*, Oxford, 1675, and *Cantabrigia illustrata*

Richard Long, *Astronomy, in Five Books*, Cambridge, 1742\*

Colin Maclaurin, *An Account of Sir Isaac Newton's Philosophical Discoveries*, London, 1748*

F. S. Maffei (see Gordon)

William Maitland, *The History of London, From Its Foundation By the Romans, to the Present Time*, London, 1739*

Daniel Marot, *Oeuvre Du Sr. D. Marot*, The Hague, *c.* 1702, 2 vols.

Jean Marot, *L'architecture françoise*, Paris, *c.* 1665

Jean Marot, *Recueil des Plans, Profils et Elevations des plusieurs Palais, Chasteaux, Eglises Sepultres Grotes et Hostels bâtis dans Paris*, Paris, *c.* 1654–60

Philip Miller, *The Gardener's Dictionary*, London, 1733 and 1739, 2 vols.

Bernard de Montfaucon, *Diarium Italicum, sive monumentorum veterum bibliothecarum, musæorum*, Paris, 1702

Bernard de Montfaucon, *L'Antiquité Expliquée et représentée en figures*, London, 1719–24, 7 vols.

Joseph Moxon, *Practical Perspective, or perspective made easy*, London, 1670

Friderick Ludvig Norden, *Drawings of some Ruins and Colossal Statues at Thebes in Egypt*, London, 1741, and 'The First part of the Painter's Heads of the Florentine. Collection, bound together, to keep them from being lost, till the Second parts are delivered to the Subscribers'

Sebastien van Noyen, *Thermæ Diocletianæ*, Brussels, 1557

Pellegrino Antonio Orlandi, *Abecedario pittorico*, Bologna, 1719

Bonaventura van Overbeke, *Les Restes de L'Ancienne Rome*, Amsterdam, 1709, 3 vols.

Andrea Palladio, *I Quattro Libri dell'Architettura*, Venice, 1601

Claude Perrault, *Les dix livres d'architecture de Vitruve*, Paris, 1684

François Perrier, *Icones et segmenta illustrium e marmore tabularum que Romæ adhuc exstant*, Rome and Paris, 1645

Pierrets le Jeune (see Bertrand)

John Pine, *Quinti Horatii Flacci Opera*, London, 1733*

Giovanni Battista Piranesi, 'Archtectura Piranese, all his Works in one Large Volume'

Jean Poldo D'Albenas, *Discours historical de l'antique et illustre cité de Nismes*, Lyons, 1560

John Potter, *Archaeologiæ Græcæ : or the Antiquities of Greece*, London, 1706, 2 vols.

Francis Price, *The British Carpenter*, London, 1735

Jonathan Richardson, *An Essay on the Theory of Painting*, London, 1725

Thomas Richers, *The History of the Royal Genealogy of Spain*, London, 1724*

Carlo Ridolfi, *Vita di Paolo Caliari, Veronese, celebre Pittore*, 1738

Cesare Ripa, *Iconologie*, Amsterdam, 1698, 2 vols.

Domenico De' Rossi, *Insignium Romæ templorum prospectus*, Rome, 1684

Domenico De' Rossi, *Raccolta di Vasi Diversi Formati da Illustri Artefici Antichi e Di Varie Targhe Soprapposte alle Fabbriche piu insigni di Roma Da celebri Architetti Moderni*, Rome, 1713

Domenico De' Rossi, *Studio D'Architettura Civile . . . di Roma*, Rome, 1702–21, 2 vols.

Giovanni Jacomo De' Rossi, *Al . . . Principe G. Cardlo Colonna . . . nova racolta degli' obelischi et colonne antiche . . . di Roma*, Rome, 1651

Giovanni Jacomo De' Rossi, *Barberinæ avlæ Fornix Romae Eq. Petri Berettini Cortonensis*, Rome, n.d.

Giovanni Jacomo De' Rossi, *Disegni Di Vari Altarie e Cappelle nelle Chiese Di Roma*, Rome, 1713

Peter Paul Rubens, *Palazzi Antichi di Genova Raccolti e Designati da Pietro Paolo Rubens*, Antwerp, 1708

Peter Paul Rubens, *Pompa introitus . . . Ferdinandi*, Antwerp, 1641

Giovanni Antonio Rusconi, *I dieci libri d'Architettura di G. A. Rusconi*, Venice, 1660

Henricus Ruse, *The Strengthening of Strong-Holds*, Amsterdam, 1654

J. J. Sandrart, *Salvator Rosa Has ludentis otij Carolo Rubeo Singularis Amicitiæ pignus*, Nuremberg, n.d.

Vincenzo Scamozzi, *L'Idea della Architettura Universale*, Venice, 1615, 2 vols.

Peter Schenk, *Roma Aeterna*, Amsterdam, 1705

Sebastiano Serlio, *Tutte l'Opere d'Architettura*, Venice, 1584

Anthony Ashley Cooper, 3rd Earl of Shaftesbury, *Characteristicks of Men, Manners, Opinions, Times*, London, 1723, 3 vols.

Israel Silvestre, 'Veues de Paris longways 2 Vol. a Paris' and 'Veues de Paris di Silvester 3 Vol. Paris' (see also Bertrand)

Joseph Smith, *Ecclesiarum Angliæ et Valliæ Prospectus or Views of all the Cathedrals in England and Wales*, London, 1719

Antoinette Bouzonnet Stella (untitled but with note: 'Cette frise a esté du stuc soubs la conduitte, et sur les desseins de Jules Romain au Palais de TE dans montouë') Paris, 1675

John Stevens, *The History of the Antient Abbeys, Monasteries, Hospitals, Cathedrals and Collegiate Churches. Being Two Additional Volumes to Sir William Dugdale's Monasticon Anglicanum*, London, 1722*

Philipp von Stosch, *Gemmæ antiquæ cælatæ sculptorum nominibus insignitæ*, Amsterdam, 1724

John Stow, *A Survey of the Cities of London and Westminster*, London, 1720, 2 vols.

Carlo Theti, *Discorsi delle fortificationi*, Venice, 1589

Filippo Titi, *Nuovo Studio Di Pittura, Scoltura, et Architettura Nelle Chiesa di Roma . . . Dell'Abbate Filippo Titi*, Rome, 1708

Pieter Van Den Bergh, *Theatrum Hispaniæ exhibens regni urbes, villas ac viridaria Magis illustria*, Amsterdam, *c.* 1700

Anthony Van Dyck, *Icones Principum Virorum Doctorum*, Antwerp, n.d.

Giorgio Vasari, *Le Vite de' piu eccellenti pittori, scultori, e architettori*, Bologna, 1647, 3 vols.

Jacob Vennekoll, *Afbeelding van 't Stadt Huys van Amsterdam, in dartigh coopere plaatenm, geordineert door Jacob van Campen en geeteeckent door Jacob Vennekool*, Amsterdam, 1661

Hieronymus Pradi and Joannis Baptista Villalpandi, *In Ezechielem Explanationes et Apparatus Urbis, ac Templi Hierosolymitani Commentariis et Imaginibus Illustratus opus Tribus Tomis Distinctum*, Rome, 1596, 3 vols.

Vitruvius (see Perrault)

Isaac Ware, *Designs of Inigo Jones and others*, London, *c.* 1733

Isaac Ware, *The Plans, Elevations, and Sections; Chimney-Pieces, and Cielings of Houghton in Norfolk*, London, 1735

Robert West, *Perspective Views Of All the Ancient Churches, and Other Buildings, In the Cities of London, and Westminster, and Parts adjacent, within the Bills of Morality. Drawn by Robert West, and Engraved by William Henry Toms*, London, 1736 and 1739, 2 vols.*

William Williams, *Oxonia depicta*, Oxford, 1732–3

Robert Wood and James Dawkins, *The Ruins of Palmyra*, London, 1753

Christopher Wren, *A Catalogue of the Churches of the City of London; Royal Palaces, Hospitals; and Publick Edifices; Built by Sr. Christopher Wren*, London, n.d.

Niccolo Zabaglia, *Contignationes, ac Pontes Nicolai Zabaglia una cum quibusdam ingeniosis praxibus, ac Descriptione Translationis Obelisci Vaticani, aliorumque per equitem Dominicum Fontana susceptæ*, Rome, 1743

Unidentified (as listed in 'A Catalogue of Mr Gibbs's Books')

'A Book of different Vases'

'Antiquitades di Sivilia, in Sivilia 1634'

'Antiquæ Romæ Splendor, Romæ 1612'

'Antiquitys of Canterbury, London 1726'

'Antiquitys of Palmira, London 1696'

'Arcus Septimij Severi Aug. Romæ 1676'

'Collection de Viues et Monuments Anciens Am. 1725'

'I Vestigij del Antiquita di Roma, a Roma 1575'

'Labratory of School of Arts'

'Le Gemme Antiche in 2 Vol. Romæ 1686' (perhaps Domenico De' Rossi, *Gemme antiche figurate*, Rome, 2 vols.)

'Maison Royalle, or Views of Versails, &c.'

'Putei Architectura et perspectiva Romæ 1702'

'Recueil de Nouveau Bastimentes' and 'Recueil de Nouvo Bastiments'

'Roma Anticha et Modierna, Roma 2 Vol. 1654'

'Tempie Antiche 2 Vol. Romæ'

'Trait de Chemins'

'Traite de Ponts, a Paris'

'Villa Pamphilia, Romæ 1612'

# ABBREVIATIONS

| | |
|---|---|
| *ABA* | J. Gibbs, *A Book of Architecture*, 1728 and 1739 |
| *AH* | *Architectural History* (periodical) |
| *AR* | Architectural Review (periodical) |
| *ASH* | Ashmolean Museum, Oxford: Gibbs Collection, including *Prints* ('A Collection of Several Prints, of different Kindes') |
| *Baker* | C. H. Collins Baker and M. I. Baker, *The Life and Circumstances of James Brydges, First Duke of Chandos*, 1949 |
| *Bart's* | The Royal Hospital of St Bartholomew, London, archives: *Corr* (Correspondence) and *Journal* (Governor's Journals) prefixed Ha |
| *Beard* | *1975* (G. Beard, *Decorative Plasterwork in Great Britain*, 1975) and *1981* (G. Beard, *Craftsmen and Interior Decoration in England, 1660–1820*, 1981) |
| *Bickham* | G. Bickham, *The Beauties of Stow*, 1750 |
| *Bill* | E. G. W. Bill, *The Queen Anne Churches*, 1979 |
| *BL* | British Library, London |
| *BM* | British Museum, London |
| *BR* | J. Gibbs, *Bibliotheca Radcliviana: or, A Short Description of the Radcliffe Library, at Oxford*, 1747 |
| *Braham* | A. Braham and H. Hager, *Carlo Fontana: The Drawings at Windsor Castle*, 1977 |
| *Burl Mag* | *The Burlington Magazine* (periodical) |
| *Burney* | British Library, London: Burney Newspapers |
| *Bodleian* | Bodleian Library, Oxford |
| *Castell* | R. Castell, *The Villas of the Ancients Illustrated*, 1728 |
| *CL* | *Country Life* (periodical) |
| *CLRO* | Corporation of London Records Office: *113B* (Committee Papers 1728–44); *113C* (Committee Minute Books, I, 1734–55); *JCCL* (Journal Committee City Lands); *CCJ* (Court of Common Council Journal, 1717 to 1736, LVII) |
| *Colvin* | H. Colvin, *A Biographical Dictionary of British Architects, 1600–1840*, 1978 |
| *Cox* | J. C. Cox and W. H. St. John Hope, *The Chronicles of the Collegiate Church or Free Church of All Saints, Derby*, 1881 |
| *Crace* | British Museum, London, Department of Prints and Drawings: Crace Collection |
| *CRO* | County Record Office |
| *Croft-Murray* | E. Croft-Murray, *Decorative Painting in England, 1537–1837*, 1962 and 1970 |
| *CUL* | Cambridge University Library, Department of Manuscripts: *CUR* (Camb. Univ. Regist. 46, Senate House 'Orders relating to the New Buildings, 1719–1769'); *LG* (Liber Gratiarium, Grace Book, I, 1718–44); *MC* (MS Misc. Collect 20); *UAB* (University Audit Book, 1660–1740); *VCV* (Vice-Chancellor's Vouchers 1718–39, Boxes 12–15) |
| *Dart* | J. Dart, *Westmonasterium. or The history and Antiquities of the Abbey Church of St. Peters Westminster*, 1723 |
| *Defoe* | D. Defoe, *A Tour Thro' the Whole Island of Great Britain*, 1724–6 (1962 edition), 1738, 1742, 1748, 1761–2 |
| *DIL* | Oxfordshire *CRO* Dillon Papers |
| *DLSL* | Derby Local Studies Library |
| *Downes* | K. Downes, *Hawksmoor*, 1959 |
| *Drummonds* | Archives of The Bank of Scotland, Drummonds Branch, London: Gibbs's account, 1722–54 |
| *Enggass* | R. Enggass, *Early Eighteenth-Century Sculpture in Rome*, 1976 |
| *Friedman* | T. Friedman, 'Foggini's Statue of Queen Anne', in *Kunst des Barock in der Toskana*, 1976 |

| | |
|---|---|
| *Friedman 1973* | J. Lever, ed., *Catalogue of the Drawings Collection of the Royal Institute of British Architects*, 1973, Vol. G–K, pp. 21–5 |
| *Gibbs MS* | Sir John Soane's Museum, London: *A Manuscri by Mr. Gibbs Memorandums, &c.*, including 'A few Short Cursory Remarks on some of the finest Antient and modern Buildings in Rome, and other parts of Italy, by Mr Gibbs while he was Studying Architectur there, being Memorandums for his own use. 1707 and not intended to be made public being imperfect' (pp. 1–70); 'A Short Accompt of Mr James Gibbs Architect And of Several things he built in England &c. affter his returne from Italy' (pp. 83–102), etc. |
| *Gillam* | S. G. Gillam, *The Building Accounts of the Radcliffe Camera*, 1958, Oxford Historical Society, NS, XIII |
| *GM* | *The Gentleman's Magazine* (periodical) |
| *Godber* | 'The Travel Journal of Phillip Yorke, 1744–63' in J. Godber, *The Marchioness Grey of Wrest Park*, 1968, Bedfordshire Historical Record Society Publications, XLVII, pp. 125–63 |
| *GSJ* | *The Grub-street Journal* (periodical) |
| *Gwynn* | J. Gwynn, *London and Westminster Improved*, 1766 |
| *HMC* | *Historical Manuscripts Commission Reports* |
| *JSAH* | *Journal of The Society of Architectural Historians* (periodical) |
| *KCL* | King's College Library and Muniments, Cambridge: *AP* (Altar-Piece, 1742–75); *CB* (Congregation Book, 1722–78); *Coll.I, KC Mun* (MS Bundle, papers relating to erection of Fellows' Building); *MB* (Mundum Book, 1721–9, Vols. 44–5). |
| *Kerslake* | J. Kerslake, *Early Georgian Portraits*, 1977 |
| *Knight* | H. Knight, *Letters Written By The Right Honourable Lady Luxborough, To William Shenstone, Esq.*, 1775 |
| *Little* | B. Little, *The Life and Work of James Gibbs, 1682–1754*, 1955 |
| *LPL* | Lambeth Palace Library, London: Commissioners for Building Fifty New Churches papers |
| *Macky* | J. Macky, *A Journey Through England*, 1714, 1722, 1732 |
| *Markham* | S. Markham, *John Loveday of Caversham, 1711–1789: The Life and Tour of an Eighteenth-Century Onlooker*, 1984 |
| *MCL* | Magdalen College Library, Oxford |
| *MLHC* | St Marylebone Public Library, London: Local History Collection, including the Ashbridge Collection and *VP* (Proceedings of the Vestry) |
| *Morrison* | H. Morrison, *Early American Architecture*, 1952 |
| *NMR* | National Monuments Record, London |
| *Park* | H. Park, *A List of Architectural Books Available in America Before the Revolution*, 1973 |
| *Perks* | S. Perks, *The History of the Mansion House*, 1922 |
| *PRO* | Public Record Office, London |
| *Rad* | Shelfmark of Gibbs's books bequeathed to the Radcliffe Library, Oxford (deposited in the Bodleian Library) |
| *Ralph* | J. Ralph, *A Critical Review Of the Publick Buildings, Statues and Ornaments In, and about London and Westminster*, 1734 |
| *RCHM* | *The Royal Commission on Ancient and Historical Monuments and Constructions Inventories* |
| *RIBA* | Royal Institute of British Architects, Drawings Collection, London |
| *SAL* | Society of Antiquaries, London |
| *Salmon* | T. Salmon, *The Foreigner's Companion Through the Universities of Cambridge and Oxford, and the Adjacent Counties*, 1748 |
| *Sherburn* | G. Sherburn, ed., *The Correspondence of Alexander Pope*, 1956 |
| *SM* | 'Palladio', 'account of the celebrated architect James Gibbs', *Scots Magazine*, September 1760, pp. 475–6 |
| *SMIF* | Westminster Public Library, Archives Department: St Martin-in-the-Fields papers (deposited by the Vestry): 419/309, pp. 1–202 (Minutes of Commissioners for Rebuilding 1720–4); 419/310, pp. 232–9 (Treasurer's Accounts 1720–7); 419/311, pp. 1–129 and back page (Accounts 1721–7) |
| *S of L* | *The Survey of London* |
| *SRO* | Scottish Record Office, Edinburgh |
| *Stowe Papers* | Henry E. Huntington Library, San Marino, California, MSS |
| *Talman* | Bodleian Library, Oxford: 'John Talman's Letter Book', MS, Eng. Letters e.34 |
| *Toynbee* | P. Toynbee, ed., 'Horace Walpole's Journals of Visits to Country Seats, &c.', *Walpole Society*, 1928, XVI |
| *VAM* | Victoria and Albert Museum, London, Department of Prints and Drawings, and the Library: MS 86 NN2 ('Voiage D'Angleterre D'Hollande Et de Flandre fait l'annee 1728') |
| *VB* | C. Campbell, *Vitruvius Britannicus*, 1715, 1717, 1725, J. Badeslade and J. Rocque, 1739, J. Woolfe and J. Gandon, 1767–71 |
| *VCH* | *The Victoria History of the Counties of England* |
| *Vertue* | *Vertue Note Books*, in *Walpole Society*, 1930–55 |
| *Wanley* | C. E. and R. C. Wright, *The Diary of Humfrey Wanley, 1715–1726*, 1966 |
| *Willis* | P. Willis, *Charles Bridgeman and the English Landscape Garden*, 1977 |
| *Willis and Clark* | R. Willis and J. W. Clark, *The Architectural History of the University of Cambridge*, 1886 |
| *WPL* | Westminster Public Library, London |
| *WS* | *The Wren Society*, 1924–43 |
| *YAS* | Yorkshire Archaeological Society, Leeds: MS 328 ('Account of my Journey begun 6 Augt 1724') |

# NOTES TO THE TEXT

## Notes to the Introduction

1. Sir John Perceval reporting in 1724 (*BL* Add. MS 47030, ff. 93–v).
2. H. Walpole, *Anecdotes of Painting in England* (1771) p. 45.
3. The Chapter of Lincoln Minster, 1726 (*Lincolnshire Architectural Society's Reports* (1954) NS, V, ii, p. 108).
4. *Anecdotes of Painting in England* (1771) p. 44.
5. 'A Hue and Cry after Four of the King's Liege Subjects, who were Lately suppos'd to be seen at Roystone in Hartfordshire,' 18 March 1721, in *WS* (1940) XVII, p. 12.
6. G. Clinch, *Marylebone and St Pancras* (1890) p. 23.
7. *Architecture in Britain 1530 to 1830* (1953) p. 357.
8. R. Morris, *The Art of Architecture, A Poem. In Imitation of Horace's Art of Poetry* (1742) p. 14.
9. J. Holloway, 'A James Gibbs Autobiography', *Burl Mag* (May 1955) pp. 147–51. The MS was apparently in existence by 1754 since it is likely to be 'A Manuscript by Mr. Gibbs, not to be Publish'd being imperfect' listed in 'A Catalogue of Mr Gibbs's Books which he has given to the Radcliffe Library at Oxford 1754' (*Bodleian* MS Eng. Misc. c.28) but with a note 'This book is not forthcoming, and I suppose not sent'. It belonged to the architect Henry Holland before passing to Soane.
10. Edward Holdsworth, architect of Magdalen College, Oxford, writing from Italy in 1743–4 (*MCL* MS 906, iii–iv).

## Notes to Chapter I

1. From Sir James Thornhill, 'A Hue and Cry after Four of the King's Liege Subjects, who were Lately suppos'd to be seen at Roystone in Hartfordshire,' 18 March 1721, in *WS* (1940) XVII, p. 12.
2. The opening is reported in *Gillam*, pp. xxii–xxv; *GM* (April 1749) pp. 164–5, (October 1749) p. 459; *London Magazine* (April 1749) p. 156.
3. *Salmon*, p. 31.
4. H. M. Petter, *The Oxford Almanacks* (1974) p. 66.
5. *Oratio in Theatro Sheldoniano habita idibus Aprilibus, MDCCXLIX. die dedicationis Bibliothecæ Radclivianæ* (1749) pp. 12–13; W. King, *A Translation Of a late Celebrated Oration, Occasioned By a Lible, entitled, Remarks on Doctor K———g's Speech* (1750) pp. 32–3.
6. P. Hume Brown, ed., *Tours in Scotland 1677 & 1681 By Thomas Kirk and Ralph Thoresby* (1892) p. 23; *Macky 1723*, p. 104.
7. The most reliable biographical information is 'A Short Accompt of Mr James Gibbs Architect' in *Gibbs MS*, discussed in J. Holloway, 'A James Gibbs Autobiography', *Burl Mag* (May 1955) pp. 147–51. In the Register of Students at the Scots College in Rome his name is entered under 12 October 1703 as 'Jacobus Gibb, filius Patritii Gibb de Fittsmyre, et Annae Gordon Aberdonensis, annorum viginti unius cum dimidio ingressus est Collegio die duodecima octobris anni millesimi septingentesimi tertii' (P. J. Anderson, ed., *Records of the Scots Colleges at Douai, Rome, Madrid, Valladolid and Ratisbon* (1906) I, p. 126, no. 246). See also *SM* and A. S. MacWilliam, 'James Gibbs, Architect, 1682–1754', *Innes Review* (Autumn 1954) V, No. 2, pp. 101–3.
8. A 'James Gibbs' appears in the officers, graduates and alumni list in the College records for 1697–1700, although not in the list of students paying graduate fees (P. J. Anderson, *Fasti Academiæ Mariscallanæ Aberdonensis*, II, p. 273).
9. *SM*, p. 475.
10. *Gibbs MS*, p. 83, mentioning an aunt, who, according to *SM*, p. 475, was Elspeth Farquhar, wife of Peter Morison, a merchant.
11. *HMC Portland*, X, p. 301 (Mar to Edward Harley, 3 August 1713).
12. *Gibbs MS*, p. 61.
13. P. Murray, 'Archer Abroad', *AR* (August 1957) p. 88; *Talman*, pp. 60–1, 84; I. Pears, 'Patronage and Learning in the Virtuoso Republic: John Talman in Italy, 1709–1712', *Oxford Art Journal* (1 May 1982) pp. 24–30.
14. *Gibbs MS*, pp. 60–1.
15. *ASH* III.129; S. Colombo, *Profilo della Architettura Religiosa del Seicento Varese e il suo Territorio* (1970) p. 18; A. Tomlinson, 'Sacri Monti', *AR* (December 1954) p. 372, fig. 11. These buildings do not appear to have been available in engravings during Gibbs's lifetime.
16. *Gibbs MS*, p. 83. For the activities of contemporary British architects in Italy, see T. Friedman, 'The English Appreciation of Italian Decoration', *Burl Mag* (December 1975) pp. 841–7; H. Honour, 'John Talman and William Kent in Italy', *Connoisseur* (August 1954) pp. 3–7.
17. A. S. MacWilliam, 'James Gibbs, Architect, 1682–1754', *Innes Review* (Autumn 1954) pp. 102–3.
18. *Gibbs MS*, p. 84.
19. *Vertue*, III, p. 15. Gibbs refers to 'Fountana' and 'Signo Abramo Paris, my old masters' as dead in 1717 (*HMC Stuart*, IV, p. 568). For Fontana and his circle (*Braham*); for Abraham Paris (O. J. Blázíček, *Baroque Art in Bohemia* (1968) p. 46, n. 9). Gibbs owned two paintings of architectural capriccios by Garroli (Rijksbureau voor Kunsthistorische Documentatie, The Hague: *A Catalogue of the Genuine and Curious Collection of Pictures, By several Eminent Masters, Of that Ingenious Architect James Gibbs, Esq.*, Langford's, 25 March 1756, lots 39–40).
20. *Gibbs MS*, p. 84.
21. *HMC Egmont*, II, pp. 218–19. Some are listed among visitors to Padua University in 1701–9 (H. F. Brown, 'Inglesi e Scozzesi all'Università di Padova dall'anno 1618 sino al 1765', in *Monografie Storiche sullo Studio di Padova* (1921) pp. 183–9; and S. Lang, 'English Architects and Dilettanti in Padua', *AR* (November 1957) p. 344). Perceval was in Padua in October 1706 and Rome by January 1707 (*BL* Add. MS 47025, ff. 66v–7; H. Sirr, 'James Gibbs

and his Friend, Sir John Perceval, 1707–8–9', *RIBA Journal* (22 April 1911) 3rd series, XVIII, pp. 429–30; J. Madge, 'A "Virtuoso" in Rome', *CL* (27 January 1983) pp. 232–3).

22. *HMC Egmont*, II, p. 217 (18 June 1707, from the Irish painter, Edward Gouge).

23. B. Ford, 'The Blathwayt Brothers of Dyrham in Italy on the Grand Tour', in *National Trust Year Book, 1975–76*, p. 24.

24. *HMC Egmont*, II, pp. 217–18.

25. *Gibbs MS*, p. 84.

26. *BL* Add. MS 47025, f. 104 (24 November 1708) and *HMC Egmont*, II, pp. 234–5, respectively. Perceval annotated a copy of the latter letter: 'Mr. Gibbs accepts my invitation to come to Ireland' (*BL* Add. MS 47025, ff. 114–v).

27. *HMC Egmont*, II, p. 236. For Burton, see *BL* Add. MS 47025, f. 68; E. Malins and The Knight of Glin, *Lost Demesnes Irish Landscape Gardening, 1660–1845* (1976) p. 7, pl. 3. Perceval also owned property at Turnham Green, London (*BM* King's Maps K.XXX, 18a–c; B. Rand, *Berkeley and Perceval* (1914) pp. 171, 174–5).

28. *Gibbs MS*, p. 84.

29. George Berkeley remarked in 1709: 'our Country seems to me the place in the World which is least furnish'd with Virtuosi' (*BL* Add. MS 47025, f. 133v). The Knight of Glin, 'New Light on Castletown, Co. Kildare', *Quarterly Bulletin of the Irish Georgian Society* (January–March 1965) p. 4.

30. *HMC Egmont*, II, pp. 235–6, annotated 'From Mr. Gibbs; that the Earl of Mar has provided for him' (*BL* Add. MS 47025, ff. 115v–16). Gibbs and Perceval remained in contact (*HMC Diary of Lord Egmont, 1739–1747*, III, pp. 233–4, 242).

31. *HMC Stuart*, V, p. 211.

32. A letter from John Drummond, 12 December 1734, regarding improvements to Quarrell, Stirlingshire (*SRO* GD 24/1/495, ff. 506–7).

33. *HMC Portland*, X, p. 301.

34. *LPL* 2690, p. 112, referring to 'Mr John Gibbs'; 2726, ff. 67–70; *HMC Portland*, X, p. 301.

35. *LPL* 2690, pp. 112, 114; 2726, ff. 71–2.

36. *HMC Portland*, V, pp. 331–2.

37. *HMC Portland*, X, p. 302.

38. *LPL* 2690, pp. 115, 117, 119, 126; 2726, ff. 73–4 (Gibbs's 8 October 1713 petition).

39. *ABA*, p. vi.

40. *Vertue*, III, p. 13, mentions in 1723 Pelham's mezzotint after a lost portrait by Hans Hysing; a version was later engraved by W. H. Worthington. An oil painting of young Gibbs holding a plan of St Mary-le-Strand (Derek Sherborne collection) attributed to both Hogarth and Dahl, in the writer's opinion is by William Aikman (compare to *Kerslake*, p. 97, pls. 263, 265). See A. Oswald, 'James Gibbs and His Portraits', *CL Annual* (1963) pp. 12–13.

41. Mar to Gibbs, 16 April 1716 (*HMC Stuart*, II, p. 92).

42. *HMC Stuart*, V, p. 27.

43. *HMC Stuart*, II, p. 92.

44. *LPL* 2726, ff. 75–6.

45. *HMC Egmont*, II, p. 235.

46. A. S. MacWilliam, 'James Gibbs, Architect, 1682–1754', *Innes Review* (Autumn 1954) p. 103. Perceval noted that Gibbs had 'Since turn'd Protestant, & is settled in London an Architect of very good note' (*BL* Add. MS 47025, f. 80), although neither he nor Michael Rysbrack, another Catholic resident of Marylebone, was a parishioner of Marylebone Chapel (*BL Portland Papers Loan* 29/42).

47. *HMC Stuart*, II, pp. 92–4.

48. *HMC Stuart*, II, p. 404, and IV, p. 568, respectively. Mar was informed on 27 August 1717, 'Your friend the architect will be with you in a few days, but very privately. I hear since that he has altered his resolution and does not come' (*HMC Stuart*, V, pp. 24, 48).

49. *HMC Stuart*, IV, p. 568; V, pp. 378–9.

50. *Anecdotes of Painting in England* (1771) IV, p. 45.

51. *BL* Misc. Add. MS 39167, ff. 74–7.

52. *Gillam*, p. 99.

53. *LPL* 2714, f. 15. The church was, however, designed by John James, 1720–5.

54. *SMIF* 419/309, pp. 16, 26–7.

55. *Vertue*, III, p. 21 (1724).

56. p. 73.

57. Edward Harley related how, journeying across Shooters Hill above Greenwich in 1723, he came upon 'a pretty ancient beggar [who] if he can in time afford it, I would recommend him to the assistance of my friend Gibbs to erect a more decent habitation than he now has on this pleasant situation' (*HMC Portland*, VI, p. 75).

58. *Drummonds* Ledgers 1722, p. 306; 1724–5, p. 70; 1726, p. 35.

59. *Vertue*, III, pp. 13, 17, 84. Gibbs presented the marble, dated 1726, to the Radcliffe Library in 1754 (P.C.C. 228 Pinfold; *Gibbs MS*, p. 101; R. Lane Poole, *Catalogue of Portraits in the Possession of The University, Colleges, City and County of Oxford* (1912) I, pp. xvi, 226, no. 685); another marble, sculptor unknown, on the Library stair-case, showing Gibbs in old age, was presented in 1845 (*Gillam*, pp. l–li); a plaster replica is in the *RIBA*.

60. *Vertue*, III, pp. 13, 56; R. de Beaumont, 'An Architect's Book Plate', *CL* (8 July 1949) p. 122; *Kerslake*, p. 97, pl. 264; *Bodleian* MS Autog. c.19, ff. 1, 3.

61. Nulty-Melcombe sale, Christie and Ansell (28 March 1783) lot 88, bought Walpole £7.7.0; *A Description of the Villa of Mr. Horace Walpole . . . at Strawberry Hill* (1784) p. 42; Strawberry Hill sale (13 May 1842) p. 177, lot 99, bought Forster £7.7.0; presented St Martin-in-the-Fields by William Boore 1865(?). This bust is signed and dated 1726 (*Vertue*, III, p. 56; *Kerslake*, p. 97, pl. 262); the marble pedestal corresponds to one in *ABA*, pl. 150; see also *VAM* E.3658-1913 and *ASH* II.14.

62. Quoted in J. McMaster, *A Short History of the Royal Parish of St. Martin-in-the-Fields* (1916) p. 85.

63. 'The Wanderer. A Vision' (1729) canto IV, lines 157–8, in C. Tracy, *The Poetical Works of Richard Savage* (1962) p. 134.

64. J. Pote, *The Foreigner's Guide* (1729) p. 48; *A New Guide to London: or Directions to Strangers* (1726) p. 26; J. W. F. Hill, 'The Western Spires of Lincoln Cathedral and their Threatened Removal in 1726', *Lincolnshire Architectural Society's Records* (1954) NS, V (ii), p. 108.

65. *KCL MB*, 1725, No. 4, p. 80.

66. Annotated preface to Johnson's copy of P. Monier, *The History of painting, Sculpture, Architecture, Graving; and Of those who Excell'd in them*, 1726 (B. Weinreb Architectural Books Ltd).

67. *SAL* Minute Book, I, pp. 26, 41, 59, 61–2, 64, 151, 170, for St Martin's references. The Treasurers Book, 1718–38, first entry under April 1726, pp. 122–3, 130, 136, 232, 268, *A General List of the Members of the Society of Antiquaries, London, from MDCCXVII inclusive to Michelmas MDCCXLVII*, p. 2.

68. Proposed 5 June, elected 16 October, admitted 20 November ('Journal Book of the Royal Society' (1726–31) XIII, pp. 341, 358, 375; *The Record of The Royal Society of London* (1940) p. 400; *The Signatures in the First Journal-Book and The Charter-Book of the Royal Society* (1980) p. 20).

69. L. Dickins and M. Stanton, *An Eighteenth-Century Correspondence* (1910) p. 236; *PRO* WO 48/68, pp. 185–6; WO 54/203, pp. 2, 6; WO 54/210, p. 11; *Colvin*, p. 979.

70. *HMC Portland*, V, p. 332; *S of L* (1963) XXXII, p. 398; (1966) XXXIV, p. 392; *Sherburn*, II, p. 298; *Building News* (18 September 1857) p. 989; J. Howgego, *Printed Maps of London circa 1553–1830* (1978) p. 157. The Marylebone houses are discussed on pp. 205–9.

71. 4 February 1731, p. 1, in connection with St Giles-in-the-Fields; the phrase is repeated, describing Gibbs, James and Leoni, with regard to the London Mansion House, in the *London Daily Post and General Advertiser* (6 March 1738, *Burney* 332b).

72. *Ralph*, pp. 31, 37–8, 69–79.

73. The 'Mr *Gibbs*, a celebrated architect' noted as recently deceased in the *Penny London Post* (26–8 September 1744) was a Brewer Street builder of the same name who had a 'considerable Business, and Good Character . . . reckon'd the best Measurer of Timber in *Eng-*

*land*' also mentioned in the *General Advertiser* (26 September 1744, *Burney* 396b) and the *Westminster Journal* (29 September 1744), perhaps the same noted in *GM* (18 January 1745) p. 52, and the *London Magazine* (January 1745) XIV, p. 49.

74. *The History of London* (1739) p. 381. Gibbs's parochial duties on the Marylebone estate during these years included dealing with the burial ground and workhouse (*MLHC* Vestry Proceedings, 1729–68).

75. *Vertue*, III, p. 133.

76. A. Cunningham, *The Lives of the Most Eminent British Painters, Sculptors, and Architects* (1831) IV, p. 294, including a portrait by W. C. Edwards of 1830 after Hogarth.

77. Compare the plan in Soldi's portrait in St Martin-in-the-Fields to *Bibliotheca Radcliffiana MDCCXL*, No. 3, dated 1737 (*Gillam*, p. 175 no. 28, pl. 38b), which differs from *BR* 1747, pl. III. Its provenance is discussed in J. Ingamells, 'Andrea Soldi—A Check-List of His Work', *Walpole Society* (1980) XLVII, p. 9, nos. 28–9, pl. 5c; *Kerslake*, p. 97, pl. 268. In Williams's portrait (*Kerslake*, pp. 96–7, pl. 266) the plan corresponds to *Bibliotheca Radcliffiana* (1737) No. 2.

78. *Kerslake*, p. 97, pl. 267. Gibbs's drawing for the surround is *ASH* I.116. For Fontana's portrait, see *Braham*, frontispiece.

79. *Knight*, pp. 139–40.

80. *BL* Add. MS 6391, f. 172; *Gibbs MS*, p. 102; G. Goodwin, *James McArdell* (1903) pp. 108–9, nos. 146–7; *Kerslake*, pp. 96–7; T. Martyn, *The English Connoisseur* (1767) II, p. 51; R. Lane Poole, *Catalogue of Portraits in the Possession of The University, Colleges, City, and County of Oxford* (1912) I, pp. 102, 104, nos. 254, 259; II, p. 88, no. 25; *Sayer and Bennett's Enlarged Catalogue of . . . Prints* (1775) under McArdell, no. 79; *Illustrated Catalogue of a Loan Collection of Portraits of English Historical Personages . . . Exhibited [at] Oxford* (1906) pp. 38–9. The Bodleian version is inscribed 'John Micha. Williams Pinxit 1752' and on verso 'Ja: Gibbs Architectus 1750'. An engraving by A. Bannerman is in R. Berry, ed., *The Works of Horatio Walpole, Earl of Orford* (1798) III, p. 432; another is a reversed version signed by J. Hopwood, *c.* 1810 (F. O'Donoghue and H. M. Hake, *Catalogue of Engraved British Portraits Preserved in the Department of Prints and Drawings in the British Museum* (1922) II, p. 327 no. 7).

81. *Bart's Journal* Ha 1/12, pp. 141–2.

82. *Vertue*, III, p. 149.

83. Scottish Portrait Gallery, no. 1373. J. Ingamells, 'Andrea Soldi—A Check-List of his Work', *Walpole Society* (1980) XLVII, pp. 9–10, no. 30; *Vertue*, III, p. 132.

84. *Bart's Journal* Ha 1/11, p. 443; Ha 1/12, pp. 46–7, 56–7, 102, 112, 120–1, 134.

85. Gibbs attended a meeting on 7 September 1749 (*Bart's Journal* Ha 1/12, p. 158).

86. He attended Radcliffe trustees meetings until March 1754 (*Gillam*, pp. 110–12), but almost certainly the Rev. James Gibbs (a subscriber to T. Lediard's *The History of England*, 1737) was the translator of *The History of the Portuguese During the Reign of Emmanuel . . . Written originally in Latin by Jerome Osorio, Bishop of Sylves. Now first translated into English by James Gibbs* (1752) rather than our architect, as suggested by *Little*, p. 155.

87. P.C.C. 228 Pinfold. The Will was proved 16 August 1754, with an abstract reprinted in *SM*, p. 476. Legacies were reported in *Bart's Journal* Ha 1/12, p. 484; Thomas Coram Foundation, Minutes of the General Committee, p. 201; *Read's Weekly Journal* (24 August 1754, *Burney* 465b, I) p. 3.

88. *GM* (August 1754) p. 387, no. 5; *Vertue*, III, p. 162; *Public Advertiser* (9 August 1754, *Burney* 467b, IV) p. 1. The *London Magazine* (5 August, 1754) XXIII, p. 380, said he was 'well known for his great genius in architecture'; *SM*, p. 476. He is not to be confused with the James Gibbes involved in a lawsuit with John, Duke of Argyll, 1733–4 (*PRO* C33/361, ff. 131v, 208v; C 11/2300/1, 12 October 1733) or Gibbs, an Old Bethlem builder, d. 1762 (*GM* (March 1762) p. 145, no. 19; *CLRO JCCL*, XXXV, p. 66b (8); XXXVI, pp. 36a, 122b).

89. Westminster Record Office: MRY1 4, St Marylebone Parish Church, County of Middlesex, Parish Registers, Burials 1749 to 1764, Vol. no. P89, under 9 August 1754.

90. p. 476, reprinted in the *European Magazine* (September 1789) pp. 168–9.

91. p. 45.

92. p. 146. An English translation, *The Present State of the Arts in England*, appeared in London in 1755 (reprinted 1970).

93. p. 402, translated as 'after the examples of the best architects of antiquity,—an example which the moderns should also imitate' (Mrs E. Cresy, ed., *The Lives of Celebrated Architects, Ancient and Modern . . . by Francesco Milizia* (1826) p. 297). By 1795 Gibbs was associated with Michelangelo, Bernini and Wren in the form of cenotaph portraits at Whitton (J. Harris, *Sir William Chambers* (1970) p. 251).

94. p. 57.

95. *Observations on English Architecture* (1806) pp. 155–6.

96. *Anecdotes of Painting in England* (1771) IV, pp. 44–5; moreover 'Gibbs like Vanbrugh, had no aversion to ponderosity; but not being enbued with much invention, was only regularly heavy'. *The Works in Architecture of Robert and James Adam* (1779) Preface to Part I, commending Jones's compartment ceilings, thought 'Vanbrugh, Campbell, and Gibbs followed too implicitly the authority of this great name'. 'Gibbs adhered scrupulously to the rules of Palladio, but nature had denied him taste' (*Anecdotes of the Arts in England* (1800) p. 109, reissued as *Les Beaux-Arts en Angleterre . . . Traduite de l'Anglois de M. Dallaway, par M\*\*\** (1807) I, pp. 114–23). M. Noble, *Biographical History of England* (1806) IV, pp. 390–2, wrote of 'his barbarous buildings for gardens, his cumbrous chimney-pieces, and vases without grace . . . striking proofs of his want of taste . . . inferior [to Jones and Wren] he did not even equal Vanbrugh'.

## Notes to Chapter II

1. p. 14.

2. *Vertue*, VI, pp. 168–9, lists Gibbs among the 18 October 1711 subscribers (W. T. Whitley, *Artists and Their Friends in England, 1700–1799* (1928) I, pp. 7–16).

3. *Vertue*, III, pp. 120, 140; V, p. 43; *BL* Add. MS 39167, ff. 73–86, recording Gibbs's membership and stewardship; *Wanley*, II, p. 261.

4. *Vertue*, III, pp. 14, 24, 120; VI, frontispiece, pp. 31–7, 137.

5. *Vertue*, III, p. 13. M. Noble, *Biographical History of England* (1806) IV, pp. 390–2, refers to it as in Harley's collection; since lost. Schröder was working in England 1718–24 (W. Nisser, *Michael Dahl and the Contemporary Swedish School of Painting in England* (1927) pp. 68–71).

6. 'A Society of Artists', *c.* 1730 (Ashmolean Museum, Oxford) and 'A Conversation of Virtuosis', 1734–5 (National Portrait Gallery, London) are discussed in *Kerslake*, pp. 340–2, pl. 951; *Vertue*, III, pp. 71–2, 81; *Willis*, pls. 19–20.

7. *Vertue*, III, p. 108, also pp. 26, 79: 'My good Lord Oxford. has at heart the promoteing of . . . Mr Gibbs'. J. Lees-Milne, *Earls of Creation* (1962) Chapter IV.

8. *Kerslake*, pp. 97–8. All three portraits are lost.

9. Art Institute of Chicago (1922.1283), annotated 'Mr Gibbs—new Church-Strand'; the posthumous representation of Prior in a portrait painting suggests a post-1721 date for this sketch.

10. H. Bunker Wright and M. K. Spears, *The Literary Works of Matthew Prior* (1959) I, p. 399; *HMC Bath*, III, pp. 483, 488.

11. *Wanley*, II, p. 271.

12. R. W. Goulding and C. K. Adams, *Catalogue of the Pictures Belonging to His Grace The Duke of Portland at Welbeck Abbey* (1936) p. xxx, listing pictures bought by Harley and sent from London to Wimpole by Gibbs on 2 February 1716.

13. Garrard to the Duke of Kent, 11 July 1716 (Bedfordshire *CRO* Lucas Papers L30/8/28/22).

14. A copy is in a bound collection of Kirkall prints belonging to

Gibbs (*Rad* a.2, no. 53). His picture collection was bequeathed to the painter, Cosmo Alexander in 1754 (P.C.C. 228 Pinfold) and sold in 1756 (Rijksbureau voor Kunsthistorische Documentatie, The Hague, *A Catalogue of the Genuine and Curious Collection of Pictures, By several Eminent Masters, Of that Ingenious Architect James Gibbs, Esq; Deceased; With some few Pictures lately consign'd from Abroad*, Langford's (25–6 March 1756). Some items are listed in *HMC Portland*, VI, p. 13; *A Catalogue of the Collection Of the Right Honourable Edward Earl of Oxford Deceas'd* (11 March 1742) p. 13, lot 49; *VAM* 86.00.18, MS 'Sale Catalogues of The Principal Collections of Pictures ... Sold by auction in England within the years 1711–1759', I, pp. 56, 208, 272, 427; II, pp. 56–9.

15. Adrian Drift told Edward Harley on 6 December 1721 about 'Two Copies of the Buste of Flora for ... Bridgman and Gibbs; which he [Prior] recommended to [Richard] Dickenson to do in perfection, as being designed to present to Two of his Brother Virtuosi ... a Debt due to Two worthy Men whom he much Esteemed' (*BL Portland Papers Loan* 29/316, f. 11v; 29/317, ff. 6v, 68, 80v–1, 149v–50v, 162, 163v, 165–v, 170; H. Bunker Wright and H. C. Montgomery, 'The Art Collection of a Virtuoso in Eighteenth-Century England', *Art Bulletin* (September 1945) p. 200, no. 36).

16. In 1725 Gibbs directed Pope to Rysbrack's studio in Vere Street, Marylebone, presumably to arrange sittings (*Sherburn*, II, p. 298). F. W. Bateson, ed, *Alexander Pope Epistles To Several Persons Moral Essays* (1951) p. 183. *The Dunciad. With Notes Variorum, and the Prolegomena of Scriblerus* (1729) 2nd ed., Book II, line 134, mentions the gentlemen of *The Dunciad* 'went so far as to libel an eminent Sculptor for making our author's *Busto* in marble, at the request of Mr. *Gibbs* the Architect'. This bust (Athenaeum Club, London) is dated 1730 (W. K. Wimsatt, *The Portraits of Alexander Pope* (1965) pp. 97–106, pls. 11.2a–b).

17. J. Butt, 'A Master Key to Popery', in J. L. Clifford and L. A. Landa, eds., *Pope and His Contemporaries* (1949) p. 50.

18. *BL* Add. MSS 18240, 18243.

19. J. Simpson, intro., *Vitruvius Scoticus* (1980) p. 29.

20. *MCL* 8 September 1729 letter. Numerous payments to Burloch or Borlach appear in Gibbs's *Drummonds* account 1724–43, the first on 17 July 1724 (Ledger 1723, p. 110). A copy of *Designs of Architecture*, with 20 numbered and signed plates, is listed in H. Kirker, *The Architecture of Charles Bulfinch* (1969) p. 387.

21. *ASH* II.15, inscribed 'to come this Evening to Mrs Boscawens In St James place and inquier for Miss Rice any time before seven o'clo[ck]'.

22. *Bart's Corr* Ha 19/29/3, also 19/29/6.

23. Northamptonshire *CRO* Fitzwilliam Papers, Milton, Map 1966 (dated 1723), nos. 78–9, 135, 150 (dated 1725), discussed in *Colvin*, p. 932.

24. *LPL* 2714, f. 15.

25. *LPL* 2690, pp. 142 (items 7–8), 209 (6); 2708, f. 7; 2712, f. 23; 2713, f. 15; 2714, f. 138; 2717, ff. 83–4; 2724, ff. 31, 35, 39–42; 2729, ff. 28v–9.

26. *Bart's Journal* Ha 1/2, pp. 141–2.

27. *Bart's Corr* Ha 19/31/1.

28. *SMIF* 419/309, pp. 175–6; 419/311, pp. 66–70, 102.

29. *LPL* 2691, p. 62; 2697, ff. 459, 461, 477; 2698, ff. 15–16; 2703, ff. 80–1; 2716, ff. 58, 62; 2721, ff. 110, 112.

30. *SMIF* 419/309, pp. 198–202; *ABA*, p. v; *Beard 1975*, pp. 201–4, 217–18, 250–1.

31. *BL* Add. MS 18238, f. 37.

32. See *ASH* II.104–6, unexecuted domestic ceilings with Gibbs's architectural framework flamboyantly ornamented in another hand; a note in Italian refers to Paolo Franchini's willingness to execute the work for £85 provided the client paid for scaffolding. Payments to 'la Franchine' totalling £105.10.0 are in *Drummonds* Ledgers 1731, p. 165; 1736, p. 105 (C. Palumbo-Fossati, *Gli Stuccatori Ticinesi Lafranchini in Inghilterra e in Irlanda nel Secolo XVIII* (1982) pls. 14–15, 19, 21 and 'The Stuccoists Lafranchini in Ireland', *Bulletin of the Irish Georgian Society* (1982) *XXV*, pp. 5–18).

33. *LPL* 2703, ff. 14v; 2716, f. 48; 2690, pp. 358, 361.

34. *SMIF* 419/309, pp. 126–8.

35. *PRO* State Papers Domestic, George I, Vol. LXIII, no. 51(3); Archives of Dean and Chapter of Lincoln: Miscellaneous Letters and Papers A.4.13 (8 March and 7 April 1776).

36. *Baker*, p. 140.

37. *BL* Add. MS 40776, f. 63.

38. *CUL CUR* 46, f. 13.

39. *Colvin*, p. 436. Horne (d. 1756) countersigned with Gibbs the carpenter's bills for building King's College Fellows' Building, 1729–30 (*KCL KCMun*), worked as measurer at St Bartholomew's Hospital, 1730–3 (*Bart's Journal* Ha 19/5(1–53)), arbitrated on the London Mansion House model, 1740–1, and for the Fishmongers Company, 1743 (see n. 77). He received a payment from Gibbs in 1744 (*Drummonds* Ledger 1743, p. 131).

40. *CUL CUR* 46, f. 17.

41. Castle Howard papers, 5 February 1737; *Vertue*, III, p. 46.

42. *Gillam*, p. 181; *Bodleian* MS Autog. c.9, f. 107, and c.19, ff. 1–3.

43. *LPL* 2690, pp. 217, 249; 2705, f. 64; 2706, ff. 80–1; 2707, f. 14.

44. *KCL AP*, p. 1.

45. *MCL* 21 April and 7 May 1728 letters.

46. *DIL* I/p/1l.

47. *Vertue*, III, p. 133. References to building payments are given under individual commissions in the Catalogue of Works.

48. *CLRO 113B*, Folder January–March 1737/8; *113C*, p. 121.

49. *CLRO 113B*, Folder 19 November 1735.

50. J. Stuart, *Critical Observations on the Buildings and Improvements of London* (1771) pp. 6–7.

51. *The Present State of the Arts in England* (1755) pp. 99–100.

52. 23 May 1734, No. 230, pp. 1–2. The series appear in Nos. 232, 236–49, 251–6, 258–9, 261, 267, 271, 289 (*Burney* 306b). E. Harris, 'Batty Langley: A Tutor to Freemasons (1696–1751)', *Burl Mag* (May 1977) p. 331. A similar brand of criticism against the '*designing Virtuosi ... Mr. Inigo Pilaster* and *Sir Christopher Cupolo*' is in *GM* (May 1732) pp. 765–6.

53. Nos. 237, p. 1; 249, p. 2; 253, p. 1; 254, p. 1. R. Wittkower, 'Pseudo-Palladian Elements in English Neoclassicism', in *Palladio and English Palladianism* (1974) pp. 168–74.

54. pp. 25–6.

55. *Stonehenge A Temple Restor'd To The British Druids* (1740) p. 15.

56. p. iii.

57. *The Art of Architecture* (1742) pp. 10, 25–6.

58. W. Herrmann, *The Theory of Claude Perrault* (1973) p. 154, n. 85, p. 159.

59. *The Family Memoirs of the Rev. William Stukeley, M.D.*, Surtees Society Publications (1883) LXXVI, II, p. 262.

60. *GM* (August–September 1732) p. 21, no. 34; *London Magazine* (September 1732) I, p. 320.

61. *Rules for Drawing*, pp. 1–2.

62. *Gibbs MS*, p. 101.

63. *Leeds Mercury* (6 and 13 June 1738). Apart from the third edition issued in 1753, facsimiles appeared in 1924 (Introduction by C. Barman) and 1968. *Rules for Drawing* is acknowledged in advertisements for Langley's *Ancient Masonry* in *GSJ* (11 July 1734) No. 237, p. 3.

64. *BL* Proposals C.116.i.4, p. 93. The 1734 recommendation was widely quoted: *GSJ* (7 February 1734) No. 215, p. 4; *The Craftsman* (12 April 1735, *Burney* 311b); *Ralph*, p. 110; and *A New Critical Review* (1736) p. 78. For Langley's criticism, see N. Lloyd, *A History of the English House* (1931) p. 135.

65. W. Elwin and W. J. Courthope, eds., *The Works of Alexander Pope* (1871–89) III, p. 174.

66. *The Art of Architecture* (1742) p. 32. F--tc--t is Henry Flitcroft.

67. *Bart's Corr* Ha 19/29/16.

68. The Duke of Montrose, a member of the St George, Hanover Square building committee (*ASH* II.38), on Gibbs's alterations to Alexander McGill's design for his Glasgow house, 5 May 1719 (*SRO* GD 220/5/829/12a–b). In 1722–4 Peter Burningham and William Langley, joiners, were the 'Arbitrators' chosen to view

and value work at St Mary-le-Strand (*LPL* 2698, f. 17).

69. H. M. Colvin, *The History of the King's Works* (1976) V, pp. 391–7.

70. *S of L* (1977) XXXIX, pp. 16, 22. The first reference to Gibbs is in Agreement No. 2, dated 2 September 1720, the last in No. 65, 12 April 1728 (*WPL* Bundles 1–20). Sir Richard Grosvenor, whose brother-in-law was Sir William Wyndham, Gibbs's client at Witham, and Thomas Grosvenor both subscribed to *ABA*.

71. *BL* Add. MS 18238, ff. 40–1. The contract for rebuilding Marylebone parish church in 1741 specified the work was 'to be approved' by Gibbs (*MLHC* Proceedings of the Vestry, 1729–40, pp. 335–41).

72. *Bart's Journal* Ha 1/10, pp. 133, 138–v, 147v.

73. These included advice on building the parish workhouse (undertaken by John Lane, 1740–53), reported frequently in *MLHC* Proceedings of the Vestry, 1729–68.

74. A fully documented history is in T. Friedman, 'The Rebuilding of Bishopsgate: A Case of Architecture and Corruption in Eighteenth Century London', *Guildhall Studies in London History* (April 1980) pp. 75–90.

75. N. J. M. Kerling, 'The Relationship between St. Bartholomew's Hospital and the City of London, 1546–1948', *Guildhall Miscellany* (October 1971) IV, No. 1, pp. 14–21.

76. *City Corruption* (1738) pp. 3–11, 16, 22, 39–46. Gibbs's reports are *CLRO JCCL* XXIV, p. 211a; XXV, pp. 108a–9a, 117a.

77. Gibbs, James Horne, Robert Morris, William Robinson and John Smallwell each received £26 for arbitrating the dispute over the model (*CLRO 113C*, pp. 296–7, 299, 301–3; D. Stroud, *George Dance Architect, 1741–1825* (1971) p. 37), illustrated in E. Hoppus, *The Gentleman's and Builder's Repository* (1737) frontispiece, and probably destroyed in 1838. Gibbs, Horne, Flitcroft, Charles Easton, Robert Morris, John Price the younger, James Steere and others were associated with the Fishmongers Company episode (Guildhall Library, London: MSS 5570/6, 5571/4, pp. 723–4; Court Ledger IV 1733–52, p. 307; P. Metcalfe, *The Hall of the Fishmongers Company* (1977) pp. 100–2).

78. City of Bristol Record Office: Chamberlain's Letters 01152(2) and Bundle J, item 41 (i). E. G. Priest, 'Building The Exchange and Markets of the City of Bristol' (1980) University of Bristol, M.Lit., pp. 124–5, 453. There is no evidence Gibbs was called.

79. Gloucestershire *CRO* Tetbury Feoffees D566 L5/4, pp. 17–27, 30–1, and 'The Report of James Gibbs Architect Concerning the Repairs done at Tetbury' (pp. 32–3); D556 L5/5–6, summarized in D556 R2/3, D1571 L30.

80. pp. 17–18, comparing Thomas Ripley's unclassical treatment of the Custom House (1718–25) and the Admiralty (1723–6), London, with work by Roger Morris, Flitcroft, Gibbs, Leoni and Ware.

81. Fontana taught Gibbs 'Architectur, geometry, and perspective [and] so by the ... reading of Books, and constant application to drawing, became a proficient in the profession' (*Gibbs MS*, p. 84). *ASH* III includes a number of likely Roman period drawings. III.9, 12–29, is a collection of illusionistic ceilings by G. P. Panini; IV.61 is inscribed by Gibbs 'The Plan of ye tene Church of Sta Maria di fiori at Florence' (described in *Gibbs MS*, p. 52). *VAM* E.3661 and 3662-1913 are copies of A. Philippon, *Curieuse Recherches De Plusieurs Beaus Morceaux D'ornemens Antiques, et Modernes, tant d'ans la Ville de Rome*; E.3655 and 3656-1913 are studies related to ceilings in S. Maria in Trastevere and the Capella Paolino in Palazzo del Quirinale (C. Ricci, *Architettura Barocca in Italia* (1922) pls. 59, 61).

82. *Gibbs MS*, pp. 34–5, 37.

83. These buildings are illustrated in books in Gibbs's library: P. Ferrerio and G. B. Falda, *Palazzi ... di Roma*, II, pl. 32, D. De' Rossi, *Studio D'Architettura Civile ... di Roma* (1702) pls. 39, 135, (1711) pl. 2; G. J. De' Rossi, *Disegni Di Vari Altarie e Cappelle nelle Chiese Di Roma* (1713) pl. 26. Other sources are suggested in S. Lang, 'Gibbs', *AR* (July 1954) pp. 26–7, (August 1954) p. 72, and J. Summerson, *Architecture in Britain, 1530–1830* (1970) pp. 306–9.

84. *Braham*, pp. 98–103, pl. 199.

85. D. De' Rossi, *Studio D'Architettura* (1702) pls. 62, 64, (1711) pls. 18–20.

86. *Gibbs MS*, pp. 3–17, 41, 60. R. Wittkower, 'A Sketchbook of Filippo Juvarra at Chatsworth', in *Studies in the Italian Baroque* (1975) p. 206. Gibbs owned Fontana's *L'Anfiteatro Flavio*, compiled by 1709 and published in 1725, in which a domed rotunda church is proposed for the arena of the Colosseum (*Gibbs MS*, pp. 27–8), and engravings of the Collège des Quatre Nations (*ASH Prints*, nos. 13–16).

87. *ASH* III.114–25 inscribed 'Invensione del Iuvarra' ('Drawings of Shields by Juvara', in 'A Catalogue of Mr Gibbs's Books', Bodleian MS Eng. Misc. c.28). Gibbs also owned *Celeberrimi ad Pacificandum Christiani Nominis Orbem* (1648), with sketch additions (*Bodleian Rad* f. 10), and various loose collections of continental engraved cartouches (*ASH Prints*, nos. 49–51, 80–8).

88. Gibbs owned 'A Book of different Vases' (unidentified); J. Berain, *Ornemens* (n.d.); François Girardon, *Galerie de Girardon* (1714); and loose engravings of vases (*ASH Prints*) of types discussed in T. Clifford, 'Polidoro and English Design', *Connoisseur* (August 1976) pp. 282–91, and E. Oechslin, *Die Vase* (1982). A design for a font or domestic buffet (*VAM* E.3646-1913) in the shape of a swan incorporates a drainage system based on Carlo Fontana's *Utilissimo Trattato Dell'Acque*. Gibbs's 'Sarcophagus's ... in the Antique Tast' (*ABA*, p. xxv, pls. 136–7) also derive from Fontana (*Braham*, pls. 32–47). The pair of horses crowning the gate piers to Villa Bolasco near Castelfranco (*The Horses of San Marco* (1979) p. 72, fig. 102) presumably inspired those in *ABA*, pl. 89.

89. *HMC Stuart*, IV, p. 568; V, pp. 24, 27, 48, 378.

90. *ASH* IV.53, 'A Rough drawght of Marly', copied from *ASH* III.49, 'Scatch of Marly taken by Mr [Alexander] Edwards on the place' (*Colvin*, p. 283). Gibbs also owned engraved views of Marly (see Gibbs's Fine Art Library, pp. 327–30) and other French buildings (*ASH Prints*).

91. *Gibbs MS*, pp. 40, 51. Gibbs owned Romano's 1733 engraving of Galilei's design (*ASH Prints*, no. 41) and a group of fine topographical views of the city drawn by Carlo Marchionni, some dated 1735 (*ASH* III.1–6).

92. Compare to Sardi's S. Pasquale Baylon, Rome, 1744–7 (N. A. Mallory, *Roman Rococo Architecture from Clement XI to Benedict XIV, 1700–1758* (1977) pp. 61–6, pls. 95–9).

93. D. De' Rossi, *Studio D'Architettura Civile* (1711) pl. 4; A. Blunt, *Borromini* (1979) pl. 61. The dome of Gibbs's 1737 design for the Library (*Gillam*, pl. 30) is based on Cortona's S. Maria in Via Lata (P. Portoghesi, *Roma barocca* (1973) I, pl. 231). The anticlassical character of the Library was noted by H. Walpole, *Anecdotes of Painting in England* (1771) p. 46, and J. Dallaway, *Observations on English Architecture* (1806) pp. 153–5.

94. *Gibbs MS*, pp. 52, 54–5. His interest in the 'tuo shells' of Florence Cathedral, based on F. Bonani's *Numismata summatoum pontificum templi vaticani* (1715) pls. 21–6, is reflected in the construction of the Radcliffe Library dome. A preliminary design for Bank Hall (c. 1750) shows Gibbs using the tripartite door and Diocletian window bound by giant pilasters of Raphael's Villa Madama (L. H. Heydenreich and W. Lotz, *Architecture in Italy, 1400 to 1600* (1974) pl. 180).

95. *Braham*, pp. 77–86, pls. 109–37. Gibbs's interest in commemorative columns and obelisks (*ABA*, pp. xx–i, pls. 85–7) stems from this source, as well as D. Fontana, *Della transportation dell'obelisco Vaticano* (1595) and N. Zabaglia, *Castelli, e ponti con alcune ingegnose pratiche, e con la descrizione del transporto dell'obelisco Vaticano* (1743), both in his library.

96. H. Hager, 'On a project ascribed to Carlo Fontana for the Facade of S. Giovanni in Laterano', *Burl Mag* (February 1975) pp. 105–7, fig. 59.

97. *VAM* 86NN2, Letter 5.

98. *Gibbs MS*, pp. 20, 29. These ideas are discussed in R. D. Middleton, 'The Abbey De Cordemoy and the Graeco-Gothic Ideal: A Prelude to Romantic Classicism', *Journal of the Warburg and Courtauld Institutes* (1962–3) XXV–XXVI, pp. 278–320, 90–123;

W. Herrmann, *The Theory of Claude Perrault* (1973); and *Laugier and Eighteenth Century French Theory* (1962).

99. *Gibbs MS*, p. 54.

100. J. Evans, *The History of The Society of Antiquaries* (1956) p. 58. Gibbs subscribed to J. Pine, *Qvinti Horatii Flacci Opera* (1733).

## Notes to Chapter III

1. *HMC Stuart*, II, p. 92.

2. *ABA*, p. vi.

3. *LPL* 2716, ff. 13–14.

4. Dickinson's Strand design of 15 July 1713 is the underplan in *WS* (1933) X, pl. 13 top; Hawksmoor's is discussed in Chapter IV.

5. *LPL* 2690, p. 157, the overplan in *WS* (1933) X, pl. 13 top. The Deptford portico was an afterthought resolved on 15 April 1714 (2690, p. 152).

6. 'Mr Van-Brugg's Proposals about Building ye new Churches' (L. Whistler, *The Imagination of Vanbrugh and his Fellow Artists* (1954) p. 250).

7. The details of this commission are discussed in the Catalogue of Works; the contributions of fellow-architects in *Bill, Downes*, pp. 156–99, and K. Downes, *English Baroque Architecture* (1966) pp. 98–105.

8. *LPL* 2690, p. 157.

9. *Gibbs MS*, pp. 24–5.

10. *Braham*, pp. 56–8, pls. 33–4.

11. *ABA*, p. vii.

12. This vista, compared to that achieved at St Martin-in-the-Fields, was praised by J. P. Malcolm, *Londinium Redivivum; or, an Ancient History and Modern description of London* (1807) IV, p. 283.

13. *LPL* 2690, pp. 42–3, 49.

14. *ABA*, p. vi.

15. *A New Guide to London: Or, Directions to Strangers; Shewing the Chief Things of Curiosity and Note In the City and Suburbs* (1726) p. 29. *GSJ* (7 November 1734) No. 254, p. 1, considered 'nothing could be worse contrived to keep out the noise of the street'.

16. pp. 1–2, pl. 27. This criticism is repeated in *Gwynn*, p. 44.

17. *Ralph*, pp. 37–8.

18. 7 November 1734, No. 254, p. 1.

19. E. W. Brayley, *Londiniana: or, Reminiscences of the British Metropolis* (1829) III, pp. 257–60; J. Gwilt, *An Encyclopedia of Architecture* (1842) p. 220, respectively.

20. *GSJ* (7 November 1734) No. 254, p. 1. John James recommended the addition of galleries in 1723, without effect (*LPL* 2713, f. 225).

21. pp. 25–6.

22. *Rules for Drawing* (1732) p. 37, pl. LV.

23. *LPL* 2724, ff. 69–70.

24. II, p. 129. The windows had 'crimson drapery, and the side inter-columnation paintings of the Passion and Annunciation, by Brown . . . The communion-cloth, of crimson velvet richly embroidered with silver' (J. P. Malcolm, *Londinium Redivivum* (1807) IV, p. 283).

25. *LPL* 2726, ff. 75–6.

26. *Defoe 1725*, II, p. 7.

27. *Baker*, p. 119. Gibbs added the New Monument Room to St Lawrence in 1735–6.

28. *Vertue*, V, p. 94.

29. *YAS* MS 328, p. 5.

30. *GSJ* (3 October 1734) No. 253, p. 1.

31. *Defoe 1738*, p. 134. *Ralph*, p. 37, called the steeple 'something very fantastick', and interesting descriptions appear in *BL* Add. MS 22926, ff. 34v–5v (1742) and 'English Architecture: or, The Publick Buildings of London and Westminster', I, p. 18, in S. Wren, *Parentalia* (1750).

32. *GSJ* (31 October 1734) No. 253, p. 1, mentions 'Corinthian columns, which support the cieling [with the] shafts . . . fluted'. G. W. O. Addleshaw and F. Etchells, *The Architectural Setting of Anglican Worship* (1948) pp. 169–71.

## Notes to Chapter IV

1. 'To Clelia, in the Country. On the pulling down St. Martin's Church', in *The Works of the late Aaron Hill, Esq.* (1753) IV, p. 56.

2. St Martin's documents quoted in this chapter are referred to in the Catalogue of Works unless otherwise stated.

3. Thornhill's design (J. Harris, *The Palladians* (1981) pl. IX) was to cost £20,000 (W. R. Osmun, 'A Study of the Works of Sir James Thornhill' (Ph.D. London University, 1950), p. 212). Dubois's, Sampson's and James's designs are lost.

4. *ABA*, p. iv.

5. *Gillam*, p. 99, pls. 3–7.

6. *Gibbs MS*, pp. 3–17.

7. *ABA*, p. iv.

8. A further irregular rectangle of 97 by 126 by 51 by 134 feet was added by a lease dated 13–14 March 1721 between the Vestry and Westminster Abbey 'to be made part of the site of the . . . Church now to be rebuilt' accompanied by a site plan (Westminster Abbey Chapter Library: 36690–91); the ground was purchased on 3 June 1724 for £472 (*SMIF* 419/311 p. 124). The difficulties in adjusting Gibbs's design to the site may be linked with his attendance on the Commissioners on 17 August 1720, when they toured St James, Piccadilly, St Clement Danes, St Andrew, Holborn, St Magnus Martyr, St Martin, Ludgate and St Stephen, Walbrook (419/309, p. 10). Gibbs made section drawings of the chancels of the first three churches (*ASH* III.94–5v).

9. By A-P. Vignon, 1807–45 (R. Middleton and D. Watkin, *Neoclassical and 19th Century Architecture* (1977) pl. 348); T. L. Donaldson, 'Some Account of the Models of Churches Preserved in Henry V's Chantry, Westminster Abbey', *Architect, Engineer and Surveyor* (1 December 1843) IV, p. 351. Gibbs's early interest in such continuously columned forms is evident in his observation on 'the fine peristylium or colonad . . . which went round the costly Monument of the Emperor Hadrian' in Rome (*Gibbs MS*, p. 1).

10. L. Whistler, *The Imagination of Vanbrugh and His Fellow Artists* (1954) pp. 250–2; *WS* (1932) IX, pp. 15–18; *LPL* 2690, pp. 42–3, 49. For a similar design of 1714, see E. Kieven, 'Galilei in England', *CL* (25 January 1973) p. 212, fig. 7.

11. Gibbs owned J. Poldo D'Albenas, *Discours historial de l'antique et illustre cité de Nismes* (1560) and called Fortuna Virilis 'the finest antient Ionick building in Rome' (*Gibbs MS*, p. 20).

12. As recommended by the Commissioners in 1712 (*LPL* 2690, pp. 42–3). Campbell introduced a '*Venetian* Window at the east end sufficiently [to] illuminate the whole Church . . . in the Vitruvian Stile' (*VB* (1717) pp. 1–2, pl. 27), also based on the Temple of Fortuna Virilis.

13. *WPL* G131(6–7) in Hawksmoor's hand, although inscribed 'For St Mary in ye Strand by J. King', presumably John King, a member of the building committee (*LPL* 2690, p. 58; 2711, f. 3; *Bill*, p. xxiii); see K. Downes, 'Hawksmoor's Sale Catalogue', *Burl Mag* (October 1953) p. 333, no. 38.

14. The church was to have 'sundry approaches [with] publick Streets on three sides' (*LPL* 2714, f. 9).

15. J. Pote, *The Foreigner's Guide* (1729) p. 120, considered St George's built 'after the same stately Manner as . . . St Martin's', whose Vestry lent the New Churches Commissioners £2,000 in 1721 'towards the Assisting and forwarding' of the former (*LPL* 2691, p. 141; 2714, f. 17).

16. *GSJ* (7 November 1734) No. 254, p. 1, suggests the portico derived from Hawksmoor's St George, Bloomsbury, 1716–31, 'the first of the kind in this city'.

17. *ABA*, p. viii, perhaps the source of Hogarth's description of St Bride's steeple, which 'diminishes sweetly by elegant degrees' (*The Analysis of Beauty* (1753) p. 47).

18. *Mouat's Journal*, 1775 (Private collection). Problems with the portico advancing too far into the Lane were discussed in 1726 (*SMIF* 419/311, p. 98).

19. *Gwynn*, pp. 45, 85, 92–3, pl. II.

20. *Ralph*, p. 31.

21. Gibbs's steeple and its relation to the body of the church has received mixed reception by architectural critics. *Gwynn*, p. 45; J. Dallaway, *Anecdotes of the Arts in England* (1800) pp. 104–5; and J. Summerson, *Architecture in Britain, 1530–1830* (1970) p. 353, regard it with suspicion. J. Murphy, *Plans Elevations and Views of the Church of Batalha* (1795) p. 16, thought it 'not undeserving of praise'.

22. *Les Dix Livres D'Architecture de Vitruve* (1684), Livre V, pp. 152–5; A. K. Placzek, ed., *Macmillan Encyclopedia of Architects* (1982) IV, p. 337; D. Nyberg, 'La sainte Antiquité', *Essays in the History of Architecture Presented to Rudolf Wittkower* (1967) pp. 159–69.

23. This motif, which Gibbs again used in the round design (*ABA*, pls. 11–12), is also found at S. Costanza, Rome (*CL* (13 November 1969) p. 1247, figs. 7–8), which he recommended as 'well worth the seeing and studying', citing A. Desgodetz, *Les Edifices antiques de Rome* (1695) pp. 63–73, as his source (*Gibbs MS*, p. 19).

24. *ABA*, p.v. On an occasion when the church was 'very full', a visitor standing 'just behind the pulpit . . . cd. not well hear' the speaker (J. L. Clifford and S. C. Roberts, *Dr: Campbell's Diary of a Visit to England in 1775* (1947) p. 71).

25. *Rules for Drawing* (1732) p. 37, pl. LV.

26. The wedding, in fact, took place in another church (R. Paulson, *Hogarth: His Life, Art, and Times* (1971) I, pp. 224–5, pl. 84). The theatricality of the arrangement was noted in *A View of London and Westminster; or, The Town Spy . . . By a Foreigner* quoted in J. McMaster, *A Short History of the Royal Parish of St. Martin-in-the-Fields* (1916) p. 85. A perspective looking towards the chancel attributed to Gibbs (Christ Church, Oxford, Inv. 1138) and later views (*WPL* F131 (31)) show these upper pews glazed.

27. A 'kind of spectacular Biblical pageant in which the church served as both auditorium and scenic setting' (P. Bjurström, 'Baroque Theatre and the Jesuits', in R. Wittkower and I. B. Jaffe, eds., *Baroque Art: The Jesuit Contribution* (1972) pp. 104–5, 108–10, pls. 59–64b). Other possible sources are Carlo Fontana's Capella dell'Assunta in the Collegio Clementino (G. J. De' Rossi, *Disegni Di Vari Altarie e Cappelle nelle Chiese Di Roma* (1713) pl. 40) and designs for the Jesuit church at Frascati (*Braham*, pp. 66–8, pls. 77–9).

28. The unconventional reversed order of the windows was commented on by Sir John Clerk in 1727 (*SRO* MS 8968, p. 7) and *Ralph*, p. 32; both Langley in *GSJ* (3 October 1734) No. 249, p. 2 and *Gwynn*, p. 45, condemned the use of Gibbs-surround windows.

29. Z. Pearce, *A Sermon Preached at the New Parish Church at St. Martins in the Fields* (1727) p. 33 (*WPL* F131 (27–32)).

30. J. Rykwerk, *The First Moderns* (1980) pp. 157–8. Gibbs owned B. Lami's *De Tabernaculo Foederis De Sancta Civitate Jerusalem, et De Templo Ejus*, 1720 (H. Rosenau, *Vision of the Temple* (1979) pp. 97–8, pls. 110–13).

31. Among Gibbs's other documented church furnishings are 'Cistern rais'd upon Pedestals, which may also serve as Fonts' (*ABA*, p. xxv, pl. 146), and a marble font at Dulwich, London.

32. St Martin's window (J. P. Malcolm, *Londinium Redivivum* (1807) IV, p. 195; J. A. Knowles, 'The Price Family of Glass-Painters', *The Antiquaries Journal* (July–October 1953) pp. 184–92) was replaced by Clayton and Bell *c.* 1867 (*WPL* 419 (313)).

33. Griffith made 'a large Scaffold at the East End to Gild Over the Altar' in June 1726 (*SMIF* 419/311, p. 71).

34. *WPL* St Martin's, Box 2, No. 18d; J. P. Malcolm, *Londinium Redivivum* (1807) IV, p. 194. An itinerant French acrobat named Gillinoe flew down a rope stretched from the top of the 178-foot tower of Derby Cathedral in 1732 (M. A. Mallender, *The Great Church* (1977) p. 24).

35. pp. 2–6.

36. pp. 3, 6.

37. p. 18. *Postscripts to the Ornaments of Churches considered* (*c.* 1760) p. 5, observed 'That the noble Arts of *Architecture, Sculpture* and *Painting* [have] an Influence on the Minds and Manners of Men, filling them with great Ideas, and spiriting them up to an Emulation of worthy Actions' (*BM* King's Maps XXIII, 24-f).

38. *HMC Bath*, III, pp. 498–9.

39. Prince's estate plan, 1719 (*Colvin*, p. 661), shows a proposed chapel on the present site, which is mentioned in letters of 21 June and 5 September 1720 (*HMC Portland*, V, pp. 598–9; *BL* Add. MS 18240, f. 28).

40. J. Pote, *The Foreigner's Guide* (1729) p. 122.

41. Anon., *Doctor H———— Vindicated, or the Case Relating to the Differences about All-Saints Church in Derby, Truly Stated* (1725?) p. 3.

42. *Ibid.*, p. 3, mentions 'so many Difficulties were started about the Architect, and the Workmen to be employ'd, that the Meetings always broke up in Confusion'.

43. Hulsberg also engraved Gibbs's design for the Cambridge Public Building in 1722; Hutchinson subscribed £21 towards this project in 1724 (*CUL MC*, f. 5).

44. *Doctor H———— Vindicated* (1725?) pp. 10, 14.

45. T. Haughton, *A Review Of the Proceedings of the Corporation of Derby, Relating to Doctor Hutchinson* (1728) p. 10.

46. *ABA*, p. viii.

47. *Cox*, pl. III. A visitor in 1742 criticized the 'one order of Dorick Pilasters, rais'd on a continued Pedestal & a Ballustrade [as] too small for the building' (*BL* Add. MS 22926, f. 73).

48. *ABA*, p. viii. Gibbs returned to the solution of Wren's St Mary Abchurch, which was admired at the time because it was 'very Airy and light, there being no Gallerys or any thing to intercept it' (*BL* Add. MS 22926, f. 26). Batty Langley criticized St Martin's because 'the ancients deemed it an absurdity to introduce two heights of rooms, within the height of one order', and galleries 'cut against the shafts . . . destroys the beauty of the columns, by hindering them from being seen clear throughout their entire height' (*GSJ* (3 October 1734) No. 249, p. 2). At Derby a critic thought the columns 'on very high Pedestals . . . do not look well' (J. Loveday, *Diary of a Tour in 1732* (1890) p. 214 and *Markham*, pp. 297, 304) and the 'Arches, springing every Way . . . has a bad Effect in the midle Isle because its Arch rise quicker than the side ones' (*BL* Add. MS 22926, f. 73).

49. *Doctor H———— Vindicated* (1725?) pp. 5–8.

50. Reported in *Doctor H———— Vindicated* (1725?); M. Hutchinson, *Exceptions Made by Dr. H. against the Corporation of Derby* (1728); T. Haughton, *A Review Of the Proceedings of the Corporation of Derby* (1728).

51. In 1732 the Countess of Exeter proposed giving a 'Curtain to the Venetian Window . . . which is thought very proper and Convenient' (Cathedral archives, Parish Order Book, III, p. 169).

52. *Doctor H———— Vindicated* (1725?) p. 5. A visitor in 1735 thought it 'the most beautifull modern Church I have seen' (*BL* Add. MS 5842, f. 134). See this chapter, n. 34.

53. *LPL* 2715, f. 14.

54. *WS* (1932) IX, p. 17.

55. *GLRO A Catalogue Of All The Materials of the Dwelling-House* (16 June 1747) p. 32, no. 68, and *A Catalogue Of all the Genuine Household Furniture, &c: Of His Grace James Duke of Chandos, Deceas'd, At his late Seat call'd Cannons* (1 June 1747) p. 41, nos. 1–2, 4.

56. Pls. 31 (left) and 98, a copy of which Turner owned. The internal Order follows closely *Rules for Drawing* (1732 and 1738) pls. X–XV.

57. J. Burke and C. Caldwell, *Hogarth: The Complete Graphics* (1968) pls. 156–7.

58. *MLHC* Vestry Proceedings, 1740–52, p. 12.

59. *Gwynn*, p. 13, regarded the church as inadequate and pressed for rebuilding. For Chambers and Woolfe, see J. Harris, *Sir William Chambers* (1970) p. 228; *MLHC* Ashbridge Collection 241 (493).

60. *Aberdeen Burgess Roll*, 8 March 1739.

61. S. Francesco della Vigna, mentioned in *Gibbs MS*, p. 54, and the Zitelle. R. Wittkower, 'Palladio's Influence on Venetian Religious Architecture', in *Palladio and English Palladianism* (1974) pp. 10–22, shows that the motif long continued to interest Venetian architects.

62. Gibbs suggested a similar composition for the unexecuted Lodge at Kiveton, Yorkshire, in 1741.

63. Gibbs here may have consulted his copy of J.-J. Granet's *Histoire de L'Hôtel Royal Des Invalides* (1736), illustrating Libérale Bruant's similar church interior, 1670–7.

64. R. Chambers, *Lives of Illustrious and Distinguished Scotsmen* (1836) II, Part. 2, p. 433, thought the exterior 'of no description of architecture under the sun' and the interior 'a degree worse', a building 'singularly repulsive to a correct taste'.

65. Thomas Foley was a New Churches commissioner present at Gibbs's election as surveyor in 1713 (*LPL* 2690, p. 126); 'Mr. Prothonotary Foley' was elected a Bart's governor in 1726 (*Bart's Journal*: Ha 1/10, p. 148v).

66. J. J. Cartwright, ed., *The Travels Through England of Dr. Richard Pococke Successively Bishop of Meath and of Ossory during 1750, 1751, and Later Years*, Camden Society (1889) NS, XLIV, pp. 229–30.

67. In 'imitation of the finest carvings' (*Ibid.*, p. 230).

68. *Knight*, pp. 223, 236–7. At Badminton in 1752 'They have just made a light fretwork cieling of Paper to the Library; it appears like stucho' (*Markham*, p. 390).

## NOTES TO CHAPTER V

1. 'Directions Concerning the Monument to be Erected in the Isle of the Church of Alloa', in 'My Legacie to My Dear Son Thomas', March 1726 (*Scottish Historical Society* (1898) XXVI, pp. 192–3, corresponding to Mar's designs of 1722 and 1730 (*SRO* Mar and Kellie deposit, RHP 13258).

2. Such activity also helped bring English taste for sculpture into the European mainstream (H. Honour, 'English Patrons and Italian Sculpture in the First Half of the Eighteenth Century', *Connoisseur* (May 1958) pp. 220–6, and M. Whinney, *Sculpture in Britain, 1530 to 1830* (1964) pp. 70–1).

3. *Braham*, figs. 32–51, 199; G. J. De' Rossi, *Disegni Di Vari Altarie e Cappelle* (1713) pl. 40.

4. Francesco Erizzo's monument in S. Marco, Rome, *c.* 1700 (E. Coudenhove-Erthal, *Carlo Fontana und die Architektur des Romanischen Spätbaroks* (1930) pl. 33).

5. *Vertue*, III, p. 49. For Bird's career, see M. Whinney, *Sculpture in Britain, 1530 to 1830* (1964) Chapter 10.

6. *Gibbs MS*, p. 33. Gibbs also admired the Pozzo-Le Gros altar of St Ignatius in the Gesù, 1695–9, for 'the elegancy of it's design, and the richness of it's materials' (p. 35). These works are discussed in *Enggass*, pp. 67–8, 131–6, pls. 1–3, 93–6, 99–107, and M. Conforti, 'Pierre Legros and the Rôle of Sculptors as Designers in late Baroque Rome', *Burl Mag* (August 1977) pp. 556–61.

7. *Vertue*, III, p. 49, calling the Newcastle monument 'a work for variety & richness of Marble beyond all others'.

8. A. Blunt, *Guide to Baroque Rome* (1982) p. 47; C. Ricci, *Architettura Barocca in Italia* (1922) pl. 113.

9. *Ralph*, p. 69.

10. *Vertue*, III, p. 108. The ducal figure is posed almost exactly as in Bird's Westminster Abbey monument to Richard Busby, 1695. The Newcastle monument was regarded in 1749 as a 'specimen [of Gibbs's] taste in Architecture [the writer] never yet could admire' (*Knight*, pp. 139–40).

11. M. Whinney, *Sculpture in Britain, 1530 to 1830* (1964) p. 77, pl. 52, discusses possible links between Gibbs and the Abbey monuments to Henry Priestman and Dr Grabe, both carved by Bird, the latter commissioned by Harley and installed in 1726 (*Mist's Weekly Journal* (17 December 1726) p. 2, Burney 249b).

12. *Vertue*, I, p. 76; III, p. 17.

13. Compare, for example, the rendering of Dr Radcliffe's statue in Gibbs's drawings *ASH* I.111 and III.82, the latter in contrasting brown pen and wash with characteristic Rysbrack touches.

14. *Remarks and Collections of Thomas Hearne*, Oxford Historical Society (1906) VII, p. 225.

15. François Girardon's Cardinal Richelieu tomb in the Church of the Sorbonne, 1675–94, of which both Gibbs and Rysbrack owned engravings (*ASH Prints*, nos. 2–7; *BL A Catalogue Of the Capital and Entire Collection of Prints, Drawings, and Books of Prints, of Mr. Michael Rysbrack* (16 February 1764) p. 5, lot 16; F. Souchal, *French Sculptors of the 17th and 18th Centuries: The Reign of Louis XIV* (1981) G–L, pp. 38–9).

16. *Gibbs MS*, pp. 34–6.

17. T. Friedman, 'Rysbrack and Gibbs', in K. Eustace, *Michael Rysbrack Sculptor, 1694–1770* (1982) pp. 16–18, 115–16.

18. *Dart*, II, pp. 94, 114; *Ralph*, p. 74. The composition may have derived from B. Cametti's Filippucci monument in S. Giovanni in Laterano, *c.* 1706 (*Enggass*, pp. 154–5, pl. 149).

19. J. Macky, *A Journey Through Scotland* (1723) p. 208.

20. *Braham*, pp. 56–60, pls. 32–51.

21. The contract and drawing is Buckinghamshire *CRO* Drake MS, D/Dr/10/11 (K. A. Esdaile, 'The Renaissance Monuments of Buckinghamshire', *Records of Buckinghamshire* (1947) XV, p. 33, pl. 13).

22. *Enggass*, p. 98, pl. 54.

23. 'I return Gibbs [*A Book of Architecture*] and cannot like Mr. Coulston's dress and full-bottomed wig on a tomb' (*Knight*, p. 167).

24. 28 January 1731, No. 56, p. 2.

25. *Ralph*, p. 74.

26. K. Lankheit, *Florentinische Barockplastik* (1962) Abb. 32; *Enggass*, pp. 144–5, pls. 143–4. Gibbs owned J. Frey's 1721 engraving of Rusconi's Gregory XIII tomb, 1715–23, in St Peter's (*ASH Prints*, no. 1). Robert Stuart's monument in St Margaret's Westminster, *c.* 1728 (see Catalogue of Works) is based on Fontana's Erizzo tomb (see this chapter, n. 4).

27. *Braham*, pp. 89–103, pls. 176, 212. The type is discussed in A. Braham, *Funeral Decoration in Early Eighteenth Century Rome* (1975).

28. *Ralph*, p. 74.

29. Anon., 'On Westminster Abbey', *GM* (September 1737) p. 565. See J. Colton, *The Parnasse François: Titon du Tillet and the Origins of the Monument to Genius* (1979), and D. Piper, *The Development of The British Literary Portrait up to Samuel Johnson* (1968).

30. *The Antiquities of St. Peter's, or, The Abbey-Church of Westminster* (1722) II, p. 29, and *Dart*, I, pp. 90, 164, pl. IX.

31. *Sherburn*, II, pp. 51–2.

32. 'With awful Eye I view great *Dryden's* Bust . . . Who has not heard of *Homer* and of thee!' (*Dart*, I, p. xli).

33. It was the subject of popular verse in *GM*: '*On the old* Bust *with a sour Air, on* Mr. DRYDEN'S Monument' (February 1733, p. 95; also November 1736, p. 674; May 1752, p. 234) and *The London and Westminster Guide* (1768) p. 52.

34. *Dart*, II, p. 61, pl. 93.

35. *Ralph*, p. 78.

36. Reprinted in *Poems on Several Occasions, by Matthew Prior* (1727) III, p. viii. The funeral, for which Gibbs was presented with a mourning ring, is reported in *BL Portland Papers Loan* 29/317, ff. 9–11v, 96v, 143v.

37. 'For his own Epitaph', lines 1–4, in H. Bunker Wright and M. K. Spears, *The Literary Works of Matthew Prior* (1959) I, p. 409.

38. Anon., 'On seeing the Funeral of Matthew Prior, Esqr: in Westminster Abbey' (*BL Portland Papers Loan* 29/317, f. 10). Gibbs appears to have associated the motif of the bust in a circular niche, perhaps derived from Pietro da Cortona's and Carlo Maratti's own tombs (A. Blunt and H. L. Cooke, *The Roman Drawings of the XVII & XVIII Centuries . . . at Windsor Castle* (1960) p. 77, no. 592, fig. 59; *Enggass*, p. 116, pl. 82), with literary figures. The type perhaps includes *ASH* III.84 and *SAL* MS 263, f. 93 (unidentified tombs presumably for Westminster Abbey).

39. The bust is dated 1714 in Prior's inventory (*BL Portland Papers Loan* 29/317, f. 17), not 1700 as given in F. Souchal, *French Sculptors of the 17th and 18th Centuries: The Reign of Louis XIV* (1977) A–F, p. 209, no. 73. Prior owned other work by Coysevox (29/316; 29/317, ff. 6–v, 16v–7, 72v, 163).

40. *Vertue*, III, p. 17.

41. *Ralph*, pp. 78–9. Pope throught the monument pretentious (*Sherburn*, II, p. 525).

42. *Vertue*, III, p. 21.

43. *BL Portland Papers Loan* 29/317, ff. 163v–4 (14 December 1721).

44. *Ralph*, p. 79.

45. Vol. I, i, pls. 104, 128, 202, particularly the Louvre *Faun with Pipes* and the Uffizi *Mercury* (F. Haskell and N. Penny, *Taste and the Antique* (1981) pp. 212–13, 266–7, pls. 110, 138).

46. *Ralph*, p. 73.
47. *Sherburn*, II, pp. 242–3.
48. *Enggass*, p. 95, pl. 43. Gibbs may have designed the monument at St Germans to Edward Elliott (d. 1722), husband of Craggs's sister Elizabeth, a Catholic friend of Pope; some features recall the Newcastle monument (N. Pevsner, *The Buildings of England: Cornwall* (1951) p. 158; *Miscellanea Genealogica et Heraldica* (1876) II, pp. 39, 46). Elliott's brother Richard supplied marble for Craggs's monument (*Sherburn*, II, pp. 217–18, 456, n. 1).
49. *Vertue*, III, p. 146 (1749). For Rysbrack's rejected Argyll designs, see K. Eustace, *Michael Rysbrack Sculptor, 1694–1770* (1982) pp. 128–32.

## NOTES TO CHAPTER VI

1. 5 August 1715 letter (Bedfordshire *CRO* Lucas Papers L 30/8/28/7); he contacted Filippo Juvarra (T. Hudson, 'A Ducal Patron of Architecture', *CL* 17 January 1974) pp. 78–81).
2. For Benson and the beginnings of eighteenth-century classicism, see J. Harris, *The Palladians* (1981) pp. 16–18, 58–63.
3. Primaticcio's 1560 project for the Valois Chapel at St Denis (which Gibbs knew from illustrations in J. Marot's *Recueil des Plans, Profils et Elevations des plusieurs Palais, Chasteaux, Eglises Sepultures, Grotes et Hostels bâtis dans Paris* and Mariette's engravings, *ASH Prints*, nos. 31–3) and Boffrand's second design, 1711, for Malgrange at Nancy, published in 1745 (L. Hautecoeur, *Histoire de l'architecture classique en France* (1950) III, p. 61, figs. 40–2) but exhibited in Paris on 22 February 1712 (H. Lemonnier, *Proces-Verbaux de L'Academie Royale d'Architecture, 1671–1793* (1915) IV, p. 4).
4. J. Macky, *A Journey Through Scotland* (1723) pp. 180–3; see also *Defoe 1725*, II, pp. 389–90; *HMC Portland*, VI, pp. 120–1.
5. Bernini's facade of Palazzo Chigi, Rome, 1664 (G. B. Falda, *Nuovi Disegni Dell'Architettura, e Piante De Palazzi Di Rome*, II, p. 15), and the court entrance to Le Vau's College des Quatre Nations, Paris, 1662 (*ASH Prints*, nos. 13–16); both are mentioned in *Gibbs MS*, pp. 47, 60.
6. *HMC Stuart*, II, pp. 404, 568; V, pp. 24, 48.
7. *Defoe 1761*, I, p. 73.
8. G. S. H. Fox-Strangways, Earl of Ilchester, *Lord Hervey and his Friends, 1726–38* (1950) pp. 70–1; Hervey refers to the 'virtuosi' as 'a true follower of Palladio and Vertuvius'.
9. *HMC Portland*, VI, p. 160.
10. *KCL Coll.I*, ff. 65, 85, and *CB*, f. 12; *CUL MC*, f. 7, and *UAB*, p. 510.
11. Horace Walpole's annotated copy of *Aedes Walpolianae* (1752) p. 38 (Pierpont Morgan Library, New York).
12. For example, the châteaux at Verneuil and Blérancourt (R. Coope, *Salomon De Brosse* (1972) pls. 19–20, 91–2); also Philips Vingboons's Amsterdam Town Hall design (W. Kuyper, *Dutch Classicist Architecture* (1980) pl. 158).
13. In April 1725 Horatio Walpole turned for architectural advice about his house at Wolterton, Norfolk, to Lord Mar, who was then living in Paris; a year earlier Mar had suggested adding huge domes to the corner pavilions of Stirling Castle (*Colvin*, pp. 295–7).
14. *VB* (1717) p. 5.
15. 'I design to make up as soon as I can the time I have lost in my building, and am therefore going immediately into the Country', a letter from Wyndham dated 30 June 1716 (Grosvenor MSS, Eaton Hall).
16. J. Hunter, ed., *The Diary of Ralph Thoresby* (1830) I, p. 275.
17. A similar solution was suggested in an anonymous design for Lowther (*VB* (1717) p. 4, pls. 78–80) which amalgamated features from the Curia Innocenziana courtyard (*Braham*, pl. 252) and the Château de Maisons, illustrated in J. Marot, *Recueil des Plans, Profiles et Elevations des plusieurs Palais, Chasteaux, Eglises Sepultures, Grotes et Hostels bâtis dans Paris*. The design may have been commis-

sioned in Italy, where various Lowthers visited between 1700 and 1716 (H. F. Brown, 'Inglesie e Scozzesi all'Università di Padova dall'anno 1618 sino al 1765', in *Monografie Storiche sullo Studio di Padova* (1921) pp. 183, 191, 195).
18. Sir John Clerk, 'A journie to Carlyle & penrith Agust 1732' (*SRO* GD18/2109, pp. 18–26). The attic was perhaps suggested by Palazzo Cantarini degli Scrigni (V. Scamozzi, *L'Idea della Architettura Universale* (1615)).
19. *Defoe 1725*, II, p. 270.
20. Annotation on J. Buckler's 1814 view of Lowther (*BL* Add. MS 36390, f. 155v).
21. Sir John Lowther's letter to 'My Dear Son', 1697 (Cumbria *CRO* D/Lons/L).
22. S. Humphrey, *Cannons. A Poem* (1728) p. 10, reprinted in T. B. Gilmore, *Early Eighteenth-Century Essays on Taste* (1972) pp. 42–63.
23. *Macky 1722*, II, p. 5.
24. *Baker*, pp. 114–15.
25. *Ibid.*, pp. 122–3.
26. *Defoe 1748*, II, pp. 158–9, refers to the estate suffering 'the Fate of sublunary Things'. Lady Newdigate remarked *c.* 1748 that 'The Remains of Cannons . . . is a melancholly object, the outside walls of that lately Magnificent House is all that now is to be seen of it' (Warwickshire *CRO* CR 1841/7, Part I, p. 20).
27. p. 10.
28. *Cannons. A Poem* (1728) p. 6.
29. *Macky 1722*, II, pp. 6, 10, and *Defoe 1725*, II, p. 7. *Vertue*, V, p. 94, also remarked on the 'noble & grand . . . square pile . . . four sides almost alike'. Gibbs owned various plans and views of Marly (see Chapter II, n. 90).
30. *Baker*, pp. 140–1.
31. Thomas Fort, Clerk of the Works at Hampton Court, was surveyor and joiner at Cannons, 1720–3 (*Baker*, pp. 146–7; *Colvin*, p. 314).
32. pp. 148–53.
33. *VAM* 86NN2, pp. 138–41.
34. Sir Edward Gascoigne's diary (Leeds City Archives: GC/F6/12b). See also *Markham*, pp. 147–8.
35. *VAM* 86NN2, pp. 102v–3.
36. *HMC Portland*, VII, pp. 294–5. Gibbs told Harley on 2 February 1715, 'I saw all your pictures safly pack'd and to morrow morning will see them put in the Cart for wimple' (*WS* (1940) XVII, p. 10).
37. *HMC Portland*, V, p. 562.
38. *Wanley*, I, pp. 49, 70, 72, 154, 178, 250; II, pp. 213, 347 (remodelled into the Gallery by Flitcroft after 1741).
39. *Defoe 1742*, I, pp. 104–5, and *BL* Add. MS 15776, pp. 43–6 (1735), respectively.
40. *BL Portland Papers Loan* 29/385, 387.
41. *BL* Add. MS 15776, ff. 43–6.
42. *Account of a journey into East Anglia*, 1728 (MS Wilton House), also mentioning 'the Gallery . . . in the middle of the house'.
43. *Sherburn*, III, p. 114.
44. As suggested in the vignette in Vertue's 1746 engraved portrait of Harley (*SAL* Harley Collection, 196H, I, frontispiece).
45. Bedfordshire *CRO* Lucas Papers L 30/8/28/11 and 15, L 30/8/33/13.
46. *BL* Add. MS 5842, f. 131v (1735) and *Markham*, pp. 173, 498.
47. *Defoe 1761*, II, pp. 272–5.
48. *The New Oxford Guide* (1759) p. 111.
49. *VB* (1717) p. 3, pl. 64.
50. *Toynbee*, p. 26.
51. Villa Giustinian, 1694, at Portobuffole, Treviso (G. Mazzotti, *Palladian and Other Venetian Villas* (1958) pl. 391).
52. Rev. J. Trapp, *The Honour and Vertue of Building, Repairing and Adorning Churches* (1723), Dedication.
53. *Bart's Journal* Ha 1/10, f. 114. Bartholomew Clarke was elected 1736 (Ha 1/11, f. 77); Young was related to Sir Peter Young, a Scottish Jacobite (H. Davidson, *The Story of Elm Grove* (1967) p. 4).

54. Rysbrack also executed Gibbs's Westminster Abbey monument to John Smith, Edward Desbouvrie's father-in-law.
55. K. Lankheit, *Florentinische Barockplastik: Die Kunst am Hofe der Letzten Medici, 1670–1743* (1962) p. 282, Doc. 340. The British Consul, Christopher Crowe, lived at Kiplin Hall, Yorkshire, which he remodelled internally in the 1730s (*CL* (4 August 1983) pp. 278–81).
56. pp. 6–7, pl. 92.
57. G. Beard, *Georgian Craftsmen and their Work* (1966) p. 50.
58. *YAS* MS 328, p. 59.
59. J. Lees-Milne, *English Country Houses: Baroque, 1685–1715* (1970) p. 241. A. Young, *A Six Month's Tour through the North of England* (1770) I, p. 127, considered it 'one of the most beautiful rooms in England'. Walpole thought it was based on the gallery of the Palazzo Colonna, Rome (P. Cunningham, ed., *The Letters of Horace Walpole* (1857) III, p. 28).
60. Journal of John or James Baker of Penn, 1728 (Buckinghamshire Archaeological Society 195/47, No. 2).
61. p. x.
62. Northamptonshire *CRO* Fitzwilliam Papers, Letters 1710 to 1744 (January 1725).
63. Sir John Clerk, 'A journie to Carlyle & penrith Agust 1732' (*SRO* GD18/2109, p. 21).
64. Sir John Lowther's letter to 'My Dear Son', 1697 (Cumbria *CRO* D/Lons/L).
65. G. Leoni, *The Architecture of A. Palladio* (1715) Book II, pp. 27–8, pl. XLV.
66. *VB* (1717) p. 4, pls. 83–4.
67. *Account of a journey into East Anglia*, 1728 (MS Wilton House).
68. J. Carswell, *The South Sea Bubble* (1960) pp. 120–1.
69. *CUL UAB*, p. 490; and *MC*, f. 3. Clarke was Headmaster, 1720–41 (*Alumni Cantabrigenses*, p. 347).
70. *Castell*, opposite p. 66. Gibbs's design also adopted Eastbury's uncommon *T*-shaped arrangement of hall, stairs and saloon (*VB* (1725) pl. 16) and his interest in this model is further evident in the unusually elaborate design represented by the plan *ASH* IV.54.
71. Quoted in *The Later Owners of the Wricklemarch Estate* (MS Page-Turner family).
72. J. Carswell, *The South Sea Bubble* (1960) pp. 122–3, 223.
73. J. H. Pye, *A Short Account, Of the Principal Seats and Gardens, In and about Twickenham* (1760) p. 52.
74. Coutts: Letter Book 9 ff.
75. *HMC Stuart*, II, p. 93.
76. *Gibbs MS*, p. 87.
77. *Castell*, pp. 1, 19–20, 39.
78. A. Palladio, *I Quattro Libri Dell'Architettura* (1570), II, pp. 59, 62, G. Mazzotti, *Palladian and Other Venetian Villas* (2nd ed., 1966) pl. 271.
79. *VB* (1715) p. 4.
80. *Toynbee*, p. 66.
81. G. Leoni, *The Architecture of A. Palladio* (1715) Book II, p. 26, pl. XL.
82. *ABA*, p. xvi.
83. *Ibid.*, pp. xvi–ii, and G. Leoni, *The Architecture of A. Palladio* (1715) Book II, pp. 22–4, pls. XXXII–XXXV.
84. The 'uncommon' front of pl. 43 may have been suggested by Vignola's Nymphaeum of the Villa Giulia (R. D. Coffin, *The Villa in the Life of Renaissance Rome* (1979) pl. 103); pl. 44 by Scamozzi's Villa Molin near Padua (*L'Idea della Architettura Universale* (1615) Part I, Book III, Cap. XIII); pl. 54 by the courtyard of the Palazzo Thiene, Vicenzi (A. Palladio, *I Quattro Libri Dell'Architettura* (1570) II, p. 15).
85. *Sherburn*, II, pp. 3–4, 44.
86. *Ibid.*, p. 125; H. Phillips, *The Thames about 1750* (1950) p. 192.
87. *Castell*, pp. 13, 24.
88. *BL* Add. MS 4808, Vol. II, f. 30v; related sketches are ff. 116, 200, and 4809, ff. 66v, 67v, 84v, 86v, 97v, 161v, 227v.
89. *Knight*, p. 170. K. Woodbridge, 'Bolingbroke's Château of La

90. Source', *Garden History* (Autumn 1976) IV, no. 3, pp. 50–64.
91. *Sherburn*, II, pp. 503, 525.
92. *Biographia Britannica*, V, p. 3576; *Croft-Murray*, II, p. 301; A. Ballantyne, *Voltaire's Visit to England, 1726–1729* (1893) p. 39. Lady Luxborough noted the hall 'painted in stone-colours, with all the implements of husbandry placed in the manner one sees . . . arms and trophies in some General's hall' (*Knight*, pp. 22–3).
93. *GM* (June 1731) p. 262, with 'An Answer to the Writer of Dawley Farm. A Poem' (July 1731) p. 306: 'Let *Dawley* triumph in the builder's art, And stand the emblem of the owner's heart'.
94. J. V. Guerinot, *Pamphlet Attacks on Alexander Pope, 1711–1744* (1969) p. 272.
95. Preface and p. 66.
96. A. R. Waller, ed., *Matthew Prior: Dialogues of the Dead and other Works in Prose and Verse* (1907) p. 187.
97. H. Bunker Wright and M. K. Spears, *The Literary Work of Matthew Prior* (1959) I, pp. 551, 556–7.
98. *HMC Bath*, III, pp. 482–3, 485.
99. *Willis*, p. 73.
100. *HMC Bath*, III, pp. 483–4, 488.
101. W. Kuyper, *Dutch Classicist Architecture* (1980) pp. 183–5, fig. 24, pls. 305, 381.
102. *HMC Bath*, III, p. 504.
103. Gibbs's source may have been Villa Molino Bragadin at Fratta Polesina, 1565–85 (*Palladio La Sua Eredita 'Nel Mondo* (1980) p. 233, pl. 2). S. Lang, 'Gibbs', *AR* (July 1954) p. 23, fig. 12, suggests Villa Tornieri. Prior's architectural library included editions of Scamozzi and Vitruvius (*BL Portland Papers Loan* 29/317, ff. 20–42).
104. *HMC Bath*, III, pp. 503–4.
105. 'A Poem On the Death of Matthew Prior Esq; of Down-Hall in Essex. By a Neighbouring Clergyman' (1721) in *Poems on Several Occasions, by Matthew Prior* (1727) III, p. 36.
106. T. Friedman, 'James Gibbs's Designs for Domestic Furniture', *Leeds Arts Calendar* (1972) No. 71, pp. 19–25, and a further group of mantle clock designs in *VAM* D.1174 and 1175–'98. Chair designs in L. Binyon, *The Catalogue of Drawings by British Artists . . . in the British Museum* (1900) II, p. 215, are unlikely to be by Gibbs.
107. N. Salmon, *The History of Hertfordshire* (1728) p. 57.
108. *Bart's Journal* Ha 1/10, p. 137.
109. Look at Kimberley Hall, Norfolk, 1712 (J. Harris, *William Talman: Maverick Architect* (1982) pp. 41–2, pl. 73). Gibbs owned a plan of William Samwell's Grange Park, Hants., *c.* 1670 (H. Colvin and J. Harris, eds., *The Country Seat* (1970) p. 48, pl. 26A).
110. Hampshire *CRO* Herriard Collection 44 M69/E83.
111. G. Leoni, *The Architecture of A. Palladio* (1715) Book II, p. 30, pl. I.
112. S. Shaw, *The History and Antiquities of Staffordshire* (1801) II, part I, p. 283.
113. *BL* Add. MS 15776, f. 171.
114. M. I. Batten, 'The Architecture of Dr. Robert Hooke, F.R.S.', *Walpole Society* (1937) XXV, pp. 100–1, from 1679–80 letters.
115. P. Toynbee, ed., *The Letters of Horace Walpole* (1903) III, p. 66.
116. p. 37, pl. LIV.
117. *GM* (December 1739) p. 641, thought there was 'something respectable in those old hospitable *Gothick* Halls, hung round with the Helmets, Breast-Plates, and Swords of our Ancestors, I entered them with a Constitutional Sort of Reverence, and look'd upon those Arms with Gratitude'. For the taste in wall busts and urns, see T. Friedman and T. Clifford, *The Man at Hyde Park Corner: Sculpture by John Cheere, 1709–1787* (1974).
118. P. Toynbee, *The Letters of Horace Walpole* (1903) III, pp. 65–6; *Beard 1975*, pp. 68–9, pl. 96; *Beard 1981*, pl. 79. In a letter of 1759 Hertford asked Walpole to meet him in London to call on Artari 'to see the design you fixed on for my Saloon in colours' (*BL* Add. MS 23281, ff. 5, 7).
119. Letter of 11 April 1734 from Hawksmoor to George Clarke regarding Magdalen College, Oxford (*MCL* MS 906 ii).

## Notes to Chapter VII

1. *BL* Add. MS 47030, f. 79v (1724). *Bickham*, p. 65, described the estate in 1750 as 'the Wonder of our Days, and the most charming Place in all *England*'.
2. *VAM* E.3627 and 3628-1913.
3. John Perceval reported in 1724 that 'Bridgman laid out the ground and plan'd the whole [of Stowe] which cannot fail to recommending him to business' (*BL* Add. MS 47030, ff. 79v–80v). In 1726–7, as if to cement their friendship, Gibbs and Bridgeman took leases on houses in Henrietta Street, Marylebone (*BL* Add. MS 18240, ff. 15–16) and they appear together in Hamilton's *Club of Artists*, 1734–5. *Willis* discusses their professional relationship.
4. *Defoe 1725*, II, p. 12. *Macky 1714*, p. 36, refers to the gardens in 1713 as for 'Elegancy and Largeness . . . much the brightest Figure [among the] abundance of Curious Seats' and James dedicated *The Theory and Practice of Gardening*, 1712, to Johnston.
5. *HMC Stuart*, II, p. 93.
6. *Macky 1722*, I, p. 63.
7. *VB* (1715) p. 6, pl. 77. Mar proposed 'adding an atique' belvedere or prospect tower to the roof in June 1721 (*SRO* Mar and Kellie deposit, RHP 13256).
8. *Defoe 1725*, II, p. 12.
9. 'Secretarie Johnsons Entertainment for the Queene & all the Royall Familie in his Octagon . . . which is a very fine Roome . . . Mr Johnson came in & paide his Honours to the Queene and all was very merrie & highlie pleased' ('Butler's Seating Plan', 13 August 1729, in Twickenham Public Library, Z.6397); J. W. Croker, *Letters To and from Henrietta, Countess of Suffolk, and Her Second Husband, The Hon. George Berkeley; From 1712 to 1767* (1824) II, p. 363, n. 3.
10. *Macky 1722*, I, p. 63.
11. *Defoe 1725*, II, p. 12.
12. The Scottish architect Sir John Clerk, visiting 16 April 1727, found the Octagon 'by Mr Gibbs . . . finely finish'd within in Stuccowork & Gilding' and thought the room 'according to the old mode [the Baroque] revived, of a whitish colour & all the carvings are gilt' (*Journey to London in 1727*, SRO GD 18/2107, pp. 24–5).
13. *Journey to London in 1727*, SRO GD 18/2107.
14. Compare this also to Burlington's 'House with an Arcade' in W. Kent, *The Designs of Inigo Jones* (1727) II, p. 12.
15. D. Croft, *A Particular of the Noble Large House . . . at Whitton* (1765) in Guildhall Library, London: Fo. Pam. 1330.
16. *SRO* GD 18/2107, pp. 18–19, and GD 18/2110, p. 38.
17. National Library of Scotland: Saltoun Papers (11 June 1736). These drawings are in *CL* (20 July 1972) p. 144, fig. 8; I. G. Lindsay and M. Cosh, *Inveraray and the Duke of Argyll* (1973) fig. 10; and Sir John Soane's Museum: Adam Drawings, Vol. 30.
18. D. Croft, *A Particular of the Noble Large House . . . at Whitton* (1765) p. 7 (Guildhall Library, London: Fo. Pam. 1330).
19. L. M.F. Bosch, 'Bomarzo: A Study in Personal Imagery', *Garden History* (Autumn 1982) fig. 1. A similar feature appears on the so-called Gunroom at Wentworth Castle, perhaps part of the improvements made by William, 2nd Earl of Strafford, who married Argyll's daughter Anne in 1741 (N. Whittaker, 'A History of The House, Gardens and Landscape Park at Wentworth Castle, Yorkshire' (B.A. Arch. Durham University, 1964), pl. XXXVII).
20. *Salmon*, pp. 10–11.
21. *BL* Add. MS 5842, f. 131v. The Blenheim Obelisk or Column of Victory, crowned by Marlborough's statue, was contracted in 1727–30 and built in 1730–1 to Lord Pembroke's design (*Colvin*, pp. 414–15, 835).
22. In the 1720s Bolton was presented with marble columns from Wren's dismantled royal palace at Winchester (E. J. Climenson, *Passages from the Diary of Mrs. Philip Lybbe Powys* (1899) p. 80).
23. C. Lazzaro-Bruno, 'The Villa Lante at Bagnaia: An Allegory of Art and Nature', *Art Bulletin* (December 1977) pp. 553–60, fig. 8.

24. P. Gazzola, *Michele Sanmicheli* (1960) pp. 144–7, pls. 123–8.
25. R. Morris, *Lectures on Architecture* (1759) p. 183.
26. J. P. Neale, *Views of The Seats of Noblemen and Gentlemen, in England, Wales, Scotland, and Ireland* (1818) I, p. 59.
27. M. H. Morgan, ed., *Vitruvius: The Ten Books of Architecture* (1914) pp. 39–40.
28. *Castell*, pp. 64–5.
29. *ABA*, p. xviii, pl. 67, 'propos'd to have been placed in the Centre of four Walks, so that a Portico might front each Walk', is based on Serlio's *Tutte l'Opere d'Architettura* (1584) II, Chap. II, f. 6, and W. Kent, *The Designs of Inigo Jones* (1727) II, pl. 13.
30. A similar temple was once at Shardeloes (*VB* (1739) pls. 100–1) but although Gibbs worked for the same family, the Drakes, at nearby Amersham, there is no evidence of his participation at the house recorded in Buckinghamshire CRO D/DR/4. See also *ASH* III.111, 'The Orthographick elivation of the fore front for ye Duke of' based on a Talman design (*RIBA* G2/11/1–3).
31. *HMC Bath*, III, pp. 483, 488, 490, 492.
32. 'A Poem On the Death of Matthew Prior of Down-Hall in Essex. By a Neighbouring Clergyman', 1721, in *Poems on Several Occasions, by Matthew Prior* (1727) III, p. 36.
33. *HMC Bath*, III, p. 504.
34. See this chapter, n. 32, p. 37.
35. Essex *CRO* Holman MS T/P195/16. Pope wrote Harley on 22 January 1726 of Down: 'I likd my Lodgings so well . . . that I am utterly against Gibbs, & all his Adherents for Demolition' (*Sherburn*, II, p. 364).
36. *Sherburn*, II, pp. 364, 369, 371. Its location is unknown although *Castell*, p. 61, recommended that 'those Parts of the Garden set aside for Bowling' should face the portico of the Villa Urbana.
37. See this chapter, n. 32.
38. G. Jackson-Stops, 'Cliveden', *CL* (3 March 1977) p. 500.
39. *BL* Add. MS 15776, ff. 118–19.
40. *SMIF* 419/309, pp. 26–7; *Bart's Journal* Ha 1/10, p. 58v. A 'Drat. of a house . . . to Wm Gore' in Marylebone is listed under 10 February 1720 (*BL* Add. MS 18239, f. 7v).
41. *YAS* MS 328, pp. 9–10. This canal is shown in Bridgeman's working drawings (*Willis*, pp. 183–4, pl. 45a).
42. *BL* Add. MS 47030, ff. 79v–80v.
43. This relationship is noted in N. Salmon, *The History of Hertfordshire* (1728) pp. 129–30. The Cestius Pyramid was 'a very fine peece of Antiquity' (*Gibbs MS*, p. 29).
44. *Willis*, pl. 138.
45. The designs are in the Badminton House archives. Beaufort's French and Italian tour, 1726–7, is discussed in O. Sitwell, 'The Red Folder', *Burl Mag* (April–May 1942) pp. 85–90, 115–18.
46. G. Leoni, *The Architecture of A. Palladio* (1715) Book II, pls. XIV–XV.
47. C. Morris, ed., *The Journeys of Celia Fiennes* (1947) p. 236.
48. *GM* (19 July 1732) p. 874.
49. *Defoe 1742*, I, p. 184.
50. J. B. Barjaud and C. P. Landon, *Description De Londres et ses Édifices* (1811) pp. 216–17.
51. pp. 72–3. The statues were copies of well-known classical works (F. Haskell and N. Penny, *Taste and the Antique* (1981) nos. 24, 43–4, 46, 88).
52. pp. 66–7. A copy of *Les Charmes de Stow* is in the Henry E. Huntington Library, San Marino, California.
53. *Stowe Papers* 14 November 1726: the 'foundation diging for the Piramid'.
54. p. 21: '*One in the Garden, the other in the Park . . . intended for a House for Colonel* Speed, *deceas'd*'.
55. *Stowe Papers* MS 'Lord Cobhams Garden 1738', p. 5, describes these as 'Lead Bronzed; all Copys after antique Originals'.
56. *Entwürff Einer historischen Architectur* (1721) I, pl. 14, a copy of which Gibbs owned.
57. G. West, *Stowe, The Gardens* (1732) pp. 6–9; the busts were removed to Kent's Temple of British Worthies in the Elysian Fields by 1735.

58. *Bikham*, pp. 7–8. From Gibbs's Building 'placed on the Top of a Mount, is a noble Prospect of the House' (*Defoe 1742*, III, p. 272).

59. *BL* Add. MS 15776, f. 2 (1735) and *Markham*, pp. 93, 204–5.

60. *Castell*, p. 39.

61. *Bickham*, pp. 2–3, 6–7.

62. From the inscription on the Temple of British Worthies. 'In *Hampden* we a second *Tully* view, A greater *Caesar*, great *Nassau* in you!' (*GM* (February 1743) p. 100). His bust appears in a chimneypiece design for Hartwell (*Bodleian* MS Top. Gen. b. 55; W. H. Smyth, *Aedes Hartwellianae* (1851) p. 105). For William III and ideas of liberty, see G. Taylor, 'The Diversity of Artistic Interests as Reported in the Gentleman's Magazine from 1731 to 1770' (B.A. Leeds University, 1981), Chapter 2.

63. M. F. du Boccage, *Letters Concerning England, Holland and Italy* (1770) I, p. 66.

64. *YAS* MS 328, p. 60.

65. *Castell*, pp. 32–8. Work required at Kiveton in 1706 specified 'bridges must bee laid in severall places' (Yorkshire Archaeological Society, Duke of Leeds Papers DD 5/24, Box 1).

66. *BL* Add. MS 15776, f. 84.

67. Letter of 5 July 1748 (Bedfordshire *CRO* Lucas Papers L30/9a/1, pp. 164–75). Yorke visited in 1744 (*Godber*, p. 125).

68. *Defoe 1762*, III, p. 51.

69. From Gilbert West, *Stowe* (1732) in J. D. Hunt and P. Willis, *The Genius of the Place* (1975) p. 215.

70. *The Seasons* (1744) Autumn, lines 1052–5. *Bickham*, p. 55, likened them to 'rural Scenes', and S. Boyse, 'The Triumph of Nature. A Poem' (*GM* (June 1742) p. 324, lines 50–8), commented on Stowe's rural character.

71. Marchioness Grey, 1748 (Bedfordshire *CRO* Lucas Papers L30/9a/1, p. 167).

72. *GM* (August 1742) p. 436, lines 391–6. A building of almost identical form, but with a central dome, called the 'Law-Temple' once existed at Wentworth Castle, Yorkshire (*VB* (1739) pls. 55–6), where Gibbs worked in 1724.

73. P. Toynbee, ed., *The Letters of Horace Walpole* (1903) III, p. 392.

74. *Bickham*, p. 54.

75. p. 36. 'Now to th' *imperial cabinet* we come, Of *cubic* form the bright *historic* room! Where *Monarchs* wholesome counsel may receive' (*GM* (August 1742) p. 436, lines 373–86).

76. *Stowe Papers* MS 'Lord Cobhams Gardens 1738', pp. 20–1.

77. W. Gilpin, *A Dialogue upon the Gardens at Stow* (1748) p. 35. Boyse appears to have been the first to associate the Stowe example with Palladio (*GM* (June 1742) p. 324, n. 3).

78. B. Seeley, *Stowe: The Gardens Of the Right Honourable the Viscount Cobham* (1751) p. 18.

79. *Bickham*, p. 51.

80. *Ibid.*, p. 48.

81. Warwickshire *CRO* CR1841/7, p. 5. *Bickham*, p. 59, thought it 'in the Taste of that of *London*', meaning Wren's Fire Monument of 1671–6.

82. Brown's letter, 22 October 1750, explains that 'The Pillar with it's Capitel and Bace are of the Tuscan Proportion, but of defert: Members, which I composed, to make it more monumentel, and to answer The Octangular forme of the Pillar' and suggests 'If you have any intention of Building a Pillar of this kind if a draught of it or any other kind will be of use to you you may comand it from me ... The Scaffolding of Buildings of this kind is the greatest Arte in The Whole, after the Foundations. The Wind has a very great effect on Buildings that stand on so small a Base' (Durham *CRO* Strathmore Collection D/St 347/37, endorsed 'Lord Cobhams Gardr').

83. Bedfordshire *CRO* Lucas Papers L30/9a/1, p. 169. 'Plac'd on the summit's lofty brow it stands, And all the wide extended view commands' (*GM* (August 1742) p. 435, lines 363–4).

84. Bedfordshire *CRO* Lucas Papers L30/9a/1, p. 169.

85. P. Toynbee, ed., *The Letters of Horace Walpole* (1903) III, pp. 191–2, 181.

86. M. R. Brownell, *Alexander Pope & the Arts of Georgian England* (1978) pp. 317–9; J. Sherwood and N. Pevsner, *The Buildings of England: Oxfordshire* (1974) pp. 781–3, pl. 45).

87. *GM* (June 1742) p. 324, lines 43–4; (August 1742) p. 435, line 361. G. Clarke, 'Grecian Taste and Gothic Virtue: Lord Cobham's Garden Programme and its Iconography', *Apollo* (June 1973) pp. 26–31; D. Watkin, *The English Vision: The Picturesque in Architecture, Landscape and Garden Design* (1982) pp. 20–1.

88. *Stowe, The Gardens* (1732) pp. 17–19. The association is elaborated by *Bickham*, pp. 17, 25; *GM* (July 1742) p. 380, lines 147–56; (March 1743) p. 154; *The Stoic* (March 1972) pp. 52, 62–8.

89. *Franco-Gallia* (1711) pp. ii–vi; (1721) pp. ii–vi. Molesworth believed the British Constitution was 'restor'd and establish'd (if not introduced) by the *Goths* and *Franks*, whose Descendants we are' (p. 1).

90. *Defoe 1762*, II, p. 228.

91. J. Evans, *A History of The Society of Antiquaries* (1956) pp. 58–60. S. Piggot, *William Stukeley: An Eighteenth Century Antiquarian* (1950) and S. Piggot, *Ruins in a Landscape: Essays in Antiquarianism* (1976). Gibbs owned the Society's engravings of the Gothic Chapel of St Thomas on London Bridge, 1747–8, and Boston church, Lincolnshire (*ASH Prints*, nos. 44–5, 93).

92. *Gibbs MS*, pp. 40, 59, and *VB* (1715) Introduction.

93. *HMC Stuart*, II, p. 404.

94. *ABA*, pp. viii–ix.

95. *ABA*, p. viii, an idea echoed in Hogarthian theory (*The Analysis of Beauty* (1753) p. 47).

96. *HMC Portland*, VI, p. 84.

97. *PRO* State Domestic, George I, Vol. 63, no. 51 (3).

98. In 1744 Philip Yorke thought this insertion 'breaks the length of the church and prevents you from having a full view of the west end, though it was perhaps the only method that could be taken' (*Godber*, p. 133).

99. See this chapter, n. 97.

100. *Defoe 1742*, II, p. 272.

## NOTES TO CHAPTER VIII

1. National Register of Archives (Scotland): Marquis of Bute (Loudoun Papers) NRA (S) survey 631, Bundles A243 and A251.

2. *HMC Stuart*, II, p. 93.

3. F. Bourget and G. Cattaui, *Jules Hardouin Mansart* (1956) pl. LVIII, and F. Blondel, *Cours D'Architecture* (1698) II, p. 563; for such doors in the Church of the Val-de-Grâce's monastic buildings, see *ASH Prints*, no. 18.

4. *Macky 1722*, I, p. 190.

5. *The Art of Painting by C. A. Du Fresnoy* (1716) 2nd ed., dedicatory epistle.

6. *Trivia: or, The Art of Walking the Streets of London* (1716) pp. 44–5.

7. *Ralph*, p. 33.

8. *VB* (1725) p. 7.

9. *Poems on Several Occasions* (1720) II, p. 306, to which Gibbs subscribed.

10. *SRO* Montrose Papers GD 220/5/824/7, 825/5, 826/23, 827/10, 828/4, 829/12 and 15, 983/3.

11. The formation of the estate as reported in *BL* Add. MS 18239, ff. 2, 3, 7r–v; 18240, ff. 7–8, 25, 28; *The Evening Post* (16 March 1715); *HMC Portland*, V, pp. 15, 550, 594, 597–9, 601, 617; *St James's Evening Post* (14–17 May 1726) No. 1718. See also *Colvin*, pp. 661–2; T. Smith, *A Topographical and Historical Account of the Parish of St Mary-le-Bon (1833) pp. 156–7;* and J. Summerson, *Georgian London* (1945) pp. 88–93.

12. p. 82.
13. *ASH* III.50–1 (*Little*, pl. 23), based on the Tuesday Market Cross, King's Lynn, 1707–10 (H. M. Colvin and L. M. Wodehouse, 'Henry Bell of King's Lynn', *AH* (1961) IV, p. 55), may be linked with the Marylebone enterprise.
14. *BL* Add. MS 18238, ff. 26–44; 18239, ff. 7v, 10, 17, 38; 18240, ff. 7–47v; J. Summerson, 'Henrietta Place, Marylebone, and its Associations with James Gibbs', *London Topographical Record* (1958) XXI, pp. 26–36; I. Toesca, 'Alessandro Galilei in Inghilterra', *English Miscellany* (1952) No. 3, pp. 201, 213, no. 10.
15. Nos. 39973 and 43800, 1 February 1750 (Guildhall Library, London: MS 8674, Vol. 75, p. 141).
16. *BL* Add. MS 18240, ff. 16, 18; 18243, ff. 8–21v; *MLHC* Minutes Church, Poor & Highway Rates, 1683–1728, pp. 416, 438, 459 and T2 to 30.
17. P.C.C. 228 Pinfold.
18. *Ralph*, p. 106, condemned the development as a 'modern plague of building [where] the rude, unfinish'd figure . . . should deter others from a like infatuation.' The attribution of work to Gibbs in Anon., 'Some English Palladian Rooms', *AR* (July 1908) pp. 38–40, is without foundation.
19. *BL* Add. MS 18238, ff. 30–2, 40–1.
20. *Ralph*, p. 33. Gibbs also worked for the Duchess at Chiswick and for other members of the Norfolk family (J. M. Robinson, *The Dukes of Norfolk* (1982) pp. 149–54).
21. Lancashire *CRO* Weld (Shireburne) of Stonyhurst Papers DD St.
22. 24 October 1734, No. 252, p. 1. The lodge, which survives in Arlington Street, was based on Burlington's design in W. Kent's *The Designs of Inigo Jones* (1727) I, pl. 59, to which Gibbs subscribed.
23. M. Maty, *Authentic Memoirs of the Life of Richard Mead, M.D.* (1755) p. 51.
24. *HMC Portland*, VI, p. 41: 'this calamity is the Nemesis of Cotton's ghost to punish the neglect in taking due care of his most noble gift to the public'.
25. M. Concanem and L. Welsted, *Of Taste* (1732) p. 3, in T. B. Gilmore, *Early Eighteenth-Century Essays on Taste* (1972) p. 7.
26. A similar cup, also dated 1734, was presented by the Earl of Pembroke to Roger Morris (Marble Hill House, Twickenham, *A Catalogue of Recent Purchases and Loans* (1969) p. 19); see also R. White, 'A Princely Present', *CL* (8 January 1981) p. 80.

## NOTES TO CHAPTER IX

1. *Bart's Journal* Ha 1/10, pp. 83, 88, 93, 154, 211v.
2. J. Harris, *Catalogue of the Drawings Collection of the Royal Institute of British Architects: Inigo Jones & John Webb* (1972) pp. 13–14, fig. 7; *Colvin*, p. 473.
3. *Bart's Journal* Ha 1/10, pp. 182, 198.
4. In *Gibbs MS*, pp. 98–9, noting also that the Capitol in Rome, having burnt down three times, was rebuilt by Michelangelo as three blocks 'detached from each other, to prevent fire' (p. 43). For the development of hospital buildings, see N. Pevsner, *A History of Building Types* (1976) Chapter 9, and J. D. Thompson and G. Goldin, *The Hospital: A Social and Architectural History* (1975).
5. p. 117.
6. *Bart's Journal* Ha 1/11, p. 15; Ha 1/12, pp. 141–2; *A List of the Benefactors to the Poor of the Royal Hospital of St Bartholomew from 1547 to 1844* (1845) p. 32; P.C.C. 228 Pinfold.
7. A 1845 survey report on replacing the eroded stone by Portland reveals Gibbs had bonded 5 to 7 inch ashlar to the brick carcass and insisted 'No alterations whatever ought to be made in the Architecture of the Building, but the whole of the cornices Architraves and Mouldings should be carefully restored as Mr Gibbs originally designed them' (*Bart's Journal* Ha 1/19, pp. 349–53).
8. *Bart's Corr* Ha 19/29/12.
9. *Bart's Journal* Ha 1/10, p. 274v.
10. *Defoe 1738*, II, p. 120. See G. Goldin, 'A Walk Through a Ward of the Eighteenth Century', *Journal of the History of Medicine and Allied Sciences* (1967) XXII, No. 2, pp. 121–38.
11. *Bart's Corr* Ha 19/31/12.
12. *Bart's Journal* Ha 1/12, p. 158.
13. *Ralph*, pp. 15–16; a similar criticism was reported in *Bart's Journal* Ha 1/12, p. 348.
14. 8 August 1734, No. 241, p. 1.
15. *Bart's Journal* Ha 1/13, p. 438 (1766).
16. *GM* (December 1741) p. 652. See also September 1741, p. 474.
17. W. H. McMenemy, 'The Hospital Movement of the Eighteenth Century and its Development', in F. N. L Poynter, ed., *The Evolution of Hospitals in Britain* (1964) pp. 43–71.
18. January 1744, p. 47. See also December 1743, p. 640, and August 1744, p. 446; *The Oxford Magazine* (1769) III, p. 283.
19. G. Whitteridge, 'The Henry VIII Gateway into Smithfield', *St Bartholomew's Hospital Journal* (July 1949) pp. 148–50.
20. *Bart's Journal* Ha 1/11, pp. 492, 523; Ha 1/12, pp. 309, 353–4.
21. *Ibid.*, Ha 1/10, pp. 307–v; Ha 1/11, p. 128.
22. *Ibid.*, Ha 1/11, p. 128; *Vertue*, III, p. 78; *Defoe 1738*, II, pp. 120–1.
23. *GM* (October 1741) p. 547, (November 1748) p. 518.
24. V. C. Medvei and J. L. Thornton, *The Royal Hospital of Saint Bartholomew, 1123–1973* (1974) pp. 19–20.
25. *Defoe 1738*, II, p. 121; *Bart's Corr* Ha 19/5/20.
26. *Bart's Journal* Ha 1/11, p. 173, as illustrated in V. C. Medvei and J. L. Thornton, *The Royal Hospital of Saint Bartholomew, 1123–1973* (1974) pl. 25; the bust has since been removed to the Rahere Ward.
27. *Bart's Journal* Ha 1/11, pp. 312, 314–15.
28. *Ibid.* Ha 1/11, p. 173.
29. B. Nicolson and J. Kerslake, *The Treasures of the Foundling Hospital* (1972).
30. St George's Hospital: 'Minute Book 19 Oct 1733 to 31 Decbr 1735', pp. 260, 266; governors and subscribers who were Gibbs's friends included Bolingbroke, Francis Farquier, Sir John Perceval and others associated with *ABA*. The attribution to Gibbs of St Thomas's Hospital (*BL* Add. MS 47025, f. 104; J. Dallaway, *Observations on English Architecture* (1806) pp. 155–6) is without foundation.
31. 28 August 1736 (*Burney* 320b). See H. M. Colvin, ed., *The History of the King's Works* (1976) V, pp. 125–341, and *Royal Buildings* (1968). In 1716 Mar asked Gibbs to send him his own drawings for Hampton Court and Kensington (*HMC Stuart*, II, pp. 94, 404); these are perhaps related to designs, 1716–30 (*SRO* Mar and Kellie deposit, RHP 13256–8; W. Adam, *Vitruvius Scoticus* (1812) pls. 109–10; *WPL* MS 728.82, 'Description of the Designe for a New Royall Palace for the King of Great Britain at London. 1726'; F. Barker and R. Hyde, *London as it Might Have Been* (1982) pp. 55–6, pl. 36), based on Versailles and Marly (*HMC Stuart*, IV, p. 123).
32. *CLRO 113B*, Box I, Folder 18 March–8 May 1735 (*Perks*, p. 165); *GSJ* (8 August 1734) No. 241, p. 1.
33. *CLRO* Court of Common Council Journal 1717–36, Vol. 57, pp. 361–3; *113C*, Box I, pp. 35–43.
34. B. R. Masters, 'The City Surveyor, the City Engineer and the City Architect and Planning Officer', *Guildhall Miscellany* (April 1973) pp. 237–55; *CLRO 113B*, Box I, Folder 19 November 1735; *113C*, I, p. 30 (*Perks*, p. 169).
35. D. R. Coffin, *The Villa in the Life of Renaissance Rome* (1979) pp. 150–74.
36. Illustrated in F. Drake, *Eboracum: or the History and Antiquities of the City of York* (1736) pp. 330–1, with the comment that it 'had the honour to be a precedent for the city of *London* to copy after'.

## NOTES TO CHAPTER X

1. 5 September 1753 (*Burney* 462b).
2. Sir John Perceval, 1724 (*BL* Add. MS 47030, ff. 93–v).
3. *HMC Bath*, III, pp. 472–3.
4. K. Downes, *Hawksmoor* (1959) pp. 117–20, pl. 36.
5. The principal benefactors in 1720 were George I, the Duke of Chandos (£800) and the Earl of Anglesey (£500), raising £6,600;

Sir Robert Walpole gave £300 in 1725, George II £2,000 in 1728 (*CUL CUR*, f. 9; *MC*, ff. 1–9; *UAB*, pp. 460, 510).

6. Vertue's 1751 engraving of the Chapel attributes it to Inigo Jones: 'The Skill of that famous Architect is shewn in [having] adapted the old Gothick way of Building to the Manner of the Tuscan Order' (*Crace*, XXVIII, no. 26). Perhaps Burrough adopted a pre-Civil War design for the Cambridge Commencement House and Library (lost), described as 'a large Square ... surrounded ... with walls & arched columnes ... fronted with Battlements ... according to [the] modell' (*CUL Baker MS*, Vol. XXX, p. 454). Burrough's involvement in the Public Building and claims of his authorship are discussed in *CUL CUR*, f. 10 (9 and 22 March 1726); *Willis and Clark*, III, p. 49; *BL* Add. MS 5832, ff. 84v, 86v; *Colvin*, p. 169.

7. *CUL CUR*, f. 10 (18 January 1724); *MC*, f. 6; *HMC Bath*, III, p. 484; *Willis and Clark*, III, p. 44.

8. See Henry Aldrich's Peckwater Quadrangle, Oxford, 1707–14 (*Colvin*, pp. 63–4).

9. *Gibbs MS*, p. 43.

10. This association was made by Samuel Dale (*CUL* Add. MS 3466, 2nd Itinerary, 22 May 1729). Wren prepared a design for the Cambridge Commencement House, 1674 (*WS* (1928) V, p. 31, pls. XIII–XIV).

11. *CUL CUR*, f. 10 (22 February 1722); *UAB*, p. 482.

12. *CUL CUR*, f. 10; *LG*, pp. 22–3; *VCV* 12(3)D.8.

13. *CUL CUR*, f. 10; *Willis and Clark*, III, pp. 48–9. T. P. Hudson, 'James Gibbs's designs for University Buildings at Cambridge', *Burl Mag* (December 1972) p. 847, n. 34, shows that true alignment would have been impossible because of the position of the existing surrounding buildings (Fig. A).

14. *Willis and Clark*, III, pp. 50–2, perhaps a reference to John James's letter to the Vice-Chancellor, 1729 (p. 54).

15. *CUL CUR*, ff. 16, 18; *Willis and Clarke*, III, p. 53.

16. *CUL CUR*, f. 17; *LG*, pp. 242–3.

17. *YAS* MS 328, p. 34; A. Palladio, *I Quattro Libri Dell'Architettura* (1570) IV, pp. 41–7.

18. There 'is little if any portland stone used in or about Cambridge' (*KCL KCMun*, 6 October 1724).

19. *VB* (1715) p. 3, pls. 12–13.

20. *Cantabrigia Depicta* (1763) p. 20.

21. *CUL VCV* 14(3)C.22.

22. *Salmon*, p. 16, and the *London Magazine* (February 1748) XVII, pp. 64–5.

23. *BL* Add. MS 15776, f. 41 (1735). Another visitor thought the ceiling 'not high enough for the Dimensions of the Room' (*Markham*, p. 91).

24. *Gibbs MS*, p. 93.

25. This document was published in *Macky 1722*, p. 148, with an expression of hope that 'some good Prince may put the Plan in Execution [to create] the noblest College in the World'. A. Doig, *The Architectural Drawings Collection of King's College, Cambridge* (1979) frontispiece, pp. 17–19. D. Loggan, *Cantabrigia Illustrata* (1690) shows the College much as Gibbs knew it in 1724.

26. *KCL Coll.I*, f. 60.

27. *Ibid.*, f. 63, mentioning 'the Duke of Chandois, who has shew'd himself so very remarkably generous upon all occasions'.

28. 'A List of Contributors to the Building of The West Wing' 1724 (*KCL Coll.I*, f. 85; *CB*, ff. 9, 12; *Willis and Clark*, I, p. 561, n. 2).

29. *KCL CB*, ff. 12–13; *Coll.I*, f. 67.

30. *KCL CB*, ff. 38, 42.

31. *KCL AP*, f. 1 (30 November 1742).

32. See this chapter, n. 25 and *KCL Coll.I*, f. 57.

33. *Defoe 1748*, p. 104; the 1738 edition (I, p. 105) mentions King's 'great Regularity, and modern Beauty'.

34. *KCL Coll.I*, f. 67; *MB* XLIV, no. 4, p. 80; XLV, no. 6, p. 81; no. 7, p. 83. The College purchased Leoni's *The Architecture of A. Palladio* (1714–21) in 1724 (no. 3, p. 80).

35. *Gibbs MS*, p. 93.

36. *ABA*, p. ix.

37. *KCL Coll.I*, f. 57.

38. *BL* Add. MS 15776, ff. 29–32 (1735).

39. *BL* Add. MS 47030, f. 93.

40. *KCL CB*, f. 12.

41. M. Whiffen, 'Academical Elysium: The Landscaping of the Cambridge Backs', *AR* (January 1947) pp. 13–18.

42. The Provost had criticized Hawksmoor's design for placing the Fellows' study and bedrooms overlooking the quadrangle rather than the river (*KCL Coll.I*, f. 57).

43. *CUL* Add. MS 3466 (22 May 1729).

44. *Salmon*, p. 38.

45. Quoted in A. A. Leigh, *University of Cambridge College Histories: King's College* (1899) p. 173.

46. Hawksmoor writing to George Clarke in 1724 (*Downes*, p. 154).

47. *MCL* correspondence (see Catalogue of Works).

48. Published in W. Williams, *Oxonia Depicta* (1732–3) and the *University Almanack* (1731). An undated design among the College papers showing an independent group of three detached blocks, each 236 feet long and with plans identical to Gibbs's Fellows' Buildings at King's, surrounding old Magdalen Hall, is endorsed 'Mr. B-'s plan', presumably referring to Borlach.

49. *MCL* undated letter.

50. *MCL* MS 906 (iii–iv), 22 October 1743 and 31 January 1744.

51. *MCL* MS 906 (i–ii), 25 March and 11 April 1734.

52. College Archives: MS All Souls D.D.c.256, No. 79.

53. W. Pittis, *Dr. Radcliffe's Life and Letters* (1736) pp. 77–82.

54. *Macky 1722*, II, p. 71.

55. *Vertue*, III, p. 78. Hawksmoor's designs are discussed in *Downes*, pp. 122–31, pls. 35–9; *Gillam*, pp. vii–xii, 148–61, pls. 1–16.

56. *BR*, p. 9.

57. *Godber*, p. 146.

58. J. Pointer, *Oxoniensis Academia: Or, The Antiquities and Curiosities of the University of Oxford* (1749) pp. 144–5, saw the Library offering 'a fine View ... of several noble Buildings round it, so that Strangers have here a curious Taste of the Beauty of Oxford'. *Gillam*, pl. 24a, shows how Gibbs's rectangular designs could not have accommodated such views.

59. *WS* (1928) V, pls. XVIII–XXI.

60. In 1774 it was reported that the 'Ratcliffe Library seems taken from [Wolfenbüttel] so they there said it was' (J. E. Ross, ed., *Radical Adventurer: The Diaries of Robert Morris, 1772–1774* (1971) p. 83). This Library was celebrated in England (*Macky 1722*, II, p. 81; N. Pevsner, *A History of Building Types* (1976) pp. 98–9, pls. 7, 15–17; H. Reuther, 'Das Gebäude Der Herzog-August-Bibliothek zu Wolfenbüttel und Ihr Oberbibliothekar Gottfried Wilhelm Leibniz', in W. Totok and C. Haase, *Leibniz* (1966) pp. 349–60).

61. W. King, *A Translation Of a late Celebrated Oration. Occasioned By a Lible, entitled, Remarks on Doctor K—g's Speech* (1750) pp. 29, 34–5; also *GM* (April 1738) pp. 215–16. The Alexandrian Library was the subject of studies for decorative paintings by James Thornhill (J. Harris, *A Catalogue of British Drawings for Architecture, Decoration, Sculpture and Landscape Gardening 1550–1900 in American Collections* (1971) p. 253, pl. 198; R. R. Wark, *Early British Drawings in the Huntington Collection 1600–1750* (1969) p. 50U).

62. *Salmon*, p. 31.

63. Pl. VI, from the English edition by T. Lediard, *A Plan of Civil and Historical Architecture ... By John Bernhard Fischer of Erlach* (1730) Book I, pp. 7–8. A history of the building type is discussed in J. S. Curl, *A Celebration of Death* (1980).

64. *Defoe 1762*, II, p. 257, the position shown in *BR*, pl. XIV. Neither the niche nor statue appears in the 1737–40 engravings.

65. *BR*, p. 9.

66. *Gibbs MS*, p. 2.

67. *Gillam*, pp. xiii–iv. James Heany seems to refer to it in *Oxford, The Seat of the Muses* (1738) p. 4: 'A Publick Library, that all must own, The like at present in the World's not known'.

68. *BR*, p. 6.

69. *Bodleian* MS Autog. c. 9, f. 107; c. 19, ff. 1–3.

70. *Gibbs MS*, p. 31. In the executed dome Gibbs added circular

Michelangeloesque windows. *A Satire Upon Physicians* (1755) p. 17, saw Radcliffe's 'aspiring lofty Dome, A rival proud to that of *Rome*'.

71. *BR*, pp. 7, 11, pls. III, XVII.

72. The 'cutting of the arches by the piers which support the gallery has a very bad effect, and might have been avoided', noted Philip Yorke in 1750 (*Godber*, p. 146).

73. *Gillam*, p. 103; *BR*, p. 12, pl. XX. Stone-coloured oil paint camouflaged the change from stone to plaster (*Gillam*, pp. 41, 55).

74. *Gillam*, pp. 105–6.

75. *BR*, pp. 7, 8, 11, pl. XVI.

76. *Gillam*, p. 53. H. Hayward and P. Kirkham, *William and John Linnell* (1980) pp. 92–4, figs. 29–32. References to the construction and decoration of the Library are in *Gillam* and the Catalogue of Works.

77. p. 13.

78. *The Lives of The Most Eminent British Painters, Sculptors, and Architects* (1831) IV, p. 294. In 1834 Macaulay wrote of Fanny Burney looking 'down from the dome of the Radcliffe Camera on the magnificent sea of turrets and battlements below' (J. Morris, *The Oxford Book of Oxford* (1978) p. 167).

# NOTES TO CHAPTER XI

1. *HMC Portland*, V, p. 332. For a comparable publication history, see T. Connor, 'The making of "Vitruvius Britannicus"', *AH* (1977) XX, pp. 14–30.

2. *LPL* 2726, ff. 77–8; 2690, p. 244(1), referring to *ASH* III.112. Gibbs's suspicions of plagerism were well founded since David Lockeley issued an almost identical print in J. Smith, *Views of all the Cathedrals in England and Wales* (1719) illustrated in T. Friedman, *James Gibbs Architect, 1682–1754: 'a man of great Fame'* (1982) cat. no. 23.

3. *Gibbs MS*, p. 54 (1707). Gibbs's aim, therefore, differed from Leoni's, who had begun his new edition of Palladio's *I Quattro Libri dell'architettura* in Dusseldorf in 1708 and published it as an English translation in London in 1715–20 (R. Wittkower, 'English Neoclassicism and the Vicissitudes of Palladio's Quattro Libri' in *Palladio and English Palladianism* (1974) pp. 79–82).

4. *The Third Volume of the Monthly Catalogue the years 1727, and 1728* (1729) No. 48, p. 48; also *Mist's Weekly Journal* (1 April 1727) No. 102, p. 3 (*Burney* 249b).

5. According to *ABA* Introduction, 'some Plates were added to what was at first intended, by the particular direction of Persons of great Distinction, for whose Commands I have the highest regard'.

6. Copies of the 15 March and 1 May 1727 *Proposals* are in Chetham's Library, Manchester (Halliwell-Phillipps Broadsides nos. 866–7).

7. *MCL* 13 January 1728. The King's College authorities paid 2 guineas by 4 May (*KCL Coll.I*, p. 67; *MB* Vol. 44, No. 6, p. 81) and Sir John Harpur on 6 May 1727 (See Calke Abbey in Catalogue of Works).

8. Payments to Heinrich Hulsberg, Elisha Kirkall and George Vertue are recorded in Gibbs's account at *Drummonds* Ledgers 1722, p. 306; 1726, p. 28; 1727, p. 28.

9. *MCL* MS 289.

10. *Vertue*, III, p. 133.

11. *The Third Volume of the Monthly Catalogue the Years 1727, and 1728* (1729) No. 61, pp. 53–4. *Gibbs MS*, p. 101, erroneously refers to *ABA* as 'printed for the author . . . anno 1726'.

12. Particularly the set represented by *ASH* II.107–18, with contemporary numbering 1–12 (*Little*, pl. 27).

13. *Vertue*, III, p. 133; *Leeds Mercury* (6 June 1738); and *London Evening Post* (14 February 1740, *Burney* 350b).

14. *A Catalogue Of Several Valuable Libraries . . . Lately Purchased; Which will be Selling for Ready Money . . . By William Cater . . . Holborn* (9 June 1783) p. 8, lot 158. A fascimile was published in 1968 (Benjamin Blom, New York).

15. *Defoe 1761*, II, p. 286.

16. Plate III, a copy of which Gibbs owned (F. Souchal, 'La Collection Du Sculpteur Girardon D'Après son Inventaire Après Décès', *Gazette des Beaux-Arts* (1973) LXXXII, pp. 8–9). In 1724 Clark issued an engraved perspective of the Cambridge Public Building based on one of Gibbs's early designs (T. P. Hudson, 'James Gibbs's designs for University Buildings at Cambridge', *Burl Mag* (December 1972) p. 842–3, n. 3).

17. T. Friedman, 'A Decorative Sculptor's Trade Card', *Leeds Arts Calendar* (1974) No. 75, pp. 29–32.

18. Leyburn was built for the Jacobite Catholic family of Yarker by an unknown architect (M. Binney, 'Leyburn Hall', *CL* (20 October 1977) pp. 1090–3). Pl. 64 (a house for 'a Gentleman in *Essex*') and pl. 96 (chimneypiece, top right) appear in slightly modified forms at Ossington Hall, Nottinghamshire, built 1729 (G. Jackson-Stops, *Vanishing Houses of England* (1982) p. 46). D. Cruickshank and P. Wyld, *London: The Art of Georgian Building* (1975), show how *ABA* doorcases were copied and reinterpreted.

19. Until recently it was thought this church had been designed by William Halfpenny on the evidence of an engraving of a 'Church . . . of my Invention for Leeds' similar to Etty's and incorporating still other Gibbsian features, published in his *Art of Sound Building*, 1725. Whatever his connection with the enterprise, Halfpenny too admired Gibbs's work, for his book includes 'a House of my Invention' (pls. 17–19) based on Witham Park and presumably taken from *VB* (1717) pl. 92; Witham was also a source for Robert Adam's Osterley Park, 1763. Halfpenny used *ABA*, pl. 54, for the front of Upton House, Tetbury, Gloucestershire (*CL* (15 February 1973) pp. 390–4). Etty's Holy Trinity drawing was published with the date 1724 in Thoresby's *Vicaria Leodiensis* (1724) p. 245 (D. Linstrum, *West Yorkshire Architects and Architecture* (1978) pp. 186–7, 376, pl. 140).

20. University of Hull Archive: DDHA 14/25–26, letter of 23 April 1725.

21. Illustrated in F. Drake, *Eboracum: or the History and Antiquities of the City of York* (1736) pp. 330–1. See also *VAM* E.3604-1913. There is a resemblance between *ASH* III.59–60 and Aldby Park near York, dated 1726, which has a hall chimneypiece based on *ABA*, pl. 94 (*CL* (9 November 1935) pp. 486–92).

22. *SRO* GD 18/4729/2, 5 May 1726 letter, and GD 18/2107 (Sir John Clerk, *Journey to London in 1727*). Adam had already begun remodelling Hopetoun House, Midlothian, for Lord Hopetoun, whose uncle James Johnston commissioned Gibbs for the Westminster Abbey Monument to the Marchioness of Annandale, 1723.

23. J. Fleming, 'John Adam's Country-House Tour', *CL* (13 July 1961) p. 66, (27 July 1961) p. 202; A. T. Bolton, 'The Shire Hall, Hertford', *AR* (1 April 1918) pp. 68–73. A copy of *ABA* (1739) is inscribed 'Mr. James Adams Brother of John Adams Architect in Edr Borrowed from Mr. Douglas Inigo Jones's workes forgot: his recept lies in my hand not being returned J :D :——Ja: Adams recept for this book lodged with Earl of Dalhousie to whom I have given the book J :D :' (author's collection).

24. A. Oswald, 'The Universities of Oxford and Cambridge', *CL* (17 October 1931) p. 425, figs. 11–12.

25. *S of L* (1980) XL, pp. 298–302, pl. 76a.

26. 'Report of y Comitt- for Rebuilding Gainsbor Church' (Lincoln Diocesan Records: Fac. 9/68). Bickerton also worked at York Mansion House (*Colvin*, p. 110). See A. Gomme, 'The Genesis of Sutton Scarsdale', *AH* (1981) XXIV, pp. 34–8, and J. Cornforth, 'Charity on a Noble Scale', *CL* (16 April 1964) pp. 902–5, for further Gibbs–Smith links.

27. J. Pote, *The Foreigner's Guide* (1729) pp. 48–50. For a detailed analysis of its steeple by a 1742 visitor, see *BL* Add. MS 22926, ff. 36r–v. J. Aheron's *A General Treatise of Architecture. In Five Books* (1754), published in Dublin, mentioned St Martin's under the subject of the 'Model'. See also D. Stillman, 'Church Architecture in Neo-Classical England', *JSAH* (1979) pp. 103–19; J. Summerson, *Georgian London* (1945) Chapter XVI; M. Whiffen, 'The Progeny of St. Martin-in-the-Fields', *AR* (July 1946) pp. 3–6; and M. Whiffen, *Stuart and Georgian Churches* (1948).

28. *Gwynn*, p. 46; P. Toynbee, ed., *The Letters of Horace Walpole* (1903) III, pp. 119–20; M. Whiffen, *Stuart and Georgian Churches* (1948) p. 42, pl. 41.

29. R. Renwick, *Extracts from the Records of the Burgh of Glasgow* (1911) VI, pp. 20–1; G. Hay, *The Architecture of Scottish Post-Reformation Churches, 1560–1843* (1957) pp. 101–2, pls. 14a, 15b. A Scottish visitor to London in 1775 found Dreghorn's portico 'not so great or lofty, & its steeple is not so fine, appearing too little tapered towards the top' but thought the interior 'excells St. Martin's [because] the Lofts are all of Mahogany & the Stucco ornaments . . . are in a finer taste' (Mouat's Journal, Private collection).

30. p. 69, pl. I, commenting that St Martin's steeple 'seen from without [appears] to stand upon the roof, and to have no other support, for which reason we have endeavoured to alter this disposition'.

31. For contemporary comments on this steeple, see *Ralph*, pp. 100–1, and *Defoe 1738*, II, p. 144; for Flitcroft's first proposal, see J. Harris, *The Palladians* (1981) pp. 86–7. Gibbs owned the 1753 Donowell-Walker engraving of St Giles (*ASH Prints*, nos. 46–7).

32. C. H. Collins Baker and K. Esdaile, 'John Sanderson and Hampstead Parish Church', *CL* (11 December 1937) pp. 610–11; *Colvin*, p. 716.

33. M. Whiffen, 'The Progeny of St. Martin-in-the-Fields', *AR* (July 1946) pp. 4–5. Baker must have had access to *ABA*, for Ludlow Butter Market, 1743–4, is based on pl. 62 (*Colvin*, pp. 83–4).

34. R. Bigland, *Historical, Monumental and Genealogical Collections, Relating to the County of Gloucester* (1791) p. 119, refers to Charles Evans as architect, although according to Eileen Harris he was merely the executor of Thomas Wright's design.

35. *MLHC* Ashbridge Collection 241(493); J. Harris, *Sir William Chambers* (1970) p. 228, pls. 144–6. Chambers's pupil Willey Reveley designed several St Martin's–like round and rectangular churches, 1776–7 (Sotheby's, 8 November 1979, lot 26, pl. III).

36. *Colvin*, pp. 227, 322, 480, 779–80. J. Morris, *Stones of Empire: The Buildings of the Raj* (1983) pp. 158–80; S. Nilsson, *European Architecture in India, 1750–1850* (1968) pp. 75, 125–30, 156–8, pls. 14–15, 53b, 55–9, noting the presence in 1801 of *ABA* at the College of Fort William, Calcutta, and also the influence of St Martin's in South Africa.

37. *Den Danske Vitruvius* (1746) pp. 64–7, plates LX–LXI, LXXXIII; *Arkitekten Lauritz de Thurah 1706–1759*, Udstilling i Kunstindustrimuseet (1981) pp. 55–8, nos. 22–3, illus.; S. Nilsson, *European Architecture in India, 1750–1850* (1968) pp. 75, 91, n.43. The Fridenchs Kirkes was erected by Frederick V but with a different steeple.

38. N. Pevsner, *The Buildings of England: Northumberland* (1975) p. 90, pl. 56b; *Colvin*, p. 220; M. Binney, 'Sir Robert Taylor's Bank of England', *CL* (13 November 1969) p. 1247. D. J. Gilson, *Books from the Library of Sir Robert Taylor in the Library of the Taylor Institution, Oxford* (1973) no. 22; he also owned *Rules for Drawing* (1732) no. 23.

39. T. Friedman, 'Rysbrack and Gibbs', in K. Eustace, *Michael Rysbrack Sculptor, 1694–1770* (1982) pp. 21–2, fig. 3; M. Whinney, *Sculpture in Britain, 1530 to 1830* (1964) pp. 96–7, pl. 75. The unusual painted monument at Alnwick, Northumberland, to Alexander Baines, dated 1737 and signed 'R. Cooper Edin Fecit', perhaps Richard Cooper, engraver of *Vitruvius Scoticus*, is a free adaption of the Prior monument published in *ABA*, pl. 112.

40. M. Whinney, *Sculpture in Britain, 1530 to 1830* (1964) pp. 126–7, pl. 101B.

41. M. Whinney, *Sculpture in Britain, 1530 to 1830* (1964) pl. 100. Carpenter advertised in the *Daily Journal* (26 January 1737, *Burney* 319b) his intention 'to leave off entirely the Casting of Lead Figures', to sell his stock and 'apply himself solely to . . . the Statuary or Carving Part in Marble or Stone'.

42. K. Eustace, *Michael Rysbrack Sculptor, 1694–1770* (1982) pp. 75–80, 106–8, 112–13. Other examples are the monuments in St Margaret's, Westminster, to Sir Thomas Crosse (d. 1738), a New Churches commissioner and St Bartholomew's Hospital governor

(*LPL* 2690, p. 124(3); *Bart's Journal* Ha 1/10, p. 144), and at Great Mitton, Yorkshire to Peregrine Widdrington (d. 1749), erected by his widow, the Dowager Duchess of Norfolk, Gibbs's client at 16 Arlington Street, London. Rysbrack's Finch monument, 1738, incorporates features from *ABA*, pl. 115 (G. E. Aylmer and R. Cant, *A History of York Minster* (1977) pl. 115).

43. The Corporation decided on 10 April 1736 to erect the monument and agreed on 19 June with Easton (d. 1786) to make it for £50 'according to the plan [lost] this day produced' (Borough of Rochester upon Medway: Meeting Day Books and Chamberlain's Accounts 1736–7; *Gunnis*, p. 138). Easton was associated with Gibbs in a Fishmongers Company dispute in London in 1743 (P. Metcalfe, *The Halls of the Fishmongers Company* (1977) pp. 100–2).

44. *Gunnis*, pp. 59, 353; H. Potterton, *Irish Church Monuments, 1570–1880* (1975) p. 10, figs. 18–19; *Little*, p. 106.

45. Adrian Drift wrote Edward Harley in 1729 that he had received loose 'Copies' of the Newcastle, Prior and Annandale monuments from Gibbs (*BL Portland Papers Loan* 29/316, f. 50).

46. H. A. Tipping and C. Hussey, *English Homes: Period IV, The Work of Sir John Vanbrugh and his School, 1699–1736* (1928) II, pp. 217–20, fig. 319; J. Lees-Milne, *English Country Houses: Baroque, 1685–1715* (1970) p. 283.

47. D. Stroud, 'The Villa Capra, Vicenza, and its English Counterparts', *CL* (8 October 1948) pp. 728–31; K. Downes, 'Chiswick Villa', *AR* (October 1978) pp. 225–36. Gibbs may have dated pl. 44 in *ABA* to 1720 (p. xii) in order to reaffirm its precedence over Burlington's Villa, first published in W. Kent, *The Designs of Inigo Jones* (1727) I, pls. 70–3, to which Gibbs subscribed.

48. *Gibbs MS*, p. 84; *HMC Stuart*, II, pp. 92, 404; IV, p. 568; V, pp. 211, 378–9. In 1754 Gibbs bequeathed £1,000, three London houses and plate to Lord Erskine, *ABA* subscriber, 'in gratitude for favours received from his father the late Earl of Marr' (P.C.C. 228 Pinfold). *Vertue*, VI, pp. 16, 19, mentions Gibbs as 'master' to the unknown 'Giovan Batista Bracelli'. William Adam's The Drum, Edinburgh, *c.* 1724–6, is another progeny of *ABA*, pl. 43 (J. Simpson, intro., *Vitruvius Scoticus* (1980) pp. 33–4, pl. 38).

49. *VB* (1725) pl. 48; *Colvin*, pp. 184–5; T. P. Connor, 'Colen Campbell as Architect to the Prince of Wales', *AH* (1979) XXII, p. 66, pls. 13c–d.

50. *Colvin*, p. 201; G. N. Wright, 'The Stony Pleasures of Purbeck', *CL* (25 July 1968) p. 212, fig. 5.

51. *Colvin*, pp. 420–1; *Friedman 1973*, pp. 130–2.

52. For example, Gibbs's proposals for the London Mansion House were displayed at Guildhall in 1737 (*CLRO 113C*, p. 97).

53. Compare *ASH* II.67–8 with C. Hussey, *English Country Houses: Early Georgian* (1955) pls. 53–7.

54. J. H. Martindale, 'High Head Castle, Cumberland', *Cumberland and Westmorland Antiquarian and Archaeological Society Transactions* (1911) NS XI, pp. 379–84. See also the similar house design in *ASH* III.45–7.

55. For a similar courtyard arrangement by an unknown architect perhaps dating 1720–5, see G. H. Kitchin, 'Lainston House', *CL* (8 March 1919) pp. 252–9. See also Kelmarsh in Catalogue of Works.

56. M. Girouard, 'Echoes of a Georgian Romantic', *CL* (2 January 1964) p. 20, figs. 1–3.

57. S. Houfe, 'A Taste for the Gothick', *CL* (24 March 1977) pp. 728–9, figs. 3, 6; *Colvin*, p. 550. The house is recorded in a 'Sketch of a Gothic Building February 1757' (Sir John Soane's Museum: 43, Set 5 'Miscellaneous Drawings of Old Houses in the Country, &c. from the Collection of Sir William Chambers, Kt', no. 5). The Stowe temple is included in a New York watercolour depicting *Jeptha's Return*, 1812 (M. Whiffen, 'James Gibbs and Betsy Lathrop', *Antiques* (September 1954) p. 212).

58. Christ Church, Oxford (Inv. 1138); the engraving, which sold at 1s., is inscribed 'Ja. Gibbs Archit.' and 'Thos Boydell delin Jno. Boydell sculp No. 43'.

59. Rouge: II, pl. 4; IV, pls. 1, 19; Hirschfield: Vol. III; Stieglitz:

pls. 53–4, 67. See also descriptions of Gibbs's London churches, Abbey monuments, St Bartholomew's Hospital, Stowe and the Radcliffe Library in *Curiosités De Londres et De L'Angleterre. Par Le Rouge* (1776) Bordeaux, pp. 19–29, 56, 98, 106–7.

60. pp. 97–100.

61. p. 402, translated as 'this admirable work, after the examples of the best architects of antiquity,—an example which the moderns should also imitate' (Mrs E. Cresy, trans., *The Lives of Celebrated Architects, Ancient and Modern ... by Francesco Milizia* (1826) pp. 296–7). The Venetian architect Selva, visiting Oxford in 1781, described the Library fully and considered it a 'buon disegno' (P. de la Ruffinière du Prey, 'Giannantonio Selva in England', *AH* (1982) XXV, p. 27). John Sanderson adapted the rotunda to a villa design of the 1750s (J. Harris, *The Palladians* (1981) p. 127). Copies of *Bibliotheca Radcliviana* (1747) were owned by the architects John Yenn (Leeds School of Architecture Library) and Thomas Hardwick (L. L. Abel, 'A Bibliography of Some 18th Century Books on Architecture', University of London M.S., p. 46), and the Library was still admired at the end of the nineteenth century by M. Schuyler, *American Architecture and Other Writings* (1961) II, p. 453.

62. *A New Guide to London: Or Directions to Strangers* (1726) p. 26, thought it 'tres belle & est aussi bien que le clocher d'un excellent bout d'Architecture'; J. Pote, *The Foreigner's Guide* (1729) pp. 48–50, 'a Master-piece'. It is also described in P. J. Grosley, *Londres* (1770) III, p. 262; *Londres et ses Environs, ou Guide des Voyageurs Curieux et Amateurs dans cette partie de L'Angleterre ... par M.D.S.D.L* (1788) I, p. 203; J. B. Barjaud and C. P. Landon, *Description De Londres et Des Ses Édifices* (1810–11) pp. 63–4. For a French appreciation of St Martin's progeny in India in 1790, see S. Nilsson, *European Architecture in India, 1750–1850* (1968) p. 128.

63. Quoting the English edition, *The Present State of the Arts in England* (1755) pp. 95–6. See also K. Woodbridge, 'Bélanger en Angleterre: son carnet de voyage', *AH* (1982) XXV, p. 9.

64. See *WPL* St Martin's Box 1 and 3. Compare them to N. Nicole's Sainte Madeleine, Besançon, 1742–66 (W. G. Kalnein and M. Levey, *Art and Architecture of the Eighteenth Century in France* (1972) p. 292, pl. 255). See W. Herrmann, *Laugier and Eighteenth Century French Theory* (1962); R. D. Middleton, 'The Abbé De Cordemoy and the Graeco-Gothic Ideal: A Prelude to Romantic Classicism', *Journal of the Warburg and Courtauld Institutes* (1962) pp. 278–320, (1963) pp. 90–123.

65. 'Gibbs and Palladio in the Colonial World' in W. H. Pierson, *American Buildings and their Architects* (1976) Chapter IV, is the fullest account of this influence.

66. J. D. Prown, *John Singleton Copley* (1966) I, p. 16, n. 3; *S of L* (1966) XXXIV, p. 387; A. Oliver, 'Peter Pelham (*c.* 1697–1751) Sometime Printmaker of Boston', in *Boston Prints and Printmakers, 1670–1775* (1973) pp. 133–73.

67. *Vertue*, III, pp. 36, 161. Smibert was admitted to the Society in 1725 and is mentioned with Gibbs in 1727 (*SAL* Minute Book, I, pp. 152, 186, 190; Treasurers Book, 1718–38, pp. 130, 136, 231, 260, 268). For his career, see D. Evans, *The Notebook of John Smibert* (1964); S. T. Riley, 'John Smibert and the Business of Portrait Painting', in I. M. G. Quimby, ed., *American Painting to 1776: A Reappraisal* (1971) pp. 159–180.

68. pp. 1, 27, pl. XXXVI. The unremodelled Fanueil Hall is discussed in H. Kirker, *The Architecture of Charles Bulfinch* (1969) pp. 232–7, and *Morrison*, pp. 439–42.

69. *Park*, p. 55.

70. B. Rand, *Berkeley and Percival* (1914) p. 171. Berkeley returned to England in 1732 but maintained his colonial contacts (A. F. Downing and V. J. Scully, *The Architectural Heritage of Newport, Rhode Island, 1640–1915* (1952) pp. 56, 438–40).

71. *An Essay Towards Preventing the Ruine of Great Britain* (1721) pp. 19–20.

72. In 1724 Perceval expressed admiration of Shoteover Park, Oxfordshire, 1713–18, for being the 'most regular [seat] I have yet seen in England ... an exact copy of that part of Somerset

house ... built by Inigo Jones' (*BL* Add. MS 47030, f. 76) as illustrated in *VB* (1715) pl. 16 (J. Lees-Milne, *English Country Houses: Baroque, 1685–1715* (1970) fig. 407).

73. B. Little, 'Norbonne Berkeley: Gloucestershire Magnate', *Virginia Magazine* (October 1955) LXII, pp. 379–409. Lord Lichfield, Gibbs's patron at Ditchley, was also a member of the circle. J. Lucas, *Kalm's Account of his Visit to England on his way to America in 1748* (1892) pp. 57–8, records a visit to Whitton, Middlesex.

74. P.C.C. 228 Pinfold; *MLHC* Vestry Minutes Church Poor, & Highways Rates, T30ff; P. M. Geddy, 'Cosmo Alexander's travels and patrons in America', *Antiques* (November 1977) pp. 972–7; G. L. M. Goodfellow, 'Cosmo Alexander in America', *Art Quarterly* (Autumn 1963) pp. 309–20; D. and F. Irwin, *Scottish Painters at Home and Abroad, 1700–1900* (1975) pp. 45–7.

75. H. Kirker, *The Architecture of Charles Bulfinch* (1969) pp. 6–7, 23–4, 387–8.

76. E. Dumbauld, 'Jefferson and Adams' English Garden Tour', in W. H. Adams, ed., *Jefferson and the Arts: An Extended View* (1976) pp. 145–6, 149–50.

77. F. Kimball, *Thomas Jefferson Architect* (1916) pp. 34, 94, figs. 232–3.

78. Fauquier was involved in the promotion of two London hospitals (B. Nicolson, *The Treasures of the Foundling Hospital* (1972) p. 81; 'Account of Proceedings of Governors of St George's Hospital Hyde Pk Corner', 1743, in *Crace*, X, no. 31), one in Bath ('The Plan and Elevation of a New General Hospital intended to be erected at Bath', 1737, in *BM* Department of Prints and Drawings, Bath Topographical folio) and one in the colonies (M. Whiffen, *The Public Buildings of Williamsburg* (1958) pp. 161–2, 174, 226; W. H. Adams, ed., *The Eye of Thomas Jefferson* (1976) p. 12; B. Little, 'Francis Fauquier and an English Architect', *William and Mary Quarterly* (July 1955) XII, 3rd series, pp. 475–6).

79. F. Kimball, *Thomas Jefferson Architect* (1968) pp. 22, 25–6, 122–3, 127, 129, 134, figs. 19–20, 35–7, 63, 72–3, 80–1.

80. *Park*, pp. 39, 54–5; C. E. Peterson, 'Liberty Hall', in *Historic Philadelphia* (1953) p. 146; C. Evans, *American Bibliography* (C. K. Shipton, ed., *Early American Imprints, 1639–1800* (1955, 1959)) nos. 9259, p. 66 (748–9); 11596, p. 6 (59–60); 22066, p. 253 (1, 296); 25915, p. 44 (3322, 4226); 30121, p. 56. Gibbs's publications were still being recommended in *GM* (March 1834) I, p. 335.

81. W. L. Warren, *Isaac Fitch of Lebanon, Connecticut: Master Joiner, 1734–1791* (1978) pp. 1, 4–5, 71.

82. Plate XXXII (*Park*, pp. 61–2; J. M. Howells, *The Architectural Heritage of the Piscataqua* (1965) figs. 6, 27).

83. This publication seems also to have made use of the Gibbs designs, reissued in Batty Langley's *A City and Country Builder's and Workman's Treasury of Designs* and Francis Price's *The British Carpenter*, which Gibbs endorsed. A copy of the latter (1735 edition) annotated 'Perfect Jan 22.1742/3 Price 0.9.0' is in the New-York Historical Society.

84. Reprinted with an introduction by C. E. Peterson, *The Carpenter's Company 1786 Rule Book* (1971). The Philadelphia sculptor William Rush consulted *ABA*, pl. 111, 116 or 118, for the source of his figure of *Wisdom*, 1812–24, which once crowned the Grand Civic Arch in that town (D. D. Thompson, 'The Public Work of William Rush: A Case Study in the Origins of American Sculpture', in *William Rush American Sculptor* (1982) Pennsylvania Academy of the Fine Arts, pp. 37–41, 139–42).

85. *Morrison*, pp. 561–2; N. Silver, *Lost New York* (1975) p. 112.

86. H. Comstock, 'Mount Pleasant', *Connoisseur* (August 1964) pp. 226–31; M. B. Tinkcom, 'Cliveden: The Building of a Philadelphia Countryseat, 1763–1767', *Pennsylvania Magazine of History and Biography* (January 1964), pp. 3–36. For other examples, see M. F. Trostel, 'Mount Clare' *Antiques* (February 1979) pp. 342–51; W. Andrews, *Architecture in New England* (1973) pp. 36–9. For discussions of the Philadelphia State House, see *Philadelphia: Three Centuries of American Art* (1976) pp. 41–2 and H. D. Eberlein and C. V. D. Hubbard, *American Georgian Architec-*

*ture* (1952) pls. 31, 33.

87. C. Bridenbaugh, *Peter Harrison: First American Architect* (1949), Appendix C, figs. 21–4, 28–9, 40–1; A. F. Downing and V. J. Scully, *The Architectural Heritage of Newport, Rhode Island, 1640–1915* (1967) pp. 46, 78–91, pls. 104–5, 108–10. *Morrison*, pp. 445–59, quotes Harrison's recommendation for woodwork 'covered on the outside with Rough-cast [and] Pine Plank worked in Imitation of Rustick', recalling techniques used in Gibbs's chapel at Sir William Turner's Hospital at Kirkleatham, Yorkshire.

88. 'Letters and Other Papers Relating to the Early History of the Church of England in Nova Scotia', in *Collections of the Nova Scotia Historical Society For the Years 1889–91* (1891) VII, pp. 107, 114, 116, 122, 124; R. V. Harris, *The Church of Saint Paul in Halifax, Nova Scotia, 1749–1949* (1949) pp. 8, 15–19, 133, 212; H. Kalman, *Pioneer Churches* (1976) pp. 88–9.

89. *SMIF* 419/309, pp. 138, 145–6. For Nicholson's architectural activities, see *Philadelphia: Three Centuries of American Art* (1976) p. 32; M. Whiffen, *The Public Buildings of Williamsburg* (1958).

90. *PRO* WO 48/68, p. 186; WO 54/203, pp. 2, 6; WO 54/210, pp. 11, 59, 109–15; WO 54/212; *Colvin*, p. 979. *GM* (14 July 1750) p. 459, speculated at the foundation-stone laying that St Paul's 'will be the handsomest [church] in America'; a similar report appeared in the *Boston Weekly News Letter* (14 July 1750).

91. R. W. Shoemaker, 'Christ Church, St Peter's and St. Paul's', in *Historic Philadelphia* (1953) pp. 187–98, figs. 1–2; *Philadelphia: Three Centuries of American Art* (1976) pp. 31–4, 72–4. See also Smith's Zion Lutheran Church, 1766–9 (G. B. Tatum, *Penn's Great Town* (1961) p. 157, pl. 13). The American architect James Bridges offered without success to rebuild St Nicholas's, Bristol (England), according to 'a Plan *I saw executed, when* on my travels through . . . *Pensilvania*' (*Four Designs for Rebuilding Bristol Bridge* (1760) pp. 45–6, in Bristol Public Library: B 10515).

92. S. L. Mims, ed., *M. L. E. Moreau de Saint-Méry, Voyage aux États-Unis de L'Amerique, 1793–1798* (1913) pp. 163–4.

93. Another example is the nearby Brick or Presbyterian Meeting House, for which builders were invited in 1793 to inspect the proposed 'plan of the steeple', inspired by Gibbs (R. Gottesman, *The Arts and Crafts in New York, 1777–1799* (1954) pp. 187–8).

94. According to their advertisement in the *New-York Advertiser*, 5 April 1796 (R. S. Gottesman, *The Arts and Crafts in New York, 1779–1799* (1954) p. 192). A. A. Gilchrist, 'John McComb, Sr. and Jr., in New York, 1784–1799', *JSAH* (March 1972) p. 13, no. 10, recording Laurence's 1794 steeple drawings; M. Dix, *A History of the Parish of Trinity Church in the City of New York* (1901) p. 145. McBean may have been among the many Jacobite emigrés to New York after 1745; the clan name, although not Thomas's, appears in W. M. MacBean, 'Notes on Members St Andrew's Society of State of New York', MS, New-York Historical Society; *Morrison*, pp. 553–5.

95. June 1753, p. 260 illus.; A. Simons and S. Lapham, *The Early Architecture of Charleston* (1927) pp. 177–9.

96. For Gibson read Gibbs. H. J. McKee, 'St Michael's Church, Charleston, 1752–1762', *JSAH* (March 1964) pp. 39–43; *Morrison*, pp. 408–10. The interior was inspired by Hawksmoor's St Alphege, Greenwich.

97. See also Aleazar Ball's design for the First Presbyterian Church, Newark, *c*. 1790 (M. D. Schwartz, 'Fine Arts in the New Jersey Historical Society', *Antiques* (April 1974) p. 246, fig. 7).

98. *Park*, pp. 33, 47, 54; P. Benes and P. D. Zimmerman, *New England Meeting House and Church, 1630–1850* (1979) pp. 28–9, 119, cat. 21; H.-R. Hitchcock, *Rhode Island Architecture* (1939) pp. 23–5; *Morrison*, pp. 461–3; A. L. Cummings, 'A Recently Discovered Engraving of The Old State House in Boston', in *Boston Prints*

*and Printmakers, 1670–1775* (1973) pp. 183–4.

99. H. Kalman, *Pioneer Churches* (1976) pp. 134–5; T. R. Millman, *Jacob Mountain, First Lord Bishop of Quebec*, University of Toronto Studies History and Economic Series (1947) X, pp. 85–91; F. C. Würtele, 'The English Cathedral of Quebec', *Transactions of the Literary and Historical Society of Quebec* (1891) No. 20, pp. 75–81.

100. R. H. Newton, *Town & Davis Architects* (1942) pp. 33–6.

101. M. Dix, *A History of the Parish of Trinity Church in the City of New York* (1901) pp. 187–9; K. N. Morgan, 'Early Nineteenth Century New York Architectural Drawings', *Columbia Library Columns* (May 1976) pp. 30–3. The interior is also based closely on St Martin's (N. Silver, *Lost New York* (1971) p. 152).

102. H. Kirker, *The Architecture of Charles Bulfinch* (1969) pp. 7–12, 19, 282–7, figs. 134–6; *Park*, pp. 33, 44, 54.

103. G. L. Wrenn, 'A Return to Solid Classical Principles', *JSAH* (December 1961) pp. 191–3. Other examples of the progeny of St Martin's are in W. Andrews, *Architecture in New England* (1973); R. N. Campen, *Architecture of the Western Reserve, 1800–1900* (1971); E. H. Ferry, *The Buildings of Detroit* (1968); T. Hamlin, *Greek Revival Architecture in America* (1964); J. M. Howells, *Lost Examples of Colonial Architecture* (1931); H. Kalman, *Pioneer Churches* (1976); R. Pare, ed., *Court House* (1978); H. W. Rose, *The Colonial Houses of Worship in America* (1963); E. W. Sinnott, *Meeting Houses & Churches in Early New England* (1963); R. G. Wilson, *McKim, Mead & White, Architects* (1983) p. 37, pl. 39. Town's Trinity Church, New Haven, 1814–17, uniquely developed the fifteenth-century tower of All Saints, Derby as illustrated in *ABA* pl. 26 (W. H. Pierson, *American Buildings and their Architects: Technology and the Picturesque* (1978) pp. 130–2).

104. Ariss did not introduce Gibbs to Virginia. The chimneypiece and flanking pilasters in James Johnston's Octagon at Twickenham (*ABA*, pl. 71) reappears in the parlour at Westover (*c*. 1726–35), built for William Byrd II, who was educated in England and owned a notable architectural library (T. T. Waterman, *The Mansions of Virginia, 1706–1776* (1945) pp. 156–7). Byrd is mentioned in a 1707 letter to John Perceval, Gibbs's early mentor (*BL* Add. MS 47025 f. 67).

105. T. T. Waterman, *The Mansions of Virginia, 1706–1776* (1945) pp. 243–7, 253–60.

106. R. R. Beirne and J. H. Scarff, *William Buckland, 1734–1774: Architect of Virginia and Maryland* (1958); W. H. Pierson, 'The Hammond-Harwood House: a colonial masterpiece', *Antiques* (January 1977) pp. 186–93. This motif, which is featured separately in *ABA*, pl. 110, and may have been suggested by Andrea Tirali's San Niccolò dei Tolentini, Venice, 1706–14 (C. L. V. Meeks, *Italian Architecture, 1750–1914* (1966) fig. 5), also appears at Norwood House, Yorkshire, *c*. 1765–70 (I. and E. Hall, *Historic Beverley* (1973) figs. 165, 167).

107. In 1789–92 Judge William Drayton's County Court House, Charleston, was being built according to *ABA*, pl. 51 (R. Pare, ed., *Court House* (1978) p. 170, pl. 160).

108. W. H. Adams, ed., *The Eye of Thomas Jefferson* (1976) pp. 234–7, 244–6.

109. J. F. Butler, 'Competition 1792: Designing a Nation's Capitol', *Capitol Studies* (1976) pp. 47–54; F. Kimball, *Mr. Samuel McIntire, Carver: The Architect of Salem* (1940), p. 144.

110. D. Gebhard and D. Nevins, *200 Years of American Architectural Drawings* (1977) pp. 86–7; T. Hamlin, *Benjamin Henry Latrobe* (1955), p. 188; C. Lancaster, 'New York City Hall Staircase Rotunda Reconsidered', *JSAH* (March 1970) pp. 33–9; D. Stillman, 'New York City Hall: Competition and Execution', *JSAH* (October 1964) pp. 129–42.

# CHRONOLOGICAL BIBLIOGRAPHY

J. Gibbs and another, 'A Manuscri by Mr. Gibbs Memorandums, &c.' (MS, Sir John Soane's Museum, London)

'Palladio', 'An account of James Gibbs, Esq ; architect', *Scots Magazine*, September 1760, pp. 475–6

J. Gwynn, *London and Westminster Improved*, 1766, pp. 45–6

F. Milizia, *Le Vite de' piu celebri Architetti*, 1768, p. 402

H. Walpole, *Anecdotes of Painting in England*, 1771, IV, pp. 44–7

Anon., 'Some Account of the Life of James Gibbs, Esq. the Celebrated Architect', *European Magazine*, September 1789, pp. 168–9

J. Dallaway, *Observations on English Architecture*, 1806, pp. 153–6, 192

M. Noble, *Biographical History of England*, 1806, IV, pp. 390–2

J. Nichols, *Literary Anecdotes of the Eighteenth Century*, 1812, II, pp. 12–13, 699

J. P. Neale, 'Architecture of Noble Mansions in the Eighteenth Century', in *Views of The Seats of Noblemen and Gentlemen, in England, Wales, Scotland and Ireland*, 1818, I, p. xviii

Mrs E. Cresy, *The Lives of Celebrated Architects, Ancient and Modern . . . by Francesco Milizia. Translated from the Italian By Mrs. E. C. With Notes and Additional Lives*, 1826, pp. 296–7

R. Stuart (R. S. Meikleham), *A Dictionary of Architecture*, 1830, II, no. 308

A. Cunningham, *The Lives of The Most Eminent British Painters, Sculptors, and Architects*, 1831, IV, pp. 284–99

T. Smith, *A Topographical and Historical Account of the Parish of St. Mary-le-Bone*, 1833, pp. 282–3

R. Chambers, *Lives of Illustrious and Distinguished Scotsmen*, 1836, II, Pt. 2, pp. 429–34

J. Gwilt, *An Encyclopedia of Architecture*, 1842, pp. 219–20

W. Papworth, ed., *The Dictionary of Architecture*, 1848–52, III, pp. 32–3

R. Chambers, *A Biographical Dictionary of Eminent Scotsmen*, 1853, II, pp. 436–41

Anon., 'Eminent Scottish Architects', *Building Chronicle : A Journal of Architecture and the Arts*, 5 June and 1 July 1854, I, nos. 2–3, pp. 22, 30

Anon., 'St Martin's Church and its Architect', *Builder*, 23 October 1858, p. 710

J. M. Graham, *An Historical View of Literature and Art in Great Britain*, 1871, p. 240

S. Redgrave, *Dictionary of Artists of the English School*, 1878, pp. 171–2

H. P. Horne, 'Some Account of the Life and Public Works of James Gibbs, Architect', *Century Guild Hobby Horse*, 1889, IV, pp. 29–36, 71–80, 110–17

A. M. Munro, 'A Note on the West Parish Church of S. Nicholas, Aberdeen, and its Architect—James Gibb or Gibbs', *Aberdeen Ecclesiological Society Transactions*, 1895, pp. 152–62

G. H. Birch, *London Churches of the XVIIth and XVIIIth Centuries*, 1898, pp. 12–13

L. Stephen and S. Lee, *Dictionary of National Biography*, 1908, VII, pp. 1146–7

E. B. Chancellor, *The Lives of British Architects from William of Wykeham to Sir William Chambers*, 1909, pp. 233–45

H. B. S. Gibbs, 'A Thesis on the Life and Work of James Gibbs', 1912 (typescript, Richmond Public Library)

V. Thieme and F. Becker, *Allgemeines Lexikon der Bildenden Künstler*, 1920, XIII, pp. 594–6

Anon., 'James Gibbs (1674–1754)', *Building News*, 2 March 1923

N. Lloyd, *A History of the English House*, 1931, pp. 129–30

J. Summerson, *Georgian London*, 1945, pp. 68–73

R. G. Chapman, 'Some Influences on the Work of James Gibbs', 1952 (typescript, School of Architecture, Cambridge)

J. Summerson, *Architecture in Britain, 1530 to 1830*, 1953, pp. 209–15

S. Lang, 'Gibbs: A Bicentenary Review of his Architectural Sources', *Architectural Review*, July 1954, pp. 20–6, and August 1954, p. 72

B. Little, 'James Gibbs', *Architect and Building News*, 15 July 1954, pp. 67–8

A. S. MacWilliam, 'James Gibbs, Architect', *Innes Review*, 1954, V, pp. 101–3

H. Colvin, *A Biographical Dictionary of English Architects, 1660–1840*, 1954, pp. 229–36

B. Little, *The Life and Work of James Gibbs, 1682–1754*, 1955 (N. Lynton review in *Burlington Magazine*, September 1957, pp. 318–19)

J. Holloway, 'A James Gibbs Autobiography', *Burlington Magazine*, May 1955, pp. 147–51

J. Field, 'The Sources of James Gibbs's Architecture and his connection with the Commissioners' Churches of 1711' 1958 (M. A. London University)

H. E. Stutchbury, 'Palladian Gibbs', *Ancient Monuments Society Transactions*, 1960, NS, VIII, pp. 43–52

D. D. Telfer, 'An Autobiography of James Gibbs, Architect 1682–1754', 1963 (typescript, Avery Library, Columbia University)

T. Friedman, 'James Gibbs, 1682–1754: The Formation of his Architectural Style', 1971 (Ph.D. London University)

T. Friedman, *James Gibbs as a Church Designer* (Derby exhibition) 1972

T. Friedman, entry in J. Lever, ed., *Catalogue of the Drawings Collection of the Royal Institute of British Architects*, 1973, Vol. G–K, pp. 21–5

T. Friedman, *In Praise of James Gibbs* (Aberdeen exhibition) 1974

J. Burke, *English Art, 1714–1800*, 1976, pp. 74–86

H. Colvin, *A Biographical Dictionary of British Architects, 1600–1840*, 2nd ed. 1978, pp. 337–45

A. Service, *The Architects of London*, 1979, pp. 48–51

T. Friedman, *James Gibbs Architect, 1682–1754: 'a man of great Fame'* (Orleans House Gallery, Twickenham, exhibition) 1982

T. Friedman, entry in A. F. Placzek, ed., *Macmillan Encyclopedia of Architects*, 1982, II, pp. 196–9

# Index

REFERENCES to books in Gibbs's fine art library, arranged alphabetically by author on pages 327–30, and in the Chronological Bibliography, pages 351–2, are not listed below. Only the most relevant references to *A Book of Architecture* are given.

# PHOTOGRAPHIC ACKNOWLEDGEMENTS